Non dilexerunt animam suam usque ad mortem.
The Latin, *Non dilexerunt animam suam usque ad mortem*, translates, "... they loved not their lives unto the death." Revelation 12:11

On The Cover: *Massacres at Salzburg* took place in 1528 when Prince-Archbishop Cardinal Matthaus Lang of Salzburg issued mandates sending police in search of Anabaptists. Many were captured and killed. This engraving illustrates the sufferings and sacrifices these Dissenters endured when their government, in conjunction with established religion, attempted to coerce and impose uniformity of religious belief. Hence, this picture is a reminder of the cost of religious liberty and the ever-present need to maintain the separation of church and state. We use this art to represent our Dissent and Nonconformity Series.

THE
HISTORY AND ANTIQUITIES
OF THE
𝔇issenting Churches

Vol. I

THE
HISTORY AND ANTIQUITIES
OF THE
Dissenting Churches
AND
MEETING HOUSES,
IN
LONDON, WESTMINSTER, AND SOUTHWARK;
INCLUDING THE
LIVES OF THEIR MINISTERS,
FROM
THE RISE OF NONCONFORMITY TO THE PRESENT TIME.

WITH
AN APPENDIX
ON THE
ORIGIN, PROGRESS, AND PRESENT STATE
OF
CHRISTIANITY IN BRITAIN.

IN FOUR VOLUMES.

BY WALTER WILSON,
OF THE INNER TEMPLE.

VOL. I.

London:
PRINTED FOR THE AUTHOR;
SOLD BY W. BUTTON AND SON, PATERNOSTER ROW;
T. WILLIAMS AND SON, STATIONERS' COURT; AND
J. CONDER, BUCKLERSBURY.
1808.

he Baptist Standard Bearer, Inc.
NUMBER ONE IRON OAKS DRIVE • PARIS, ARKANSAS 72855

Thou hast given a *standard* to them that fear thee;
that it may be displayed because of the truth.
-- *Psalm 60:4*

*Reprinted
by*

THE BAPTIST STANDARD BEARER, INC.
No. 1 Iron Oaks Drive
Paris, Arkansas 72855
(501) 963-3831

THE WALDENSIAN EMBLEM
lux lucet in tenebris
"The Light Shineth in the Darkness"

ISBN #1-57978-615-4

PREFACE.

When an author appears before the bar of the public, he puts himself in a situation of great responsibility, which is increased in proportion as his facts or opinions are liable to be disputed. A writer of history should be, above all other people, an attentive observer of human nature. Facts derive their principal value from their application to character. Revolutions in empires may become important by an exhibition of the baser passions; but they are only valuable in as much as they conduce to the welfare of the people. So, in the history of individuals, those traits of character are to be pointed out, and chiefly insisted upon, which are calculated to subserve the benefit of society. Perhaps no subject requires to be treated with so much judgment as ecclesiastical history; and yet there is no branch of knowledge that has been more shamefully perverted to the baleful purposes of priestcraft and superstition. The history of the Church is any thing rather than a history of Christianity. Clothed in the venerable garb of antiquity, the grossest delusions have been imposed upon the understanding; and the greatest crimes have been sheltered behind the presumed sacredness of the clerical character. It is only of late years that the veil has been drawn aside, and that pretended saints have been shown in their true colours. In the hands of a skilful writer, endowed with judgment, and acquainted with the spirituality of religion, ecclesiastical history is a topic that might be treated upon with much interest, as affording a variety of incidents that are calculated both for amusement and instruction. Much has been done towards clearing away the rubbish of former writers by Mr. Milner; but a church-history of our own country, written upon really Christian principles, is still a *desideratum*.

It is quite natural that popish writers should bend the facts of ecclesiastical history to support the vast fabric of clerical dominion, so essential to the existence of their church; but that Protestant writers should have fallen into the same error is not a little extraordinary. Unfortunately, the subject has been handled principally by persons who have been more concerned to exalt the dignity of the priesthood than to promote the kingdom of Christ. Hence the insufferable pride, the sectarian bigotry, and the malicious representations of churchmen, when they are writing concerning those who do not belong to their communion. In support of these charges, we need only refer to the writings of Heylin, Collier, Wood, Echard, Kennett, and a thousand more that might be named, who, whatever may be their merits as valiant champions for the hierarchy, failed in the principal requisites as historians. It is the record of christian principles, not the prosperity of a sect, that constitutes the beauty of ecclesiastical history.

The attainment of truth is the only legitimate end of history. If destitute of this ingredient, it may delude mankind, but cannot instruct them; it may serve the interests of a party, but strikes at the foundation of religion and virtue. To arrive at truth, we must divest ourselves of sectarian prejudices, weigh well the opinions of others, and be diffident of our own judgment. True wisdom is always allied to modesty; and whilst it becomes us to be decided in our own opinions, a recollection of human fallibility will teach us a lesson of candour to others. As there is hardly any thing more destructive to the peace of society, so there is nothing more contemptible than bigotry. History is full of its evil consequences, and we heartily despise those narrow minds in which it was an inhabitant. In denouncing this disturber of the christian world, truth makes no distinction of sects. The mind of an Edwards was no less deformed than that of a Wood, and whilst we use their facts, we reject their opinions, and pity their bigotry.

A difference of opinion as to rites and ceremonies, and forms of worship, has been the source of endless divisions amongst Christians. But all the schisms that have taken place in the church would have been as harmless as the picture drawn of them by the frightful mind of a non-juror, if Christians had cultivated the spirit of their religion, and aimed at a greater likeness to the temper of its founder. Unfortunately, every sect has seated itself by turns in the chair of infallibility, and imposed its peculiar dogmas with as much confidence as if they had descended from heaven with a strict commission to persecute all who would not embrace them. Uniformity has been the grand idol of ecclesiastics in all ages, and the civil power has assisted them to proclaim its worship. Till the period of the Reformation men bent their necks to the yoke in submissive silence; but the progress of knowledge, consequent upon that event, has burst the fetters; and, in spite of the most cruel persecutions, the mind has continued to assert its liberty.

The failure of every attempt to force opinion ought to be a sufficient lesson of its absurdity. Upon this point enlightened men of all sects are now pretty well agreed; but there is still a difference of opinion as to the propriety of exalting one sect, by civil distinctions, at the expence of another. If the sentiments advanced in the ensuing work be correct, civil establishments of religion are utterly incompatible with the nature of a christian church. How injurious they have been to the interests of religion and liberty is abundantly illustrated in the history of our own country. In the present day they may be deemed needful for pageantry and other state purposes, but no one can, for a moment, identify them with the kingdom of Christ, which is declared to be "not of this world." Public opinion has already done much towards disarming them of power, and will probably, without any use of violence, effectuate their downfal. Did not experience warrant the conclusion, the nature of the thing would be sufficient to decide that civil governments may exist, and answer all the great purposes of society, without the patronage of any particular sect. I know that great pains have been taken to inculcate the idea that church and state are so closely interwoven, that they must live or fall together. This opinion, however, is at variance with our history; and I take it to be a libel upon our civil constitution to place its existence at the mercy of a few priests. In all states the civil power should be sufficiently strong to protect public morals, and to set the priesthood at defiance. The clergy can only be formidable in proportion as they are secularized and rendered independent of the people. In their proper station they will be useful instructors, and harmless members of society.

In offering the present work to the public, the author has no wish to kindle animosities: If he has made some free remarks upon men and things, they are such only as he apprehended to result from his facts. Liberal minds will have no desire to screen the characters, nor palliate the crimes of persecutors: This is by no means necessary to the defence of the cause which they espoused. An Episcopalian or a Presbyterian may still maintain the divine right of his respective church, and so long as he argues with decency and temper, shall be attended to with respect; but when he outsteps the boundaries of good manners, and uses railing instead of arguments, he will be considered an unworthy advocate, and pitied for his bigotry. If any of my readers should think me mistaken in my conclusions, let them follow out their convictions, and I shall freely give them the same liberty of judgment that I have taken myself. Christians who cannot debate their differences without being angry, should leave the path of controversy, and confine themselves to the cultivation of the christian graces.

History is a branch of knowledge so admirably adapted both to delight and instruct, that it is no wonder enlightened people should consider it a necessary branch of education. Of the different classes into which it may be divided, none has been held in greater estimation than biography. Accordingly, numerous have been the tributes given in favour of this branch of study, and it has been cultivated with an ardour and success unknown at any former period. One of the first writers who gave a polish to this class of composition was Dr. Johnson, who possessed an almost unbounded controul over our language; and had his liberality been as comprehensive as the powers of his mind, he would have been as much entitled to our esteem as he must be to our respect. Since his time, we have had a host of writers devoted to the same pursuit, and the public voice has borne witness to the interest and utility of their labours. If religion should be the principal study of man's life, as involving interests that affect his future destiny, christian biography must be a subject peculiarly interesting to our feelings. But this, like many other excellent things, is capable of being perverted. Prejudice on the one hand, and partiality on the other, have made sad havoc with the characters of men. To draw them with accuracy requires temper and judgment, and a thorough acquaintance with the motives as well as actions of individuals. A laboured panegyric is as useless as it is often untrue; but the faithful delineation of a life devoted to the cause of literature and religion, will furnish ample topics both for reflection and improvement.

The task which the author proposed to himself in the ensuing work was one of no common difficulty. To write concerning so great a variety of persons and opinions without giving offence to some, seemed a very hopeless undertaking; more especially as he was not at all disposed to countenance that temporizing spirit which, under the fair name of charity, so extensively prevails amongst the professors of religion. He can honestly say that truth has been the grand object of his inquiries, and if he has mistaken it in any instance, he shall not be displeased with any candid attempts to set him right. As the work was not undertaken at the instance of any denomination, so no party is liable for the sentiments it avows. These, whether they be right or wrong, rest wholly with the author, who has neither disguised the truth, nor wilfully misrepresented it from fear or affection, towards any party or individual whatsoever.

The foundation of the present performance was laid many years ago, although without any view to publication till within a few weeks of its appearance. It originated in a perusal of Mr. Neal's life, drawn up by Dr. Toulmin, and prefixed to his edition of the History of the Puritans. Successive inquiries added to his stock of materials, till it reached the form and bulk, in which it is now presented to the public.

Upon the utility of such an undertaking, it will be unnecessary to enlarge. " I have often thought it a debt due to the churches, (says Dr. Latham,) as well as to the memory of those who have deserved well of them, if some faithful hand would discharge it, to transmit some account of those, who have devoted themselves to the cause and interest of the naked truth, or gospel, in that way wherein they could have no temptation from the rewards of this world : It would be only a proper continuation of Mr. Baxter's and Dr. Calamy's account of our ministers brought down to to the present time, and might serve some valuable purposes in several respects; nor could any unkind construction be justly put upon it, if from a sincere regard to the command of Christ, *not to call any one Master upon earth*, they modestly declined paying that deference, that hath been expected, to human authority in matters of religion. One would think it must recommend them to the esteem of an age, that pretends to such a strong sense of liberty; for the rights of conscience, though they have been forgotten in some late remonstrances on that head, have the best plea for it, and in the exercise of them, there is the most glorious enjoyment of it."*

It is greatly to be lamented that the idea of a similar work did not occur to some person acquainted with the affairs of the Dissenters, at least half a century ago; many facts might then have been recovered which are now buried in oblivion. That a task of so much consequence, seeming to require long experience, extensive information, and no mean influence, should have been undertaken by the present writer, may seem an act of singular temerity; and he must confess, that could he have foreseen the difficulties he has experienced, and the little encouragement afforded by Dissenters to works of labour and research, he should have hesitated in entering upon so arduous an undertaking. A spirit of inquiry as to the distinguishing features of nonconformity, has, with the exception of the Bap-

---

* Dr. Latham's Sermon on the death of the Rev. Matthew Bradshaw, p. 33, 34.

tists, wholly fled from the different sects. The Presbyterians have either deserted to the world, or sunk under the influence of a lukewarm ministry; and the Independents have gone over in a body to the Methodists. Indifference and enthusiasm have thinned the ranks of the old stock, and those whe remain behind are lost in the croud of modern religionists.

In the composition of the work, the author has adopted the topographical order, as best suited to his subject; and in ascertaining the limits of his divisions, has followed the best writers upon the history of London. After describing the situation of his places, he has given a particular account of the different revolutions that each has undergone, detailing the succession of pastors in each church, the variation in numbers, doctrinal sentiment, and such other particulars as were deemed necessary, or could be ascertained. The lives that follow the introductory matter, will be found, perhaps, not the least interesting part of the performance. In drawing them up, the author has paid a particular attention to facts, and as far as his materials would permit, has rendered them subservient to the cause of literature. There being a great sameness in character, he has usually compressed that part of biography, and in the application of its leading features has sometimes consulted his own judgment in preference to the indiscriminate adulation of partial or injudicious friends. To serious persons, christian biography has always been a source of profitable amusement, and in this part of his work, the author trusts he has not neglected the great interests of religion. In order to this, he has not thought it necessary to make any sacrifice of principle, nor to compromise the leading features of nonconformity. The power of religion never shone in brighter lustre than it did in many of the worthies here recorded; and the talents they displayed in defending the great truths of Christianity, raised them to an equal eminence with their conforming brethren. If these excellent characters are to be construed by modern Dissenters into formalists and bigots, the author cannot expect a treatment much different, nor is he desirous of better company. The truth is, that bigotry and charity are terms but little understood, though artfully noised abroad till they delude the passions of the multitude.

As there is some appearance of novelty attached to this performance, persons unacquainted with Dissenters, may annex to it notions of singularity. But they should recollect that our ideas are comparative; and as the author writes for Dissenters, he expects the same latitude for them, that would be granted to an antiquarian in compiling any local history. The subject he has chosen, has been strangely passed over by all who have undertaken to write concerning the history of London. This can only be attributed to those sectarian prejudices that always abound amongst national Christians; but it is high time that they should be laid aside, and that the human character should be estimated by a more accurate standard. The parochial churches, and other public buildings in the metropolis, have received ample illustration from the pen of the historian, and the pages of our biographies are crouded with the lives of churchmen. But no one has hitherto explored the sanctuaries of Dissenters, nor recorded the biography of their pastors. To supply this chasm the present undertaking was attempted; and it is presumed, that the facts recorded in these volumes will afford sufficient evidence that learning, talents, and piety, are not confined to any party or denomination of Christians.

It was an object with the author to make his work a repository of useful information. For this purpose, he has brought together a large collection of facts, for which, in all material cases, he has quoted his authorities. If he has sometimes descended to a minuteness more acceptable to the antiquarian than to the general reader, he has not forgotten the entertainment of the latter, for whose sake he has occasionally enlivened his pages with anecdote. In the course of his inquiries it will be found that he has brought to light many places which were scarcely known to be in existence, and has recorded the lives of many excellent persons, whose names are not to be found in any other publication. Some apology may, perhaps, be deemed necessary for inserting so many of the ejected ministers, whose lives are to be met with in the Nonconformists' Memorial. But, as the work would not be complete without them, so it will be found that the accounts here inserted interfere very little with that performance, which he has but seldom consulted. The whole of such lives are re-written, most of them considerably enlarged from other sources, and some of them entirely new. Even in this view, therefore, the two works illustrate each other. But those worthies occupy only a small portion of these volumes. It is their successors whose lives the author has most laboured, and he hopes they will be found not altogether destitute of interest. That a work consisting almost wholly of facts and dates should be free from errors, is not to be expected: That they are so numerous the author greatly regrets, and must cast himself upon the reader's indulgence.

In the ensuing pages, the reader will meet with frequent references to places of which he will not find any account. To explain this, it is necessary to inform him, that the author designed, originally, to extend his work through the whole of the British metropolis, and the circumjacent villages; but finding that he could not comprise the whole in four volumes, he has restricted himself to those places that are within the cities of London and Westminster, and the Borough of Southwark. If those who feel interested in the performance, regret that it is not extended to another volume, so as to include all the places they could wish, they must not blame the author, but those to whom it appertains to encourage such an undertaking. Posterity will, perhaps, think that it reflects no credit upon Dissenters of the present day that they can scarcely muster three hundred persons who feel interested in what concerns the affairs of their own churches. That the work is not better deserving their patronage is matter of regret to the author, who wishes it had fallen into abler hands.

For the facts upon which this history is founded, the author has had recourse to a variety of sources, both printed and manuscript, as well as to oral information. The valuable records belonging to the societies in White's-alley, Barbican, Devonshire-square, New-court, and Stepney, have afforded him many useful particulars relating to contemporary churches. That the Dissenters in general have not been more careful in preserving their records, and in noting down the transactions relating to their body seems very surprising, and argues a carelessness that merits censure. In the infancy of their societies they were more particular; but as their discipline relaxed, they grew remiss in the registry of events, and their early records having fallen into private hands are, in most cases, lost. Most of our old churches know little more of their history than what is derived from tradition; a defect which the present work is intended to supply. Amongst the persons to whom he has been most indebted, he has to acknowledge his obligations, primarily, to the late Rev. Josiah Lewis, who took much pains in making similar collections, which he communicated to the author. For many useful facts relating to the General Baptists he has been indebted to the late venerable Mr. Stephen Lowdell, who also permitted him to examine some ancient manuscripts belonging to that denomination. That ornament to the Dissenters, the late Rev. Samuel Palmer, whose long standing, and extensive acquaintance, gave him great facilities for information, communicated to the author a number of facts, as also, a manuscript account of the Dissenters in London from 1695 to 1731, which has been of considerable use. His obligations are next due to Dr. Toulmin, of Birmingham; Dr. Rees and Dr. Winter, of London, for much collateral information; but there is no one from whom he has received more valuable communications as from Mr. Isaac James of Bristol, whose extensive researches into the history of Dissenters has, perhaps, never been exceeded. To Mr. Joseph Meen, of Biggleswade, he is indebted for the loan of a valuable manuscript; and to the Rev. G. Burder, R. Burnside, G. Greig, J. Martin, T. Tayler, T. Thomas, T. Morgan, J. Evans, S. Hacket, J. Stewart, and Mr. B. Coxhead, of London; the Rev. J. Philipps, of Clapham; B. Brook, of Tutbury; R. Frost, of Dunmow; T. P. Bull, of

Newport Pagnell; J. Jefferson, of Basingstoke; W. Kingsbury, of Southampton; J. Sutcliff, of Olney; J. Townsend, of Ealand; J. Barker, of Towcester; J. Hickman, of Wattesfield; Mr. James Conder, of Ipswich; Mr. J. Whittuck, of Bristol; also, to the late Rev. J. Barber, Dr. R. Young, and S. Girle, of London, for a variety of communications, too numerous to particularize, and to whom the author desires publicly to return his thanks. Also to the trustees of Dr. Williams's Library, Red Cross-street, for liberty to consult the valuable library of that institution, and to take engravings from the portraits deposited there.

To the patronage of the public, he now commits his labours with becoming deference, not insensible of many imperfections that attend them, but still not without hope that they will receive the approbation of the liberal and judicious of all denominations.

CAMDEN TOWN,
May 1, 1814.

CONTENTS

OF

VOLUME I.

RISE OF THE FIRST NONCONFORMING CHURCHES.

	Page
Protestant Congregation in London, in the reign of Queen Mary,	3
First *Presbyterian* Church in England	9
The *Brownist* Congregation about London,	13
First *Independent* Church in England,	36

CITY OF LONDON, EASTERN DIVISION.

Crutched Friars, *Baptist*,	53
Poor Jewry-lane, *English Presbyterian*,	55
Jewry-street, *Calvinistic Methodist*,	128
Mark-lane, *Independent*,	134
Turners'-Hall, *General Baptist*,	135
———— *Reformed Quakers*,	137
———— *Independent*,	139
———— *Particular Baptist*,	143
———— *Independent*,	146
Weigh-House, *Independent*,	148
Grace-church-street, *Particular Baptist*,	205
Pewterers'-Hall, *Independent*,	208
Lime-street, *Independent*,	212
Bury-street, *Independent*,	251
Crosby-square, *Presbyterian*,	329
———— *Rellyanists*,	358

CONTENTS.

	Page
Great St. Helen's, *Particular Baptist*,	362
Little St. Helen's, *Presbyterian*,	363
Camomile-street, *Independent*,	387
Hounsditch, *Particular Baptist*,	392
Gravel-lane, Hounsditch, *Presbyterian*,	397
Bishopsgate-street, *Presbyterian* and *Independent*,	398
Hand-alley, *Presbyterian*,	399
Devonshire-square, *Particular Baptist*,	400

SOUTHERN DIVISION.

	Page
Great Eastcheap, *Particular Baptist*,	457
Miles's-lane, *Independent*,	462
———— *ditto*,	467
———— *Scotch Seceders*,	519
Dyers' Hall, Extinct,	525
Joyners'-Hall, *Particular Baptist*,	526
Plumbers'-Hall,	533
Tallow-Chandlers'-Hall, *Particular Baptist*,	535

THE
HISTORY AND ANTIQUITIES
OF THE
𝔇issenting Churches

Vol. I

THE

HISTORY AND ANTIQUITIES

OF

DISSENTING CHURCHES,

&c. &c.

PROTESTANT CONGREGATION IN LONDON, IN THE REIGN OF QUEEN MARY.

THE Churches of this kingdom had been overspread, for many centuries, with the darkest mist of ignorance and superstition; and, as far as appears, without any considerable opposition, till the famous John Wickliffe arose, the Morning Star of the Reformation. The sanguinary laws enacted by our Monarchs after his death, prevented a public avowal of his opinions, till the time of Henry VIII. who having quarrelled with the Pope, revenged himself by becoming the open patron of the Reformed. The absurd and capricious conduct of this King occasioned a great fluctuation of Religion during the whole of his reign. Under his excellent son, Edward VI. the Reformation made a rapid progress, but was suddenly arrested by the immature death of that amiable young Prince, after a short reign of six years. There are few persons but have been made acquainted from their infancy with the shocking barbarities that disgraced the reign of Queen Mary, and will transmit her name with infamy to the latest period of time. Popery having regained the ascendancy, and become the religion of the State, many Protestants withdrew into foreign countries. Of those who remained at home, congregations were formed in different parts of the country, but the most considerable met in and about London.

This Church, which there seems great propriety in placing at the head of our history, was formed soon after Queen Mary's accession, and consisted of about 200 members. Their meetings were held alternately near Aldgate, and Blackfriars, in Thames-street, and in ships upon the river. Sometimes they assembled in the villages about London, and especially at Islington, that they might the more easily elude the Bishop's officers and spies. To screen themselves from the notice of their persecutors, they often met in the night, and in secret places, and experienced some remarkable providential deliverances.*

The public devotions of this society were conducted successively by the following ministers, whose names are preserved by the industrious Mr. Clark.

EDMUND SCAMBLER, D. D. This excellent prelate was born at Gressingham in Lancashire, and received his education in the University of Cambridge. In the beginning of Queen Mary's reign, he united himself to the Protestant congregation, and became their first pastor. Persecution, however, compelled him in a little time to relinquish this situation; when he probably retired abroad. Soon after the accession of Elizabeth, he was made chaplain to Parker, Archbishop of Canterbury, through whose interest he rose to high preferment in the church. In 1560, he was consecrated Bishop of Peterborough, and translated to Norwich in 1584.† It should be recorded to his credit,

---

* Clark's Martyrology, p. 515, 516.
† Godwin de Præsulibus Angliæ, p. 441.

Protestant Congregation in London in the Reign of Queen Mary.

that in his exalted state, he conducted himself with great prudence and moderation. He was a learned man, and very zealous against the Papists. His concern for the diffusion of religion, led him to encourage associations among the clergy for that desirable end.* But as they were countenanced and attended by persons who were stigmatized as Puritans, the Queen put an immediate stop to their proceedings. Dr. Scambler died May 7, 1597, aged 85 years, and was buried in the cathedral church at Norwich.†

Mr. FOWLER.---Dr. Scambler was succeeded by a Mr. Fowler, of whom no account has reached us.

JOHN ROUGH, a native of Scotland, came into England for freedom of religion, in the preceding reign. Upon the accession of Queen Mary, he retired into Frizeland, where he laboured hard for his living; but meeting with many difficulties, he returned to London, joined the Protestant congregation, and after a short time was chosen their pastor. He continued faithfully to execute his office, teaching and confirming them in the truth of the Gospel, till, by the treachery of a false brother, he was betrayed into the hands of the Romanists. He was apprehended with Mr. Cuthbert Simpson and several others, at a house in Islington, where the church were about to assemble, as was their custom, for prayer and preaching the word; and being taken before the council, after several examinations, he was sent prisoner to Newgate, and his case committed to the management of Bonner. The character of this man, whose hands were so deeply stained with innocent blood, needs no colouring in this place; the faithful page of history will always hold it up to the execration of mankind. In his hands, Mr. Rough met with the most relentless cruelty. Not contented with degrading and delivering him over to the

---

* Neal's History of the Puritans, vol. i. p. 183.
† Wood's Athenæ Oxon. vol. i. p. 697.

secular power, the furious prelate flew upon him, and plucked the very beard from his face. At length, after much *rough* usage, he ended his life joyfully in the flames, Dec. 1577.*

AUGUSTINE BERNHER, whose name indicates him to have been a foreigner. He resided some time with the excellent Bishop Latimer, and witnessed his martyrdom. He also imbibed much of the spirit of that extraordinary man, whose sermons he introduced to the public with a long dedication to the Lady Katherine, Duchess of Suffolk, of whose remarkable preservation during the Marian persecution, a particular account is preserved by Mr. Fox. Mr. Bernher had the satisfaction to witness the re-establishment of the Reformed religion under Queen Elizabeth; and afterwards resided at South-Ham in Warwickshire, from whence he dates his dedication, October 2, 1570.

THOMAS BENTHAM, D. D. born at Sherbourne in Yorkshire, and educated at Magdalen College, Oxford. Upon Queen Mary's accession, he was deprived of his Fellowship; when he retired to Zurich, and then to Basil, where he became preacher to the English exiles. Afterwards, being recalled by his Protestant brethren, he was made Superintendent of their congregation in London. In this situation he continued till the death of the Queen, encouraging and confirming his people in their faith by his pious discipline, constant preaching, and resolute behaviour in the Protestant cause. Under his care and direction, they often met by hundreds for divine worship, without discovery, notwithstanding they were under the nose of the vigilant and cruel Bonner.† Upon the accession of Elizabeth, he was nominated to the Bishopric of Litchfield and Coventry; which he filled with great moderation till his death, Feb. 21, 1578-9.‡ Dr. Bentham

---

* Fox's Acts and Monuments, vol. iii. p. 722.—Clark's Martyrology, p. 495-6.   † Heylyn's History of the Reformation, p. 79, 80.
‡ Wood's Athenæ Oxon. vol. i. p. 192, 704.

Protestant Congregation in London in the Reign of Queen Mary.

was held in great repute for learning and piety. It was with considerable reluctance that he complied with the Queen's injunctions for suppressing the prophecyings. His letter to his Archdeacon upon this subject,* bears strong marks of a pious mind; but at the same time shows the extent to which the Queen carried her prerogative, and the blind obedience she exacted from her subjects. The Prophecyings, were religious meetings instituted by the clergy, for explaining the scriptures, and promoting knowledge and piety. One very important benefit arising from them was, that they occasioned a familiar intercourse between the clergy and their people, and excited a laudable emulation in watching over their respective flocks. The Queen complained of them to the Archbishop,† as nurseries of Puritanism; she said that the laity neglected their secular affairs by repairing to these meetings, which filled their heads with notions, and might occasion disputes and seditions in the state. She moreover told him, that it was good for the church to have but few preachers, three or four in a county being sufficient; and peremptorily commanded him to suppress them. The Archbishop, however, instead of obeying the commands of his royal mistress, thought that she had made some infringement upon his office, and wrote her a long and earnest letter, declaring that his conscience would not suffer him to comply with her injunctions. This so inflamed the Queen, that she sequestered the Archbishop from his office, and he never afterwards recovered her favour.‡

CUTHBERT SIMPSON.---Before we close this article, it will be proper to make some mention of Mr. Cuthbert Simpson, a deacon of the church now under consideration. He was a pious, faithful and zealous man, labouring incessantly to preserve the flock from the errors of popery, and to secure them from the dangers of persecution. His apprehension at Isling-

---

* See Neal's Puritans, vol. i. p. 239.
† Dr. EDMUND GRINDAL, ‡ Neal, ubi supra, p. 239—40.

ton at the same time with Mr. Rough, has been noticed above. Indeed, at this time the whole church was in the utmost danger. It was the office of Mr. Simpson to keep a book containing the names of the persons belonging to the congregation, which book he always carried to their private assemblies. But it happened through the good providence of God, that on the day of his apprehension, he left it with Mrs. Rough, the minister's wife. (A) Two or three days after this, Mr. Simpson was sent to the Tower. During his confinement there, the Recorder of London examined him strictly as to the persons who attended the English service; and because he would discover neither the book, nor the names, he was cruelly racked three several times, but without effect. The Lieutenant of the Tower also caused an arrow to be tied between his two fore-fingers, and drew it out so violently as to cause the blood to gush forth. These marble-hearted men not being able to move the constancy of our Confessor, consigned him over to Bonner, who bore this testimony concerning him before a number of spectators: " You see what a personable man this is; and for his patience, if he were not an heretic, I should much commend him; for he has been thrice racked in one day, and in my house he hath endured some sorrow, and yet I never saw his patience once moved." But notwithstanding this, Bonner condemned him, ordering him first into the stocks in his coal-house, and from thence to Smithfield, where with Mr. Fox and Mr. Devenish, two others of the church taken at Islington, he ended his life in the flames.*

(A) A few nights before his apprehension, Mr. Rough had the following remarkable dream. He thought he saw Mr. Simpson taken by two of the guard, and with him the book above-mentioned. This giving him much trouble he awoke, and related the dream to his wife. Afterwards, falling asleep, he again dreamt the same thing. Upon his awaking the second time, he determined to go immediately to Mr. Simpson, and put him upon his guard; but while he was getting ready, Mr. Simpson came in with the book, which he deposited with Mrs. Rough, as above related.——*Clark's Martyrology, ubi supra.*

* Clark's Martyrology, p. 497.

FIRST PRESBYTERIAN CHURCH IN ENGLAND.

THE first Presbyterian Church in England was erected at *Wandsworth,* near London, in the year 1572.

The Reformation as established in England by Queen Elizabeth was materially defective, and came far short of what was designed by those who had the chief hand in promoting it. The Queen imbibed much of her father's temper; she was vain, cruel and intolerant, fond of Popish rites and ceremonies, and affected great magnificence in her devotions. Her own arbitrary will was the supreme law of the land, from which she would suffer no deviation. By sanguinary laws she attempted to bring all her subjects to one uniform opinion in religious matters, but this being impossible, persecution followed, and fines, bonds and imprisonment, and sometimes death itself, awaited those who presumed to differ from her.

Most of our English Reformers were much averse to every thing that savoured of Popery, and aimed to abolish gradually all the remaining vestiges of it from the church. Those who were exiles for religion in Queen Mary's days, returned home upon Elizabeth's accession, hoping to obtain such a form of worship as they had observed in the best reformed churches abroad. But in this they were disappointed, the Queen had modelled the church according to her own fancy, and preferred those only who would fall in with her establishment; leaving the rest in the same threadbare, starving condition they exhibited, when first returned from abroad. Among these were the learned and industrious John Fox the Martyrologist, (B) old father Miles Coverdale, and many other

(B) Mr. Fox in a letter to his friend Dr. Humphreys, writes thus : "I still wear the same clothes, and remain in the same sordid condition that

VOL. I.

First Presbyterian Church in England.

excellent divines, who were some of the greatest ornaments of our church. These desired a further reformation; but not being able to obtain it, petitioned the Queen for an indulgence in things that were indifferent. This being denied, the heads of the Puritans held a solemn consultation, in which after prayer, and a serious debate about the lawfulness and necessity of separation, they came to this conclusion, that " since they could not have the word of God preached, nor the sacraments administered without *idolatrous geare,* and since there had been a separate congregation in London, and another at Geneva, in Queen Mary's time, which used a book and order of preaching, administration of the sacraments and discipline, that the great Mr. Calvin had approved of, and which was free from the superstitions of the English service; that therefore it was their duty in their present circumstances, to break off from the public churches, and to assemble as they had opportunity, in private houses, or elsewhere, to worship God in a manner that might not offend against the light of their consciences."* This was the æra of the separation, A. D. 1566. After which they continued to hold private assemblies for worship; but the Queen and her Bishops soon made them feel their vengeance; their meetings were disturbed, and those who attended them apprehended, and sent in large numbers to Bridewell, and other prisons, *for conviction.*

There being no further prospect of a reformation by the legislature, some of the leading Puritans agreed to attempt it in a more private way; for this purpose they erected a Presbytery at Wandsworth, a village five miles from London, conveniently situated for the brethren, as standing on the

---

England received me in, when I first came home out of Germany; nor do I change my degree or order, which is that of the *mendicants,* or if you will, of the *friars preachers.* Thus pleasantly did this grave and learned Divine reproach the ingratitude of his times.——*Neal, ubi supra, p.* 116.

* Neal's Puritans, vol. i. p. 154.

First Presbyterian Church in England.

banks of the river Thames. The heads of the association were Mr. Field, lecturer of Wandsworth, Mr. Smith of Mitcham, Mr. Crane, of Roehampton, Messrs. Wilcox, Standen, Jackson, Bonham, Saintloe and Edmonds; to whom afterwards were joined Messrs. Travers, Clarke, Barber, Gardiner, Crook, Egerton, and a number of very considerable laymen. On the 20th of November, 1572, eleven elders were chosen, and their offices described in a register entitled, " The Orders of Wandsworth." This, says Mr. Neal, was the first Presbyterian Church in England. All imaginable care was taken to keep their proceedings secret, though without success; for the Bishop, whose eye was upon them, gave immediate intelligence to the *High Commission,* upon which the Queen issued out a proclamation for putting the act of Uniformity in execution. But though the Commissioners knew of the Presbytery, they could not discover the members, nor prevent others being erected in neighbouring counties.*

Most of the above persons were Divines of considerable eminence, beneficed in the Church of England, and much esteemed by the people for their useful preaching, and exemplary lives. But this could not protect them from the fury of the Queen and her Bishops, who were infinitely more concerned to preserve a few unprofitable rites and ceremonies, than to promote the instruction of the people and the peace of the church. A rigorous conformity was the idol they set up, and those who would not worship that idol, were deprived of their livings, and hurried to jails, as wholesome methods to remove their scruples. But the harder the Puritans were pressed, the more were they disaffected to the national establishment, and the more resolute in their attempts for a reformation of discipline. There was a book in high esteem among them, entitled, *Disciplina Ecclesiæ sacra ex Dei verbo descripta;* that is, " The holy discipline of the Church described in the word of God." It was drawn

---

* Neal, ubi supra, p. 202.

up in Latin by Mr. Travers, a learned Puritan, and printed at Geneva about the year 1574. Afterwards, being reviewed and corrected, it was translated into English, in 1584. A preface was added by Mr. Cartwright, for general use; but, while printing at Cambridge, the Archbishop* ordered it to be seized, and advised that all the copies should be burnt as factious and seditious. After Mr. Cartwright's death, a copy was found in his study, and reprinted in 1644, under this new title, " A Directory of Government anciently contended for, and as far as the times would suffer, practised by the first Nonconformists in the days of Queen Elizabeth; found in the study of the most accomplished Mr. Thomas Cartwright, after his decease, and reserved to be published for such a time as this. Published by authority." This book contains the substance of those alterations in discipline, which the Puritans of those times contended for, and was subscribed by a number of their most eminent Divines.† A copy of it may be seen in the Appendix to Neal's History of the Puritans.

The history of the Church during the reign of Elizabeth, presents a melancholy picture of discord, bigotry and intolerance. It is much to be lamented that the Bishops of those times, many of whom were men of learning and piety, should condescend to become so far the tool of the prerogative, as to oppress their brethren, and be the instruments of sowing divisions in the Church. If the Reformation had been formed upon a broader basis, the confusions that followed would in all probability have been prevented. The rights of conscience, however, were not then fully understood, nor indeed, were they publicly asserted for above a century afterwards. Though the doctrines of the Reformed were established by law, that most objectionable part of popery, which erected an inquisition into the consciences of men, was still retained. The supremacy of the Pope was abolished together with his infallibility; but the name only was discarded—not the thing. A woman became

---

* Dr. WHITGIFT. † Neal, ubi supra, p. 301.

First Presbyterian Church in England.

the head of the church; her opinions were the infallible rule of faith, and she was declared the supreme arbiter of the consciences of her subjects. The monstrous absurdity of these claims was left for subsequent times to explode, and it was not till above a century afterwards, that the genuine principles of religious liberty were throughly discussed and explained. (c) A faithful and elegant delineation of those times may be found in " The History of the Puritans," by the Rev. Daniel Neal, who has done ample justice to his subject. This is a work that does honour to the Dissenters, and will perpetuate the name of its worthy author, as long as just notions of liberty shall be entertained by mankind.

THE BROWNIST CONGREGATION ABOUT LONDON.

THE violent measures pursued by the court, instead of reconciling the Puritans to the Church, drove them further from it. Men who act upon principle, as Mr. Neal judiciously observes,* are not easily moved by the artillery of canons, injunctions, subscriptions, fines, imprisonments, &c. much less will they esteem a church that fights with such weapons. Multitudes, by these methods, were carried away to a total separation, and so far prejudiced as not to allow

(c) The first of our countrymen who discussed this subject upon real Protestant principles, was the learned Dr. John Owen. The track pursued by that great man, was followed, after a few years, by the immortal Locke; since whose time, hosts of able advocates have arisen in the same cause.

* Neal's Puritans, vol. i, p. 251.

the Church of England to be a true church, nor her ministers true ministers; they renounced all communion with her, not only in the prayers and ceremonies, but also in hearing the word and sacraments. These were the people called Brownists, from one Robert Brown, of whose history and principles, we shall here give a brief account.

Robert Brown descended from an ancient and honourable family in Rutlandshire, (D) and was nearly related to the Lord Treasurer Cecil. He received his education in Corpus Christi College, Cambridge, and preached sometime in Bennet Church, where the vehemence of his delivery gained him reputation with the people. Afterwards he became a schoolmaster in Southwark, and then a lecturer at Islington. Having embraced the principles of the Puritans, he resolved to refine upon them, and produce something more perfect of his own. Accordingly, about the year 1580, he began to inveigh openly against the dicipline and ceremonies of the Church of England, which he held up to the people as antichristian. In 1581, he settled at Norwich, where the Dutch having a numerous congregation, many of them imbibed his principles. Growing confident by success, he called in the assistance of one Richard Harrison, a country schoolmaster, and planted churches in different places. It was not long, however, before he was noticed by Dr. Freake, Bishop of Norwich, who committed him to the custody of the Sheriff of the county. After his release, Brown left the kingdom, and settled at Middleburgh in Zealand. There, with the leave of the magistrates, he formed a church after his own model, which he explained in a book he published in 1582, entitled, *" A Treatise of Reformation without tarrying for any, and of the wickedness of those preachers*

(D) His grandfather obtained the singular privilege of wearing his cap in the King's presence, by a charter of Henry viii.

The Brownist Congregation about London.

who will not reform them and their charge, because they will tarry till the Magistrate command and compel them. By me Robert Brown." (E) After he had resided some little time at Middleburg, his people began to quarrel among themselves, and split into parties; insomuch, that Brown growing weary of his office, returned to England in 1585. The same year, he was convened before Archbishop Whitgift, to answer to one of his books; but the prelate having by force of reasoning brought him to submission, dismissed him a second time at the intercession of the Lord Treasurer Burleigh. He then went home to his father's house, and continued there four years. But this lenity making little or no impression upon his mind; his father gave him up to his wandering course of life, and discharged him the family. After travelling up and down the country with his assistant, preaching against the rulers and forms of the church, he went to reside at Northampton. Here his preaching soon gave offence, and he was cited before Lindsell, Bishop of Peterborough, who upon his refusing to appear, publicly excommunicated him for contempt. The solemnity of this censure made such an impression upon Brown, that he renounced his principles of separation, and having obtained absolution, was preferred to the rectory of Achurch, near Oundle, in Northamptonshire. This was about the year 1590. Fuller* does not believe that he ever formally recanted his opinions; but that his promise

---

(E) Besides the above, Brown published two other pieces; one entitled, " A Treatise upon the 23d chapter of Matthew, both for an order of studying and handling the scriptures, and also for avoiding the popish disorders, and ungodly communion of all false christians, and especially of wicked preachers and hirelings."—The title of the other is, " A book which sheweth the life and manners of all true christians, and how unlike they are unto Turks and Papists, and heathen folk. Also the points and parts of all divinity, that is, of the revealed will and word of God, are declared by their different divisions and definitions following.——*Biog. Brit. Art. Brown.* Note E.

* Church History, B. 9. p. 168.

The Brownist Congregation about London.

of a general compliance with the Church of England, improved by the countenance of his patron and kinsman, the Earl of Exeter, prevailed upon the Archbishop to procure him this favor. He adds, that Brown allowed a salary for another person to discharge his cure; and though he opposed his parishioners in judgment, yet agreed in taking their tythes. Brown was a man of good parts and some learning, but his temper was imperious and uncontrolable; and so far was he from the Sabbatarian strictness espoused by his followers, that he seemed rather a libertine than otherwise. In a word, continues our author, he had a wife with whom he never lived, a church in which he never preached, and as all the other scenes of his life were stormy and turbulent, so was his end. For being poor and proud, and very passionate, he struck the constable of his parish, for demanding the payment of certain rates; and being beloved by nobody, the officer summoned him before Sir Rowland St. John, a neighbouring justice, in whose presence he behaved with so much insolence, that he was committed to Northampton gaol. The decrepid old man not being able to walk, was carried thither upon a feather bed in a cart; where not long after, he sickened and died, A. D. 1630, in the 81st year of his age, boasting, "That he had been committed to thirty-two prisons, in some of which he could not see his hand at noon day." Such was the unhappy life and tragical end of Robert Brown, founder of the famous sect, from him called BROWNISTS.[*]

As the principles of these people were greatly misrepresented by their adversaries, it will be proper here to give some account of them. They thought that the form of Church government should be democratical; that every distinct society was a body corporate, having full power within

---

[*] Biog. Brit. vol. ii. Art. Brown.—Fuller's Church History, B. 9. p. 168.—Neal's Puritans, vol. i. p. 252.—Collier's Ecclesiastical History, vol. ii. p. 581.

The Brownist Congregation about London.

itself to admit or exclude members, to choose and ordain officers, and when the good of the society required it, to depose them, without being accountable to any other jurisdiction. They did not allow the priesthood to be a distinct order; any lay brother had the liberty of prophesying, or giving a word of exhortation in their church assemblies; and it was usual after sermon, for some of the members to propose questions, and confer with each other upon the doctrines that had been delivered. They declared against all prescribed forms of prayer; and as for church censures, they were for an entire separation of the ecclesiastical and civil sword. Some of their reasons for withdrawing from the church are not easily answered. They alleged, that the laws of the realm, and the Queen's injunctions, had made several unwarrantable additions to the institutions of Christ: that there were several gross errors in the Church service: that these additions and errors were imposed and made necessary to communion: that if persecution for conscience sake was the mark of a false church, they could not believe the church of England to be a true one. They apprehended further, that the constitution of the hierarchy was too bad to be mended; that the very pillars of it were rotten, and that the structure should be raised anew. Since, therefore, all Christians are obliged to preserve the ordinances of Christ pure and undefiled, they resolved to lay a new foundation, and keep as near as they could to the primitive pattern, though it were at the hazard of all that was dear to them in the world. Such were the principles of the Brownists, whose chief error seems to have been their uncharitableness, in unchurching the whole Christian world but themselves.*
It is apprehended that some of their sentiments bore a near affinity to those adopted in more modern times by the followers of Mr. Glas.

* Neal's Puritans, vol. i. p. 253-4.

The Brownist Congregation about London.

Though the revolt of Brown, broke up his congregation abroad, it was far from destroying the seeds of separation at home. His followers rapidly increased, insomuch that Sir Walter Raleigh declared in the Parliament-house, they were not less than 20,000, divided into several congregations, in Norfolk and Essex, and in the parts adjacent to London. There were, at this time, some persons of considerable learning and piety at their head; as the two Johnsons, Mr. Smith, Mr. Jacob, the learned Mr. Ainsworth, the *rabbi* of his age, and many others.[*]

The congregation about London being pretty numerous, formed themselves into a Church; Mr. Francis Johnson being chosen pastor by the suffrage of the brotherhood, Mr. Greenwood, doctor or teacher, Messrs. Bowman and Lea, deacons, and Messrs. Studley and Kinaston, elders. This service was performed in one day at the house of Mr. Fox, in Nicholas-lane, in the year 1592. At the same time, seven persons were baptized, without godfathers, or godmothers, Mr. Johnson only washing their faces with water, and pronouncing the form " I baptize thee in the name of the Father, &c." The Lord's supper was also administered in this manner: five white loaves being set upon the table, the pastor implored the blessing of God, and having broken the bread, he delivered it to some, and the deacons to the rest, some standing and others sitting about the table, using the words of the Apostle, 1 Cor. xi. 24. Take eat, &c. In like manner he gave the cup, saying, This cup is the New Testament, &c. At the close they sung an hymn, and made a collection for the poor. When any one entered into the church, he made this single protestation or promise, that " he would walk with them so long, as they did walk in the way of the Lord, and as far as might be warranted by the word of God."[†]

The congregation being obliged to meet in different places,

---

[*] Neal's Puritans, vol. i. p. 363.   [†] Neal, ubi supra.

The Brownist Congregation about London.

to hide themselves from the Bishop's officers, was at length discovered on a Lord's day at Islington, in the very same place, where the protestant congregation met in Queen Mary's reign. About 56 were taken prisoners, and sent two by two, to the gaols about London, where several of their friends had been confined for a considerable time. On their examination, they acknowledged to have met in fields, in the summer season, at five o'clock in the morning of the Lord's day, and in winter at private houses; that they continued all day in prayer and expounding the scriptures, dined together, and afterwards made a collection for their diet, and sent the remainder of the money to their brethren in prison; and that they did not use the Lord's prayer, apprehending it not to be intended by our blessed Saviour, to be used as a form after the pouring out of the Spirit on the day of Pentecost. Their adversaries charged them with many extravagancies about baptism, marriage, lay preaching, &c. from which they vindicated themselves in a very solid and judicious reply, shewing how far they disowned, and with what limitations they acknowledged the charge.* Notwithstanding their artless confession, Mr. Smith, one of their ministers, was remanded to the Clink, and his brethren to the Fleet, where, by order of Mr. Justice Young, they were confined in solitary cells. Here they died in great numbers, some for want, and others of infectious diseases. Among those who thus perished, was one Roger Rippon, who dying in Newgate, his fellow-prisoners wrote the following inscription upon his coffin.

" This is the corps of Roger Rippon, a servant of Christ,
" and her Majesty's faithful subject; who is the last of 16 or
" 17, which that great enemy of God, the Archbishop of
" Canterbury, (Dr. John Whitgift) with his high commis-
" sioners, have murdered in Newgate, within these five
" years, manifestly for the testimony of Jesus Christ. His
" soul is now with the Lord, and his blood cries for ven-

* Neal, ubi supra.

"geance against that great enemy of the saints, and against
"Mr. Richard Young, (a justice of peace in London,) who
"in this and many like points, hath abused his power for
"the upholding of the Romish Antichrist, prelacy, and
"priesthood. He died A. D. 1592."*

But the severities against these pious and conscientious persons, did not end here; six of them were publicly executed as felons,(F) and others proscribed and banished their country. Among the latter were Mr. Francis Johnson, Mr. Henry Ainsworth, Mr. John Smith, Mr. John Robinson, Mr. Henry Jacob and others, who with leave of the States of Holland, erected churches after their own model at Amsterdam, Arnheim, Middleburg, Leyden, and other places.† Of Mr. Jacob we shall have occasion to speak in the next article; the other names require some biographical notice in this place.

FRANCIS JOHNSON. Of Mr. Johnson's early life, no particulars have reached us. He was, probably bred up at Cambridge, and had a living in the establishment; but embracing the sentiments of the Brownists, became one of their principal leaders. The Puritans of those times despairing of any further reformation, published a book, entitled, "The holy discipline of the Church, described in the word of God;" which being revised, was subscribed with the names of above five hundred Divines, all beneficed in the Church of England. Among these, occurs the name of Johnson.‡ About 1591, he was apprehended and committed to prison, together with some leading ministers among the Puritans, for refusing the oath *ex officio*; but after some time, upon compliance, they were released.§ The formation of

---

* Neal, ubi supra, p. 366-7.

(F) These were Edmund Coppinger, Elias Thacker, John Greenwood, Henry Barrow, John Penry, and —— Dennis.

† Neal, ubi supra, p. 386.   ‡ Neal's Puritans, vol. i. p. 234.

§ Ibid. p. 358.

the Brownist congregation, in 1592, and the choice of Mr. Johnson for pastor has been already noticed. The following year, he was convicted upon the statute of 31 Eliz. " To retain the Queen's subjects in their obedience."* This act condemned the Puritans to indiscriminate banishment. Johnson retiring to Amsterdam, there erected a church after the model of the Brownists, having the learned Mr. Henry Ainsworth for doctor or teacher.† In 1598, they drew up a confession of their faith in Latin, and dedicated it to the universities of Leyden, St. Andrews, Heidelberg, Geneva, and the other seminaries of Holland, Scotland, Germany, and France. It was afterwards translated into English, and does not differ much in doctrine from the harmony of confessions.‡

Johnson was a learned man, but rigid in his principles, and his people entertaining discordant sentiments, it was not long before they split into parties. Three principal subjects of debate, appear to have divided them. The first was occasioned by the marriage of Francis Johnson to a widow of competent fortune, whom his brother George and his father thought an improper match in those times of persecution.(G) Frequent disputes took place from 1594, the time of the marriage, till 1598 or 1599, when George Johnson, his father, and some members of the church attached to them, were put away on account of their behaviour in this affair. The greater number took part with Francis the pastor.§ The next subject of dispute, related to matters of doctrine, more especially baptism, which occasioned a schism in the church, headed by Mr. John Smyth, who settled with his followers at Amsterdam, and afterwards at Leyden.||

* Neal's Puritans, vol. i. p. 380.   † Ibid. p. 436.
‡ Life of Ainsworth prefixed to his " two treatises," 1789.
(G) George Johnson represents her as addicted to luxurious living, excess of finery in dress, and a lover of ease.——*Life of Ainsworth, ubi supra.*
§ Life of Ainsworth, ubi supra. || Ibid.

The Brownist Congregation about London.

The third controversy is confounded by Mr. Neal,* with the first, but it happened many years afterwards, and was occasioned by a dispute between Johnson the pastor and Ainsworth the teacher, on the question of discipline, which caused another division. Francis Johnson placed the government of the church in the eldership alone; Ainsworth in the church of which the elders are a part. The event was, that Johnson excommunicated Ainsworth and his half of the church; and the common account is, that Ainsworth returned the compliment upon the opposite party; but there seems no foundation for the latter charge. On the contrary, Mr. Cotton of New England observes, that "Mr. Ainsworth and his company did not excommunicate Johnson and his party, but only withdrew, when they could no longer live peaceably."† Ainsworth and his adherents held a separate assembly in Amsterdam, and the two congregations were afterwards distinguished as Franciscan and Ainsworthian Brownists. Johnson appears to have removed soon after to Embden, where he died, and his congregation dissolved. (H)

HENRY AINSWORTH. It is much to be regretted that we can say so little concerning a man, whose uncommon skill in Hebrew learning, and whose excellent commentaries on the sacred scriptures, have justly gained him a large share of reputation. Though a native of England, we know of him only as residing in Holland; but at what time he

---

* Hist. of the Puritans, vol. i. p. 406.
† Cotton's Way of Congregational Churches, p. 6.

(H) Mr. Johnson published several pieces in vindication of his particular sentiments; as, "An Answer to White's Discoverie of Brownism, 1606."—"Certayne Reasons and Arguments, proving that it is not lawful to hear, or have any spiritual communion with the present ministry of the Church of England, 1601," &c. &c. He also wrote against Smyth, in defence of infant baptism; and published some other pieces upon the controversies of the times, the titles of which have not reached us.——*Life of Ainsworth*, *ubi supra.*

The Brownist Congregation about London.

removed thither is not exactly ascertained. It is probable, however, that he accompanied the Brownists in their general banishment, about 1593, having previously shared in their persecutions. Mr. Neal enumerating some books written against the Church of England, and seized by authority in 1589, notices one under the title of " Counter Poison," &c.* The author of this book, though not mentioned, was our Ainsworth; and as it probably drew him into danger and difficulties, so it hastened his departure. Ainsworth was certainly in Holland in 1596, when he corresponded with the celebrated Junius. Hoornbeck relates, that he made a voyage from thence to Ireland, and left some disciples there.† His external circumstances at Amsterdam, like those of the church in general, were very abject. He is said to have been porter to a bookseller, who first discovered his skill in the Hebrew language, and made it known to his countrymen. Roger Williams, the founder of Providence Plantation in New-England, in whose testimony we have reason to confide, informs us, that " he lived there upon ninepence a week, and some boiled roots."‡ The account the Brownists give of themselves is, that " they were almost consumed with deep poverty; loaded with reproaches; despised and afflicted by all."§ The reception they met with, from a people just emerging from civil and religious oppression, was very different to what might have been expected. The civil power, commonly in every state, more friendly to toleration than the ecclesiastic, does not, indeed, seem to have troubled them. But the Dutch clergy regarded them with a jealous eye; and they appear to have been screened from persecution chiefly by their own insignificance.|| During this season of trial, Mr. Ainsworth did not remain idle; for most of his books were written at this period, and are evi-

* Neal, ubi supra, p. 338.   † Summa Controversiarum, p. 740.
‡ Cotton's Reply to Williams, p. 119.
§ Epist. Frat. Ang. F. Junio, apud Epist. Præstant. et Erudit.
|| Life of Ainsworth, ubi supra.

dently the fruit of great reading and application. The first work in which we find him engaged was, a translation of the Brownist Confession of Faith into the Latin language. It appeared in 1598, and was dedicated to the universities of Leyden, &c. as noticed before.* In this confession the Brownists did not intend to erect a standard for the faith of others, but merely to vindicate themselves from that odium under which they rested, as discontented and factious sectaries. How different was their conduct in this respect from that of the most famous councils and synods, which, while compiling systems of faith and tests of orthodoxy for other nations and ages, have sown the seeds of discord, and rendered man the enemy of man.

We have already noticed the unhappy divisions that afflicted the Brownist church at Amsterdam. In the first, Ainsworth took part with Johnson the pastor; but was so much grieved at the unnatural heats which the controversy excited, that he spoke of laying down his office as teacher. In the next controversy, Ainsworth took an active part against Smyth, who had espoused some sentiments afterwards maintained by Arminius, and added to them a rejection of infant-baptism. Of the third division, in which Ainsworth was personally concerned, he published a particular account in a book with the following title: " An animadversion to Mr. Richard Clifton's advertisement, who under pretence of answering Chr. Laune's book, hath published another man's private letter, with Mr. Francis Johnson's answer thereto. Which letter is here justified; the answer thereto refuted; and the true causes of the lamentable breach that hath lately fallen out in the English exiled church at Amsterdam, manifested. 1713." The occasion of this breach seems to have been a difference of opinion with respect to church discipline.† A second congregation was formed at Amsterdam under the superintendence of Ainsworth, who is said to have

---

* Life of Ainsworth, ubi supra.   † Ibid.

The Brownist Congregation about London.

been succeeded by the well known Mr. John Canne, author of marginal references to the Bible.* Of this celebrated person we shall have occasion to speak hereafter.†

It is a circumstance that deserves to be recorded to the honour of Ainsworth, that in the midst of the various controversies that employed his pen, he preserved a meek and christian spirit, and cultivated those studies which were more congenial to his profession, as they were more beneficial to the interests of mankind. His great work, the " Annotations on the Five Books of Moses, the Psalms, and the Song of Songs," was published separately in quarto, in 1612, and some following years. In 1627, they were collected together and reprinted at London, in one volume folio, and again in 1639. This last edition is said to be very rare, and is inserted in all the catalogues of scarce books. As to the execution of the work, its merit has been established by the strongest testimonies of foreign as well as British Divines. Succeeding critics have adopted his remarks, and he is frequently cited by modern commentators. Dr. Doddridge observes, " Ainsworth on the Pentateuch is a good book, full of very valuable Jewish learning; and his translation in many places to be preferred to others, especially in the Psalms."‡ The whole work was translated into Dutch, and printed at Leuwarden, in 1690; as was a German translation of the Song of Solomon, at Frankfort, in 1692. It should be remarked, that Ainsworth's works are more valued abroad than in his own country, insomuch that it is not easy to produce an English writer oftener quoted, or with greater testimonies to his merit, and this by the learned of all sects and opinions.§

The manner of Ainsworth's death, as related by Mr. Neal, was sudden and singular, and not without strong

* Neal's Puritans, vol. i. p. 437. † See Art. *Deadman's Place.*
‡ Doddridge's Preaching Lectures. § Biog. Brit. Art. Ainsworth.

suspicion of violence. For it is reported, that having found a diamond of great value in the streets of Amsterdam, he advertised it in print; and when the owner, who was a Jew, came to demand it, he offered him any acknowledgment he desired. Ainsworth, however, though poor, would accept of nothing but a conference with some of the Rabbies, upon the prophecies of the Old Testament relating to the Messiah, which the other promised; but not having interest sufficient to obtain, it is thought he caused him to be poisoned.* Other accounts say, that he obtained this conference, and so confounded the Jews, that from spite and malice they in this manner put a period to his life.† A modern writer,‡ however, seems to doubt the truth of the whole account, from the circumstance of its not being mentioned by any of the editors of his posthumous pieces. Mr. Ainsworth's death, by whatever cause it was produced, happened at the end of the year 1622, or beginning of 1623.§

Besides the pieces already mentioned, he published a treatise " Of the Communion of Saints;" and another entitled, " An arrow against idolatry." These were reprinted together at Edinburgh in 1789; and to this edition was prefixed a very copious and interesting account of the author. He also wrote some other pieces of a controversial nature, the titles of which are specified below. (1)

---

* Neal's Puritans, ubi supra.   † Account of his Life, ubi supra.
‡ Dr. Stewart, author of his Life.   § Life of Ainsworth, ubi supra.

(1) " A Defence of the Holy Scriptures, Worship and Ministry, used in the Christian churches separated from Antichrist, against the challenges, cavils and contradictions of M. Smyth, in his book entitled, ' The Differences of the churches of the separation.' Whereunto are annexed, a few animadversions upon some of M. Smyth's censures in his answer made to M. Bernard. By Henry Ainsworth, Teacher of the English exiled church at Amsterdam. 1690."—" The trying out of the truth, begun and prosequuted in certain letters and passages between John Aynsworth and Henry Aynsworth : the one pleading for, the other against the present religion of the church of Rome. 1615."—" Reply to the pretended Christian plea for *the antichristian church of Rome, published against Francis Johnson.* 1620."—

The Brownist Congregation about London.

Whatever engaged the pen of Ainsworth, was received with proper respect, even by his adversaries; who, while they disapproved his sentiments, could not fail to admire his abilities. The worthy Dr. Hall, Bishop of Norwich, who wrote against the Brownists, always speaks of him as the greatest man of his party; and refers to him as their Doctor, their Chief, their Rabbi.* He was unquestionably a person of profound learning, exquisitely versed in the scriptures, and deeply read in the Rabbins. He possessed a strong understanding, a quick penetration, and wonderful diligence. His temper was meek and amiable, his zeal for divine truth fervent, and he conducted himself with great moderation towards his adversaries. With the character of Ainsworth, drawn by the editor of one of his posthumous pieces,† we shall close this account of him. " For the life of the man, myself being an eye-witness, living some while with him at Amsterdam, of his humility, sobriety, and discretion, setting aside his preposterous zeal in the point and practice of separation, he lived and died unblamable to the world; and I am thoroughly persuaded that his soul rests with his Saviour."‡

" *An advertisement touching some objections against the sincerity of the Hebrew text; and the allegations of the Rabbins.*" This piece was reprinted in his Annotations. Ainsworth also published, " The Book of Psalms, Englished both in prose and metre; with annotations opening the words and sentences by conference with other Scriptures." An edition of this book was printed at Amsterdam in 1644. A large treatise entitled " A Guide to Sion," is also attributed to our author. His posthumous pieces are, " A seasonable discourse; or, a Censure upon a Dialogue of the Anabaptists, entitled, A Description of what God hath predestinated concerning man. 1643." This piece was reprinted in 1644.—" Certain Notes of Mr. Ainsworth's last Sermon on 1 Pet. ii. 4, 5. 1630."—" The old orthodox foundation of religion, *long since collected by that judicious and eloquent man, Mr. Henry Ainsworth, for the benefit of his private company, and now divulged for the public good of all that desire to know that Corner Stone, Jesus Christ crucified.* By S. W. London. 1641."——*Life of Ainsworth, ubi supra.*

* Bishop Hall's Apology for the Church of England.
† " The old orthodox foundation of religion," &c.
‡ Neal's Puritans, vol. i. p. 436.—Biog. Brit. Art. Ainsworth.—Account of his Life, ubi supra.

The Brownist Congregation about London.

JOHN SMYTH, of whom mention has been made in the preceding account, seems to have been beneficed at Gainsborough in Lincolnshire. At what precise period he embraced the principles of the Brownists we are not informed; but he is spoken of as one of their leaders in 1592. Before he separated, he spent nine months in studying the controversy;[*] and held a disputation with Mr. Hildersham, and some other Divines, on conformity to the ceremonies, and the use of prescribed forms of prayer.[†] In the above county, and on the borders of Nottinghamshire and Yorkshire, the principles of the separation made an extensive impression.[‡] Two churches were formed, in one of which Mr. Smyth presided; in the other Mr. Robinson and Mr. Clifton. Being harassed by the High Commission Court, they removed to Holland. Mr. Smyth and his followers settled at Amsterdam, A. D. 1606, and joined themselves to the English church of which Johnson was pastor, and Ainsworth teacher. It was not long, however, before a very serious breach took place. The subjects of debate that gave rise to this division, were certain opinions very similar to those afterwards espoused by Arminius. Smyth maintained the doctrines of free-will and universal redemption; he opposed the predestination of particular individuals to eternal life; as also the doctrine of original sin; and maintained that believers might fall from that grace which would have saved them had they continued in it. He seems also to have entertained some absurd and enthusiastic notions; such as the unlawfulness of reading the scriptures in public worship; that no translation of the Bible was the word of God; that singing the praises of God in verses, or set words, was without authority; that flight in time of persecution was unlawful; that the new-creature needed not the

---

[*] Life of Ainsworth prefixed to his two treatises.
[†] Crosby's History of the English Baptists, vol. i. p. 265.
[‡] Neal's Hist. of New England, v. i. p. 75.

support of scriptures and ordinances, but is above them; that perfection is attainable in the present life, &c.*

Smyth differed from his brethren likewise on the subject of baptism. The Brownists, as we have already remarked, denied the Church of England to be a true church, or her ministers as acting under a divine commission; consequently, every ordinance administered by them, was null and void. They were guilty, however, of this inconsistency, that while they re-ordained their pastors and teachers, they never thought of repeating their baptism. This defect was easily discovered by Smyth; whose doubts concerning the validity of baptism as administered in the natural church, paved the way for his rejecting the baptism of infants altogether. Upon a further consideration of the subject, he saw grounds to consider immersion as the true and only meaning of the word baptism, and that it should be administered to those alone who were capable of professing their faith in Christ. The absurdity of Smyth's conduct appeared in nothing more conspicuous than in this: That not choosing to apply to the German Baptists, and wanting a proper administrator, he baptized himself, which procured him to be called a Se-Baptist.† Crosby, indeed, has taken great pains to vindicate him from this charge, though it seems with little success.‡ His principles and conduct soon drew upon him an host of opponents, the chief of whom were Johnson, Ainsworth, Robinson, Jessop and Clifton.§ The controversy began in 1606, about the time Smyth settled at Amsterdam. Soon afterwards he removed with his followers to Leyden, where he

---

* Life of Ainsworth, ubi supra.—Crosby, ubi supra, p. 92, 267.
† Life of Ainsworth, ubi supra —Neal's Puritans, vol. i. p. 437.
‡ Hist. English Baptists, vol. i. p. 95.
§ Smyth wrote several books in vindication of himself and his opinions; as " Parallels and Censures. 1609."—" Character of the Beast."—" Differences of the Churches of the separation."—" A Dialogue of Baptism."—" Reply to Mr. Clifton's Christian Plea;" and probably others, the titles of which have not reached us.——*Life of Ainsworth, ubi supra.—Crosby, ubi supra, p.* 268.

continued to publish various books in defence of his opinions, till his death in the year 1610. The following year appeared " The Confession of Faith, published in certain conclusions, by the remainder of Mr. Smyth's company:" with an appendix giving some account of his last sickness and death.* A few articles of this confession are preserved by Crosby.†

Mr. Smyth was succeeded in the pastoral office by Mr. THOMAS HELWISSE, a member of his congregation; who, after sometime began to reflect on the conduct of himself and his friends in deserting their country on account of persecution. He resolved, therefore, to return home, that he might share the same lot with his suffering brethren. Being accompanied by the greater part of his congregation, they settled in London, where they gained many proselytes, and became, as is not improbably conjectured, the first *General-Baptist* Society in this kingdom.‡ How long Mr. Helwisse continued the elder of this church, or who succeeded him, we are no where informed. It is greatly to be lamented that no authentic records are preserved of the early state of many of our churches. For want of these, the reader will find many chasms in the subsequent part of our history; and where he may look for certain information, we shall be often guided by the dubious hand of conjecture.

JOHN ROBINSON. This excellent Divine received his education in the University of Cambridge. He was afterwards beneficed near Yarmouth in Norfolk,§ in which neighbourhood he had a separate congregation, which assembled in private houses, for about seven or eight years. But, being frequently disturbed by the Bishop's officers, and his friends almost ruined in the ecclesiastical courts,|| he remo-

---

* Crosby,—and the Life of Ainsworth, ubi supra.
† Appendix to vol. i. and ii.   ‡ Crosby, vol. i. p. 269—276.
§ Neal's Puritans, vol. i. p. 427.
|| Neal's Hist. New-England, vol. i. p. 72-3.

The Brownist Congregation about London.

ved with his congregation to Amsterdam, in 1608,* having encountered great dangers in their passage at sea, as well as at their embarkation.† There, with the leave of the magistrates, they hired a meeting-house; and Mr. Robinson having formed a church upon the model of the Brownists, they worshipped God publicly in their own way.‡ At this time, the English exiles were greatly embroiled among themselves: the controversy between Smyth and the other Brownists was carried on with great warmth, insomuch, that Amsterdam proved too hot for the gentle spirit of Robinson, who, after a year's residence there, removed with his congregation to Leyden.§

Robinson set out upon the most rigid principles of Brownism; but after he had seen more of the world, and conversed with learned men, particularly Dr. Ames, he became more moderate, and struck out a middle way between the Brownists and Presbyterians. Though he always maintained the lawfulness and necessity of separating from the Reformed Churches where he resided, yet he was far from denying them to be true Churches. He even admitted their members to occasional communion, and allowed his own people to join with the Dutch churches in prayer and hearing the word, though not in the sacraments and discipline. This procured him the character of a Semi-Separatist.‖ He maintained that every church or society of Christians, had complete power within itself to choose its own officers, to administer all gospel-ordinances, and to exercise all acts of authority and discipline over its members; consequently that it was independent upon all classes, synods, convocations and councils. He allowed, indeed, the expediency of these grave assemblies for reconciling differences among churches, and giving them friendly advice; but not for the exercise of any authority without the free consent of

* Life of Ainsworth, ubi supra. † Prince Chronology, p. 5, 6, &c.
‡ Neal, ubi supra. § Life of Ainsworth, ubi supra.
‖ Neal's Puritans, ubi supra.

the churches themselves.* These are some of the principles by which the *Independents* are distinguished in the present day.

When Mr. Robinson had been settled some years at Leyden, his congregation, through the death of some aged members, and the marriage of their children into Dutch families, began to decline. This put them upon consulting how to preserve their church and religion, then likely to be lost in a strange land. At home there was not the least prospect of a reformation, nor even of a toleration for such as dissented from the establishment. At length, after spending many days in solemn addresses to heaven for direction, it was resolved that part of the congregation, should transport themselves to America, where they might enjoy liberty of conscience, and be capable of encouraging their friends and countrymen to follow them. They accordingly, sent over agents into England, who having obtained a patent from the crown, agreed with several merchants to become adventurers in the undertaking. Several of Mr. Robinson's congregation sold their estates, and made a common bank, with which they purchased a small ship of sixty tons, and hired another of one hundred and eighty. The agents sailed into Holland with their own ship, to take in as many of the congregation as were willing to embark, while the other vessel was freighting with necessaries for the new plantation. All things being ready, Mr. Robinson observed a day of fasting and prayer with his congregation, and preached an excellent sermon from Ezra viii. 21. *I proclaimed a fast there, at the river Ahava, that we might afflict our souls before God, to seek of him a right way for us, and for our little ones, and for all our substance.*

He then took leave of them with the following truly generous and christian exhortation.

* Neal's New-England, ubi supra.

The Brownist Congregation about London.

" Brethren,

" We are now quickly to part from one another, and whether I may ever live to see your faces upon earth any more, the God of heaven only knows; but whether the Lord has appointed that or no, I charge you before God and his blessed angels, that you follow me no farther than you have seen me follow the Lord Jesus Christ. If God reveal any thing to you by any other instrument of his, be as ready to receive it as ever you was to receive any truth by my ministry; for I am verily persuaded, the Lord has more truth yet to break forth out of his holy word. For my part, I cannot sufficiently bewail the condition of the Reformed Churches, who are come to a period in religion, and will go at present no farther than the instruments of their reformation. The Lutherans cannot be drawn to go beyond what Luther said; whatever part of his will our God has revealed to Calvin, they will rather die than embrace it; and the Calvinists, you see stick fast where they were left by that great man of God, who yet saw not all things. This is a misery much to be lamented, for though they were burning and shining lights in their times, yet they penetrated not into the whole council of God, but were they now living, would be as willing to embrace further light as that which they first received. I beseech you remember, it is an article of your church covenant, that *you be ready to receive whatever truth shall be made known to you from the written word of God.* Remember that, and every other article of your sacred covenant. But I must herewithal exhort you to take heed what you receive as truth; examine it, consider it, and compare it with other scriptures of truth, before you receive it; for it is not possible the Christian world should come so lately out of such thick anti-christian darkness, and that perfection of knowledge should break

" forth at once. I must also advise you to abandon, avoid,
" and shake off the name of BROWNISTS; it is a mere
" nick-name, and a brand for the making religion and the
" professors of it odious to the Christian world."

On the first of July, 1620, this small band of Christian adventurers (in number about one hundred and twenty) went from Leyden to Delfthaven, whither Mr. Robinson and the elders of his congregation accompanied them. They continued together all night; and next morning, after mutual embraces, Mr. Robinson kneeled down on the sea-shore, and with a fervent prayer committed them to the protection and blessing of heaven.* The leader of the Colony was Mr. William Brewster, a wise and prudent man, of whom the reader will find some account in the note below.(k) Mr.

* Neal's Puritans, ubi supra. p. 490.—New-England, p. 78-79.

(k) Mr. William Brewster received a learned education in the University of Cambridge. His first employment was in the service of Mr. Davison, Secretary of State to Queen Elizabeth, with whom he went over to Holland, and was entrusted with affairs of great importance, particularly with the keys of the cautionary towns. He afterwards lived much respected in his own country, till the severity of the times obliged him to return to Holland, where he became first a member, and afterwards a ruling elder of Mr. Robinson's congregation at Leyden. When he was sixty years of age, he had the courage and resolution to put himself at the head of the colony, which first peopled New-England. They sailed from Delfthaven August 5, and, after a long and dangerous voyage, arrived at Cape Cod, November 9, 1620. Upon their landing they divided the ground by lot, according to the number of persons in each family; and having agreed upon some laws, chose a governor, and named the place of their settlement NEW-PLYMOUTH. Inexpressible were the hardships they underwent the first winter. The fatigues of their late voyage, the severity of the weather, and the want of necessaries occasioned a sad mortality, which swept away half the colony; and of those who remained alive, not above six or seven at a time were capable of helping the rest. But as the spring returned they began to recover, and receiving some fresh supplies from England, they maintained their station, and laid the foundation of one of the noblest settlements in America, which after that time proved an asylum for the Protestant Nonconformists under all their oppressions. Mr Brewster shared the fatigues and hardships of the infant colony with the utmost bravery. He was not an ordained minister,

The Brownist Congregation about London.

Robinson designed to accompany the remaining part of his congregation to America, in person, but before he could fulfil his intention, it pleased God to remove him to a better world, in the fiftieth year of his age, A. D. 1626. The life of this amiable man, both in public and private, exhibited a fair transcript of those numerous virtues that elevate and adorn the human character. In his younger days, he was distinguished for good sense and solid learning; and as his mind began to expand, he acquired that moderate and pacific temper for which he was greatly celebrated among Christians of different communions. His uncommon probity and diffusive benevolence recommended him highly to the Dutch ministers and professors, with whom he lived in the most perfect harmony. They lamented his death as a public loss; and as a testimony of their esteem and affection, though he was not of their communion, honoured with their presence his funeral solemnities. Mr. Robinson wrote several learned treatises to justify his separation from the Church of England, which were universally esteemed, and reprinted after his death. (L) He was indeed an admirable disputant, as appears by his public disputations in the University of Leyden, when the Arminian controversy agitated and divided

but being a man of learning and piety, he preached to them above seven years, till they could provide themselves with a pastor. He was held in the greatest respect both by the magistrates and people; and after a long life, in which he suffered much on account of religion, he died in peace, April 18, 1643, in the 84th year of his age.——*Neal's Hist. New-England*, vol. i. p. 79 and 211.

(L) The following are the titles of such of Mr. Robinson's pieces as have come to our knowledge: " A Justification of Separation from the Church of England, against Bernard. 1610."—" A Treatise on Communion, &c. 1614."—" Apologia justa et necessaria quorundam Christianorum, æque contumeliose ac communitæ dictorum *Brownistarum* ac *Barrowistarum*, per Johannem Robinsonum, Anglo-Leidensem, suo, et ecclesiæ nomine, cui præficitur. 1619."—A Translation of the same book by himself. 1644.—An Appendix to Mr. Perkins's Six Principles of Christian Religion. 1641.—He also wrote some pieces against Smyth in the controversy concerning Baptism, and on some points of christian doctrine.——*Life of Ainsworth, ubi supra.*

the churches of Holland. The death of this excellent man proved a serious loss to the remaining branch of the church at Leyden, which immediately separated. Most of the members retired to Amsterdam; but, after a few years, joined their brethren in New-England.* This Mr. Robinson was the father of the *Independents,*

FIRST INDEPENDENT CHURCH IN ENGLAND,

IN the preceding article, we have traced the origin of the Independents to Mr. Robinson; it will be proper now to observe, that Mr. Jacob having embraced his sentiments of discipline and Church government, transplanted them into his own country, and laid the foundation of the FIRST INDEPENDENT CHURCH IN ENGLAND.

HENRY JACOB was a native of Kent, and born about the year 1563. At sixteen years of age, he became a commoner of St. Mary-Hall, Oxford, and took the degrees in arts. Entering into holy orders, he was made precentor of Christ Church College, and afterwards beneficed at Cheriton in his native county; but he must have quitted this living before 1591. Wood describes him as a most zealous Puritan.† It was about this time that he embraced the principles of the Brownists; though he never carried them to that uncharitable extent which was the worst feature in their character. Upon the general banishment of that people, in

* Neal's New-England, vol. i. p. 110.—Morse's American Geography, p. 157. † Wood's Athenæ, vol. j. p. 464,

First Independent Church in England.

1593, Mr. Jacob retired to Holland,* but must have returned to England before 1597. In that year, a controversy arose concerning the true interpretation of that article in the Apostle's Creed which related to the descent of Christ into hell. Bishop Bilson, in some sermons at Paul's Cross, maintained the literal sense of the passage; and affirmed that he went thither not to suffer, but to wrest the keys of hell and death out of the hands of the devil. This seems to have been the prevailing doctrine of the times.† The first of our countrymen who ventured to oppose it was the celebrated Mr. Hugh Broughton, who fully demonstrated that the word *hades* did not mean hell, the abode of the wicked; but the state of the dead, or the invisible world.‡ The Bishop's sermons had not made their appearance long in the world, before Mr. Jacob drew up a reply, which he published under the following title; " A Treatise of the Sufferings and Victory of Christ in the work of our Redemption, &c. written against certain Errors in these points, publicly preached in London, 1597. *Lond.* 1598. oct." The points defended by Mr. Jacob, in the above treatise, were (1.) That Christ suffered for us the wrath of God, which we may well term the pains of hell, or hellish sorrows. (2.) That the soul of Christ, after his death, did not actually descend into hell. In 1600 he published his " Defence of a treatise touching the Sufferings and Victory of Christ in the work of our Redemption."§ The writings of Mr. Jacob and other Puritans upon this subject, roused the attention and indignation of Queen Elizabeth, who commanded the Bishop " Neither to desert the doctrine, nor to let the calling which he bore in the Church of God to be trampled under foot by such unquiet refusers of truth and authoritie."‖ This occasioned him to write his " Survey of

* Neal's Puritans, vol. i. p. 386.   † Ibid. p. 391.
‡ Biog. Brit. vol. ii. Art. Broughton.
§ Wood's Athenæ Oxon. vol. i. p. 465.
‖ Biog. Brit. vol. ii. Art. Bilson.

Christ's Sufferings for Man's Redemption: and of his descent to Hades, or Hel, for our deliverance. *Lond.* 1604."*
Prior to the publication of his last treatise, Mr. Jacob appears to have removed to Amsterdam, where he was engaged in some disputes with the Brownists. The question agitated was, " Whether the Church of England be a true Church." This the Brownists generally denied; but was affirmed and defended by Mr. Jacob, who was much less rigid in his opinions. The particulars of this controversy may be gathered from a book he published in 1599, entitled, " Of the Church and Ministry of England, written in two Treatises against the Reasons and Objections of Mr. Francis Johnson. *Middleburg.* 1599. 4to." It was during these debates, and about the year last mentioned, that he settled at Middleburg in Zealand, where he gathered a church among the English exiles, over whom he continued pastor several years. Though Mr. Jacob considered the Church of England to be a true church, yet he believed there were several things appended to her discipline and worship that needed Reformation. Accordingly, in 1604, he published his thoughts upon this subject, in a treatise entitled, " Reasons taken out of God's word and the best human Testimonies, proving a Necessity of Reforming our Churches of England, &c." The same year, he gave to the public, " A position against vain-glorious, and that which is falsely called, learned preaching." This piece was designed to expose the quibbling and scholastic method of preaching, so prevalent in his time. About 1609 or 1610, Mr. Jacob performed a journey to Leyden, where conversing with Mr. Robinson, he embraced his opinions of church-government, since known by the name of Independency.† This change in his sentiments appears to have been the result of cool and deliberate inquiry; and he published to the world the result of his convictions in a treatise

---

* Biog. Brit. vol. ii. Art. Bilson.
† Neal's Puritans, vol. ii. p. 438, 476.

First Independent Church in England.

entitled, " The Divine beginning and institution of Christ's true, visible, and material Church. *Leyden*, 1610. 8vo." Soon after the publication of this piece he returned to his congregation at Middleburg. The following year he drew up a treatise, designed to explain and confirm the former one, entitled, " A Declaration and opening of certain Points, with a sound Confirmation of some others, in a treatise entitled, *The Divine beginning, &c. Middleburg.* 1611."*

Mr. Jacob, after being absent several years from his native country, returned to London in the year 1616. Here he formed a design of raising a separate congregation, similar to those in Holland; and imparted his intention to Mr. Dod, and some other learned Puritans, who foreseeing no prospect of a national reformation, expressed their entire approbation of his conduct. He accordingly summoned several of his friends together; and having obtained their consent to unite in church-fellowship, for a purer administration of Christian Ordinances, laid the foundation of the first Independent or Congregational Church in England. The method of proceeding upon this occasion was as follows :—Having observed a day of solemn fasting and prayer for a blessing upon their undertaking, each member of the society, towards the close of the solemnity, made a public confession of his faith in Jesus Christ. Then standing together, they joined hands, and *solemnly covenanted with each other, in the presence of Almighty God, to walk together in all God's ways and ordinances, according as he had already revealed, or should further make known to them.* Mr. Jacob was chosen their pastor by the suffrage of the brotherhood, and proper persons were appointed to the office of deacons, with fasting and prayer, and imposition of hands. The same year, (1616) Mr. Jacob published " A Protestation, or Confession, in the name of certain Christians, shewing how far they agreed with the

---

* Wood's Athenæ Oxon; ubi supra.

First Independent Church in England.

Church of England, and wherein they differed, with the reasons of their dissent drawn from Scripture." To this piece was added, a petition to the King for the Toleration of such Christians. This was followed soon after, by another piece, entitled, " A Collection of sound Reasons, shewing how necessary it is for all Christians to walk in all the ways and ordinances of God in purity, and in a right way."—Mr. Jacob continued with his congregation about eight years, but in 1624, being desirous to extend his usefulness, he went with their consent to Virginia, where he soon after died.*

JOHN LATHORP. Upon Mr. Jacob's retiring to America, the congregation chose for his successor a Mr. John Lathorp, of whose history but few particulars have reached us. He was trained to the ministry in the Church of England, and received his education, most probably, in the University of Cambridge. Afterwards he had a living in Kent, but renouncing his orders, became pastor of this little society. The congregation, which had hitherto assembled in private, and shifted from house to house, began now to assume courage, and ventured to shew themselves in public. It was not long, however, before they were discovered by Tomlinson the Bishop's pursuevant, at the house of Mr. Humphrey Barnet, a brewer's clerk, in Black-Fryars; where, on April 29, 1632, forty-two of them were apprehended, and only eighteen escaped. Of those who were taken, some were confined in the Clink, and others in New Prison and the Gate-House, where they continued about two years. They were then released upon bail, except Mr. Lathorp, for whom no favour could be obtained. He therefore petitioned the King for liberty to depart the kingdom; which being granted, he went in the year 1634, to New-England, being accompanied thither by about thirty of his congre-

* Neal's Puritans, vol. i. p. 446-7.

First Independent Church in England.

gation. Mr. Lathorp was a man of learning, and of a meek and quiet spirit; but met with some uneasiness from his people, upon the following occasion. It appears that some of the society entertained doubts as to the validity of baptism performed by their own minister; and one person who indulged these scruples, carried his child to be re-baptized at the parish-church. This giving offence to several persons, the subject was discussed at a general meeting of the society; when the question being put, it was carried in the negative, and resolved by the majority, not to make any declaration at present, *Whether or no parish churches were true churches?* This decision being unacceptable to the more rigid, they desired their dismission; and uniting with some others who were dissatisfied about the lawfulness of infant-baptism, formed a new society, which was the earliest of the Baptist denomination, in London. This separation took place in the year 1633.* The remainder of Mr. Lathorp's Church renewed their covenant, *to walk together in the ways of God, so far as he had made them known, or should make them known to them, and to forsake all false ways;* and so steady were they to their vows, that hardly an instance can be produced of one that deserted the church, under the severest persecutions.† Mr. Lathorp, being driven from his native country, settled at Barnstable, in New-England, where he formed a congregation; but how long he survived, or what became of him afterwards, we are no where informed.

HENRY JESSEY, M. A.—After Mr. Lathorp's removal, the congregation chose for his successor the learned Mr. Henry Jessey. This amiable and pious divine, was born Sept. 3, 1601, at West Rowton, in the North Riding

---

* Crosby's History of the English Baptists, vol. i. p. 148.
† Neal's Puritans, vol. i. p. 662-3.

of Yorkshire, near which place his father was minister. At seventeen years of age, he was sent to St. John's College, Cambridge, where he continued six years. During this time he made a rapid progress in the languages, particularly the Hebrew, Syriac and Chaldee, and acquainted himself with the writings of the Rabbins. In 1624, he removed into the family of old Mr. Brampton Gurdon, of Assington in Suffolk, where he lived as chaplain about nine years, and applied himself to the study of physic.

In 1627, he received episcopal ordination, and became very useful in his neighbourhood, by preaching and distributing good books among the poor. At this time he had some considerable offers of preferment, but waved compliance till 1633, when he accepted the living of Aughton, nine miles from York, in the room of Mr. Alder, who had been removed for nonconformity. But Mr. Jessey was not likely to continue there long, as he could not conform, even so far as his predecessor. Accordingly, the next year, he was ejected for not using the ceremonies, and for presuming to take down a crucifix. On this, he was received into the family of Sir Matthew Boynton, of Barneston, in Yorkshire, by whose encouragement he preached there and at Rowsby, a neighbouring parish, and was much noticed for his piety, humility, and excellent preaching.

In 1635, Mr. Jessey removed with his patron to London, and the next year to Hedgley-House, near Uxbridge. He had not been long there before he was earnestly solicited to take the pastoral charge of a congregation in London, lately under the care of Mr. Lathorp. They had often heard him preach to their satisfaction; and it was well known, that, in the present order of things, he would accept no preferment in the national church. His great modesty for some time prevented his compliance; but, at length, after much consideration and prayer, he accepted their call about Midsummer, 1637, and laboured among them with great faithfulness till his death. In London, frequent storms of per-

First Independent Church in England.

secution awaited him. The congregation being assembled at Queenhithe, Feb. 21, 1637-8, the greater part were seized and carried away by the bishop's pursuivants. In May following, they met with a similar disturbance in another place. On April 21, 1640, several congregations being assembled on Tower-hill, to seek God by fasting and prayer, they were interrupted and imprisoned in the Tower; but being bound over by Archbishop Laud to answer at the next sessions, they were soon released, and the prosecutors did not think it advisable to proceed any further. On August 22, 1641, Mr. Jessey, with five of his congregation, were seized by order of the Lord Mayor, and committed prisoners to Wood-street Compter; but, on appealing to Parliament, they were released.

Hitherto, Mr. Jessey must be considered as a Pædo-Baptist, but some circumstances now took place, that led to an alteration of his sentiments. The year after his settlement with his congregation, several persons left it and joined the Baptists. In 1639, and some following years, a much greater number followed their example. This put Mr. Jessey upon studying the controversy. The result was, that he himself also changed his sentiments; though not without great deliberation, many prayers, and frequent conferences with pious and learned men of different persuasions. His first conviction was about the *mode* of baptism; and though he continued two or three years to baptize children, he did it by immersion. About the year 1644, the controversy with respect to the *subjects* of baptism was revived in his church, when several gave up *infant*-baptism, and among the rest Mr. Jessey. He would not, however, absolutely determine the point, till he had consulted some learned and judicious ministers, as Dr. Goodwin, Mr. Nye, Mr. Burroughs, Mr. Cradock, &c. but these giving him no satisfaction, in June, 1645, he submitted to immersion, which was performed by Mr. Hanserd Knollys. Notwithstanding this change in his sentiments, he maintained the same christian love and charity for good men of all denominations. As a proof of this, he had always some Pædo-Baptists in his church, whom he admitted to communion. He could not think that any particular sentiments concerning baptism, should be the boundary of church fellowship; and took great pains to promote a like catholic spirit among others. Mr. Jessey divided his labours in the ministry according to the catholicism of his principles. Every Lord's-day afternoon, he was among his own people. In the morning, he usually preached at St. George's church, Southwark, where he seems to have been rector. He also preached once a week at Ely-House, and in the Savoy to the wounded soldiers.

Besides his constant labours in the ministry, Mr. Jessey was employed many years upon a new translation of the Bible, in which he was assisted by many learned men, both at home and abroad. This, he made the great master-study of his life; and, in order to evince its necessity, observed, that Archbishop Bancroft, who was supervisor of the present translation, altered it in fourteen places, to make it speak the language of prelacy. (M) Mr. Jessey had nearly completed this great work when the Restoration took place; but the subsequent turn to public affairs, obliged him to lay it aside, and this noble design, eventually, proved abortive. The year 1657 afforded Mr. Jessey a favourable opportunity of displaying his benevolence. The Swedes and Poles being engaged in war, the poor Jews at Jerusalem were in a most distressed state; all supplies from their rich brethren in other countries, upon whom they depended for subsistence, being cut off. This induced Mr. Jessey to raise a collection for their relief; and he sent them £300, with letters, strongly persuading them to embrace christianity.

(M) Dr. Miles Smith, afterwards Bishop of Glocester, who was one of the Translators of the Bible, and wrote the Preface, complained of the Archbishop's unwarrantable alterations; "But" says he, "he is so potent, there is no contradicting him."

First Independent Church in England.

Upon the Restoration, in 1660, he was ejected from his living at St. George's, and silenced from his public ministry. This, however, was only the forerunner of other troubles. He was seized Nov. 27, 1661, and kept in the messenger's hands till released by the privy council, after a month's illegal imprisonment. On August 30, 1662, he was again apprehended, upon false information; and confined six months in the messenger's house, till, by an order of council, he was again released Feb. 20th following. An account of his examinations before the Privy Council, was drawn up and published by the celebrated Gadbury.* Crosby says, he died while under imprisonment;† but this is a mistake. About five or six months after his release, he was taken ill of the distemper which put a period to his labours and sufferings; and having experienced much of the consolations of religion, was at length, gently dismissed from the prison of the body, Sept. 4, 1663, when he had just completed his 63d year. (N) The character of this venerable man was of that estimable nature, as greatly to distinguish him in his day. His benevolence was diffusive, and of the most disinterested kind. Above thirty families depended upon him for their subsistence; nor did he confine his charity to persons of his own persuasion. That he might have the more extensive means of doing good, as well as be more entirely devoted to his sacred work, he chose a single life; thereby sacrificing his individual happiness to the public

---

* Kennet's Chronicle, p. 858.   † History of the Baptists, vol. i. p. 320.

(N) That grand libeller of the Nonconformists, Anthony Wood, gives the following farcical account of Mr. Jessey's death and burial. "At length, (says he) paying his last debt to nature, Sept. 4, 1663, being then accounted the oracle and idol of the faction, was on the seventh of the same month laid to sleep with his fathers, in a hole made in the yard joining to Old Bedlam, near Moorfields, in the suburbs of London, attended with a strange medley of fanatics, mostly Anabaptists, that met upon the very point of time, all at the same instant, to do honour to their departed brother. Some years after, came out a short account of his life and death, but full of ridiculous and absurd cantings, &c."—*Fasti Oxon.* vol. i. p. 239.

welfare. His piety was of the most ardent as well as rational nature; and effectually supported him under the severest trials, and in the prospect of dissolution.* As an author, he is at present but little known, though he published several pieces, the titles of which are specified below. (o)

It is not certainly known where Mr. Jessey's meeting-house was situated; but as he was buried from Woodmonger's-Hall, Duke's-Place, it is highly probable that he preached there during some of the latter years of his life. From a manuscript quoted by Crosby,† we learn, that Mr. Jessey's congregation being too numerous to meet together in one place, without danger of being discovered, divided by mutual consent in 1640, and, henceforward, became two churches. " Just half," says the manuscript, " being with Mr. Praise-God Barebone, and the other half with Mr. Henry Jessey." Mr. Barebone's name appears with some celebrity on the page of history as reputed godfather

* Wood's Fasti, Oxon. vol. i. p. 238.—Crosby's Hist. of the Baptists, vol. i. p. 307--323.—Calamy's Cont. p. 45--51.—Nonconformist's Memorial, vol. i. p. 129--135.—Life and Death of Mr. Henry Jessey. 1671.

(o) His Works are, 1. A Catechism for Children.—2. A Scripture Kalendar from 1645 to 1660.—3. The exceeding Riches of Grace advanced in the Experience of Mrs. Sarah Wright. 1647.—4. Storehouse of Provision for resolving Cases of Conscience. 1650.—5. Scripture Motives for Kalendar Reformation, partly urged formerly by Mr. J. B. renewed and enlarged by H. Jessey. 1650.—6. Description and Explanation of 268 Places in Jerusalem, and the Suburbs thereof, with a large Map. 1653.—7. Lord's loud Call to England : being a true Relation of some late, various and wonderful Judgments, or handy Works of God, by Earthquakes, Lightning, &c. 1660. —8. Miscellanea Sacra : divers necessary Truths seasonably published, &c. 1665.—9. A Looking-glass for Children : being a Narrative of God's gracious Dealings with some little Children. 1674.—He wrote a Preface to Grayle's " Modest Vindication of the Doctrine of Conditions in the Covenant of Grace ;" and another to " The English-Greek Lexicon ; containing the Derivations and Significations of all the Words in the New Testament. 1661." In this Work he had a capital concern.—He is also supposed to be the Author of " Mirabilis Annus ; or the Year of Prodigies and Wonders, &c. 1662."

† Hist. of the English Baptists, vol. iii. p. 41.

First Independent Church in England.

to one of Cromwell's parliaments. Though we know very little of him in the character of a divine, yet as he appears to have been pastor of a congregation in London, he is entitled to some notice in this place.

Praise-God Barebone was by occupation a leather-seller, in Fleet-street, and, according to Rapin, passed among his neighbours for a notable speaker, being used to entertain them with long harangues upon the times.* This pointed him out to the notice of Cromwell, who nominated him a member of the legislative body that succeeded the long parliament in 1653. In this assembly, he greatly distinguished himself for his activity; insomuch that the members, who were but little skilled in politics, received from him, in derision, the appellation of Barebone's Parliament.† Upon the dissolution of this body, about five months afterwards, Barebone appears to have retired from any concern in the government; and we hear nothing further of him till February 1659-60.‡ Monk being then in London with a view of restoring the King, and intent upon the re-admission of the secluded members, Barebone appeared at the head of a numerous rabble, alarming even to that intrepid general, and presented a petition to parliament against the regal interest. Monk, who knew the popularity of Barebone, was obliged to make a general muster of his army, and wrote a letter to the parliament, expostulating with them " for giving too much countenance to that furious zealot and his adherents."§ The petitioners, however, received the thanks of the house for the expression of their good affections to the parliament.∥ The same year, he was concerned in the publication of a book against the Court of Charles the Second, entitled, " *News from Brussels, in a letter*

* Rapin's Hist. of England, vol. ii. p. 590.
† Granger's Biog. Hist. of England, vol. iii. p. 68.
‡ Kennet's Chronicle, p. 52.   § Granger, ubi supra.
∥ Kennet's Chronicle, p. 52.

from a near attendant on his Majesty's person, to a person of honour here. Dated March 10, 1659, O. S." A reverend prelate* stiles this " a rascally piece against the " King to expose him to the hatred of his people." It ought to be observed, that the reputed author of this book was Marchmont Needham, and Barbone only his agent in conveying it to the printer or bookseller.† On the thirtieth of the foregoing month, Mr. Barebone was summoned before the council of state, to answer to some matters objected against him; but on signing an engagement not to act in opposition to the existing government, or to disturb the same, he was discharged from further attendance.‡ After the Restoration he was looked upon with a jealous eye, and on Nov. 26, 1661, was apprehended, together with Major John Wildman, and James Harrington, Esq. and committed prisoner to the Tower, where he was confined for some time.§ On the meeting of parliament early in the following year,|| the Lord Chancellor¶ thought fit to alarm the house with the noise of plots and conspiracies, and enumerated the names of several persons whom he reported to be engaged in traiterous designs against the government. Among these were Major Wildman, Major Hains, Alderman Ireton, Mr. Praise-God Barebone, &c.** How far the charge against these persons was substantiated, or whether it was only a political engine of government to get rid of suspected individuals, we will not take upon us to say. Certain it is, that Mr. Barebone had now to contend with the strong arm of the civil power, which was directed with all the acrimony of party prejudice against persons of his stamp.

The principles and conduct of this man are not sufficiently detailed in history, to form a just estimate of

---

* Op. Kennet apud Chronicle, p. 80. † Ibid.
‡ Bp. Kennet apud Chronicle, p. 101. § Ibid. p. 567.
|| January 10, 1661-2. ¶ Lord Clarendon.
** Kennet's Chronicle, p. 602.

First Independent Church in England.

their real nature and tendency. It seems probable, however, from the preceding facts, connected with the history of the times in which he lived, that he drank somewhat into the wild enthusiastic notions that disgraced some prevailing sects in his day. This might lead him into certain extravagancies of conduct, which are not otherwise to be accounted for. The time of Mr. Barebone's death is not mentioned by any author we have met with, nor are we acquainted with any further particulars of his history. It may be observed, however, for the amusement of the reader, that there were three brothers of this family, each of whom had a sentence for his christian name, viz. Praise-God Barebone; Christ-came-into-the-world-to-save Barebone; and If-Christ-had-not-died-thou-hast-been-damned Barebone: some are said to have omitted the former part of the sentence, and to have called him only " Damned Barebone."* This stile of naming individuals was exceedingly common in the time of the civil wars. It was said that the genealogy of our Saviour might be learnt from the names in Cromwell's regiments; and that the muster-master used no other list than the first chapter of Matthew. (P) It should be observed, however, that the absurdity of naming children after this manner, was not peculiar to that period; but was in use long before, and the practice continues, in some measure, even to the present day.

* Granger's Biog. Hist. of England, vol. iii. p. 68.

(P) A jury was returned in the county of Sussex of the following names:

Accepted Trevor, of Norsham.
Redeemed Compton, of Battle.
Faint-not Hewet, of Heathfield.
Make-peace Heaton, of Hare.
God-reward Smart, of Fivehurst.
Stand-fast-on-high Stringer, of Crowhurst.
Earth Adams, of Warbleton.
Called Lower, of Warbleton.
Kill-Sin Pimple, of Witham.
Return Spelman, of Watling.
Be-faithful Joiner, of Britling.
Fly-Debate Robert, of Britling.
Fight-the-good-fight-of-faith White, of Emer.
More-fruit Fowler, of East-Hadley.
Hope-for Bending, of East-Hadley.
Graceful Harding, of Lewes.
Weep-not Billings, of Lewes.
Meek Brewer, of Okeham.

First Independent Church in England.

HENRY FORTY.—After the death of Mr. Jessey, some disputes arose in his church on the subject of mixed communion, which produced a separation. Those who opposed it withdrew, and chose for their pastor Mr. Henry Forty, then a member of the congregation. After some years, he accepted a call from the Baptist church at Abingdon, in Berkshire. He was a man of eminent piety, and underwent great trials and sufferings on account of religion; but, it pleased God to make him an honoured instrument in his hands for the conversion of many, particularly his own father and mother. In the reign of Charles the Second, he was imprisoned in Exeter jail, for the testimony of a good conscience; and, to the disgrace of the times, was suffered to continue in confinement twelve years. At length, having lived an unspotted life, he finished his course peaceably, in the 67th year of his age, A. D. 1692. He seems to have been buried in Southwark, so that it is probable he died there. Mr. Benjamin Keach preached his funeral sermon, and afterwards published it, with an elegy on his death. When Mr. Forty retired to Abingdon, his people joined with Mr. Kiffin's congregation in Devonshire-square.* What became of the other branch of Mr. Jessey's church we have not been able to discover.

* Crosby's Hist. of the English Baptists, vol. iii. p. 100.—and Mr. Keach's Sermon on the death of Mr. Forty.

Dissenting Churches

IN THE

CITY OF LONDON.

EASTERN DIVISION.

CONTAINING,

1. CRUTCHED FRIARS.
2. POOR JEWRY LANE.
3. JEWRY-STREET.
4. MARK-LANE.
5. TURNERS'-HALL, PHILPOT-LANE.
6. WEIGH-HOUSE, LITTLE EAST-CHEAP.
7. GRACECHURCH-STREET.
8. PEWTERER'S-HALL, LIME-STR.
9. PAVED ALLEY, DITTO.
10. BERRY-STREET, ST. MARY AXE.
11. CROSBY-SQUARE.
12. GREAT ST. HELEN'S.
13. LITTLE ST. HELEN'S.
14. CAMOMILE-STREET.
15. HOUNDSDITCH.
16. GRAVEL-LANE, DITTO.
17. BISHOPSGATE-STREET.
18. HAND ALLEY, DITTO.
19. DEVONSHIRE-SQUARE, DITTO.

CRUTCHED FRIARS.

BAPTIST, EXTINCT.

CRUTCHED, Crouched, or Crossed Friars, the first place that falls under our notice, according to the division we have adopted, is situated in Aldgate Ward, at the eastern extremity of the city. It is so called from the *Fratres Sancti Crucis*, or Brethren of the Holy Cross, who had a house at the south east corner of Hart-street. It was founded about 1298, by Ralph Hosier and William Sabernes, who became friars on their own foundation. Originally they carried in their hands an iron cross, which was afterwards changed for one of silver. On their garments they wore a cross of red cloth. Towards the beginning of the reign of Henry VIII. some lands were granted to this fraternity, on condition that they should pray for the prosperity of the city. The unlucky detection of a friar, in the commission of a fact that was *contra bonos mores*, hastened the dissolution of the monastery, which was granted by King Henry VIII. to Sir Thomas Wyatt, who built a handsome mansion on the site. The friars' hall was converted into a glass-house, the first manufactory of that article in England. On the fourth of September, 1575, it was destroyed by fire. The site is now occupied by the East India Company's Tea Warehouse.*

In an early state of the Baptist interest, there was a congregation of that persuasion, whose place of meeting was in Crutched Friars. They had been part of a society of Independents, under the care of Mr. John Lathorp, and afterwards of Mr. Henry Jessey, but peaceably withdrew, in 1639, upon an alteration in their sentiments with respect to baptism. A manuscript of Mr. Kiffin's quoted by Crosby,† notices the separation in the following terms. " In

---

* Maitland's Hist. of London. vol. ii. p. 782.
† Crosby's Hist. of the Baptists, vol. iii. p. 82.

CRUTCHED-FRIARS.—*Baptist*, Extinct.

the year 1639, another congregation of Baptists was formed, whose place of meeting was in Crutched-Fryars; the chief promoters of which were Mr. Green, Mr. Paul Hobson, and Captain Spencer."—Concerning the first and last of these names we are wholly in the dark. Crosby mentions a Mr. John Green, who, soon after the Restoration, was imprisoned in Lincoln jail, for half a year, along with Mr. Grantham.* Possibly he might be the person intended here. In Kennet's Chronicle, Captain Spencer is noticed as one of the leaders of a plot to dethrone the King.† Of Mr. Paul Hobson, we are enabled to speak with greater certainty.

PAUL HOBSON was a Captain in the army during the civil wars; and Mr. Robinson relates some scandalous indecencies committed by his soldiers, in contempt of infant-baptism. In 1645, he was taken into custody by the governor of Newport-Pagnel, for preaching against infant-baptism, and for reflecting upon the ordinance of parliament against lay-preachers. After being confined there a short time, Sir Samuel Luke, (Q) the governor, sent him prisoner to London. His case was soon brought before the committee of examination; and having some powerful friends, upon being heard, he was immediately discharged. After this, he preached publicly at a meeting-house in Moorfields. In 1646, he subscribed the Confession of Faith, set forth by the seven Baptist Churches in London. At the Restoration, he was chaplain of Eton College, from whence he was ejected for nonconformity.‡ What became of him afterwards we are no where informed.—It is probable this is the same society that afterwards met in Houndsditch.

* Crosby's Hist. of the Baptists, vol. iii. p. 82.
† Kennet's Chronicle, p. 840.

(Q) The hero of Hudibras, the celebrated poem of Butler, was the above-mentioned Sir Samuel Luke, with whom the poet resided during the interregnum.——*Biog. Brit. Art. Butler.*

‡ Crosby's Baptists, vol. i. p. 226. and iii. 26.—Noncon. Memorial. vol. i. p. 300.

POOR JEWRY LANE.

ENGLISH PRESBYTERIAN, EXTINCT.

POOR JEWRY LANE, now called Jewry-street, was so denominated from the number of Jews who inhabited the neighbourhood. The meeting-house, which is at present occupied by the Methodists, is of ancient date, and was probably erected in the reign of King Charles II. but for whom is uncertain. A society of Presbyterians met there statedly for upwards of a century, and enjoyed the labours of some of the most considerable Divines among the Dissenters. With our utmost researches, we have not been able to trace the origin of the church. The first pastor upon record is Mr. Timothy Cruso, who settled here a little before the Revolution. In his time, there was a flourishing church and congregation. After the death of Mr. Cruso, there were two candidates for the pastoral office, Mr. (afterwards Dr.) William Harris, and Mr. Timothy Shepherd, afterwards of Braintree, who had a majority of the church by one voice; but by art and management the election was overruled. This circumstance occasioned a large breach in the society, which it never recovered. In the time of Dr. Lardner and Dr. Benson, the church was in a very low state; for though they were men of learning and talents, and deserve honourable mention, on account of their labours in defending christianity against infidels, yet their sentiments and mode of preaching were extremely unpopular, and but ill adapted to preserve the church from a languishing state. After some feeble attempts to revive the expiring interest, the society dissolved in the year 1774, and the meeting-house was disposed of to the Methodists.

In conformity to our plan, we shall now present the reader with some biographical sketches of the several Ministers who have officiated at this place, whether as pastors, or

POOR JEWRY LANE.—*English Presbyterian*, Extinct.

assistants, whose names together with the time of their settlement and removal, may be gathered from the following table:

Ministers' Names.	As Pastors.		Assistants.	
	From	To	From	To
Timothy Cruso, M. A.	16	1697	-	-
Francis Fuller, M. A.	-	-	16	1701
William Harris, D. D.	1698	1740	-	-
Samuel Rosewell,	-	-	1701	1705
John Billingsley,	-	-	1706	1722
Samuel Harvey,	-	-	1722	1729
Nathaniel Lardner, D. D.	-	-	1729	1751
George Benson, D. D.	1740	1762	-	-
Ebenezer Radcliffe,	1762	1774	1760	1762
Richard Price, D. D.	-	-	1763	1770
John Calder, D. D.	-	-	1770	1774

TIMOTHY CRUSO, M. A. This learned divine, and very eminent preacher, was born about the year 1657. We have no materials that furnishes us with any particulars concerning his parentage, or the place of his birth. It appears from a manuscript he left behind him, that, when a youth, he was favoured with the friendship and counsel of that pious and venerable Divine, Mr. Oliver Bowles, father to Mr. Edward Bowles, a Nonconformist Minister at York. Mr. Cruso attended him during his last illness, and received the following affectionate advice from him, the day before his death, which happened Sept. 5, 1674.—" Have a care of
" yourself, Timothy, in this evil world; and be not so en-
" tangled with the vanityes of it, as to lose the substance for
" the shadow. Seeing that thou designest thyselfe for the
" work and office of the ministry, I would advise you never
" to trouble your hearers with uselesse or contending noti-
" ons; but rather preach all in practicalls, that you may set
" them upon doing, and more advance a holy life. I would

Timothy Cruso M.A.

From an original Picture.

London Publish'd Aug.t 1.st 1808 by Maxwell & Wilson Skinner S.t

POOR JEWRY LANE.—*English Presbyterian*, Extinct.

" not any longer live that idle and unserviceable life which
" I have lately done; and therefore if God hath some work
" for mee yet to do here, hee will continue mee yet here;
" but if not, I am sure there is better work for mee in hea-
" ven, whereby I shall act for his praise and glory more.
" When I took my last leave of him, hee said, Farewell
" Timothy; and if I see thee not any more in this world
" (as indeed he did not) I hope I shall in the next, which is
" a better! (and so I hope also, said Mr. Cruso) Only
" remember (continues Mr. Bowles) to keep a good con-
" science, and walk close with God. Which last words he
" twice repeated with a considerable emphasis, that it might
" work a deeper impression, and the greater observation."*
The above Mr. Oliver Bowles was a member of the Westminster assembly, and is said by Dr. Calamy † to be " of Sutton in Bedfordshire;" but whether he died there we are not informed.

Mr. Cruso received a liberal education for the ministry, first at a private academy among the Nonconformists; and afterwards in one of the universities of North-Britain, where he resided some years, and took the degree of Master of Arts. Before he entered upon his ministerial employment, it is probable he spent some time as chaplain, or tutor, in a private family, a very usual practice for young ministers at that time; and it is certain the Dissenters have derived no advantage by discontinuing so laudable a custom. It does not appear whether Mr. Cruso preached any where stately before he settled in London; which we suppose to have been about the time of King James's Indulgence, in 1687. After the division in the Pinners'-Hall lecture, occasioned by the exclusion of Mr. (afterwards Dr.) Daniel Williams, in 1694, Mr. Cruso was chosen to fill up one of the vacancies. This argues him to have been in high repute as a preacher,

* Theol. Bib. Mag. vol. iv. p. 138-9.   † Account, p. 779.

that distinction being conferred only upon the most eminent Divines, in and about the metropolis. At that lecture he delivered many elaborate discourses, which he wrote at full length in long-hand, accurately composed, and very judicious. From these a sufficient number was selected after his death to form a moderate size volume, which was published in 1699, with a recommendatory Preface by the Rev. Matthew Mead.

Mr. Cruso's qualificatious for the ministry were very considerable. He had laid in a large stock both of divine and human learning, which he cultivated with care, and improved by close application and industry. He possessed a sound mind, and a steady judgment in the great doctrines of the gospel, which he explained with clearness and precision, and enforced with a becoming solemnity. His views of the nature and importance of the ministerial office, would never snffer him to enter the pulpit in an unprepared and careless manner; for though he looked up with becoming reverence to the promised presence and assistance of the Holy Spirit, he thought this was only to be obtained in the use of means, and, therefore, never neglected a diligent preparation in his study. He was a minister that excelled in pulpit talents. His compositions were judicious, exact, serious, and practical. He possessed a solid judgment, and a rich and lively invention. His voice was clear and melodious; his manner eloquent and persuasive; and his deportment in every respect so agreeable, that he could hardly fail of commanding the attention of the most dull and inconsiderate of his hearers. These qualifications were happily directed to the noblest purposes. Mr. Cruso esteemed it his highest honour to be a faithful minister of Jesus Christ; he took great delight in his work, and consecrated all his efforts to the best interests of the souls of men. And his labours were attended with a remarkable degree of acceptance and success. He was justly esteemed one of the greatest preachers of the age

POOR JEWRY LANE.—*English Presbyterian*, Extinct.

in which he lived; and presided over a numerous and flourishing church to the day of his death.

Mr. Cruso was a hearty friend to civil and religious liberty. No man rejoiced more at the downfal of despotism and popery, and the re-establishment of British freedom by the glorious revolution, under the immortal King William. In commemoration of that happy event, he preached and published a discourse, in which, after gratefully acknowledging the interposition of Providence, he expresses his admiration for the hero, our deliverer. With regard to the religious disputes which agitated the nation in his time, Mr. Cruso, from a principle of conscience, sided with the Nonconformists; but he inculcated love and forbearance among christians of all denominations. He entertained a strong sense of the injustice and barbarity of that fatal act, which, in one day, extinguished so many burning and shining lights, and may be considered as a step to all the calamities which obscured that and the succeeding reign. The anniversary of the Bartholomew ejectment, he never failed to commemorate by a sermon on the 24th of August, when he took occasion to enforce strongly the necessity of a national repentance for that great national sin. Mr. Cruso's religious sentiments harmonized, entirely, with those of the Assembly of Divines at Westminster; and for the doctrines contained in their celebrated confession, he was a strenuous and able advocate.

This truly great and excellent man, to use an expression of Mr. Mead, "lived too fast;" not like many, who shorten their days by sinful excesses, but as a taper which wastes itself to give light to others. His bodily constitution, naturally weak, was greatly impaired by constant study and incessant labours. His extraordinary zeal for the interest of Christ and the souls of men, animated him to increasing desires for usefulness; and his ardent mind continually aspiring to greater knowledge and higher attainments, at length overreached his strength, and brought him to the grave, in the midst of his days.* His death was hastened by an asthmatic complaint, which deprived the church of one of her brightest ornaments, on November 26, 1697, in the 41st year of his age. The celebrated Mr. Matthew Mead preached and published a sermon upon his death, from Rom, viii. 11. *If the Spirit of him that raised up Jesus from the dead dwell in you, he that raised up Christ from the dead, shall also quicken your mortal bodies by his Spirit that dwelleth in you.* It is a very curious discourse, upon an uncommon subject, and treated in an able and perspicuous manner. The drift of the author is to prove, that the Spirit of God dwells in believers, not only by his gifts and graces, but in a *real personal* manner. This union he supposes to continue equally after death, and that the bodies of the saints are the dwelling-places of the Holy Ghost, even while they are dead and lying in the grave. As a consequence of this, they will be reanimated and raised at the last day, by the energy of that same Spirit, which dwells in their dust as a principle of resurrection power. Mr. Mead has not a single word concerning Mr. Cruso's history, but contents himself with the following brief account of his character and death.

—— " I know you expect (says Mr. Mead) that I should say something of the person deceased, and not pass him by in silence. But I acknowledge myself very unfit for this province, it being a work I rarely engage in; as having no authority to take the commission out of the hands of his own works, they are to praise him in the gates, and not I. And yet it is not fit, when every mean virtue in others hath its funeral trumpet, that so much excelling worth as was in him should be forgotten, and the memory of it buried with him. Should I speak of his carriage and behaviour in the various relations he stood in—as a son to his surviving mother—as a husband to his wife—as a father while he had

* Mr. Mead's Pref, to Mr. Cruso's Sermons at Pinners'-Hall.

POOR JEWRY LANE.—*English Presbyterian*, Extinct.

children—as a master to servants—as a friend to his friend. I might herein propound him as a pattern to many, for he excelled most. And that is a good man indeed, who is good in all relations. But his great and chief care was to fill up his relation to God in Christ, and that not only as a christian and a believer, but as a minister of Christ, and a pastor to that flock which the Holy Ghost had committed to his charge. I must say, God had fitted him for this work and service above many of his brethren, in betrusting him with such gifts and talents as but very few have received. And how diligent and faithful was he in laying them out, and so improving them in his master's service? How zealous was he for Christ! How laborious in his work! How sound in the faith! How great in prayer! How apt to teach! And how all was crowned with success, is evident in the many comfortable seals which God gave to his ministry among you. And though his natural parts were great, and made much greater by the blessing of God upon his unwearied industry; yet that he neither leaned upon them, nor trusted to them, appeared by his constant labour and study for every sermon. They that were discerning christians, and did wisely observe the suitable matter he prepared, the exact method in which it was ordered, the taking dress with which it was clothed, the charming manner in which it was uttered, could not but say, that he did not offer to God that which cost him nothing. His great delight was in his work, for he knew how well it becomes a disciple to be as his Lord, whose delight was to do the will of God. And therefore he was fervent in spirit, serving the Lord. And this made him willing to spend, and to be spent, till by degrees he wasted and consumed himself—I would have said no more of him, were it not to obviate some false and malicious whispers; as if he died in great darkness, and under much trouble of conscience. I was with him the day before he died, and among other things I asked him, how it was with him concerning his spiritual state. He told me, " That he

POOR JEWRY LANE.—*English Presbyterian*, Extinct.

had a firm confidence of hope in the infinite righteousness of Jesus Christ." I then asked him (and desired that he would be as plain with me, as I desired to be faithful to him) if there was any particular thing that lay as a burden upon his conscience. He replied, " No, he blessed God, there was not. But that which troubled him in general was, that in the course of his ministry he had not honoured God as he ought to have done ; nor had he been so faithful to the souls of men as he should have been : but yet in this he could appeal to God, that whatever by-ends might come in, and mingle themselves, which he renounced, yet the glory of God in the conversion and salvation of souls was the great end he aimed at in the whole course of his ministry." And blessed is that servant (adds Mr. Mead) whom his Lord when he comes shall find so doing."*

Mr. Cruso's remains were interred in Stepney Churchyard, where a handsome tomb was erected over his grave, with a Latin inscription to his memory. This we shall insert, together with a translation, for the benefit of the English reader. It appears from the same stone that Mr. Cruso had a brother named Nathaniel, who was a valuable person. Of the two brothers it is said, they were " Lovely and pleasant in their lives and in their deaths." It was probably a daughter of this Nathaniel, who was mother to the late excellent Dr. Wilton. A list of Mr. Cruso's works is inserted in the note below.†

* Mr. Mead's Sermon on Mr. Cruso's death, p. 30, 31.

† WORKS.—1. The Duty and Support of Believers in Life and Death : Funeral Sermon for Mrs. Smith. 1638.—2. The Period of Human Life determined by the Divine Will : a Funeral Sermon on the Death of Mr. Henry Brownsword, who deceased April 27, 1688 ; on Psa. iii. 2.—3. The mighty Wonders of a Merciful Providence : in a Sermon preached Jan. 31, 1688-9, being the Day of Public Thanksgiving to God for the great Deliverance of this Kingdom, by his Highness the Prince of Orange. On Numb. xxiii. 29.—4. The Usefulness of Spiritual Wisdom with a Temporal Inheritance : in a Sermon preached March 11, 1688-9, at the Entrance of a young Man upon his Habitation and particular Calling. On Eccles. vii. 11.—5. The

POOR JEWRY LANE.——*English Presbyterian*, Extinct.

M. S.
TIMOTHEI CRUSO,
Evangelii Ministri egregiè fidelis.
Tam eximia pietate quam prædara eruditione ornati,
Concionatoris ad persuadendum compositi canori copiosi judicio subtili
atque limato ingenio acerrimo,
Industria incredibili,
Conjugis amantissimi,
Patris Clementissimi,
Amici Firmissimi,
Propter lenitatem suis,
Propter singularem humanitatem omnibus,
Jucundi, qui gregem Christi pascendo exaturando vigilis, curis,
Laboribus Fractus.
Quod sui est Mortale Asthmaticus
Deposuit
et
Ad summi Pastoris ædes concionemque Beatorum anhelans
Ascendit die Nov: 26, 1697.
Ætat. suæ 41.

Church's Plea for the Divine Presence to prosper human Force: in a Fast Sermon, June 5, 1689.—6. The Excellency of the Protestant Faith, as to its Objects and Supports: in a Sermon preached Nov. 5, 1689.—7. The Christian Laver: or a Discourse opening the Nature of Participation with, and demonstrating the Necessity of Mortification by Christ: in two Sermons on John xiii. 8. 1690.—8. The Duty and Blessing of a tender Conscience plainly stated, and earnestly recommended to all that regard Acceptance with God, and the Prosperity of their Souls: the Substance of several Sermons on 2 Kings, xxii. 19.—9. God the Guide of Youth: briefly opened and urged in a Sermon preached with a special relation to young Persons, Jan. 1, 1694-5. On Jer. iii. 4.—10. An earnest Plea for constant Attendance at the Lord's Table: in a Sermon preached June 4, 1696. On 1 Sam. xx. 27.—11. Eleven Discourses upon Dives and Lazarus. 1697.—12. The three last Sermons of the late Rev. Mr. Cruso; to which is added, his Sermon on Nov. 5, 1697, with a Preface by the Rev. Francis Fuller. 1698.—13. Twenty-four Sermons preached at the Merchants' Lecture, at Pinners'-Hall. By the late Rev. T. Cruso, M. A. with a Preface by the Rev. Matthew Mead. 1699. The two last pieces were posthumous.

POOR JEWRY LANE.——*English Presbyterian*, Extinct.

Translation.

Sacred to the Memory
Of TIMOTHY CRUSO,
A minister of the gospel
Of extraordinary faithfulness,
Who adorned his character
No less by his eminent piety, than by his excellent learning.
He was an eloquent, melodious, and persuasive preacher,
Of a rich and penetrating judgment,
With which he united a polished and lively invention.
He was a man of indefatigable industry,
A most affectionate husband,
A most indulgent father,
A most steady friend;
To whom he endeared himself by the gentleness of his manners,
As well as by his uncommon benignity to all.
He took great delight in feeding the flock of Christ,
But his constitution was at length broken
By incessant watchings, studies and labours.
An asthmatic complaint
Consigned his mortal part to this Tomb;
and
His soul aspiring towards the abode of the Chief Shepherd,
And the Assembly of the Blessed,
Took its flight Nov. 26, 1697,
In the 41st year of his age.

FRANCIS FULLER, M. A.—Mr. Cruso enjoyed for some time, the stated assistance of the Rev. Francis Fuller, son to Mr. John Fuller, a pious and eminent minister in London, who was ejected, in 1662, from St. Martin's, Ironmonger-lane.* He trained up three sons to the ministry, all of whom proved scholars and celebrated preachers. The two eldest, Dr. Thomas, and Dr. Samuel Fuller, conformed at the Restoration; but Mr. Francis Fuller, the youngest, continued a Nonconformist till his death.† He

* Calamy's Account, p. 46.
† Jer. White's Serm. on the Death of Mr. Fr. Fuller, 12mo.

POOR JEWRY LANE.——*English Presbyterian*, Extinct.

received his education in Queen's College, Cambridge, where he proceeded Master of Arts; and in 1663, he was incorporated in the University of Oxford.* Dr. Calamy mentions him as ejected from Warcup, or, as it should be, from Werkworth, in Northamptonshire, where he was curate to Dr. Temple.† He afterwards preached sometime in the West of England; but, at length, settled in London, as colleague with Mr. Cruso, at Crutched-Friars.

Mr. Fuller was a man of considerable learning, which descended to him as an hereditary accomplishment; for, as Mr. Jer. White observes, it belonged to his family to be learned. The same author also remarks, that, though he was the youngest of the three brothers, he was excelled by the other two, only in age and fortune; his conscience not allowing him to make that advantage of his education which they did. As a preacher, he was serious, judicious and evangelical; and he lived in the practice of what he preached. To a sound judgment he united much genius, and oftentimes mixed with his instructions some lively and pleasant remarks, which greatly tended to captivate and delight his hearers. His observations also, were often pertinent, and left great impressions upon their minds. The subjects he discussed were weighty and sublime, and he delivered them in a chaste, easy and perspicuous style. Though he connected himself chiefly with the Presbyterians, he never espoused any party as such, but gave the right-hand of fellowship to good men of all denominations. He measured spiritual persons and things, not by a consent in opinions, or a conformity to this or that outward form; but by the influence of religion, upon the character and conduct. Love to real goodness was the principle that pre-

* Wood's Fasti, vol. ii. p. 158.   † Calamy's Acc. p. 497.

POOR JEWRY LANE.—*English Presbyterian*, Extinct.

dominated in his breast, and gave a colouring to all his concerns in life, whether civil or sacred. He was a true lover of his country, and heartily asserted our civil liberties, as the best bulwark of our religious privileges. In private life, he had the art of pleasing his friends by a certain facetiousness of conversation, for which his family was remarkable. But while this rendered his company desirable, he was careful to mix with it that instruction which made him a no less profitable than pleasant companion.* Mr. Fuller died in London, July 21, 1701, aged 64. His friend, Mr. Jeremiah White, preached his funeral sermon, on 2 Thess. iv. 14. and afterwards published it, with some account of his character. (R)

WILLIAM HARRIS, D. D.—This eminent Divine was born, most probably, in London, about the year 1675. Though we have no account of his parents, it should seem they were pious persons, and instructed him, betimes, in the principles of religion. From a child, he is said to have known the holy scriptures. In his youthful days, he joined himself to a society of young men, who met once a week for prayer, reading, and religious conversation; for the mutual communication of knowledge; and with a view of strengthening each other against the solicitations of evil company. Of this society, the excellent Dr. Grosvenor was likewise a member. It is somewhat extraordinary that we find no mention made of the names of Dr. Harris's tutors. There is, however, some reason for supposing, that he pursued his studies for the ministry under the

---

* Mr. White's Sermon on the Death of Mr. Fuller, p. 110—118.

(R) He published the following WORKS. Rules how to use the World.—A Treatise of Faith and Repentance. 1684.—Of the Shortness of Time.—Words to give the young man knowledge and Direction. 1685.—A Treatise of Grace and Duty. 1688.—Peace in war by Christ the Prince of Peace: a Fast Sermon, June 26, 1696.—Mr. Orton pronounces some of these pieces to be very excellent, entertaining and useful.

Pickersgill del.　　　　　　　　Hopwood Sculpt

William Harris, D.D.

From an original Painting,

in Dr Williams Library Red Cross Street.

London Publish'd Sept.r 1.st 1808 by Maxwell & Wilson Skinner St.

POOR JEWRY LANE.—*English Presbyterian,* Extinct

tuition of the celebrated Mr. Timothy Jollie, at Attercliffe, in Yorkshire. But, be this as it may, there is abundant evidence that, he made a very considerable progress in the languages, philosophy, divinity, history, and other branches of learning. He began to preach when very young; but entered the pulpit with an unusual degree of furniture, and with that solidity of judgment, for which he was remarkable throughout life. His first appearance in public, was as assistant to Mr. Henry Read, in Gravel-lane, Southwark. From thence, in 1698, he was called to succeed the Rev. Timothy Cruso, in the pastoral care of the congregation at Crutched-Friars. His great modesty and humility, made him hesitate, for some time, upon his acceptance of this call; being diffident of his fitness to fill up the place of so excellent and popular a preacher. His anxiety he sometimes expressed in the words of Jeremiah,* *Ah, Lord God! behold I cannot speak, for I am a child.* But then, he received encouragement from what immediately follows: *And the Lord said unto me, Say not I am a child, for thou shalt go to all that I shall send thee, and whatsoever I command thee, thou shalt speak. For I am with thee.*† The result of this debate with himself, after consultation with his friends, was to accept the invitation of the church; and, in a little time, he was set apart to the pastoral office, with fasting and prayer, and the laying on of the hands of the Presbytery, which he always thought a scriptural mode of ordination. It was about this time that he obtained the keys of the meeting-house, and spent there, by himself, a whole day in fasting and prayer to God for his direction, and blessing in the work he had just undertaken. The efficacy of the prayers of that day, was very visible in his growing abilities, in his acceptance as a preacher, and in his eminent usefulness both in the civil and sacred concerns of life.

* Chap. i. ver. 6.   † Ver. 7, 8.

POOR JEWRY LANE.—*English Presbyterian*, Extinct.

As a preacher, the compositions of Dr. Harris are allowed by judges to be very accurate. His method was always clear and distinct. The orderly division of his discourses greatly assisted the memory, and was the fruit of much study and serious deliberation. His language was compact and concise, sententious, and nervous, clothed with strong sense, carrying conviction to the mind, and bearing down opposition with irresistible force. He discovered a fine imagination in the choice of his similies, and regulated it with judgment His delivery was grave and manly, and his voice strong, though somewhat interrupted by a hoarseness at the outset of his speaking; this, however, gradually cleared itself as he proceeded, till he made his audience glow with the same warmth he himself felt towards the application, which was always pathetic and affecting. His preaching was adapted to the several states and exigencies of mankind. The subjects he discussed, comprised the most important points of religion, with their grounds and evidences, and the various duties of the Christian life. These he enforced by the strongest motives.

The celebrity which Dr. Harris acquired as a preacher, often called him from his own pulpit, not only to stated lectures, but also, to officiate on public and particular occasions. He was, for above thirty years, one of the preachers of the Friday evening lecture at the Weigh-house, in Little Eastcheap. The design of this service, which was set on foot at the commencement of the seventeenth century, was to encourage the delightful exercise of psalmody, and promote in our assemblies a greater harmony and devotion in conducting that important part of divine worship. His colleagues in this lecture, were Dr. Jabez Earle, Dr. Benjamin Grosvenor, Mr. Thomas Reynolds, Mr. John Newman, and Mr. Thomas Bradbury. On the death of the Rev. William Tong, Dr. Harris was chosen, April 12,

POOR JEWRY LANE.——*English Presbyterian*, Extinct.

1727, one of the six preachers of the Merchants' Lecture, at Salters'-Hall. In 1735, when there was an alarm concerning the increase of Popery, he united with several ministers in conducting a course of sermons against the principal errors of the Church of Rome. The subject allotted for his discussion, was the absurd doctrine of Transubstantiation. On funeral occasions, and at the public ordination of ministers, his assistance was frequently required, and his performances always met with great acceptance. Of this, the many single sermons he published are a convincing proof.

But it was not merely as a preacher that Dr. Harris distinguished himself. The other branches of the pastoral office, he performed in a manner that was highly creditable to him as a minister of the gospel: for, with fidelity and tenderness, he admonished, warned, advised and comforted his flock, in private, as the circumstances of things required. His skill as a casuist is abundantly evident in some of his printed discourses; and he rendered it subservient to the instruction of his people, in their monthly exercises on the Monday evening after the administration of the Lord's-supper, when he spoke to a question given in before. It was a mark of Dr. Harris's good sense, that, notwithstanding the exactness of his own compositions, he was a candid hearer of others. To younger ministers he proved a good friend and patron, and exhibited both in his preaching and conversation, an excellent model for their imitation.

As the ground-work of all his attainments and usefulness, Dr. Harris acquired, from early life, an intimate acquaintance with the sacred scriptures. These he read, not only as a Christian, for the daily bread of his spiritual life, but as a Christian minister and critic. This, he was enabled to do, by a familiar acquaintance with the original languages. It was an observation of his, with regard to scripture criticism, that " without some knowledge of it,

POOR JEWRY LANE.—*English Presbyterian*, Extinct.

no man can thoroughly understand his Bible, or make a proper use of it." From the Scriptures alone, as the fountain of truth, he derived all his notions on subjects of religion; and having once formed his judgment, it was difficult to move him. Should the reader inquire, to what party he belonged? Dr. Grosvenor shall answer, " To me he seemed to be of no party. Men might call him by what name they pleased; he was fond of no denomination but that of a Christian. Truth had him of her side, and he embraced her as heartily as if she brought along with her a dowry of worldly emolument." If this description be thought too indefinite, we will add, that Dr. Harris was a firm Protestant Dissenter, of the Presbyterian denomination, but a hearty lover of good men of every persuasion, and a decided assertor of evangelical *truth*; equally opposing those who denied the peculiar doctrines of the gospel, or exhibited it as consisting wholly of promises without any commands. His high veneration for the oracles of God, inclined him always to encourage the labours of learned men, who endeavoured to explain them. Of such writings he made a very extensive collection, which, with the remainder of his books, consisting of a very large and valuable assortment, in various branches of learning, he bequeathed by will, to Dr. Williams's library, in Redcross-street; where is likewise preserved a very fine painting of the Doctor. But, however useful literature may be, and undoubtedly is, to a public instructor, there are, at the same time, other qualifications that ought always to be joined with it. A preacher of the Christian religion who is not himself a Christian, who has never tasted the grace of God, nor received Christ Jesus the Lord, so as to walk in him, is a very unfit person to instruct others. While Dr. Harris attended to the fields of other men, he did not neglect to cultivate his own vineyard.

In private life, his character appeared equally amiable. He was a watchful guardian over his own family, a faithful

POOR JEWRY LANE.—*English Presbyterian*, Extinct.

monitor, an affectionate friend. He had a great command over his temper and words; was scarcely ever seen to be angry; and seldom spoke to the disadvantage of any one. His friendship was uniform and steady; not deserting, but liberally relieving, those who were in distress; and administring consolation suited to their necessities. He was happy in the esteem and respect of numbers of his brethren in the ministry, and in other stations; being fitted, by his extensive attainments, to associate with persons of knowledge and judgment, in the higher walks of life. At the same time, he could condescend to meaner persons, and was equally happy in their society, provided they discovered an inquisitive temper, and a good understanding in the things of religion. In the congregation to which he stood related for the space of forty-two years, he enjoyed much comfort, and experienced some particular tokens of their regard; nor was he wanting in constancy and zeal to promote their best interests, both in public and private. Indeed, when we consider the number and variety of his engagements; his zeal and assiduity for the public service; the large epistolary correspondence he maintained with a numerous acquaintance; the abundance of good offices he performed in private, together with his concern in many great and useful designs of a more public nature, it may be difficult to conceive how he could have sufficient time and strength for what he did. But he loved employment, could endure long and close application, and was blessed with a quick apprehension, which fitted him for dispatch.

Dr. Harris had an uncommon veneration for the elder ministers of the seventeenth century. He highly valued their character and great usefulness, from a grateful sense of his obligations for their countenance and assistance; for the pleasure of their conversation; and for the benefit he received from their learned labours. From these worthies, he acquired a knowledge of many things, that enriched his

POOR JEWRY LANE.—*English Presbyterian*, Extinct.

memory, and, of which, he was always very communicative. This made his company both entertaining and instructive. And yet, he was above being enslaved by an attachment to human authority. It was, doubtless, from this consideration, that he declined uniting with the subscribing ministers, at the Salter's-Hall Synod, in 1719. His name, therefore, appears among the non-subscribers. As a just testimony to his merit, the universities of Aberdeen and Edinburgh conferred on him, without his knowledge, and in the most respectful manner, the highest literary honours.

At length, after an useful and laborious life, spent in the service of God, and the souls of men, being mercifully exempted from the painful sufferings of a lingering and tedious sickness, he slumbered only a few days, and then fell asleep in Jesus, May 25, 1740, aged 65 years.* His remains were interred May 30, in Dr. Williams's vault, Bunhill-Fields; and his friend, Dr. Obadiah Hughes, delivered a very suitable address at the grave. On the following Lord's-day, an excellent sermon was preached on the occasion of his death, by Dr. Benjamin Grosvenor, from Psa. cii. 17. Dr. Lardner, also, delivered a suitable discourse, upon the same melancholy event, from 2 Thess. i. 10. They were both published, and are the principal sources from whence we have taken the present article.

Dr. Harris's character as an author stands high in the literary as well as the religious world. He was reckoned the greatest master of the English tongue among the Dissenters. His style was plain and easy, and his thoughts substantial. Dr. Grosvenor ranks his works among the standards of the English language, which he considers as having derived some embellishments from his manner of writing. He published a variety of single ser-

* Dr. Grosvenor's Sermon on the Death of Dr. Harris—and Dr. Lardner's Sermon on the same occasion.

POOR JEWRY LANE.—*English Presbyterian,* Extinct.

mons ; (s) besides which he was the author of several publications of a larger size. The first of these was a practical

(s) The following are the titles of them. 1. A Sermon at Salter's-Hall to the Society for Reformation of Manners, June 29, 1702.—2. A fast Sermon, Jan. 29, 1703-4, with a special Reference to the late dreadful Storm and Tempest. Isa. xxix. 6. 1706.—3. A Wedding Sermon.—4. The Mischief of Evil Company, preached on Easter Monday, April 14, 1707, Prov. i. 10.—5. On the General Mourning for the Death of Prince George. Eccles. xii. 5. 1708.—6. On the Excellence of Singing; at the Eastcheap Lecture. Psa. cxlvii. 1. 1708.—On Prayer; at the same Lecture. 2 Tim. ii. 1. 1711.—8. Directions for Hearing the Word ; at the same. Luke viii. 18. 1713.—9. On the Pope's Supremacy, Nov. 5, 1713. Matt. xvi. 18.—10. The Nature and Reasonableness of Consideration ; preached at the Old Jewry, to a Society of Young Men, June 28, 1716. 2 Tim. ii. 7.—11. A Thanksgiving Sermon for the Suppression of the late unnatural Rebellion, June 7, 1716. Psa. lxviii. 20.—12. Objections against Reading the Scriptures considered ; at the Eastcheap Lecture. Matt. xxii. 29. 1717.—13. Consolations in the Death of aged Christians ; preached at Crouched-Fryars on the Death of Mrs. Dorcas Billingsley, Dec. 29, 1717. Job v. 26.—14. Of the Sin against the Holy Ghost, Matt. xii. 31, 32. 1718.—15. Consolations in the Death of good Men ; preached at Hackney on the Death of Mrs. Bathshua Barker, Sept. 18, 1719. 1 Thess. iv. 8.—16. Readiness for the coming of the Lord ; preached at Cheshunt, on the sudden Death of Mr. Thomas Pickard, Feb. 14, 1719-20. Matt. xxiv. 44.—17. On the Coronation. Psa. xcvii. 1. 1721. —18. A Christian's Groans in the mortal Body, and Desires of the heavenly Happiness ; preached at Crouched-Fryars on the Death of the Rev. John Billingsley, May 13, 1722. 2 Cor. v. 2.—19. On the Nature of the Pastoral Office: or, The Apostle Peter's Exhortation to the Elders of the Church, briefly considered ; preached at Ongar in Essex, May 7, 1725, at the Ordination of Mr. John Tren, and Mr. Benjamin Owen.—20. The happy End of a useful Life ; preached at Crouched-Fryars, May 16, 1725, on the Death of Mr. John Mercer. Acts xiii. 26.—21. The Reasonableness of believing in Christ, and the Unreasonableness of Infidelity ; two Sermons preached at Salter's-Hall, May 21 and 28, 1728. John ii. 45, 46. With an Appendix, containing brief Remarks on the Case of Lazarus, relating to Mr. Woolston's fifth Discourse on Miracles. 1729.—22. Consolations in the Death of good Men in the midst of their Days ; preached at Crouched-Fryars, April 27, 1729, on the Death of the Rev. Samuel Harvey, Psa. cii. 23, 24.—23. The Love of Christ's Appearance, the Character of a sincere Christian ; preached in Southwark, on the Death of the Rev. Joshua Oldfield, D. D. Nov. 23, 1729. 2 Tim. iv. 8.—24. Faithfulness in the treatise, entitled, "Self-Dedication, personal and sacramental, explained and enforced." 12mo. This passed through more than one edition. In 1717, he published a small piece, entitled, "Two Questions of present Importance, briefly stated and argued." In 1724, there appeared from the press, a large volume of sermons, under the title of "Practical Discourses on the principal Representations of the Messiah, throughout the Old Testament." These Discourses, soon after their publication, were handsomely spoken of by Dr. Watts, and have been held in great reputation. They were composed with reference, though not as a direct answer, to Mr. Collins's Discourse on the Grounds

Christian Ministry, briefly represented and argued; at the Ordination of Mr. Thomas Payne, at Stratford by Bow, Essex, Oct. 2, 1729. 1 Cor. iv. 2.—25. Finishing the Christian Course considered and argued; preached in New Broad street, Petty-France, on the Death of the Rev. John Evans, May 23, 1730, in the 51st Year of his Age. Oct. 20, 1724.—26. Of Despising Young Ministers; preached at Haberdasher's-Hall, Dec. 18, 1730, at the Ordination of Mr. William Ford, and Mr. Samuel Parks. 1 Tim. iv. 12. —27. Of Deliverance by Christ from the Fears of Death; preached at Wapping, on the Death of Mrs. Sarah Bush, wife of the Rev. William Bush, June 13, 1731. Heb. ii. 15.—28. Lukewarmness in Religion represented and reproved; in two Sermons at Salter's-Hall, Nov. 2 and 16, 1731; with a Discourse on False-Zeal. 1732.—29. Diligence in the Christian Life, necessary to be found in Peace; preached at Kingston-upon-Thames, on the Death of the Rev. Daniel Mayo, June 24, 1733. Acts vii. 59.—31. On Transubstantiation; at Salter's-Hall, Feb. 18, 1734-5. Luke xxii. 19, 20.— 32. A second Discourse concerning Transubstantiation, in which the sixth Chapter of John's Gospel is particularly considered; preached at Salter's-Hall, April 22, 1735. John vi. 53.—33. A Christian's Desire to depart, or Willingness to die; preached at the Old Jewry, on the Death of Mrs. Lydia Leavesley, Wife of the Rev. Thomas Leavesley, June 29, 1735. Philip. i. 23.—Consolations in the Death of Wicked Relations. 2 Sam. xiii. 33. 1736. —35. Consolations in the Death of Infants. Matt. iii. 18. 1736.—36. The Nature of the Lord's Supper, and the Obligations to it, briefly considered; with a serious Exhortation to a due Attendance upon it; in four Discourses preached at Salter's-Hall, Nov. and Dec. 1736.—37. A Discourse, preached August 1, 1737.—38. The Case of Sodom and Gomorrah, and of the Israelites in the Wilderness, practically considered; in two Discourses. 1739 and 1740. Gen. xviii. 32. 1 Cor. x. 11.

POOR JEWRY LANE.—*English Presbyterian*, Extinct.

and Reasons of the Christian Religion. In the Preface, he recommends them to the people of his charge, with whom he observes " he had long lived in uninterrupted peace, and with many marks of distinguished respect." At the conclusion, he observes of the constant aim of his labours, " Such as they are, I make a humble sacrifice of them to the honour of the blessed Redeemer, and lay them at his feet; having no higher ambition in this world, than to serve his interest, and to be accepted of him; nor higher expectation of hope, than to be with him, and behold his glory." In 1736, he gave to the public, a volume of " Funeral Discourses; in two parts: containing, (1.) Consolations on the Death of our Friends. (2.) Preparations for our own Death." They had been preached at distant times, and on different occasions; many of them had been published singly, and they were now brought together in one view. Dr. Harris also published, " A Practical Illustration of the Book of Esther." In 1703, he was entrusted by the executors of Mr. Nathaniel Taylor, with the publication of the posthumous pieces of that celebrated preacher, to which he prefixed a Preface; " an example, (says Dr. Lardner) of that excellent manner by which all his writings are distinguished." In 1725, he was employed to revise the second edition of Dr. Manton's Sermons on the 119th Psalm, to which he prefixed, Memoirs of the Author. These were afterwards printed separately in octavo. He was also concerned with Dr. Evans, in the publication of two volumes of Sermons, by the great Mr. John Howe, on " The Spirit's Influence on the Church, and on Particular Persons." It ought not to be omitted, that Dr. Harris was one of the continuators of Matthew Henry's Exposition; and wrote the Commentary upon the Epistles to the Philippians and Colossians. (T)

(T) Besides the above Dr. William Harris, there was another writer of the same names, also a Dissenting Minister, and a celebrated historian. The latter was a native of Salisbury, and received his academical learning under

POOR JEWRY LANE.—*English Presbyterian*, Extinct.

SAMUEL ROSEWELL, M. A.—Dr. Harris had various ministers successively to assist him. The first, was the pious and excellent Mr. Samuel Rosewell, who was chosen

Mr. Grove, and Dr. Amory, at Taunton. At that period, he was remarkable for pregnant parts, and a love of books. He began to preach when very young; it is apprehended, before he was nineteen years of age. His first settlement was with a dissenting congregation at St. Loo, in Cornwall. From thence he removed to the city of Wells, were he was ordained April 15, 1741. Mr. Samuel Billingsley, of Ashwick, and Dr. Amory, of Taunton, assisted on the occasion. Mr. Harris did not continue many years at Wells; but, on marrying Miss Bovet, of Honiton, he removed to that town, to reside with two uncles of that lady, and preached the remainder of his life to a small society, at Luppit, in the neighbourhood. In September 1765, the University of Glasgow conferred upon him the degree of Doctor of Divinity, through the interest of his friend, the late Thomas Hollis, Esq.

Dr. Harris's first essay in the walk of literature, in which he afterwards made a distinguished figure, was the Life of Hugh Peters, after the manner of Bayle. In 1753, he published " An historical and critical Account of the Life and Writings of James I." upon the model of the fore-mentioned writer; drawn from State Papers and original documents. This was followed in 1758, by the Life of Charles I. upon the same plan. These publications attracted the notice, and secured him the friendship, of the munificent Mr. Thomas Hollis, who, from time to time, assisted him with many valuable books and papers, for the furtherance of his design. In the year 1762, he gave to the public, the Life of Oliver Cromwell, in one large volume octavo; and in 1766, the Life of Charles II. in two volumes octavo. Both were executed in the same manner, and gained the Author increasing reputation. The characteristic qualities of Dr. Harris as an historian, are diligence in collecting materials; exact fidelity in quoting authorities; impartiality in stating facts; and an ardent zeal for civil and religious liberty. It has been justly observed, that while Eachard, Hume and Smollet, and other writers of their stamp, composed their histories for the use of Kings, or rather tyrants, to instruct them how to rule at pleasure; Rapin, Harris, Wilson, Osborne, &c wrote for the use of the people, to show them that they could claim an equal protection in their privileges and liberties, by a right anterior to the authority conferred upon Kings.* Dr. Harris adopted the manner of Bayle, as it gave him an opportunity to enter into disquisitions, and to indulge reflections in the notes, which, in the text, would have interrupted the narrative. His abilities and merits as an historian, introduced him to an acquaintance and correspondence with some of the most eminent

* Memoirs of Thomas Hollis, Esq. vol. i. p. 210.

POOR JEWRY LANE.—*English Presbyterian*, Extinct.

about 1701, in the room of Mr. Francis Fuller, before-mentioned.* In this connexion he continued a few years, preaching with great acceptance, till 1705, when he accepted an invitation to assist the learned Mr. John Howe, pastor of a congregation in Silver-street, to which article we refer for a further account of Mr. Rosewell. The vacancy at Crutched-Friars, occasioned by his removal, was filled up the following year, by the Rev. John Billingsley, from Hull.

JOHN BILLINGSLEY was born at Chesterfield, in Derbyshire, about the year 1657. His father, the Rev. John Billingsley, M. A. was the ejected minister of that place; a man of great piety and worth, and a faithful industrious preacher. He died May 30, 1684. A particular account of him may be seen in Dr. Calamy's Abridgment,† together with a handsome Latin epitaph, drawn up by this his only surviving son. After passing through a preparatory course of education, he was admitted a member of Trinity College, Cambridge; but, when neither his inclination nor circumstances, allowed his longer continuance at the University, he was placed under the care of the famous Mr. Edward Reyner, of Lincoln. He afterwards had considerable assistance in his studies, from his worthy father, and

---

characters in his day; as Lord Orford, Archdeacon Blackburn, Dr. Birch, Mrs. Macauley, Dr. Mayhew of Boston, Mr. Theophilus Lindsey, &c. Besides the foregoing works, it is conjectured that he was the author of a tract, without his name, in answer to " An Essay on Establishments in Religion;" which passed as the work of Mr. Rotherham, but was suspected to have been dictated, or at least revised, by Archbishop Secker. He was, likewise, the editor of a volume of Sermons, by the late Mr. William West, of Exeter. An ill state of health, brought on by nocturnal studies, when the mornings had been spent in relaxation, and converse with neighbouring friends, impeded his application to further historical investigations, and terminated his life, on February 4, 1770, when he was only 50 years of age. *Monthly Magazine for August*, 1800.

* MS.   † Vol. ii. p. 169.

POOR JEWRY LANE.—*English Presbyterian*, Extinct.

his uncle Whitlock, of Nottingham. He was ordained to the ministry by fasting and prayer, and imposition of hands, at the same time with Mr. Joshua Oldfield, Mr. Samuel Cotes, and Mr. Samuel Rose: the ministers engaged in the service, were his father Mr. John Billingsley, Mr. Robert Porter, Mr. John Oldfield, Mr. Edward Prime, and Mr. William Cotes, all names of renown in that part of the country.

Mr. Billingsley entered upon the ministry in the darkest part of the reign of King Charles the Second, as did several other worthy ministers, though without any prospect of worldly advantage, or, even opportunity of public service; but under the greatest difficulties and discouragements. His first services were at Chesterfield, where he was engaged only on the evening of the Lord's-day. After the death of his father, it is probable he resided some time with Mr. Edward Prime, at Sheffield, of whom he says, " This excellent person was to me many years as a father, instructing, counselling and comforting me; and his name and memory will always be most precious to me."* Afterwards he preached for seven years at Selston, to a plain but serious auditory. From thence he removed to Kingston-upon-Hull, where he lived ten years with as great usefulness and reputation, as any minister in those parts. About the year 1706, the providence of God directed Mr. Billingsley to London, and he was chosen colleague with Dr. William Harris, at Crutched-Friars. This service he undertook with the advice and opinion of several worthy ministers, his particular friends; and continued preaching about fifteen years, as constantly as the frequent returns of bodily disorder would admit. " I ever esteemed him (says Dr. Harris) a great blessing to the congregation; and I believe he was thought so by every one in it. We lived together, through that course of time, in a most perfect un-

---

* Preface to Mr. Fern's Sermon on the Death of Mr. Prime.

POOR JEWRY LANE.—*English Presbyterian*, Extinct.

interrupted friendship and endearment: his labours and his memory will be always precious in my account."*

For several years, during the winter season, Mr. Billingsley spent his Lord's-day evenings in a catechetical exercise to a numerous congregation at the Old Jewry. On these occasions, he expounded both the shorter and larger catechism of the assembly of Divines, and went over the principal points of the popish controversy. Many persons, especially of the younger sort, who attended this lecture, afterwards remembered it with pleasure; and God remarkably owned and blessed his endeavours for sound instruction, and saving conversion. When the controversy concerning the Trinity was so warmly agitated in the West of England, at the beginning of the eighteenth century, the Dissenting ministers in London, with a view of composing the differences, convened a synod at Salter's-Hall in 1719; but unhappily split upon the rock of subscription, and still further widened the breach. Mr. Billingsley divided with those who were against subscribing; not from any disaffection to the doctrine, but because he apprehended it interfered with that fundamental principle of Protestant Dissent, The unlawfulness of requiring subscription to human tests in matters of religion. In this affair, no man was more anxiously careful to see his way clear, or more throughly satisfied in the judgment he had formed with so much deliberation.

Mr. Billingsley laboured under the great infelicity of a crazy constitution, which, he used to say, he brought into the world with him; and was much exercised with weakness and pain. He has often gone into the pulpit without any comfortable rest the preceding night, and groaning under the burthen of the mortal body. On such occasions, he used to repeat an expression he heard from the mouth of that excellent man, Mr. Richard Baxter, who was greatly afflicted in a similar way; " When we are sick we groan,

---

* Harris's Funeral Discourses, p. 253.

POOR JEWRY LANE.—*English Presbyterian*, Extinct.

when we are well we lust; sickness is our burthen, health is our snare." During his long and various exercises, he expressed a patient submission, and humble resignation to the Divine will; and was only solicitous that his faith and patience might hold out to the end. It was a great disadvantage to him under his afflictions, that his natural temper was melancholy and timorous; this circumstance, however, made his humility shine with the more distinguished lustre. "When I discoursed with him (says Dr. Harris) concerning his spiritual state, and future prospects in his last sickness, he spake to this sense; 'I hope my heart has been right with God: I think I have made it the business of my life to please him. I have an humble confidence in the covenant faithfulness of a gracious God, and the precious merit of the Redeemer's blood; but pretend not to transports of affection, and rapturous joys; for, says he, you know my temper and make."* During his illness, he preserved a most profound reverence of the glorious majesty of God; the highest thoughts, and most ardent affection to the blessed Redeemer; and his soul was full of love to all good men. He possessed a settled peace and composure of mind; nor did his bodily weakness, or fearful temper, which ever made him cautious and humble, appear to disturb his peace, or give him uneasiness of mind. This excellent and useful minister departed to the world of spirits May 2, 1722, in the 65th year of his age. His remains were interred in Bunhill-Fields; and on Lord's-day, May 13, Dr. Harris delivered the funeral sermon at Crutched-Friars, from 2 Cor. v. 2. *For in this we groan, earnestly desiring to be clothed upon with our house which is from heaven.*

To the above remarks upon Mr. Billingsley's life, we will subjoin a few particulars of his character. As a preacher, his discourses were solid and judicious, the result

---

* Harris's Funeral Discourses, p. 257.

POOR JEWRY LANE.—*English Presbyterian*, Extinct.

of mature thought and diligent preparation. It is recorded to his honour, that he never satisfied himself with loose or sudden composures; nor allowed any idle neglects, or unguarded liberties in what concerned the honour of divine truth, and the welfare of the souls of men. His manner was grave and serious; and sometimes, upon awakening and important subjects, very solemn and awful; such as exceedingly engaged the attention, and affected the heart. The subjects he handled were the peculiar doctrines of the Gospel, by which he enforced the duties of religion. His usual method was, to reduce his subject into propositions, and then apply it to the cases of different hearers. In prayer, he greatly excelled; and upon particular occasions, was remarkable for the pertinence as well as fulness of his matter. " The many opportunities we have had of praying together (says Dr. Harris,) in private families, and upon particular emergencies, have given very affecting and instructing instances of it." As to his personal character, he was a man of great sincerity and plainness of heart; and of a very serious spirit. His highest care and ambition was to please God, and be accepted of him. He was a diligent inquirer after knowledge, and used great application to inform his mind, and fit himself for his sacred work. In the study of the ancient and modern languages he took particular pleasure, and acquired considerable skill as a critic. But, under all his attainments he was exceedingly modest and humble, paid great deference to the judgment of others, and was always ready to receive information from the meanest person. He was remarkable for a peculiar tenderness of mind, and a scrupulous conscientiousness in all his concerns; and through a long course and many trials, his conversation was unblamable and exemplary. Of the reputation of younger ministers he was extremely tender; greatly delighted in their conversation; and rejoiced much in the serious spirit, and excellent accomplishments, with which many of them were

POOR JEWRY LANE.—*English Presbyterian*, Extinct.

endowed. He had a large acquaintance among serious and judicious people of all denominations; and possessed a general love and esteem. " I believe (says Dr. Harris) he is thought by all who knew him, a loss to the world, and to the church of God."*

Mr. Billingsley had the singular happiness of seeing five children grown up and disposed of in the world, who were all dutiful and religious. One of these was a Dissenting minister at Dover, where, after several years, marrying a sister of Sir Philip Yorke, afterwards Lord Chancellor Hardwicke, he was induced to conform, and accept a good living in the church, together with a prebend in Bristol Cathedral. In this station he continued till the day of his death. He was a moderate conformist, and maintained a friendly intercourse with the Dissenters to the last. He left two sons; one of whom was made clerk of the patents in the reign of George the Second; and the other was bred a clergyman.† (u)

SAMUEL HARVEY.—This pious and excellent young minister was a native of Birmingham, and born about the

---

* Dr. Harris's Sermon on the Death of Mr. Billingsley, p. 35—42.
† Nonconformist's Memorial, vol. i. p. 402, note.

(u) The following is a list of Mr. Billingsley's publications.—1. The Believer's Daily Exercise; or the Scripture Precept of being in the Fear of God all the Day long: Explained and urged in four Sermons. 1690.—2. A Reformation Sermon preached at Hull, Jan. 10, 1699-1700. Jude 22, 23. 3. Two Sermons upon 2 Peter, v. 6. 1700.—4. A Reformation Sermon preached in London, July 1, 1706. Ezra v. 2.—5. A Sermon on the 5th of November, preached at Crutched Fryars. 1710.—6. Doing Good to all encouraged and directed; in a Sermon on Gal. vi. 10. 1710.—7. A Call to Prayer from the City to the Country. 1712.—8. A Thanksgiving Sermon, Jan. 20, 1714-15.—9. A Brief Discourse of Schism.—10. A Funeral Sermon upon the premature Death of Mr. John Dudley, who departed this Life at Leicester, Jan. 5, 1715-16.—11. An Exposition of the Epistle of Jude; in the Continuation of Matthew Henry's Exposition.—12. A Volume of Sermons against Popery. 1723.

POOR JEWRY LANE.—*English Presbyterian*, Extinct.

year 1699. Almost as soon as he could speak, he gave manifest indications of a very serious spirit; and by the gravity of his deportment in the first years of life, exhibited something superior to the manners of a child. He told a worthy minister, his dear and intimate friend, (w) " That as long as he could remember any thing, he remembered his being concerned for the salvation of his soul; and he always preferred his books and his closet, to the diversions of childhood." This serious disposition was productive of the most happy consequences, even while a school-boy; for conversing with one of his companions upon religious subjects, it proved the means of his conversion, and he afterwards became a preacher. We are informed, that from the fifth year of his age, the impressions of the best things were never effaced from his mind. He loved the conversation of ministers and Christians, especially when it turned upon religious subjects; and he received great assistance from an elder sister of eminent piety. His habits of seriousness, coupled with a natural love of learning, engaged much of his time in reading the works of our best practical Divines; and fitted him for the ministry, to which he had a strong inclination.

He pursued his studies sometime under the care of the pious and ingenious Mr. John Reynolds, of Shrewsbury. From thence he removed to be under the tuition of the celebrated Mr. Samuel Jones, of Tewkesbury; but he appears to have finished his studies at Findern, in Derbyshire, under Mr. Thomas Hill, and Dr. Ebenezer Latham. Though this change of tutors could not have operated to his advantage, he is said, nevertheless, to have made great improvements in the most useful parts of learn-

(w) The Rev. Edward Brodhurst, a very valuable minister and tutor at Birmingham, who was removed by death, in the midst of his usefulness, July 21, 1730, in the 39th year of his age. He was the intimate friend and correspondent of the celebrated Dr. Watts, who drew up his epitaph in Latin, which may be met with in the Doctor's " Reliquiæ Juveniles," and contains a full delineation of his excellent character.

POOR JEWRY LANE.—*English Presbyterian*, Extinct.

ing, and to have acquired a critical skill in the Greek tongue. But he applied himself chiefly to the study of divinity; both as more agreeable to the temper of his mind, and to his future prospects in life. From this, he was not to be diverted by any worldly motives. When his tender and prudent father feared lest his stature should render him despicable, and be an obstruction to his acceptance and usefulness in the world; he declared to a friend, as his deliberate judgment, " That he was willing to undergo any pains or reproach for the term of life, if he might be the instrument of saving one soul." And it pleased God to grant him his desire for usefulness, without being subject to those inconveniences which his father apprehended. While at the academy, he used to have set meetings with a select number of his fellow-students designed for the ministry, to implore the blessing of God upon their studies; a custom, which, after his settlement in London, he proposed to some younger ministers of his particular acquaintance. He spent many hours, and sometimes parts of a day, in solemn prayer to God, and in delightful communion with him. Such was the ardent zeal of this extraordinary young man, such the specimens of his early piety!

Soon after the death of Mr. Billingsley, in 1722, Mr. Harvey was chosen assistant to Dr. William Harris, at Crutched-Fryars. Having now taken upon him the ministry, he resolved to study over the church-controversy, and not rest in the first impressions of education. With this view, he read with close application and impartiality, the *London Cases*, and other principal books on both sides the question. At length, upon mature deliberation, he became fixed in moderate nonconformity; which he thought grounded upon the fundamental principles of the Reformation, the perfection of the Scriptures, the sole authority of Christ in his church, and the unalienable right of every man to judge for himself, according to the best light and advantages afforded him. Mr. Harvey stood firm upon

POOR JEWRY LANE.—*English Presbyterian*, Extinct.

this basis. He did not, however, confine religion to a party; but freely owned and embraced all who loved Christ, and held the essentials of religion, however they were distinguished among men.

When Mr. Harvey had been settled almost seven years at Crutched-Fryars, he received an invitation to become pastor of the Independent congregation at Sudbury, in Suffolk, in the room of the Rev. Joshua Foster, who removed to Basingstoke, Hants, at the latter end of 1728. This call produced great anxiety in Mr. Harvey's mind; being desirous to know the will of God, by carefully weighing the circumstances attending his removal, before he finally determined. His friends, in general, apprehended his abilities fitter for London, where there was the greatest sphere of service. But the uncommon affection of the people at Sudbury, and the value they expressed for him; together with the apprehensions he entertained of greater usefulness among a considerable number of very serious persons, at length, inclined him to settle there. When he was admonished by an elder minister, of the weakness of his constitution, he said, " He was willing to venture his life in the service of God, wherever he should call him; that it was a good work, and he served a good Master, and was not solicitous about the event." It pleased God, however, to disappoint the expectations of the good people at Sudbury; for before Mr. Harvey could remove thither, he was taken to a better world.

When he was attacked with his last sickness, he was reading over the Christian Writers of the three first centuries. His disorder was a slow fever, which proved fatal, through the weakness of his constitution, before he was apprehended to be in danger. Venturing abroad while the fever was upon him, he much exhausted his spirits in a conversation with some younger persons, who greatly valued his ministry. At the beginning of his illness, when his books were packed up for his removal, he said to a friend,

POOR JEWRY LANE.—*English Presbyterian,* Extinct.

" Perhaps I have a longer journey to go than to Sudbury." And so it proved; for he died the day previous to the one he had fixed for his journey thither. He designed to have taken a solemn leave of the congregation at Crutched-Fryars, for whom he had always expressed a sincere value, in a farewell sermon, which he had nearly composed for the purpose. The subject he fixed upon was, The Apostolical Benediction, in 2 Cor. xiii. 14. and he designed to have published it, as a mark of respect to his late hearers; but the ill state of his health would not allow him to finish it. The slow advance of his distemper at first, and the sudden turn of it afterwards, prevented him from expressing his thoughts concerning death, and giving those advices, which, doubtless, he would have done, greatly to the edification of those about him. The night before he died, he was often heard to pray fervently, till nature being at length exhausted, he resigned his spirit into the hands of his Redeemer, April 17, 1729, in the 31st year of his age. Dr. Harris preached his funeral sermon at Crutched-Fryars, on Psa. cii. 23, 24.

The character of this excellent man appears in the most amiable light. His natural abilities were above the common rate. He possessed a sound judgment, a quick apprehension, and a tenacious memory. As he read much, so he digested and retained what he read; and he had a surprising faculty of repeating the sermons he heard. In conversation, he discovered great justness and compass of thought, a natural ease and propriety of expression, and in his countenance and speech was exhibited a happy mixture of liveliness and gravity. In his ministerial capacity, he was furnished greatly beyond his years. His discourses were always upon the most weighty and serious subjects, composed with great judgment, and arranged in the best order. He delivered himself with a manly decency, and with becoming warmth and zeal; which while they engaged attention and gave delight, procured him the esteem of the serious and

POOR JEWRY LANE.—*English Presbyterian*, Extinct.

judicious. Instead of displaying in the pulpit a vain ostentation of learning and wit, he chose, rather, to appear serious; as one who was in good earnest himself, and intent upon doing good to the souls of men. He took great pains to press upon his hearers the vast importance of the mediation of Christ, and the standing influences of the Holy Spirit, as the grand peculiarities of the Christian dispensation; and feared that the want of due regard to them, was one great reason of the languishing state of religion, and of the frequent revolts from the Christian interest. How far his apprehensions have been justified, in the state of many of our churches, for the last half century, deserves the most serious consideration. In private life, Mr. Harvey exhibited all the graces of the christian character. He was a man of strict integrity, a stranger to artifice and deceit, and remarkably conscientious in all his words and actions. It is recorded to his honour, that he was never head to speak evil of any man. His mind was deeply tinctured with religion, and he ever discovered an uncommon degree of genuine, unaffected piety.(x) Religious conversation was his great delight, and he seldom cared to bear part in any other; being strongly persuaded of the good that might be done by it, when managed with discretion. Here he shone to great advantage; being free, communicative, and cheerful. He was ever inquisitive after truth; zealous for what he thought important, especially in what related to vital and practical religion; and greatly lamented the visible decays of it, among Christians of different communions. A worthy minister, who was intimately acquainted with him from his youth, declared, " That in the latter part of his life, he considered him as a Christian fully grown, and arrived to

(x) It appears that he kept a diary of the state of his soul, and of the most remarkable providences of God, for more than sixteen years together; in which are many wise and judicious remarks, and the most devout reflections and ejaculations, bewailing the disorders of his mind, imploring the Divine aid, adoring the Divine mercy, &c.

POOR JEWRY LANE.—*English Presbyterian*, Extinct.

the most advanced steps of the Divine life, which are to be found among men on earth." Dr. Harris observes of him, " I must bear this testimony to his memory from the most intimate acquaintance, and I know I have the concurrence of my brethren, who best knew him; That I never knew any young minister of so serious a spirit, and so earnestly set for doing good. He was indeed ripe for service, and ripe for heaven betimes. I can truly say, that I never heard him without pleasure, and often with admiration."* The excellent Dr. Watts, who had a great esteem for Mr. Harvey, drew up the following epitaph to his memory.

>Here lie the ruins of a lowly tent,
>Where the seraphic soul of Harvey spent
>Its mortal years. How did his genius shine,
>Like heaven's bright Envoy clad in powers divine!
>When from his lips the grace or vengeance broke,
>'Twas majesty in arms, 'twas melting mercy spoke.
>What worlds of worth lay crowded in the breast!
>Too strait the mansion for th' illustrious guest.
>Zeal, like a flame, shot from the realms of day,
>Aids the slow fever to consume the clay,
>And bears the Saint up thro' the starry road
>Triumphant: So Elijah went to God.
>What happy Prophet shall his mantle find,
>Heir to the double portion of his mind?

NATHANIEL LARDNER, D. D.—This learned and eminent Divine, was born at Hawkehurst, in Kent, June 6, 1684. Of his father, the Rev. Richard Lardner, who was a respectable and worthy minister among the Protestant Dissenters, we shall have occasion to make distinct mention, in the course of the present work. His mother was one of the daughters of Mr. Nathaniel Collyer, formerly of the borough of Southwark, but who afterwards retired to

* Dr. Harris's Sermon on the Death of Mr. Harvey, p. 37—45.

POOR JEWRY LANE.—*English Presbyterian*, Extinct.

Hawkehurst, a large village, south of Cranbrook, and lying in that part of Kent which borders upon Sussex. It was probably at his grandfather's house that young Lardner was born. Where he received his grammatical education cannot now be ascertained; though, from his father's residence at Deal, it is supposed to have been at that place. From the grammar-school, he was removed to an academy in Hoxton-square, under the superintendance of those eminent Divines, Messrs. Spademan, Lorimer, and Oldfield. Here he must have continued but a short time; for towards the latter end of 1699, being then only in his sixteenth year, he was sent to prosecute his studies at Utrecht. He was accompanied thither by Mr. Martin Tomkins, afterwards a Dissenting minister, and a writer of some eminence; and they found there the celebrated Mr. Daniel Neal. The Professors of the University at that time were D'Uries, Grævius, and Burman, names of no small celebrity in the literary world. Under such tutors, Mr. Lardner made suitable improvements in various branches of learning; and brought back with him a testimonial from Professor Burman to that purpose. After spending somewhat more than three years at Utrecht, Mr. Lardner removed to Leyden, where he studied about six months. In 1703, he returned to England, in company with Mr. Tomkins and Mr. Neal, and joined himself to the Independent Church in Miles's-lane, under the pastoral care of the Rev. Matthew Clarke. The six following years he spent in close study, and diligent preparation for the sacred profession he had in view.*

Mr. Lardner did not hastily press himself into the ministry, for it was not till he was above twenty-five years of age that he entered the pulpit. He preached his first sermon for his friend Mr. Martin Tomkins, at Stoke-Newington. The subject of his discourse was, Rom. i. 16. *For I am*

* Memoirs of the Life and Writings of the late Rev. Nathaniel Lardner, D. D. p. 1—7

POOR JEWRY LANE.—*English Presbyterian*, Extinct.

not ashamed of the gospel of Christ, &c. We have no information concerning him during the four years that succeeded this event; but, it is probable he preached frequently for his father, who was then pastor of a congregation in London. In the year 1713, he was invited to reside in the family of Lady Treby, widow of Sir George Treby,(y) in quality of chaplain to her ladyship, and tutor to her youngest son, Brindley Treby. To this proposal he acceded; and it need not be said, how well qualified he was, by his knowledge, judgment and learning, to undertake such a trust. After he had superintended the studies of Mr. Treby for three years, he accompanied him in an excursion into France, the Austrian Netherlands, and the United Provinces, which employed four months. From a journal which Mr. Lardner kept of this tour, it was evident that he did not lose the opportunity it afforded him of making exact and judicious observations on the manners and customs of the inhabitants whom he saw and visited, and on the edifices and curiosities of the countries through which he passed. After his return, he continued to reside in the family of Lady Treby, till 1721, the time of her ladyship's death. By this event, he was removed from a situation which seems to have been an agreeable one, and was thrown into circumstances of perplexity and suspense. His own remarks will show the state of his mind at that time. " I am yet at a loss, (says he) how to dispose of myself. I can say I am desirous of being useful in the world. Without this, no external advantages relating to myself will make me happy; and yet I have no prospect of being serviceable in the work of the ministry; having preached many years without being favoured with the approbation and choice of any one congregation."*

(y) Sir George Treby, Knight, was appointed Lord Chief Justice of the Court of Common Pleas, in 1692, and sustained that high office with great ability and integrity, till his decease in 1702.

* Memoirs, *ubi supra*, p. 4.

POOR JEWRY LANE. - *English Presbyterian*, Extinct.

That such a man as Dr. Lardner should be suffered to lie so long neglected, has been matter of surprise to some persons, who have been inclined to censure the Dissenters upon that account. It should be observed, however, that he had not then commenced author, and his talents were only known in the private circle of his acquaintance. But, besides this, there were some material circumstances that contributed to render him unpopular. In his best days, he possessed but an indifferent elocution; and he dropped his words greatly in the pulpit. To this may be added, that the matter of his discourses, as well as his mode of composition, was not calculated to strike the multitude. It was also about this time that he became afflicted with a deafness that increased upon him as he advanced in years. This calamity was not a little heightened by the death of his pupil Mr. Treby,(z) for whom he entertained the highest affection and esteem. On the subject of his deafness, he writes thus in the beginning of the year 1724, " Mr. Cornish preached; but I was not able to hear any thing he said, nor so much as the sound of his voice. I am, indeed, at present so deaf, that when I sit in the pulpit, and the congregation is singing, I can hardly tell whether they are singing or not."*

It is a circumstance not generally known, that Mr. Lardner commenced his stated labours in the ministry, at an ancient meeting-house in Hoxton-square. Here he preached for a few years, as assistant to his father, Mr. Richard Lardner.† At the time of his leaving Lady Treby's family, he was a member of a literary society, consisting of ministers and lay gentlemen, who met on Monday evenings, at Chew's Coffee-house, in Bow-lane, Cheapside. He was also a member of another society, which met at the same place, on a Thursday, and consisted entirely of ministers. One of

---

(z) This event happened in 1723.
* Memoirs, *ubi supra*, p. 11.   † MS.

POOR JEWRY LANE.—*English Presbyterian*, Extinct.

the objects they had in view, was to compose a Concordance to the Bible; and they began to methodize the book of Proverbs for that purpose. But by some means or other, the design was never completed. In the year 1723, he was concerned, with several other ministers, in conducting a course of lectures, on a Tuesday evening, at the Old Jewry. In his turn, on these occasions, he delivered three admirable discourses on the Credibility of the Gospel History; which, probably, laid the foundation of his great work. Certain it is, that, from this time, he was diligently engaged in writing the first part of his Credibility. His modesty, however, was such, that he was doubtful about the publication of it, and greatly regretted, that, by the decease of his friend and pupil, Mr. Treby, he was deprived of his advice, on this and other occasions. At length, getting the better of his diffidence, he published in 1727, in two volumes octavo, the first part of " The Credibility of the Gospel History; or, the facts occasionally mentioned in the New Testament confirmed by passages of ancient authors, who were contemporary with our Saviour, or his Apostles, or lived near their time." An appendix was subjoined, concerning the time of Herod's death. It is scarcely necessary to say how well this work was received by the learned of all denominations. It is, indeed, an invaluable performance; replete with admirable instruction, sound learning, and just criticism; and it hath rendered the most essential service to Christianity. A second edition was soon called for, and a third was published in 1741.*

In the beginning of February, 1728, the course of Mr. Lardner's studies was interrupted, and his life threatened by the attack of a violent fever, which proved of long continuance. For some time his recovery was despaired of by his relatives and friends; but he was relieved, and at length, happily restored to health, by the divine blessing on the

---

* Kippis's Life of Dr. Lardner, prefixed to his works, p. 12.

POOR JEWRY LANE.—*English Presbyterian*, Extinct.

prescriptions of Dr. (afterwards, Sir Edward) Hulse, who was called in to consult with the other physicians. It was not long after his recovery, that he settled at Poor Jewry Lane, Crutched-Fryars. For preaching a casual sermon there on the 24th of August, 1729, he was unexpectedly invited to become assistant to Dr. William Harris; and entered upon his office on the 14th of September following.*

At this time, the religious world was engaged in an important controversy, relative to the Christian revelation. Mr. Woolston, by reading Origen, and other mystical writers, had been led to embrace an allegorical mode of explaining the scriptures, which he carried to a most extravagant and ridiculous excess. After several absurd publications, he contended, in a tract entitled, " The Moderator between an Infidel and an Apostate," that the Miracles of our Saviour were not real, or ever actually wrought. For this work, a prosecution was commenced against him, in 1726, by the Attorney General; but, in consequence of Mr. Whiston's intercession, it was laid aside. Mr. Woolston was not induced by this indulgence, to continue in silence. He pursued the subject through the following years, till 1730, in six discourses, and two defences of them; in which he not only maintained his former principles, but treated the Miracles of our Saviour with a licentiousness, buffoonery, and insolence, that was strongly indicative of malignant infidelity. The prosecution, therefore, was renewed against him; and, being tried before Lord Chief Justice Raymond, he was condemned in one year's imprisonment, and a fine of a hundred pounds. But a far better method of confuting Mr. Woolston, was adopted by many learned Divines, who wrote against him. Among these, Mr. Lardner appeared to no small advantage. His work upon this occasion, published at the latter end of

* Memoirs, *ubi supra*, p. 11, 12.

POOR JEWRY LANE.—*English Presbyterian*, Extinct.

1729, was entitled, "A Vindication of Three of our Blessed Saviour's Miracles, viz. The Raising of Jairus's Daughter, the Widow of Nain's Son, and Lazarus." This Vindication, which was composed with reference to Mr. Woolston's fifth discourse, was undoubtedly one of the best treatises which appeared in that controversy. It abounds with admirable and judicious observations, and contains a complete defence of three of the most important of our Lord's miracles. Accordingly, it was very favourably received by the learned world, and soon came to a second edition. Mr. Lardner was not one of those who approved of the prosecution which was carried on against Mr. Woolston by the civil magistrate. In his preface, therefore, he has made some excellent remarks on the subject of free inquiry and discussion. If men be permitted to deliver their sentiments freely in matters of religion, and to propose their objections against Christianity itself, he declares it to be his opinion, that there would be no reason to be in pain for the event. He justly observes, that all force on the minds of men, in matters of belief, is contrary to the spirit of Christianity; and that severity instead of doing good, has always done harm. The force of this remark, is abundantly verified by matter of fact. Dr. Waddington, at that time Bishop of Chichester, who was highly pleased with Mr. Lardner's Vindication, did not equally approve of the preface; and, therefore, wrote to him upon the subject. Several letters passed between them on the occasion, and they are couched in terms of mutual civility and respect.*

In 1733, appeared the first volume of the second part of "The Credibility of the Gospel History; or the principal Facts of the New Testament confirmed by Passages from ancient Authors, who were contemporary with our Saviour, or his Apostles, or lived near their time." The testimonies

* Kippis's Life of Dr. Lardner, p. 15—18.

POOR JEWRY LANE.——*English Presbyterian,* Extinct.

produced and considered, in this volume, were those of Barnabas, Clement, Hermas, Ignatius, Polycarp, Papias, Justin Martyr, Dionysius of Corinth, Tatian, Hegesippus, Melito, Ireneus, and Athenagoras. Our author also treats on a fragment called, Clement's Second Epistle, the relation of Polycarp's Martyrdom, the Evangelists in the reign of Trajan, the Epistle to Diognatus, and the Epistle of the Churches of Vienne and Lyons. In the Introduction, he has given an admirable summary of the history of the New Testament. The testimonies of approbation he received, in consequence of this work, were exceedingly numerous; and it was so highly valued abroad, as to be translated by two learned foreigners, into Latin and Low Dutch. The second volume of the second part of the Credibility, appeared in 1735. The subjects of this volume were, Miltiades, Theophilus of Antioch, Pantæneus, Clement of Alexandria, Polycrates, Heraclitus, and several other writers near the end of the second century; also Hermias, Serapion, Tertullian, together with a number of authors who required only to be shortly mentioned, and certain suppositious writings of the second century; such as the Acts of Paul and Thecla, the Sibylline Oracles, the Testaments of the Twelve Patriarchs, the Recognitions, the Clementine Homilies, and the Clementine Epitome. Among these different articles, those which relate to Clement of Alexandria and Tertullian, are peculiarly important, and the remarks on the Apocryphal works are very curious and useful. The farther Mr. Lardner proceeded in his design, the more did he advance in esteem and reputation among learned men of all denominations.*

In November 1736, our author was attacked by another severe and dangerous fever; and the effects of it were such, that he did not recover his health, so far as to be able to preach, till late in the spring of 1737. In that year, he

* Kippis, *ubi supra*, p. 20—23.

POOR JEWRY LANE.—*English Presbyterian*, Extinct.

published his " Counsels of Prudence for the Use of Young People; a Discourse on the Wisdom of the Serpent, and the Innocence of the Dove: in which are recommended general Rules of Prudence; with particular Directions relating to Business, Conversation, Friendship, and Usefulness." This discourse was generally and justly admired; and it received the particular commendation of Dr. Secker, then Bishop of Oxford. In 1738, Mr. Lardner gave to the public, the third volume of the second part of the Credibility. This volume carried the evidence down to the year 233, and included Minucius Felix, Apollonius, Caius, Asterius Urbanus, Alexander Bishop of Jerusalem, Hippolytus, Ammonius, Julius Africanus, Origen, and Fermilian. Some of these articles are of interesting importance, particularly that of Origen. The following year, our author published two discourses, entitled, " A Caution against Conformity to this World." These may justly be considered as a sequel to the Counsels of Prudence. Early in January, 1740, appeared the fourth volume of the second part of the Credibility. This volume commences with an account of various writers of less note in the former part of the third century. Our author then proceeds to the consideration of Noetus, and others who were called heretics at that period; such as the Valesians, the Angelics, the Apostolics, and the Origenists. But the volume is chiefly devoted to Gregory Bishop of Neocesarea; Dionysius of Alexandria; and Cyprian of Carthage. The two last articles are very copious and curious.*

In the year 1740, Mr. Lardner suffered a severe domestic affliction, in the death of his venerable father, in the 87th year of his age. With his worthy parent he had resided ever since he quitted Lady Treby's family; and this event affected him in a very sensible manner. The same year, he sustained another loss in the death of his respectable and

---

* Kippis, *ubi supra*, p. 24—28.

POOR JEWRY LANE.——*English Presbyterian,* Extinct.

highly valued colleague Dr. William Harris; on which occasion, he preached and printed a suitable discourse. Soon after this event, he had an unanimous invitation to undertake the pastoral charge of the Society in Poor Jewry Lane, in conjunction with some other minister, of whom they should make choice. To this he was strongly urged by his friend Mr. Joseph Hallet, of Exeter, whom he consulted upon the occasion; but for reasons at present unknown, he declined taking a share in the pastoral office. It is probable that his deafness contributed, among other causes, to this determination. In November, Mr. (afterwards Dr.) George Benson, was chosen sole pastor of the Society, and our author continued assistant preacher.*

It was not till the year 1743, that Mr. Lardner was enabled to give to the public, the fifth volume of the second part of the Credibility. This volume comprehended Cornelius Lucius, and Dionysius, bishops of Rome; Novatus, Commodian, Malchion, Anatolius, and three others, bishops of Laodicea; Theognostus; Theonas, bishop of Alexandria; Pierius, presbyter of the same church; two Doritheuses; Victorinus, bishop of Pettaw; Methodius, bishop of Olympus in Lycia; Lucian, presbyter of Antioch; Hesychius, bishop in Egypt; Pamphylius, presbyter of Cæsarea; Phileas, bishop of Thumis in Egypt; Philoromus, receiver-general at Alexandria; Peter, bishop of Alexandria, and the Miletians. In an advertisement, prefixed to the volume, our author expresses his apprehensions that some persons might be ready to charge him with prolixity; but he offers, at the same time, very satisfactory reasons for the method he has pursued. Among other things, he observes, that the particular design of his work was to enable persons of ordinary capacities, who had not an opportunity of reading many authors, to judge for themselves concerning

* Memoirs, *ubi supra,* p. 86—95.

POOR JEWRY LANE.—*English Presbyterian*, Extinct.

the external evidence of the facts related in the New Testament. This volume of his great work was followed, the same year, by another valuable performance, entitled, " The Circumstances of the Jewish People an Argument for the Truth of the Christian Religion." It consists of three discourses on Rom. xi. 11. and is handled with great perspicuity and success.* It was in the year last mentioned, that death made another inroad in his family, by the decease of the Rev. Daniel Neal, who had married his sister. And the following year (1744) he lost another distant relation by marriage, Dr. Jeremiah Hunt, who was one of his most intimate and beloved friends. This latter event, he improved in a funeral discourse, which he afterwards published.

In 1745, Mr. Lardner favoured the public with another volume of his great work, being the sixth of the second part. Excepting one chapter, relating to Archelaus, bishop in Mesopotamia, the whole volume was devoted to the Manichees; and the account of them is both curious and instructive. The same year, he revised and published a volume of posthumous sermons of the Rev. Mr. Kirby Reyner, of Bristol; to which he prefixed a brief account of the author. It was in the beginning of this year, that Mr. Lardner received a diploma from the Marischal College of Aberdeen, conferring upon him the degree of Doctor in Divinity. This was an honour which our author did not solicit, but which, when bestowed in so obliging a manner, he did not think it became him to refuse; preserving herein the due medium, between seeking for such a distinction, and despising it when offered. In 1746, Dr. Lardner was appointed one of the correspondent members at London, of the Society in Scotland, for propagating Christian Knowledge, and Protestant Principles, in the northern parts of that country, and the adjacent islands. In 1748, he was

* Kippis, *ubi supra*, p. 31—33.

POOR JEWRY LANE. — *English Presbyterian*, Extinct.

engaged in superintending a new edition of the two first volumes of the second part of the Credibility; and in the same year, he published the seventh volume of that part. The persons of whom an account was given, and whose testimonies were recited in this volume, were Arnobius, Lactantius; Alexander, bishop of Alexandria; Arius and his followers, and Constantine the Great, the first Christian Emperor. There were, likewise, two chapters on the Donatists, and on the burning of the Scriptures in the time of the Dioclesian persecution. It will appear from these names, that most of the articles are of peculiar importance. The character of Constantine is drawn with equal judgment and candour; and he discusses the fable of the *cross*, in the most sagacious and convincing manner.*

A new edition of the third volume of the second part of the Credibility was called for in 1750; and in the course of the same year appeared the eighth volume. It began with the council of Nice, and then proceeded to Eusebius, bishop of Cæsarea. The other persons and subjects treated of were, Marcellus, bishop of Ancyra in Galatia; Eustathius, bishop of Antioch; Athanasius, bishop of Alexandria; a dialogue against the Marcionites, Juvencus, Julius Firmicus Maternus, Cyril of Jerusalem, the Audians, Hilary of Poictiers, Aerius, the council of Laodicea, Epiphanius, Bishop in Cyprus; and the Apostolical Constitutions and Canons. In this volume, the two first articles are of peculiar importance. At the conclusion of the account of the council of Nice, are some admirable reflections on the conduct of that council, and on the pernicious effects of introducing subscriptions, authority, and force into the Christian Church. The history of Eusebius is very copious, and contains many excellent observations concerning the divisions of the sacred books, the character of the writers of them, and the employment of the Apostles, and aposto-

* Kippis, *ubi supra*, p. 35—89.

POOR JEWRY LANE.—*English Presbyterian.* Extinct.

lical men.* In the same year, our author published a volume of sermons, the subjects of which are entirely of a practical nature. In 1751, he resigned the office of morning preacher at Crutched-Fryars. His reasons for this determination were, the continuance and even increase of his deafness, the smallness of the morning auditory, and the importance of redeeming time for carrying on his long work. He preached his last sermon on the 23d of June; having been assistant at Poor Jewry Lane nearly, twenty-two years. The subject of his farewell discourse was, 2 Cor. iv. 18. *While we look not at the things which are seen, but at the things which are not seen; for the things which are seen are temporal, but the things which are not seen are eternal.*†

The ninth volume of the second part of the Credibility appeared in 1752. The persons treated of, were Rheticius, bishop of Autun; Triphyllius, Fortunatianus, Photinus; Eusebius, bishop of Vercelli; Lucifer, bishop of Cagliari in Sardinia; Gregory, bishop of Elvira; Phœbadius, bishop of Agen; Caius Marius Victorinus Afer; Apollinarius, bishop of Laodicea; Damasus, bishop of Rome; Basil, bishop of Cæsarea in Cappadocia; Gregory Nazianzen; Amphilochius, bishop of Iconium; Gregory, bishop of Nyssa in Cappadocia; Didymus of Alexandria, Ephrem the Syrian, Ebedjesu; Pacian, bishop of Barcelona; Optatus of Milevi; Ambrose, bishop of Milan; Diodorus, bishop of Tarsus; Philaster and Gaudentius, bishops of Brescia; Sophronius, and Theodore, bishop of Mopsuestia in Cilicia. There is also a long and curious chapter concerning the Priscillianists, and a shorter one relative to a commentary upon thirteen of Paul's Epistles, ascribed by many to Hilary, deacon of Rome. To this volume were subjoined, " Remarks upon Mr. Bower's Account of the Manichees, in the second volume of his History of the

* Kippis, *ubi supra*, p. 40. † Memoirs, *ubi supra*, p. 107.

POOR JEWRY LANE. — *English Presbyterian*, Extinct.

Popes." In this year, a second impression was called for of the Discourses on the Circumstances of the Jewish People. The next year produced the tenth volume of the second part of the Credibility; in which the persons treated of are few in number, but very important with respect to their character, works and testimony. They are Jerome; Rufinus; Augustin, bishop of Hippo; and John Chrysostom, bishop of Constantinople. A short chapter is introduced, on the third council of Carthage. Two other publications came from the pen of Dr. Lardner the same year. The first was, " A Dissertation upon the two Epistles ascribed to Clement of Rome, lately published by Mr. Wetstein; with large Extracts out of them, and an Argument showing them not to be genuine." The other production of Dr. Lardner appeared without his name, and was entitled, " An Essay on the Mosaic Account of the Creation and Fall of Man." In this piece, our author adopts the literal sense of the history of our first parents, and, after having critically explained the narration, deduces from it a variety of important observations.*

Dr. Lardner was now drawing to the conclusion of the second part of the Credibility. In 1754, the eleventh volume of it was published, containing a succinct history of the principal Christian writers from the fifth to the twelfth centuries, inclusive; with their testimony to the books of the New Testament. The persons introduced in this volume were more than forty in number, it not being necessary to make the articles so large and particular, as had been requisite at a more early period. An appendix was added, giving an account of the ecclesiastical histories of Socrates, Sozomen, and Theodoret. As such a quantity and variety of matter was comprehended in this great work, an epitome of it became very desirable, to assist the memory, and to display, at one view, the force of the argu-

* Kippis's Life of Lardner, p. 44—47.

POOR JEWRY LANE.—*English Presbyterian,* Extinct.

ment. Accordingly this was undertaken by the author himself, who, in the twelfth and last volume of the second part, which was published in 1755, gave a general review of his design, and an admirable recapitulation of the eleven preceding volumes, with some new additional observations. Lists were added of various readings, and of texts explained; together with an alphabetical catalogue of Christian authors, sects and writings, and an alphabetical table of principal matters.*

About this time, Dr. Lardner, in conjunction with Dr. Chandler, Dr. John Ward, and Mr. Edward Sandercock, was engaged in perusing, and preparing for the press, some posthumous dissertations of the Rev. Moses Lowman, a learned dissenting minister at Clapham. In 1756, he published the first and second volumes of " The Supplement to the Credibility of the Gospel History;" and the following year a third volume, which completed the work. The first volume of the Supplement contained general observations upon the Canon of the New Testament, and a history of the four Evangelists, with the evidences for the genuineness of the four Gospels, and the Acts of the Apostles, and an examination of the times in which these books were written. There is, likewise, a chapter concerning the time when the Apostles left Judæa, to preach the Christian religion in other countries; which event, our author thinks, could not have taken place until after the council at Jerusalem. The volume concludes with a discussion of the question, whether either of the first three Evangelists had seen the gospels of the others before he wrote his own ; and is determined in the negative. The second volume comprehended the history of the Apostle Paul, displayed the evidences for the genuineness of his fourteen Epistles, particularly that to the Hebrews, and ascertained the times in which they were written. Through the whole were interspersed many curious remarks;

* Kippis, *ubi supra,* p. 48—50.

POOR JEWRY LANE.—*English Presbyterian*, Extinct.

and the two concluding chapters were employed in shewing, that the Epistle inscribed to the Ephesians, was actually addressed to them, and that the churches of Colosse and Laodicea were planted by Paul. In the third volume the seven catholic Epistles, and the Revelation of John, was considered, and histories given of James, Peter, and Jude. The order of the books of the New Testament is examined, and proofs afforded that they were early known, read, and made use of by Christians. In conclusion it is shewn, that there is no reason to believe that any of the sacred books of the New Testament have been lost. It would not be easy to say too much in praise of this work. The different questions are discussed with a depth of investigation, and an accuracy of judgment, which are worthy of the highest admiration. Dr. Watson, bishop of Landaff, has inserted this Supplement in his valuable collection of Theological Tracts. The execution of this work, completed one grand part of Dr. Lardner's design, which was, to produce, at large, the testimonies of Christian writers to the books of the New Testament. It was a work of thirty-three years, and must have cost him immense labour. He had a design of publishing another volume of testimonies to the principal facts of the New Testament; but for some reason, it was never carried into effect. Perhaps, upon reflection, he might judge, that almost every thing he might wish to say upon this subject, would be found in the volumes already published.*

In the year 1757, Dr. Lardner, in conjunction with the Rev. Caleb Fleming, revised for publication, and introduced with a preface, a posthumous tract of Mr. Thomas Moore, entitled, " An Inquiry into the Nature of our Saviour's agony in the garden."(z) In the following year ap-

---

* Kippis's, *ubi supra*, p. 50—55.

(z) Mr. Moore was a woollen-draper, in Holywell-street, Strand; a thinking man, and studious in the scriptures. The design of his pamphlet

POOR JEWRY LANE.—*English Presbyterian*, Extinct.

peared two productions from his own pen. The first was, " The case of the Demoniacs, mentioned in the New Testament; being four Discourses upon Mark v. 19, with an Appendix for the further Illustration of the Subject." In this work, Dr. Lardner maintains the hypothesis formerly supported by Mr. Joseph Mede, and more lately by Dr. Sykes, and the celebrated Mr. Hugh Farmer. This scheme, which supposes the demoniacs to have been only diseased, or lunatic persons, and not actually possessed by evil spirits, has gained ground of late years; but it has been considered by many persons as involving the most injurious consequences; being not only contrary to the whole tenor of scripture evidence, but subversive even of Christianity itself. The subject is certainly an important one, and deserves the serious attention of every inquisitive reader. (A) The other publication of Dr. Lardner's this year, was anonymous, and entitled, " A Letter to Jonas Hanway, Esq. in which some reasons are assigned why houses for the reception of penitent women, who have been disorderly in their lives, ought not to be called Magdalen Houses." Mary Magdalen, as our author shows, was not the sinner recorded in the seventh chapter of Luke, but a woman of distinction and excellent character, who, for a while, laboured under some bodily indisposition, which our Lord miraculously healed. To stamp infamy upon her name, therefore, is not only highly injurious, but a direct violation of the sacred history.*

was to account for our Lord's agony, from the series of events which befel him during the latter part of his ministry, without supposing it to have been the result of any præternatural inflictions. It is certainly an ingenious performance ; but how far it is calculated to do honour to the Redeemer, must be left to the reader's judgment.

(A) Those who wish to inform themselves upon this subject, may consult the writings of Sykes, Lardner and Farmer, on the one side ; and of Fell and Worthington, who answered them. Fell's book is a master-piece of acute criticism.

* Kippis, *ubi supra*, p. 56, 57.

POOR JEWRY LANE.—*English Presbyterian*, Extinct.

In the year 1759, Dr. Lardner published, but without his name, " A Letter written in the year 1730, concerning the question, Whether the Logos supplied the place of a human Soul in the person of Jesus Christ." The reason why this did not appear sooner, perhaps, was because the author had not fully made up his mind on the subject. There were now added, " Two Postscripts: The first, containing an Explication of the words, the Spirit, the Holy Ghost, the Spirit of God, as used in the Scriptures: The second, containing Remarks upon the third Part of the late Bishop of Clogher's Vindication of the Histories of the Old and New Testaments." In this treatise, Dr. Lardner opposes the Arian hypothesis, to which he acknowledges he had once, for a while, been much inclined; but which he now thought irreconcileable to reason.* Instead of this, he labours to support a scheme, which we apprehend to be much more irreconcileable, we will not say to reason, but to the sacred scriptures, the only touchstone of a doctrine that is purely a matter of Revelation. It is with extreme concern, that we place so great a man as Dr. Lardner on the list of Socinian authors, who, however respectable, on account of their labours in the cause of literature, have contributed by their writings to poison the streams of divine truth, and promote an universal scepticism in matters of belief. (B)

A second volume of Sermons, on various subjects, was published by our author in 1760. They are of a more critical nature than those he gave to the world ten years

---

* Kippis, *ubi supra*, p. 58, 59.

(B) We have somewhere met with an observation of the celebrated Dr. Taylor of Norwich, which is much to our present purpose. The Doctor, who was a zealous Socinian, and a learned tutor at Warrington, expressed his surprise " how it happened that most of his pupils turned Deists." The fact, it seems, he admitted; but he never thought of accounting for it from the sceptical tendency of Socinian principles.

POOR JEWRY LANE.—*English Presbyterian*, Extinct.

before. The same year, the eleventh volume of the Credibility, and the two first volumes of the Supplement came to a second edition. The fifth volume had been reprinted in 1756, and the fourth and sixth in 1758. About this time, he revised the manuscript of a Treatise on the True Doctrine of the New Testament concerning Jesus Christ; written by the Rev. Paul Cardale, (c) a Dissenting Minister at Evesham, in Worcestershire. It is introduced by a long discourse on Free Inquiry in Matters of Religion, and contains a particular defence of the Socinian scheme. In 1761 and 1762, Dr. Lardner communicated four papers to a periodical work, called, " The Library." The tenth volume of the Credibility came to a new edition in the former year, as did the eleventh in 1762, and the eighth in 1766. It was in 1762, that our author published his " Remarks on the late Dr. Ward's Dissertations on several Passages of the Sacred Scriptures; wherein are shown, beside other things, that John computed the hours of the day after the Jewish manner; who are the Greeks, John xii; who the Grecians, Acts vi; the design of the Apostolic decree, Acts xv; that there was but one sort of Jewish proselytes; wherein lay the fault of Peter; and how Paul may be vindicated." In 1764, he published some

---

(c) Mr. Cardale was educated for the ministry under Dr. Latham, at Findern, in Derbyshire. About the year 1735, he settled at Evesham, where he preached about forty years, till his death, early in 1775. At the last, he had about twenty people to hear him, having ruined a fine congregation by his very learned, dry, and critical discourses, an extreme heaviness in the pulpit, and an almost total neglect of pastoral visits and private instruction.† He wrote several pieces in a dull, tedious way, in favour of Socinianism. In common with other writers of his stamp, he endeavours to impress his readers with an idea that every creed promulgated under the name of Christian, is equally acceptable to the Divine Being; or in other words, that there is no such thing as religious truth. His publications, according to Dr. Kippis,‡ had considerable influence in drawing over persons to his own opinions.

† Orton's Letters to Dissenting Ministers, vol. i. p. 154.
‡ Life of Lardner, p. 67.

POOR JEWRY LANE.—*English Presbyterian*, Extinct.

strictures on Dr. Macknight's Harmony of the Four Gospels, so far as related to the History of our Saviour's Resurrection.*

Amidst these various productions of a smaller nature, Dr. Lardner continued the prosecution of his grand object. Accordingly, in 1764, he gave to the world, in quarto, the first volume of " A large Collection of ancient Jewish and Heathen Testimonies to the Truth of the Christian Religion." This volume contained the authors of the first century. The heathen testimonies were, the pretended Epistle of Abgarus, King of Edessa; the Knowledge which the Emperor Tiberius had of our Lord; a monumental inscription concerning the Christians in the time of Nero; Pliny the elder; Tacitus; Martial; Juvenal; and Suetonius. But the volume is chiefly occupied with the Jewish testimonies, the principal of which is that of Josephus. He has taken great pains in examining the celebrated passage in that historian relating to Jesus Christ; which he pronounces an interpolation. The learned Dr. Chandler, who was convinced of its genuineness, addressed a letter on the subject to our author, who returned a written reply. In more recent times, the passage has been defended with great strength of reasoning, by the late Mr. Jacob Bryant. The second volume of our author appeared in 1765, containing the Heathen Testimonies of the Second Century. The persons treated of are Pliny the younger, and Trajan; Epictetus the Stoic, and Arrian; the Emperor Adrian; Bruttius Præsens; Phlegon, Thallus, and Dionysius the Areopagite; the Emperor Titus Antoninus the Pious; the Emperor Marcus Antoninus the Philosopher; Apuleius; the early adversaries of Christianity, and particularly Celsus; Lucian of Samosata; Aristides the Sophist; Dion Chrysostom, and Galen. The third volume of the Collection of Testimonies was published in 1766, and contains an account

* Kippis, *ubi supra*, p. 63—70.

POOR JEWRY LANE.—*English Presbyterian*, Extinct.

of the Heathen Writers of the Third Century. This volume, which extended to the conversion of Constantine the Great, abounded like the two former ones, with much valuable information. The persecution to which the professors of the Gospel were exposed, and particularly that under the Emperor Dioclesian, are here amply considered. A peculiar attention is likewise paid to Porphyry, and to his objections against the authenticity of the book of Daniel. In the chapter that relates to Diogenes Laertius, our author has introduced a very curious criticism on the altar to the unknown God, at Athens, mentioned in the Acts of the Apostles. The fourth volume of the Testimonies appeared in 1767, and contained the Heathen Writers of the Fourth, Fifth, and Sixth Centuries; to which was added, the State of Gentilism under the Christian Emperors. Among the persons mentioned, Julian, Ammianus Marcellinus, and Libanus are particularly distinguished. He has also introduced to our notice, not a few persons of great learning, and fine abilities, who were still tenacious of the pagan rites, and fond of all the fables upon which they are founded. In the copious article concerning Julian, a very important point came under Dr. Lardner's consideration; this was the attempt of that Emperor to rebuild Jerusalem, and the frustration of it by a miraculous interposition. The miracle is recorded, not only by three contemporary Christian writers, Gregory Nazianzen, Chrysostom, and Ambrose, but also by the heathen historian Ammianus Marcellinus. It is mentioned, likewise, by Rufinus, Socrates, Sozomen, Theodoret, and other ancient authors. Bishop Warburton also, wrote a very elaborate treatise in defence of the miracle; and scarcely any learned man suggested a doubt concerning it; excepting M. Basnage, in his history of the Jews. Dr. Lardner, however, after the fullest examination, was obliged to hesitate upon the subject. This fourth volume completed our author's original de-

POOR JEWRY LANE.—*English Presbyterian*, Extinct.

sign, at the period of forty-three years from its commencement.*

Providence spared the life of Dr. Lardner to a long term; and, his hearing excepted, he retained to the last, the use of his faculties in a very perfect degree. At length, in the summer of 1768, and the 85th year of his age, he was seized with a decline, which carried him off in a few weeks, at Hawkehurst, the place of his nativity, where he had a small paternal estate. He had been removed thither, in the hope that he might recruit his strength by a change of air, and relaxation from study. At his particular request, no funeral sermon was preached upon his death. His remains were conveyed to town, and deposited in Bunhill-Fields, in the vault belonging to the family of the Neals. He gave strict orders that his funeral should be as private as possible. Four coaches and a hearse constituted all the funeral appearance. There were no pall-bearers, and he even forbad feathers; but that was not complied with. Four ministers preceded the corpse. These were Mr. Ebenezer Radcliff, and Doctors Price, Amory, and Fleming. Mr. Radcliff delivered the oration.§ Sometime afterwards, the following inscription was placed upon his tomb.

The REV NATHANIEL LARDNER, D. D.
Author of the Credibility of the Gospel History,
Antient Jewish and Heathen Testimonies
To the Truth of the Christian Religion,
And several other smaller pieces;
Monuments of his
Learning, Judgment, Candour, Impartiality, Beneficence, and true Piety.
He was born at Hawkehurst in the County of Kent,
June the 6th, 1684,
And died on a visit there
July 24, 1768,
In the 85th Year of his Age.
An Israelite indeed, in whom is no guile!

* Kippis, *ubi supra*, p. 71—89.
§ Prot. Diss. Mag. vol. iv. p. 434.

POOR JEWRY LANE.—*English Presbyterian*, Extinct.

In the parish church at Hawkehurst is a neat marble slab, fixed to a pillar near the pulpit, containing the following inscription:

>NATHANIEL LARDNER, D. D.
>Drew his first and latest breath at Hall-House
>In this Parish.
>Benevolent as a Gentleman,
>Indefatigable as a Scholar,
>Exemplary as a Christian Minister,
>Wherever he resided.
>His usefulness was prolonged to his 85th Year,
>When
>Having established the Credibility of the Records
>Of our Common Salvation,
>Without partiality and beyond reply,
>Their promises became his eternal inheritance,
>July 24, 1768.

From reverence to the Memory of his Uncle, these truths were inscribed by David Jennings, 1789.

The length to which we have extended the life of Dr. Lardner, leaves but little room to dilate upon his character: and this is the less necessary, as his merits have been appreciated by the wise and learned, of all denominations. His proficiency in that branch of learning to which he turned his principal attention, as well as his extraordinary diligence, will recommend him to the esteem and veneration of posterity. The most learned advocates for revelation in modern times have been greatly indebted to his labours; and his writings have been translated into the principal modern languages. In his private deportment, his manners were polite, gentle and obliging. He had seen much of the world in the early part of life, which was of singular use to him, as he possessed great sagacity of observation. Notwithstanding his deafness, he was continually visited by persons of various professions and countries, who were supplied with pens, ink and paper, through which medium they communicated their thoughts, with any questions they wished to propose. To these, as they were severally written, he replied with

POOR JEWRY LANE.—*English Presbyterian*, Extinct.

great freedom and cheerfulness, and in a way that was both instructive and entertaining. The benevolence of Dr. Lardner's temper has been highly spoken of, together with the candour and moderation with which he maintained his sentiments.* These, most certainly, were amiable features in his character. We wish it could be added, that his zeal for the peculiar doctrines of the gospel, corresponded with his other excellent qualities, and especially with the ability he discovered, in defending the outworks of Revelation. His writings, certainly, would not have been the less valuable, but they would have been infinitely more useful to mankind. It is greatly to be regretted that a writer of our author's ability and worth, should have lent his assistance to the dissemination of principles so derogatory to the honour of our blessed Redeemer, as well as so destructive to the faith and hope of Christians. Alas, of what value is Christianity when stripped of her brightest ornaments, and left with nothing but naked walls! Should our moderation be questioned in what concerns the present remarks, our shelter is the certainty and importance of Divine Truth. Charity, for a system that stabs at the very vitals of Christianity, is no longer a virtue, but a crime.

Before we close the present article, it will be proper to take some notice of Dr. Lardner's posthumous publications. There came out, in 1769, Memoirs of his Life and Writings; to which were annexed eight sermons upon various subjects. In 1776, was published, A short Letter, which our author had sent, in 1762, to Mr. Caleb Fleming, upon the Personality of the Spirit. When Dr. Lardner began his great work, he declined writing the history of the Heretics of the two first centuries, on account of the difficulty of the subject, and for some other reasons. He intended, however, to take it up on a future occasion; and when he had finished his Jewish and Heathen Testimonies, began to make collections for the purpose; but he did not live to

* Kippis, *ubi supra*, p. 90, 91.

OOR JEWRY LANE.—*English Presbyterian*, Extinct.

finish them. Some parts of the work, indeed, were fitted for the press, having received his last corrections; but others were so imperfect, that it was doubted for a considerable time whether they were proper to be laid before the public. However, upon mature deliberation, his papers were put into the hands of the Rev. John Hogg, a Dissenting minister at Exeter, who having revised and completed them, they were published in 1780, in one volume, quarto, under the title of " The History of the Heretics of the two first Centuries after Christ: containing an Account of their Time, and Opinions, and Testimonies to the Books of the New Testament. To which are prefixed, General Observations concerning Heretics." Though this volume is not, upon the whole, so valuable and important as some of the former ones, it is possessed, nevertheless, of very considerable merit. The last posthumous publication of Dr. Lardner, appeared in 1784. It is entitled, " Two Schemes of a Trinity considered, and the Divine Unity asserted." This work consists of four discourses upon Philippians ii. 5—11. The first represents the commonly received opinion of the Trinity; the second describes the Arian scheme; the third treats on the Nazarean doctrine; and the fourth explains the text according to that doctrine. Our author had himself transcribed these sermons for the press, with particular directions to the printer; but they lay concealed till this year, when they were given to the public, by the Rev. John Wiche, a Dissenting minister of the General Baptist persuasion, at Maidstone in Kent.* In the year 1788, the whole of our author's works were collected together and reprinted in seven volumes, octavo, under the superintendence of the Rev. Baxter Cole. To the first volume was prefixed a very copious life of the author, drawn up by Dr. Kippis. They are now become scarce and fetch a high price.

* Kippis, *ubi supra*, p. 83—86.

POOR JEWRY LANE.—*English Presbyterian*, Extinct.

GEORGE BENSON, D. D.—This learned and eminent Divine, was born of respectable and pious parents, (D) at Great Salkeld, in Cumberland, on the first of September, 1699. He was early distinguished for seriousness of temper, and a great attachment to books; and he applied himself so closely to study, that, at eleven years of age he is said to have been able to read in the Greek Testament. This induced his parents to dedicate him to the ministry. After having passed through a course of grammar-learning, he was sent to an academy, kept by Dr. Dixon, at Whitehaven, where he continued about a year. From thence he was removed to the University of Glasgow, where he completed his academical studies.*

About the close of the year 1721, Mr. Benson came to London, and having been examined and approved by several of the most eminent Presbyterian ministers, he began to preach, first at Chertsey, and afterwards in the metropolis. At this time, the learned Dr. Calamy took him into his family, and treated him with great kindness and friendship. By the recommendation of that great man, he afterwards went to Abingdon, in Berkshire, and was chosen pastor of

---

(D) The family of the Bensons was originally from London. Towards the latter end of the reign of Queen Elizabeth, John Benson, the Doctor's great grandfather left the metropolis and settled at Great Salkeld, where the family made a considerable figure. He had thirteen sons, from the eldest of whom the late Lord Bingley descended. In the civil wars, occasioned by the mal-administration of King Charles the First, George Benson, the Doctor's grandfather, and the youngest of these sons, engaged on the side of liberty and the Parliament, and suffered considerably in his fortune, particularly from the Scots, previous to the battle of Worcester. He was a Puritan Divine, and had the living of Bridekirk, in his native county, from whence he was ejected at the Restoration. He afterwards retired into Lancashire, where he preached privately till his death, in 1691, aged 76 —— *Amory's Memoirs of the Life, Character and Writings of Dr. Benson, prefixed to his History of the Life of Christ*, p. 3, 4.

* Mr. Pickard's Sermon on the Death of Dr. Benson, p. 26.

POOR JEWRY LANE.—*English Presbyterian*, Extinct.

a congregation of Protestant Dissenters in that town. He was ordained on the 27th of March, 1723, Dr. Calamy, and five other ministers, officiating on the occasion. At Abingdon he continued seven years, and spent that time in a diligent application to study. It appears that Mr. Benson had, in early life, been instructed in those principles that are usually termed Calvinistical; and that he preached them during the first years of his ministry. While at Abingdon, he published three practical discourses, addressed to young persons, which were well received. These, however, on account of their evangelical tendency, he afterwards caused to be suppressed. In 1726, he married Mrs. Elizabeth Hills, widow, with whom he lived very happily, for fourteen years. After his marriage, he seems to have had a design of studying physic, but laid it aside. Mr. Benson continued at Abingdon till 1729, when he was obliged to leave that place on account of the Arminian sentiments he had lately embraced, which were very generally disapproved by his people.* He then removed to London, and accepted an invitation to become pastor of a congregation in King John's Court, Southwark. Here he continued eleven years.†

The light which the celebrated Mr. Locke had thrown on some of the most obscure and difficult parts of Paul's Epistles, by his close attention to the original design with which they were written, and by carefully pursuing the thread of the author's reasoning, induced and encouraged Mr. Benson, as it had before done Mr. Pierce, to attempt the illustration of the other Epistles of Paul, in a similar method.‡ Accordingly, in 1731, he published, in quarto, " A Paraphrase and Notes on St. Paul's Epistle to Philemon. Attempted in Imitation of Mr. Locke's Manner.

---

* MS. *penes me*.
† Amory's Memoirs of the Life, Character and Writings of Dr. Benson, prefixed to his History of the Life of Christ.
‡ Amory, *ubi supra*, p. 8.

POOR JEWRY LANE.—*English Presbyterian*, Extinct.

With an Appendix, in which is shewn, That St. Paul could neither be an Enthusiast, nor an Impostor: And consequently, the Christian Religion must be (as he has represented it) Heavenly and Divine." It is well known that the argument in this Appendix was afterwards improved and illustrated with great force and elegance, by the celebrated Lord Lyttleton. Mr. Benson's first publication on the Epistles meeting with a very favourable reception, he proceeded in his design with great diligence, and in the same year published his Paraphrase and Notes on Paul's first Epistle to the Thessalonians. This was followed, the next year, by his labours on the second Epistle. To the last were annexed, two Dissertations; 1. Concerning the Kingdom of God. 2. Concerning the Man of Sin. In 1733, he gave to the public, his thoughts on the first Epistle to Timothy, to which was subjoined, an Appendix concerning inspiration. The same year appeared the Paraphrase and Notes upon Titus, accompanied by an Essay concerning the Abolition of the Ceremonial Law. In 1734, our author produced his observations upon the second Epistle to Timothy. To this was annexed, an Essay, in two parts: 1. Concerning the Settlement of the primitive Church: 2. Concerning the Religious Worship of the Christians, whilst the Spiritual Gifts continued.

Mr. Benson having completed his design, as far as related to Paul's Epistles, proceeded to explain, after the same manner, the seven Catholic Epistles. In 1738, appeared the Paraphrase and Notes on the Epistle of James; with an Essay to reconcile that Apostle with the writings of Paul, on the subject of justification. Our author proceeded next to the two Epistles of Peter. To the former was annexed, a Dissertation, to explain what is meant by Christ's preaching to the spirits in prison. To the Paraphrase upon the second Epistle of Peter, published in 1745, was annexed the author's observations upon the Epistle of Jude. In the year 1749, he gave to the public his Paraphrase and Notes upon the three

POOR JEWRY LANE.—*English Presbyterian*, Extinct.

Epistles of John; including two Dissertations: 1. On the genuineness of that disputed text, 1 John, v. 7, 8. *For there are three that bear record in heaven, &c.* 2. On 1 John, 16, 17. concerning *a sin unto death, and a sin not unto death.* This completed our author's design, after he had been employed upon it for the space of nineteen years. The Paraphrase and Notes upon the six Epistles of Paul were collected together and reprinted in one volume, in 1752. They were followed, in 1756, by the seven Catholic Epistles; forming together, two handsome volumes in quarto. To this edition were added, for convenience of reference, five separate indexes; containing the Hebrew and Greek words, the different readings, texts incidentally explained, and a table of English words.*

During the time that Mr. Benson was engaged in this arduous undertaking, he found time to compose, and present to the public, other works of an important nature. In 1738, he published in three thin volumes, quarto, " The History of the First Planting of the Christian Religion, taken from the Acts of the Apostles, and their Epistles. Together with the remarkable Facts of the Jewish and Roman History, which affected the Christians during this period." In the preface Mr. Benson observes, that " it had been the care and study of some years, as far as his health, and other affairs, would permit." Dr. Amory observes,† that, " in this work, besides illustrating the history of the Acts, and most of the Epistles, by a view of the history of the times, the occasion of the several Epistles, and the state of the churches to whom they were addressed, he hath established the truth of the Christian Religion on a number of facts, the most public, important and incontestable; the relations of which we have from eye-witnesses of unquestionable integrity, and which produced such extensive alterations

---

* Benson on the Epistles, *first and second editions.*
† Memoirs, *ubi supra*, p. 10.

POOR JEWRY LANE.——*English Presbyterian*, Extinct.

in the moral and religious state of the world, as cannot be rationally accounted for, without admitting the reality of these facts, and the truth of these relations." At the end of the second volume, the author has added a Dissertation, designed to show, " That Luke was the author of the Acts of the Apostles ; that he published that book while many of the Apostles and primitive Christians, who knew the facts, were alive, to attest the same. And, supposing that it is an authentic history, Christianity must certainly, and of course be a divine revelation, and worthy of the highest regard."* This work came to a second edition in 1756, and received some considerable additions from the author.

In the year 1740, Mr. Benson was chosen pastor of the congregation of Protestant Dissenters, in Poor Jewry Lane, Crutched-Friars, in the room of Dr. William Harris ; and in this situation he continued till his death. It has been noticed in the preceding article, that he enjoyed for several years the assistance of the very eminent and learned Dr. Nathaniel Lardner. Notwithstanding the difference of their opinions upon several subjects, which they debated with great freedom and good humour, they lived together in the greatest harmony and friendship, which was only interrupted by death. Mr. Benson having the misfortune to lose his first wife in 1740, was married a second time in 1742, to Mrs. Mary Kettle, daughter of Mr. William Kettle, of Birmingham. (E) About the same time, he received an unanimous invitation to become joint-pastor of the Presbyterian congregation at Birmingham, with Mr. Samuel Bourn. But this he declined. In 1743, he published, in octavo, his treatise on " The Reasonableness of the Christian Religion, as delivered in the Scriptures." This book was at first published as an answer to " Christianity not founded on Argument." But the author's design extended

---

* Preface, p. 4.

(E) She was a Lady of a very amiable temper, and died in 1754. Dr. Benson had no children by either of his wives.

POOR JEWRY LANE.—*English Presbyterian*, Extinct.

farther, and may be regarded, as Dr. Leland observes, " not merely as an argument to that pamphlet, but as a good defence of Christianity in general."* A second edition was published in 1746, to which was added an appendix, containing a vindication of some things which had been objected against in the work. A third edition, revised and corrected, with alterations and additions, was published in 1759, in two volumes, octavo. In the year 1744, in consideration of our author's great learning and abilities, the University of Aberdeen conferred on him the degree of Doctor in Divinity. It appears that a similar honour was designed him from the University of Glasgow, but was opposed by some persons who considered him unsound in the faith. When the scheme was mentioned, one of the members spoke of him with abhorrence as an avowed Socinian.† It was in the same year that our author published, " A summary View of the Evidences of Christ's Resurrection," in answer to " The Resurrection of Jesus considered;" written by one who stiles himself " A Moral Philosopher."

In the year 1745, our author was employed in revising for the press, in two volumes quarto, the work of a late learned friend, entitled, " A Critical and Chronological History of the Rise, Progress, Declension, and Revival of Knowledge, chiefly Religious: In two Periods. 1. The Period of Tradition from Adam to Moses. 2. The Period of Letters from Moses to Christ." By Dr. Thomas Windor, of Liverpool. To this work, Dr. Benson prefixed some memoirs of the author's life. In the following year, he was engaged in preparing for the press, " A plain Account of the Nature and End of the Sacrament of the Lord's Supper, adapted to the Use of such Protestants as do not Use the Book of Common-Prayer." This was a

---

* Leland's View of the Deistical Writers, vol. i. p. 164. 5th edition.

† Biographia Britannica, vol. ii. *Art. Benson.*

POOR JEWRY LANE.—*English Presbyterian*, Extinct.

slight alteration of Bishop Hoadley's Treatise on the same subject.

In 1747, Dr. Benson published a volume of Sermons on various subjects. A copy of these he presented to Dr. Thomas Herring, Archbishop of Canterbury, with congratulations on his elevation to that See. The letter of thanks which the Archbishop wrote to him upon this occasion, on account of the excellent spirit it breathes, shall be inserted below.(F) In 1748, our author collected into one volume, octavo, several Tracts which he had formerly printed separately, and had passed to a second edition. Their titles are, 1. A Dissertation on 2 Thess. ii. 1—12. In which it is shown, that the Bishop of Rome is the Man of Sin, &c. 2. A Letter to a Friend concerning the End and Design of Prayer: or the Reasonableness of praying to an unchangeably wise, powerful and good God. In Answer to the Objections of the modern Infidels. 3. A Postscript to the

(F) " Reverend Sir,

" I cannot satisfy myself with having sent a cold and common answer of thanks, for your volume of most excellent and useful Sermons. I do it in this manner with great esteem and cordiality. I thank you, at the same time, as becomes me to do, for your very obliging good wishes. The subject on which my friends congratulate me, is, in truth, matter of constant anxiety to me. I hope I have an honest intention, and for the rest I must rely on the good grace of God, and the counsel and assistance of my friends.

" I think it happy, that I am called up to this high station at a time, when spite and rancour, and narrowness of spirit, are out of countenance; when we breathe the benign and comfortable air of liberty and toleration; and the teachers of our common religion make it their business to extend its essential influence, and join in supporting its true interest and honour. No times ever called more loudly upon Protestants for zeal, and security, and charity.   " I am,
                                                " Reverend Sir,
Kennington,   " Your assured friend,
Feb. 2, 1747-8.   " T. CANTUAR."*

* Memoirs, *ubi supra*, p. 15.

POOR JEWRY LANE.—*English Presbyterian*, Extinct.

Letter on Prayer, concerning the Views which we ought to have in Praying; the drawing up proper Forms; the Use of Scripture Language; the Confession of such Sins only, as we are conscious we have been guilty of. 4. The 30th Dissertation of Maximus Tyrius, concerning this question, Whether we ought to pray to God, or no? Translated from the Greek. 5. Remarks on the foregoing Dissertation of Maximus Tyrius. 6. The Doctrine of Predestination reviewed: or the Nature of the Councils and Decrees of God; and the Rise and Occasion of the Scripture Language concerning them. 7. A brief Account of Calvin's causing Servetus to be burned at Geneva, for an heretic. To this edition, which is called the third, is added a Supplement, containing, (1.) A Defence of the brief Account of Calvin's Treatment of Servetus. (2.) A brief Account of Archbishop Laud's cruel Treatment of Dr. Leighton. (3.) An Essay concerning the Belief of Things, which are above Reason. These Tracts came to another edition in 1753. It may be remarked, that the account which our author gives of Calvin's conduct towards Servetus, gave great offence, and we apprehend justly; for it contains a very exaggerated statement of what must ever be considered the worst feature in the character of that Reformer.(G)

Dr. Benson's labours in the cause of sacred literature, met with a very favourable reception both at home and in foreign countries; (H) and procured him the friendship and

---

(G) Besides the above works, Dr. Benson published, a small tract entitled, " Second Thoughts concerning the Sufferings and Death of Christ, as a propitiatory Sacrifice for the Sins of the World, and a Satisfaction to Divine Justice."—Also two Sermons: one occasioned by the Death of the Rev. James Read, preached at New Broad-street, Petty-France, Aug. 24, 1755, on 2 Cor. v. 4. The other entitled, " The Gospel Method ot Justification."

(H) In Germany, the reputation of the Paraphrases and Notes on the Epistles, was so great, that John David Michaelis, one of the Professors of Hebrew and Philosophy, in the University of Gottingen, in the Electorate of Hanover, a gentleman of distinguished learning, and still superior judg-

POOR JEWRY LANE.—*English Presbyterian*, Extinct.

esteem of many persons of eminence and distinction, both in and out of the establishment. Among his friends and correspondents, were Lord Chancellor King, Lord Barrington, Bishop Hoadly, Bishop Butler, Bishop Coneybeare, Dr. Taylor of Norwich, Mr. Bourn of Birmingham, Dr. Wishart of Edinburgh; Dr. Duchal, and Dr. Leland, of Dublin; Dr. Mayhew of New-England, Professor Michaelis of Gottingen, besides many other learned and ingenious persons. Dr. Edmund Law, Bishop of Carlisle, was also his particular friend; and as a proof of his friendship, at Dr. Benson's request, permitted his Dissertation on Mark ix. 49, 50, to be inserted in the *Appendix to the Life of Christ*, though not prepared by him for the press. Dr. Benson appears, likewise, to have been upon very friendly terms with Dr. Watts, though their difference of sentiment in some points was considerable. They occasionally corresponded together; and some of Dr.

---

ment, undertook the laborious task of translating them into Latin, beginning with Mr. Pierce's Paraphrase on the Epistle to the Hebrews, and Dr. Benson's on the Epistle of James, both which were published in 1746, with additional notes of the translator. There was also prefixed a recommendatory preface of another eminent German Professor, Sigismund James Baumgarten. The Dissertation annexed to the Paraphrase of the first Epistle of John, on the authenticity of verses seven and eight of the fifth chapter, was translated into Latin by Andrew Goetlib Marsch, a learned Divine of the Lutheran persuasion, in the Duchy of Mecklenburg, who added large notes; in which he defended the genuineness of the text against the Doctor's objections.* Mons. Bamberger, a Protestant Divine at Berlin, also translated into his own language, the Doctor's Treatise upon the Resurrection of Jesus Christ;" his " Essay concerning the Belief of Things, which are above Reason;" and, his " Plain Account of the Lord's Supper." It seems he also began his Paraphrase and Notes upon the Epistles.† His Letter on Prayer was translated into High Dutch, by Dr. Kortholt, then of Vienna, but afterwards Professor of Divinity, in the University of Gottingen.‡

  * Amory, *ubi supra*, p. 12, 13.   † Biog. Brit. *ubi supra*.
   ‡ Benson's Collection of Tracts, preface.

VOL. I.   R

POOR JEWRY LANE.—*English Presbyterian*, Extinct.

Benson's earlier pieces were submitted to Dr. Watts's perusal.*

An indefatigable application to his studies, together with the constant exercise of preaching, at length, so impaired the constitution of Dr. Benson, that he found it necessary to quit his public ministry. He intended to devote the remainder of his days to a peaceful retirement; and it was the general hope of his friends, that he might have been enabled to continue the prosecution of his studies for some years, though he was not capable of the fatigues of the pastoral charge. But the rapid manner in which he declined, disappointed their expectations. Happily, he was not suffered to linger on the bed of sickness, under tormenting pains; but was removed after a very short cessation from his public labours. He died in a very composed and resigned manner, on the 6th of April, 1762, in the 63d year of his age.† The Rev. Ebenezer Radcliff delivered the oration at his interment in Bunhill-Fields, and on Lord's-day, April the 18th, his funeral sermon was preached at Crutched-Friars, by the Rev. Edward Pickard, from Matt. xxv. 21. *Well done, thou good and faithful servant*, &c.

Dr. Benson was a remarkable instance of the happy effects of a learned industry. It is well known that he was not a man of great original genius; that he had small powers of invention and fancy; and that he had not applied to the cultivation of elegance and taste in composition. When at the University, we are assured that he was thought to be but a dull lad by his fellow-students, and that they expected nothing considerable from him. But, by the force of application, he outstripped his more lively companions, and produced works of real and lasting utility and merit.‡

Dr. Benson was a firm Protestant Dissenter, and a zea-

---

* Biog. Brit. *ubi supra.*
† Mr. Pickard's Sermon, and Biog. Brit. *ubi supra.*
‡ Biog. Brit. *ubi supra.*

POOR JEWRY LANE ——*English Presbyterian*, Extinct.

lous advocate for free inquiry, and the right of private judgment. His regard to the dissenting interest, he testified by his will; leaving one hundred pounds to the fund for the relief of poor ministers and students, and the same sum to that for widows and orphans.* His religious sentiments are well known to have harmonized with those of Socinus; and the freedom with which he expressed his opinions, exposed him to much censure. This has been attributed to narrowness of mind and a want of candour; while others, perhaps, will call it a zeal for truth. It is certain that Socinianism had not then made that rapid progress among the Dissenters, which it did afterwards. Dr. Benson's usual method of preaching was critically to explain the Scripture, and then to inculcate duty. His being short-sighted was a great inconvenience to him, in the public delivery of his discourses; and his natural temper prevented his excelling in a warm and pathetic address to the passions of his hearers. But his appearance was grave and venerable, and he is said to have had " an air of seriousness and sincerity in his manner, which had a very good effect upon his auditors."† It is certain, however, that he was very unpopular as a preacher. His peculiar sentiments gave a certain cast to his sermons, and rendered them devoid of that energy which is so well calculated to interest the feelings and warm the heart. That he took great pains in studying the Scriptures, is evident from his own writings, as well as from the testimony of others; and of his ability and zeal in defending Christianity against Infidels, there can be no doubt. His integrity, also, was unquestioned, " I believe no earthly consideration (says Mr. Pickard) could have tempted him to speak or act contrary to the dictates of his judgment and conscience; or to what he apprehended to be the will of

* Pickard's Sermon, *ubi supra*, p. 30.
† Biog Brit. *ubi supra*.

POOR JEWRY LANE.—*English Presbyterian*, Extinct.

God."* What a pity is it, therefore, that so much good sense, learning, and worth, should be directed to undermine those doctrines of Christianity, which the bulk of Christians in all ages, have considered the bulwarks of religion, and upon which they have rested all their earthly consolation, as well as their hopes of future happiness. The anomaly of this procedure in the divine government can only be satisfactorily explained at a future day. Dr. Benson loved the conversation of men of letters, especially those whose studies were similar to his own. He belonged many years to a society, in which he took much pleasure, consisting of Divines and other literary persons, who met once a week, during the winter season, and debated freely upon some of the most important and curious subjects of critical and theological learning. Among the members of this society were Dr. Jeremiah Hunt, Dr. Lardner, Professor Ward, Dr. Avery, Philip Glover, Esq. author of " An Inquiry concerning Virtue and Happiness," and other gentlemen of similar views.† Besides his constant labours in preaching and writing, Dr. Benson employed a portion of his time in assisting the studies of young Divines; and for many years, he had one or more living with him, who applied themselves to the critical study of the Scriptures under his immediate eye. Some of these, by the figure they afterwards made, did honour to their tutor; particularly Dr. Macknight, author of the Harmony of the Gospels, and Mr. John Alexander, a Dissenting Minister at Birmingham.‡

Dr. Benson left behind him, in manuscript, " The History of the Life of Jesus Christ, taken from the New Testament, with Observations and Reflections proper to illustrate the Excellence of his Character, and the Divinity of his Mission and Religion." To which were added, several critical dissertations. The whole was published

---

* Sermon on the Death of Dr. Benson, p. 30.
† Amory, *ubi supra*, p. 17. ‡ Ibid.

POOR JEWRY LANE.—*English Presbyterian,* Extinct.

together, in 1764, in one volume, quarto, to which was prefixed a fine mezzotinto print of the author. Dr. Amory, who was the editor, also added some memoirs of the life, character, and writings of Dr. Benson, to which we are indebted for much of the preceding account. Dr. Newcome, late Primate of Ireland, in the Appendix to his Harmony of the Gospels, printed in 1778, inserted Dr. Benson's manner of harmonizing the accounts of Christ's Resurrection, from his Life of Christ. In the Appendix to the first volume of the Theological Repository, second edition, are inserted two curious letters from Dr. Shaw to Dr. Benson, relative to the passage of the Israelites through the Red Sea."*

EBENEZER RADCLIFF.—Upon Dr. Lardner's resignation of the office of assistant preacher at Poor Jewry Lane, Dr. Benson undertook the whole service for about eight years and a half; till his growing infirmities obliged the church to look out for an assistant, and the Rev. Ebenezer Radcliff was chosen to that service. As this gentleman is still living, our readers will not expect that we should enter into a minute detail respecting his history and character. Some few particulars will, however, be expected. Mr. Radcliff is a native of Yorkshire, and received his education for the ministry under the celebrated Dr. Philip Doddridge. His first settlement, we believe, was at Stamford, in Lincolnshire, in 1750, as successor to the Rev. Timothy Laugher, who removed to Nailsworth, in Glocestershire, and afterwards to Hackney, near London. In December, 1751, he removed to Boston, in the same county, and continued there till December, 1759. He then removed to Walthamstow, in Essex, as Afternoon-preacher to the congregation of Protestant Dissenters, and colleague with the celebrated Mr. Hugh Farmer. Shortly after, he

* Biog. Brit. *ubi supra.*

POOR JEWRY LANE.—*English Presbyterian*, Extinct.

was chosen Morning-preacher to the congregation in Poor Jewry Lane; and, upon the resignation of Dr. Benson, early in 1762, sole pastor. In this relation, he continued upwards of twelve years, still preserving his connexion at Walthamstow. Mr. Radcliff was one of those ministers who strenuously supported the application to Parliament, for the repeal of the Test Act, in 1772. The denial of redress, in the matter of subscription, at that time, roused his indignation in a sermon composed expressly upon the occasion, and afterwards published, dedicated to His Grace the Duke of Richmond. Though this discourse was characterized by many just remarks, and a manly assertion of religious liberty, yet, at the same time, it contained some exceptionable passages, and was considered at the time as much too violent. The congregation in Poor Jewry Lane being in a very reduced state, dissolved in the year 1774. After this, Mr. Radcliff continued to preach for a short time at Walthamstow; but, at length, wholly declined the ministry. Since then, he has resided in the above village, in the style of a private gentleman. Mr. Radcliff is one of the Trustees of Dr. Williams's Library, in Redcross-street.*

RICHARD PRICE, D. D.—Not long after the choice of Mr. Radcliff to succeed Dr. Benson, the celebrated Dr. Price, then pastor of a congregation at Newington-green, was elected Afternoon-preacher at Poor Jewry Lane. This situation he retained till the year 1770, when, being chosen pastor of the congregation at the Gravel-Pit meeting, in Hackney, he resigned, in favour of the same service at Newington-green.† As we shall have occasion to mention Dr. Price in other parts of this work, we wave entering into further particulars respecting him in this place.

* Private Information.
† Priestley's Sermon on the Death of Dr. Price, p. 39.

POOR JEWRY LANE.——*English Presbyterian*, Extinct.

JOHN CALDER, D. D.—Upon the resignation of Dr. Price, the afternoon service in Poor Jewry Lane was undertaken by Dr. Calder. This gentleman (who is still living) is a native of Scotland, and received his education in the University of Aberdeen, from whence he received his degree. He was settled some time with a congregation at Alnwick, in Northumberland, where he married a lady of considerable fortune. From thence he removed to London, and succeeded Dr. Price as already mentioned. After the dissolution of the society in Poor Jewry Lane, Dr. Calder retired to Hammersmith, where he devoted himself chiefly to his literary labours. Since that time he has not undertaken any stated work in the ministry; and he is now a member of Mr. Belsham's congregation in Essex-street.[*]

Thus we are brought to the close of a society, which we have traced through successive changes, for nearly the period of a century. From the facts that have passed under our observation, we may derive some lessons of profitable instruction. We shall not, however, detain the reader any further than by reminding him, that, though individual churches may experience those changes which are common to every thing in the present life, yet, that the church of Christ is perpetual. It withstands equally the blasts of persecution, and the snares of worldly grandeur; nor is it at all affected by the errors and prejudices of mistaken friends, or the open attacks of avowed enemies. And happy is every one who shall be honoured with a name and a place within the gates of the heavenly Jerusalem.

[*] Private Information.

JEWRY-STREET.

CALVINISTIC METHODISTS.

THOUGH the present article has respect to the same place as the preceding one, yet as we are now to speak of a different society, and the old name of Poor Jewry Lane has given place to that of Jewry-street, we have adopted the latter as the name by which it is at present most known. Upon the dissolution of the old Presbyterian Society, the meeting-house was shut up for a short time; but, in 1775, Sir William Plomer, the proprietor of the premises, granted a lease for twenty-one years, to three persons, who fitted up the place for the late Mr. Henry Mead, who died a short time since at Reading. Mr. Mead, however, being then in orders in the Church of England, did not think fit to take upon him the charge, and never preached there. (1)

(1) The Rev. Henry Mead was born in the year 1745, in or near the city of Bath. When a youth, he was put apprentice to a low mechanic; but left his master and went off to London. Here he soon became immersed in all the dissipations of a gay metropolis. Being led on one occasion to Tottenham Court Chapel, with a view of diverting himself at the expence of that man of God, Mr. George Whitefield, it happened that Mr. Howell Davis was the preacher. Mr. Mead being greatly affected by the awakening discourse of that faithful minister, went home and assumed a profession of religion. Afterwards, being desirous of engaging in the ministry, he applied, through Mr. Whitefield, for admission into the Countess of Huntingdon's College at Trevecca; and went there in 1767. It appears that he did not preach long in that connection, having taken orders in the Church of England prior to his marriage in 1776. Previous to this he became minister of Ram's Chapel, Hackney, and was chosen lecturer of St. John's, Wapping. Afterwards, he preached a morning lecture at the German Chapel in Goodman's-Fields, and had a weekly lecture at Little Trinity Church in the Minories. He was very near becoming minister of Jewry street Chapel, and had purchased the organ, which was built for the Little Minories Church; but he is said to have been dissuaded from it by the late Mr. Romaine. After this, he preached a morning lecture at St. Pancras, and took a small chapel at Somer's-Town. At length, his health beginning to

JEWRY-STREET.—*Calvinistic Methodists.*

After this, the late Mr. Aldridge was appointed. Upon the expiration of the lease in 1796, it was renewed for another twenty-one years, by the present trustees. Jewry-street Chapel, as it is now called, carries the appearance of an ancient building, and does not seem materially altered from its former state. When it was opened upon the present plan, an organ was erected in the front gallery, and the liturgy of the Church of England introduced. Though the present minister professes himself an Independent, the people cannot with strict propriety be called Dissenters; indeed many of them avow their preference to the national establishment, for which reason we have termed them Calvinistic Methodists. Besides the usual services on the morning and evening of the Lord's-day, there is a lecture here on a Thursday, and a prayer-meeting on a Monday evening.*

The ministers of this chapel since it was opened upon its present plan, are as follows.

MINISTERS' NAMES.	From	To
William Aldridge, ...	1776	1797
Richard Povah, ...	1797	1801
John Ball, ...	1801	18

WILLIAM ALDRIDGE, was born at Warminster, in Wiltshire, in the year 1737. His youth appears to have been spent in the pursuit of pleasure and worldly gratifica-

decline, he went in 1797, to Henley upon Thames, where he experienced great benefit from the air. Unable, however, to recover his spirits, he did not resume his stated labours, but visited various parts of Yorkshire, Hampshire, &c. About 1802, he retired to Reading, where he occasionally assisted the Rev. Herbert Marsh. His death, occasioned by the rupture of a blood vessel, happened on the 29th of October, 1807, when he was 62 years of age. Mr. Mead was not a man of the first rate abilities, but he was generally esteemed as a preacher. His views of divine truth were, what are usually termed Calvinistic, and to them he continued firmly attached to the last.—*Evang. Mag. for January and April*, 1807.

* Private Information.

JEWRY-STREET.—*Calvinistic Methodists.*

tion, and it was not till his twenty-fourth year that he received those first serious impressions that produced a saving change in his mind and conduct. At this time, he was under great distress of soul, his sins appeared in a most awful light, and it was a considerable time before he experienced deliverance. Having a strong inclination to the ministry, he was introduced to the Countess of Huntingdon's College, at Trevecca, in South Wales, and became one of her senior students. Having continued there the usual time allotted to study, he preached some years in her Ladyship's connexion, which gave him an opportunity of visiting various parts of England.*

In September, 1771, Lady Huntingdon receiving an anonymous letter, requesting her to send a minister to Margate, in the Isle of Thanet, describing it as a licentious place, particularly at the watering season, she made known the contents of it to Mr. Aldridge, giving him the liberty to select any student in the College, to accompany and assist him in this important work. Mr. Aldridge fixed upon a Mr. Joseph Cook, who died in 1790, a missionary in South Carolina. Being utterly unknown to any person at Margate, they began to preach out of doors. Many attended, and meeting with success, they extended their labours to other places. About this time, many persons in Dover having left Mr. Wesley's Societies, gave them a pressing invitation, which they accepted. Mr. Aldridge preached at Dover, for the first time, in the market-place, on a Lord's-day, but met with great opposition. The Presbyterian meeting-house, which had been shut up a considerable time, was therefore procured, and Mr. Aldridge continued to preach in it while he resided at Dover. Afterwards it was agreed, that Mr. Aldridge, and his colleague should supply Dover and Margate alternately, changing every week.†

* Bryson's Sermon on the death of the Rev. W. Aldridge, p. 14.—and private Information.
† Baptist Register, vol. i. p. 501, 502.

JEWRY-STREET.—*Calvinistic Methodists.*

The Countess of Huntingdon, who never suffered her students to continue long in one place, afterwards appointed Mr. Aldridge to supply the Mulberry-Garden Chapel, in Wapping. There, his ministry was so well received by the congregation, that they united in a petition to the Countess, to have his labours continued for some time longer; but, it being a maxim with her Ladyship, never to comply with the wishes of her congregations in this particular, she peremptorily refused. This occasioned his leaving her connexion in 1776, and Jewry-street Chapel being then vacant, Mr. Aldridge was invited to settle there as the stated officiating minister. In this connexion he continued upwards of twenty years, and was greatly beloved by an affectionate congregation.*

As a preacher, Mr. Aldridge was extremely popular. He delivered his discourses with perspicuity and ardour; his ideas were generally arranged with propriety, and his subjects mostly selected with judgment. His ministerial labours, especially in the younger part of his life, were very successful; and he had the singular felicity of introducing into the ministry, no less than sixteen or seventeen young men, from his own communion. Mr. Aldridge's health began to decline visibly for a considerable time before his death. Early and continued exertions, joined to advanced years, at length, made rapid depredations on his life, and hastened his final illness. This seems to have been a complication of disorders, which he bore with the same placid serenity which distinguished him in health. His dying expressions discovered a steady peace, arising from a conscious interest in his Redeemer, and a well founded hope of a blissful immortality.† He died on Tuesday morning February the 28th, 1797, in the sixtieth year of his age. The Rev. George Gold delivered the address at his interment in Bunhill-Fields, on March the 7th; and on the

* Private Information.
† Bryson's Sermon on the Death of the Rev. W. Aldridge, p. 16.

JEWRY-STREET.—*Calvinistic Methodists.*

following Lord's-day, two funeral sermons were preached for him at Jewry-street Chapel: that in the morning by the Rev. Anthony Crole, and that in the evening by the Rev. Thomas Bryson. The three services were afterwards printed. Mr. Aldridge published " The Doctrine of the Trinity, stated, proved, and defended;" and a funeral sermon on the death of the Countess of Huntingdon. (k)

RICHARD POVAH.—During his last illness, Mr. Aldridge had the occasional assistance of the Rev. Richard Povah. This gentleman, is son to a minister, formerly in the Countess's connexion, but since then, pastor of a congregation at Kennington. He was educated at Corpus Christi College, Cambridge. After he left the University, he preached occasionally in the Countess of Huntingdon's Chapels, and at various other places, till he settled at Jewry-

(k) It will be expected that we should not pass over altogether in silence, a Mr. Bryan, who preached at Jewry-street along with Mr. Aldridge, during the early part of his ministry in that place. This gentleman was a native of Yorkshire, and pursued his studies for the ministry in the Countess of Huntingdon's College, at Trevecca. It seems he did not itinerate long in that connexion. Erasmus, a Greek bishop, having visited London, in 1763, laid his hands upon several persons who could not procure ordination from the English bishops. Mr. Bryan being desirous of episcopal ordination, applied to him for that purpose, and easily obtained it. After this, he became minister of a congregation at Sheffield. Having contracted an acquaintance with Mr. Aldridge while at College, it was afterwards maintained by a mutual correspondence; and when Mr. Aldridge settled at Jewry-street, Mr. Bryan constantly spent three months of the year in London, preaching in the pulpit of his friend, who, during that interval, supplied the chapel at Sheffield. Mr. Bryan was afflicted for many years, at intervals, with an unhappy dejection of spirits, which bordered upon derangement. To such a height did his disorder sometimes proceed, that he has attempted, in the frenzy of despair, to make away with himself. Nevertheless, his friends considered him to be a truly good man, and he was enabled, eventually, to overcome the temptations of the adversary. He died many years ago, and was buried under his own pulpit at Sheffield.—*Private information.*

JEWRY-STREET.—*Calvinistic Methodists.*

street, where he was chosen to succeed Mr. Aldridge. As Mr. Povah had not hitherto been ordained to the work of the ministry, he now applied for orders in the Church of England. These he speedily obtained, and it was no great while before he took an opportunity of discovering his zeal for the national establishment. When he had been settled nearly four years at Jewry-street, he communicated to the Trustees, his desire to have the chapel consecrated, and placed under the jurisdiction of the bishop of London. But the managers, though many of them decidedly attached to the Church of England, declined placing themselves under the episcopal care, as they well knew, that by so doing, they should deprive themselves of the right to choose their own minister. After some debate upon the subject, it was agreed that Mr. Povah should resign his ministry at Jewry-street, which he did, at Midsummer 1801. Since then he has become curate and lecturer of St. James's, Duke's-place.*

JOHN BALL, the present minister of Jewry-street Chapel, is a native of Windsor, and was born about the year 1770. Being designed for the water, he spent a part of his youth upon the river Thames; but Providence intending him for a higher and more important employment, he entered the newly instituted academy at Mile-End, under the superintendence of Dr. Addington. Soon after his entrance upon the ministry, he went over to Ireland, where he had a meeting-house, and preached several years. Afterwards, he returned to England, and settled with a congregation at Westbury, in Wiltshire; from whence, after a few years, he removed to London, to succeed Mr. Povah at Jewry-street. Being recommended to that congregation by the Rev. Matthew Wilks, of the Tabernacle, he was requested in the month of July, 1801, to pay them a visit for a few weeks upon

* Private Information.

trial; and his ministry being approved, he was invited, in October following, to take upon him the pastoral office. Though Mr. Ball professes himself a strict Independent, he has continued to read the Common Prayer, and, a few years ago, united with the Methodist associated congregations. Since his removal to London, Mr. Ball has enjoyed but an indifferent state of health; and we are sorry to add, that he is now in that disordered condition, that it is hardly expected he will ever be able to preach again.*

In 1807, Mr. Ball took up the cudgels in defence of the Rev. Rowland Hill, in a pamphlet entitled, " Animadversions on a late Pamphlet, entitled, An admonitory Epistle to the Rev. Rowland Hill, A. M. occasioned by the Republication of his Spiritual Characteristics, or most curious Sale of Curates." It is written in an ill temper, and has been severely censured by the Reviewers.

MARK-LANE.

INDEPENDENT.

AT the time of the Revolution, in 1688, the Independent church under the pastoral care of the Rev. Dr. Chauncey, is said to have assembled at the house of a Dr. Clarke, in Mark-lane. It was there that the celebrated Dr. Watts was ordained to the pastoral office; and he preached there during the first two or three years of his ministry. At Midsummer 1704, the church removed to Pinner's-Hall; and from thence, in 1708, to the present meeting-house, in White-Horse-Yard, Duke's-Place, St. Mary Axe. To that place we refer the reader for a particular account of Dr. Watts's church.

* Private Information.

TURNERS'-HALL, PHILPOT-LANE.

PHILPOT-LANE reaches from Fenchurch-street North, to Little Eastcheap South, and is situated in Langbourn Ward, but the greatest part is in Billingsgate Ward. The Company of Turners, it seems, formerly had their Hall here; but their present one is situated on College Hill. At the time of the Revolution in 1688, Turners'-Hall was used as a meeting-house for Nonconformists. This is the earliest account we have of it in that connexion. It was occupied successively by several different societies, for upwards of half a century. After this, it was shut up for some time, but at length taken down; and the memory of it has, for many years, been entirely effaced from the neighbourhood. The first Dissenting society we find mentioned as meeting here, was of the General Baptist persuasion. The people who occupied it next in succession can scarcely be placed under any denomination. They were followed by another society likewise of a peculiar cast. A congregation of Particular Baptists next occupied it; and they were followed by a people of the Independent persuasion. We shall consider them separately in this order, beginning with the

GENERAL BAPTISTS.

THIS Society was collected, in the year 1688, by the Rev. RICHARD ALLEN, a respectable minister among the General Baptists. The occasion of its formation was this. The church at White's Alley, with which Mr. Allen was connected, both as a member and a preacher, adhered with rigid tenacity to the practice of laying on of hands on baptized believers. This, indeed, formed an essential article in their constitution. Any deviation, therefore, from this practice was considered as an infringement upon the rules of the society, and subjected the offending person to exclusion. Mr. Allen, it seems, had his doubts with respect to the

TURNERS'-HALL, PHILPOT-LANE.—*General Baptists.*

divine right of this institution; at least, he thought the matter should be left indifferent, and not made an indispensable requisite to church communion. This opinion, as opportunity offered, he declared publicly in the church; which giving offence, it occasioned some debates, and a separation ensued. The matter was deemed of so much consequence, that several other churches, who adhered to the practice in question, were invited, by their representatives, to attend at White's Alley, to discuss the subject, and sanction by their presence whatever proceeding the church should think fit to adopt. Accordingly, a church-meeting was held at White's Alley, June 18, 1688, when the following resolution was passed, and signed by six elders of sister churches.

" For as much as Brother Allen hath this present day,
" and at several other times, and upon several occasions,
" denied the ordinance of laying on of hands upon baptized
" believers to be a principle of Christ's doctrine, whereof
" complaint having been made, and the matter several times
" debated, at several church meetings, and adjourned to
" this day, whether Brother Allen having declared his opinion
" against this ordinance, it be for the preservation of the
" truths of the gospel, and for the peace of the church,
" that Brother Allen shall continue in the ministry as a
" preacher amongst us, upon debate of the matter by the
" elders of the several congregations in communion with us,
" and of the church now assembled about this matter, the
" Church of Christ do hereby unanimously agree, That
" Brother Allen be for the present suspended from being a
" minister amongst us."*

Mr. Allen being excluded the ministry at White's Alley, in consequence of the above resolution, proceeded to gather a separate church at Turners'-Hall, where he preached about seven years to a small, but affectionate people, and was much respected by his brethren. In 1695, on a

* MS. *penes me.*

TURNERS'-HALL, PHILPOT-LANE.—*Reformed Quakers.*

vacancy in the General Baptist church in Paul's-Alley, Barbican, occasioned by the death of the Rev. Thomas Plant, Mr. Allen was unanimously invited to take upon him the pastorship of that society. His attachment to the people at Turners'-Hall, caused him to hesitate, and he refused to desert his little flock. However, on union between the two churches being agreed upon, Mr. Allen removed to Barbican, where the union was publicly recognized, June 12, 1695.* A further account of Mr. Allen, will be given under the article " Paul's-Alley."

REFORMED QUAKERS.

AFTER the removal of Mr. Allen's congregation, the meeting-house at Turners'-Hall was occupied for some time by a Mr. GEORGE KEITH, who seems to have been a singular character, and his congregation as much so. In 1698, there was published a pamphlet, entitled, " A friendly Epistle to Mr. George Keith, and the Reformed Quakers at Turners'-Hall: with some Animadversions on a Discourse about a right Administrator of Baptism, &c. and of Episcopacy: with a Postscript about the Education of Children, &c. By Calvin Philanax." From the title of this piece, the reader will be led to infer considerable eccentricity in the sentiments of Mr. Keith. (J) After continuing several years among the Nonconformists, he thought fit, in

---

* MS. *penes me.*

(J) In the " View of all Religions," by Hannah Adams, there is the following article, but whether it refers to the above person, does not seem quite certain. " KEITHIANS, a party which separated from the Quakers, in Pennsylvania, in the year 1691. They were headed by the famous George Keith, from whence they derived their name. Those who persisted in their separation after their leader deserted them, practised baptism, and received the Lord's-Supper. This party were also called Quaker Baptists, because they retained the language, dress, and manners of the Quakers.

TURNERS'-HALL, PHILPOT-LANE.—*Independents.*

the year 1700, to go over to the Church of England. On May the 5th he preached his farewell sermon at Turners'-Hall; and on the Lord's-day following, May 12, he delivered two initiatory discourses amongst his new friends, at St. George's, Botolph-lane, near Billingsgate, from Luke i. 6. *And they were both righteous before God, walking in all the commandments and ordinances of the Lord blameless.* A most singular text for such an occasion, and conformable with his other sigularities. After a while, Mr. Keith was presented to the rectory of Edburton in Sussex; but what became of him afterwards, we no where learn.* (L)

* MS. *penes me.*

(L) In the continuation of Granger's Biographical History of England, published a short time since, some mention is made of a George Keith, who is styled Minister of the Gospel. Of this person there is a wooden cut, in the title to his " Guide, or the Christian Pathway to Everlasting Life." 1700, 8vo. In the book above-mentioned, there is the following account of him. " This disgrace to the clerical character was, at one time, the most active of the marrying parsons in the Fleet. Driven from Scotland for his attachment to episcopacy, he settled in London; and to procure a maintenance, commenced the same trade since so successfully carried on by the Blacksmith of Gretna Green. Few persons so much injured the public morals, or so much distressed families, as this unworthy man, and his brethren the priests of Hymen; who even had their setters to ask people passing, whether they wanted a clergyman to marry them: and the ceremony was frequently still further profaned by the intoxication of the priest and the parties. Keith and his journeymen, it was said, in one morning, during the Whitsun-holidays, at May-Fair Chapel, locked together a greater number of couples than had been married at any ten churches within the bills of mortality. He had transferred his practice to this place, and continued to officiate there for many years, till he was again obliged to take refuge in the Fleet. At length the Bishop of London, taking cognizance of the abuse, excommunicated him, and the sentence was repeated in May-Fair Chapel."* From some eccentricities recorded of this man, we strongly suspect him to be the same with the person above-mentioned. The chief difficulty regards his being driven from Scotland on account of episcopacy. Perhaps this may be incorrect.

* Noble's continuation of Granger, vol. iii. p. 144.

TURNERS'-HALL, PHILPOT-LANE.—*Independents.*

INDEPENDENTS.

AFTER the conformity of Mr. Keith, his congregation at Turners'-Hall was soon dispersed. The place was then taken by Mr. Joseph Jacob, a person of considerable note in his day, but of no less eccentricity; and concerning whom we are happy to have it in our power to lay before the reader the following particulars, which have never appeared in print, and may be considered authentic.

JOSEPH JACOB.—This singular person was born about the year 1667, but the place of his birth is not mentioned. His parents belonged to that denomination of people called Quakers, and trained him up in the same principles; but he appears to have renounced them pretty early in life. He was bred to the trade of a linen-draper, and followed that profession for sometime in London. At an early period, he seems to have discovered those singular traits of character, which distinguished him throughout life. He was warm in the cause of civil and religious liberty; and was an utter enemy to the designs and practices of those who were plotting the overthrow of our constitution, in the reign of King James the Second. At the Revolution, he discovered his zeal by mounting a horse, and going to meet King William in the West. The storm blowing over, and the affairs of the nation putting on a favourable aspect, Mr. Jacob began to profess himself a Protestant Dissenter, of the congregational persuasion; and being desirous of becoming a preacher, he, with a view to qualify himself for that profession, put himself under the tuition of the Rev. Robert Traile, a learned and eminent Divine, at that time, in the metropolis. Upon his first appearance in public, he manifested that he was no ordinary person, and soon gathered a numerous congregation.

About 1697, Mr. Jacob set up a weekly lecture at Mr. Gouge's meeting-house, near the Three Cranes, Thames-

TURNERS'-HALL, PHILPOT-LANE.— *Independents.*

street, where he was much followed. Being naturally of a bold daring spirit, and having an unaccountable propensity to find fault with his betters, in which he seems to have much delighted, he took occasion frequently, at this lecture, to interfere more than he ought to have done, with the public affairs of the government. His conduct in this respect, drew upon him, as might be expected, much censure, and was certainly calculated to bring him into no small trouble. The matter soon reached the Parliament-house; and Mr. Shallet, one of Mr. Gouge's people, being then a member of Parliament, took up the business at a church meeting, complained loudly of Mr. Jacob's behaviour, and insisted upon his being dismissed from his lecture at that place; which was complied with. This resolute proceeding, however, served only to exasperate Mr. Jacob, who, before he took leave of the place, fell foul upon several very worthy ministers, and amongst others, upon the valuable Mr. Matthew Mead. At the same time, he produced in the pulpit, one of Mr. Mead's books, out of which he read what he thought proper, and then ridiculed and lampooned it as served his pleasure. And this being his farewell sermon at that place, he concluded with telling the people, that he shook off the dust of his feet as a testimony against them, because they would not receive his gospel; and this he actually attempted in the literal sense.

Notwithstanding the singularities which marked his character, Mr. Jacob still had numerous friends; and when he was deprived of his lecture at the Three Cranes, they proceeded to build him a new meeting-house, in Parish-street, Southwark. This was in 1698. Here he soon had a numerous audience; and he set about forming his people into a regular church, which he was determined should be more pure than any that had been before him. For this purpose, he drew up a church-covenant, which he obliged all his members to sign; but of what particulars it was composed, cannot, at this distance of time, be recovered. However,

TURNERS'-HALL, PHILPOT-LANE.—*Independents.*

we may form some judgment of the leading features of it, from certain singular customs observed in his church, which have come to our knowledge. He passed an order, obliging the whole of the congregation to stand during the time of singing. This, though by no means an uncommon thing in the present day, was then looked upon as a great novelty. In this reformed church all periwigs were discarded; the men members wore whiskers upon their upper lips, in which Mr. Jacob set them an example; and an order passed for the regulation of the women's garb. The members of this church were not allowed to attend public worship at any other place, not even if their business occasionally called them to a distance; nor were they suffered to intermarry with other churches. The relations of life could be filled up only from this perfect society; nor could any person, excepting Mr. Jacob, be safely employed to solemnize the marriage union. These articles, *cum multis aliis,* were the distinguishing features of this very singular church, which stood aloof from the other bodies of Dissenters. Some persons not conforming to the new rules, were forthwith excommunicated. But this harsh usage only offended others, who withdrew in consequence. This proved a great detriment to Mr. Jacob; and, in the end, his church dwindled away so far that he was obliged to quit his meeting-house. This was about the year 1702. However, he still went on in his usual way; for being of a courageous temper, and having always a number of admirers, he made shift to stand his ground. The next place he occupied as a meeting-house, was Turners'-Hall. Here he proceeded, as formerly, to pollute his pulpit, by animadverting upon public characters; reflecting particularly upon King William, and ridiculing many worthy ministers in the metropolis; such as Mr. Howe, Mr. Traile, Mr. Clarke, Mr. Bragge, &c. From Turners'-Hall he removed to Currier's-Hall, Cripplegate, which was the last stage of his performance. There he went on much in the same way, till his followers gra-

TURNERS'-HALL, PHILPOT-LANE.—*Independents.*

dually deserted him, and he was taken away by death, June the 26th, 1722, when he was 55 years of age; and with him died the Reformed Church of which he was pastor.*

As to the character of Mr. Jacob, the reader will be enabled to form a pretty correct idea of it, from the preceding sketch of his history. He was a man of considerable natural talents, and possessed some learning. His zeal was ardent, and his courage undaunted. He despised danger, ridiculed the idea of singularity, and set himself above the reach of vulgar prejudice. He had, for many years, an uncommon influence over his followers, and, had he possessed sufficient discretion to govern his conduct, he would not only have ensured respect, but have acquired considerable weight with his brethren, and his name would have been handed down with credit to the Dissenting cause. But like Ishmael of old, and not unlike one of his descendants in the present day, it might be said of him, that *his hand was against every man, and every man's hand against him.* However, we must leave him, and his defects, to the scrutiny of that day, when *every man's work shall be made manifest: For the day shall declare it, because it shall be revealed by fire; and the fire shall try every man's work of what sort it is.* We have seen two or three single sermons of Mr. Jacob, preached at Turners'-Hall, which we believe is all that he has in print. This extraordinary man lies buried in Bunhill-Fields, beneath a handsome tomb, containing the following inscription:

In hopes of a part in the first resurrection.
To the Memory
Of Mr. JOSEPH JACOB,
An Apostolic Preacher,
Who died the 26th of 4 mo. 1722,
Aged 55.

Also, SARAH JACOB, his wife; and two of their Daughters.

* MS. *penes me.*

TURNERS'-HALL, PHILPOT-LANE.—*Particular Baptists.*

PARTICULAR BAPTISTS.

After the death of Mr. Jacob, the meeting-house at Turners'-Hall was taken by a congregation of Particular Baptists. This society originated in the following circumstance. Upon the death of Mr. William Collins, pastor of an ancient Particular Baptist Church, in Spitalfields, the majority of that Society agreed to unite with another church, of the same persuasion, that met at Lorimer's-Hall. They also agreed to bring in the practice of singing psalms, which was beginning, just then, to be introduced among the Baptists; and was not received without considerable opposition. It appears that several members disliking this innovation, separated from the rest, claiming to themselves the title of the Old Church, because they adhered to their ancient constitution and settlement. These resolving to keep up their church-state, and conduct public worship upon their former plan, hired the meeting-house at Turners'-Hall, and chose Mr. Ebenezer Wilson for their pastor. They continued to assemble there for about twenty-three years; but, in 1727, removed to Devonshire-square, and united with one of the congregations which met in that place.* The following persons were pastors of this Society while they met at Turners'-Hall.

Ministers' Names.	From	To
Ebenezer Wilson, - - - - - - - -	1704	1714
Thomas Dewhurst, - - - - - - -	1716	1723
Sayer Rudd, - - - - - - - - -	1725	1727

Ebenezer Wilson.—He was son to the Rev. John Wilson, many years pastor of the Baptist congregation at

MS. *penes me.*

TURNERS'-HALL, PHILPOT-LANE.—*Particular Baptists.*

Hitchin, Herts. Part of his education he received under the Rev. John Shuttlewood, an ejected minister, who kept his seminary at Sulby, near Welford, in Northamptonshire.* It appears from Crosby, that he was, also, sometime under the tuition of the celebrated Mr. Timothy Jollie, at Attercliffe, in Yorkshire.† At the close of his studies, he settled at Bristol, as assistant minister to one of the Baptist congregations in that city. It is not quite certain whether he preached at Broadmead, or the Pithay. We had some notion that it was at the latter place, as assistant to old Mr. Andrew Gifford; but a memorandum before us mentions a Mr. Wilson, a learned man, who kept a school in that city, and was assistant to Mr. Thomas Vauxe, pastor at Broad-mead. While at Bristol, Mr. Wilson married the daughter of the Rev. George Fownes, who was minister at High-Wycombe, and afterwards preached at Broadmead. By this lady, he had five or six children, one of whom was the Rev. Samuel Wilson, a respectable minister in Goodman's-Fields. About the year 1704, Mr. Wilson removed to London, to take charge of the congregation at Turners'-Hall, and continued in that situation till his death, in 1714. He was a very worthy man, and a good scholar; but not popular as a preacher. On this account, his congregation was but small; nevertheless, it consisted of some wealthy persons, so that he had a tolerable maintenance, and being greatly respected, they contributed largely to his support. His funeral sermon was preached by the Rev. Edward Wallin, but not printed.‡

THOMAS DEWHURST.—After a vacancy of about two years, Mr. Wilson was succeeded by a Mr. Thomas Dewhurst. This gentleman came from Backop in Lancashire,

---

* Nonconformist's Memorial, vol. ii. p. 398.
† Crosby's Hist. of the English Baptists, vol. iv. p. 316.
‡ Crosby, *ubi supra.*

TURNERS'-HALL, PHILPOT-LANE.—*Particular Baptists.*

where he was member of a Baptist church under the care of the Rev. Richard Ashworth. He was received a member at Turners'-Hall, Aug. 19, 1716, and after a further trial of his ministerial gifts, was ordained to the pastoral office on the 29th of the same month. Mr. Wallin opened the work of the day, and was the mouth of the church upon the occasion; two members of the church prayed; Mr. Mark Key gave a word of exhortation to the minister, and Mr. John Skepp preached to the church; Mr. Dewhurst then closed the work of the day with prayer. He continued at Turners'-Hall about seven years, till 1723, when he either died, or removed to some other place.* Mr. Dewhurst was one of the subscribing brethren at the Salter's-Hall Synod in 1719.

SAYER RUDD.—Mr. Dewhurst was succeeded, after a considerable interval, by the Rev. Sayer Rudd, then a member of Mr. Wallin's church at the Maze-Pond, Southwark. He was publicly set apart, with laying on of hands, July 2, 1725. The following year, upon the death of the Rev. Mark Key, the church at Devonshire-square, expressed a desire of putting themselves under the care of Mr. Rudd, and invited him to preach for them several times, with that view. At length an union between the two churches was agreed to, upon condition that the people at Devonshire-square should dissolve their church state, and join Mr. Rudd's congregation, which was to remove from Turners'-Hall, and meet henceforward in Devonshire-square. After several letters had passed between them on the subject, the union was publicly recognized June 27, 1727.† As Mr. Rudd will again fall under our notice more than once in the course of the present work, we shall omit any further mention of him in this place.

* MS. *penes me.* † Ibid.

TURNERS'-HALL, PHILPOT-LANE.—*Independents.*

INDEPENDENTS.

Upon the removal of Mr. Rudd's congregation, Turners'-Hall was taken by a society of Independents, who were a branch of Mr. Hussey's church in Petticoat-lane. After the death of that celebrated man, which happened in 1726, the discontents which had for sometime subsisted in his church, greatly increased, and all attempts for the restoration of harmony proving ineffectual, a separation followed. The majority having withdrawn, assembled for public worship, for a short time, in a private house, which they licensed for that purpose. About 1727, they removed into Turners'-Hall, where they continued to conduct the worship among themselves, with the occasional assistance of such ministers as they could procure to preach for them. They afterwards experienced some considerable difficulties, and began to fall to pieces among themselves; insomuch that several persons left them. (M) After this they were compelled to lay aside preaching altogether; and met only on the latter part of the Lord's-day. On these occasions, they spent their time in imploring the divine countenance and blessing; praying earnestly, that God would send them a pastor after his own heart. At this time, Mr. William Bentley, a very active deacon of the church, received a call to exercise his preaching gifts, and many persons were extremely desirous of introducing him to the ministerial office. If we may believe his own account, he was not a little backward in attending to the request of the church. How-

(M) From an entry in the church books belonging to the Society in Collier's Rents, Southwark, it appears that propositions were made for an union with the church at Turners'-Hall, and several messages passed upon the subject. The correspondence took place in the spring of 1730, and it seems as if the union had been effected. But, if so, the church at Turners'-Hall must have been different from the one of which we are now speaking.

TURNERS'-HALL, PHILPOT-LANE.—*Independents*.

ever, having got the better of his modesty, he had a further call to a more public display of his preaching talents, by conducting the whole worship as usual, on the Lord's-day. He was then sent forth to preach the gospel, and being set apart by the church, with solemn prayer, he entered upon his public work, Dec. 7, 1729. But the members of this society, being still debarred from the Lord's-Supper, and the ordinance of baptism, for want of a proper administrator, set themselves to inquire how they might overcome this difficulty. At length after searching the scriptures, and consulting the writings of Dr. Goodwin, Dr. Owen, and Dr. Chamey, who confirmed them much in their opinion, they determined to have a ruling-elder, and gave Mr. Bentley a call to that office. After continuing for sometime in this state, with comfort and satisfaction on both sides, the church began to think it would be better for them to have a proper pastor. For this purpose, they spent several days in imploring the divine direction, and at length, came to an unanimous resolution, that Mr. Bentley should be fixed in the pastoral office. Having signified his acceptance of this call, a day was appointed to set him apart by fasting and prayer. As they were not in connexion with any board, and the London ministers did not notice them, the service was conducted entirely among themselves. Mr. Bocket, one of the deacons was deputed by the church to be their mouth upon the occasion; and he transacted the chief service of the day. After some of the brethren had engaged in prayer, Mr. Bocket desired the church to renew their call, which was done accordingly. Mr. Bentley then declared his acceptance of the pastoral office, and gave a short account of his call to the ministry. After this, Mr. Bocket exhorted the minister, from Col. iv. 17; and the church, from 1 Thess. v. 12, 13. Some of the brethren then went to prayer, and the service concluded with singing.* Mr.

* " The Lord the helper of his people;" by Mr. Bentley, p. 1—32.

Bentley continued to preach at Turners'-Hall, till 1740, when his congregation having grown numerous, removed to a larger meeting-house, in Crispin-street, Spitalfields.† Under that article we shall give a further account of Mr. Bentley. (N)

WEIGH-HOUSE, LITTLE EASTCHEAP.

INDEPENDENT.

THE King's Weigh-House is situated at the corner of Love-lane, in Little Eastcheap. On the same site formerly stood the church of St. Andrew Hubbard, which was burnt in the fire of London, and the parish united to that of St. Mary-Hill. The King's Weigh-House then stood in Cornhill; but after this catastrophe, was removed to the spot where it now stands. The object of this building was, (for the prevention of frauds,) to weigh merchandise brought from beyond sea, by the King's beam; but of late years, little has been done in this way, as there was no compulsive power, and the merchants alleged it to be an unnecessary

---

† MS. *penes me.*

(N) Mr. Wesley, in one of his Journals, has the following paragraph : " Thursd. Sept. 27, 1739. I went in the afternoon to a society at Deptford, and then at six came to Turners'-Hall, which holds by computation two thousand persons. The press, both within and without, was very great. In the beginning of the expounding, there being a large vault beneath, the main beam which supported the floor broke. The floor immediately sunk, which occasioned much noise and confusion among the people. But two or three days before, a man had filled the vault with hogsheads of tobacco; so that the floor, after sinking a foot or two, rested upon them; and I went on without interruption."

WEIGH-HOUSE, LITTLE EASTCHEAP.—*Independent.*

trouble and expence. It was under the government of a master, and four master-porters, with labouring-porters, who used to have carts and horses to fetch the merchants' goods to the beam, and to carry them back. The appointments were in the gift of the Grocers' Company. Over this building stood the former meeting-house; from which circumstance it derived its name. It was built in 1697, for Mr. Thomas Reynolds, and after standing nearly a century, was taken down, when many human bones were dug from the foundation. The Weigh-House being discontinued, a large warehouse was erected in its room, and over it the present meeting-house, which was finished in 1795. It is a large, handsome, oblong building, with three deep galleries, and an upper one for a charity-school. The pews, in the body of the meeting, are raised one above the other, in a very tasty manner. The pulpit stands somewhat higher than customary, but has a light appearance, and is very handsome. In short, the whole is fitted up in an expensive manner, and in a style of great elegance.

The Society assembling at the Weigh-House is of early origin, being collected in the reign of King Charles the Second, soon after the Act of Uniformity, by Mr. Samuel Slater. It met originally at St. Katherine's, and afterwards in Cannon-street, or rather, in Great Eastcheap; and removed from thence to the Weigh-House. From a small this became a large and flourishing Society, and having many wealthy persons belonging to it, made, for many years, the largest collection for the fund of any congregation in London, Salter's-Hall excepted. The pastors of the church before the present one, carried their contributions for country ministers to the Presbyterian fund, but Mr. Clayton, soon after his settlement, joined the Independents. In point of religious sentiment, there has been but little variation; and for numbers, and affluence, it is at present one of the most respectable of our Dissenting Churches. During the greatest part of the last century, a lecture was preached at

WEIGH-HOUSE, LITTLE EASTCHEAP —*Independent.*

the Weigh-House, on a Friday evening, by some of the most eminent ministers, of different denominations, in London. Four volumes of sermons, on singing, praying, hearing the word, and reading the scriptures, delivered in an early stage of the lecture, were afterwards published. An annual sermon in commemoration of the great fire, in 1666, which began near this place, was also preached here for a century afterwards. The following table will give the reader, at one view, the names of the different ministers who have been connected with the church, at the Weigh-House, both as pastors and assistants.

Ministers' Names.	As Pastors.		As Assistants.	
	From	To	From	To
Samuel Slater, Sen.	1662	1670	—	—
Richard Kentish,			1662	16—
Thomas Kentish,	1670	1695	—	—
John Knowles,	—	—	1672	1685
Thomas Reynolds,	1695	1727	—	—
Jabez Earle,	—	—	1699	1707
James Read,	—	—	1707	1720
James Wood,	1727	1742	1720	1727
Samuel Sanderson,	—	—	1730	1736
William Langford,	1742	1775	1736	1742
Samuel Palmer,	—	—	1763	1766
Edward Vennor,	—	—	1767	1775
Samuel Wilton,	1776	1778	—	—
John Clayton,	1779	18—	—	—

SAMUEL SLATER, Sen.—Of this venerable Divine, but little information is now to be obtained. As he is not mentioned by Wood, it is probable that he received his education in the University of Cambridge. After preaching about

WEIGH-HOUSE, LITTLE EASTCHEAP.—*Independent.*

ten years at some place in the country, he removed to London, and became minister of the collegiate chapel of St. Katherine's, in the Tower. He continued in the city during the time of the plague, in 1625, when many others left it, and endeavoured by his good offices to alleviate the miseries of the suffering inhabitants. Though his income did not exceed forty pounds a-year, he lived upon it very contentedly, being happy in the esteem and affection of his parishioners. After preaching nearly forty years at St. Katherine's, this venerable man was deprived of his small living, in 1662, for not violating his conscience by subscribing the Act of Uniformity. Something of his disposition and strain of preaching may be learnt from his farewell sermon, on 1 John, v. 1 and 21. *Whosoever believeth that Jesus is the Christ is born of God, and he that loveth him that begat, loveth him also that is begotten of him. Little children keep yourselves from idols.* The discourse is plain and practical, and addressed to the conscience. Concerning the immediate occasion of it, he remarks, " I suppose you all know there is an act come forth by supreme authority, and it is not for us to quarrel at it, but to submit as far as we can with a good conscience; there being many besides myself who cannot comply with the injunctions, but are willing rather to submit to the penalty. You have had the benefit of my poor labours for nearly forty years; during which I have performed my service to God, Christ, and his people, and I bless his name, not without acceptance and success. My work, so far as I know, in this course, as in the weekly course, is now at an end. My desire is, that you whose hearts have been inclined to wait upon God in the way of my ministry, may be kept faithful, and that you may have the blessing of the everlasting covenant upon your souls: that you may have the power of this doctrine, held forth in this sermon, put forth upon your hearts, that as you believe that Jesus is the Christ, the Son of God, you may carry it suitably to your profession: that you may walk in love to

WEIGH-HOUSE, LITTLE EASTCHEAP.—*Independent.*

God, love to Christ, and love to one another: that you may labour to manifest a noble generous spirit, in overcoming the world, its errors, corruptions, false doctrines, and unwarrantable worship: that you may in all things labour to approve yourselves. And *little children keep yourselves from idols. Amen.*" *

After his ejectment, Mr. Slater collected a small society at St. Katherine's, and continued to exercise his ministry in private, as he had opportunity. This venerable man died about the year 1670, when he must have been between eighty and ninety years of age. He had been a preacher sixty years, and was considerably above seventy years old, when he was silenced. Dr. Calamy speaks of him as a man of eminent piety, of great plainness, and remarkable sincerity.† He left a son in the ministry of the same name, who was likewise one of the Bartholomew Confessors, and afterwards preached to a congregation in Crosby-square. Under that article we shall have occasion to give a particular account of him.

Mr. Slater published a metrical version of the Songs of Moses, Deborah, Hannah, and Solomon, and of the Church in the xxvi of Isaiah. 8vo. 1653. Also, "The Plague Check'd; in a Letter to a Friend." 8vo. 1665. He was also the author of several other pieces, the titles of which have not reached us. After his death, appeared his "Treatise of Growth in Grace; in nineteen Sermons." 8vo. 1671.‡ The editor of this volume, in an address to the reader, speaks of Mr. Slater as "A Reverend, laborious and judicious preacher, whose growth in grace was well known."

RICHARD KENTISH.—He was fellow-labourer with Mr. Slater at St. Katherine's in the Tower, and ejected at

---

* Farewell Sermons, p. 469.
† Calamy's Continuation, p. 39, 40.   ‡ Ibid.

WEIGH-HOUSE, LITTLE EASTCHEAP.—*Independent.*

the same time.* This is all the account that is left us concerning him. Some circumstances, however, lead us to think that he continued to assist Mr. Slater in his nonconforming society, after Bartholomew-day. It does not appear what relation he was to the other ejected ministers of the same name. Probably he was brother to Mr. Thomas Kentish, who was deprived of the living of Middleton, in the bishopric of Durham, soon after the Restoration. If this be correct, he was uncle to the person mentioned in the next article. Mr. Richard Kentish published nothing, we believe, excepting a sermon, preached before the long parliament, Nov. 24, 1647, on Rev. ii. 2.

THOMAS KENTISH.—This excellent and useful minister was son to the Rev. Thomas Kentish, who was ejected soon after the Restoration, from Middleton, in the bishopric of Durham. He brought up three sons to the ministry, and died in London full of years.† Of the three sons just mentioned, the subject of the present biographical sketch, is the only one of whom we find the least notice; and the memorials concerning him are extremely scanty. He is not mentioned by the Oxford historian, though a member of that University; the probable reason of which is, that he was never graduated. He was, also, living when the first edition of Wood's work made its appearance. Dr. Calamy informs us, that he received his education in Pembroke College.‡ At the Restoration, he was rector of Overton, in Hampshire, but did not enjoy it long afterwards, being deprived by the Act of Uniformity, in 1662. He then retired to London, and succeeded Mr. Slater as pastor of the Society at St. Katherine's, which removed soon afterwards to Cannon-street. This good man suffered much

* Calamy's Continuation, p. 40. † Calamy's Account, p. 290.
‡ Calamy's Continuation, p. 518.

WEIGH-HOUSE, LITTLE EASTCHEAP.—*Independent.*

from the persecuting spirit of the times. Being on one occasion in Mr. Janeway's pulpit, at Rotherhithe, he was seized by the troopers, and taken to the Marshalsea, where he was some time confined a prisoner. Mr. Kentish died in 1695, and was succeeded in his congregation by Mr. Thomas Reynolds. Dr. Calamy gives him the character of a very serious, useful, friendly, candid person.* He left two sons in the ministry, one in Southwark, and the other at Bristol; but they neither of them long survived their father. It does not appear that Mr. Kentish ever published any thing.

JOHN KNOWLES, sometime colleague with Mr. Thomas Kentish. He was a native of Lincolnshire, and pursued his studies at Magdalen College, Cambridge, where he was chamber-fellow with Mr. Vines. In 1625, he was chosen Fellow of Katherine-Hall, where he had full employment as a tutor. He had forty pupils under his care at one time, many of whom became persons of consideration and worth. About the year 1650, twelve of them were members of parliament, and no less than thirty eminent preachers. Before the death of Dr. Sibbes, who was master of Katherine-Hall, a fellowship became vacant in Magdalen College, for which archbishop Laud recommended one of his bell-ringers at Lambeth. This was a great stretch of authority, and designed to promote a quarrel if he was refused, or to have a spy there if accepted. Dr. Sibbes, who was not for provoking persons in power, told the fellows that Lambeth-House would be obeyed; that the person was young, and might prove hopeful; so he was chosen accordingly. But fifty years afterwards, Mr. Knowles observed, that nothing troubled him more than the vote he gave upon that occasion. The man thus forced upon them, proved a mere timeserver. He went thither of the Lambeth cast;

* Account, p. 351.

WEIGH-HOUSE, LITTLE EASTCHEAP.—*Independent.*

but as the times changed, became a Presbyterian, an Independent, every thing that prevailed; and in every way violent. At last, he wrote a book, called, " St. Austin imitated in his Retractations;" but this he was ready enough to retract upon a fresh change in the government.*

Upon the death of Dr. Sibbes, there was a great contest about a successor to the vacant Mastership; but the choice, at length, fell upon Dr. Brownrig, who proved a most worthy and exemplary person. While Mr. Knowles was, with great pleasure and usefulness, leading a college-life, he received an invitation from the Mayor and Aldermen of Colchester, to be their lecturer. This he accepted, and applied himself to his work with great acceptance and success. While at this place, he became intimately acquainted with the famous Mr. John Rogers of Dedham, whose eyes he closed, and whose funeral sermon he preached. He also recommended to them his worthy successor, Mr. Matthew Newcomen. The schoolmaster's place at Colchester becoming vacant, Mr. Knowles and the Mayor carried the election for a person in opposition to the recommendation of archbishop Laud; who was so incensed, that he would not suffer Mr. Knowles to continue there any longer. His licence being revoked in 1639, he went to New-England, and became teacher to the church at Watertown, of which Mr. George Philips was pastor. There he continued about ten years, when he was sent to Virginia, to preach the gospel, in conjunction with Mr. Thompson of Braintree. At their first coming, the governor entertained them courteously; but when he found they were inimical to the surplice, common prayer, &c. he would not allow them to preach in the places of public worship. They, however, continued to preach there privately, for some time, and did

* Dr. Calamy's Account, p. 605, 606.

WEIGH-HOUSE, LITTLE EASTCHEAP.—*Independent.*

much good. Mr. Knowles has often been heard to say, that he never saw so much, of the blessing of God upon his ministry as there, and at Colchester. At length, they were forced to remove; and it was to them a remarkably kind providence: for no sooner were they on board the ship, in which they were to have sailed, than there was a general rising of the Indians, who massacred all the English, sparing neither old nor young. Mr. Knowles then returned to Watertown, when he made but a short continuance.

After an absence of more than eleven years, Mr. Knowles returned back to England, about the year 1650. Soon after, he became a preacher in the cathedral at Bristol, where he lived in great credit and usefulness. At the Restoration, he was ejected from this place; and in 1662, silenced with the rest of his brethren. He then returned to London, where he continued preaching in private as he had opportunity. During the great plague, in 1665, he was very useful to such as continued in the city; visiting rich and poor, without distinction, and regardless of danger. Upon King Charles's Indulgence, in 1672, he preached statedly to a people at St. Katherine's, as colleague with Mr. Thomas Kentish. In London, he underwent some severe persecutions, and experienced as many remarkable deliverances. When some of his friends dissuaded him from preaching, lest he should be cast into prison, he answered, " In truth, I had rather be in a jail, where I might have a number of souls, to whom I might preach the truths of my blessed Master, than live idle in my own house, without any such opportunities." Like his Redeemer, he made it the business of his life to go about doing good; and so fervent was he in his work, that he sometimes preached till he fell down. His discourses in company, concerning the dealings of God with him, his temptations and afflictions, his deliverances and supports, were so many affecting ser-

WEIGH-HOUSE, LITTLE EASTCHEAP.—*Independent.*

mons. This valuable man lived to a good old age, and died April 10, 1685.*

THOMAS REYNOLDS.—This eminent and useful minister, was born in London, about the year 1667. His father was a protestant Dissenter, a religious man, and a member of Mr. Howe's church in Silver-street. Our author, who was his eldest son, he designed for the profession of the law. Accordingly, he was placed betimes, under the care of Mr. Singleton, of Clerkenwell-Close, who made a considerable figure at that time, for classical literature. Having continued with this gentleman a proper time, he was sent to prosecute his studies at Oxford. But there things did not answer his expectation. The tutor under whom he studied being particularly disagreeable to him, he desired that he might be recalled, and was gratified in his request. Soon after his return to London, the court revived the persecution against the Dissenters.† Not being allowed to worship publicly, agreeably to his own choice, he was compelled to hear as he could, and attended the ministry of Mr. Smithy's, at Cripplegate church. Under the preaching of that gentleman, Mr. Reynolds received great satisfaction and profit. It pleased God to work effectual conviction upon his mind, insomuch that he received a new bias; all his thoughts about the law vanished at once; and he resolved to devote himself to God in the work of the ministry, even though bonds and imprisonment might attend it. His father observing the uncommon concern of spirit which he now discovered, together with the influence it produced, endeavoured to divert him from his purpose; urging the difficulties that attended the ministry among the nonconformists at that period. To

* Calamy's Account, p. 605—608.——Nonconformist's Memorial, vol. iii. p. 173—175.——Mather's History of New-England, B. III. p. 216.

† This must have been about 1681, or 1682, when Dr. Stillingfleet's mischief of separation so provoked the papal fury.

WEIGH-HOUSE, LITTLE EASTCHEAP.—*Independent.*

this, young Mr. Reynolds replied, " That he foresaw these discouragements, and acknowledged that the advantage as to this world, lay in the other scale : yet upon this view of the case, he preferred being a minister of Jesus Christ ; and if he might be successful in bringing one soul to him, it would yield him more satisfaction than thousands of gold and silver." The force of this reasoning, doubtless, yielded secret satisfaction to the heart of Mr. Reynolds's father, though it disappointed his original intentions.*

Mr. Reynolds having chosen the ministry among the nonconformists, the next care of his father was to give him a suitable education for that profession. With this view, he placed him under the care of Mr. Charles Morton, at Newington-green; a gentleman, who, for a considerable course of time, taught university learning, with applause. Mr. Reynolds was admitted a member of his academy, March 27, 1683, before he had completed his sixteenth year. At this seminary, he chose for his companions the most solid and serious ; such as had the best taste for learning, as well as the greatest emulation to excel. And, as he came behind none in real piety, so, he had his share of reputation as a scholar. The troubles of the nonconformists increasing, and their seminaries being looked upon by the government with an evil eye ; some young persons engaged in the same studies, and with the same views, judged it prudent to retire abroad, and fixed upon Geneva as the most eligible place, where they might not only pursue their studies unmolested, but likewise have the benefit of a public university. Mr. Reynolds, sensible of these advantages, requested his father, that he might make one of the number, which was readily granted. There, they attended the lectures of the deservedly celebrated Dr. Francis Turretine.†

---

* Mr. Wood's Sermon on the Death of the Rev. Thomas Reynolds, p. 30, 31.   † Ibid. p. 32.

WEIGH-HOUSE, LITTTE EASTCHEAP.——*Independent*

Mr. Reynolds had not been long at Geneva, before it pleased God to suffer him (the better to fit him for the work of the ministry) to be exercised with great doubts as to his spiritual state. Darkness and fears continued to grow upon him, and his spiritual troubles ran so high, that he seemed to be not many removes from despair. But the clouds scattered by degrees; and it pleased God to bless the conversation of a worthy person, providentially there at the time, by which means he was restored to a solid, settled peace of mind.*

Having spent some time at Geneva, he removed to the United Netherlands; and studied at the University of Utrecht. Here the philosophy professor was the famous De Vries, and Witsius the professor of divinity; men who shone among the first lights, in their more private characters as Christians, as well as in the faculties which they publicly professed. Under the disadvantage of ill health, he made a good proficiency in useful learning; and it has been remarked to his honour, by those who knew him abroad, that the seriousness of his spirit was beyond what was ordinarily seen in such a stage of life, and his ability in prayer as extraordinary.†

Having passed through the requisite preparatory studies, Mr. Reynolds returned home, and preached occasionally about the metropolis. He had not been long there before his fame as a solid, judicious, edifying preacher, was so noised abroad, that the congregation under the pastoral care of the learned Mr. John Howe, in Silver-street, being then in want of an assistant, invited him to serve them in the work of the gospel. In this station he behaved with so much modesty, that he gained an high interest in the esteem both of pastor and people.‡ While in this situation, Mr. Reynolds was ordained at the first public meeting held for that

---

* Mr. Wood's Sermon on the Death of Mr. Thomas Reynolds, p. 33.
† Ibid. ‡ Ibid. *ubi supra*, p. 34.

WEIGH-HOUSE, LITTLE EASTCHEAP.—*Independent.*

purpose, among the Dissenters, after the act of Uniformity. The service was conducted at Dr. Annesley's meeting-house, Little St. Helen's, June 22, 1694. Six other young men were ordained at the same time, and the work was performed by several aged nonconforming ministers.*

Sometime after, upon the death of Mr. Thomas Kentish, a worthy ejected minister, in 1695, he was invited to succeed him in the pastoral care of a small congregation, in Cannon-street. This application was made, not without fears as to the issue. The church consisted of not more than sixteen or seventeen men; the auditory in proportion. The encouragement therefore, to a reflecting person, could not be very great. Besides, he was then in a church of principal note, had a respectable and flourishing audience, and was amidst a number of hearty generous friends: so that, to an eye of sense, it could not but appear that he must be a considerable loser by falling in with the proposal. His removal was strongly opposed by some persons of the first rank and influence in the church at Silver-street; as also by his father, who was a member of that society. They also promised to enlarge his income, though it was already above what he had any rational prospect of receiving from the other congregation. But notwithstanding these circumstances, he resolved to accept the call, observing that there was so much of the hand of God in the unanimity and affection expressed by the people who had invited him, that he would take his lot with them, and leave the event.†

Mr. Reynolds had not been settled long in this new situation before things began to assume a better appearance. His ministry met with very general acceptance, and the congregation rapidly increased. This greatly encouraged him in his labours, and made him acquiesce the more in his removal. In a short time, his church became so numerous

* Calamy's Continuation, p. 635.
† Mr. Wood's Sermon, *ubi supra*, p. 34, 35.

WEIGH-HOUSE, LITTLE EASTCHEAP.—*Independent.*

that it was found necessary to provide a larger meeting-house; and having obtained leave to build a new one, over the King's Weigh-House, they removed thither, in 1697. Here we cannot help remarking as somewhat extraordinary, and much to the credit of Mr. Reynolds, that his people should be so much augmented both in numbers and influence, in such a short time, as to be able to enter upon so large a concern as the one we have just mentioned. And we would here observe, that those persons strangely miscalculated the matter who supposed that the interest of nonconformity would die with the more immediate sufferers for it. On the contrary we have seen the same thing exemplified in this case which has been remarked in many others, that the more any particular opinions have been persecuted and held up to derision, so much the more have they flourished and gained ground. The reason is obvious; injured innocence will always obtain admirers, and the cause for which people are persecuted will naturally be sought out: thus free inquiry will be promoted, and truth obtain her admirers, notwithstanding the opposition of self-interested zealots. But to return.

Mr. Reynolds continued labouring with his congregation for above thirty years, much to his own reputation and the public benefit. He was a plain, serious, and affectionate preacher, and had many seals to his ministry. In discharging the duties of the pastoral office, he was an example of great diligence and fidelity. His public discourses were solid and judicious, remarkably adapted to strike the consciences of men, to persuade them of the reality of religion, and rouse them to a serious concern for the salvation of their souls. The subjects he insisted upon were the important points of faith and practice, and he endeavoured to interest his hearers in the glorious truths of the gospel revelation.*

* Wood's Sermon, *ubi supra*, p. 37.

WEIGH-HOUSE, LITTLE EASTCHEAP.——*Independent.*

The zeal he discovered for some important doctrines of Christianity, exposed him to much obloquy from persons who held them with a looser hand; or at least did not lay that stress upon them which he did. For the cause of Christ, and especially for poor country ministers, he was a remarkable pleader; and God gave him in a liberal manner, the hearts and purses of his people.

The reputation which Mr. Reynolds acquired as a preacher, often called forth his talents upon funeral and other public occasions. The many discourses he was prevailed upon to print, afford a good specimen of his pulpit abilities, as well as of the seriousness of his spirit. He was called to fill up the place of lecturer in some of the most considerable pulpits, in and about London. At the commencement of the Friday evening lecture at the Weigh-house, early in the eighteenth century; Mr. Reynolds was one of the first six ministers chosen to conduct it. He was also elected one of the preachers, on a Tuesday morning, of the merchant's lecture at Salter's-Hall. His people, for many years, kept up a friendly union with the churches under the care of Dr. John Evans, and Mr. Benjamin Robinson, in their monthly preparations for the Lord's-Supper, and, also, in their quarterly meetings for fasting and prayer; till the harmony of this association was disturbed by the affair of Mr. James Read, which shall be noticed presently.

In the year 1719, the Dissenting churches in the West of England, were thrown into a flame, in consequence of some of their ministers having embraced Arianism. This produced a long controversy, which was carried on with great bitterness on both sides. At length, the matter being referred to the London ministers, they met together in a synod at Salter's-Hall, to consider of advices to be sent to their brethren in the West, with a view of composing the differences. But it so happened that they could not agree among themselves; and, as is generally the case with large bodies,

WEIGH-HOUSE, LITTLE EASTCHEAP.—*Independent.*

they split into parties, and still further widened the breach. It being proposed in this assembly, that, in order to support their orthodox brethren in the West, the ministers present should make a declaration of their own sentiments with regard to the Trinity, by subscribing the first article of the Church of England, and the answers to the fifth and sixth questions in the Assembly's Catechism, the matter was violently opposed, as an infringement of Christian liberty, and they divided into two parties of subscribers and non-subscribers. Mr. Reynolds, from a motive of conscience, united with the former; and justified their conduct with great zeal and ability. To a belief of the doctrine of the ever blessed Trinity, he attached very great importance. The true eternal Godhead of the Son, and Spirit, he looked upon as the corner-stone of Christianity; all our hopes of happiness depending upon a practical belief of this doctrine. He was one of the four London ministers, who wrote a pamphlet, entitled, " The Doctrine of the Blessed Trinity stated and defended." The part he undertook was, Some Heads of Advice relating to that Doctrine. This was just before their unhappy differences, which ended in the division above-mentioned. Mr. Reynolds continued steadfast to the last, in the doctrine which he had thus publicly defended. On all proper occasions, he took care to warn his people against those who would draw them off, in this point, to another gospel. And he died in the same faith which he preached; rejoicing in having thus borne his testimony to a doctrine so essential to the comfort and hope of Christians.*(o)

* Mr. Wood's Sermon, *ubi supra*, p. 39.

(o) It appears that some unfavourable reports were spread by Mr. Reynolds's enemies, concerning the share he had taken in the business of subscription at Salters'-Hall; as if he had altered his mind on that subject. He has, however, publicly exposed the falsehood of those aspersions. " I take this opportunity (says he) to wipe off a foul reproach from myself, as if I had repented of what I had done, and that I should go mourning for it

WEIGH-HOUSE, LITTLE EASTCHEAP.—*Independent.*

Not long after the disputes just mentioned, Mr. Reynolds was engaged in another controversy, of a very unpleasant nature, with his assistant, the Rev. James Read. This gentleman, during the debates at the Salters'-Hall Synod, had taken the opposite side to Mr. Reynolds. He had, also, given some reason to suspect that, in his notions concerning the Trinity, he had deviated from the interpretation generally received by those who are reputed orthodox. This produced some heats in Mr. Reynolds's church, and occasioned Mr. Read's dismission, July 20, 1720. Some time after, a particular account of this affair was laid before the public, and produced much recrimination on both sides; but we reserve any further mention of it till we come to speak of Mr. Read in a separate article.

The fatigue and anxiety experienced by Mr. Reynolds during this troublesome and perplexing affair, greatly injured his health, so that he preached and administered the Lord's-Supper only one Lord's-day after Mr. Read's dismission, before he fell into such indisposition of body, as gave but little hopes of his life. He was confined above three months, during which time, his character was much insulted and abused; artful methods were made use of to entice away his people; and every mean devised, that could possibly distress him. His enemies spread a malicious report as if his disorder had affected his senses, and he would never be able to appear again in the pulpit; but through the goodness of God, he was wonderfully restored, and his church preserved from divisions. So that, out of three

to the grave. I declare it utterly false; but, believe, That, indeed, so it would have been if I had omitted what I have judged, and do still judge, to have been my duty. I pray God most heartily to forgive those, who, by this, and many other false reports, and subtle methods, have endeavoured to injure my reputation, and to lessen the small use, which God is pleased to make of me. I bear ill will to none, and have a great deal of comfort to find I dare not treat others as some have treated me."—*Life of the Rev. William Hocker, affixed to the Sermon upon his death, by the Rev. Thomas Reynolds, p.* 52.

WEIGH-HOUSE, LITTLE EASTCHEAP—*Independent.*

hundred communicants, of which Mr. Reynolds's church consisted, there were not more than ten or twelve who left it upon Mr. Read's account.*

In the year 1723, Mr. Reynolds was engaged in another controversy with the Rev. Simon Browne. This gentleman had taken some offence at a passage in a sermon preached by our author, upon the death of the pious and excellent Mr. Samuel Pomfret; as also to the preface prefixed to that discourse. The subject in dispute, related to the Salters'-Hall controversy, and the old affair of subscription. Mr. Browne's pamphlet, it must be acknowledged, is written with great keenness and show of argument, but, the unceremonious manner in which he treats Mr. Reynolds, and his subscribing brethren, ought to be spoken of in terms of severe reprobation. In the answer to Mr. Browne's Letter, published by Mr. Reynolds, he points out some gross misrepresentations of facts, and vindicates himself from the injurious reflections cast upon his character. " I have suffered long (says he) by false reports, though whilst my opposers did content themselves with more private methods of defamation, I only defended myself against them, as they came in my way; but since Mr. Browne has thought fit to attack me in print, and to renew the assault again in his late postscript, (to the second edition of his letter) I must stand condemned before the world, or be thought perfectly stupid, if I do not answer for myself in a manner as public as that in which I am accused."† Mr. Reynolds then gives a particular account of the transactions between himself and Mr. Read, and closes his pamphlet with the following reflections. " I have not imitated Mr. Browne in his abusive way of writing, as never daring to break through the boundaries of religion, truth, and good manners, to shew a little

---

* Mr. Reynolds's Answer to the Rev. Simon Browne, p. 52, 53.

† Answer to the Rev. Mr. Simon Browne's Letter. By Thomas Reynolds, p. 8.

WEIGH-HOUSE, LITTLE EASTCHEAP.—*Independent.*

wit. If he will be profane, prostitute his character, belie and defame a brother minister to make sport, and gain reputation among wanton scoffers, I can assure him he is far from being the object of my envy. My business is to slight his wit, and to see what he has of truth or argument, which, when examined into, is but of small account."* We thought it necessary to introduce the above extracts in vindication of Mr. Reynolds, because the several writers of Mr. Browne's Life, have noticed the pamphlet of that gentleman in such terms of unqualified praise as must lead the reader to form a very unfavourable idea of his opponent.

The health of Mr. Reynolds had been declining for some years. His constant labours, and public cares, the load of business upon his hands, and the frequent returns of acute bodily pain, together with the unkindnesses he met with from some persons who ought to have treated him with more honour, tended in a very considerable degree to break his constitution. It was his frequent prayer that he might not outlive his usefulness. And it pleased God to grant him his request; for, the last time he appeared in public, which was at the Lord's-Table, it was remarked, that he had never been more lively and affectionate, more enlarged and edifying than upon that occasion. It was also his desire, that he might not die under a cloud, and thereby bring dishonour upon Christ, or cast a stumbling-block in the way of his people. In this particular he was also heard. Mr. Wood, his assistant, who visited him at this period, observes, " I have often been called to attend on God's people in their dying hours, have been more than once with dying ministers, but remember not to have seen more of God's special and gracious presence, or so much of the light of his countenance."† He died in the possession of

---

* Answer to the Rev. Mr. Simon Browne's Letter. By Thomas Reynolds, p. 102.

† Mr. Wood's Sermon, *ubi supra*, p. 26.

WEIGH-HOUSE, LITTLE EASTCHEAP.—*Independent.*

a clear and strong judgment. One of his last acts, was to pray for his church; and bless them in the name of the Lord. And how the Spirit of God helped him under his infirmities of body, when he had the sentence of death in himself, the reader will be able to judge by the following brief narrative of his last day's conversation with some of his friends.

To his sorrowful wife he said, " My dear, had I power with God as Abraham; I would improve it to secure the best of blessings for you, for my children, and for the whole church of Christ. Let *my* God be *your's*; be faithful unto death; it will not be long till we meet where we shall never part, never more be sad." Quickly after he said, " O the joys I feel! my heavenly Father is carrying me to heaven in his arms; I am going thither *on a bed of roses*. I feared this hour, lest my pains should extort an impatient word, or cause that I should seem to be uneasy under his hand; I have often wished to die praising God, how kind is he who gives me leave so to do! Trust my God, he will not fail those who put their trust in him. O the comforts I feel! what blessed company shall I soon be in! what a mercy to be taken hence amidst my sympathising friends!" Having blessed particularly the branches of his family, he ordered one who was present, to tell his people as opportunity offered, that their dying minister sent his love and thanks to them, for their kindness to him. " Tell them (said he) that I send them my dying blessing; and if I were in the pulpit, and all my people about me, I would as far as a minister of Jesus Christ can do it, bless them in the name of my great Lord." When he was cautioned against speaking too much, as what did sensibly weaken him, in his low condition, he replied, " I have served my Lord living, and I am now doing it dying."* No cloud sullied his countenance to the last; his end was peace, and

* Mr. Wood's Sermon, *ubi supra*, p. 26, 27.

WEIGH-HOUSE, LITTLE EASTCHEAP.—*Independent.*

he finished his course with joy, August the 25th, 1727, aged about sixty years. The Rev. James Wood preached his funeral sermon, from 2 Cor. i. 12. *For our rejoicing is this, the testimony of our conscience, &c.*

Thus lived and died the Rev. Thomas Reynolds, a minister of no ordinary reputation for zeal, piety and ministerial usefulness; and, who, on account of his attachment to some peculiar doctrines of revelation, endured as large a share of obloquy as almost any minister in his day, the famous Mr. Bradbury, perhaps, excepted. By the divine blessing upon his skilful and diligent labours, he raised his congregation from a low state, to one of the most flourishing and wealthy societies among the Presbyterians. His fidelity and zeal procured him honour and acceptance in many churches of Christ, but more especially in the affections of his own people. But, though highly valued by others, he thought meanly of himself; and lived under a prevailing sense of his weakness and deficiency, in the performance of religious duties. In his last will, made a few years before his death, he says, " If Mr. Wood shall consent to preach a sermon on the occasion of my death, and shall think fit to say any thing of me therein, let it be no more than this; that the not being able to do more good, was the greatest burthen which attended me throughout my whole life; and the incomprehensible, infinite mercy of God, through the Lord Jesus Christ, is my only refuge, my chief support under the prospect of death."*

Mr. Reynolds was no less remarkable for prudence, than zeal, affection, and faithfulness, in the discharge of the ministerial office. He was well acquainted with mankind, and understood the world as well as most men in his station. In short, he lived, in as full reputation as most ministers of his age, and few died more sincerely or generally lamented.†

* Mr. Wood's Sermon, *ubi supra*, p. 40.
† *Ibid.*

WEIGH-HOUSE, LITTLE EASTCHEAP. *Independent.*

His writings, which consist chiefly of single sermons, shall be enumerated in the note below. (P)

JABEZ EARLE, D. D.—This venerable Divine, who died within the memory of many persons still living, when he had attained, almost, to the years of a patriarch, commenced his stated ministry, in 1699, as assistant to the Rev. Thomas Reynolds. He preached at the Weigh-House about eight years; but, in 1707, removed to Hanover-street, Long Acre, where his labours were prolonged to more than sixty years. To that place we refer the reader for a more particular account of this extraordinary man.

JAMES READ.—Upon the removal of Mr. Earle, the place of assistant-preacher, at the Weigh-House, was filled

(P) WORKS.—1. Sermon preached to the Societies for Reformation of Manners, in London and Westminster, Feb. 19, 1699, Prov. ix. 7, 8.—2. A Sermon on the Death of the Rev. John Ashwood, with an Account of his Life and Character; and an Address to the Orphans of Religious Parents. 1706.—3. Objections against Singing considered: In the Eastcheap Lectures. Psa. lxvii. 3, 4. 1708.—4. An Account of the Life of Mrs. Mary Terry, who died Dec. 8, 1708, in the 18th year of her age; together with her Funeral Sermon, on Prov. viii. 17. 1709. Dedicated to Mrs. Mary Terry, the author's mother-in-law.—5. Directions to the Gift and Grace of Prayer: In the Eastcheap Lectures. Luke xi. 1. 1711.—6. An Account of the Life of Mrs. Clissold, who departed this Life Dec. 12, 1711, in the 29th year of her age; together with her Funeral Sermon. Luke i. 45.—7. Exhortation to hearing the Word: in the Eastcheap Lectures. Heb. iii. 7. 1713.—8. A Funeral Sermon for Mr. Thomas Clissold, who died May 24, 1713, in the 31st Year of his Age. Eccles. ix. 10. 1713.—9. A Funeral Sermon for Mrs. Eleanor Murdin, who died May 31, 1713.—10. The Nature of Reading the Scriptures: In the Eastcheap Lectures. Acts xiii. 15. 1717.—11. Some Advices relating to the Doctrine of the Trinity. 1719.—12. A Funeral Sermon for the late Reverend and pious Mr. William Hocker, who died Dec. 12, 1721; with some Account of his Life. Acts xx. 37, 38. 1722.—13. A Funeral Sermon for the late Rev. and pious Mr. Samuel Pomfret, who deceased Jan. 11, 1721-2. Acts xx. 31, 32. 1722.—An Answer to the Rev. Mr. Simon Browne's Letter to Mr. Thomas Reynolds. 1723.

WEIGH HOUSE, LITTLE EASTCHEAP.—*Independent.*

up by the Rev. James Read, brother to Mr. Henry Read, of St. Thomas's, Southwark. He was appointed to this situation in 1707, and continued his ministry with acceptance, both to pastor and people, till the fatal Salters'-Hall controversy caused a separation. Mr. Read, as we have hinted above, joined the non-subscribing ministers, and thereby, took the opposite side to Mr. Reynolds. This gave much dissatisfaction to the congregation at the Weigh-House, many of whom discontinued their attendance upon Mr. Read's ministry. Mr. Reynolds, it seems, so far from countenancing this neglect, used his endeavours to restore him to their good opinion; expressing for him great personal regard, as well as the highest idea of his integrity and friendship. At this time, a few persons in the church endeavoured to raise a party against Mr. Reynolds; and these having espoused the cause of Mr. Read, attempted a division. Several church meetings were held upon the business; and, it being thought expedient, that pastor and assistant should be of one mind in religious matters, Mr. Reynolds was desired to wait upon Mr. Read, to know his sentiments, particularly as to what regarded the truth and importance of the doctrine of the Trinity. Two questions more especially, were pressed home upon Mr. Read's consideration. 1. Whether a person that pays religious worship to Christ, but at the same time disowns him to be truly and properly God, (that is, in the strictest and strongest sense of the word) be chargeable with downright idolatry? 2. Whether such a one has forfeited his claim to Christian communion? After some delay, Mr. Read, at a church meeting, held July 15, 1720, and convened expressly for the purpose, publicly declared that he could not agree with Mr. Reynolds in the affirmative of those questions.

This gave great dissatisfaction to the whole company, which soon afterwards broke up. From this time, it appeared pretty evident that Mr. Read could not continue much longer in connexion with the church at the Weigh-

WEIGH-HOUSE, LITTLE EASTCHEAP.—*Independent.*

House. Accordingly, at a meeting held July 20, the following resolution was agreed to: " We, the underwritten, " finding Mr. Read to differ in his sentiments from Mr. " Reynolds, in some points that we hold of consequence in " religion, do not see how they can discharge the office of " the ministry together consistent with the peace and edifi- " cation of our church. And, therefore, we are of opinion, " that Mr. Reynolds, our pastor, do part with Mr. Read, " and desire it may be done as speedily, and in as friendly " a manner as may be." With this resolution, Mr. Reynolds acquainted Mr. Read, in a letter, dated July 26, in which he observes, "Your disagreement with me in sentiment about matters of so great consequence, and your way of managing, have given me and my people a world of trouble and grief, both on your own and many other accounts that are obvious. I have always testified a just esteem and love for you, and have had a great deal of ease and pleasure in the concurrence of your labours with mine, and should have rejoiced as much as any man in the continuance of them, had not this difference rendered it utterly inconsistent with my own, and the peace and edification of my people. But these things, and the concern I have for truth, must take place of personal regard. However, as the resolution that has been taken by me and my people, has not proceeded from any private pique, but from conscience and necessary self-defence; so I shall endeavour to be as much your friend as I can consistent with these, and the duties I owe to God and those he hath placed under my care."*

The above is a brief, but, we believe, faithful account of a very unpleasant transaction, which drew much censure upon Mr. Reynolds, at the time, nor, are we disposed, entirely, to justify his conduct. That a religious society has a right at any time to inquire into the principles as well as

* Mr. Reynolds's Letter to the Rev. Simon Browne, p. 12—51.

WEIGH-HOUSE, LITTLE EASTCHEAP.—*Independent.*

practice of its minister, and to choose whether they will continue him in that relation, we are fully of opinion. And while we think Mr. Read must be acquitted of any attempts to divide the church, we do not know how far any jealousies that crept in, might render it prudent in Mr. Reynolds to retain him any longer as his assistant. At the same time, we quite disapprove the means that were made use of, to accomplish his dismission. There was no direct charge of heterodoxy against Mr. Read, nor does Mr. Reynolds intimate a suspicion that he had embraced the Arian heresy. To entangle him, therefore, with such abstract propositions as those above-mentioned, was neither friendly nor ingenuous. Though Mr. Reynolds had made up his mind for the affirmative of those questions, we are not quite clear that Mr. Read's hesitation upon the point, was a sufficient ground for depriving him of the ministry, much less for casting him out of the society. To start such questions, was calculated to promote jealousy and division; and appears quite unnecessary even though the circumstances of the church might render a separation expedient. We strongly suspect the latter to have been the case. Immediately after his dismission from the Weigh-House, Mr. Read was invited to Mr. (afterwards Dr.) Evans's pulpit, and proposed for his assistant. To this office he was, soon afterwards, chosen; and upon the death of that excellent person, succeeded to the pastoral charge. A more particular account of Mr. Read's life and character, will be given under the article New Broad-street, Petty-France.

JAMES WOOD.—Of this worthy and excellent minister our information is extremely confined. His own modesty forbad any funeral sermon; and though his request was not exactly complied with, the one that was published, contains not a single fact of his personal history. The time and circumstances of his birth, together with the particulars of his education, therefore, we are compelled to leave in the same

WEIGH-HOUSE, LITTLE EASTCHEAP.—*Independent.*

obscurity that we find them. In the year 1713, he was ordained pastor of the Presbyterian congregation in New-court, Cary-street, Lincoln's-inn-fields. The principal part of the service upon that occasion, fell upon the Rev. Matthew Henry; and it was the last work of the kind, in which that excellent person engaged. In this church, Mr. Wood succeeded to the celebrated Mr. Daniel Burgess. Upon the dismission of Mr. James Read, in 1720, Mr. Wood was called to fill up the place of morning-preacher at the Weigh-House; and, having an assistant appointed for him at New-court, he continued, for about seven years, to supply both places, alternately.*

It must have been about this time that he was called to assist a senior minister, in a catechetical lecture at the Old Jewry. This service, it is apprehended, he did not conduct any great length of time ; but resigned early in 1723-4. He preached his farewell sermon February 23, in that year, and afterwards committed it to the press. It is entitled, " Steadfastness in Religion recommended;" and the text is, 2 Pet. iii. 17, 18. Upon his services at this exercise, he has the following remarks. " I do sincerely profess, that I reckon myself with the meanest of those who have served you. Yet, can say, that however unworthy, I have endeavoured to be faithful. As I never forbore what I judged to be the truth of God, through fear of displeasing any ; neither have I ever offered what appeared to me to be such, with a view to the soothing or gratifying any creature. Your practice in attending to the explication of it, shews the esteem you have, of the excellent composure, of the Reverend Assembly of Divines, at Westminster. While I heartily approve your judgment, I must remind you that I always endeavoured to found your faith of the doctrines contained in it, upon the scriptures themselves, no where short of them ; and as far as I have gone in the practical part, I have laboured to convince

---

* MS. *penes me.*

WEIGH-HOUSE, LITTTE EASTCHEAP.——*Independent.*

you, that I laid no burthen upon any man, which God himself did not bind upon him; leaving you after all, to judge for yourselves."*

The discourse just mentioned, was followed by the publication of another, in the same year; preached at New-court, June 14; it was occasioned by the death of Mrs. Anne Kelley, daughter of Ellis Crisp, of the county of Surry, Esq. the eldest son of Tobias Crisp, D. D. minister of Brinkworth, in Wiltshire, and well known on account of the peculiar strain of his writings. The text of this discourse, is Matt. xxiv. 44. and Mr. Wood has given a particular account of the excellent character of the deceased. In the year 1726, a weekly lecture, on a Friday morning, was founded at the meeting-house in Little St. Helen's, by the well known William Coward, of Walthamstow, Esq. It was opened by the excellent Mr. Matthew Clarke, of Miles's-lane, and was conducted originally by six ministers. Mr. Clarke's first coadjutors were, Mr. Hubbard, of Stepney; Mr. Godwin, of St. Helen's; Mr. Hall, of Moorfields; Mr. Gibbs, of Hackney; and Mr. Wood.

In the year 1727, Mr. Wood sustained a heavy loss by the death of his highly esteemed friend, the Rev. Thomas Reynolds. Upon this occasion, he preached a suitable discourse to the bereaved church, from 2 Cor. i. 12. It was afterwards published, and contains a particular account of the deceased. Soon afterwards, our author was called to succeed his departed friend, as pastor of the congregation at the Weigh-House; and he entirely resigned his connexion with the church at New-court. Soon after he settled in this situation, he left the Presbyterian board, and carried the contributions of his church to the Independent fund.†
Early in 1729, there appeared a volume of sermons, preached at Mr. Coward's Friday lecture, at Little St.

---

* Mr. Wood's Farewell Sermon at the Old Jewry, p. 21, 22.
† MS. *penes me.*

WEIGH-HOUSE, LITTLE EASTCHEAP.—*Independent.*

Helen's. In this collection, there were two by Mr. Wood. The subject is, " The Redeemer's Concern for the Sinner's Salvation considered and applied ;" and the text, John vii. 27. In the same year, Mr. Wood appeared again before the public, in a funeral sermon, on the death of the Rev. Joseph Hill, preached at Haberdashers'-Hall, Feb. 9. The title of the discourse is, " The Believer's committing of his Soul to Christ considered ;" the text 2 Tim. i. 12. At the close, there is some account of the life and character of the deceased. His next publication was a sermon for the benefit of the Gravel-lane Charity-school, entitled, " Readiness to good Works, and largeness of Mind in them, recommended ;" preached in Gravel-lane, Southwark, Jan. 1, 1731-2. The text is, 1 Tim. vi. 17—19. In 1733, Mr. Wood was called to perform the last office of respect for that faithful and useful minister, the Rev. Daniel Wilcox. The funeral sermon which he preached upon this occasion at Monkwell-street, was afterwards published. It is entitled, " The Returning our Spirits to him that gave them, considered ;" the text Psa. xxxi. 5.

In the year 1737, Mr. Wood was called to sustain a loss of a severer nature than any we have yet mentioned. On the 14th of October, in that year, his wife, Mrs. Honor Wood, was taken to her everlasting rest. She was the daughter of Dr. William Dawes, President of the Royal College of Physicians; and grand-daughter to Dr. John Littleton, Master of the Temple, whose brother was the famous Lord-Keeper of that name. She was a woman of universal piety, and shone in all the relations of domestic life.* Dr. Langford, who preached her funeral sermon, gave a particular account of her amiable character. It pleased God to exercise Mr. Wood with some heavy afflictions in the latter part of his life. These he bore with great patience and resignation, often expressing his gratitude to

* Langford's Sermon on the Death of Mrs. Honor Wood, p. 27.

WEIGH-HOUSE, LITTLE EASTCHEAP.—*Independent.*

God for inward supports, and consolations. In his last illness, and in the near views of death, he declared his joyful hope of that rest which remains for the people of God; and expressed an earnest desire to be with Christ. With his dying breath, he bore his testimony to the truth and power of the gospel he had preached, which was his support in the afflictions of life, and in the prospects of eternity.* He finished his work before he had past the meridian of life, and received the reward of the promised inheritance, May 15, 1742. Mr. (afterwards Dr.) Langford, his assistant, improved his death, in a funeral discourse to the congregation at the Weigh-House, from Phil. i. 21. *For me to live is Christ, and to die is gain.*

Mr. Wood was a man of excellent ministerial abilities, and a lively, good preacher. He possessed popular talents, and met with great acceptance and success in various places, particularly in the church to which he stood related for nearly twenty-two years. His spirit was deeply impressed with the great truths of the gospel, and he contended earnestly for the faith once delivered to the saints. His printed discourses, which afford a good specimen of his pulpit compositions, are highly evangelical and scriptural. The great points of faith and practice he connected together, without exalting one to the prejudice of the other. For the supreme Godhead of Jesus Christ, and his claims to divine worship, he was a strenuous advocate ; and, in other points of doctrine, his sentiments harmonized strictly with those of the Reverend Assembly of Divines, as expressed in their confession of faith. That he did not encourage a merely speculative faith, however, is evident from the following passage. " Let not that knowledge satisfy you, which is not sanctifying. If you only learn here to out-talk other people, while your righteousness is far from exceeding theirs, this head knowledge will only make you more like the devil,

---

* Langford's Sermon on the Death of the Rev. James Wood, p. 28.

WEIGH-HOUSE, LITTLE EASTCHEAP.—*Independent.*

who is very intelligent, yet a devil still. Many a man has gone down to hell very orthodox; has thought justly, but perished because he did not act accordingly. A right way of thinking, if it is not accompanied with a right way of living, will but greaten our guilt, and inflame our reckoning."* Besides the sermons already mentioned, Mr. Wood was the author of some excellent discourses on the parable of the ten virgins, in which there is a remarkable spirit of piety, and a rich variety of the most serious and useful reflections, adapted to the cases of saints and sinners.†

SAMUEL SANDERSON.—This pious and amiable man, was born at Sheffield, in Yorkshire, about the year 1702. He received his grammar learning under Mr. Clarke of Hull; the well known author of several school-books. Under this gentleman, he acquired a good knowledge of both the Latin and Greek classics. He commenced his academical studies under the celebrated Mr. Timothy Jollie, tutor of a flourishing academy at Attercliffe, in Yorkshire. He, also, became a member of Mr. Jollie's church at Sheffield. (Q) Mr. Sanderson finished his studies in London, under the learned Mr. John Eames, F. R. S. the colleague of Dr. Ridgley. After completing the course of his education, he resided for some time at Kensington, as chaplain to the family of —— Birch, Esq. cursitor-baron of the Ex-

* Mr. Wood's Farewell Sermon at the Old Jewry, p. 22, 23.
† Mr. Langford's Sermon, *ubi supra.*

(Q) In the list of members of Mr. Jollie's church at Sheffield, are also the names of the celebrated Mr. THOMAS BRADBURY, and Mr. THOMAS SECKER, who was, afterwards, under the care of Mr. JONES, of *Tewkesbury,* and became archbishop of Canterbury. Hence, it is evident, that the bishop of London was mistaken in saying, as he does in his Life of SECKER, that " he never was in communion with the Dissenters." So far from this being the case, that eminent man actually preached among the Nonconformists, and delivered a probationary sermon in the meeting-house at Bolsover, in Derbyshire.

VOL. I.   A A

WEIGH-HOUSE, LITTLE EASTCHEAP.—*Independent.*

chequer. He also preached occasionally in and about the metropolis. From a manuscript list of Dissenting Ministers, in and about London, in 1727, it appears that Mr. Sanderson preached, in that year, to an Independent congregation at Kensington. About the year 1732, he was chosen assistant to the Rev. James Wood, minister at the Weigh-House, in Eastcheap; from whence he removed, Feb. 26, 1737, to be assistant to the Rev. Ebenezer Chandler, (R) pastor of the Dissenting congregation at Bedford.

Mr. Sanderson's labours were so highly approved by the congregation at Bedford, that, on May 14, 1740, he was ordained co-pastor with Mr. Chandler; and that venerable man becoming blind and superannuated, about four years after, the whole service devolved upon him. At Bedford, he married a daughter of Mr. Thomas Woodward, a respectable brewer, who enjoyed great esteem and influence in the town, as well as in the congregation. She was a lady of excellent sense, as well as great piety; in whom he was exceedingly happy, but had no children. Her eldest sister was married to the Rev. James Belsham, (father to the Rev. Thomas Belsham,) who resided many years at Bedford, and preached at Newport-Pagnel; but before he took the charge of that congregation, used, on the sacrament-day, to assist his brother Sanderson. The whole family lived in great harmony and friendship. Mr. Sanderson always expressed great satisfaction in his situation at Bedford,

(R) Mr. Chandler was the immediate successor of the famous Mr. John Bunyan. He was a Pœdobaptist, and a member of an Independent church in London, under the pastoral care of the Rev. Richard Taylor. Being invited down to Bedford, his ministerial services proved acceptable; and he was ordained there, Nov. 3, 1691. Under his ministry, the congregation increased so much as to require a larger meeting-house, which was erected in the year 1707. With this congregation, he laboured almost sixty years, to a good old age. In the latter part of his life, increasing infirmities greatly unfitted him for public work. In March, 1744, he was totally laid aside, and on June the 24th, 1747, was gathered to his fathers.——*Dr. Ryland's Sermon on the Death of the Rev. Joshua Symonds. Appendix.*

WEIGH HOUSE, LITTLE EASTCHEAP.—*Independent.*

not only on account of his connexions with an amiable family there, and the general respect he met with in the town, but the very considerable success which attended his ministerial labours. Under him, the church and congregation continued in a very flourishing condition; and the meeting-house, though a very large one, was completely filled to the last. Peace and harmony were preserved in the society notwithstanding some diversity of sentiment, particularly about baptism, a subject which he never brought forward for discussion, nor did he ever baptize any children in public, through fear of moving that controversy. He always dreaded a division, and studied the things that made for peace. By his prudence and good temper, he preserved the congregation from those animosities which took place after his death.

Mr. Sanderson was diligently attentive to the duties of his station, very seldom absenting himself from his flock. He constantly preached twice on the Lord's-day; and, in the evening, encouraged some of his hearers, who took down the substance of his sermons, in short-hand, to repeat them in the meeting. This exercise was accompanied with prayer, and designed chiefly for those who could not attend both the other services, or who had not families to occupy them at home. During the winter season, he had a lecture every Tuesday evening; and, in the summer, he catechised the children, for which service he was peculiarly qualified, and in which he was eminently useful. He addressed his catechumens in so familiar, condescending, and affectionate a manner, as was adapted to secure their love both to him and to religion. In the summer, he also preached occasionally in the neighbouring villages, whither it was esteemed a privilege by some of his young friends to attend him. Every Thursday evening, he had a meeting for prayer at his own house, for the space of one hour, when he was particularly solicitous to have the prayers of the brethren, with a view to the work of the following sabbath.

WEIGH-HOUSE, LITTLE EASTCHEAP.—*Independent.*

Mr. Sanderson was blessed with a good constitution, and enjoyed such a considerable share of health, that he was but rarely interrupted in his public work. The disorder that proved fatal to him, was a nervous fever, by which he was confined but eight days, and debarred from preaching only one sabbath. In this respect his wishes were gratified; for, he had always desired that he might not outlive his usefulness. The last time he appeared in the pulpit, he preached from these words; *Neither count I my life dear unto me, so that I may finish my course with joy.* The manner in which he finished his course, is thus described by the Rev. Samuel Palmer, who was an eye-witness of his faith and christian joy. " As soon as I heard of his illness, I went to see him. And though it was to me a melancholy visit, it was a truly edifying one. I never before, or since, saw so much of the power and excellence of religion. I sat up with him one whole night, great part of which he spent in prayer and praise, or in conversation with me, giving me his fatherly counsel, and relating the state of his mind on the review of life, and in the prospect of another world, to which he considered himself as near; for he expected from the first that his sickness would be unto death. He bore it with the greatest patience and resignation to the divine will, often repeating those words of Job, *Though he slay me, yet will I trust in him.* And those of Paul, on which he commented in a striking manner, *These light afflictions which are but for a moment, work out for us a far more exceeding and an eternal weight of glory.* He blessed God he was not slavishly afraid of death, nor yet greatly desirous of living; and added, ' were I permitted to chuse for myself, I would refer it to God and say, *Lord, not as I will, but as thou wilt.*' After this, he conversed with several of his other friends, with great freedom, almost to the last, much to their edification, who took down some of his memorable sayings. He spent much of his time in prayer, particularly in intercession for the world, for this

WEIGH-HOUSE, LITTLE EASTCHEAP.——*Independent.*

kingdom, for the church of Christ, and for his nearest friends; but more especially for his church and congregation, among whom, he reflected with satisfaction, he had laboured many years with great pleasure, and not without some success. He desired his hearers might know that he died in the same faith which he had professed, and that he felt the power of those blessed truths which he had preached, in supporting and comforting his soul on his dying bed. He continued in prayer till his breath was exhausted, and gently fell asleep in Jesus, Jan. 24, 1766, aged 63 years."* Mr. Sanderson was buried January 29, in the ground belonging to his own meeting-house. The Rev. Samuel Palmer, of Hackney, spoke at the grave, and afterwards preached the funeral sermon, from 1 Pet. v. 4. *And when the chief Shepherd shall appear, ye shall receive a crown of glory that fadeth not away.* This discourse was afterwards printed.

The character of Mr. Sanderson was amiable in every point of view; and, perhaps, few ministers have exhibited a brighter model of Christian excellence. He was a man of polite behaviour, of great humility and candour, and of uncommon benevolence and sweetness of temper, accompanied with habitual cheerfulness. This secured him the respect and esteem of all who were acquainted with him, whether among the Dissenters or in the establishment. He possessed a happy method of ingratiating himself with children and young persons; was eminent for piety and devotion; and had a singular talent for introducing serious discourse, even in mixed company, so as not only to avoid giving offence, but to leave a favourable impression of his character, on the minds of those who were no friends to his principles, or to religion itself. As a minister of the gospel, he was highly exemplary; being conscientious and diligent in all the duties of the pastoral office. Though he did not possess

* Theol. Bib. Magazine, for April, 1806.

WEIGH-HOUSE, LITTLE EASTCHEAP.—*Independent.*

any shining or popular talents as a preacher, yet, his discourses were acceptable and useful. Indeed, in this particular, he scarcely did himself justice. For, being prevailed upon by his people, to preach without notes, contrary to his former custom, his great diffidence was a bar to that fluency in public speaking, which was enjoyed by many of his inferiors. In point of sentiment, he was strictly Calvinistic; but his preaching was seldom very doctrinal, much less controversial: it was chiefly practical and experimental. His voice was clear, though not strong; so that he was distinctly heard by a large congregation, without any exertion. His manner of address was plain, easy, and unaffected; much in the conversation style; so that he was understood by the most illiterate. In prayer, he possessed great variety, both as to matter and order. His language was plain and simple, his expressions scriptural and pertinent, and his delivery grave and solemn, well suited to the purposes of devotion. He had, also, this great excellence in his prayers, that they were never long and tedious, twenty minutes being their utmost extent. As he was careful to guard his flock against errors in general, so he was particularly strenuous against Antinomianism. In this view, he much recommended Flavel on Mental Errors. Being a man of learning himself, though he was candid to his uneducated brethren in the neighbourhood, and admitted some of them into his pulpit, he was zealous for a learned ministry. He, therefore, encouraged young men, who were inclined to the ministerial office, to pass through a course of academical studies. Several, who were in necessitous circumstances, he materially assisted, with the help of a few friends, in the expence of their education; and he, himself, previously initiated them, at his own house, in the Latin and Greek languages. He used particularly to inculcate upon his young friends lessons of humility, (of which he was a bright pattern,) and strongly cautioned them against being too forward to appear in public. But, when the

WEIGH-HOUSE, LITTLE EASTCHEAP.——*Independent.*

proper time came for their entering the pulpit, he took a pleasure in putting them into his own, heard them with candour, and gave them the kindest encouragement. Mr. Sanderson brought up a nephew to the ministry, Mr. John Hall, now preacher to the English church at Rotterdam. He was succeeded in his congregation at Bedford, by Mr. Joshua Symonds, on whose becoming a Baptist, a separation took place, and Mr. Thomas Smith was chosen pastor of the new interest. His great modesty prevented him from ever publishing any thing, and he ordered all his sermons and manuscripts to be burnt.*

WILLIAM LANGFORD, D. D.—This respectable Divine was born Sept. 29, 1704, at Westfield, near Battle, in Sussex. He descended from pious parents, and his father died when he was not more than three or four years old. Soon afterwards, his mother removed to Tenterden, in Kent, where the Doctor received his grammar learning under one Mr. Hammond, who, it is apprehended was a clergyman as well as a schoolmaster. Under this gentleman, our young scholar made uncommon proficiency in the classics, and on one occasion, by the appointment of his master, he committed to memory the whole poem of *Horace de Arte Poetica,* consisting of nearly five hundred verses. From Tenterden, in the year 1721, or 1722, he went for academical learning to the University of Glasgow. In March, 1723, he drew up what he styles a Covenant-Transaction with God, in our Lord Jesus Christ. It is dated Glasgow-College, and may be seen in the sermon preached upon his death by Dr. Gibbons. At Glasgow, he continued to prosecute his studies, conducting himself in the most exemplary manner till May 1727, when he quitted the College, having previously taken the degree of *Master of Arts.*

* Theol. Bib. Magazine, *ubi supra,*—and Mr. Palmer's Sermon on the Death of Mr. Sanderson.

WEIGH-HOUSE, LITTLE EASTCHEAP.—*Independent.*

Upon his return from Scotland, Mr. Langford was soon fixed with a congregation at Gravesend, in Kent, where he was ordained to the pastoral office, and continued about seven years. In the year 1734, upon the decease of the Rev. Daniel Mayo, he removed to London, to become co-pastor with the Rev. Thomas Bures, at Silver-street. In the following year, he was chosen into the Lord's-day morning lecture at Little St. Helen's; and he published two discourses, preached on the first of August, in different years, to the society that support that service. As he was engaged at Silver-street only on one part of the Lord's-day, he was invited, in 1736, to become assistant to the Rev. James Wood, at the Weigh-House. This invitation he accepted, and continued to preach alternately at both places till June 1742, when he succeeded Mr. Wood in the pastoral office, and relinquished his services at Silver-street. Mr. Langford continued sole pastor of the church at the Weigh-House, till his death; being a period of nearly thirty-three years. During the chief part of the time, he performed the whole service himself; but latterly he had some young ministers to assist him. Soon after his settlement at the Weigh-House, he was chosen one of the preachers of the Friday-lecture, at that place, in conjunction with Dr. Chandler, Dr. Lawrence, and Mr. Godwin. And, in 1762, the King's-College, at Aberdeen, at the motion, unknown to himself, of a brother in the ministry, conferred on him the degree of Doctor in Divinity.

For some time before his decease, Dr. Langford seemed, as one expresses it, " to be on the borders of heaven." There was a remarkable spirituality in the temper of his mind, which discovered itself particularly in the administration of baptism, and of the Lord's-Supper. As for his departure from our world, it was easy and gentle. His constitution had been evidently declining for some time before. An hoarseness which compelled him to whisper, rather than speak, had hung upon him for some years, and, at

WEIGH-HOUSE, LITTLE EASTCHEAP.—*Independent.*

last heavily oppressed him, and greatly hindered his public usefulness. He was never heard to murmur, or complain, under the divine dispensations, though, to him, it was doubtless a severe trial. With a view of alleviating the burthen of his afflictions, and the hope, in some measure, of reviving his health, he retired to a friend's house at Croydon. He removed thither on the afternoon of Saturday, April 22, 1775, walked in the garden, and was cheerful in the evening. At the usual time, he retired to bed, passed some hours in a restless manner, and, at about four o'clock on the Lord's-day morning, was evidently struck with death. At six, without a sigh or a groan, as if he had been literally falling asleep, he breathed his last, and, having just lived to begin another sabbath on earth, entered on his everlasting sabbath in glory. He was heard to say in the night, though, as it is supposed, not apprehending that he was heard by any, " I have been in pain through fear and unbelief, but now all is removed by faith." Dr. Langford was in his 71st year. He was removed to town, and interred in Bunhill-fields, May the 3d. (s) Dr. Gibbons delivered the address at the grave, and also preached the funeral sermon at the Weigh-House, from Rev. xiv. 13. *And I heard a voice from heaven, saying unto me, write, Blessed are the dead which die in the Lord, from henceforth.*

Dr. Langford was a man of good abilities. He possessed a clear understanding, and a sound judgment. His reason-

(s) The following inscription is recorded upon his grave-stone in Bunhill-fields.

The Remains
Of the Rev. WILLIAM LANGFORD, D. D.
Are here deposited.
Who, beloved by his family
And the Churches of which he was successively Pastor,
Departed this life April 23, 1775,
Aged 71.

WEIGH-HOUSE, LITTLE EASTCHEAP.—*Independent.*

ings and observations upon subjects were just, pertinent, and weighty; his compositions easy, orderly, and substantial, not without the mixture, at times, of a lively and beautiful description, and some remarks that were rather new and surprising. His views of the doctrines of the Gospel were what are generally termed Calvinistical. Not that he called any man master on earth, but, the sentiments, which appeared to him to be contained in the Bible, and which he deduced thence, agreed with the tenets of that eminent Reformer. He maintained a strict watch over his own heart, and the whole of his behaviour was exemplary.* Dr. Langford published several single sermons, the titles of which shall be specified below. (T)

SAMUEL PALMER.—Dr. Langford was assisted, for a short time, by the Rev. Samuel Palmer, now of Hackney. He delivered his first sermon at the Weigh-House, June 10, 1763; from which time he preached occasionally till Jan. 20,

---

* Dr. Gibbons's Sermon on the Death of Dr. Langford, p. 18—31.

(T) 1. The best Improvement of public Mercies and Deliverances; or, England's Duty and Interest: represented in a Sermon to the Society that supports the Lord's-day morning lecture at Little St. Helen's, August 2, 1736.—2. A Sermon, occasioned by the Death of Mrs. Honor Wood, who departed this Life, Oct. 14, 1737. Psa. xxiii. 4.—3. The Life and Death of a Christian opened and applied, in a Sermon occasioned by the Death of the Rev. James Wood, May 15, 1742. Phil. i. 21.—4. The Improvement of the Death of faithful Ministers: a Sermon preached at Silver-street, Oct. 11, 1747, on the Death of the Rev. Thomas Bures. 2 Cor. iv. 12.—5. A Sermon for the Benefit of the Charity-School in Gravel-lane, Southwark, 1747-8.—6. A Sermon at the Ordination of the Rev. John Sheldon, at Canterbury, Aug. 9, 1749. 2 Cor. v. 18.—7. A Sermon occasioned by the Death of the Rev. Edward Godwin; preached at Little St. Helen's, April 8, 1764. John xii. 26.—8. A Charge at the Ordination of the Rev. Thomas Prentice. 1764.—9. A Sermon at the Admission of the Rev. John Trotter, D. D. to the pastoral office in Swallow-street, Jan. 10, 1770. Acts xxiii. 11.—10. Truth and Love united: a Sermon to the Correspondent Board in London of the Honourable Society in Scotland for propagating Christian Knowledge. 1774.—11. A second Sermon to the Society that supports the Morning Lecture at Little St. Helen's.

Samuel Wilton, D.D.
Copied from an Original Painting
In the Possession of his eldest Son.

London Pub. Nov. 1, 1808, by Maxwell & Wilson Skinner Street.

WEIGH-HOUSE, LITTLE EASTCHEAP.—*Independent.*

1765, when he was appointed regular assistant and morning preacher at this place. In the following year, Mr. Hunt, of Hackney, being laid aside from his public work, Mr. Palmer, who was their afternoon-preacher at that place, removed thither entirely, and relinquished his services at the Weigh-House. He preached his farewell sermon there, Dec. 28, 1766. Though he had the choice of both places, he wisely preferred the retreat of a country village, to the bustle and caprice of the metropolis.* This venerable minister has distinguished himself by some valuable publications in behalf of Nonconformity; on which account, as well as in some other respects, he will be entitled to the esteem of all true Protestant Dissenters. We shall have to notice some further particulars concerning him, under the article MARE-STREET, HACKNEY.

EDWARD VENNOR.—Upon Mr. Palmer's removal to Hackney, Mr. Edward Vennor, who married Dr. Langford's daughter, was appointed his assistant. This gentleman, who is still living, is a native of Warwick, and received his academical education at Mile-End, under Doctors Walker, Conder, and Gibbons. Upon the death of Dr. Langford, he removed to Ware, in Hertfordshire, as assistant to the Rev. William Lister; upon whose death, in 1778, the congregation divided. A new meeting-house was built, in which Mr. Vennor became the fixed pastor, and where he still preaches. Both interests are in a very low state.†

SAMUEL WILTON, D. D.—This excellent minister was born in London, in the year 1744. He was the eldest son of Mr. Samuel Wilton, an eminent hosier, in Newgate-street, in partnership with the very respectable Mr. Thomas

* Private Information.   † *Ibid.*

WEIGH-HOUSE, LITTLE EASTCHEAP.—*Independent.*

Holmes, whose wife's sister he married. This lady, whose christian name was Grace, was the daughter of a Mr. Avery, and a descendant of the celebrated Mr. Timothy Cruso. (u)

During his earliest years, Mr. Wilton was placed under the care of a maiden aunt, his father's eldest sister, Mrs. Elizabeth Wilton, who, in connexion with Mrs. Rachael King, sister to Dr. William King, of Hare-court, for many years, kept a boarding-school for young ladies in Hackney. There is reason to believe that her early instructions, in connexion with those of his pious parents, were of use to form his tender mind to that lively sense of divine things which he early discovered. She expressed the warmest affection for him, so long as he lived, and the highest respect for his memory to the

(u) Both the parents survived their son, whose death, though an inexpressible affliction, they bore with a truly christian patience and resignation. They were, indeed, persons of an amiable spirit as well as of exemplary piety. Mr. Wilton was many years member, and a deacon of the church in Old Gravel-lane, Wapping, under the pastoral care of the learned Dr. David Jennings. He died at Homerton, Jan. 21, 1779, aged 68. The Rev. Noah Hill, now pastor of the same church, preached and printed a sermon upon his death, containing a just and striking account of his amiable character. Besides Dr. Wilton, these excellent persons had another son, and three daughters, all of whom they had the pleasure to see following them to heaven. Mr. Thomas Wilton, the son, was engaged in the same business as his father, but died at an early period, of a most painful and lingering disorder. He was a youth of distinguished piety, who had promised great usefulness in the world, and the church of Christ. Dr. Gibbons, of whose church he was a member, preached and printed a sermon upon occasion of his death, which happened August 5, 1776, in the 31st year of his age. It contains an edifying account both of his character, and his manner of leaving the world. One of the daughters above-mentioned, was admitted Feb. 1, 1765, at the same time with her brother just mentioned, a member of the church at Haberdashers'-Hall. She was early married to Mr. Joseph Parker, son to the Mr. Parker, who was Dr. Watts's Amanuensis.——*Theological Magazine for July* 1801.—*Mr. Hill's Sermon for Mr. Samuel Wilton*—*and Dr. Gibbons's Sermon for Mr. Thomas Wilton.*

WEIGH-HOUSE, LITTLE EASTCHEAP.—*Independent.*

day of her death, which took place many years afterwards.* (w)

Mr. Wilton received his classical learning, in which he was a great proficient, in the grammar-school of Christ-Church Hospital, in the precincts of which his father lived. (x) His tutor was the Rev. Mr. Townley, a learned man, and a clergyman of the established church, who ever manifested the most respectful regard to his pupil, as one who did him singular honour. He entered upon academical studies under the direction of the eminent Dr. David Jennings, who dying before they were finished, he completed them under the Doctor's assistant and successor, Dr. Samuel Morton Savage, of whose church he also became a member. Soon afterwards, the academy was removed to Hoxton, and the students were boarded by Dr. Abraham Rees, who was chosen mathematical tutor, and Dr. Andrew Kippis, teacher of the Belles-Lettres.† Mr. Wilton conducted himself, in every respect, suitably to his character, as a candidate for the sacred ministry, so as to enjoy the respect and love of his fellow-pupils, as well as the distinguished regard of his pastor and tutors.‡ (y)

* Theological Magazine for July, 1801.

(w) Mrs. Elizabeth Wilton died at Hackney, May 13, 1799, at the advanced age of 91. She retained her faculties in a remarkable degree to the last; and, like most of her family, was eminent for faith and piety.—*Prot. Diss. Magazine*, vol. vi. p. 240.

(x) His house stood on the spot where a new grammar-school was erected a few years ago.

† Orton's Letters to Dissenting Ministers, vol. ii. Appendix.

‡ Mr. Palmer's Sermon on the Death of Dr. Wilton, p. 23.

(y) Dr. Rees observes, that, " Mr. WILTON, who was his pupil in Mathematics, Astronomy, and Philosophy, made considerable proficiency in those departments of science, and that his talents, attainments and character deserve high commendation."—One of his fellow-pupils, also, added the following testimony: " He had the fullest claim to their esteem and love, for he was most exemplary for his assiduity and attainments; for a respectful attention to his tutors, and for his courteousness and unaffected kindness to his fellow-pupils. One trait, in particular, of his disposition

WEIGH-HOUSE, LITTLE EASTCHEAP.—*Independent.*

While he pursued his academical studies, he continued to reside in his father's house, where he was a comfort and a blessing to the whole family. As this was a very hospitable mansion, to which a number of worthy ministers, both in town and country, had frequent access, he formed with many of them an early acquaintance. This was of no small advantage to himself, and afterwards proved, in some respects, a blessing to several of them, particularly those settled in the country, whose circumstances rendered that assistance acceptable, which he had afterwards the ability, and which it was one of his highest gratifications, to bestow. Here also, several of his fellow-students, and some of his contemporaries in another academy, met with a kind entertainment from his friends, and established a friendship with him, to their mutual pleasure and profit. (z) As was, also, the case with some young scholars of good characters and abilities, who were on the foundation of the school to which his father's house was so contiguous.*

Mr. Wilton having finished his studies, came forth to the discharge of ministerial duties, with a mind richly furnished,

towards them is worthy of being recorded. His ardour in the pursuit of knowledge, and of every qualification for the important work to which he had consecrated himself, was entirely free from jealousy and selfishness. He was solicitous to excite and cherish the same ardour in his associates. He was, at that early period of his life, modestly communicative, and a zealous promoter of useful conversation. At his father's house, and at the apartments of his fellow-students, he would join with them in reading the classics, and in pursuing other branches of literature: and though a reciprocal communication was the idea under which he represented the design of those meetings, his liberality in imparting information was equal to his superior abilities and furniture. On such occasions, too, and at every suitable opportunity, he would, in the most amiable, and unoffending manner possible, suggest hints respecting the spirit, conduct and views, which became those who were under a course of education for the Christian Ministry.—*Orton's Letters to Dissenting Ministers*, vol. ii. *Appendix.*

(z) One of this number was the respectable and well known Mr. Kingsbury, of Southampton.

* *Theological Magazine, ubi supra.*

WEIGH-HOUSE, LITTLE EASTCHEAP.—*Independent.*

both with knowledge and piety. He entered upon the pastoral office at Lower Tooting, in Surry, where he succeeded the learned Dr. Henry Miles, F. R. S. whose widow erected a new meeting-house, at her own expence. He was ordained June 18, 1766. Dr. Kippis delivered the introductory discourse; Dr. Savage gave the charge; and Dr. Furneaux preached to the people. Though his talents qualified him for a larger sphere, and he might have settled in the city, he prudently preferred this retired situation, that he might improve his ministerial furniture. As the interest at Tooting was greatly declined, he wished to be instrumental in reviving it; and was speedily gratified. He no sooner undertook the care of the church, than he applied himself in earnest to the duties of his office. Besides the ordinary services on the Lord's-day, he statedly preached a lecture on the Wednesday evening. He, also, immediately undertook the useful, but too much neglected, work of catechising children, and was very diligent in visiting his flock; especially the poor, and those who were in afflicting circumstances. Nor did he confine his labours to the people of his charge. He frequently engaged in occasional services in the neighbourhood; besides more stated ones, in concurrence with several of his brethren, on the Lord's-day evening. And he did not labour in vain; his ministry being succeeded, in many instances, for promoting the great ends which he always kept in view. He not only found the number of his stated hearers increase, but had the satisfaction of seeing many additions to his church, several of whom were effectually converted to God by his means.*

Besides the schemes for usefulness just mentioned, Dr. Wilton united with a select society of his brethren, who met once a month at each other's houses, with a view to their mutual improvement and usefulness as Christian ministers. One principal object which they had in view was to promote

* Mr. Palmer's Sermon, *ubi supra*, p. 24, 25.

WEIGH-HOUSE, LITTLE EASTCHEAP.——*Independent.*

the preaching of the gospel in villages, and to furnish poor country congregations with plain and zealous preachers. For this purpose, they contributed, with the assistance of some of their benevolent hearers, and other Christian friends, towards the expence of maintaining lectures in such places in the country as had no stated preaching in the ordinary season of divine worship. By this means, the usefulness of some of their brethren was promoted, in devoting their Lord's-day evenings to preaching, in adjacent villages. They likewise assisted in the expence of supporting a few pious young men, disposed to the work of the ministry, in a short course of studies, sufficient to qualify them for serving such societies as did not require ministers of profound learning. To their maintenance, also, they contributed, for a short time after they went forth to preach; in the hope of their being instrumental towards the revival and increase of such congregations as were so much reduced, or so small and poor, as to be unable to support a minister themselves. Several such young persons were trained up under the late Mr. Gentleman, then pastor of a new Independent church at Shrewsbury; and some of them are, at this day, blessings to the churches. The members of this friendly society proposed, likewise, to unite in carrying on lectures themselves, at their own expence, on the Lord's-day evenings, in places where their help might be acceptable, and a door opened for their admission. The first place of this kind which offered, and, indeed, the only one where they themselves personally appeared, was Mortlake, in Surry; a village, but a few miles from Tooting, and where Mr. Wilton procured their welcome reception. Here, Mr. Lowe, one of Dr. Gibbons's church, fitted up a room, in his own house, (A) in a very commodious manner, and ge-

(A) A good meeting-house was then, and is yet standing at Mortlake; but the congregation having become extinct, the son of the last minister let it, upon a lease, for a low secular purpose, and all attempts to recover it proved fruitless. A striking instance, among many, to show the necessity of a proper deed of trust, where new meeting-houses are erected.

WEIGH-HOUSE, LITTLE EASTCHEAP.——*Independent.*

nerally entertained those preachers, who continued, in their turns, to bestow their labours here, with considerable encouragement, till this gentleman removed to a distance. As Mr. Wilton was one of the most zealous members of this friendly and truly useful society, while he resided at Tooting, so he continued the same after his removal to London.

Soon after his settlement at Tooting, he married Mrs. Mary Mattick, niece of the above-mentioned Mr. Holmes. She was a lady of many excellent endowments, and possessed a handsome fortune, which enabled him to gratify, to a greater extent, his benevolent disposition. By her, he had three sons and a daughter, who, at the time of his decease, were too young to estimate the worth of such a father, and to be fully sensible of the loss they sustained by his death. The daughter was cut off at an early period; but all the sons survive.

In consequence of Mr. Wilton's intimate acquaintance with Dr. William Gordon, who succeeded Dr. Jennings in the church to which his father had belonged, and his correspondence with him after his removal to America, he received a Doctor's diploma from the College in New Jersey. This was a title of distinction which he had no ambition to possess, and which he would hardly have accepted from any other quarter. For, if in any thing he discovered what approached to an enthusiastic zeal, it was for the success of America, in her struggle for independence. With this, he thought, the interest of liberty, civil and religious, both in that, and the mother country, was intimately connected. His zeal for liberty was, indeed, great, but not so great as for the interest of vital religion; and he shewed himself ever ready to adopt such measures as appeared likely to promote it. He approved himself a truly evangelical and laborious minister of the glorious gospel, and was instant in season and out of

WEIGH-HOUSE, LITTLE EASTCHEAP.—*Independent.*

season, to promote the cause of Christ, and the good of souls.

Dr. Wilton discovered a warm and laudable zeal for the support of the Dissenting Interest. Upon occasion of the application to parliament, in the years 1772 and 1773, for the relief of Protestant Dissenting Ministers, Tutors, and School-masters, in the business of subscription, he was appointed one of the members of the committee who conducted that application. To this situation he was chosen in the room of Dr. Conder, who resigned. If in any thing the zeal of Dr. Wilton seemed to carry him beyond the bounds of moderation, it was in the glorious cause of civil and religious liberty. But, in defending these he must be acquitted of any sinister design, and especially of any thing like malevolence towards the persons of those against whom he wrote. Wherever he thought the interest of truth or justice concerned, he possessed spirit equal to his ability, to defend himself and the cause he espoused. When several ministers about London, who opposed the application to parliament, circulated a printed paper, containing their reasons for so doing,(B) Dr. Wilton became the able apologist of his brethren who supported the application. The

(B) As some of our readers may be desirous to know who it was that opposed the application, we shall here insert their names.

David Muir,
John Rogers,
Thomas Towle,
Samuel Brewer,
Edward Hitchin,
Thomas Oswald,
John Potts,

John Trotter,
John Macgowan,
George Stephens,
Joseph Popplewell,
Henry Hunter,
John Kello.

It is deserving remark, that, of these thirteen ministers, seven were Scotchmen, who, from their educational prejudices, might be supposed favourable to church establishments. It need not, therefore, be wondered at, that they should unite in the support of penal laws, which are considered their best bulwarks.

WEIGH-HOUSE, LITTLE EASTCHEAP.—*Independent.*

title of his pamphlet was, " An Apology for the Renewal of an Application to Parliament by the Protestant Dissenting Ministers. Addressed to the Thirteen Ministers who protested against it. In which the Evidence and Force of their Reasons are fairly examined, and the Application is shown to be neither inconsistent with the Principles of Orthodoxy, or Loyalty. 1773." In an advertisement prefixed to this pamphlet, the author observes, that " It being always his sincere wish, to live in brotherly love and union with all the ministers of the gospel, he was extremely sorry for the sad occasion, of thus opposing the sentiments of any of his brethren; and especially, of those with whom he has long been personally acquainted. But,. as those reasons were printed, and distributed among the members of parliament, with a view of obstructing the success of an application, in which, he thinks, not only his own personal security, but that of many of his brethren are particularly interested ; but the cause of truth and religious liberty in general equally concerned; and that they had likewise a tendency to prejudice the minds of Christians against the petitioners ; on these accounts he could be no longer silent." In 1774, Dr. Wilton published, " A Review of some of the Articles of the Church of England, to which a Subscription is required of Protestant Dissenting Ministers." Both these publications met with a cordial reception from the public, and are drawn up with much good temper, as well as great force of argument.

As Dr. Wilton's zeal was founded upon knowledge, so it was regulated by charity. He maintained a friendly intercourse with several worthy members and ministers of the established church, whom he was ever ready to embrace as brethren. In what he said and wrote upon the controversy between them and us, he was actuated by a pure regard to truth, to the sacred rights of conscience, and the best interests of mankind. Though he thought nothing small, in which the honour of Christ,

WEIGH-HOUSE, LITTLE EASTCHEAP.—*Independent.*

and the interest of religion were concerned; yet, the grand objects of his zeal were, the great matters of faith and practice, concerning which all good men are agreed. These, he devoted his life to promote; nor did he think his life dear to him so that he might be instrumental to so glorious an end.*

Upon the death of the worthy Dr. William Langford, Dr. Wilton was invited to undertake the pastoral charge of the church and congregation at the Weigh-House, which he accepted in the year 1776. Here he was highly esteemed; and, though not attended by a great crowd of admirers, the interest which had been sunk very low, began gradually to revive, and some valuable additions, especially of young persons, were made to the church. His heart was much set upon doing good; and he formed several schemes of usefulness, which had his life been prolonged, would have yielded essential benefit to the cause of Christianity at large.†

The last public service in which Dr. Wilton engaged, was a labour of love, at an evening lecture, March 29, 1778, in the pulpit of his highly esteemed friend and neighbour, (c) the Rev. Samuel Palmer. His subject was, Psa. cxix. 125. *I am thy servant, give me understanding, that I may know thy testimonies;* words very expressive of his own character, and the prevailing desire of his heart. On the Saturday following, he found himself much indisposed, but having to preach a funeral sermon the next day, for the improvement of a very distressing providence, he was fully bent upon performing that friendly office. Instead, therefore, of providing any assistance, or taking that care of himself which his own situation required, he sat up late to study, (which was his prevailing fault,) and when he retired to rest, many hours beyond the time he ought to have done, he

* Mr. Palmer's Sermon, *ubi supra*, p. 29, 30.   † *Ibid.* p. 26.
(c) Upon his leaving Tooting, Dr. Wilton went to reside at Hackney.

WEIGH-HOUSE, LITTLE EASTCHEAP.—*Independent.*

found himself in a high fever, which, for want of timely assistance, made so rapid a progress, as to baffle all medical attempts to extinguish the flame. The disorder proved putrid, and its effects were soon apprehended to be fatal. He, himself, considered it as the message of death; which, however, he viewed without the least dismay, and he was not only willing, but even desirous to depart and be with Christ.* He, therefore, with great calmness, set his house in order, by settling some temporal affairs; for his eternal ones had been settled long before. For several days, he was a good deal delirious, but, in the afternoon of the day in which he died, he had a lucid interval, and gave delightful evidence to his mourning friends that he was ripe for glory. He said to an intimate friend, who came from the city to visit him, (after having spoken with great composure upon some secular affairs,) " You now see me in the near view of death, and rejoice in the prospect. It has been my delight to preach the gospel of Christ and promote his glory. I am not afraid to die, for *I know whom I have believed, and am persuaded that he is able to keep that which I have committed unto him against that day.*" He then said, " You will go to prayer with me. Let us offer a few more petitions to God before we enter the world of praise, from which I am at no great distance." Soon after, some other friends coming into the room, he, with a pleasing smile on his countenance, broke out into an affectionate prayer for them, which he concluded with saying, " Come Lord Jesus, come quickly." One of them expressing some hope and desire that he might yet be recovered, he asked, in the language of reproof, " Do you wish me to come back again into the wilderness? No, I do not wish to return one step. I am not afraid to die." He humbly lamented his imperfections; but at the same time expressed his confidence.

* Theological Magazine, *ubi supra.*

WEIGH-HOUSE, LITTLE EASTCHEAP.—*Independent.*

"I have had my doubts, (says he) but my hope is well founded. I have had such manifestations of the love of God, that I do not, I cannot doubt." He then expressed the most lively and delightful views and foretastes of the heavenly happiness, in such transporting language, as greatly astonished the by-standers, who were not able fully to describe it. Having expressed a desire to see his intimate friend, the Rev. Samuel Palmer, " once more (as he expressed it) before they met in glory," he was immediately sent for. On approaching his bed, and saying, " This is the most painful meeting we have ever had," he very cheerfully answered, " We shall soon meet again." Upon Mr. Palmer's congratulating him on the strong consolation he enjoyed, he expressed the continuance of it, and then repeated those words of the Apostle, *I know in whom I have believed, &c.* Hereupon, his delirium returned, and the symptoms of his dissolution drew on apace. For a considerable time he struggled hard, apparently under great agony, attended at times with doleful groans; but even these were mingled with *hallelujahs*, which he frequently repeated, till, at length, nature being entirely spent, his breath gradually failed, and at midnight, April 3, 1778, after an illness of only six days, and in the 34th year of his age, he gently fell asleep in Jesus. His funeral sermon was preached at the Weigh-House, at his own request, by the Rev. Samuel Palmer, on 2 Tim. i. 12. being the last words that he spoke.

Dr. Wilton's remains were interred in the family vault, in Bunhill-Fields, where a vast concourse of sincere mourners were assembled to lament his loss. His pastor and tutor, Dr. Savage, delivered the address at the grave, which was printed at the end of the funeral discourse, and discovers strong emotions of grief, as well as the highest esteem for the memory of the deceased. Upon his tomb-stone is the following inscription:

WEIGH-HOUSE, LITTLE EASTCHEAP—*Independent.*

Underneath are deposited the Remains
Of SAMUEL WILTON, D. D.
Some time Pastor of a Christian Church at Tooting, in Surry,
And afterwards at the Weigh-House, Eastcheap.
He was an honest man,
A Christian of primitive simplicity,
A Minister of uncommon talents, natural and acquired,
A Pastor most affectionate, vigilant and faithful:
While a bold assertor of what appeared to him truth,
He always shewed a mild and catholic spirit towards gainsayers,
In no character were Christian zeal and charity more happily united
As he lived esteemed, beloved and honoured,
So he died universally lamented,
3d April, 1778,
Aged 34.

Dr. Wilton was eminently formed for usefulness, both by nature and religion. With regard to natural endowments he was greatly distinguished by a retentive memory, which was called forth upon some important occasions. He could not only recollect what, at any time, he had premeditated for the pulpit, but likewise what he heard from other persons, so as to be able to repeat a speech or sermon, if he thought it worth retaining, almost verbatim. When the city of London attempted to invade the privileges of Dissenters, it was partly from his memory, as well as that of Dr. Furneaux, that the celebrated speech of Lord Mansfield was published, for establishing their rights upon that occasion. To this important faculty he united a lively imagination, a solid judgment, and a ready utterance. So that, though he always studied, he seldom wrote his discourses; which, however, when he retained the full possession of himself, often had the appearance of elaborate composures. He had a wonderful readiness in composition, whatever subject he took in hand, and a rich fund of ideas; so that his chief difficulty in writing was that of moving his pen with a rapidity equal to the flow of his thoughts and expressions. His acquired abilities were, also, considerable. Though he made no parade of his learning, he was by no means deficient in that

WEIGH-HOUSE, LITTLE EASTCHEAP.—*Independent.*

particular. His mind was richly stored with sentiments of all the several subjects of practical and experimental divinity. With controversial matters his acquaintance was not inferior; but he knew too well the great design of the Christian ministry, and the worth of souls, to shew it in his public discourses. There was an uncommon savour, fervency, and affection in his preaching, which was not adapted to amuse the fancy, much less irritate the passions, but to touch the conscience, to warm the affections, and comfort and animate the soul. His prayers were copious and highly devotional, evidently flowing from a heart deeply affected with a sense of divine things. In this part of divine worship, he possessed an uncommon variety, as well as an unusual fluency of language and readiness of utterance. But his delivery was too rapid, both in prayer and preaching; his sentences too long; and, in consequence of his uncommon flow of ideas, his whole services too prolix. On these accounts, together with a habit he had contracted, of keeping his eye fixed upon his Bible, as if he was reading, and his too great uniformity of pronunciation, he was less popular than a person of his talents would otherwise have been. In his private character, the several virtues of the Christian life eminently shone in his habitual temper and conversation. He possessed the social affections as strongly as any man. This led him to cultivate a very general acquaintance with ministers, and others, of different denominations and religious sentiments. Towards them he discovered such an amiable sweetness and cheerfulness of temper, and so much candour towards their distinguishing opinions, and yet, at the same time, such an openness in declaring, as well as truly Christian spirit in maintaining his own, as greatly endeared him to all whose good opinion was worth securing, and as did honour to the evangelical sentiments which he espoused. With regard to his own views of Christianity, he might be pronounced an Independent, and a moderate Calvinist. And while he was very candid towards those

WEIGH-HOUSE, LITTLE EASTCHEAP.—*Independent.*

who dissented from him, he was not indifferent to his own principles. Upon the whole, Dr. Wilton was a man in whose character were combined as many excellencies as are usually to be met with among mortals; and his removal, at so early a period, was a singular loss to the interests of religion, particularly among the Dissenters.*

Dr. Wilton laboured under some habitual complaints which indisposed him for an intense application to study, and especially to the use of his pen, from which, otherwise, the public might have expected something important. From what he did publish, which was extorted by temporary occasions, and written with great haste, the reader will form no mean idea of his mental powers. Two of his publications, upon the affair of subscription, have been already noticed. Besides these, he published only three single sermons. One was occasioned by the death of Mr. Joseph Longhurst; preached at Lower Tooting, in Surry, June 18, 1769. It contains a very particular and instructive account of the life and death of a very worthy man, in an obscure situation. The other sermons of Dr. Wilton were preached upon charitable occasions: one at Mr. Towle's meeting-house, London Wall, for the benefit of the charity-school in Bartholomew-close; the other at St. Thomas's, for the charity-school in Gravel-lane, Southwark. They are both calculated for general utility.†

JOHN CLAYTON.—Upon the death of Dr. Wilton, the Rev. Robert Gentleman, of Shrewsbury, was invited to succeed him in the pastoral office, but declined. After a short interval, the vacancy was filled up by the Rev. John Clayton, the present minister at the Weigh-House. This gentleman was born about the year 1753, at a small village,

* Palmer's Sermon,—Theological Magazine,—and Orton's Letters, *ubi supra*.
† Orton's Letters to Dissenting Ministers, *ubi supra*.

WEIGH-HOUSE, LITTTE EASTCHEAP.—*Independent.*

called Clayton, near Chorley, in Lancashire. His parents were reputable persons, and strongly attached to the Church of England. Being designed for the medical profession, he spent part of his youth at Manchester; and, afterwards followed the same line of business, for a short time, in London. It appears, that his first serious impressions were received under the preaching of the late excellent Mr. Romaine. Some time after, having a strong inclination to the ministry, he was admitted a student in the College of Trevecca, in South-Wales, under the patronage of the late Countess of Huntingdon. Here he possessed some advantages for learning above the other students, being appointed steward of the house; which office required his constant attendance. At the close of his academical course, he continued to preach for some time in her ladyship's chapels, and also at the Tabernacle in Moorfields. It seems that he was at one time upon the eve of receiving episcopal ordination; but upon further investigation, was led to dissent for reasons that appeared to him of sufficient weight, particularly that he might avoid a prostitution of the Lord's-Supper, to unworthy persons and purposes. The reading of Towgood's Letters are said to have had great weight with him in this decision. This was when he was about twenty-three years of age. Upon his quitting the Countess's connexion, he was chosen assistant to the Rev. Sir Harry Trelawney, (c) who was pastor of an In-

(c) Sir Harry Trelawney, descended from Sir Jonathan Trelawney, one of the seven bishops who were committed to the Tower, in the reign of King James the Second. He was educated at Christ-Church, Oxford. Afterwards, deserting the Church of England, he became pastor of an Independent congregation at West Loo, in Cornwall. He was ordained at Southampton, April 22, 1777. In a little time he left the orthodox, and attached himself to those whom he called rational Dissenters. Sir Harry vindicated his nonconformity in " A Letter addressed to the Rev. Thomas Alcock, M. A. vicar of Runcorn, in Cheshire, and of St. Budeaux, Devon." In this pamphlet, he insists chiefly upon these two points ; 1. That subscription to articles that we do not believe, is a dishonest, and

WEIGH-HOUSE, LITTLE EASTCHEAP.—*Independent.*

dependent congregation, at West Loo, in Cornwall. An alteration taking place, in the sentiments of that gentleman, Mr. Clayton removed to London, and preached a short time as probationer at the Weigh-House. In November, 1778, he was ordained to the pastoral office. The service was conducted in the following order: Mr. Jennings, of Islington, began with reading and prayer; Dr. Gibbons delivered the introductory discourse; Mr. Richard Winter prayed the ordination prayer; Dr. Trotter gave the charge; Dr. Hunter prayed; and Mr. Brewer preached and concluded. Soon after his settlement in London, Mr. Clayton was united in marriage to Miss Flower, eldest daughter of the late Mr. George Flower, of Cannon-street. With this lady, he possessed a handsome fortune.

Mr. Clayton, at his entrance upon the ministry, did not excite very great expectations, but, in a little time, discovered considerable abilities, and has obtained an established reputation as a preacher. In point of religious sentiment, he is thoroughly orthodox. Many years ago, he was chosen into the Merchants' lecture, on a Tuesday morning, formerly at Pinners'-Hall, but now, at New Broad-street. Of the force of example, and the excellence of Mr. Clayton's domestic discipline, we cannot have a stronger proof, than by taking a survey of his family. Though it often happens, from what cause we will not

---

prevaricating business: 2. That by remaining a Dissenter, he secured that freedom of mind, which is the birthright, and unalterable privilege of every rational creature. Notwithstanding this declaration, so inconsistent is the conduct of human beings, Sir Harry, immediately after returns to Oxford, procures ordination in the national establishment, and is made a country rector in the West of England; in which station he is likely to remain. Robinson's words upon hearing that Trelawney had conformed, should hold out a caution to those Dissenters who are ambitious of imitating his example. He observes, " That they rarely obtain preferment by conforming that when their ministers are ordained in the church, they usually become stationary, and receive little but mortification and disappointment."—— *Dyer's Life of Robinson,* p. 181.

WEIGH-HOUSE, LITTLE EASTCHEAP.—*Independent.*

stay to inquire into, that the sons of the Prophets, more commonly than others, prove sons of Belial; yet, we have here a noble confutation of that scandal. Mr. Clayton has the honour of enumerating three sons, all Dissenting ministers, of promising expectations, and two of them pastors of congregations in London, or the vicinity. This is a circumstance that will always be mentioned to his praise.

Mr. Clayton has appeared several times before the public in the character of an author, though chiefly as a sermon writer. In 1786, he published, " A Charge at the Ordination of the Rev. Joseph Brooksbank." In 1789, " A Discourse on the Snares of Prosperity; to which was added, An Essay on Visiting." In 1791, " A Charge at the Ordination of the Rev. James Knight. And, in the same year, " A Sermon occasioned by the late Riots at Birmingham : with a prefixed Address to the Public, intended to remove the Reproach lately fallen on Protestant Dissenters." This last discourse gave general offence at the time, and met with severe reprehension from several Divines of approved orthodoxy, particularly Mr. Fell. But by none was it opposed with greater ability and force of argument, than by the Rev. Robert Hall, in a pamphlet, entitled, " Christianity consistent with a Love of Freedom." Besides these, Mr. Clayton has published some other single sermons, as " A Thanksgiving Sermon for the Peace, 1802;" and " two Charges at the Ordination of each of his Sons." A few years ago, he was engaged in a controversy with a member of his own church, on the unlawfulness of public amusements; in the course of which he published two pamphlets. But it will not be necessary to state the particulars, as the subject is still fresh in the minds of the religious public.*

---

* Some of the facts in the above narrative, are taken from the Spiritual Magazine, for 1783.. The remainder are derived from private information, or from the author's own observation.

GRACECHURCH-STREET.

PARTICULAR BAPTISTS.

IN the reign of King Charles the Second, the Particular Baptists had a meeting-house in Grace-church-street, but the precise spot where it was situated, cannot now be ascertained. Respecting the history of the Society that occupied it, but little, likewise, is known. The interest appears to have been but small. We learn from Crosby, that, at the period above-mentioned, the pastor of this church was Dr. De Veil, a foreign Divine. The same author also informs us, that the former minister renounced his religion through fear of persecution, and soon after destroyed himself in the greatest horror.* We find this church referred to, in an old manuscript, under the year 1692, but how long it existed after that period, we cannot take upon us to say. Of Dr. De Veil's history, we shall present the reader with a brief abstract.

CAROLUS MARIA DE VEIL, D. D. was born at Metz, in Lorrain,† of Jewish parents, and educated in that religion. But, by perusing the prophetical part of the Old Testament, and comparing it with the New, he was led, while very young, to embrace Christianity. This so enraged his father, that, with a drawn sword, he attempted to kill him; but was prevented by some persons present. His great abilities soon advanced him to considerable preferment in the Gallican church. He became a canon-regular of St. Augustin, prior of St. Ambrose, at Melun, and professor of Divinity in the University of Anjou, where he proceeded

* Crosby's History of the English Baptists, vol. iii. p. 109.
† Birch's Life of Archbishop Tillotson, p. 76.

Doctor of Divinity. In the year 1672, he published a commentary on the gospels of Mark and Luke, in which, besides a literal exposition of the text, he took opportunity to defend the errors and superstitions of the Church of Rome. This so advanced his reputation, that he was appointed to assist in writing against the Hugunots, the then main adversaries of the Catholics in France. This employment led him to examine the controversies between the Papists and Protestants, to whose principles he had been hitherto a stranger; and finding the truth on their side, he freely followed the dictates of his mind. However, to prevent the consequences that were likely to attend a change of his principles, he fled to Holland, where he abjured Popery, in 1677, and soon after, came over to England. Here he soon became acquainted with Bishop Stillingfleet, Bishop Compton, Bishop Lloyd, Dr. Tillotson, Dr. Sharp, Dr. Patrick, and other clergymen of the greatest dignity and worth. He was soon admitted into orders in the church, and became chaplain and tutor, in a family of distinction.

In 1678, he revised his commentary on Matthew and Mark; and in the following year, published a literal explication of Solomon's Song, which he dedicated to Sir Joseph Williamson, President of the Royal Society. This work was so well received by the clergy, both at home and abroad, that they encouraged him to proceed in expounding the other parts of the sacred writings. Upon this, he published, in 1680, his literal exposition of the Minor Prophets, which he dedicated to Lord Chancellor Finch. These publications strongly recommended him to Dr. Compton, bishop of London, who gave him all possible encouragement, and granted him free admittance, at all times, into his library. There, he met with some writings of the English Baptists; and the arguments they made use of, appearing to him to be founded on the word of God, he, without hesitation, embraced their opinions. After this, he obtained an interview with the famous Mr. Hansord Knollis;

GRACECHURCH-STREET.—*Particular Baptists*.

and became intimately acquainted with Mr. John Gosnold, with whose learning and conversation, he was so much taken, that he soon became a member of his congregation. Such a proselyte as Dr. De Veil, brought no small honour to the Baptists. But he lost all his old friends, as well as his employments, with the exception of Dr. Tillotson, who valued men for their merits, not their opinions. Not long after this change in his sentiments, he wrote his literal explanation of the Acts of the Apostles. It was printed at London in 1684, and the following year translated by the author from the Latin, into the English language.* In this piece, he vindicates the principles and practices of the Baptists, with much learning and good judgment. After this, Dr. De Veil practised physic for his maintenance, and he received an annual stipend from the Baptists till his death. As he was not a perfect master of the English language, he never succeeded as a preacher. He was, however, a grave and judicious Divine, a skilful grammarian, and a pious good man.† He had a brother, Lewis De Compeigne De Veil, who, also, embraced the Protestant religion. He was a learned man, and, before he came to England, interpreter of the Oriental languages to the King of France.‡

* Birch's Life of Tillotson, p. 76, 77.
† Crosby, *ubi supra*, vol. iv. p. 252—259.
‡ Birch's Life of Tillotson, p. 75, 76.

PEWTERERS'-HALL, LIME-STREET.

INDEPENDENT, EXTINCT.

PEWTERERS'-HALL is situated on the West side of Lime-street, nearly opposite Cullum-street; and is in Langbourn Ward. It was one of the city halls appropriated to the use of the Nonconformists in the reign of Charles the Second, when they were prohibited preaching in the churches. An Independent congregation assembled here, soon after the Bartholomew ejectment, under the pastoral care of the Rev. Robert Bragge, who was deprived of a living in the neighbourhood. But he, most probably, gathered the church before the Restoration. After continuing several years in a flourishing state, it became extinct under his successor, the Rev. John Wowen, in 1715. What became of Pewterers'-Hall, after this event, we no where learn, but it was, most probably, never afterwards occupied as a meeting-house. Of the above ministers, and, also, of another, who was colleague with Mr. Bragge, we shall here present the reader with a brief account.

ROBERT BRAGGE.—He was born in the year 1627, and was son to a gentleman, who, upon the breaking out of the civil wars, became a captain in the parliament army. Upon the surrender of Oxford, in 1646, he was sent to Wadham College, of which Dr. Wilkins was Warden. After studying there the regular time, he was chosen fellow. Coming, afterwards, to London, he settled in the parish of Alhallows the Great, Thames-street, where he gathered a church, upon the Independent plan, of which he continued pastor till the day of his death.* It does not seem quite certain whether Mr. Bragge ever held the living of Alhallows. If he did, he

* Calamy's Account, p. 51.

PEWTERERS'-HALL, LIME-STREET.—*Independent*, Extinct.

must have quitted it some time before Bartholomew-day, as Mr. John Blemell was instituted to that living, June 12, 1662.* However, he was certainly silenced by the Bartholomew Act, as effectually as if he had been ejected. In Kennet's Chronicle we find mention of the following resolution of the Rump parliament, February, 1659-60. " Ordered, that it be referred to the committee for plundered ministers, to put Mr. Brague into the place formerly conferred on Mr. Burgess."† The place vacated by the latter, appears to have been a living at Portsmouth, in consequence of his appointment as chaplain to the regiment of Colonel Sir John Lenthal. Whether this person be the same as our Mr. Bragge, and if so, whether he was ever appointed to the living above-mentioned, appears quite uncertain. After the Restoration, Mr. Bragge's congregation met at Pewterers'-Hall, Lime-street, where he preached till his death, April 14, 1704, aged 77 years. He was a man of great humility and sincerity, and of a very peaceable temper.‡ His remains were interred in Bunhill-Fields, in the same vault, where the celebrated Mr. John Bunyan had been buried above fifteen years before. Mr. Bragge left a son in the ministry among the Dissenters, of both his names, who succeeded Mr. Nathaniel Mather, and whom we shall have occasion to notice under the next article. His only publications, were two single sermons, upon funeral occasions. One for the Rev. Ralph Venning, in 1673; the other for the Rev. Thomas Wadsworth, in 1676. He also joined with some other ministers, in an epistle before Mr. Faldo's book against Quakerism.§ Mr. Bragge's name is also affixed to the renunciation of Venner's plot, published by the Independent ministers in London, in 1660.||

* Newcourt's Repertorum, vol. i. p. 249. † Kennet's Chronicle, p. 54.
‡ Calamy's Account, p. 51. § Continuation, p. 74.
|| Neal's Puritans, vol. ii. p. 592.

PEWTERERS'-HALL, LIME-STREET.——*Independent*, Extinct.

RALPH VENNING.—Mr. Bragge enjoyed for some years the assistance of the Rev. Ralph Venning. This excellent Divine was born about the year 1620, and pursued his academical studies in Emmanuel College, Cambridge. Dr. Calamy speaks of him as ejected from the lectureship of St. Olave, Southwark, which, it seems, was all the preferment he enjoyed when the Bartholomew Act took place. After his ejectment, he preached as colleague with Mr. Bragge, at Pewterers'-Hall. He was a person of eminent ministerial gifts, an excellent and powerful preacher, very popular, and much followed. For the poor, he was a most importunate and prevalent pleader, having such a way of recommending charity as frequently prevailed with people to give, who had gone to church with resolutions to the contrary. He accordingly collected for the poor, some hundreds of pounds annually. Mr. Venning died March 10, 1673, aged 53 years.* He was buried in Bunhill-Fields, in the presence, (as Wood informs us) of very many Nonconformists.† His funeral sermon was preached by his colleague, the Rev. Robert Bragge, from Matt. ix. 38. It was afterwards published, but contains scarcely a single particular relating to the life and character of the deceased. (D) After the death of Mr. Venning, Mr. Bragge, most probably, had other ministers to assist him; but their names have not reached us. He was succeeded by the person next mentioned.

* Calamy's Account, p. 22. Continuation, p. 18.
† Wood's Athenæ, vol. ii. p. 514.

(D) WORKS.—Mr. Venning published the following treatises: 1. Orthodox and Miscellaneous Paradoxes: or, a Believer clearing Truth by seeming Contradictions. 1647. 12mo.—2. A Warning to Backsliders: a Sermon before the Lord Mayor and Aldermen of London, Rev. ii. 5. 1654.—3. The Way to Happiness.—4. Mercies' Memorial.—5. Canaan's Flowings; or Milk and Honey.—6. The New Command renewed.—7. Mysteries and Revelations.—8. Things worth thinking on, or Helps to Piety.—9. Sin the Plague of Plagues; or, sinful Fear the worst of Evils.—10. His Farewell Sermon at St. Olave's, Southwark, Heb. x. 23. 1663.—11. His Re-

PEWTERERS'-HALL, LIME-STREET.—*Independent*, Extinct.

JOHN WOWEN, or JONATHAN OWEN, for there seems to be some difficulty with regard to his real name. A manuscript, to which we shall have frequent occasion to refer in the course of the present work, speaks of him under the former name, as the founder of the Independent church in Deadman's-Place, Southwark. There he had a numerous congregation, and was very popular. But falling out with his people, he left them about 1702, and, after a short time, was chosen to succeed Mr. Bragge, at Pewterers'-Hall.* He continued to preach there till 1715, when he embraced the principles of the Baptists, and went down to Bristol, where he assisted the Rev. Andrew Gifford, at the Pithay-meeting.† Crosby records the same facts of a Mr. Jonathan Owen,‡ from whence there can be no doubt but he was the same person. Calamy mentions a Mr. John Wowen,§ who was silenced by the Act of Uniformity, and appears to be the person of whom we are speaking. But we defer entering into a discussion of this subject, as we shall have some further particulars to relate under the article DEADMAN'S-PLACE. Upon Mr. Wowen's leaving Pewterers'-Hall, his church broke up, and the people separated into other societies.

mains. To this Book is prefixed, the Author's Portrait, by Hollar.—
12. A Spiritual Garden of sweet-smelling Flowers; or, Mr. Ralph Venning's Divine Sentences. This is in a Book, entitled, Saints' Memorials: or, Words fitly spoken, like Apples of Gold in Pictures of Silver. Being a Collection of Divine Sentences, written and delivered by those late Reverend and eminent Ministers, Mr. Edmund Calamy, Mr. Joseph Caryl, Mr. Ralph Venning, and Mr. James Janeway. London. 1674. 8vo. In the Frontispiece to this Book, there is a Portrait of each of these Ministers, in four squares. Mr. Venning, also, had a hand in the English-Greek Lexicon, published in 1661.

* MS. *penes me.*
† Crosby's History of the Baptists, vol. iv. p. 168. ‡ *Ibid.*
§ Calamy's Account, p. 777. Contin. p. 896.

PAVED-ALLEY, LIME-STREET.

INDEPENDENT.

PAVED-ALLEY, of which, at present, no traces remain, was situated at the upper end of Lime-street, towards Leadenhall-street, and the site has been many years covered by a wing of the East India-House. The meeting-house, which was a large building, with three capacious galleries, was erected about the time of King Charles's Indulgence, in 1672. The congregation that assembled in it was of early origin; being gathered by the celebrated Dr. Thomas Goodwin, soon after his return from Holland, at the beginning of the long parliament, in 1640. Their first place of meeting was in the parish of St. Dunstan in the East, but the exact spot cannot be ascertained. Suffice it to say, that it was somewhere about Thames-street. The congregation was for many years very considerable both for numbers and opulence, and made the largest collection for the fund of any church in London. The meeting-house being conveniently situated, was made use of for the purpose of several lectures. Mr. Bragge preached one on the Lord's-day evening for several years. There was, also, a catechetical lecture here on a Wednesday evening, which was removed to Little St. Helen's. In 1730, Mr. Coward fixed upon it as a proper place for carrying on a course of lectures on the most important doctrines of the gospel. They were twenty-six in number, and were preached by nine ministers* of approved character and abilities. The lecture was opened November the 12th, 1730, and continued weekly till April 8, 1731. The discourses delivered at it were afterwards published, in two volumes octavo, and are esteemed among the best defences of Calvinism. The church

---

* There were Mr. ROBERT BRAGGE, Dr. ABRAHAM TAYLOR, Mr. JOHN SLADEN, Mr. PETER GOODWIN, Mr. JOHN HURRION, Mr. THOMAS BRADBURY, Mr. THOMAS HALL, Mr. SAMUEL WILSON, and Dr. JOHN GILL. The two last were of the Baptist denomination.

PAVED-ALLEY, LIME-STREET.—*Independent.*

in Lime-street continued to flourish under a succession of valuable ministers, till Christmas, 1755, when the East India Company having purchased a large plot of ground, including the spot where the meeting-house stood, the congregation was compelled to quit. Soon after, it was taken down, to make way for the enlargement of the Company's premises. Mr. Richardson, who was the pastor, at that time, having relinquished his charge, the congregation divided into two branches. One of these went off to Artillery-street, where Mr. Richardson resumed the pastoral office. The remaining branch removed to Miles's-lane, and chose for their pastor the Rev. William Porter. After assembling there about ten years, they built the present meeting-house in Camomile-street. The history of these two branches we shall take up in their proper order. We now proceed to give the succession of ministers at the old church, in Lime-street, distinguishing pastors from assistants.

Ministers' Names.	As Pastors.		As Assistants.	
	From	To	From	To
Thomas Goodwin, D. D.	1640	1650	—	—
Thomas Harrison, D. D.	1650	165.	—	—
Thomas Mallery,	165.	16..	—	—
John Collins, Sen.	16..	1687	—	—
Francis Howel, M. A.	—	—	16..	1679
John King,	—	—	1680	1688
Nathaniel Mather, M. A.	1688	1697	—	—
Robert Trail, M. A.	—	—	1688	1697
John Collins, Jun.	1698	1714	—	—
Robert Bragge,	1698	1738	—	—
Philip Gibbs,	—	—	1715	1729
John Atkinson,	—	—	1732	1735
John Hill,	—	—	1735	1736
John Richardson,	—	—	1736	1755

PAVED-ALLEY, LIME-STREET.—*Independent.*

THOMAS GOODWIN, D. D.—This learned and eminent Divine, who was one of the principal leaders of the Independents, during the reign of Charles the First, was born October 5, 1600, at Rolesby, in Norfolk. His parents, who were religious persons, devoted him early to the work of the ministry, and gave him a suitable education with that view. After obtaining a competent knowledge of the Latin and Greek languages, he was sent, at thirteen years of age, to Christ's College, Cambridge; where his good natural abilities were so improved by diligent study, as to secure him great esteem in the University.

In 1616, he took the degree of Bachelor of Arts.* After continuing at Christ's College about six years, he removed, in 1619, to Katherine-Hall, under the tuition of the famous Dr. Sibbes. In the following year, he proceeded Master of Arts,† was chosen fellow, and a lecturer in the University. After some time, he proceeded Doctor in Divinity.‡

During the first six years which he spent at College, he walked in the vanity of his mind. Ambitious designs entirely engrossed his attention, and his whole aim was to obtain preferment and applause. But God, who had designed him to higher purposes was pleased to change his heart, and turn the course of his life to his own service and glory. It appears from his own account of his conversion, and of his experience both before and after, that, from the time he was six years old, he had strong impressions of religion upon his mind, which led him to the performance of common duties. At his first going to College, he constantly attended the Lord's-Supper; but, his good inclinations were often overcome, and he relapsed into sin. At one time, having made uncommon preparation for the Lord's-Supper at Whitsuntide, expecting to be thereby so confirmed, as never again to fall away, his tutor observing

---

* Kennet's Chronicle, p. 935.   † *Ibid.*
‡ Dr. Goodwin's Life, prefixed to the fifth volume of his works.

PAVED-ALLEY, LIME-STREET.—*Independent.*

him come to receive, sent to forbid him. To this, he seems to have been actuated on account of his youth. It was such a disappointment, however, to young Goodwin, as to discourage him from attending the ministry of the Puritans. From that time, he left off prayer, gave himself up to a worldly course of life, and followed such studies as were merely calculated to display the wit and learning of the preacher. At length, on a certain day, (Oct. 16, 1620,) while at Cambridge, his attention was engaged by the tolling of a bell for a funeral, and a sermon being expected, one of his companions persuaded him to stay and hear it. Being then averse to serious preaching, he was not much inclined to follow this proposal; but finding Dr. Bambridge, a witty man, was to preach, he staid to hear him. The Doctor preached from Luke xix. 41, 42. *And when he was come near, he beheld the city and wept over it, saying, If thou hadst known, even thou at least in this thy day, the things which belong unto thy peace! But now they are hid from thine eyes.* Though Mr. Goodwin had heard the sermon before, yet the preacher's manner greatly engaged his attention. The observations he made were " That every man has his day, or a time in which grace is offered him—that if he neglects it, God is just in hiding it from his eyes— and that it behoves every man to pray against blindness of mind, and hardness of heart." The sermon was closed with a warm exhortation to an immediate repentance and return to God. Though the remarks he had heard were far from being uncommon, yet, he was so much affected, that he told his companions, he hoped he should be the better for that sermon as long as he lived. Instead of spending the evening in mirth as he intended, he returned to his own College, and passed it in retirement. His mind was now greatly oppressed with a sense of the evil of sin, and its dreadful consequences. He saw the vanity of his former religion, and the deficiency there was in the root of all his devotion, the flowers of which had withered because they

PAVED-ALLEY, LIME-STREET.—*Independent.*

wanted moisture in the heart to afford them nourishment. He now found the disposition of his mind entirely changed. Instead of vain-glory, and the love of academic praise, he proposed the glory of God as the end of all his actions ; and, in his preaching, wholly discarded the affectation of wit, and a flimsy eloquence.*

After his conversion, Dr. Goodwin became a celebrated preacher in the University, and was instrumental in turning many to the love and practice of serious religion. In 1628, he was chosen to the lectureship of Trinity Church, in Cambridge, though not without opposition from Dr. Buckridge, bishop of Ely. It also appears, that, in 1632, he was presented by the King to the vicarage of the same church. Afterwards, being in his conscience dissatisfied with the terms of conformity, he quitted the University, together with his preferments, in 1634. Though this step was contrary to his worldly interest, yet, as he acted with sincerity, he often expressed great joy and thankfulness ; and received great encouragement in the acceptance and success of his ministry.†

The persecution in England growing hot, under the guidance of Archbishop Laud, Dr. Goodwin, that he might enjoy liberty of conscience, retired to Holland, in 1639, and settled as pastor of the English church an Arnheim, in Guelderland. (E) At the beginning of the long parliament,

---

* Life of Dr. Goodwin, *ubi supra*,—and Nonconformist's Memorial, vol. i. p. 237—239.   † *Ibid.*

(E) In 1638, a year before he retired abroad, he married Elizabeth, daughter of Mr. Alderman Prescot. This lady dying, he was espoused, in 1649, to Miss Mary Hammond, then only in her seventeenth year. Dr. Goodwin was very happy in both these ladies. By the former, he had an only daughter, who was married to Mr. John Mason, a citizen of London. By his second wife, he had two sons and two daughters. Of the eldest son, who bore both his names, and was a Dissenting minister first in London, and afterwards at Pinner, in Middlesex, we shall have occasion to speak in the progress of this work. Richard, the second son, died on a voyage to the East Indies, where he was going as one of the Company's factors. Both the daughters died in their infancy.—*Life of Dr. Goodwin, prefixed to the fifth volume of his works.*

PAVED-ALLEY, LIME-STREET.—*Independent.*

he returned to England; and, coming to London, gathered an Independent congregation, in the parish of St. Dunstan in the East, Thames-street. In 1643, he was chosen a member of the Assembly of Divines, at Westminster, and by his modesty and meekness, gained the esteem of that venerable body, notwithstanding he was one of the Dissenting brethren. Of the transactions of this assembly he took notes, which he left in fourteen or fifteen volumes. In 1647, he had invitations from Mr. John Cotton, and other worthy ministers, to remove to New-England, which he was so much inclined to do, as to put a great part of his library on shipboard. But the persuasions of friends, to whose advice he paid great deference, made him alter his resolution.* By an order of parliament, dated Jan. 8, 1649-50, he was appointed President of Magdalen College, Oxford, with the privilege of nominating fellows and demies, in such places as should become vacant by death, or by the possessors refusing to take the engagement.† Being in high favour with Oliver Cromwell, he was nominated, in 1653, upon a committee of Divines, to draw up a catalogue of fundamentals, to be presented to parliament; and, the same year, was made one of the Triers for the approval of Ministers.‡ In the following year, he was appointed one of the assistants to the Commissioners of Oxfordshire, for the removal of scandalous and insufficient preachers.§ He was, also, one of the principal ministers who composed the synod of congregational churches, which met at the Savoy, in 1658, for the purpose of framing a confession of faith for the Independent churches. ||

Upon his appointment to the Presidentship, Dr. Goodwin applied himself diligently to promote learning and piety

---

* Life of Dr. Goodwin, *ubi supra*. † *Ibid.*
‡ Neal's Puritans, vol. ii. p. 443, 447.
§ Wood's Fasti, vol. ii. p. 104. || Neal's Puritans, vol. ii. p. 506.

PAVED-ALLEY, LIME-STREET.—*Independent.*

in his College. His candid and ingenuous behaviour, and his catholic charity for good men of different persuasions, gained him the esteem of those who had been most averse to his promotion. In conferring places of preferment, he was not biassed by party motives; real merit being the sole standard of his conduct. He preached constantly at St. Mary's, and sometimes in the College chapel; and set up a weekly meeting for religious purposes, at his own lodgings. Here he also formed a church, upon the Independent plan, of which, among others, Mr. Thankful Owen, Mr. Francis Howel, Mr. Theophilus Gale, and Mr. Stephen Charnock, were members.* The learned Mr. John Howe was, at that time, a member of the same College. As he had an established reputation, and did not offer to join the society, Dr. Goodwin took occasion to speak to him upon the subject, expressing, at the same time, his surprise and concern at his neglect. Mr. Howe told him very frankly, " The only reason was, that he understood they laid a great stress upon some peculiarities for which he had no fondness, though he could give others their liberty, without any unkind thoughts of them; but, if they would admit him into their society upon catholic terms, he would readily join them." The Doctor embraced him, saying, he would do it with all his heart, and that he knew it would be much to the satisfaction and edification of the rest. A proof that Dr. Goodwin was not so narrow minded as some have represented him.†

Soon after the Restoration, he was dismissed from his Presidentship, when he retired to London, whither many of his church followed him. Here, he continued in the faithful discharge of his ministry, living a retired life, which he spent in prayer, reading and meditation. The authors he most valued and studied were, Augustine, Calvin, Musculus, Zanchius, Paræus, Waleus, Gomarus, Altingius, and

* Life of Dr. Goodwin, *ubi supra.* † Calamy's Life of Howe, p. 10, 11.

PAVED-ALLEY, LIME-STREET.—*Independent.*

Amesius; and among the schoolmen, Suarez and Estius. And, as he had furnished his library with a good collection of commentators, so he made good use of them. But the scriptures, as containing an inexhaustible treasure of divine knowledge, were what he chiefly studied. Upon the glorious doctrines contained in the inspired volume, his mind soared with the greatest delight. In the dreadful fire of London, which consumed a considerable part of the city, A. D. 1666, he lost above half his library, to the value of five hundred pounds. Upon this he observed, that God had struck him in a very sensible part, and acknowledged it as a rebuke of Providence, for having loved his library too much. He was thankful, however, that the loss fell chiefly upon books of human learning, those on divinity being preserved, though they were exposed, apparently, to the greatest danger. As the exercise of faith and patience reconciled him to this providence, so he wrote a discourse upon the subject, which he soon afterwards printed. The labours of this eminent man were terminated by means of a rapid fever, which carried him off in a few days, Feb. 23, 1679-80, in the 80th year of his age. In his last moments, he enjoyed the fullest assurance of faith, and expressed himself with so much joy, thankfulness, and admiration of the free grace of God, as extremely affected all who heard him.*

Dr. Goodwin was a very considerable scholar, a man of extensive reading, and an eminent Divine. Mr. Wood styles him and Dr. Owen, " the two Atlasses and Patriarchs of Independency." He was, however, by no means equal to Dr. Owen. In the common register of the University, he is said to be, *In scriptis in re theologicâ quam plurimis orbi notus;* that is, " well known to the world by many theological writings." His works, which consist of five folio volumes, besides many single pieces, published in his lifetime, and since his death, have been much read and esteemed,

* Life of Dr. Goodwin, *ubi supra.*

PAVED-ALLEY, LIME-STREET.—*Independent.*

particularly by Calvinists of the supra-lapsarian cast, to which our author belonged. His style is plain and familiar; but very diffuse, homely and tedious. He had a remarkable talent at exposition, in which he made great use of his critical learning; and was very successful in explaining abstruse and difficult texts. The least particles of speech came under his notice, and, in numberless instances, he has made it appear, how much depends upon little words, which are too generally overlooked. He had a genius to dive into the bottom of a subject, " to study it down," as he used to express it, not contenting himself with a superficial knowledge. As from the extent of his own library he was enabled to consult the best authors, so he had the advantage of an intimate acquaintance with some of the greatest Christians of his age. This enabled him to treat his subjects in an experimental manner, and to appear with advantage when he discussed cases of conscience. He was much addicted to retirement and deep contemplation, had been much exercised in the controversies that agitated the age in which he lived, and had a deep insight into the grace of God, and the covenant of grace. In the course of his ministry, he went over the grand points of religion, and thoroughly dijested them in his own mind. His observations were clear, genuine and natural, often above common observation, and he confirmed them by pertinent scripture references. He discovered a deep insight into the sublime mysteries of the gospel, and by a plain and familiar method, brought them down to the level of common capacities. He was in high esteem with Oliver Cromwell, and visited him on his dying bed.* Of Dr. Goodwin, and his writings, we shall have occasion to make further mention, in the course of the present work.*

---

* Life of Dr. Goodwin, prefixed to the first volume of his works.—Nonconformist's Memorial, vol. i. p. 236--241.——Calamy's Account, p. 60, 61.—Neal's Puritans, vol. ii. p. 716.——Wood's Fasti, vol. ii. p. 104.

PAVED-ALLEY, LIME-STREET.—*Independent.*

THOMAS HARRISON, D. D. was born at Kingston-upon-Hull, in the East Riding of Yorkshire. While a youth his parents removed to New-England,* where they trained him up to the ministry, and gave him the best education which the country, at that time, afforded. In the early part of his ministry, he was chaplain to the governor of Virginia, who appears to have been a great enemy and persecutor of the Puritans. When Mr. Knowles of Watertown, and Mr. Thompson of Braintree, undertook a mission to the Indians of Virginia, the governor finding them disaffected to the rites and ceremonies of the Church of England, ordered them to depart the country immediately. Mr. Harrison, though he seemed openly to plead for their continuance, and liberty to preach; yet, secretly wished their dismission. This, he afterwards owned, with shame and contrition. But the departure of the missionaries was followed by a most dreadful occurrence, which some persons looked upon as a retaliation of Providence. The good men were no sooner embarked, than there was a general rising of the Indians, who miserably massacred the English, sparing neither old nor young. Those whom they met in the streets they deliberately murdered, and burned such as thought themselves secure in their own houses. No less than five hundred persons are reported to have been killed upon this occasion; besides other mischief done to the plantations. Among those who escaped the massacre, some were gathered into church order by Mr. Harrison, who, after this providence, became quite another man. Indeed, it was a signal warning to the despisers of the gospel. But the governor was only the more hardened, and dismissed his chaplain, who was now grown too serious for him. This circumstance induced him to leave the country.†

Upon his return to England, Mr. Harrison settled in London, where he soon became a celebrated preacher.

* Calamy's Account, p. 121.   † *Ibid.* p. 607.

PAVED-ALLEY, LIME-STREET.—*Independent.*

About 1650, he was chosen to succeed Dr. Goodwin, in his gathered church, at St. Dunstan's in the East, and was extremely followed. In this situation he continued but a few years, when he left the city, but, upon what occasion, does not appear. He then went to reside at Brombrough-Hall, in Wirral, where he preached constantly. In 1657, he went over to Ireland with Henry Cromwell, youngest son to Oliver, Lord Protector, who appointed him Lord Lieutenant of that kingdom. In his family, Mr. Harrison lived with great respect, and preached some years at Christ-Church, in Dublin, with universal applause. He continued there till the turn of the times, when he returned back to England, and fixed his residence in the city of Chester. There he preached for some time in the cathedral, to a large and attentive auditory, till he was silenced by the Act of Uniformity.* From a list of graduates at Cambridge, by virtue of his Majesty's letters mandatory, from Oct. 10, 1660, to Oct. 10, 1661, it seems that Mr. Harrison obtained his Doctor's degree from that University.† Dr. Calamy, however, says that he received it from the University of Dublin.‡ It is possible both may be right.

Dr. Harrison being silenced in England, again crossed the sea to Dublin, where he had before met with unusual respect. In that city, he continued the exercise of his ministry in private, having a flourishing congregation, and many persons of quality for his constant auditors. His popularity, however, did not fail to stir up much envy. He was, indeed, a most agreeable preacher, and had a peculiar way of insinuating himself into the affections of his hearers. Though he wrote his sermons at full length, yet, he took great pains to impress them upon his memory, so that he could deliver them without the use of his notes. He had also an extraordinary gift in prayer; being noted for such a

---

* Calamy's Account, p. 121, 122.   † Kennet's Chronicle, p. 546,
‡ Calamy's Account, p. 607.

PAVED-ALLEY, LIME-STREET.—*Independent.*

wonderful fluency, as well as peculiar flow of eloquence, as excited the admiration of all who heard him. In his manners, he was a complete gentleman; and while his conversation was courted by the greatest persons, he could condescend to be free with the meanest. Lord Thomond, who had a sincere value for him, as well as a high opinion of his abilities, used to say, " That he had rather hear Dr. Harrison say grace over an egg, than hear the bishops pray and preach." He was congregational in his judgment as to church discipline; and though his people were universally of another stamp, yet he managed matters with such discretion, temper and moderation, that there never was the least clashing, or danger of a division. When he died, the whole city of Dublin seemed to lament the loss of him, and there was a general mourning. His funeral was attended by persons of all ranks; and the sermon upon the occasion was preached by Mr. (afterwards Dr.) Daniel Williams, then pastor of another congregation in the same city. The time of Dr. Harrison's death is not mentioned. He left behind him a valuable library, and among other manuscripts a large folio, containing a whole system of Divinity. His only publications were " Topica Sacra; or, Spiritual Pleadings: and a Funeral Sermon, for Lady Susannah Reynolds, preached at Lawrence Jewry, Feb. 13, 1654, on Gen. xlvii. 9."*

THOMAS MALLERY.—Of this person, but few biographical particulars can be obtained. It is likely that he was descended from a member of parliament in the reign of King James the First, who, for talking with too great liberty upon state affairs, was committed to prison, together with some other leading members; as Sir Edward Coke, Sir Robert Philips, Mr. Selden, and Mr. Pym. This was

* Calamy's Account, p. 122, 123. Contin. p. 169.

PAVED-ALLEY, LIME-STREET.—*Independent.*

in 1621.* As he is not mentioned by Anthony Wood, it is probable that he received his education in the University of Cambridge. We find no mention of Mr. Mallery in any lists of ministers who were appointed to manage ecclesiastical matters during the inter-regnum; so that, it is probable, he took no active part in the transactions of those times. Upon the removal of Dr. Harrison, he was chosen to succeed him as pastor of the congregational church, at St. Dunstan's in the East, gathered by Dr. Goodwin. He was, also, chosen lecturer of St. Michael's, Crooked-lane, and preached a lecture at Deptford.† These were all the preferments he held at the Restoration. In Kennet's Chronicle there is the following entry. " Thomas Mallory, S. T. P. presented July 30, 1660, to a prebend of Chester, void by the death of Essex Clark, last incumbent."‡ Though this must have been a different person from our author, it is probable he was some relation. After the insurrection of Venner, the Independents, with a view to vindicate themselves from all suspicion of having a share in that mad transaction, published " A Renunciation and Declaration of the Congregational Churches, and public Preachers of the said Judgment, living in and about the City of London, against the late horrid Insurrection and Rebellion, acted in the said City." Dated Jan. 1660-1. Mr. Mallery's name is affixed to this declaration, which disowns the principle of a fifth monarchy, or the personal reign of King Jesus upon earth, as dishonourable to him, and prejudicial to his church. It also speaks with abhorrence of propagating this, or any other opinion, by force, or blood.§ After this, we hear nothing further of Mr. Mallery, nor is even the time of his death mentioned. It is probable, however, that this event took place before King's Charles's Indulgence in 1672, when Mr. Collins appears to have been pastor of

* Neal's Puritans, vol. i. p. 494.   † Calamy's Account, p. 36, 391.
‡ Kennet's Chronicle, p. 333.   § Neal's Puritans, vol. ii. p. 592.

PAVED-ALLEY, LIME-STREET.—*Independent.*

the church now under consideration. Dr. Calamy has no account of him excepting this short character, "He was a person of an exemplary conversation, and very faithful in his ministry."* He was congregational in his judgment with regard to church-government, and had a considerable congregation to the day of his death. Mr. Mallery has a sermon in the Morning Exercise at Cripplegate, on "The Conceptions we should form of God in Duty." There is, also, a small volume of his in print, entitled, "The inseparable communion of a Believer with God in his Love;" being the substance of several Sermons on Rom. viii. 38, 39. 8vo. 1674. He also joined with Mr. Greenhill and Mr. Caryl, in a preface to Mr. Malbon's Discourse on Life and Death.†

JOHN COLLINS.—Of this excellent Divine and eminent preacher, the accounts that are preserved are extremely defective. We are not acquainted even with the place of his birth; but it appears that, in early life, he went over with an English colony to America. In the churches of New-England, his family was in considerable repute. Of his father, Cotton Mather gives this simple account. "There was a good old man, called Collins, the deacon of the church at Cambridge, who is now gone to heaven; but, before he went thither, had the satisfaction to see several most worthy sons become very famous persons in their generation: sons, that having worthily served their generation, are now gone thither as well as he."‡ The following anecdote is related of Mr. Collins, during his youth. Having received a wound by a fall, which had nearly cost him his life, that famous Divine, Mr. Thomas Shepard, happened to come up to him just as he lay gasping for breath. He im-

* Calamy's Contin. p. 53. † *Ibid.*
‡ Mather's History of New-England, B. iv. p. 199.

PAVED-ALLEY, LIME-STREET.—*Independent.*

mediately addressed him in the following consolatory terms: " I have just now been wrestling with the Lord for thy life, and God hath granted me my desire; young man, thou shalt not die but live; but remember that now the Lord says, Surely thou wilt now fear him, and receive instruction."* The life thus preserved, proved, afterwards, a considerable benefit to the churches in Great-Britain, but especially in London, where he spent the chief part of his public ministry.

Mr. Collins pursued his studies for the ministry in Harvard College, Cambridge. Cotton Mather mentions him in a list of graduates thus: " 1649, Joannes Collins, *Socius;*" from whence it appears that he became a fellow of Harvard College, in that year. The President of the College at that time was Mr. Henry Dunstar, of whom the reader will find some account in Mather's History of New-England.† Here Mr. Collins made considerable progress in his studies, was eminent for diligence and piety, and soon after he left the University, became an admired preacher.

It does not appear that Mr. Collins was ever settled with a congregation in America. Soon after he commenced preacher, he returned to England, and found Cromwell at the summit of his power. Afterwards, he became chaplain to General Monk, whom he accompanied in his march from Scotland into England.‡ At the Restoration, he was not in possession of any benefice, and therefore, not ejected; but he was silenced by the Act of Uniformity in 1662. He, afterwards, succeeded Mr. Mallery, as pastor of a considerable Independent church in London.§ Upon the establishment of the Merchant's lecture, at Pinners'-Hall, in 1672, Mr. Collins was chosen one of the first six lecturers. And it is observable, that he, and Dr. Owen, were the only Independents selected for this purpose; the

* Mather, *ubi supra*, p. 200. † B. iii. p. 99. B. iv. p. 128.
‡ Calamy's Account, p. 837, 838. § *Ibid.*

PAVED-ALLEY, LIME-STREET.——*Independent.*

other preachers being chosen from the Presbyterian denomination.* In these situations Mr. Collins continued till his death, which happened Dec. 3, 1687, but at what age, we are no where informed. When this good man lay upon his dying bed, that eminent minister, the Rev. Matthew Mead, being to preach in his turn at Pinners'-Hall, poured out such an affectionate prayer for his recovery, that there was scarcely one dry eye to be seen in the numerous congregation.†

Mr. Collins was a minister of uncommon abilities, and greatly signalized himself as a preacher. Such were the charms of his eloquence, that few persons could go from under his preaching displeased, or unaffected.‡ With the sacred scriptures he possessed a thorough acquaintance, and applied himself with great diligence, to the several duties of the pastoral office. In private life, he discovered a most amiable temper, and was very charitable to all good men, without confining himself to a party.§ He left a son in the ministry, who succeeded Mr. Nathaniel Mather, in his own congregation, as joint-pastor with the Rev. Robert Bragge. Mr. Collins was interred in Bunhill-Fields. Cotton Mather has preserved his Latin epitaph,|| which, as our character of him is so short, we shall here subjoin, together with an English translation. (F)

* Neal's Puritans, vol. ii. p. 688.
† Mather's History of New-England, B. iv. p. 200.
‡ Mather, *ubi supra.*   § Calamy's Account, p. 838.
|| History of New-England, *ubi supra.*

(F) WORKS.—Mr. Collins has a sermon in the third volume of the Morning Exercise, upon this question : " How are the religious of a nation the strength of it." Also, another in the second volume of the London Collection of Farewell Sermons, on Jude 3. Besides these, he has nothing, we believe, in print, excepting a preface to Mr. Venning's Remains, and another to Mr. Michael's Treatise on Eternal Glory.*

* Calamy's Account, p. 838. Contin. p. 962.

PAVED-ALLEY, LIME-STREET.—*Independent.*

JOANNES COLLINS,
Indolis Optimæ Puerulus, Patrem Pietate insignem,
Castiorem Dei cultum, et Limatiorem
Ecclesiæ disciplinam, anhelantem,
In Americanum Anglorum, secutus est Colonium,
Ubi quà Gymnasiis, quà Cantabrigiensi isthic collegio,
(Deo inderessis adspirante studiis)
Scriba factus ad Regnum cœlorum instructissimus,
Antiquæ cum fœnore, rependitur Angliæ.
Scotiæ etiam celebrium Ministrorum Gens fertilis,
Et audivit, et mirata est concionantem.
Utrobiq; multos Christo lucrifecit;
Plures in Christo ædificavit.
Præsertim hac in Metropoli, Gregis gratissimi Pastor;
Nil segnis Otii gnavo indulgens Animo;
Nec laboribus, morbisq; fracto parcens Corpori;
Meditando, Prædicando, Conferendo, Votaq; faciendo,
Vitam insumpsit fragilem,
Ut æternæ aliorum Vitæ consuleret;
Quo Ecclesiarum itaq; nulla pastorem optimum,
Aut vivum magis Venerata est,
Aut magis indoluit morienti.
M. Dris Die IIIº. Anno Æræ Christianæ.
M.DC.LXXXVII.

Translation.

Here rest the Remains
Of the Rev. JOHN COLLINS,
Who, when a child discovered the most promising disposition.
When a Father, he excelled in Piety;
A sincere worshipper of God,
Ardently promoting the pure discipline of the Church.
He followed an English Colony to America,
Where he entered as a Student in Cambridge College.
God assisting him in his unwearied studies,
He became a scribe well instructed in the kingdom of heaven,
When he returned to Old England richly compensated for his labours.
He also went to Scotland,
A country fruitful in celebrated preachers,
Whom he heard and admired in the Assembly.
In both which places he turned many to Christ,
And built up more in their most holy faith;
Especially in this Metropolis, where he was Pastor of a most grateful flock.
He did not indulge himself in indolence,
But diligently improved the powers of his mind,
Not sparing his body, which was broken by labours and diseases.
By meditation, by preaching, by conversation, and by prayer,
He greatly impaired a weakly constitution,
That he might attend to the eternal concerns of others;
For which he was held in such high esteem by the churches,
Being considered the best of Pastors,
That it is difficult to say, Whether he was most respected whilst living,
Or regretted now dead.
He departed Dec. 3, 1687.

PAVED ALLEY, LIME-STREET.—*Independent.*

FRANCIS HOWEL, M. A. Fellow of Exeter College, Oxford, also one of the Proctors of the University, and Reader of Moral Philosophy. In 1654, he was appointed by the Protector Oliver, one of the New Visitors of that University; and soon afterwards Principal of Jesus College. After the Restoration, he was deprived of his preferments by King Charles's Commissioners. Upon this, he retired to London, and being congregational in his judgment, became fellow-labourer with Mr. John Collins, to whose congregation he preached one part of the Lord's-day with great acceptance. He died at Bethnal-green, on the 8th or 10th of March, 1679, and was buried in Bunhill-Fields, in the presence of a great number of Nonconformists.*

JOHN KING.—After the decease of Mr. Howell, a Mr. John King was invited to become assistant to Mr. Collins; and he preached in this connexion about seven years. In January, 1687-8, he was invited to become assistant teacher to the Independent church at Yarmouth, and accepted the call. The following year, he had an invitation to the pastoral office in the same church, but declined; and in 1690, he was discharged from that connexion.† What became of him afterwards, we no where learn.

NATHANIEL MATHER.—There have been few families in the Christian church that have contributed more essentially to serve its best interests, by their pious and diligent labours, than that of the Mathers. The father of this numerous family, was the Rev. RICHARD MATHER, an eminent Puritan Divine, in Lancashire, who, for the sake of a good conscience, and the undisturbed exercise of his ministry, was compelled to leave his country. He removed to America in 1635, and having a call from a con-

---

* Calamy's Account, p. 59.—Wood's Fasti, vol. ii. p. 64.
† Baptist Annual Register, vol. iv. p. 641, 642.

PAVED-ALLEY, LIME-STREET.—*Independent.*

gregation at Dorchester, continued to labour there, with great usefulness, till his death, April 22, 1669, in the 73d year of his age.* Many years before his death, he had the comfort of seeing four sons, preachers of no mean consideration. 1. SAMUEL MATHER, who, at nine years of age, went over with his father to New-England, and was educated in Harvard College. Afterwards, removing to Ireland, he became a senior fellow of Trinity College, Dublin, and a preacher at St. Nicholas church; but, at the Restoration, he lost all his preferments, and continued the exercise of his ministry in private till his death, Oct. 29, 1671, in his 46th year.† 2. NATHANIEL MATHER, the subject of the present memoir. 3. ELEAZAR MATHER, who was also educated in Harvard College, and became pastor of a church at Northampton, in New-England, where he laboured eleven years, till his death, July 24, 1669, aged 32 years.‡ 4. INCREASE MATHER, who was born, educated, and spent the chief part of his life in New-England. He was many years President of Harvard College, and pastor of a church at Boston, where he died August 23, 1723, at the great age of 84.§ By a daughter of Mr. John Cotton, a famous New-England Divine, he had three sons. 1. COTTON MATHER, D. D. pastor of a church at Boston, and well known to the world by his many valuable writings. 2. NATHANIEL MATHER, who died in New-England, at the age of nineteen, Oct. 17, 1688; and of whose early piety an account was published by his elder brother.|| 3. SAMUEL MATHER, who had a small congregation at Witney, in Oxfordshire, and published several pieces of a valuable nature.¶

* Mather's History of New-England, B. iii. p. 122—130.
† *Ibid.* B. iv. p. 143—153.   ‡ *Ibid.* B. iii. p. 130.
§ Calamy's Continuation, p. 494—500.
|| Mather's History of New-England, B. iv. p. 208.
¶ Calamy, *ubi supra.*

PAVED-ALLEY, LIME-STREET.—*Independent.*

NATHANIEL, the second son of Richard Mather abovementioned, was born in the county of Lancaster, March 30, 1630.* When his father removed to New-England, he was only five years of age. In 1647, he became a graduate of Harvard College,† where he made a considerable proficiency in literature. But, he finished his studies in England, where he also commenced preacher. His first preferment was the living of Harberton, near Totness, in Devonshire. In 1656, he was presented by Oliver Cromwell, to that of Barnstaple, in the same county. This was the sequestered living of Mr. Martin Blake, a pious, learned and moderate man, who, it seems, met with much ill usage. But to this, Mr. Mather cannot be chargeable with being in the least accessary. At the Restoration, he lost all his preferments; and, retiring to Holland, became pastor of the English congregation at Rotterdam.

Upon the death of his brother, Mr. Samuel Mather, in 1671, he went over to Ireland, and succeeded him as pastor of a congregation, in Dublin. There he continued several years. Some time after his settlement in Ireland, he published a valuable manuscript left behind by his brother, being a course of Sermons upon the Types of the Old Testament. It was printed in 1683, and has been considered one of the best treatises upon the subject. In 1688, Mr. Mather removed to England, to take the pastoral charge of a numerous congregation in Lime-street, in the room of Mr. John Collins, deceased. It appears that the celebrated Dr. Daniel Williams, also, preached as a candidate, at the same time, and had a considerable number of votes. Mr. Mather was likewise chosen one of the Merchants' lecturers at Pinners'-Hall. Several sermons which he delivered in his turn at that lecture, were afterwards printed. At length, after a diligent and faithful discharge of the ministerial duties, for the space of forty-seven years, this excel-

---

* Watts's Epitaph for the Rev. Nathaniel Mather, apud " Lyric Poems."
† Mather's History of New-England, B. iv. p. 136.

PAVED-ALLEY, LIME-STREET.—*Independent.*

lent man was taken to his rest, July 26, 1697, aged 67 year.*

Mr. Mather was tall in stature, and of a mildly majestic aspect. To a penetrating genius, he united solid and extensive learning. But above these advantages, his piety shone with a distinguished lustre. He possessed a most amiable spirit, and gave the most striking proofs of an unaffected modesty. Having himself imbibed much of the temper of Jesus Christ, and experienced largely of that grace which bringeth salvation, he was anxious that it might be communicated to others. Of the Christian faith, he was an able defender, as well as a bright ornament. He was a judicious, zealous, and affectionate preacher; his aspect was venerable, his gesture pleasing, and his pronunciation agreeable. In his public discourses, there was neither a lavish display, nor an inelegant penury of oratorial excellence; while the dignity of his subjects superceded the necessity of rhetorical embellishments. In addressing sinners, he possessed an awfulness in his manner, that was greatly calculated to strike the arrows of conviction, and interest the feelings of the mind. And he was equally skilful in administering those consolations which flow from a believing view of the gospel. Nevertheless, he possessed a certain heaviness in the pulpit, which rendered him unpopular. In his private visits to his people, he adapted his conversation to their several cases; always aiming at their spiritual instruction, and to diffuse the savour of the Redeemer's name, wherever he went. He sustained the attacks of corporal pain, and a tiresome affliction, with invincible fortitude, and, at length, in full assurance of faith, made a triumphant departure to his everlasting reward.†

Mr. Mather was interred in Bunhill-Fields, where a Latin inscription was placed upon his monument; which we

* Calamy's Account, p. 238. Contin. p. 157.—Nonconformist's Memorial, vol. ii. p. 4.
† Epitaph for the Rev. Nathaniel Mather, by Isaac Watts, *ubi supra*,—and MS. *penes me.*

PAVED-ALLEY, LIME-STREET.—*Independent.*

shall insert, together with an English translation. Dr. Watts, also, drew up an epitaph to his memory. It is very descriptive; but on account of its extraordinary length, must be omitted in this place. Those who are desirous of reading it, may have recourse to the Doctor's Lyric Poems.(G)

> Sub hoc reconditur tumulo Vir admodum Reverendus
> NATHANAEL MATHER,
> Richardi Mátheri Filius,
> Utriusq; ANGLIÆ Decus.
> Edidit hæc nostra, in agro Lancastriensi:
> Imbuit Literaturâ, & Magistri Laurea honestavit
> Altera illa transmarina.
> Quâ propter temporum acerbitatem
> Parvulus adhuc cum patre recesserat.
> Inde reversus, Ecclesiæ quæ est DUBLINII apud Hibernos,
> Communi suffragio præficitur.
> Unde ad hanc urbem accersitus,
> Pastorali munere cum vita defunctus est.
> Si laudes quæris, paucis accipe;
> Animi dotibus fuit dives, Literis eruditissimus
> Judicio perpolitus, ingenio acer,
> Cujusque Muneris Naturæ & Doctrinæ potens:
> Sacravit omnia in serviendo Deo.
> Omnino instructissimus ad officium,
> Beati servatoris Evangelium sincere promulgavit;
> Ornavitque vita decora;
> Comitate, Modestia, Patientia mixta.
> Pietatis Exemplar maxime illustre;
> Semper sibi par, & sibi constans.
> Christianus Religiosissimus,
> Maritus indulgentissimus,
> Conscionator aptus & operosus,
> Pastor Fidelis & Vigilans.
> In sacræ Functionis Exercitiis, arte pia celavit hominem,
> Ut solus conspiceretur Deus,
> Omni deniq; Virtute præditus & Laude dignissimus.
> Sed ah! Quantus Dolor? mortuus est.
> Plerophoria tamen Fidei, cœlestem adiit Gloriam,
> Et triumphum 26 Julii,
> Æræ Christianæ M.DC.XCVII.
> Ætat. LXVII.

(G) WORKS.—1. The Righteousness of God by Faith, upon all, without difference, who believe. In two Sermons, preached at Pinners'-Hall. Rom. iii. 22.—2. A Discussion of the Lawfulness of a Pastor's acting as an Officer in other Churches, besides that of which he is called to take the oversight.—3. Twenty-three select Sermons, preached at Pinners'-Hall, and Lime-street. Wherein several Cases of Conscience, and other weighty Matters are propounded and handled. 1701.—4. A Fast Sermon, on 1 Cor. xi. 30. 1711.

PAVED-ALLEY, LIME-STREET.—*Independent.*

Translation.

Under this tomb is laid
The Rev. Mr. NATHANIEL MATHER,
The honour of both *Englands.*
The county of *Lancaster,* in our *England,*
Gave him birth:
And the *American England*
Trained him up in literature,
And honoured him with the degree of Master of Arts:
To which country, when he was very young,
Through the severity of the times,
He fled with his father.
Returning thence,
He was unanimously chosen Pastor
Of a church at *Dublin,* in *Ireland ;*
Whence being called by a Christian Society
To this city,
He here closed his life and pastorship.
If you inquire his merits,
Take his character in a few words:
He had rich endowments of mind,
Was profoundly learned,
Had an exact judgment,
And a most piercing understanding:
In a word, Nature and Science
Enriched him with all their stores,
And all were consecrated to the service of his God.
He was well qualified
For all the branches of his work.
He faithfully preached
The Gospel of his blessed Redeemer,
And adorned it with a most exemplary life.
In him benevolence, modesty and patience
Mingled their glories,
And he was a most illustrious pattern of holiness.
He was always equal, and constant to himself ;
A most pious Christian,
A most tender husband,
An able and laborious minister,
And a faithful and vigilant Pastor.
In the exercise of his sacred office
He with an holy art concealed the man,
That the Lord alone might be exalted :
In fine, he was ennobled with every virtue,
And was meritorious of the highest praise.
But, alas! how severe the affliction, " he is gone."
But with a full sail of faith,
He entered his port of glory,
And began his everlasting triumph.
He died July 26, 1697,
Aged 67.

PAVED-ALLEY, LIME-STREET.—*Independent.*

ROBERT TRAIL, M. A.—This excellent Divine descended from an ancient family in the county of Fife. Walter Trail, Bishop of St. Andrew's, in the reign of Robert the Third, A. D. 1385, purchased the estate of Blebo, in the above county, and bequeathed it to his nephew. Andrew Trail, the great grandfather of our author, was a younger brother of the family of Blebo. Following the profession of a soldier, he rose to the rank of a colonel, and was for some time in the service of the city of Bruges, and other towns in Flanders, in the wars which they carried on in defence of their liberties, against Philip II. King of Spain; when he left this service, his arrears amounted to 2,700l. for which he received a bond secured upon the property of the States. He then served under the King of Navarre, afterwards Henry IV. of France, in the civil wars of that kingdom; and had occasion to do that prince considerable service in taking a town by stratagem. Upon his return to Britain, he was made a gentleman of Prince Henry's privy-chamber. His son, James Trail, endeavoured to recover the sum due to his father by the cities of Flanders; and, upon a petition to King James, which was referred to Sir Harry Martin, Judge of the Admiralty, he obtained a warrant to arrest a ship belonging to the city of Bruges, which was done accordingly. But the Duke of Buckingham being gained by the adverse party, the ship was soon released; nor could he ever afterwards recover any part of the debt. This circumstance, together with the expence of the prosecution, brought him into such difficulties, that he was obliged to dispose of a small estate in the parish of Deninno, in the county of Fife. His son, Robert Trail, the father of our author, was minister, first of Ely in Fife, and afterwards of the Grey-Friars church, Edinburgh. This excellent man, who was much distinguished for his fidelity and zeal in discharging the duties of his function, suffered greatly from the persecuting spirit of the times. After a cruel imprisonment, he was banished his country, and took

PAVED-ALLEY, LIME-STREET.—*Independent.*

refuge in Holland. By Jean Annan, of the family of Auchterallan, he had three sons and three daughters. William, minister of Borthwick; Robert, the subject of the present memoir; James, a lieutenant of the garrison in Stirling Castle; Helen, married to Mr. Thomas Paterson, minister of Borthwick; Agnes, married to Sir James Stewart, of Good-trees, Lord Advocate of Scotland; and Margaret, married to James Scot, of Bristo, writer in Edinburgh.*

ROBERT TRAIL was born at Ely, in the county of Fife, in the month of May, 1642. After the usual preparatory course of grammatical education, he was sent to the University of Edinburgh. There, he recommended himself to his tutors, by his excellent capacity, and diligent application to study. Having resolved to devote himself to the work of the ministry, he applied closely, for some years, to the study of divinity. Afterwards, having undergone with approbation, the different trials required by the Scotch Presbytery, he was licensed by an association of Nonconformist ministers of the Presbyterian persuasion, to preach the gospel.†

Episcopacy being at that time the established religion of Scotland, the most injurious measures were adopted, in order to exact a rigorous conformity. Mr. Trail's father being then in banishment, his family, which he left behind in Scotland, was reduced to great straits, so that our author had no settled residence. In 1666, he was obliged to conceal himself for some time, as were his mother and elder brother, because some copies of a book, entitled, " An apologetic Relation, &c." which the privy council had ordered to be publicly burnt, were found in Mrs. Trail's house. At that time the Presbyterians were treated with the greatest severity. The privy council, at the instigation

* Life of the Rev. Robert Trail, prefixed to his works, in 3 vols. 8vo. vol. i.
† *Ibid.*

PAVED-ALLEY, LIME-STREET.—*Independent.*

of the bishops, was continually harassing them by tyrannical edicts; enjoining conformity to the established church, under civil pains and penalties, and enforcing their arbitrary and intolerant decrees, by the terror of military execution. These harsh and unjustifiable methods provoked many of that oppressed and unhappy people to such a degree, that they took up arms in despair, and advanced the length of Pentland-hills, near Edinburgh. There they were totally defeated, and dispersed in an engagement with the King's troops. Mr. Trail being suspected of having joined those who were in arms, a proclamation for apprehending him was issued by the council. This obliged him to retire into Holland, to his father, where he arrived in the beginning of 1667. There, he was employed, for some time, in assisting Nethenus, professor of divinity in the University of Utrecht, in the publication of Rutherford's Examen Arminianismi. In the preface, Nethenus speaks of Mr. Trail as a learned, pious, prudent, and industrious young man, worthy the praise and admiration of every lover of sound doctrine and true eloquence.*(H)

How long Mr. Trail continued abroad we are no where informed; but we find him in London, in 1670, when he was ordained to the ministry of the gospel, after the Presbyterian model. Soon after, he returned into Scotland, where he preached publicly, but the persecuting fury of the prelatical party soon broke out against him with increased violence. On the nineteenth of July, 1677, he was appre-

* Life of Mr. Trail, *ubi supra.*

(H) The words of Nethenus are thus: " Attulit mihi manuscriptum autoris, doctus, pius, prudens, et industrius juvenis vir D. Robertus Trallius, patris cognominis ob Christi causam veritatisque confessionem exulis, haud degener filius, sacræ theologiæ et ministerii evangelici candidatus, mihi, in procuranda & promovenda hijus libri editione, adjutor destinatus; qui et partes suas diligenter, fideliter, et constanter, ad finem usque obiit, dignus proinde laude & amore omnium, orthodoxæ veritatis, & clarissimi Rhetorfortis p. m. amatorum & cultorum.—*Life of the Rev. Robert Trail, prefixed to his works.*

PAVED-ALLEY, LIME-STREET.—*Independent.*

hended and brought before the council; where, being accused of having held field-conventicles, he acknowledged that he had held meetings in a private house. On being questioned, whether he had not preached at field-conventicles, he referred it to proof, the law having made it a criminal offence. He owned that he had conversed with Mr. Welch, when on the English border, and that he was ordained to the ministry, by Presbyterian ministers at London, in 1670. But refusing to clear himself by oath, he was committed prisoner to the *Bass*. Major Johnston, who apprehended him, obtained a thousand pounds for his trouble. We have no account at what time he was released. But he was afterwards an useful minister in London, where he laboured many years, with great diligence, zeal, and success.*

Mr. Trail was a preacher in London, (though it does not appear to what congregation) in 1682. In October of that year, he delivered a sermon from 2 Tim. iv. 16. upon the following question: " By what means may ministers best win souls?" This discourse was published in the Continuation of the Morning Exercises, in the following year. After the Revolution, Mr. Trail was chosen colleague with the Rev. Nathaniel Mather, and continued to preach statedly in Lime-street, till Mr. Mather's death. After this event, he gathered a separate congregation, of which he was pastor several years.

Mr. Trail, who was warmly attached to those doctrines that are usually called Calvinistic, took a zealous concern in the controversy that followed the publication of the works of Dr. Crisp. In 1692, he published his " Vindication of the Protestant Doctrine of Justification, and of its first Preachers and Professors, from the unjust Charge of Antinomianism. In a Letter from the Author to a Minister in

---

* Biographia Scoticana, *preface.*—Woodrow's History of the Church of Scotland.

PAVED-ALLEY, LIME-STREET,—*Independent.*

the Country." In this piece, our author discovers great zeal against *Arminianism*, and is not a little displeased with those Divines who took what was then called *the middle way*, and wrote against Dr. Crisp. At the same time, he vindicates himself, and his brethren who took the same side, from the charge of Antinomianism. At the latter end of 1694, and the beginning of 1695, he preached a course of sermons on Heb. x. 20—24, entitled, " A steadfast Adherence to the Profession of our Faith." They were not published till after the author's death; and when they made their appearance, in 1718, were introduced with a recommendation by the Reverend William Tong, John Nesbit, and Matthew Clarke. To a subsequent edition recommended by the Rev. James Hervey, and dated Weston-Favel, July 8, 1755, there were added, Two Letters to his wife and children; both written by him in the time of his banishment. Also some advices relating to some important duties. In 1696, Mr. Trail published " Thirteen Sermons upon the Throne of Grace; from Heb. iv. 16." From the preface to these discourses, it appears that the author was not in the habit of reading his sermons; but made use, only, of short notes, containing the heads of doctrines, and scriptures confirming them. His Sixteen Sermons on the Lord's-Prayer, (John xxvii. 24.) made their appearance in 1705. Mr. Trail's writings have been held in great esteem by pious persons, particularly in Scotland, where they have passed through several impressions.

Mr. Trail lived to witness several vicissitudes in the civil and religious concerns of his country. He had seen the hierarchy and regal power overthrown, and rise again with greater power and splendour from their ruins. After this, he had observed an overstrained prerogative giving birth to liberty, and toleration taking the place of a persecuting spirit. Of the blessings that attended the glorious Revolution, he was duly sensible; and rejoiced in the prospect of their continuance, by the settlement of the Protestant suc-

PAVED-ALLEY, LIME-STREET.—*Independent.*

cession in the illustrious house of Hanover. Mr. Trail died in the month of May, 1716, aged 74 years.*

Mr. Trail's works were collected together, and published at Glasgow, in three volumes, octavo, in 1775. But besides these, two small volumes have been since published in addition; one containing seven, and the other eleven sermons. The simple and evangelical strain of Mr. Trail's writings have been useful to many, and will continue to be so, while a taste for scriptural religion is in request. We understand that a new edition of his works is now in the press.

JOHN COLLINS, Jun. son to the before-mentioned Mr. Collins, was born in the city of London, about the year 1673. After passing through a course of preparatory studies at home, he removed to Holland, and spent some time in the University of Utrecht. There he had the advantage of sitting under the instructions of some of the most eminent Professors, which, at that time, adorned the several branches of literature. Upon his return from abroad, he was chosen to succeed Mr. Nathaniel Mather, as minister of a very considerable congregation in Lime-street. He was ordained co-pastor with the Rev. Robert Bragge, some time in the year 1698; and, not long after, was elected one of the Merchants' lecturers at Pinners'-Hall. In 1702, he was engaged at the ordination, in Mark-lane, of the celebrated Dr. Isaac Watts.

Mr. Collins was a good preacher, and a serious Christian, but his discourses not being well connected, and his delivery singular, he had not a large auditory. Such, however, was the general excellence of his character, that he was held in great esteem by the churches.† He died in the prime of life, and very suddenly, on March 19, 1714, when he was little more than forty years of age. The excellent Mr. Matthew Henry, who was upon terms of intimate friendship with Mr. Collins, takes notice of his death with more

* Life of Mr. Trail, *ubi supra.* † MS. *penes me.*

PAVED-ALLEY, LIME-STREET.—*Independent.*

than ordinary concern of mind. In his diary, is found the following memorandum: " March 20, 1714. Mr. Collins, co-pastor with Mr. Brague, and one of the lecturers of Pinners'-Hall, a serious, holy person, aged, I suppose, somewhat above forty, preached in his turn the last Tuesday lecture, and was here in Hackney yesterday, with Mr. Powell, about some of his uncle's charities, and dined at Mr. Lydes', prayed with Mrs. Lydes, and went home between three and four. In the evening, some young men of the congregation used to meet at his house for prayer and religious conference. He went to his study, and ordered to be called when they came. His maid, after some time, went and told him they were come. He answered, " He would come to them presently ;" was heard to unlock his study door, and come out, but immediately fell down dead. This providence is very affecting to me," adds Mr. Henry.*— " It is very remarkable, says Mr. Tong, that when he was going out of Mrs. Lydes' chamber, who was then in a dying condition, he turned again and desired the servant to tell her mistress, he should soon meet her in heaven ; and, about ten days after, March 20, that good gentlewoman finished her course in her sleep."†

ROBERT BRAGGE, a minister of great respectability, and of some note in his day, among the Dissenters of the Independent denomination, was born in London, about the time of the great plague, in 1665. His grandfather was a captain in the parliament army; and his father, the Rev. Robert Bragge, a worthy and respectable minister in London, of the congregational persuasion ; but silenced by the black Bartholomew act, in 1662.‡ Under the fostering care of a pious and intelligent father, Mr.

* Tong's Life of Matthew Henry, p. 367, 368. † *Ibid.*
‡ Calamy's Account, p. 51.

PAVED-ALLEY, LIME-STREET.—*Independent.*

Bragge made early progress in the paths of knowledge and piety.

Being designed for the work of the ministry, to which his own views were directed, he was placed under the care of suitable tutors; but the names of those who directed his youthful studies, have not reached us. It is probable that, after passing through a course of preparatory education at home, he went over to the University of Utrecht, and there finished his academical course. The Nonconformists of that period being excluded the English Universities, on account of the oaths and subscriptions introduced at the Restoration, were compelled to have recourse to more private methods of instruction. It was fortunate for them that there were so many Divines of learning and piety, who had the courage, as well as ability, to undertake so arduous an employment. By this means, the ejected ministers left behind them a race of Divines as fully qualified for their work, as if they had been bred up under the wings of the establishment. It was also, a considerable advantage that the foreign universities were accessible, free from those shackles that were imposed at home. For, though this method of education was expensive, yet the opportunities for improvement were commensurate, and afforded them the advantage of sitting under the most eminent Professors of that day.

Upon his return home, Mr. Bragge began to preach in various places about the metropolis. He entered upon the ministry with considerable advantages. His father was then a senior minister in London, and being much respected, his countenance and patronage was of considerable service in introducing young Mr. Bragge to the notice of other ministers, whose preaching and conversation tended much to form his mind, and to qualify him for future usefulness. He had not begun to preach long before some of his friends invited him to undertake a lecture on the Lord's-day evening at Salters'-Hall. This meeting-house was conveniently situated

PAVED-ALLEY, LIME-STREET.—*Independent.*

for the citizens, and the use of it being kindly granted by Mr. Nathaniel Taylor, the minister of the place, Mr. Bragge preached there, for some time, with great acceptance and popularity, to a crowded audience.*

Upon the death of Mr. Nathaniel Mather, pastor of the congregational church, in Paved-alley, Lime-street, Mr. Bragge was invited to succeed him in the pastoral charge, in conjunction with Mr. John Collins. They were ordained together to the pastoral office, in the year 1698. It is somewhat remarkable, that Mr. Bragge's father, who was living at that time, was pastor to another congregation in the same street. Soon after his ordination, Mr. Bragge removed his lecture from Salters'-Hall, to his own place; and it was observed that this proved a nursery to his church, his labours in this occasional service being owned to the conversion of many souls. Besides the evening lecture, Mr. Bragge preached at Lime-street statedly, in the morning, till the death of Mr. Collins, when, at the unanimous request of the church, he undertook the whole pastoral charge. This he executed with great diligence and fidelity, and with various assistants, till the day of his death.†

A few years after his settlement at Lime-street, Mr. Bragge was chosen one of the Merchants' lecturers, on a Tuesday morning, at Pinners'-Hall. In 1719, when the disputes concerning the Trinity were so warmly agitated, and occasioned the famous synod at Salters'-Hall, Mr. Bragge took a part in the debates of that assembly; and, being a zealous advocate for the doctrine of the Trinity, as likewise for subscribing to the truth of it, he was one of the ministers who signed the roll, and took his lot with the subscribers. Some years after this event, a scheme having been formed for setting up a lecture, at which a course of sermons was to be preached upon the most important doctrines

* MS. *penes me.*   † Ibid.

PAVED-ALLEY, LIME-STREET. — *Independent.*

of the gospel, Mr. Bragge's meeting-house was fixed upon as most conveniently situated for carrying on such a design. It was instituted chiefly under the patronage of William Coward, of Walthamstow, Esq. and nine ministers of considerable abilities, and of known Calvinistic sentiments, of whom Mr. Bragge was one, were selected to preach in their turn. The lecture was opened November 12, 1730, when Mr. Bragge preached an introductory discourse, from Isaiah lix. 19. *When the enemy shall come in like a flood, the Spirit of the Lord shall lift up a standard against him.* In the course of the lecture, he also delivered four sermons upon the doctrine of Justification, from Gal. ii. 16. *Knowing that a man is not justified by the works of the law, but by the faith of Jesus Christ, even we have believed in Christ, that we might be justified by the faith of Christ, and not by the works of the law; for by the works of the law, shall no flesh be justified.* These discourses were afterwards printed in the Lime-street collection.

Mr. Bragge had the felicity of enjoying a good constitution, and was continued in his usefulness, till the infirmities of age grew upon him, and gave warning of his dissolution. At length, after a long course of unwearied labours in the service of his Divine Master, he was taken peacefully to rest, February 12, 1737-8, when he was 72 years of age; having been pastor of the church in Lime-street, almost forty years. His remains were interred in Bunhill-Fields, beneath a handsome tomb, where the remains of the celebrated Mr. John Bunyan, author of the Pilgrim's Progress, are likewise deposited. (1)

(1) Over the vault has been erected a handsome tomb-stone, containing an account of the several persons buried there. As the inscriptions afford us some information relating to Mr. Bragge's family connections, we shall insert them for the satisfaction of the curious reader.

PAVED-ALLEY, LIME-STREET.—*Independent.*

Two discourses were preached and published upon the occasion of Mr. Bragge's death, by the Rev. Thomas Bradbury, from Philip. iii. 8, 9. *That I may win Christ, and*

Here lies the body of Mr. JOHN STRUDWICK,* who died the 15th January, 1697, aged 43 years.

Also the body of Mrs. PHŒBE BRAGGE,† who died the 15th of July, 1718 aged 49 years.

Here also lies the body of the Rev. ROBERT BRAGGE, Minister of the Gospel, who departed this life, February 12, 1737, ætatis 72.

Mr. THEOPHILUS BRAGGE, died September the 25th, 1768, aged 29 years.

Dr. ROBERT BRAGGE,‡ died June 13, 1777, aged 77 years.

Also, Mrs. ANNE JENNION, great grand-daughter of the Rev. ROBERT BRAGGE, died the 9th of February, 1780, aged 62 years.

Also, Mrs. SARAH POOLE, daughter of Mrs. Anne Jennion, died the 9th of September, 1784, aged 32 years. Also lyeth here two of their infant Children.

On the Right Side.

Here also lieth the Remains of Mrs. ANNE HOLYHEAD, Sister of the above-mentioned Mrs. Sarah Poole, who, after having laboured above twelve-months through much pain and weakness, from a fatal fall, calmly resigned her breath, the 2d Nov. 1788, aged 33 years.

Here also lies the precious Remains of a most affectionate Sister, Mrs. ELIZABETH JENNINGS, who died in the Lord the 11th of June, 1798, aged 61 years.

On the Left Side.

Mr. JOHN BUNYAN, author of the Pilgrim's Progress, Ob. 12th August, 1688, æt. 60.

Undisturbed rests here the unfettered clay of Mr. JOHN JENNINGS, late of Newgate Street, who, after many wearisome days and nights, finished well his course the 6th of March, 1800, aged 57 years.

Entombed in this vault the Remains of that once blooming young man, Mr. JOHN LONG, late of Abbott's-Langley, Herts, (a cousin of Mr. Jennings's) who, after enduring the pains of a deep consumption, a few months, willingly resigned his departing spirit, in view of a better state, the 16th of August, 1804, aged 24 years.

At the Foot.

Here rests in hopes of future bliss, the once amiable and much admired youth, Ensign JOSEPH JENNINGS POOLE, of the 3d Regiment of Royal East India Volunteers, who, through a rapid consumption, fell asleep in Jesus, the 31st January, 1799, aged 22 years, and was interred with military honours.

---

* Mr. Strudwick was a grocer on Snow-hill. It was at his house that the celebrated Mr. John Bunyan breathed his last. Hence we account for his being buried in this vault. There feems to have been some family connexion between Mr. Strudwick, and Mr. Bragge. It is probable that the latter married a daughter of the former.

† Probably the Wife of the Rev. Robert Bragge.

‡ A physician, and son to the Rev. Robert Bragge. He seems, also, to have had another son, a portrait-painter.

PAVED-ALLEY, LIME-STREET.—*Independent.*

be found in him. The only mention made of the deceased, is to be found in the following short paragraph. " Our deceased friend, who made it his last request that I should serve you in this place, upon this occasion, has been so well known, that, as you cannot be supposed to want his character, I cannot be expected to give it. Nor would I at all run into the popular vanity now, because that was never his practice, and was always my abhorrence. Very often, funeral enlargements are full of partiality and hypocrisy, and are no less than offering incense to the dead, and no better than laying a snare for the living. I need not mention his affability; his generous and charitable carriage; his easiness of temper under great and uncommon afflictions. Neither he, nor any other, can have a good report, but through faith. But, let me only observe, that this doctrine lived in his soul, and his soul in that. They were pleasant together in life, and at death were not divided. But I will keep my word, and stop short of those enlargements, which he and I have often talked of with a mutual satisfaction."*

In order to supply, in some measure, Mr. Bradbury's deficiency, we shall add a few farther particulars relating to Mr. Bragge's public character. He possessed good advantages for the acquisition of human learning, which he diligently improved by close application to study. To a critical knowledge of the learned languages, he united a familiar acquaintance with the best writers, ancient and modern. He had thoroughly digested the arguments advanced in support of divine revelation, and took great pains in coming at an accurate knowledge of the doctrines of the gospel. His religious sentiments, after mature investigation, came nearest to those of Calvin; but he maintained them with a becoming moderation, and was never transported beyond the rules of decency and good manners. Though his attachments were strong, and he would never sacrifice what he

---

* Mr. Bradbury's Sermon on the death of Mr. Bragge, p. 26.

PAVED-ALLEY, LIME-STREET.—*Independent.*

apprehended to be truth, out of deference to the opinions of others, yet he always maintained the most enlarged charity towards those who differed from him, and honoured the image of his Lord and Master, wherever it was to be found. Amongst those of his own denomination, he was held in considerable repute, and enjoyed the esteeem of many worthy persons of other communions. As a preacher, he was plain, familiar, and serious; and, though his discourses were not the most laboured, yet they were attended with great success; so that he had a flourishing church and congregation to the last. This is the more remarkable, as his method of preaching is said to have been somewhat tiresome. It was his custom, as we are informed, to make the most of his subject, by preaching several discourses upon the same text. There is a story related of him, but for the truth of which we cannot be responsible, that, in one part of his life, he was employed no less than four months in developing the mysteries of Joseph's coat, from Genesis xxxvii. 3. *And he made him a coat of many colours.* In allusion to this circumstance, Mr. Bragge was thus characterized, in some lines descriptive of the Dissenting ministers, at that period:

> Eternal Bragge, in never-ending strains,
> Unfolds the wonders Joseph's Coat contains;
> Of every hue describes a different cause,
> And from each patch a solemn mystery draws.

In reply to the above lines, the following were handed about soon afterwards:

> The unwearied Bragge, with zeal, in moving strains,
> Unfolds the mysteries Scripture-book contains;
> Marks every truth, of error shews the cause,
> And from each mystery useful doctrine draws.

The characters of men have been often misrepresented by the strength of partiality on the one hand, and by the

PAVED-ALLEY, LIME-STREET.——*Independent.*

force of prejudice on the other: in such cases it is safest to steer a middle course. Though we cannot admire the poetic genius displayed in either of the above stanzas, yet, we may conclude from their contents, that there is some foundation for the anecdote above-mentioned. The method of preaching here described, though it might suit the taste of people, at that time, would be extremely unpopular in the present day, when it is customary to exhaust a subject in a single discourse. However, it is certain that Mr. Bragge had a numerous congregation, and it was one of the wealthiest in London, collecting, annually, for the congregational fund, the sum of three hundred pounds. This exceeded what was raised by any other church in London, of either denomination. It was further observed of Mr. Bragge, that he used often to preach against Atheism, Deism, Arminianism, Arianism, Socinianism, Neonomianism, and Antinomianism. But, though he took this freedom in the pulpit, from whence some concluded he was of a censorious temper, yet, it was remarked, that he could never be drawn to speak evil, or to the prejudice of any man's personal character. In private life, he maintained a close walk with God, and was himself an exemplary pattern of the Christian character.*

Besides the five sermons published in the Lime-street collection, Mr. Bragge was the author of " A brief Essay concerning the soul of man; shewing what, and how noble a Being it is. To which is added, A Short Answer to that weighty Inquiry, *Watchman, what of the night?* Occasioned by the cruelty of the Jesuits at Thorn." This tract came to a second edition, in 1725. He left corrected for the press, a small treatise, which appeared after his death, in one volume octavo, entitled, " Church Discipline according to its ancient standard, as it was practised in primitive times. 1739." An appendix was added, containing a short Scriptural Account of a Teaching Elder. It was dedicated

* MS. *penes me.*

PAVED-ALLEY, LIME-STREET.——*Independent.*

to the Manager's of the Pinners'-Hall Lecture, at whose request it was written. In Dr. Williams's Library, Red Cross-street, there is preserved a fine picture of Mr. Bragge, painted by his son. It was copied in mezzotinto, by Faber, in 1738. He is represented sitting in a chair, with his morning gown, and a velvet cap.

PHILIP GIBBS.—Mr. Bragge having succeeded to the whole pastoral charge, after the death of Mr. Collins, the church thought it necessary to provide him an assistant; and the Rev. Philip Gibbs was chosen to that service in 1715. This gentleman continued his connexion with the church in Lime-street, about fourteen years; but, in 1729, he removed to Hackney, to be colleague with the Rev. John Barker. At that place, the reader will find some further account of him.

JOHN ATKINSON.—After the departure of Mr. Gibbs, Mr. Bragge undertook the whole service for about three years; but, in consequence of his growing infirmities, it was judged expedient to appoint him an associate in the ministerial office. The Rev. John Atkinson, a young minister, who had not long finished his studies, which he pursued under Dr. Ridgley, and Mr. Eames, was chosen to the office of teaching-elder, December 4, 1732. It may not be amiss to observe, in this place, that Mr. Bragge looked upon the office of *teaching-elder*, as of divine appointment, and equivalent to that of co-pastor. But he disliked the latter term as unscriptural. His opinion upon this subject may be seen in the Appendix to his Treatise upon Church Discipline. Mr. Atkinson's labours in this office were but of short continuance; for he was removed by death, in the prime of life, in the month of April, 1735.*

* MS. *penes me.*

PAVED-ALLEY, LIME-STREET.—*Independent.*

JOHN HILL.—But a short time elapsed after the death of Mr. Atkinson, before his place was supplied by the Rev. John Hill, who removed from Stoke-Newington. He was ordained to the office of teaching-elder, in Lime-street, May 19, 1735; but, in the following year, accepted a call to become co-pastor with Dr. Ridgley, at the Three-Craues.† Under that article, we shall present the reader with a more particular account of Mr. Hill.

JOHN RICHARDSON.—The vacancy occasioned by the removal of Mr. Hill, was filled up the same year, by the Rev. John Richardson. This gentleman received his academical education under Dr. Ridgley and Mr. Eames. Upon the death of Mr. Bragge, he succeeded to the whole pastoral office. At his first setting out in the ministry, he was much followed, but his popularity afterwards declined. He possessed but slender talents, nor was he, as a preacher, remarkably judicious. He continued to preach in Lime-street, till Christmas 1755, when he resigned the pastoral charge. After this, the meeting-house being taken down, the congregation divided. Mr. Richardson, with part of the people, went to the meeting-house in Artillery-street, then vacant, by the removal of Mr. Hitchin's congregation to White Row.* He continued to preach there till his death; but, for further particulars we refer the reader to that place.

Thus, this ancient church, after subsisting under one form for about a hundred and fifteen years, separated into two branches. Their separate histories will be taken up, in the order we have prescribed to ourselves in the present work.

* MS. *penes me.*

BURY-STREET, St. MARY AXE.

INDEPENDENT.

Duke's-Place, Bury-Street, St. Mary Axe, stands on the site of the dissolved Priory of the Holy Trinity, called Christ Church. It was founded A. D. 1108, by Matilda, Queen of Henry I. through the persuasions of Anselm, Archbishop of Canterbury, and Richard Beaumeis, Bishop of London. After bestowing upon it considerable endowments, she gave the church to Norman, the first Canon Regular in all England, for Canons of the order of St. Augustin. In process of time, this convent swallowed up four parishes, became rich in lands and ornaments, and surpassed all the priories in the same county. It is even reported to have been the richest in England. The prior was always an alderman of London, of Portsoken-Ward; who, if he happened to be exceedingly pious, appointed a substitute to transact temporal matters. On solemn days, he rode through the city, with the other aldermen, but in his monastic habit. At the dissolution of monasteries in the reign of Henry the Eighth, the Priory of the Holy Trinity, on account of its riches, was fixed upon as an early spoil. It was given by that Monarch (July 1531) to Sir Thomas Audley, Speaker of the House of Commons, and afterwards Lord Chancellor. On the site, he erected a noble mansion, in which he resided till his death, in 1544. By the marriage of his daughter and sole-heiress, Margaret, to Thomas Duke of Norfolk, the estate descended to the Howard family, and received the name of Duke's-Place. The Duke losing his head upon Tower-hill, the mansion passed to his eldest son, Thomas Howard, Earl of Suffolk, who sold it, A. D. 1592, to the mayor, commonalty and citizens of London. Some remains of this edifice may still be traced, enveloped in

BURY-STREET, ST. MARY AXE.—*Independent.*

more modern buildings, from which it appears, that the architecture was of the Saxon style. Out of this priory arose the present church of St. James, so called from King James I. in whose reign it was built, A. D. 1622. Formerly, some persons of consideration had their houses in this neighbourhood; such as the Abbots of Bury, corruptly called Bevis Marks; Sir Francis Walsingham; Sir Thomas Wyat; the Earl of Northumberland, &c. The Jews, who form the principal inhabitants, and have four synagogues, settled here, principally, in the time of Oliver Cromwell.*

The meeting-house in Duke's-Place was erected in the year 1708, for the congregation under the care of the celebrated Dr. Isaac Watts. It does not exactly appear where they originally assembled; though it must have been in this neighbourhood. Mr. Caryl, who was the first pastor, resided in Bury-street; and during the latter part of his time, at least, his meeting-house was in Leadenhall-street. In Dr. Chauncey's time, they assembled at the house of a Dr. Clark, in Mark-lane. At Midsummer 1704, they removed on account of the decayed state of the building, to Pinner's-Hall, which they occupied in the afternoon only till 1708, when they took possession of their new meeting-house in Duke's-Place. It was opened on Lord's-day, October the 3d, with suitable exercises of devotion; and the celebrated Mr. Thomas Bradbury preached upon the occasion. The expence of the building was not quite £650. The original contract was with Mr. Charles Great, who leased a part of his garden, viz. forty feet front, and fifty feet in depth, for a term of fifty years, at a ground rent of twenty pounds per annum. It is a large substantial square building, with three galleries of considerable dimensions. A short time since, it underwent a thorough repair, and two new fire-places were built.

The church was collected soon after the Black Bartholo-

---

* Strype's, Maitland's, and Pennant's Histories of London.

BURY-STREET, ST. MARY AXE.—*Independent.*

mew Act, in 1662, by the celebrated Mr. Joseph Caryl, and consisted of some of his former hearers at St. Magnus, London-Bridge. After his death, his people invited the learned Dr. John Owen, then pastor of another society, at no great distance. Both congregations having agreed to unite, they assembled together for the first time, June the 5th, 1673. At the time of their coalescing, the united church consisted of one hundred and seventy-one members; amongst whom were Lord Charles Fleetwood, Sir John Hartopp, Colonel Desborough, Colonel Berry, and other officers of the army; also Lady Abney, Lady Hartopp, Lady Vere Wilkinson, Lady Tompson, Mrs. Bendish, granddaughter of Oliver Cromwell, &c. &c. This church is remarkable for the number of ejected ministers who have presided over it. We have an account of no less than eight of those worthies in this connexion. There has been a considerable variation in the state of the Society for the last century and upwards. Prior to Dr. Chauncey, it appears to have been in a flourishing condition; but in his time it declined. There was a great revival under Dr. Watts, who had a large and respectable audience. During the latter part of Dr. Savage's time, the interest was in a very low state. Though a learned man, and a judicious, as well as evangelical preacher, his labours were not attended with that success which frequently accompanies meaner abilities. At the settlement of the present pastor, it was expected that his popular talents would have a considerable influence in reviving the congregation; but they have failed of that desired effect.

During the year 1733, a course of sermons by several ministers, (K) was preached at this meeting-house, under the patronage of the well-known Mr. William Coward, of Walthamstow. They were published in 1735, under the title

(K) These were Dr. ISAAC WATTS, Dr. JOHN GUYSE, Dr. DAVID JENNINGS, Mr. SAMUEL PRICE, Mr. DANIEL NEAL, and Mr. JOHN HUBBARD.

BURY-STREET, ST. MARY AXE.—*Independent.*

of "Faith and Practice represented in Fifty-four Sermons on the principal Heads of the Christian Religion." Few of our readers need be informed of the merit of the Bury-street Sermons. In January 1798, a lecture to the Jews was set on foot at this place by some ministers of the Calvinistic persuasion, and several discourses delivered here were afterwards printed. But the descendants of Abraham turning a deaf ear to the admonitions of their benevolent instructors, the lecture was discontinued. At present the place is open only for those services usual among Dissenters.

We shall now lay before the reader, a list of those ministers who have been connected with the church in Bury-street, distinguishing pastors from assistants.

Ministers' Names.	As Pastors.		As Assistants.	
	From	To	From	To
Joseph Caryl, M. A.	1660	1673	—	—
William Bearman,	—	—	16..	16..
John Owen, D. D.	1673	1683	—	—
Robert Ferguson,	—	—	16..	16..
David Clarkson, B. D.	1682	1687	—	—
Isaac Loeffs, M. A.	168.	1689	—	—
Isaac Chauncey, M. D.	1687	1702	—	—
Edward Terry, M. A.	—	—	16..	1697
Isaac Watts, D. D.	1702	1748	1698	1702
Samuel Price,	1713	1756	1703	1713
Meredith Townshend,	—	—	1742	1746
Samuel Morton Savage, D. D.	1753	1787	1747	1753
Thomas Porter,	17.	1764	17..	1764
Josiah Thompson,	1765	17..	1765	17..
Thomas Beck,	1788	18..	—	—

BURY-STREET, ST. MARY AXE.——*Independent.*

Joseph Caryl, M. A.—This excellent Divine was born in the city of London, A. D. 1602. His parents were respectable persons; and intending him for the ministry, sent him, at seventeen years of age, to Exeter College, Oxford. There he had the benefit of a good tutor, and in a short time, became a noted disputant. In 1627, he proceeded Master of Arts, and entering into holy orders, preached, for some time, in and about the city of Oxford. Afterwards, removing to London, and being " puritanically affected," as Wood terms it, he was chosen preacher to the honourable Society of Lincoln's-Inn, where he continued several years with good applause. In 1643, he was appointed a member of the assembly of Divines, at Westminster, and became a frequent preacher before the Long Parliament. About the same time, he was constituted one of the licencers of the press. In 1645, he was presented to the living of St. Magnus, near London-Bridge, became a zealous preacher, and continued to do much good till he was ejected soon after the Restoration.*

Mr. Caryl was employed several times by the parliament to attend upon King Charles the First. In January, 1646, he was nominated, together with Mr. Stephen Marshall, chaplain to the Commissioners, who were sent to the King at Newcastle, in order to an accommodation for peace. Removing thence, by easy journies, to Holmby-house, in Northamptonshire, the two chaplains performed divine worship in the chapel there; but the King never attended. He spent his Sundays in private; and though they waited at table, he would not so much as admit them to ask a blessing. (L)

* Wood's Athenæ Oxon. vol. ii. p. 512.

(L) Wood, who mentions this circumstance, relates the following curious anecdote. " 'Tis said that Marshall did on a time put himself more forward than was meet to say grace, and, while he was long in forming his chaps, as the manner was among the saints, and making ugly faces, his Majesty said grace himself, and was fallen to his meat, and had eaten up some part of his dinner, before Marshall had ended the blessing: but Caryl was not so impudent."—*Wood's Athenæ, vol. ii. p. 512. 513.*

BURY-STREET, ST. MARY AXE.—*Independent.*

In September, 1648, Mr. Caryl attended the Commissioners at the treaty of Newport, in the Isle of Wight; and on the 30th of January following, a few hours before the King suffered death, was ordered, with several other ministers, to visit that unhappy prince, and afford him such consolations as were suited to his condition. But he declined their services. In April, 1649, Mr. Caryl, Mr. Nye, and Mr. Marshall were employed by the officers of the army to invite the secluded members to resume their places in the parliament-house. When Oliver Cromwell was sent to Scotland in 1650, Mr. Caryl accompanied him thither, by order of parliament, along with Dr. John Owen. At the latter end of 1653, he was nominated one of the triers for the approbation of public ministers; and, in the following year, an assistant to the commissioners of London, appointed by parliament for displacing ignorant and scandalous ministers, &c. He was also a member of the committee of Independent Divines, who met at the Savoy in 1658, in order to prepare and publish to the world an uniform confession of their faith.* In November, 1659, he accompanied Major-General Whalley, and Colonel Goffe into Scotland, to acquaint General Monk with the true state of affairs in England, and prevent the further effusion of blood. On the 14th of March following, he was again nominated upon the committee for the approval and admission of ministers.† In 1660, soon after the Restoration, he joined with several other ministers in protesting against Venner's plot.‡

Mr. Caryl continued at his living of St. Magnus, till Bartholomew-day, 1662, when he was ejected for nonconformity. After this, he gathered a separate congregation amongst his former hearers, to whom he preached as the times would permit, till death, the great silencer, removed

* Neal's Puritans, vol. ii. p. 506. † Wood's Athenæ Oxon, *ubi supra.*
‡ Neal's Puritans, vol. ii. p. 592.

BURY-STREET, ST. MARY AXE.—*Independent.*

him to his everlasting rest. He died at his house in Bury-street, Feb. 7, 1672-3, aged 71 years.*

Mr. Henry Dorney, in a letter to his brother, gives the following account of Mr. Caryl's death. " That famous and laborious minister, Mr. Joseph Carril, your ancient friend and companion, is departed this life, aged about seventy-one years; his death greatly lamented by the people of God throughout this city. About the beginning of his sickness I was with him, and he inquired concerning you, as he was wont to do; and perceiving him to be somewhat weak, though he did not then keep his chamber, I desired him, while he was yet alive, to pray for you; which motion he cheerfully and readily embraced. And coming to him again, about three days before his death, found him very weak, and past hope of life. He then told me, as well as I could understand him, (for his speech was low), that he had remembered his promise to me concerning you. I think good to mention this particular passage, to provoke you to all seriousness in reference to your own soul, whose eternal welfare lay so much upon the heart of this servant of Christ. His labours were great, his studies incessant, his conversation unspotted, his sincerity, faith, zeal, and wisdom gave a fragrant smell among the churches and servants of Christ. His sickness, though painful, borne with patience, and joy in believing; and so he parted from time to eternity, under full sail of desire and joy in the Holy Spirit. He lived his own sermons. He did at last desire his friends to forbear speaking to him, that so he might retire to himself; which time they perceived he spent in prayer; oftentimes lifting up his hands a little, and at length, his friends seeing not his hands to move, drew near and perceived he was silently departed from them, leaving many mournful hearts behind."†

* Wood, *ubi supra*,—and Noncon. Mem. vol. i. p. 146.
† Dorney's Contemplations, Letter 113. p. 292, 293.

BURY-STREET, ST. MARY AXE.—*Independent.*

Mr. Caryl was a moderate Independent, a very pious and humble man, and of indefatigable industry. Even Wood calls him "a learned and zealous Nonconformist."* He was author of a considerable number of sermons; but his great work is, "A Commentary on the Book of Job," in two folio volumes of a very large bulk. It is also printed in 12 vols. quarto. Though this work possesses very great merit, yet its formidable size has been a great obstruction to its usefulness. One just remark, however, has been made upon its utility, that it is a very sufficient exercise for the virtue of patience, which it was chiefly intended to inculcate and improve.† There is a good abridgment of it in the second volume of Poole's Synopsis. (M)

* Athenæ Oxon. vol. ii. p. 515.

† Granger's Biog. Hist. of England, vol. iii. p. 313.

(M) HIS WORKS.—Several Sermons, as 1. The Works of Ephesus explained in a fast Sermon before the House of Commons, April 27, 1642. Rev. ii. 2, 3.—2. David's Prayer for Solomon. 1643.—3. The Nature, Solemnity, Grounds, Property and Benefit of a Sacred Covenant, &c. preached at Westminster, Oct. 6, 1643. Nehem. ix. 38.—4. The Saint's Thankful Acclamation at Christ's Redemption, of his great Power, and the Initials of his Kingdom: a Thanksgiving Sermon before the House of Commons, April 23, 1644, for the Victory gained by Lord Fairfax at Selby, in Yorkshire. Rev. xi. 16, 17.—5. Arraignment of Unbelief as the grand Cause of our National Non-establishment: a Fast Sermon before the House of Commons, May 28, 1645. Isa. vii. 9.—6. Heaven and Earth embracing, or God and Man approaching: a Fast Sermon before the House of Commons, Jan. 28, 1645. Jam. iv. 8.—7. Joy out-joyed, &c. a Thanksgiving Sermon at St. Martin's in the Fields, Feb. 19, 1645, for the Reduction of Chester by the Parliament Forces under the command of Sir William Brereton. Luke x. 20.—8. England's *plus ultra*, both of hoped Mercies and required Duties: a Thanksgiving Sermon before the Houses of Parliament, Lord Mayor and Aldermen, and Assembly of Divines, April 2, 1646, for the Recovery of the West, and the disbanding 5000 of the King's Horse, &c. Psa. cxviii. 17.—9. A Fast Sermon before the House of Commons, July 29, 1646.—10. A Thanksgiving Sermon before the Parliament at St. Margaret's, Westminster, Oct. viii. 16. Psa. cxi. 1—5. —— 11. A Fast Sermon before the Parliament, Sept. 24, 1656. Jer. iv. 9.—12. A Sermon. 1657.—13. A Fast and Thanksgiving Sermon before the Parliament, in August and October, 1659.—14. Farewell Sermon at St. Magnus, on Rev. iii. 4. 1662.—Expo-

BURY-STREET, ST. MARY AXE.—*Independent.*

WILLIAM BEARMAN.—Our information respecting this gentleman is very confined. Wood takes no notice of him amongst the Oxford writers, so that it is probable he received his education in the University of Cambridge. When the act of Uniformity took place, in 1662, he was Lecturer of St. Thomas's, Southwark. Upon his leaving the congregation at that place, he preached a most affectionate farewell discourse, from Acts xx. 17—38, printed in the London Collection. It is accurately drawn up, and seems to have been his only publication. After his ejectment, he joined himself to Mr. Caryl's congregation, of which he became one of the first members. It is probable that he, also, assisted Mr. Caryl in the ministerial office. We have certain information of his preaching occasionally to this church, as well as to another upon the Pavement, in Moorfields; but, we believe he never undertook any pastoral charge. At the next church-meeting, after the resignation of Dr. Chauncey, April 15, 1701, he was desired to take the chair, and to preach during the church's vacancy; but the latter he declined, probably through age and weakness. Mr. Bearman continued a member of this Society, through its successive changes, till called away by death, October 7, 1703, when he must have been considerably advanced in life.* Dr. Calamy gives him this character: "He was a very pious and sober person, and a good preacher;"† which

---

sition, with practical Observations, on the Book of Job, delivered in several Sermons and Lectures in St. Magnus Church, 2 vols. folio. 1676—1677. with a Portrait of the Author.—The Nature and Principles of Love, as the End of the Commandment, declared in some of his last Sermons. With a Preface by Dr. Owen. 8vo. 1674.—Gospel-Love, Heart-Purity, and the flourishing of the Righteous: being his last Sermon. Lond. 1674-5.—He had a principal hand in the English-Greek Lexicon, containing the Derivations, and various Significations of all the Words in the New-Testament, 8vo. 1661.—Also, in the Saints' Memorial; or Collection of Divine Sentences, by several Presbyterian Ministers. 1674.——*Wood's Athenæ Oxon.* vol. ii. p. 513, 514.

* MS. *penes me.* † Calamy's Account, p. 25.

BURY-STREET, ST MARY AXE.——*Independent.*

is all the Doctor says of him, excepting that he lived many years after his ejectment, in Hoxton-square. In addition to this it may be observed, that he was a man of considerable fortune, and equal benevolence. He left his estate to charitable purposes, but did not defer his charity till after his death. What Cotton Mather says of Mr. John Eliot, the renowned apostle of the Indians, may, with justice, be applied to Mr. Bearman. " He did not put off his charity to be put in his last will, as many, who therein shew that their charity is against their will : but he was his own administrator, he made his own hands his executors, and his own eyes his overseers."* Mr. Bearman erected, in his lifetime, eight alms-houses for poor women, at Hoxton, which he endowed with a yearly stipend, besides a quantity of coals. These have, of late years, been increased. In one of the apartments of these alms-houses, better fitted up than the rest, and which had an opening into his own garden, he used, at stated times, to attend and pray with the poor women, and give them a word of exhortation. The door through which he used to enter is still to be seen, though fastened up. But a much more extensive charity was devised by his will, and left to the discretion of his trustees. From the produce of his estate, the value of which has considerably increased, many necessitous persons in private life, as well as poor Dissenting ministers, have been essentially relieved, and several students for the ministry greatly assisted in their academical studies ; as also, some in grammar-learning, a charity which the Dissenters greatly needed.†

JOHN OWEN, D. D. the prince of modern Divines, derived his pedigree from Lewis Owen, of Kwyn, near Dollegelle, Esq. who was lineally descended from a younger

---

* Mather's History of New-England, B. iii. p. 181.
† Nonconformist's Memorial, vol. i. p. 192.

BURY-STREET, ST. MARY AXE.—*Independent.*

son of Kewelyn ap Gwrgan, prince of Glamorgan, and Lord of Cardiff; this being the last family of the five regal tribes of Wales. From Susan, the daughter of Griffith, the fifth son of the above Lewis Owen, who was married to Humphrey Owen, of the same family, but another line, descended Henry Owen, the youngest of fifteen children. This Henry was bred a scholar, and having passed through his academical studies at Oxford, was, after some time, chosen minister at Stadham, in that county. On account of his extraordinary zeal in the cause of Reformation, he was reckoned a strict puritan. At length, after many years of reputation and usefulness, he died in a good old age, leaving several children, our author being the second son.

JOHN OWEN was born at Stadham, in the year 1616. He received his grammar-learning chiefly under Mr. Edward Sylvester, in All-Saints' parish, Oxford; and made such proficiency in his studies, that at twelve years of age, he was admitted a student in Queen's College. There, he pursued his studies with incredible diligence, allowing himself, for several years, not above four hours sleep in a night; so that he soon made a considerable progress in learning. However, his whole aim at that time, as he himself afterwards confessed, was to raise himself to some eminence in church or state, to either of which he was then indifferent. His father having a large family, could not afford him any considerable maintenance at the University, but he was liberally supplied by an uncle, one of his father's brothers, a gentleman of a good estate in Wales; who having no children of his own, designed to have made him his heir. In 1635, being only nineteen years of age, he proceeded Master of Arts; and continued in the College about two years longer.

About this time, Dr. Laud, Archbishop of Canterbury, and Chancellor of Oxford, having imposed several superstitious rites on the University, under pain of expulsion, they were resisted by Mr. Owen, who having received some

BURY-STREET, ST. MARY AXE.—*Independent.*

impressions of a religious nature, was inspired with a zeal for the purity of divine worship, and a reformation in the church. This change of his judgment soon discovered itself, and his friends immediately forsook him as one infected with Puritanism. Upon the whole, he was become so much the object of resentment to the Laudensian party, that he was forced to leave the College. It was about this time that he became exercised with many perplexing thoughts concerning his spiritual state, which, with his outward troubles, threw him into a deep melancholy that lasted three months; and it was near five years before he attained to a settled peace.

At the commencement of the civil wars, he espoused the cause of the Parliament, which was so strongly resented by his uncle, a zealous loyalist, that he withdrew his favour, and settled his estate upon another person. At this time Providence interposed in his favour. Sir Robert Dormer, of Ashcot, in the parish of Great Milton, took him into his family as chaplain, and tutor to his eldest son, in which employments, he acquitted himself with reputation. He, afterwards, became chaplain to John Lord Lovelace, of Hurley, in Berkshire, who, though a loyalist, treated him with great civility; but going, at length, into the King's army, Mr. Owen came up to London, and took lodgings in Charter-House Yard. On one Lord's-day, going to Aldermanbury church, with a view of hearing Mr. Calamy, it happened that a stranger preached; and though he could never afterwards learn his name, notwithstanding the most diligent inquiry, the discourse was made singularly useful in removing his doubts, and restoring him to that peace and comfort which he enjoyed as long as he lived.

Mr. Owen's bodily health, as well as mental peace being restored, he applied himself to write his " Display of Arminianism," which appeared in 1642, and met with great acceptance from the public. In such esteem was this book held by the ruling party at that time, that it recommended the author to the committee for ejecting scandalous minis-

BURY-STREET, ST. MARY AXE.—*Independent.*

ters, who, through Mr. White, their chairman, presented him to the living of Fordham, in Essex. In this situation he continued about a year and a half, to the great satisfaction of the parish, and adjoining country. During his residence at Fordham, he married his first wife,(N) by whom he had several children, all of whom he outlived. Upon a report that the sequestered incumbent was dead, the patron, who was not well-affected towards Mr. Owen, presented another person to the living. Upon this, the people at Coggeshall, about five miles distant, earnestly invited him to be their minister; and the Earl of Warwick readily gave him the living. There he preached to a more numerous, as well as judicious, congregation, (having seldom fewer than two thousand hearers,) with great success.

Hitherto Mr. Owen had followed the Presbyterian model of church-government, but, upon further inquiry, he became convinced that the congregational plan was most agreeable to the New Testament. His judgment upon this point, he communicated to the world in two distinct publications.(o) At Coggeshall, he formed a church upon con-

(N) Her maiden name is said to have been Rooke; but this is not certain. She was a person of excellent character, and died at the Doctor's house in Charter-House Yard, though in what year is not known. By this lady he had eleven children, who all died young, excepting one daughter, who married a Welch gentleman; but this proving an unhappy match, the Doctor took her home to his own house, where she died of a consumption. He married, for his second wife, the widow of Thomas D'Oyley, Esq. brother to Sir John D'Oyley, of Chishelhampton, near Stadham, Oxfordshire. Her maiden name was Michel, and she descended from a family of eminence at Kingston-Russel, in Dorsetshire. She was a lady of extraordinary piety and good sense; of an affectionate temper; and brought him a considerable fortune, which with his own plentiful income, enabled him to keep his carriage, and country-house at Ealing, near Acton, in Middlesex, where he lived in a very hospitable manner. Mrs. Owen survived the Doctor several years. Her funeral sermon was preached by Dr. Watts, Jan. 30, 1703-4.

(o) See his " Inquiry into Evangelical Churches." 1681, and his " True Nature of Gospel Churches." 1689.

BURY-STREET, ST. MARY AXE.—*Independent.*

gregational principles, which continued in a flourishing condition under a succession of pastors, for many years. But so great a man could not be long concealed. In 1646, he was sent for to preach before the Parliament, as he did frequently afterwards, upon particular occasions, particularly the day after the death of Charles the First. In 1649, previous to his intended departure for Coggeshall, calling to take leave of General Fairfax, with whom he became acquainted at the siege of Colchester, he met with Lieutenant-General Cromwell. As this was their first interview, Cromwell laid his hands upon Mr. Owen's shoulders in a familiar way, saying, " Sir, you are the person I must be acquainted with." Mr. Owen modestly replied, " That will be much more to my advantage than yours." To this Cromwell answered, " We shall soon see that." He then took him by the hand, and leading him into Lord Fairfax's garden, from that time contracted an intimate friendship, which continued till his death. Cromwell being then about to sail with an expedition to Ireland, to take vengeance for the blood barbarously shed in that kingdom, desired Mr. Owen to accompany him thither, and reside in the College at Dublin. Though he would willingly have excused himself from this journey, being desirous of returning to his people at Coggeshall, yet he was obliged to comply. He went to Ireland in a private manner, and continued there about six months, preaching, and superintending the affairs of the College. Afterwards, with Cromwell's leave, he re-embarked for England, and returning to Coggeshall, was received joyfully by his people. But he had scarcely arrived there before he was ordered to London, to preach at Whitehall.

In September, 1650, Mr. Owen was desired by Cromwell to accompany him into Scotland, along with Mr. Caryl; but being averse to the journey, an order of parliament was procured to enforce his compliance. He staid at Edinburgh about half a year, and then returning to England, went once more to Coggeshall, in the hope of spending

BURY-STREET, ST. MARY AXE.—*Independent.*

there the remainder of his days. But Providence had designed him for a more public station, and he was eventually called to preside over the University of Oxford. The first intelligence he had of his preferment was, from one of the weekly newspapers at Coggeshall, which contained the following paragraph: " The House taking into consideration the worth and usefulness of Mr. John Owen, student of Queen's College, Master of Arts, has ordered that he be settled in the deanery of Christ-Church, in Oxford, in the room of Dr. Reynolds." Soon afterwards he received a letter from the principal students of that College, inviting him thither, and expressing their satisfaction in his appointment, which took place March 18, 1651.—Oliver Cromwell, Chancellor of the University, being then in Scotland, and finding it inconvenient to attend to the duties which that office imposed, by an instrument dated Oct. 16, 1652, delegated his authority for the time being, to Mr. John Owen, and some other Divines, who were to hear causes, and take into consideration other matters which required his consent. In the following year (Sept. 26,) he was chosen Vice-Chancellor of the University; and on Dec. 23, 1653, diplomated Doctor of Divinity. (p) About the same time, he was appointed one of the Commissioners for the appro-

(p) Dr. Owen expressed a very great indifference to all titles of distinction. Upon a certain high-churchman refusing to style him *Reverend*, he wrote thus: " For the title of *Reverend*, I do give him notice, that I have very little valued it ever since I have considered the saying of Luther: *Nunquam periclitatur Religio nisi inter Reverendissimos.* (Religion never was endangered except among the most Reverends.) So that he may, as to me, forbear it for the future, and call me as the Quakers do, and it shall suffice. And, for that of *Doctor*, it was conferred on me by the University in my absence, and against my consent, as they have expressed it under their public seal: nor doth any thing but gratitude and respect unto them, make me once own it; and freed from that obligation, I should never use it more: nor did I use it, until some were offended with me, and blamed me for my neglect."—*Defence of Review of Schism, prefixed to* Mr. Cotton's *Defence against* Cawdry, p. 97, 98.

BURY-STREET, ST. MARY AXE.—*Independent.*

bation of public preachers; and a member of the committee for ejecting scandalous and insufficient ministers. In 1654, he was elected burgess for the University of Oxford; but did not sit long in parliament.

For these preferments, Dr. Owen was indebted to the favour and friendship of Oliver Cromwell, who, having eclipsed the power of the Presbyterian party, raised the Independents upon its ruins. The honourable trust now committed to him, he managed with singular prudence for the space of five years. He took care to restrain the vicious, to encourage the pious, and to prefer men of learning and industry. Under his administration, the whole body of the University was reduced into good order, and furnished with a number of excellent scholars, as well as persons of distinguished piety. Towards the Presbyterians as well as Episcopalians, he discovered great moderation. To the former he gave several vacant livings at his disposal, and the latter he was ever ready to oblige. A large congregation met statedly under his eye, to celebrate divine service according to the liturgy of the Church of England, but, though frequently urged, he never gave them the least disturbance. At home, he was hospitable and generous; charitable to the poor, especially to poor scholars; some of whom he took into his family, maintained at his own charge, and gave an academical education. The moderation and gentleness of temper he discovered while in power, gained him universal love and respect; but when occasion required, he could exercise that degree of authority which was necessary to preserve a proper discipline. Such was the high character sustained by Dr. Owen while he presided over the University. As for the ridiculous libels retailed against him by Anthony Wood, they can serve only to expose the folly of that poor illiberal writer. (q) The Rev. James Granger, a

(q) Mr. Wood represents him as a perjured person, a time-server, a hypocrite whose godliness was gain, and a blasphemer; and as if this was

BURY-STREET, ST. MARY AXE.—*Independent.*

worthy conforming clergyman, entertained a more just sense of our author's worth. He speaks of him as a man of more learning and politeness than any of the Independents; and as exceeded by none of that party in probity and piety. "Supposing it necessary (says he) for one of his persuasion to be placed at the head of the University, none was so proper as this person; who governed it several years with much prudence and moderation, when faction and animosity seemed to be a part of every religion."*

Notwithstanding his engagements as Vice-Chancellor, Dr. Owen still redeemed time for his studies; preached every other Lord's-day at St. Mary's, and often at Stadham, as well as other places; and employed himself in writing many excellent books. At the earnest request of the University, he published, in 1653, his *Diatriba de Justitiâ Divinâ*, against the authors of the Racovian Catechism, particularly Crellius and Socinus. In the preface to the Reader, he takes notice, that he was but just returned from the farthermost parts of the island; and from an expedition to foreign countries, whither he had been sent for the sake of the gospel: As also, that his health was somewhat impaired. He dedicated this book to Oliver Cromwell, and mentions

not sufficient, he has also made him a fop. All which means no more than this: That when Dr. Owen entered himself a member of the University of Oxford, he was of the established church, and took the usual oaths; that he turned Independent, preached and acted as other Independents did, took the oath called the Engagement, and accepted of preferment from Cromwell; that he was a man of a good person and behaviour, and liked to go well dressed.—" We must be extremely cautious (says Mr. Granger) how we form our judgment of characters at this period; the difference of a few modes or ceremonies in religious worship, has been the source of infinite prejudice and misrepresentation. The practice of some of the splenetic writers of this period, reminds me of the painter well known by the appellation of *Hellish Brueghel*, who had so accustomed himself to painting of witches, imps, and devils, that he sometimes made but little difference betwixt his human and infernal figures."——*Granger's Biog. Hist. of England*, vol. iii. p. 301, 302.

* *Granger's Biog. Hist. of England*, vol. iii. p. 301.

BURY-STREET, ST. MARY AXE.—*Independent.*

his being advanced, by his means, to the post of Vice-Chancellor. But as he speaks very modestly of himself and his book, so he abstains from those fulsome compliments which it is usual for authors to bestow upon their patrons, especially when so high in power. In 1654, appeared his treatise on "The Saints' Perseverance," in answer to Mr. John Goodwin's book, entitled, "Redemption Redeemed." It is a valuable performance, full of strong reasoning, and written with an admirable spirit. In the preface is to be found a variety of useful matter, describing the reception which this doctrine has met with in various ages of the church. He has, also, some remarks upon Dr. Hammond, and the primitive episcopacy; points out the interpolations in the Epistles of Ignatius; and the forgery of the *Apostolical Constitutions*. In the following year appeared his " Vindiciæ Evangelicæ; or, The Mystery of the Gospel vindicated, and Socinianism examined." This book was chiefly written against Biddle the Socinian, who had published two catechisms upon the plan of the Racovian, drawn up by Valentius Smalcius, which the Doctor likewise examines. It is an accurate and elaborate performance, and was undertaken at the desire of the Council of State. In a large preface, he gives a particular history of the opposition that has been made to the doctrine of the Trinity, especially the Deity of Christ, beginning at Simon Magus, down to his own time. He also points out the disingenuous subterfuges resorted to by the enemies of this doctrine, and the means they made use of to deceive the people.

Dr. Owen continued Vice-Chancellor of the University of Oxford till 1657, when he gave place to Dr. Conant. At the Savoy conference in 1658, he took an active part, and had a principal hand in drawing up the confession of faith of the Congregational Churches. In 1659, not long after Richard Cromwell succeeded to the Protectorate, he was cast out of his deanery, and succeeded by Dr. Edward Reynolds, afterwards bishop of Norwich. The changes in the

BURY-STREET, ST. MARY AXE.—*Independent.*

government that rapidly followed, are well known to every reader of English history. It may be proper to observe, that Dr. Owen has been charged by Mr. Baxter, and some other writers, with having had a considerable hand in Richard's downfal. This, however, he denied, and the writer of his life has taken no small pains in endeavouring to invalidate the charge. After he quitted his public employments in Oxford, he went to reside at Stadham, the place of his birth, where he possessed a good estate; and continued to live there privately till the Restoration. During this recess, his time was employed in preaching, and in writing many useful books, calculated to serve the common interests of religion and learning.

At the accession of Charles the Second, Dr. Owen was not in possession of any preferment in the church, but had collected a congregation at Stadham, where he continued to preach till persecution forced him from place to place, and he, at length, settled in London. Here he contracted an acquaintance with some of the most eminent persons in Church and State, and might have risen to considerable preferment had he chosen to conform. In 1661, was published his Latin treatise, " De Natura, Ortu, Progressu, & Studio veræ Theologiæ." It is a learned and elaborate performance, and was afterwards reprinted at Bremen, in Germany. The next year there came out a book, called, *Fiat Lux*, written by John Vincent Lane, a Franciscan Friar, who, under the pretence of recommending moderation and charity, laboured to draw over his readers to the church of Rome, as the only infallible cure of church divisions. Two impressions of this book were printed before it fell under the Doctor's notice; but it was, at length, sent him by a person of quality, with a desire that he would write a reply. This he readily undertook, and, in the same year, sent forth his " Animadversions on *Fiat Lux*. By a Protestant." This piece meeting with very general acceptance, greatly irritated the friar, who published a sheet or two by

BURY-STREET, ST. MARY AXE.—*Independent.*

way of reply. This produced the Doctor's answer, entitled, "A Vindication of Animadversions on *Fiat Lux.*" 1664. There was some difficulty in obtaining a licence for this performance. The bishops, who were appointed by act of parliament, the principal licencers of books in divinity, having examined it, started two objections. 1. That whenever the Doctor had occasion to mention the evangelists and apostles, even Peter himself, he left out the title of saint. 2. That he endeavoured to prove in this book, that it could not be determined whether Peter was ever at Rome. To the first the Doctor replied, that the title of Evangelist or Apostle, given to them in scripture, was much more glorious than the appellation of saint; for in that name all the people of God were alike honoured: nevertheless, to please them, he yielded to that addition. But, as to the other objection, he would by no means consent to any alteration, unless they could prove him mistaken. Indeed, he rather preferred suppressing the book altogether; and, it is probable, it would never have seen the light, had it not been for the interference of Sir Edward Nicholas, Secretary of State, who wrote to the Bishop of London to grant his licence without any further restraint. This book recommended him to the esteem of the Lord Chancellor Clarendon, who sent for him, through Sir Bulstrode Whitlocke, and after acknowledging the service he had rendered by his late books, assured him, " That he had deserved the best of any English Protestant of late years." He moreover declared, that the church was bound to own and advance him; and, at the same time, offered him preferment if he would conform. The Chancellor also observed, that there was one thing which greatly surprised him, " That he, being so learned a man, and so well acquainted with church-history, should embrace the novel opinion of Independency, for which, in his judgment, so little could be said." The Doctor replied, " That, indeed, he had spent some part of his time in reading over the history of the church; and offered to prove against

BURY-STREET, ST. MARY AXE.—*Independent.*

any bishop whom his lordship might select, that this was the plan of government practised in the church for several hundred years after Christ."—" Say you so (said the Chancellor), then I am much mistaken." They had some farther discourse concerning liberty of conscience, during which the Doctor expressed the most enlarged views upon the subject.

Notwithstanding the service which Dr. Owen had rendered to the Church of England, in his late controversy, he was still persecuted from place to place, so that he began to entertain serious thoughts of leaving his native country. At this period, he received an invitation from his brethren in New-England, who pressed him to remove thither, and take upon him the Presidency of Harvard College. This call, after mature deliberation, he thought fit to accept, and actually made preparations for his voyage: but the court getting scent of his design, he was stopped by particular orders from the King.

About this time, it pleased God to visit the nation with the dreadful calamities of pestilence and fire. These heavy judgments happening at a juncture when religion was banished the court, and some of its brightest ornaments persecuted into corners, was considered by some persons as not a little remarkable. Even Clarendon himself, who was banished his country, in 1667, could not help observing that " his affairs never prospered after the Oxford Act." The laws against nonconformists being somewhat relaxed, Dr. Owen preached in London to a congregation of his own gathering, consisting, among other persons, of many officers in the army. He also set up a lecture to which many persons of quality, as well as eminent citizens, resorted. Taking a journey, upon one occasion, to visit his old friends at Oxford, and look after his family estate, he narrowly escaped being taken by some troopers. After this, he had fresh invitations to New-England, and also to the United Provinces, where he was strongly solicited to become Professor of Divinity in one of the Dutch Universities.

BURY-STREET, ST. MARY AXE.——*Independent.*

In the year 1668, he published his Exposition of the hundred and thirtieth Psalm, in which he treats largely of gospel-forgiveness. It is an excellent performance, and well calculated to afford consolation under distress of mind. In the same year, he gave to the world the first volume of his Exposition upon the Epistle to the Hebrews; the fourth and last volume appeared in 1684. It is not easy to convey to the reader a just idea of the value and usefulness of this laborious and extensive work. It is filled with a great variety of rabbinical and other learning; he has thrown considerable light upon some obscure and difficult texts; and adapted the whole to the faith and comfort of Christians. In several parts, he has enumerated the main arguments of Socinian writers, and obviated their principal objections.

At the latter end of 1669, Mr. Samuel Parker wrote his " Discourse of Ecclesiastical Polity; and the Power of the civil Magistrate in Matters of Religion." It was first preached in the chapel at Lambeth, and afterwards printed by order of the Archbishop of Canterbury. This so inflated his mind that he said to the Earl of Anglesey, " Let us see, my Lord, whether any of your chaplains can answer it." Upon which, Dr. Owen published, in the same year, his " Truth and Innocence vindicated." The publication of this book greatly advanced his reputation, and mortified the pride of his antagonist. Parker was a man of violent passions, without any sense of religion, and of as little decency as virtue. His writings inculcated the most slavish principles of passive obedience, and he shews himself as little acquainted with the rights of conscience, as with the feelings of humanity. Besides Dr. Owen, he met with another formidable opponent in Mr. Andrew Marvel, a gentleman of good sense, remarkable wit, and uncommon integrity. The " Rehearsal Transprosed," which he wrote in answer to Parker, brought down his high spirit, and set him completely at rest.

BURY-STREET, ST. MARY AXE.—*Independent.*

The parliament which met in 1670, fell upon the Nonconformists more furiously than ever. The act against conventicles was revived, and carried through both houses, with a high hand. Dr. Owen was desired to draw up some reasons against it, which were laid before the lords by several eminent citizens and persons of distinction. The paper was entitled, " The State of the Kingdom, with Respect to the present Bill against Conventicles." The whole Bench of bishops voted for this inhuman act, with only two exceptions—Dr. Wilkins, Bishop of Chester, and Dr. Rainbow, Bishop of Carlisle; whose names, on account of their Christian moderation, ought always to be mentioned with honour. (ǫ) This barbarous act was executed with the greatest rigour, to the utter ruin of many families, as well as private individuals.

Upon the death of the Rev. Joseph Caryl, in 1673, Dr. Owen was invited to succeed him in the charge of a very numerous congregation in Leadenhall-street, of which several persons of quality were stated members. As the Doctor was then pastor of another congregation, they both agreed to unite; and the union took place, June 5, 1673. In the following year he published, in folio, " A Discourse concerning the Holy Spirit." This work met with great acceptance at its first appearance, and has, ever since, been held in the highest esteem by serious and judicious Christians. It is indeed, an admirable performance, and the subject managed " with that depth of judgment, solidity of argument, and fervour of piety, which characterize his

---

(ǫ) Bishop Wilkins having spoken against the bill in the house, the King sent for him, and desired him to be quiet. Dr. Wilkins replied, " he thought the act to be an ill thing both in conscience and policy; therefore, as he was an Englishman and a bishop, he was bound to oppose it: and since by the laws and constitution of England, and by his Majesty's favour, he had a right to debate and vote, he was neither afraid nor ashamed to own his opinion in that matter."—*Neal's Puritans, vol* ii. *p.* 671.

theological performances."* A new edition of this work, in three volumes octavo, was published in Scotland, in 1791. About three years afterwards, there appeared a very good abridgment of it, by the Rev. George Burder; and a second impression, with improvements, has very lately be given to the public. Another work of importance and merit produced by our author, made its appearance in 1677, under the title of " The Doctrine of Justification by Faith, through the Imputation of the Righteousness of Christ, explained, confirmed, and vindicated." In this treatise, he pursued a method that evinced more than ordinary judgment and skill. After laying down the scripture doctrine by numerous citations, he applies the whole to the experience of real Christians, and effectually removes the stale objection against its moral tendency. In 1679 appeared his excellent treatise on " The Glorious Mystery of the Person of Christ;" in which he considers his two-fold nature of God and Man, the relation he bears to his church, and the exercise of his Mediatorial office; together with the grounds and reasons of his Incarnation, and the divine honours that are due to him from every real Christian. The piety, zeal, and learning, which run through the whole of this performance, cannot fail to raise the admiration of all who love our Lord Jesus Christ in sincerity.

Thus we see with what faithfulness and diligence this great man employed his talents for the service of the church. He was continually writing something that might contribute to that noble design; and, though it would be tedious, in this place, to give a particular account of every book he published, yet, those we have enumerated, are sufficient to gain him the esteem of every wise and good man. They procured him, at the time, the admiration and friendship of many persons of quality and worth, who took great delight in his conversation. Among these may be enumerated the

* Preface to Burder's Abridgment.

BURY-STREET, ST. MARY AXE.—*Independent.*

Earl of Orrery, the Earl of Anglesea, the Lord Willoughby of Parham, the Lord Wharton, the Lord Berkley, Sir John Trevor, one of the Principal Secretaries of State, &c. &c. Even King Charles himself, and the Duke of York, paid particular respect to him. When the Doctor was at Tunbridge, drinking the waters, the Duke sent for him to his tent, and entered into a long conversation on the subject of Nonconformity. After his return to London, the King did him the like honour, conversed with him for the space of two hours together, and, after assurance of his favour and respect, told him that he might have access to his person as often as he pleased. At the same time the King assured him how sensible he was of the wrong he had done to the Dissenters, declaring himself a friend to liberty of conscience; and, as a proof of his sincerity, gave him a thousand guineas to distribute among those who had suffered most by the late severities. The Doctor had, also, some friends among the dignified clergy, particularly Doctor Wilkins, Bishop of Chester, and Dr. Barlow, Bishop of Lincoln, formerly his tutor. It is well known that Dr. Owen applied to the latter for the release of the celebrated Mr. John Bunyan, who had been confined in jail twelve years upon an excommunication for nonconformity. When the bishop received the Doctor's letter, he told the person who delivered it, that he had a particular kindness for Dr. Owen, and would deny him nothing he could do legally; and desiring his service, said, he would strain a point to oblige him. In this particular, however, he scarcely fulfilled his word. The same bishop, upon one occasion, asked him, " What can you object against our liturgical worship, that I cannot answer?" The Doctor's reply, it seems, occasioned the bishop to pause; upon which the former said, " Don't answer suddenly, but take time till our next meeting," which never happened.

It is not surprising that a life so actively employed, should decline under the weight of growing infirmities. His hard studies, and indefatigable labours in preaching and writing, brought upon him the stone, a distemper common to the studious. This, together with an asthma, made great inroads upon his constitution; frequently laid him aside from public work, and some times confined him to his chamber. During these intervals, he was employed in writing several excellent books. One of these " The Grace and Duty of being Spiritually Minded," appeared in 1681, and was the result of his own meditations not long before his death. He wrote it, as he informs us, " in a season wherein he was every way unable to do any thing for the edification of others, and far from expectation that he ever should be able any more in this world." Great was the attention paid to him by his friends, in his declining years. He had frequent invitations to the country houses of persons of quality, particularly that of Philip Lord Wharton, at Woburn, in Buckinghamshire, where he was visited by many persons of rank, and enjoyed the company of several of his nonconforming brethren; the seat of that nobleman, being an asylum for persecuted ministers. He afterwards resided sometime at Kensington. One day, when coming to town, he was overtaken in the Strand, by two informers, who immediately seized his carriage. Upon this a mob gathered around him; but he was discharged by the interposition of Sir Edmundbury Godfrey, a justice of peace, who happened to be passing at the time. From Kensington, Dr. Owen removed to a house of his own, at Ealing, where he finished his course. He there employed his thoughts on a future state, and composed his excellent " Meditations on the Glory of Christ," in which he breathes the devotion of a soul that was daily ripening for the heavenly world.

As the Doctor was of a cheerful temper, he bore the racking pains which usually accompany the stone, with that patience and resignation which became so great a man, and so excellent a Christian. He was confined above a month, and suffered much by violent pains in his head. His con-

BURY-STREET, ST. MARY AXE.——*Independent.*

versation during this time, was agreeable to the main course of his life, heavenly and spiritual. He expressed much concern on account of the calamitous times, particularly the afflictions of the Nonconformists, which threatened the Protestant churches over Europe. On the morning of the day in which he died, Mr. Thomas Payne, an eminent tutor, and dissenting minister, at Saffron-Walden, in Essex, who was entrusted by the Doctor with the publication of the performance last mentioned, came in to see him, and said, " Doctor, I have just been putting your book, On the Glory of Christ, to the press :" To which Dr. Owen answered, " I am glad to hear that that performance is put to the press ;" and then lifting up both his hands and eyes, as in a kind of rapture, he said, " But Oh! brother Payne, the long looked-for day is come at last, in which I shall see that glory in another manner than I have ever done, or was capable of doing in this world." (R)

(R) The above is a sufficient confutation of the vile calumny propagated by Anthony Wood, who says, " At length, he, the said Dr. Owen, having spent most of his time in continual agitation to carry on the cause, to promote his own interest, and gain the applause of people, he did very unwillingly lay down his head and die, having, a little before, been knowing of, and consenting to the Presbyterian plot, &c." Though the character of Dr. Owen can suffer no injury from the foul pen of this scandalous writer, nevertheless, the following letter, dictated to a friend, will show the temper of his mind in the prospect of dissolution, only two days before his death.

To CHARLES FLEETWOOD, *Esq.*

DEAR SIR,

Although I am not able to write one word myself, yet I am very desirous to speak one word more to you in this world, and do it by the hand of my wife. The continuance of your entire kindness, knowing what it is accompanied withal, is not only greatly valued by me, but will be a refreshment to me, as it is even in my dying hour. I am going to him whom my soul has loved, or rather, who has loved me with an everlasting love ; which is the whole ground of all my consolation. The passage is very irksome and wearisome, through strong pains of various sorts, which are all issued in an intermitting fever. All things were provided to carry me to London to-day, according to the advice of my physician ; but, while the great pilot is in it,

BURY-STREET, ST. MARY AXE.—*Independent.*

In this pious and heavenly frame he departed to the world of glory, on Bartholomew-day (August 24) 1683, in the 67th year of his age. He was speechless for some hours before his death, but very sensible, frequently lifting up his eyes and hands with great devotion. Dr. Cox and Dr. (afterwards Sir Edmund) King, who attended as his physicians, ascribed his dying agonies to the strength of his brain. He was removed from Ealing to Bunhill-Fields, Sept. 4 ; his funeral being attended by sixty-seven carriages belonging to noblemen and gentlemen of his acquaintance, besides many mourning coaches and gentlemen on horseback. Over his vault was erected a monument of freestone, containing the following Latin inscription drawn up by the Rev. Thomas Gilbert, of Oxford :

>JOHANNES OWEN, S. T. P.
>Agro Oxoniensi Oriundus;
>Patre insigni Theologo Theologus ipse Insignior;
>Et seculi hujus Insignissimis annumerandus:
>Communibus Humaniorum Literarum Suppetiis,
>Mensura parum Communi, Instructus;
>Omnibus, quasi bene Ordinata Ancillarum Serie,
>Ab illo jussis suæ Famulari Theologiæ:
>Theologiæ Polemicæ, Practicæ, et quam vocant Casunm
>(Harum enim Omnium, quæ magis sua habenda erat, ambigitur)
>In illa, Viribus plusquam Herculeis, serpentibus tribus,
>Arminio, Socino, Cano, Venenosa Strinxit Guttura:
>In ista suo prior, ad verbi Amussim, Expertus Pectore,
>Universam Sp. Sti Œconomiam Aliis tradidit:
>Et, missis Cæteris, Coluit ipse, Sensitque,
>Beatam quam scripsit, cum Deo Communionem :
>In terris Viator comprehensori in cœlis proximus:
>In Causum Theologia, Singulis Oraculi instar habitus;
>Quibus Opus erat, et copia, Consulendi:
>Scriba ad Regnum Cœlorum usquequoque institutus;
>Multis privatos infra Parietes, a Suggesto Pluribus,

the loss of a poor under-rower will be inconsiderable. Live and pray, and hope and wait patiently, and do not despond ; the promise stands invincible, that he will never leave us nor forsake us. I am greatly afflicted at the distemper of your dear Lady. The good Lord stand by her, and support and deliver her. My affectionate respects to her, and the rest of your relations, who are so dear to me in the Lord. Remember your dying friend with all fervency. I rest upon it that you do so, and am your's entirely,

August 22, 1683. J. OWEN.

BURY-STREET, ST. MARY AXE.—*Independent.*

A Prelo omnibus, ad eundem scopum collineantibus,
Pura Doctrinæ Evangelicæ Lampas Præluxit ;
Et sensim, non sine aliorum, suoque sensu,
    Sic prælucendo Periit,
    Assiduis Infirmitatibus Obsiti,
    Morbis Creberrimus Impetiti,
Durisque Laboribus potissimum Attriti, Corporis,
(Fabricæ, donec ita Quassatæ, Spectabilis) Ruinas,
   Deo ultrà Fruendi Cupida, Deseruit ;
Die, à Terrenis Protestatibus, Plurimis facto Fatali ;
   Illi, à Cœlesti Numine, felici reddito ;
Mensis Scilicet Augusti XXIVº. Anno à Partu Virgineo.
   M.DC.LXXXIIIº. Ætat. LXVIIº,

Translation.

JOHN OWEN, D.D.
Born in the County of Oxford,
The son of an eminent Minister,
Himself more eminent,
And worthy to be enrolled
Among the first Divines of the age.
Furnished with human literature
   In all its kinds,
   And in all its degrees,
He called forth all his knowledge
   In an orderly train
To serve the interests of Religion,
And minister in the Sanctuary of his God.
In Divinity, practic, polemic, and casuistical,
He excelled others, and was in all equal to himself.
The Arminian, Socinian, and Popish errors,
Those Hydras, whose contaminated breath
And deadly poison infested the Church,
He, with more than Herculean labour,
Repulsed, vanquished, and destroyed.
The whole economy of redeeming grace,
Revealed and applied by the Holy Spirit,
He deeply investigated and communicated to others,
Having first felt its divine energy,
According to its draught in the Holy Scriptures,
Transfused into his own bosom.
Superior to all terrene pursuits,
He constantly cherished, and largely experienced,
That blissful communion with Deity
He so admirably describes in his writings.
While on the road to Heaven
   His elevated mind
   Almost comprehended
   Its full glories and joys.
When he was consulted
   On cases of conscience
   His resolutions contained

BURY-STREET, ST. MARY AXE.—*Independent.*

>The wisdom of an Oracle.
>He was a scribe every way instructed
>In the mysteries of the kingdom of God.
>In conversation he held up to *many*,
>In his public discourses to *more*,
>In his publications from the press to *all*,
>Who were set out for the celestial *Zion*,
>The effulgent lamp of evangelical truth
>To guide their steps to immortal glory.
>While he was thus diffusing his divine light,
>With his own inward sensations,
>And the observations of his afflicted friends,
>His earthly tabernacle gradually decayed,
>Till at length his deeply sanctified soul,
>Longing for the fruition of its God,
>Quitted the body: in younger age
>A most comely and majestic form;
>But in the latter stages of life,
>Depressed by constant infirmities,
>Emaciated with frequent diseases,
>And above all crushed under the weight
>Of intense and unremitting studies,
>It became an incommodious mansion
>For the vigorous exertions of the spirit
>In the service of its God.
>He left the world on a day
>Dreadful to the Church
>By the cruelties of men,
>But blissful to himself
>By the plaudits of his God,
>August 24, 1683, aged 67.

Dr. Owen was formed by nature to command attention, and his personal as well as mental accomplishments eminently qualified him to be the leader of a party. Tall in stature, he possessed a grave aspect, a comely and majestic figure, and his deportment was every way that of a gentleman. His large capacity of mind, ready invention, and good judgment, being improved by education, rendered him a person of incomparable abilities. Of the university, over which he presided, he was one of the brightest ornaments; a perfect master of the languages, and thoroughly versed in the ancient writers. Even Anthony Wood, after much abuse, speaks of him, from his own knowledge, as " a person well skilled in the tongues, rabbinical learning, Jewish rites and customs; that he had a great command of his English pen, and was one of the most genteel and fairest writers who have appeared against the

BURY-STREET, ST. MARY AXE.—*Independent.*

Church of England." Dr. Stillingfleet observes, " Our author treated him with civility and decent language, for which he thanked him;" and Mr. Dodwell, who would not allow the Nonconformists to be Christians, says, that " he was of a better temper than most of his brethren, as abstaining from personal slanders, and confining himself wholly to the cause." His numerous writings afford convincing proof of his abilities as a divine; that he was well skilled in polemical divinity, and familiarly acquainted with the writers of the primitive church. He was an excellent preacher, possessed a persuasive elocution, and could move the affections of his hearers at pleasure. Though his sermons were mostly delivered without notes, they were studied and well digested; so that he could at any time, without premeditation, deliver himself pertinently upon any subject. With his immense stores of learning, he possessed a remarkable facility in resolving cases of conscience, and addressing persons under temptation, desertion, and affliction. As to his temper, he was affable, courteous, and sociable; a great master of his passions, and of such a moderate healing spirit, that, had others been like-minded, the divisions which then agitated the church, would easily have been prevented. It ought to be mentioned to the honour of Dr. Owen, that he seems to have been one of the first of our countrymen who entertained just and liberal notions of the right of private judgment, and of toleration. His sentiments on these subjects he was honest enough to avow, when he was at the summit of preferment, as he continued to do afterwards in his writings; and he supported the generous principles afterwards maintained by Mr. Locke. His singular worth engaged the respect of many considerable persons at home and abroad. Some foreign divines having read his Latin discourses, applied themselves to learn the English language, that they might enjoy the benefit of his other Works; and not a few took journies to England, on

BURY-STREET, ST. MARY AXE.—*Independent.*

purpose to converse with him.* His labours as a minister and a writer were incredible: Of the latter, the reader will form some judgment by the list of his printed Works inserted below. (s)

* Life of Dr. Owen prefixed to his Sermons in folio and octavo.—Wood's Athenæ, Oxon. vol. ii. p. 737-747.—Nonconformist's Memorial, vol. i. p. 198-208.

(s) HIS WORKS.—*Folio.* 1. The Doctrine of the Saints' Perseverance explained and confirmed. 1654.—2. An Exposition of the Epistle to the Hebrews. 4 vols. 1668-1684.—3. A Discourse of the Holy Spirit. 1674.— 4. A complete Collection of his Sermons formerly published, with others never before printed: Also several Tracts now first published from MSS. with others grown very scarce; viz. 1. Several practical Cases of Conscience resolved. 2. Of Marrying after Divorce in Case of Adultery. 3. Of Infant Baptism. 4. A Word of Advice to the Citizens of London. 5. The State of the Kingdom. 6. An Account of the Grounds and Reasons why Protestant Dissenters desire their Liberty. 7. The Case of Present Distresses on Nonconformity examined. 8. A Letter concerning the Matter of the present Excommunications. 9. An Answer to this Question: May a true Church Err or Mistake in administering Church Censures? 10. Some short Reflections on a slanderous Libel against the Doctor. 11. Five *Latin* Orations when he was Vice-Chancellor of Oxford. To this Volume are prefixed, some Memoirs of the Doctor's Life, with several of his Letters; and his Funeral Sermon, preached by Mr. Clarkson. *Lond.* 1721.

Quarto. 1. A Display of Arminianism. 1643.—2. The Duty of Pastors and People distinguished. 1644.—3. Salus Electorum, Sanguis Jesu: Or, The Death of Death, in the Death of Christ. 1648.—4. Of the Death of Christ. 1650.—5. Vindiciæ Evangelicæ: Or, The Mystery of the Gospel vindicated, &c. in Answer to J. Biddle. 1655.—6. Of Communion with God; Father, Son, and Holy Spirit. 1657.—7. Θεολογουμενα: Sive de Naturâ, Ortu, Progressu, & Studio Veræ Theologiæ. 1661.—8. An Exposition of the 130th Psalm. 1668.—9. The Doctrine of Justification by Faith through the imputed Righteousness of Christ, explained, &c. 1677.—10. The glorious Mystery of the Person of Christ, God and Man. 1679.—11. The Grace and Duty of being Spiritually-Minded. 1681.—12. An Enquiry into the Original, Nature, Institution, Power, Order, and Communion of Evangelical Churches. 1681.—13. The true Nature of a Gospel Church, and its Government. 1689.—14. A Review of the Annotations of Grotius. 1656.—— 15. A Discourse concerning Liturgies and their Imposition. 1662.—16. Indulgence and Toleration considered, in a Letter. 1667.—17. A Peace Offering, or Plea for Indulgence. 1667.—18. The Church of Rome no safe Guide. 1679.—19. Some Considerations about Union among Protestants. 1680.—20. A Vindication of the Nonconformists from the Charge of

BURY-STREET, ST. MARY AXE.—*Independent.*

ROBERT FERGUSON was a native of Scotland. It does not appear when he came into England; but at the Restoration he was in possession of the living of Godmarsham, in Kent, which he was obliged to relinquish on Bartholomew-Day, 1662. After his ejectment, he taught university-learning at Islington, and preached as assistant to Dr. Owen; but, at length, ran so far into political matters as to fall under general censure. He was very intimate with Lord Shaftes-

Schism. 1680.—21. An Account of the Nature of the Protestant Religion. 1682.—22. Three Sermons in the Morning Exercises.

Octavo. 1. Two Catechisms. 1645.—2. Eshcol: Or, Rules for Church-Fellowship. 1648.—3. Diatriba de Justitia Divina. 1653.—4. Of the Mortification of Sin in Believers. 1656.—5. A Discovery of the true Nature of Schism. 1657.—6. A Review of the true Nature of Schism, with a Vindication of Congregational Churches. 1657.—7. Of the Nature and Power of Temptation. 1658.—8. A Defence of Cotton against Cawdry. 1658.—9. Exercitationes Quatuor pro Sacris Scripturis. 1658.—10. The Divine Original and Authority of the Scriptures. 1659.—11. A Primmer for Children. 1660.—12. Animadversions on Fiat Lux. 1662.—13. Vindication of those Animadversions. 1664.—14. A brief Instruction in the Worship of God. 1667.—15. The Nature of indwelling Sin. 1668.—16. Truth and Innocence vindicated; in a Survey of a Discourse of Ecclesiastical Polity. 1669.—17. A brief Vindication of the Doctrine of the Trinity. 1669.—18. Of the Sabbath, and the Divine Institution of the Lord's Day. 1671.—19. Of Evangelical Love, Church Peace, and Unity. 1673.—20. A Vindication of his Book of Communion with God, from the exceptions of Sherlock. 1674.—21. The Nature of Apostacy from the Profession of the Gospel. 1676.—22. The Reason of Faith in the Scriptures. 1677.—23. The Ways and Means of Understanding the Mind of God in the Scriptures. 1678.—24. An humble Testimony to the Goodness and Severity of God in his dealing with sinful Churches and Nations. 1681.—25. The Work of the Holy Spirit in Prayer. 1682.—26. Meditations on the Glory of Christ in his Person and Offices. 1684.—27. Of the Dominion of Sin and Grace. 1688.—28. Two Discourses of the Work of the Spirit. 1693.—29. Evidences of the Faith of God's Elect. 1695.——30. Thirteen Sermons, from a MS. in the possession of Mrs. Cooke, of Newington, and never before printed. Besides these, he had a hand in the English Annotations begun by Matthew Poole; and wrote Prefaces to several other Works, as Clark's Annotations; the Works of Dr. Thomas Taylor; Durham on Solomon's Song; Scudder's Christian's Walk; Powel's Concordance; Gale on Jansenism; Caryl's Sermons; Ashwood's best Treasure, &c.

BURY-STREET, ST. MARY AXE.—*Independent.*

bury, whom he followed into Holland; but returned with the Duke of Monmouth in 1685, and was with his army in the West. After the defeat of that unfortunate prince, Mr. Ferguson made shift to escape, and retired again to Holland. He continued there till the Revolution, in 1688, when he came over with King William, who gave him a good place. In a little time, however, he became disgusted, plotted against his benefactor, and was ever after the boldest and most active man of the Jacobite party. He was, indeed, a man by himself, and behaved so that his brethren in the ministry were ashamed of him. Always plotting, he found a way to escape : it is somewhat singular, that though he was in the first proclamation published by King Charles the Second, upon occasion of what was called *The Presbyterian Plot*, and warrants were issued to seize the accused persons, yet Legat the messenger had strict charge from Mr. Secretary Jenkyns, not to take Mr. Ferguson, but to let him escape. This is a mystery not to be unravelled without supposing him a state intelligencer, employed to betray others. The latter part of his life he spent in the same continual agitation; embroiled himself with the government of Queen Anne; and, at length, died very poor and low, in the year 1714.* Bishop Burnet, who was well acquainted with the history of those times, gives him the following character. " Ferguson was a hot and bold man, whose spirit was naturally turned to plotting : he was always unquiet, and setting people on to some mischief: I knew a private thing of him, by which it appeared he was a profligate knave, and could cheat those that trusted him entirely. He was cast out by the Presbyterians, and then went among the Independents, where his boldness raised him to some figure, though he was at bottom a very empty man. He had the management of a secret press, and of a purse that maintained it, and gave about most of the pam-

* Calamy's Account, p. 383, 384. Contin. p. 544.

BURY-STREET, ST. MARY AXE.—*Independent.*

phlets wrote on that side. With some, he passed for the author of them; and such was his vanity, because this made him more considerable, that he was not ill-pleased to have that believed, though it only exposed him so much the more"* (T)

DAVID CLARKSON, B. D.—This excellent Divine, who succeeded Dr. Owen in the pastoral charge of the Society now under consideration, was born at Bradford, in Yorkshire, in the month of February, 1621-2. At an early age, he was sent to the University of Cambridge, where he made great proficiency in his studies, became Fellow of Clare-Hall, and a noted tutor in his College. Among others whom he had under his care, was the celebrated Dr. John Tillotson, who always maintained for him that singular respect which he had contracted while under his tuition.† In a course of time, he was presented to the living of Mortlake, in Surry, which he held till Bartholomew-day, 1662, when he was ejected for nonconformity. After this, he gave himself up to reading and meditation, shifting from one place of obscurity to another, till the times suffered him to appear openly. He was chosen co-pastor with Dr. Owen, in July, 1682, and upon the Doctor's death, in the following year, succeeded to the whole charge. In this situation, he continued till his own death, which was sudden and unexpected; yet, as he declared, no surprise to him; for he was entirely resigned to the will of God, and desired to live no longer than he could be serviceable. " His soul (says

---

* Burnet's History of his own Time, vol. i. p. 542.

(T) Mr. Ferguson published, A sober Inquiry into the Nature, Measure, and Principle of Moral Virtue. 1673.—The Interest of Religion; with the import and use of Scripture Metaphors, and some Reflections on Mr. Sherlock's Writings, particularly his Discourse on the Knowledge of Christ. 1675.—A Discourse concerning Justification.—And many political Pamphlets; among the rest, The Duke of Monmouth's Manifesto, on his landing at Lyme. 1685.

† Birch's Life of Tillotson, p. 4.

BURY-STREET, ST. MARY AXE.—*Independent.*

Dr. Bates) was supported with the blessed hope of enjoying God in glory. With holy Simeon, he had Christ in his arms, and departed in peace to see the salvation of God above," June 14, 1686, in the 65th year of his age. His funeral sermon was preached by Dr. Bates, on John iv. 2. *In my Father's house are many mansions, &c.* *

Mr. Clarkson's character is thus drawn by the Doctor. " He was a man of sincere godliness, and true holiness, which is the divine part of a minister, without which all other accomplishments are not likely to be effectual for the great end of the ministry, that is, to translate sinners from the kingdom of darkness, into the kingdom of God's dear Son. That he might be thoroughly furnished for his work, he diligently improved his time for the acquisition of knowledge; being very sensible (to use his own words), *That the blood of the soul runs out in wasted time.* In humility and modesty he greatly excelled. These noble qualities led him to conceal his name from the public in some excellent publications, which discovered his learning and judgment. He was well satisfied to serve the church, and illustrate the truth, while he remained in his beloved secrecy. His temper was calm, not ruffled with passions, but gentle and kind; and in his controversial writings, he displayed an equal tenor of mind. In his conversation a comely gravity, mixed with an innocent cheerfulness, attracted universal respect and love. In the discharge of his sacred work, his intellectual abilities, and holy affections were very evident. He discovered a striking solemnity in prayer, and his preaching was very instructive, and persuasive. The matter of his sermons was always judiciously derived from his text, and remarkable for depth and clearness. In his language, there was neither a rude neglect, nor gaudy display of eloquence. Whilst

---

* Calamy's Account, p. 667.—Continuation, p. 813, 814.—Nonconformist's Memorial, vol. iii. p. 109, 304.—Neal's History of the Puritans, vol. ii. p. 776.

BURY-STREET, ST. MARY AXE.—*Independent.*

opportunity continued, with alacrity and diligence, and constant resolution, he served his blessed Master, till a languishing distemper extinguished the lamp of life, and removed him to a more noble employment in heaven."* The excellent Mr. Richard Baxter speaks of Mr. Clarkson as " A Divine of extraordinary worth for solid judgment, healing moderate principles, acquaintance with the fathers, great ministerial abilities, and a godly upright life."†

As an author, Mr. Clarkson gained most celebrity by his treatise entitled, " No Evidence of Diocesan Episcopacy in the primitive Times;" 1681, 4to. in answer to Dr. Stillingfleet. " This book (says Mr. Granger) shows him to have been a man of great reading in church-history."‡ He also published a discourse against the Romanists, in 4to. entitled, " The Practical Divinity of the Papists proved destructive of Christianity and Men's Souls." Likewise two Sermons in the Morning Exercises, one at Cripplegate, the other against Popery; and a funeral sermon for Dr. Owen, prefixed to the collection of the Doctor's sermons. After his death was published, A Discourse on *Free Grace;* another on *Episcopacy;* and a third against *Liturgies.*§ In 1696, there came from the press a collection of his sermons in one large volume folio; to which was prefixed, a fine portrait of the author, engraved by White. Mr. Rowe and Mr. Mead introduced them to the world with the following short preface: " The Rev. Mr. Clarkson was so esteemed for his excellent abilities, that there needs no adorning testimony, to those who knew him; and the following sermons, wherein the signatures of his spirit are very conspicuous, will sufficiently recommend his worth to those who did not know him. They are printed from his original

---

* Funeral Sermon for the Rev. David Clarkson, *apud,* Bates's Works, p. 749, 750.
† Reliquiæ Baxtrianæ, P. iii. p. 97.
‡ Granger's Biog. Hist. of England, vol. iii. p. 310.
§ Calamy's Account, p. 667, 668.

BURY-STREET, ST. MARY AXE.—*Independent.*

papers, and, with the divine blessing, will be very useful to instruct and persuade men to be seriously religious."* Mr. Granger, above quoted, says, " These sermons are esteemed judicious; are written in an unaffected syle and good method."†

Isaac Loeffs, M. A. educated in Peter-House, Cambridge, of which he became Fellow. Dr. Calamy has preserved the following testimonial to his character, while at the University, by Dr. Lazarus Seaman, Master of the College. " These are to certify whom it may concern, that Isaac Loeffs, M. A. of the last year, and Fellow of Peter-House, Cambridge, is of a godly life and conversation, orthodox in judgment, and well affected to the parliament. In witness whereof I have subscribed my hand, La. Seaman, Magr. C. S. P." Dated Sept. 9, 1648. After this follows the Latin testimonial of Henry Rich, Earl of Holland, Chancellor of the University of Cambridge, dated Dec. 9, in the same year; certifying that Mr. Isaac Loeffs was admitted to the degree of Master of Arts, at the appointed time, and annual commencement, in 1648, and that he was a discreet person, whose learning, good life, and laudable conversation, qualified him for that degree, and could not be called in question by the envy of slanderous, or malice of insidious persons, &c. In the year 1652, Mr. Loeffs was presented to the living of Shenley, in Hertfordshire, vacant by the resignation of Mr. Stephen Jones, in 1650. The patron of the living was John Crew, of Crew, in the county of Chester, Esq. who had transferred his right of nomination to three of the parishioners, from whom Mr. Loeffs received a legal presentation. Mr. Loeffs continued in possession of this living till the Restoration, when he was ejected for nonconformity. Some time afterwards he came to London, and was chosen lecturer of St. Magnus, London-

---

* Preface to Mr. Clarkson's Sermons. † Granger, *ubi supra.*

BURY-STREET, ST. MARY AXE.—*Independent.*

Bridge, but was deprived of this situation also, by the act of Uniformity, in 1662. After this, as Dr. Calamy informs us, he became assistant to Dr. Owen, in his gathered church. It is probable, however, that he was co-pastor with Mr. Clarkson, whom he succeeded. In the church-book, his name stands in the list of pastors, immediately after the latter. We know nothing further concerning him, excepting that he died July 10, 1689.* Mr. Loeffs published a treatise on " The Soul's Ascension in a State of Separation." 8vo. 1670.

ISAAC CHAUNCEY, M. A. and M. D. eldest son of Mr. Charles Chauncy, minister of Ware, in Hertfordshire, of whose sufferings in the High Commission Court, Rushworth has preserved a particular account.† He was suspended and silenced by Archbishop Laud, for refusing to read the book of sports; and having suffered for nonconformity by fines and imprisonment in his own country, became an exile in New-England. He arrived there in 1638, and upon the removal of Mr. Dunstar, was made President of Harvard College, in which office he continued till his death, Feb. 2, 1671, leaving six sons, all bred to the ministry. Their names were Isaac, the subject of the present memoir; Ichabod, one of the ministers silenced by the Bartholomew Act, and afterwards an eminent physician in Bristol; Barnabas, Nathaniel, Elnathan, and Israel, all ministers in New-England. It was observed of all the sons, that, like their excellent father, they had a skill in medicine added to their other accomplishments.‡

Isaac Chauncey was born at Ware, in Hertfordshire, but

* Calamy's Account, p. 33, 360.—Contin. p. 36, 524.—Nonconformist's Memorial, vol. ii. p. 312, 313.
† Rushworth's Historical Collections for the year 1629.
‡ Mather's Hist. of New-England, B. iii. p. 140.

BURY-STREET, ST. MARY AXE.—*Independent.*

in what year is not mentioned. He could not, however, have been more than two or three years of age when his father removed to New-England. His mind having been formed by a preparatory course of education, he was entered a student at Harvard College, in the year 1651, at the same time with his brother Ichabod Chauncey. It is probable that he finished his studies in England, either at Oxford or Cambridge. Some little time before the Restoration, he was presented to the living of Woodborough, in Wiltshire, where he continued till the act of Uniformity ejected him, in 1662. After this he removed to Andover, where he was pastor of a congregational church, which met in the same place of worship with another congregation under the pastoral care of the Rev. Samuel Sprint. This latter gentleman attempted a coalition between the two churches, and had brought Dr. Chauncey to give his consent; but some of the people opposed and frustrated the design. Having quitted Andover sometime after the recalling of King Charles's Indulgence, he came to London, with a design of acting chiefly as a physician. Here, in the month of October, 1687, he had a call to succeed Mr. Clarkson in the pastoral office, in conjunction with Mr. Loeffs. In this situation he continued fourteen years; and during his time, the church met at the house of a Dr. Clark, in Mark-lane.

Dr. Chauncey was a Divine of considerable learning; but rigid in his principles, and very unpopular as a preacher. He greatly distinguished himself in the controversy that followed the publication of Dr. Crisp's works, by his zeal against Dr. Williams, and what was then called the Neonomian doctrine. This he frequently made the subject of his ministry. But what rendered him chiefly unpopular, was his frequent preaching upon the order and discipline of gospel churches, by which he, at last, preached away most of his people.* This determined him, at length, wholly to

* MS. *penes me.*

BURY-STREET, ST. MARY AXE,—*Independent.*

quit the ministry, and no entreaties could prevail with him to the contrary. He resigned his charge, April 15, 1701, and, not long afterwards, Mr. (afterwards the celebrated Dr.) Isaac Watts, was chosen his successor. After his removal to London, Dr. Chauncey was chosen tutor of a new academical institution, among the Nonconformists of the Congregational persuasion, over which he presided till his death, Feb. 28, 1712. (u) He was succeeded by those learned persons Dr. Thomas Ridgley, and Mr. John Eames.* The institution still exists, at Homerton, under the superintendence of the Rev. John Pye Smith, D. D. and is known by the name of the Fund-board Society.

EDWARD TERRY, M. A. was son to the Rev. Edward Terry, rector of Great Greenford, in Middlesex, who accompanied Sir Thomas Roe, in his embassy to the Great Mogul, at whose court he resided for more than two years. Wood speaks of him as "An ingenious and polite man, of a pious and exemplary conversation, a good preacher, and much respected by the neighbourhood where he lived." He died Oct. 8, 1660.†

Greenford was probably the birth-place of his son Edward Terry, who pursued his studies in University College, Oxford, of which he became fellow, and where he took his degree of M. A. Here he devoted himself, for many years, to the instruction of youth, in which employment he was made very useful. He also obtained great fame for his

(u) Dr. Chauncey published, The Divine Institution of Congregational Churches.—The Interest of Churches: or, a Scripture Plea for Steadfastness in Gospel Order. 1690.---Neonomianism Unmasked: or, the ancient Gospel pleaded against the other called, A new Law or Gospel. 1692.---An Essay on the Interpretation of the Angel Gabriel's Prophecy, Daniel ix. 24.— Christ's Ascension to fill all Things; a Sermon at Horsleydown, &c.—The Doctrine according to Godliness; in the Way of Catechism. 1700.

* Calamy's Account, p. 761. Contin. p. 877. Nonconformist's Memorial, vol. iii. p. 380.

† Wood's Athenæ Oxon. vol. ii. p. 253.

BURY-STREET, ST. MARY AXE.—*Independent.*

exercises in the University; particularly for his funeral oration at the interment of Dr. Joshua Hoyle, the Master of his College, Regius Professor of Divinity in the University, and a Member of the Assembly of Divines. Mr. Terry succeeded his father in the living of Great Greenford, to which he was admitted, Feb. 27, 1661.* He did not, however, enjoy it long, being ejected for nonconformity, on Bartholomew-day, in the following year. After this, we hear nothing further of him till the time of the Revolution; when he was assistant to Dr. Chauncey. He continued a member of the church after he was incapacitated for preaching, which was several years before his death; but he took great pleasure in hearing others read to him. Dr. Calamy gives him the character of a man " Of a very mild disposition, of a blameless life, and very charitable; much honoured for his work's sake, and a lover of peace and truth." After enjoying a greater measure of health than most men, he was suddenly removed in a lethargic fit, which seized him about ten o'clock at night, on March 7, 1715-6, and carried him off at two o'clock the next morning.† He must have been considerably advanced in life.

ISAAC WATTS, D. D.—This illustrious Divine was born July 17, 1674, at Southampton, where his father kept a respectable boarding-school, for young gentlemen. He was an intelligent and pious man, a Dissenter from principle, and deacon in the congregation at Southampton. It appears that he possessed some paternal property; but was much injured in his circumstances by the persecutions of the times, having been more than once imprisoned for nonconformity. During his confinement, Mrs. Watts has been known to sit on a stone near the prison-door, suckling her infant son Isaac. Notwithstanding this, Mr. Watts reared a large family with much respectability, and died in a good old

* Newcourt's Repertorum, vol. i. p. 615.
† Calamy's Account, p. 472. Contin. p. 614.

BURY-STREET, ST. MARY AXE.—*Independent.*

age, Feb. 10, 1736-7;* " having the happiness indulged to few parents, of living to see his son eminent for literature, and venerable for piety."†

The Doctor was the eldest of nine children, and given to books from his infancy. Before he could speak plain, when he had any money given him, he would run to his mother and cry, " A book! a book! buy a book!" At four years old he began to learn Latin; and about seven, to lisp in poetic numbers. Good Mrs. Watts, it seems, sometimes employed the pupils, after school hours, in writing a few lines, for which she rewarded them with a farthing. On one of these occasions, her son Isaac being required to do the same, his aspiring muse indited the following couplet:

" I write not for a farthing, but to try
How I your farthing writers can outvie."

At an early age, he was placed under the care of Mr. Pinhorne, a clergyman of the establishment, and master of the free-school in Southampton; (x) to whom, at the age of twenty, his grateful muse dedicated an elegant Latin ode. His early proficiency in learning, being noticed by Dr. Speed, the physician, and some other gentlemen, they proposed to raise a subscription for his support at one of the universities; but, notwithstanding the disadvantages of the times, Mr. Watts chose rather to take his lot with the Dissenters. " Such he was (observes Dr. Johnson) as every Christian church would rejoice to have adopted."

At sixteen years of age, he was sent to an academy in the vicinity of London, under the superintendence of the

* Gibbons's Life of Watts, p. 1.
† Johnson's Lives of the English Poets; art. Watts.
(x) Mr. Pinhorne was Rector of All-Saints in the same town, Prebendary of Leckford, and Vicar of Eling in the New-Forest, Hants. He was held in repute for learning, and bore the character of a worthy man. A monument was erected to his memory at Eling, bearing this inscription: Here lies the body of the Rev. Mr. John Pinhorne, Prebendary of Leckford, and Vicar of Eling, who died June 8, 1714, aged 62."

BURY-STREET, ST. MARY AXE.—*Independent*.

Rev. Thomas Rowe, pastor of an Independent-church, then meeting at Girdlers'-Hall, of which his pupil became a member, in 1693; being then in his nineteenth year. " I have been credibly informed, (says Dr. Jennings) that while he resided in this college of learning, his behaviour was not only so inoffensive that his tutor declared he never gave him any occasion of reproof, but so exemplary that he often proposed him as a pattern to his other pupils for imitation."* Among his fellow-students were Mr. John Hughes, the poet; Mr. Josiah Hort, afterwards Archbishop of Tuam; and Mr. Samuel Say, a Dissenting minister in Westminster. " Some Latin essays, supposed to have been written as exercises at this academy, (according to Dr. Johnson) shew a degree of knowledge, both philosophical and theological, such as very few attain by a much longer course of study." While at the academy, he cultivated an acquaintance with the muses; or as himself modestly expresses it, was " a maker of verses from fifteen to fifty;" and, in his youth, he appears to have paid attention to Latin poetry. Some of his productions at this period, are remarkably easy and elegant. His method of study was to impress upon his memory the contents of the books he read, by abridging them; and by interleavements to amplify one system with supplements from another. The reader may form a correct idea of his manner of reading by having recourse to the very instructive specimens adduced by Dr. Gibbons and Mr. Palmer.(y)

Mr. Watts having finished his academical studies at the age of twenty, returned to his father's house, where he con-

* Funeral Sermon for Dr. Watts, p. 21.

(y) It was customary with Dr. Watts to make remarks in the margin of his books, and in the blank leaves to write an account of what was most distinguishing in them, to insert his opinion of the whole, to state his objections to what he thought exceptionable, and to illustrate and confirm what appeared to him just and important.——*Palmer's Life of Watts*, p. 5. *note.*

BURY-STREET, ST. MARY AXE.—*Independent.*

tinued two years. Instead of entering immediately on his public work, he employed this period in study and devotion, following those pursuits that were more immediately connected with his intended profession. At this time, a circumstance occurred which laid the foundation of his future popularity as a Christian poet. The composures sung by the congregation at Southampton, being of a very humble class, and so little to our author's taste, he could not forbear representing the matter to his father, who, knowing his poetical turn, desired him to try if he could do better. He did so: one hymn after another was produced and approved; and he was encouraged to proceed till, in process of time, there was a sufficient number to fill a volume.*

From under the roof of his father, he was invited to reside in the family of Sir John Hartopp, Bart. at Stoke-Newington, as tutor to his son. In this employment he spent five years; and, during that time, devoted himself to a diligent study of the sacred Scriptures. He preached his first sermon on the birth-day that completed his twenty-fourth year, A.D. 1698, and his ministry meeting with acceptance, he was, in the same year, chosen assistant to Dr. Chauncey, pastor of the Independent congregation in Mark-lane. His ministerial labours, however, were soon interrupted by a painful illness, of five months continuance; in which he learned that patience in suffering was a part of Christian duty no less important than activity in labour. His health being gradually restored, he received a call to succeed Dr. Chauncey in the pastoral office, which he accepted the very day on which King William died—a day very discouraging and alarming to the dissenting interest. Ten days after, being the 18th of March, 1702, he was solemnly ordained to the pastoral office.† The ministers engaged on this occasion were, the Rev. Matthew Clarke, Thomas Collins, Thomas Ridgley, Benoni Rowe, and Thomas Rowe, his tutor.‡

* Gibbons's Life of Watts, p. 254.   † *Ibid.* p. 92---97.
‡ Baptist Annual Register, vol. iv. p. 554.

BURY-STREET, ST. MARY AXE.—*Independent.*

Not long after his entrance on this charge, he was again visited by a painful and alarming illness, which threatened an early period to his usefulness. His confinement was long, his recovery slow, and his constitution considerably impaired. It was, therefore, judged necessary to provide him an assistant, and the Rev. Samuel Price was chosen to that office in July, 1703. Mr. Watts's exertions, however, kept pace with his recovery; and he was enabled to preach more than ever to the edification of his hearers. In the prosecution of his various plans of usefulness, he met with no material interruption till September, 1712, when he was seized again with a fever of such violence, that shook his constitution, and left a weakness upon his nerves, from which he never wholly recovered. For more than four years he was entirely laid aside from the exercise of his ministry, and it was not till October, 1716, that he was enabled to resume his public labours. The affection of his people during this season of trial, was strikingly exemplified in their solicitude for his recovery. Particular days were set apart to intercede with God in prayer for so desirable an event, and many of his brethren in the ministry assisted upon those occasions. At Mr. Watts's desire, Mr. Price, his assistant, was now associated with him in the pastoral office; to which he was ordained in March 1713. Between these amiable men there existed an inviolable friendship, which continued through life.*

The painful and distressing state to which Mr. Watts was reduced by this sickness, inspired his friends with a tender and becoming sympathy, and particularly engaged the benevolent attention of Sir Thomas Abney, Knt. and Alderman of London, (z) who received him into his house; where,

* Gibbons's Life of Watts, p. 98-101.

(z) Sir Thomas Abney was descended from an ancient and honourable family at Wilsley, in the County of Derby. He was born in January 1639; and his mother dying when he was young, his father sent him to a school at Loughborough, in the County of Leicester, that he might be under the eye of a pious aunt, whose instructions were conducive to those serious impressions which ever after remained upon his mind. In 1693 he was elected

BURY-STREET, ST. MARY AXE.—*Independent.*

with a constancy of friendship, and uniformity of conduct not often to be found, he was treated for thirty-six years, with all the kindness that friendship could prompt, and all the attention that respect could dictate. Sir Thomas died about eight years afterwards, but he continued with his lady and her daughter to the end of his life. " A coalition like this (says Dr. Johnson) a state in which the notions of patronage and dependence were overpowered by the perception of reciprocal benefits, deserves a particular memorial." In this family he experienced all the tenderness and care which the languishing state of his health required. Whatever wealth could supply, or affection suggest, to alleviate his afflictions, he enjoyed to the full extent of his wishes. The following anecdote, related by Mr. Toplady, who received it from the Countess of Huntingdon, will serve to confirm what is said of the happy terms upon which he lived with this benevolent family. The Countess being on a visit to Dr. Watts, at

Sheriff of London and Middlesex, and, before the expiration of his year, Alderman of Vintry-Ward. He also received the honour of Knighthood from King William. In 1700 he was chosen Lord Mayor, some years before his turn; and, the same year, procured an Address to the King against the Pretender, which gained him considerable popularity. In 1701 he was chosen a Member of Parliament for the City of London, and continued the ornament of religion and his country till his death, Feb 6, 1721-2, in the 83d year of his age. Sir Thomas, in early life, cast his lot with the Nonconformists; and joined the church in Silver-street, under the care of Dr. Jacomb, and afterwards of the learned Mr. John Howe. For his first wife he married the daughter of the famous Mr. Joseph Caryl, who lived with him very happily above twenty years. In 1700 he married his second wife, Mrs. Mary Gunston, eldest daughter of Mr. John Gunston, of Stoke-Newington, who survived till Jan. 12, 1749-50. The following anecdote places the piety of Sir Thomas Abney in so striking a light, that it cannot fail to interest the serious reader. It was his custom to keep up the duty of prayer in his family, during the whole of his Mayoralty. On the evening of the day he entered upon his office, he withdrew, without any notice, from the public assembly at Guildhall, after supper, went to his house, there performed family worship, and then returned to the company.---*Jer. Smith's Funeral Sermon for Sir T. Abney—and Gibbons's Life of Watts.*

Stoke-Newington, was thus accosted by him: " Your ladyship is come to see me on a very remarkable day." " Why is this day so remarkable?" answered the Countess. " This very day thirty years (replied the Doctor) I came to the house of my good friend Sir Thomas Abney, intending to spend but a single week under his friendly roof; and I have extended my visit to the length of thirty years." Lady Abney, who was present, immediately said, " Sir, what you term a long thirty years visit, I consider as the shortest visit my family ever received."* His gratitude, in the review of his obligations, during a thirty-six years residence with her Ladyship, is strongly marked in a passage of his will, where he speaks of " the generous and tender care shewn him by her Ladyship and her family, in his long illness many years ago, when he was capable of no service, and also, her eminent friendship and goodness during his continuance in the family ever since.†

It has been observed of literary men, and particularly Divines, that from the even tenor of their lives they afford but little interesting matter for the biographer. This may be true of some persons, but will not apply to such characters as Watts, whose writings have instructed as well as delighted thousands, and will continue to produce the same happy effects to the end of time. We are not indeed to look for those surprising events which characterize the intrigues of the statesman, or the deeds of the hero, but for something vastly more adapted to the great purposes of intellectual and moral improvement. This is effected by reviewing the lives of those who have exemplified the beauties of unaffected devotion, and shewn the way to substantial happiness, and immortal honour. " Extraordinary incidents, and curious anecdotes, are not to be expected in the life of a man, whose excursions were bounded by a few miles in the neighbourhood of the metropolis; who had formed no domestic relations;

* Gospel Magazine, 1776, p. 41.
† Dr. Jennings's Sermon on the Death of Dr. Watts, p. 26.

BURY-STREET, ST. MARY AXE.—*Independent.*

whose bodily afflictions often, and after long seasons, incapacitated him for every duty, and for every pleasure, but such as were purely intellectual and spiritual; and who, when in health, perhaps rather shunned social intercourse, as incompatible with his literary pursuits and his ministerial obligations. But whoever is capable of appreciating the importance of learning and philosophy, when sanctified by an ardent zeal for the glory of God, by gentleness, humility, and unremitted exertions for the best interests of the world; or whoever possesses the noble ambition of attaining such eminence in wisdom, piety, and usefulness, and of imbibing any degree of that elevation of mind, so conspicuous in this great man, may anticipate more substantial rarities, the zest of which he will never lose, while he needs the aid of instruction, or the animating influence of an example so full of grace and beauty."*

From the time of Mr. Watts's reception into the above family, his life, when not interrupted by sickness, was constantly employed upon some scheme for advancing the improvement of mankind. This is evidenced by his successive publications. " Their number and variety (says Dr. Johnson) shew the intenseness of his industry and the extent of his capacity." In reviewing the writings of Dr. Watts, and his character as an author, we shall consider him as a poet, as an instructor of youth, as a philosopher, and as a divine.

The first fruits of his genius were given to the public in his " *Horæ Lyricæ;* or Lyric Poems," published in 1706. Of the merit of these composures Dr. Johnson was so thoroughly convinced, as to insert them in his edition of the English Poets. Concerning the Author he observes, " As a poet, had he been only a poet, he would probably have stood high among the authors with whom he is now associated. For his judgment was exact, and he noted beauties and faults with very nice discernment; his imagination, as the Dacian

---

* Life of Dr. Watts prefixed to his Works. *Leeds edition.*

BURY-STREET, ST. MARY AXE.—*Independent.*

battle proves, was vigorous and active, and the stores of knowledge were large by which his fancy was to be supplied. His ear was well tuned, and his diction was elegant and copious." This commendation is followed by an extraordinary assertion with respect to devotional poetry; that " the paucity of its topics enforces perpetual repetition, and the sanctity of the matter rejects the ornaments of figurative diction." But, so far from this being true, there is nothing whatever that supplies a greater variety of topics, or is better adapted to admit of poetical images, as religion. Witness the sublime composures of many of the sacred writers, particularly the prophets, in which the loftiest images and boldest figures are introduced in almost every line. The Preface to the Lyric Poems contains an ample defence of this species of composition. The author shews that the sacred poet possesses advantages almost infinite in the variety, as well as the dignity of his topics; and that they reject no embellishments, though they require them to be used with judgment. Of the comparative merits between our author and other writers of the same class, Dr. Johnson observes, " It is sufficient for Watts to have done better than others, what no man has done well."

It was no small testimony to the poetic talents of Watts, that was shewn him by Mr. Cave, the original printer and proprietor of the Gentleman's Magazine, who, in order to excite emulation, and procure for his work productions of real genius, proposed to give certain rewards to his poetical correspondents, and wrote to Dr. Watts, requesting him to decide upon their respective merits. His natural modesty revolted at the idea of becoming a literary judge; but, on being pressed, he gave his opinion with so much candour, and judicious discrimination, that all parties expressed their gratitude, and cheerfully acquiesced in his decision.

The year after the publication of the Lyric Poems, appeared his volume of HYMNS, to the occasion of which we have before alluded. The copyright was sold to Lawrence

BURY-STREET, ST. MARY AXE.—*Independent.*

the bookseller, for only ten pounds!* though, could now it be re-assumed, it would probably be worth as many thousands. This production meeting with a rapid sale, and being very generally approved, the author was encouraged to attempt a version of the PSALMS. His long cessation from public labour, occasioned by the severe illness before-mentioned, enabled him to follow up this design, which, as his health gradually amended, he completed in 1719, when they were first published, and four thousand sold within the year. These are generally allowed to excel all his other poetical performances. Considered as a composition for the use of Christian societies, they may be justly pronounced superior to every other work of the kind; and they have given the name of Watts a kind of immortality in our worshipping assemblies. Whatever defects may be noticed in the manner of conducting public worship in our dissenting congregations, in the delightful exercise of psalmody they far outstrip their brethren of the Establishment. Who that has a taste for this sublime part of devotion, does not prefer the elegant composures of Watts, before the jingling rhymes that are constantly chaunted in the parish churches? Though the volume of *Hymns* composed by our author, are not equal to the *Psalms*, yet they contain many specimens of sublime and devotional piety, well calculated for the edification of Christian societies; and which are highly recommended by the plainness of the composition and the smoothness of the verse. If in some instances they may be thought less judicious than the *Psalms*, it should be remembered that many of them were composed when a youth. With respect to the reports propagated by some Arian and Socinian writers, that the author revised these composures a little before his death, in order to render them as they say, " wholly unexceptionable to every Christian professor," they deserve not the least attention. Dr. Watts possessed two extensive a knowledge of human nature to entertain so chimerical a project.†

* Life of Watts prefixed to his " Practical Works," p. 14.
† Palmer's Life of Watts, p. 26—28, note.

BURY-STREET, ST. MARY AXE.——*Independent.*

It could not have been long after this period that our author published his " Divine and Moral Songs for Children ;" a work admirably adapted to entertain and instruct the infant mind. The number in constant circulation throughout Great Britain and America is prodigious. In England alone, the consumption exceeds 50,000 annually.* As to the merit of these composures, it has been estimated by the wise and good of all denominations, and received the stamp of extensive usefulness. Besides the Songs for Children, he composed some other pieces adapted to juvenile minds. One of these, " The Art of Reading," published in 1720, was compiled for the use of the younger branches of the family under whose benevolent roof he resided. This was followed, in 1725, by " The Elements of Geography and Astronomy," dedicated to Mr. John Eames ; " A Book of Catechisms ;" " Prayers for Children ;" " A Discourse on the Education of Children and Youth ;" and " A short View of Scrpture History." These several pieces, all adapted for the use of younger minds, are so many monuments of the author's benevolence and piety, in stooping from the higher branches of literature, to converse with the lisping infant. " For children (says Dr. Johnson) he condescended to lay aside the scholar, the philosopher, and the wit, to write little poems of devotion, and systems of instruction adapted to their wants and capacities, from the dawn of reason through its gradations of advance in the morning of life. Every man, acquainted with the common principles of human nature, will look with veneration on the writer who is at one time combating Locke, and at another, making a catechism for children in their fourth year. A voluntary descent from the dignity of science is perhaps the hardest lesson that humility can teach."

The philosophical writings of Dr. Watts, which next fall under our notice, have justly gained him no small share of reputation. The immortal discourse on " Logic," pub-

* Life of Watts prefixed to his " Practical Works," p. 19.

BURY-STREET, ST. MARY AXE.——*Independent.*

lished in 1724, while it exhibited the true system of reasoning, rejected that wretched system of quibbling, which had hitherto disgraced the schools. Though other authors had written upon the subject, and prepared many of the materials, yet, it remained for Watts to simplify the system, and reduce it to general use. The Logic was soon received into the English Universities; and in the year 1741, Bishop Secker tells the author, " It was by no means the only piece of his read there with high esteem."* Lord Barrington calls it a book by which, not only the youth of England, but all who are not too lazy, or too wise to learn, may be taught to think and write better than they do; and adds, " I intend, as some have done Erasmus, or a piece of Cicero—to read it over once a a year."†

In 1733, appeared his " Philosophical Essays" on various subjects; to which was added, " A System of Ontology," which has been much admired. In one of his disquisitions he has been charged with confounding the idea of *space*, with that of *empty space* ; but chiefly, we believe, by those metaphysicians who have pleaded for a vacuum in nature. The most useful lesson to be derived from this volume, however, is, that it impresses upon the reader a conviction of the contracted limits of the human mind, and the uncertainty attending the mere deductions of reason, unaided by revelation.

The next work that falls under our notice, was one of the most important, not only of those produced by Dr. Watts, but that ever appeared in the English language. We allude to the first part of " The Improvement of the Mind; or, a Supplement to the Art of Logic, containing a Variety of Remarks and Rules for the Attainment of useful Knowledge in Religion, in the Sciences, and in common Life." It made its appearance in 1741, and as the author

* Gibbons's Life of Watts, p. 353. † *Ibid.* p. 405.

BURY-STREET, ST. MARY AXE.——*Independent.*

confesses, had been the labour of more than twenty years: The second part was left in MS. and published by the editors of his works. Dr. Johnson says of this treatise, " Few books have been perused by me with greater pleasure than his Improvement of the Mind, of which the radical principles may indeed be found in Locke's Conduct of the Understanding; but they are so expanded and ramified by Watts, as to confer upon him the merit of a work in the highest degree useful and pleasing. Whoever has the care of instructing others, may be charged with deficiency in his duty if this book is not recommended."

We are now to take some notice of the Doctor's Theological writings, which for their number and value, have not been exceeded by any Divine of modern times. The perspicuity and elegance of his expression, and the richness of his imagination, enliven the most common subjects, and add lustre to the most interesting. The multiplicity and diversity of his native and acquired talents are every where conspicuous; and the application of these talents uniformly discovers an accurate knowledge of human nature, a high veneration of the gospel, an unshaken attachment to the cause of Christian liberty, and an habitual readiness for any sacrifice to the virtue and happiness of mankind. " Whatever he took in hand (says Dr. Johnson) was, by his incessant solicitude for souls, converted to theology. As piety predominated in his mind, it is diffused over his works; it is difficult to read a page without learning, or at least, wishing to be better. The attention is caught by indirect instruction, and he that sat down only to reason, is on a sudden compelled to pray."

During the first years of his ministry, he delivered a set of discourses to a number of young persons, who associated for prayer in the vestry of his meeting-house. These were afterwards corrected, and arranged in a little volume entitled, " A Guide to Prayer," in which the subject is scientifically considered, and we are taught to pray by rule, without a

BURY-STREET, ST. MARY AXE.——*Independent.*

form. The method pursued in this discourse is extremely judicious, and the author's directions full of piety and wisdom. In 1721, appeared the first volume of his *Sermons.* The occasion of writing them he has himself explained. His repeated afflictions had very much circumscribed his public labours; for a long time he was unable to preach at all, and when he did, it was with such weakness and pain, that he was often obliged to retire immediately to bed, and have the room closed in darkness and silence. And, as he was incapacitated for public labour, so he was also for the more private duties of the pastoral office; such as visiting the sick, and conversing with his flock at their habitations. This filled him with anxiety and regret, and induced him to present his people with a volume of discourses from the press, that they might read in their families the same truths which they had heard from his lips.* Though these discourses contain some slight inaccuracies, as well as redundancies of expression, yet they abound with many just remarks. The originality of thought, and many happy illustrations that run through them, discover the genius of the writer; and the perspicuity as well as simplicity of their style, render them familiar to the meanest capacities. To this may be added, that they contain a rich display of evangelical truth and Christian experience. A second volume of sermons on the Christian Morals, appeared in 1723, and a third volume in 1734. Lady Hertford mentions a pleasing instance of the utility of our author's sermons, in the case of a man who had been a bad husband, and a drunkard twenty years; but, by reading them was converted to a course of life just the reverse.†

In 1722, he published his excellent discourses on " Death and Heaven," preached upon the death of Sir John Har-

---

* Preface to his Sermons, vol. i.
† Life of Dr. Watts, prefixed to his " Practical Works."

BURY-STREET, ST. MARY AXE.—*Independent.*

topp and his lady. These sermons, which contain many ingenious conjectures concerning the employment of heaven, were so highly esteemed by the celebrated Professor Frank, that he caused them to be translated into German; and his successor, Dr. Rambach, wrote a recommendation in very strong and emphatic language.* But the principal work of this year was " The Christian Doctrine of the Trinity, or Father, Son, and Spirit, three Persons and one God, asserted and proved, with their Divine Rights and Honours vindicated by plain Evidence of Scripture, without the Aid or Incumbrance of human Schemes." This was his first piece upon the subject, and was followed, soon after, by " Seven Dissertations relating to the Christian Doctrine of the Trinity: in two Parts." (A)

* Life of Watts, prefixed to his " Practical Works."

(A) As Dr. Watts deviated from what is called the Orthodox Doctrine of the Trinity, it may not be improper briefly to state what were his views upon the subject. In the treatises above-mentioned, he discovers his partiality to the doctrine of the pre-existence of Christ's human soul, which laid the foundation of his future system, called the *Indwelling Scheme.* This supposes " That the Godhead, the Deity itself, personally distinguished as the *Father,* was united to the man Christ Jesus, in consequence of which union, or indwelling of the Godhead, he became properly God." This union he supposes to have existed anterior to our Saviour's appearance in the flesh, and that the human soul of Christ existed with the Father from before the foundation of the world." In his " Useful and important Questions concerning Jesus the Son of God," published in 1746, he labours to shew that the term *Son of God,* does not expressly relate to his Deity, but to his mediatorial character and human nature. With regard to his Divine nature, he supposes the Godhead of Christ, and the Godhead of the Father, to be one and the same. At the latter end of the year beforementioned, he gave to the public his three Discourses on " The Glory of Christ as God-Man," which was his last publication on the subject, and goes over the same ground as his former pieces. With respect to the *Holy Spirit,* the Doctor seems not to have held the common notion of his real personality, as distinct from the Father, supposing it to mean the Divine Power, or Influence, or God himself exerting his influence. It is no part of our design to confirm, or condemn, the Doctor's opinions upon these points. Every human scheme of so sublime a doctrine as that of the Trinity, is liable to difficulties; and the unmeaning jargon that has been in-

BURY-STREET, ST. MARY AXE.—*Independent.*

In the year 1731, the Doctor gave to the public his valuable " Essay on the Strength and Weakness of Human Reason." A copy of this work, presented to Dr. Gibson, Bishop of London, was the occasion of his opening a correspondence with that prelate. About the same time appeared his " Discourses on the Love of God, and the Use and Abuse of the Passions in Religion." The object of these discourses was to lead men from the frigid zone of Christianity (mis-named rational religion), into the warmer region of Divine love, which is here shewn to be the proper climate of the Christian. The Doctor proves that Christianity not only admits, but demands the warmest of our affections ; and that the cool and cautious religionist errs just as far from true reason as from piety.* " The Redeemer and Sanctifier; or the Sacrifice of Christ, and the Operations of the Spirit, vindicated," was published about 1735. Bishop Gibson, to whom the Doctor presented a copy, says, " He read it with great satisfaction and delight." He adds, " The seeing so shameful a departure from true Christianity, on the two points which are the subject of your book, has long been a sensible concern and grief to me, and especially when I see it countenanced and propagated by many who call themselves Christians, but are in reality little more than Deists ; for (says he) if the great work of our Redemption, and the blessed fruits of it are to be laid aside, I cannot see that the Christian name signifies much." The good bishop particularly laments this defection among some of the

vented in order to explain it, has only added to its obscurity, and been the source of endless contentions and divisions in the church. If those who preach, or write, upon this doctrine, would confine themselves to the simple language of scripture, they would not only be more intelligible, but more successful in *putting to silence the ignorance of foolish men*, who would fain set up their own *fallible reason* in opposition to the *Wisdom of God.* Those who wish for a more particular account of Dr. Watts's sentiments with respect to the Trinity, may have recourse to his own writings, or to his Life by the Rev. Samuel Palmer.

* Life of Watts, prefixed to his " Practical Works."

BURY-STREET, ST. MARY AXE.—*Independent.*

Dissenters, who, he confesses, "had been hitherto, without exception, zealous for them."*

In 1739, appeared his valuable " Discourses on the World to come ; or, the Joys and Sorrows of departed Souls at Death, and the Glory or Terror of the Resurrection. To which is prefixed, An Essay towards the Proof of a separate State of Souls after death ;" a subject which he has treated in the most awful yet affectionate manner, adapted to every age and situation in life. Another of his publications was, " The Ruin and Recovery of Mankind ; or, an Attempt to Vindicate the Scriptural Account of these great Events upon the plain Principles of Reason ; with an Answer to various Difficulties relating to Original Sin, the Universal Depravation of Nature, and the overspreading Cause of Death ; general Offers of Grace to all Men, and the certain Salvation of some ; the Case of the Heathen Nations, and the State of dying Infants." This long title will give the reader an idea of the curious subjects discussed in this book, which contains some new and remarkable sentiments. Among others is the following singular opinion, as Dr. Doddridge terms it : " That the sin of Adam has subjected all his posterity not only to death, but to the utter *extinction of being ;* the consequence of which is, that all those who die in their infancy fall into a state of *annihilation,* excepting those who are the seed of God's people, who by virtue of the blessings of the covenant made with Abraham, and the promise to the seed of the righteous, shall through the grace and power of Christ, obtain part in a happy resurrection, in which other infants shall have no share."* Since the time of Dr. Watts, the subject of the Divine conduct towards infants, has been treated in a manner far more scriptural, as well as more satisfactory, to the parental feelings.

* Gibbons's Life of Watts, p. 359, 360.
† Doddridge's Lectures, vol. ii. p. 216.

BURY-STREET, ST. MARY AXE.—*Independent.*

The last of his publications we shall notice was, " Orthodoxy and Charity United." The great object of this piece, and of the Doctor's life, was to place the doctrines of the fall—the atonement—divine influence—the necessity of repentance, faith, and holiness, (which formed his system of orthodoxy) in a point of view consistent with their truth and importance; at the same time endeavouring to lessen the smaller differences among Christians respecting inferior points of sentiment, or rather forms of expression, and to promote charity and forbearance. The Doctor thought (and who does not think?) that the chief difference between real believers lies rather in terms than things. Habits of education and of reading, create these differences; but in the exercises of devotion, they are melted down in the beautiful language of scriptural piety. It was not only in his book (says Dr. Johnson) but in his mind that orthodoxy was united with charity." To this work was appended an ingenious Essay, entitled, " Self-Love and Virtue reconciled only by Religion."*

Besides the works already mentioned, our author published a variety of other pieces, all excellent in ther nature, but too numerous to be here described. Such as we have not noticed shall be enumerated in the note below. (B)

---

* Life of Watts, prefixed to his " Practical Works."

(B) A Sermon, preached at Salters' Hall, to the Societies for Reformation of Manners. 1707.—Defence against the Temptations to Self-Murder. 1726.—A Sermon at Bury-street, occasioned by the Death of George I. 1727.—A Discourse on Charity Schools. 1728.—A Caveat against Infidelity, or, the Danger of Apostacy from the Christian Faith. 1729.—An humble Attempt towards the Revival of Practical Religion among Christians, particularly Protestant Dissenters. 1731.—Reliquiæ Juveniles ; Miscellaneous Thoughts in Prose and Verse, on natural, moral and divine Subjects.—Written chiefly in younger Years. 1734.—Nine Sermons in the Bury-street Collection. 1735.—Remnants of Time employed, in Prose and Verse. 1736.—An Essay on Humility, as exemplified in the Character of St. Paul. 1737.—Essay on the Holiness of Times and Places, &c. 1738.—An Essay on Civil Power in Things Sacred. 1739.—The Doctrine of the Passions explained and improved.—Questions proper for Students in Divinity.—A short Essay towards

BURY-STREET, ST. MARY AXE.—*Independent.*

The reputation acquired by our author, in the various departments of literature, resounded far beyond the limits of his own country; and procured him a large correspondence with learned and worthy persons, both at home and abroad. It was, therefore, with great propriety that he received, in 1728, from the Universities of Edinburgh and Aberdeen, an unsolicited diploma, creating him Doctor of Divinity. "Academical honours (says Dr. Johnson) would have more value if they were always bestowed with equal judgment." Another writer (Mr. Toplady) has this observation upon the subject: "Learned seminaries would retrieve the departing respectability of their diplomas, were they only presented to (I will not say, such men as Dr. Watts; for few such men are in any age to be found: But to) persons of piety, orthodoxy, erudition, and virtue."* "The presenting such titles to people who either can pay for them, (observes another writer) or whose silly vanity prompts them to have their names ushered in with a sound, without any just qualification in the world beside, exposes the honours of a University to contempt, and the persons who bear them to ridicule. The name of Doctor, though it cannot make a man intuitively

the Improvement of Psalmody.—The Harmony of all Religions. 1742.—An Essay on the Freedom of the Will. 1746.—Evangelical Discourses on several Subjects: To which is added, An Essay on the Powers and Contests of Flesh and Spirit. 1747.—The rational Foundation of a Christian Church. 1747.—Besides these, the Doctor wrote several Prefaces to the Works of others. He left the care of his Papers and Manuscripts to Dr. Doddridge and Dr. Jennings, who published a complete Edition of his Works in Quarto. 1749. These having become exceeding scarce and valuable, a new Edition was published in 1802, in 7 vols. 8vo. under the superintendance of the Rev. Edward Parsons, of Leeds, and the Rev. Dr. Williams, of Rotherham. This Edition has, also, been some time out of print. Many years after his death, were published what is called his "Posthumous Works." The first volume consisting of Poetry, is considered a gross imposition upon the public. The Letters between the Doctor and his friends, contained in the second volume, are curious, and probably authentic.

* Gospel Magazine for 1776.

BURY-STREET, ST. MARY AXE.—*Independent.*

learned or wise, should give the world a just expectation not to find him at least either weak or illiterate."*

The closing scenes of Dr. Watts's pilgrimage were such as might be expected from a life of such exalted piety and devotion. The delicacy of his constitution and repeated sickness soon brought upon him the infirmities of age; and these were greatly promoted by midnight studies. He was for several years together greatly distressed with insomnia, or continual wakefulness. Very often he could obtain no sleep for several nights successively, excepting such as was forced by medical preparations; and, not unfrequently, opiates lost their virtue, and served only to aggravate his malady. Yet, through the goodness of God, and the kind attention of friends, his feeble frame was lengthened out to a period beyond the common lot of mortals. But though the taper of life burned slowly to the socket, its flame was brilliant to the last. He beheld his approaching dissolution with a mind perfectly composed, without the least dismay, or shadow of a doubt as to his future happiness. His trust in God, through Jesus the Mediator, remained unshaken to the last. With application to himself he often repeated the words of Paul to the Hebrews: " Ye have need of patience, that after ye have done the will of God, ye may receive the promise." When he has found his spirit tending to impatience, he would thus check himself, " The business of a Christian is to bear the will of God as well as to do it. If I were in health I could only be doing that, and that I may do now. The best thing in obedience is a regard to the will of God, and the way to that is to get our inclinations and aversions as much mortified as we can." When almost worn out and broken down by infirmities, he observed, in conversation with a friend, " That he remembered an aged minister used to say, that the most learned and knowing Christians, when they come to die, have only the same plain promises of the gospel for their support

* Middleton's Biographia Evangelica, vol. iv. p. 279.

BURY-STREET, ST. MARY AXE.—*Independent.*

as the common and unlearned; and so (said he) I find it. They are the plain promises of the gospel which are my support, and I bless God they are plain promises, which do not require much labour or pains to understand them, for I can do nothing now but look into my Bible for some promise to support me, and live upon that." Again, " I should be glad to read more, yet not in order to be confirmed more in the truth of the Christian religion, or in the truth of its promises, for I believe them enough to venture an eternity upon them." On retiring to rest, he would declare with the sweetest composure, " That if his master was to say to him he had no more work for him to do, he should be glad to be dismissed that night." At other times he would say, " I bless God I can lie down with comfort at night, not being solicitous whether I awake in this world or another."*

Mr. Joseph Parker, a person of most respectable character, and for about twenty-one years the Doctor's amanuensis, sent the following intelligence concerning him to his brother, at Southampton, the day before his death, Nov. 24, 1748, " I wrote to you by the last post that we apprehended my master very near his end, and that we thought it not possible he should be alive when the letter reached your hands; and it will no doubt greatly surprise you to hear that he still lives. We ourselves are amazed at it. He passed through the last night in the main quiet and easy, but for five hours would receive nothing within his lips. I was down in his chamber early in the morning, and found him quite sensible. I begged he would be pleased to take a little liquid to moisten his mouth, and he received at my hands three tea-spoonfuls, and has done the like several times this day. Upon inquiry he told me he lay easy, and his mind peaceful and serene. I said to him this morning that he had taught us how to live, and was now teaching us how to die by his patience and composure, for he has been remarkably in this frame for several

* Gibbons's Life of Watts, p. 311—316.

BURY-STREET, ST. MARY AXE.—*Independent.*

days past. He replied, ' Yes.' I told him, I hoped he experienced the comfort of these words, ' I will never leave thee nor forsake thee." He answered, ' I do.' The ease of body and calmness of mind which he enjoys is a great mercy to him and to us. His sick chamber has nothing terrifying in it. He is an upright man, and I doubt not but his end will be peace. We are ready to use the words of Job and say, ' We shall seek him in the morning but he shall not be.' But God only knows, by whose power he is upheld in life, and for wise purposes, no doubt. He told me he liked I should be with him. All other business is put off, and I am in the house night and day. I would administer all the relief that is in my power. He is worthy of all that can be done for him. I am your faithful and truly afflicted servant." On the 26th of November, the day after the Doctor's decease, Mr. Parker wrote again to the same person, " At length the fatal news is come. The spirit of the good man, my dear master, took its flight from the body to worlds unseen and joys unknown, yesterday in the afternoon, without a struggle or a groan. My Lady Abney and Mrs. Abney are supported as well as we can reasonably expect. It is an house of mourning and tears, for I have told you before now that we all attended upon him, and served him upon a principle of love and esteem. May God forgive us all that we have improved no more by him, while we enjoyed him."*

Thus died, after an honourable and useful life, the truly great and excellent Dr. Watts, Nov. 25, 1748, in the 75th year of his age. His remains were deposited in Bunhill-Fields; and as a testimony to his affection and liberality, his pall was supported by six Ministers, selected equally from the three denominations. Dr. Samuel Chandler delivered the oration at the grave, and Dr. Jennings preached the funeral sermon to his bereaved church, from Heb. xi. 4. Similar testimonies of respect were paid to his memory by several

* Gibbons's Life of Watts, p. 318, 319.

other Ministers in different parts of England. But while his various excellencies procured him these honours, he, in his lifetime, was concerned to prevent whatever might be considered as inconsistent with the humility of his character. A handsome tomb-stone was erected over his grave, bearing the following humble inscription, composed by himself:

" ISAAC WATTS, D.D. Pastor of a Church in London, Successor of the Rev. Mr. JOSEPH CARYL, Dr. JOHN OWEN, Mr. DAVID CLARKSON, and Dr. ISAAC CHAUNCEY, after Fifty Years of feeble Labours in the Gospel, interrupted by four Years of tiresome Sickness, was at last dismiss'd to Rest, Nov. 25, A.D. 1748, Æt. 75.

2 Cor. v. 8. *Absent from the Body, present with the Lord.*

Col. iii. 4. *When Christ, who is our Life, shall appear, I shall also appear with him in Glory.*

IN VNO IESV OMNIA.

This Monument, on which the above modest Inscription is placed, by order of the Deceas'd, was erected, as a small Testimony of Regard to his Memory, by Sir John Hartopp, Bart. and Dame Mary Abney."

To the foregoing account of Dr. Watts's life, we will subjoin a few particulars illustrative of his character. In his personal appearance there was little that could interest the admirers of external comeliness. He was low of stature, (c) (not much above five feet) and his bodily presence weak; yet

---

(c) The Doctor being once in a Coffee-room with some friends, he overheard a Gentleman asking, rather contemptuously, " What, is that the great Doctor Watts?" When turning round suddenly, and in good humour, he repeated a stanza from his Lyric Poems, which produced a silent admiration:

" Were I so tall to reach the pole,
" Or mete the ocean with my span,
" I must be measured by my soul:
" The mind's the standard of the man."

HORÆ LYRICÆ, *False Greatness.*

BURY-STREET, ST. MARY AXE.—*Independent.*

there was a certain dignity in his countenance, and such piercing expression in his eyes, as commanded attention and awe. As a preacher he ranked with the most eminent. Though he used very little action, his manner was animated. In his preparations for the ministry, he wrote and committed to memory the leading features of his sermons, amplifying as he found occasion, with the utmost ease and freedom. Such were his flow of thoughts, as well as promptitude of language, that he never failed to acquit himself with credit. At the conclusion of weighty sentences it was his custom to pause, that he might quicken the attention, and add greater solemnity to the weighty truths he delivered. The correctness of his pronunciation, the elegance of his diction, and the grandeur of his sentiments, obtained him an uncommon share of popularity. " I once mentioned (says Dr. Johnson) the reputation which Mr. (Dr.) Foster had gained by his proper delivery to my friend Dr. Hawkesworth, who told me, that in the act of pronunciation he was far inferior to Dr. Watts." Though it is much to be questioned whether this information be accurate, yet, it is certain that the discourses of Dr. Watts were far better to general edification.

In health he was remarkable for vivacity in conversation, and for ready wit; though he never shewed a fondness for displaying it, especially in satire, to which his amiable temper was naturally averse. " Wit fell from him (says Dr. Gibbons) like occasional fire from heaven; and, like the ethereal flame, was ever vivid and penetrating." By his natural temper he was quick of resentment; but by his established and habitual practice, he was gentle, modest, and inoffensive. His tenderness appeared in his attention to children and to the poor. Though his long and repeated illnesses gave him little opportunity for visiting, yet, when those occasions occurred, he would always fill his pockets with hymns and catechisms; and where he was known and expected, the young people would flock around him to receive them. A third part of his income he devoted to the purposes of charity,

BURY-STREET, ST. MARY AXE.—*Independent.*

and when laid aside from public labours, he refused to receive his salary. As the Doctor was free and cheerful in conversation, so his remarks were constantly directed to some valuable end. On his last visit to his father at Southampton, Richard Ellcock, a servant in the family was ordered to accompany him a day's journey homeward. On this occasion, the Doctor entered into such a serious discourse with him, as proved the means of his conversion, and he ever after lived an ornament to his character. In early life, Dr. Watts is said to have formed an attachment to the pious and amiable Miss Singer, afterwards Mrs. Rowe; but if this was ever any thing more than a platonic passion, it subsided into a pure and sincere friendship; in consequence of which that lady, at her death, committed her papers to his care.

As an author, no man's posthumous claim upon the gratitude of the church, and of his country, can be urged with a more imperative tone. The natural strength of his genius, which he cultivated and improved by a very considerable acquaintance with the most celebrated writers, both ancient and modern, had enriched his mind with a large and uncommon store of just sentiments, and useful knowledge of various kinds. His soul was too noble and large, to be confined within narrow limits; he could not be content to leave any path of learning untried, nor rest in a total ignorance of any science, the knowledge of which might be for his own improvement, or might in any way tend to enlarge his capacity of being useful to others. Though that which gave him the most remarkable pre-eminence was the extent and sublimity of his imagination, how few excelled, or even equalled him in quickness of apprehension, and solidity of judgment; and having also a faithful memory to retain what he collected from the labours of others, he was able to pay it back again into the common treasury of learning with a large increase. It is a question whether any author before him ever appeared with reputation on such a variety of subjects, as he has done, both as a prose writer, and a poet. However, this we may

BURY-STREET, ST. MARY AXE.—*Independent.*

venture to say, that there has been no writer of late years, whose works have been so widely dispersed both at home and abroad, in such constant use, and translated into such a variety of languages; many of which will remain more durable monuments of his great talents, than any representation that can be made of them, though it were graven on pillars of brass.*

It would be easy to adduce testimonies in abundance to the talents and piety of Dr. Watts, two however shall suffice; and these selected from enemies. (c) Dr. Vicessimus Knox, in his " Christian Philosophy," says, " For my own part, I cannot but think this good man approached as nearly to Christian perfection as any mortal ever did in this sublunary state; and therefore I consider him as a better interpreter of the Christian doctrine than the most learned critics, who, proud of their reason and their learning, despised or neglected the very life and soul of Christianity; the living, everlasting gospel, the supernatural influence of divine grace; and be it ever remembered, that Dr. Watts was a man who studied the abstrusest sciences, and was as well qualified to become a verbal critic, or a logical disputant on the scripture, as the most learned among the Doctors of the Sorbonne, or the greatest proficients in polemical divinity. I mention this circumstance for the consideration of those who insinuate that the doctrines of grace cannot be entertained but by ignorant, as well as fanatical persons; by persons un-initiated in the mysteries of philosophy."

" Few men (says Dr. Johnson) have left behind such

* Dr. Jennings's Sermon on the Death of Dr. Watts, p. 27, 28.

(c) Dr. Johnson's high-church principles are well known : A remarkable instance of his bigotry will be noticed above. To call Dr. Knox an enemy may seem strange, after the panegyric above quoted ; but for a solution of the difficulty, we refer to his Sermon at the opening of the Chapel belonging to the Philanthropic Reform, Nov. 9, 1806 ; which, however, contains not a tenth part of the contemptible bigotry and nonsense, expressed in the delivery.

BURY-STREET, ST. MARY AXE.—*Independent.*

purity of character, or such monuments of labrious piety. He has provided instruction for all ages, from those who are lisping their first lessons, to the enlightened readers of Mallebranche and Locke ; he has left neither corporeal nor spiritual nature unexamined ; he has taught the art of reasoning and the science of the stars. His character, therefore, must be formed from the multiplicity and diversity of his attainments, rather than from any single performance ; for it would not be safe to claim for him the highest rank in any single denomination of literary dignity ; yet perhaps there was nothing in which he would not have excelled, if he had not divided his powers to different pursuits." The same author, after a critique upon his poetry, before noticed, conclude thus : " And happy will be that reader whose mind is disposed by his verses or his prose, to imitate him *in all but his nonconformity,* to copy his benevolence to man, and his reverence to God."* (D)

SAMUEL PRICE, whose name is identified with that of Watts, as having been his colleague in the ministry for

* Life of Watts by Gibbons, Johnson, Palmer, prefixed to his Work, *Leed's edition* ;---and to his Practical Works. Also funeral Sermons for him by Jennings, Milner, and Ashworth.

(D) The exception taken by Dr. Johnson to the nonconformity of Watts, discovers a littleness of mind unworthy so great a man. After the warm eulogium upon his talents, benevolence and piety, who could expect so unnecessary a caution, and so miserably out of place? Was the caveat here introduced a diminution of his literary, or a blot upon his religious reputation ? Or was the mind of Dr. Johnson so debased by a churlish bigotry, that he supposed a conformity to certain rites and ceremonies, the criterion of true excellence ? Certain it is, that the character of Dr. Watts was so singularly irreproachable, that, excepting in a matter of conscience, nothing could be alleged against him. In his liberal soul were united all those excellencies that form the very reverse of a party-zealot ; and if a meek and lowly mind could shield the memory of any man from the envenomed influence of this detestable spirit, his nonconformity had never been mentioned but with a view of recommending the virtues by which it was so greatly adorned. It is probable that Dr. Johnson never studied the grounds of Nonconformity, otherwise he would have entertained a better opinion of the understandings, as well as integrity, of its advocates.

BURY-STREET, ST. MARY AXE.—*Independent.*

more than forty years, was a native of Wales, and pursued his academical studies under the celebrated Mr. Timothy Jollie, at Attercliffe, near Sheffield, in Yorkshire. In July, 1703, he was chosen assistant to Dr. Watts; and during the long illness of that great and excellent man, was, upon his recommendation, and at his express desire, chosen by the church to the office of joint-pastor, to which he was ordained March 3, 1713; Messrs. Nesbitt, Bragge, Collins, Ridgley, and Foxon, assisted on the occasion. This connexion subsisted with the utmost harmony during a long course of years, till dissolved by death. Mr. Price survived his amiable colleague but little more than seven years, and died lamented by persons of various persuasions, April 21, 1756, having been connected with the church in Bury-street, almost 53 years. He was uncle to the late celebrated Dr. Richard Price.

During a long life Mr. Price supported an exemplary character for probity and virtue. He was a man of sound and solid sense, a judicious, useful preacher, and eminent for his gift in prayer. He possessed great sagacity; was very able, faithful, and ready to advise, and communicate his mind in serviceable hints and cautions to his friends. His disposition was friendly and peaceable, and he laid himself out to do good, in which he much delighted. He was highly esteemed by his excellent friend Dr. Watts, who, in his will, styles him " his faithful friend and companion in the labours of the ministry ;" and mentions a legacy he bequeaths him " as only a small testimony of his great affection for him on account of his services of love during the many harmonious years of their fellowship in the work of the gospel."

Mr. Price lies buried in Bunhill-Fields, when a handsome tomb-stone is erected to his memory, containing the following modest lines, which he himself directed in his last will, and also desired that he might be buried as near as possible to his honoured colleague.

BURY-STREET, ST. MARY AXE.—*Independent.*

" Here lies the body of Mr. SAMUEL PRICE, who served with the truly Rev. Dr. Watts in the gospel, under the character of his assistant and co-pastor 45 years, to whose uninterrupted goodness and candour he has been highly obliged so great a part of his life. He died in hopes of being together for ever with the Lord, the 21st April, 1756."

Mr. Price's publications are not numerous: they consist, we believe, only of the following sermons. To the Society who support the Morning Lecture at Little St. Helen's, August 1, 1724.—To the Societies for Reformation of Manners: preached at Salters'-Hall, June 28, 1725.—Nine Sermons in the Bury-street Collection, 1735.—A Charge at the Ordination of the Rev. John Angus, at Bishop's-Stortford, 1748.—A Sermon on the Death of Dame Mary Abney. 1750.*

MEREDITH TOWNSHEND.—Mr. Price feeling the infirmities of age growing upon him, found it necessary to have an assistant, and Mr. Meredith Townshend was chosen to that service, February 5, 1742. He continued in this situation till June, 1746, when he settled at Hull, in Yorkshire, from whence he removed to Stoke-Newington. He was held in high esteem by the church in Bury-street, on account of his excellent preaching and exemplary character.†

SAMUEL MORTON SAVAGE, D. D.—This learned and respectable Divine was born in London, July 19, 1721. His grandfather on the paternal side, was the Rev. John Savage, pastor of the seventh-day Baptist church, in Millyard, Goodman's-fields; and on the maternal, Mr. Abraham Toulmin, who, though educated in the medical line, kept a school in Old Gravel-lane, Wapping. He derived his name Morton from his father's mother; and from pater-

* Gibbons's Life of Watts, p. 151. *note.*
† MS. *penes me.*

BURY-STREET, ST. MARY AXE.—*Independent.*

nal claims had the honour of very noble connexions. The family of the Savages was related to Dr. Hugh Boulter, Primate of Ireland; and he considered himself as the direct lineal descendant of John Savage, the first Earl of Rivers of that family, to whose estate, when the title became extinct, he had an undoubted right, though he never claimed it.*

By a religious education, Dr. Savage was led into an early acquaintance with the Holy Scriptures; and the reading some books on practical religion, was the means of awakening in him an earnest concern for his eternal interests. " The great things of salvation shone into his mind in so forcible and convincing a manner, as not only to bear down all objections and command the assent, but so as to carry away his soul with joy, mixed with such an awful admiration as if God himself had been personally speaking to him."† His religious views and impressions ran much into that train of thought which distinguishes the writings of our old Divines on the subject of conversion; and their effects were lasting.

It was the design of his friends to place him in the national church, under the patronage of his relative, the Lord Primate of Ireland; but this scheme was dropt in deference to his own judgment, which determined him for nonconformity. Encouraged and assisted by Dr. Watts, to whose acquaintance he had introduced himself, by means of a letter, he entered on academical studies under the learned Mr. John Eames; on whose death, in 1744, Dr. David Jennings being chosen Divinity Professor, made it a condition of his filling that post, that Mr. Savage, who had not then finished his academical course, should be his colleague, to lecture on mathematics, natural philosophy, and other branches

---

* Life of Dr. Savage, prefixed to his Sermons, by Dr. Toulmin, p. 1, 2.
† Bennet's Sermons on the Death of Dr. Savage, p. 34.

BURY-STREET, ST. MARY AXE.—*Independent.*

of literature and science, This province he supported with reputation till 1762, when Dr. Jennings died, and the seminary, under the direction of Mr. Coward's trustees, assumed a new form, and was removed to Hoxton. Mr. Savage was placed in the divinity chair, and had for his colleagues in the other branches of science, the late Dr. Kippis, and Dr. Rees.

After preaching some time occasionally, he was chosen, in December, 1747, assistant to the justly esteemed Mr. Samuel Price, and was afterwards associated with him in the pastoral office; to which he was ordained in 1753. On the death of Mr. Price, in 1756, he became sole pastor, which office he held with various assistants, till he resigned it, after a connexion of forty years, at Christmas, 1787. Previously to this, at Midsummer, 1785, he quitted the academy, not of necessity, as he expressed it, but of choice, chiefly that he might have time to employ himself, then late in the evening of life, (above 64,) in studies for his own personal satisfaction and improvement. He received the degree of Bachelor in Divinity, from the Royal College of Aberdeen, in April, 1764; and the degree of Doctor in Divinity, from the Marischal College of the same university, in November, 1767. (D)

Besides his pastoral connexion with the Independent church in Bury-street, Dr. Savage officiated, for some years, as afternoon preacher to the Presbyterian congregation in Hanover-street, under the ministry of the venerable Dr. Earle. He entered on this office at Christmas, 1759, and continued in it till Lady-day, 1766. He was also one of the preachers of the Thursday lecture in that place from November, 1760, till Christmas, 1767, when it was dropped. Of Mr. Coward's Friday lecture, at Little St. Helen's,

---

(D) In 1752, he married Miss Houlme, only daughter of Mr. George Houlme, stock-broker, in Hoxton-square; by whom he left two daughters. This lady dying in 1763, he continued a widower till 1770, when he married Miss Hannah Wilkin, who survived him.

BURY-STREET, ST. MARY AXE.—*Independent.*

he was likewise a lecturer from July, 1761, to November, 1790. From October, 1769, to January, 1775, he preached constantly at Clapham, in the afternoon of those Lord's-days, on which Dr. Furneaux was even lecturer at Salters'-Hall. It ought also, to be mentioned to his honour, that he was one of the gentlemen with whom originated, in 1772, the design of applying to parliament for relief in the matter of subscription, and by whose active exertions the affair was brought to a favourable termination.*

Close application to study, in the early period of life, protracted far beyond midnight, greatly affected the health of Dr. Savage, and injured his constitution; which, as it was strong, held out to an advanced period. Towards the close of life, his health gradually declined ; but his death was occasioned by a singular obstruction in his throat, thought, by the physician who attended him, to be an internal swelling of the œsophagus, which gave the painful apprehension that he must be starved to death. The œsophagus gradually became so contracted, that he was unable to swallow any nourishment, except by single drops ; so that his family and friends had the mortification of seeing him dying by inches, and at length reduced to a skeleton, till he was literally starved to death. He was at last so emaciated, that the bones absolutely fretted the skin to soreness, and all but came through it.† As a natural consequence of the lingering nature of his disease, the dark valley was for a considerable time open before him, but he was not terrified by the prospect: " I am descending (said he, with the greatest serenity,) gradually into it ; the face of death is smooth to me." He acknowledged, indeed, that he did not feel those joys, which some have experienced in their last moments, and that there were seasons when he was sensible of fear ; but it was transient. Though he possessed a nervous habit, and had formerly laboured under great fears of death, yet

---

* Toulmin's Life of Savage, *ubi supra*, p. 4—9.
† Gentleman's Magazine, Feb. 1791, p. 191.

BURY-STREET, ST. MARY AXE.—*Independent.*

now his habitual frame was serene and cheerful; his fears were scattered; and a divine peace filled his mind: he supported his illness in a manner that became the man and the Christian. Not one impatient repining, or discontented, word proceeded out of his lips. His calm and cheerful acquiescence in the will of God was highly pleasing and instructive; and his conversation well adapted to fill those who heard it with an holy veneration and love of true piety. A little before his dissolution, being asked whether he wished for any thing? He replied, " I only long for my release;" which was granted him in the most gentle manner, without a sigh or a groan, February 21, 1791, in the 70th year of his age.*

Dr. Savage possessed good natural abilities, which were improved by close study, and an intimate acquaintance with the various branches of literature. As a preacher, his discourses were distinguished by good sense, perspicuity, precision and accuracy; and they were pervaded by a serious evangelical spirit. Though his delivery was not adorned by a studied eloquence, it was warm and energetic. His preaching, however, though highly esteemed by some, was never encouraged by a large auditory; nor was his apparent success in proportion to his learning, abilities, and piety. Whatever were the causes, " no criminality (observes Mr. Towle) rested with him. Most earnestly did he desire that the great ends, in order to the attaintment of which he was advanced to the stations he filled, might be faithfully and punctually accomplished. For this purpose, he laboured with indefatigable zeal and diligence. When he had reason to fear his labours were not successful, the thought pierced his heart with an anguish peculiarly pungent, but when there was ground to hope that success crowned them, his whole soul was filled with sensations exquisitely delightful."† In

* Mr. Bennet's Sermon, and Mr. Towle's Address at the grave.
† Mr. Towle's Address, p. 44.

BURY-STREET, ST. MARY AXE.——*Independent.*

the capacity of a tutor, besides the many acts of friendship which he performed for particular students, he acted with a truly generous spirit, recommended the cause of learning and piety, and encouraged free inquiry. He possessed a valuable library, of which he made a proper use. His reading was careful and diligent; and his books by the references and remarks written in the margin, bore on almost every page, strong proofs of the care and judgment with which they were perused. As an instance of his patient assiduity, it is recorded that he read over the folio and octavo editions of "The Antient Universal History" together, to compare and note the variations between them. By extensive reading he acquired much valuable knowledge; particularly excelled in mathematical science, and had a taste for poetry. His great love of retirement gave him opportunities for his literary pursuits; but rendered him the less amiable in social converse. In point of religious sentiment, he was an Independent, and a moderate Calvinist; and in his intercourse with other denominations behaved with the greatest candour. Evangelical principles commanded his assent, engaged his love, and governed his actions.* His publications consist of a few single sermons, which shall be specified below.(E)

* Toulmin's Life of Savage, p. 13—19.

(E) 1. An Introductory Discourse at the Ordination of the Rev. William Ford, Jun. at Miles's lane, Dec. 14, 1757.—2. The Duty of Subjects to honour the King: a Sermon on the Accession of George III. Nov. 30, 1760. 1 Pet. ii. 17.—3. Good men dismissed in Peace: a Sermon on the Death of the Rev. David Jennings, D. D. Sept. 26, 1762. Luke ii. 29, 30.—4. The Wisdom of being Religious: a Sermon at St. Thomas's, Jan. 1, 1763. Job xxviii. 28.—5. A Discourse on the Lord's Supper, 12mo. 1763.—6. A Charge at the Ordination of the Rev. Samuel Wilton, June 18, 1766, at Lower Tooting, in Surry.—7. An Oration at the Interment of the Rev. Dr. Samuel Wilton, in Bunhill-Fields, April 10, 1778.—8. National Reformation the Way to prevent National Ruin: a Sermon at the Monthly Exercise on Account of the State of public Affairs; preached at Haberdashers'-Hall, Feb. 20, 1782. Jer. xviii. 7, 8.—After Dr. Savage's death, several Sermons which he had transcribed for the press, were published in one volume octavo, with some memoirs of his life, drawn up by his relative Dr. Joshua Toulmin, then of Taunton, but now of Birmingham.

BURY-STREET, ST. MARY AXE.—*Independent.*

Dr. Savage was interred in Bunhill-Fields, beneath a handsome tomb-stone, bearing the following inscription.

Sacred
To the Memory of the
REV. SAMUEL MORTON SAVAGE, D.D.
Forly Years Pastor of
A Congregational Church among Protestant Dissenters
In BURY-STREET, LONDON;
Formerly under the care of
The eminently pious and learned Dr. ISAAC WATTS;
And Professor of Divinity
In the Academy late at Hoxton,
Founded by William Coward, of Walthamstow, Esq.
His superior natural abilities, extensive literature, and uniform piety,
Rendered him greatly respected by those who knew him,
And enabled him with honour and fidelity
To discharge the duties of private and public life.
The approach of death,
Though attended with circumstances peculiarly trying,
He met with exemplary patience,
And Christian fortitude,
And joyful hope.
He died the 21st February, 1791,
In the 70th year of his age.

As Dr. Savage preached only in the morning at Bury-street, he had various ministers to assist him in the afternoon. The first statedly engaged in this service was the Rev. THOMAS PORTER, for about four or five years. He was followed by the late Rev. JOSIAH THOMPSON, who preached several years at Bury-street, in the afternoon, after he went to reside in St. Mary Axe. Of both these ministers we shall have occasion to speak elsewhere, and therefore, forbear enlarging upon their characters in this place. After Mr. Thompson's removal to Clapham, the afternoon service in Bury-street was discontinued till 1779, when the use of the place for that portion of the Lord's-day was granted to the General Baptist Societies under the care of Mr. Joseph Brown, and Dr. Joseph Jeffries, till they removed to Worship-street, in 1781.

BURY-STREET, ST. MARY AXE.—*Independent.*

THOMAS BECK, the present minister of Bury-street meeting, was born in Bermondsey parish, Southwark, about the year 1755. His first serious impressions are said to have been received under the preaching of the Rev. John Langford, minister of a meeting in Blacksfields; but while he was an apprentice, he frequently attended public worship at the places in connexion with the late Rev. John Wesley. He began to preach before he was out of his time, and the sphere of his early labours is said to have been Kennington, near Newington, in the county of Surry. At his setting out in the ministry, he was extremely popular; and very soon had an invitation to Morpeth, in Northumberland. But this he declined, intending at that time to go to the Countess of Huntingdon's College at Trevecca; though through some means or other, his intention was never fulfilled. About 1776, or 1777, he had a chapel taken for him in Hermitage-street, Wapping; where he preached about a twelvemonth. After this, he was introduced to Mr. Whitefield's connexion, preached sometimes at the Tabernacle, and under the patronage of Mr. Keene, went frequently to Mitcham, and occasionally to Bristol. He also became acquainted with Dr. Peckwell, for whom he sometimes preached at Westminster chapel. From the Tabernacle connexion, he had a call to Gravesend, which he accepted, and continued there about nine years. While at this place, he published a sermon occasioned by the death of Mrs. Susannah Link, who died Jan. 30, 1781, aged 22 years. This we believe was the only sermon he ever printed. While at Gravesend, he also published an allegorical poem, entitled, "The Three Youths;" and an Elegy on the death of Dr. Peckwell.

In the month of April, 1788, Mr. Beck was invited to succeed Dr. Savage, at Bury-street. The congregation was then in a very low state, and notwithstanding the attempts that have been made to revive it, has continued so ever since.

BURY-STREET, ST. MARY AXE.—*Independent.*

Some time after his settlement at Bury-street, Mr. Beck had an invitation from the church in East-Lane, Walworth, before Mr. Swain was chosen pastor. But this he declined. A few years ago he built a small chapel in his own garden at Deptford, where there is service every Lord's-day in the winter season, and three times in summer.

Since his settlement in London, Mr. Beck has given to the public several specimens of his abilities as a poet. In 1795, he published, " The Passions taught by Truth; an allegorical Poem :" in which " the excellence of evangelical truth, in its application to the passions and interests of mankind, is clearly demonstrated, and embellished with much fertility and vivacity of imagination."* In the following year appeared " The Mission, a Poem;" and since then several Elegies: as one for Dr. Hunter; another for Cowper, the poet; and a third for the late Rev. John Newton. In 1806, he presented the public with a small volume, of a satirical nature, entitled, " The Age of Frivolity; by Timothy Touch'em;" which came to a second edition in the following year. We understand he has another volume of Poems in the press, nearly ready for publication.

There is a good endowment belonging to this church, and it would have been still more considerable had not part of the principal been sunk in the time of Dr. Savage, to defray the expences of repairs.†

* Evangelical Mag. for June, 1795, p. 256.   † Private Information.

CROSBY-SQUARE.

INDEPENDENT.—EXTINCT.

CROSBY-SQUARE, situated on the East side of Bishopsgate-street, takes its name from Sir John Crosby, grocer and woolman, who erected a magnificent mansion on the site; Alice Ashfield, Prioress of St. Helen's, having granted him a lease of certain lands and tenements, for ninety-nine years, from 1466, at an annual rent of 11l. 6s. 8d. The house was built of stone and timber, very large and beautiful, and the highest at that time in London. Sir John was sheriff and alderman of London, in 1470, knighted by Edward III. in the following year, and died in 1475— so short a time did he live to enjoy this stately structure! In the reign of Edward V. it was the city residence of Richard Duke of Glocester, afterwards Richard III. who here contrived the measures that eventually secured him the crown, by dethroning his nephew, and murdering the two innocents in the tower. In 1542, Henry VIII. made a grant of these premises to Antonio Bonvici, a rich Italian merchant, who made them his residence. In the reign of Elizabeth, Crosby-House was appropriated to foreign ambassadors. Henry Ramelius, chancellor of Denmark, resided here in 1586, as did the ambassador of France. It was afterwards purchased by Sir John Spencer, alderman of London, who kept his mayoralty here, in 1594. The chief part of this noble structure has been long since pulled down, and the site built upon; the hall mis-called Richard the IIId.'s chapel, still remains, and is very entire. It is a beautiful Gothic building, with a bow window on one side;

CROSBY-SQUARE.—*Independent*, Extinct.

the roof is of timber and much to be admired. In the reign of Charles the Second, it was appropriated to the Nonconformists, who occupied it as a meeting-house for upwards of a century. For the last thirty years it has been used for inferior purposes; and is at present occupied by a woolpacker.*

The Society assembling in Crosby-Square was collected soon after the act of Uniformity, by the Rev. Thomas Watson, the ejected minister of St. Stephen's, Walbrook. He was an eminent Presbyterian Divine, and laid the foundation of a very flourishing society. During the early part of the ministry of Dr. Grosvenor, the congregation was very large and rich, and, at one time, made the largest annual collection for the fund, of any Presbyterian church in London. But as the Doctor grew in years, he became incapacitated for active exertion, and a disorder in his palate contributed not a little to lessen his popularity, so that the congregation gradually declined; nor did the preaching of his successors ever succeed in causing a revival. At length, upon the expiration of the lease, in 1769, the church not finding itself in a condition sufficiently prosperous to warrant a renewal of it, agreed to dissolve; and the remaining members joined themselves to other societies. After this, a lease of the meeting-house was taken by the well-known Mr. James Relly, who preached here to a Society of his own formation, till his death. With respect to the Presbyterian church, the following is, we believe, a pretty accurate list of the ministers who have been connected with it, whether as pastors or assistants.

* Histories of London, by Strype, Maitland, and Pennant.

CROSBY-SQUARE.——*Independent*, Extinct.

Ministers' Names.	As Pastors.		As Assistants.	
	From	To	From	To
Thomas Watson, M. A.	1662	16..	—	—
Stephen Charnock, B. D.	1675	1680	—	—
Samuel Slater, M. A.	1680	1704	—	—
John Reynolds,	—	—	16..	1691
Daniel Alexander,	—	—	1693	1704
Benjamin Grosvenor, D. D.	1704	1749	—	—
Samuel Wright, D. D.	—	—	1705	1708
John Barker,	—	—	1708	1714
Clerk Oldsworth,	—	—	1715	1726
Edmund Calamy, Jun.	—	—	1726	1749
John Hodge, D. D	1749	1762	—	—
Richard Jones,	1763	1769	—	—

THOMAS WATSON, M. A. received his education in Emmanuel College, Cambridge, where he was noted for being a hard student. In the time of the civil wars, A. D. 1646, he became rector of the parish of St. Stephen's, Walbrook, where he executed the office of a faithful pastor, with great diligence and assiduity, for nearly sixteen years. His pious and useful labours soon spread his fame in the city, and procured him very general respect, which he carried with him to his grave.* During the commotions that agitated the nation in his time, Mr. Watson discovered great loyalty and attachment to the person of King Charles the First, and totally disapproved the methods made use of by the army to bring him to trial. He also joined the Presby-

* Calamy's Account, p. 37.

CROSBY-SQUARE.—*Independent*, Extinct.

terian ministers in a remonstrance to General Cromwell, and the Council of War, against the death of that monarch.* After this, in 1651, he was concerned with some other persons in carrying on a correspondence with the Scots, for the purpose of bringing in King Charles II. which being discovered, he was apprehended and committed prisoner to the Tower, along with Dr. Drake, Mr. Jenkins, Mr. Jackson, Mr. Robinson, Mr. Blackmore, and Mr. Haviland. These, after some time, on their petitioning for mercy, and promising submission to the government, were released; but Mr. Christopher Love, an eminent Presbyterian minister, was publicly executed as a terror to others.†

Mr. Watson continued at his living till Bartholomew-day, 1662, when he was ejected for nonconformity. There are three farewel sermons of his in the London collection; and another, printed separate, but without the author's knowledge, said to have been preached at St. Stephen's, Walbrook, August 17: it is entitled, " The Pastor's Love expressed to a loving People," from Acts xx. 28. *Sorrowing most of all for the words that he spake, that they should see his face no more.*‡ Notwithstanding the rigorous execution of this unnatural act, Mr. Watson continued the exercise of his ministry in private as Providence gave him opportunity. After the fire of London, in 1666, when the churches were burnt, and the parish-ministers unemployed for want of places of worship, the nonconformists fitted up large rooms with pulpits, seats and galleries, for the reception of those who had an inclination to attend. Of this number was Mr. Watson.§ Upon the Indulgence in 1672, he licenced the great hall in Crosby-House, then belonging to Sir John Langham, who patronized the Nonconformists. There he preached for several years; till, at length, his strength wearing away, he retired into Essex, where he died

---

* Neal's Puritans, vol. ii. p. 363.   † *Ibid.* p. 404.
‡ Kennet's Chronicle, p. 744.   § Neal's Puritans, vol. ii. p. 686.

CROSBY-SQUARE.—*Independent*, Extinct.

suddenly in his closet at prayer.* The time of Mr. Watson's death is not mentioned; but we apprehend it to have happened about a year after the Revolution.

Mr. Watson was a man of considerable learning, a popular but judicious preacher, and eminent in the gift of prayer. Of the latter, the following anecdote affords a sufficient proof. Once on a lecture-day, before the Bartholomew Act took place, the learned Bishop Richardson came to hear him, and was so well pleased with his sermon, but especially with the prayer after it, that he followed him home, returned him his thanks, and desired a copy of it. "Alas! (said Mr. Watson) that is what I cannot give, for I do not use to pen my prayers; it was no studied thing, but uttered *pro re nata*, as God enabled me, from the abundance of my heart and affections." Upon this, the good bishop went away, wondering that any man could pray in so excellent a manner extempore.† Mr. Watson published a variety of books upon practical subjects, and of a useful nature; the titles of which shall be specified below.(F) But his principal work was a body of divinity, in 176 sermons upon the Assembly's Catechism, which did not appear till after his death. It was published in one volume folio, in 1692, and

* Calamy's Account, *ubi supra*. † Ibid.

(F) HIS WORKS.—Sermons and Works, 2 vols. 12mo. 1657.—Discourses on the Beatitudes. 1660.—The Christian's Charter, shewing the Privileges of a Believer. 1661.—The Art of Divine Contentment. 1661.—A Discourse of Meditation; with several occasional Sermons. 1661.—The Godly Man's Character.—A Word of Comfort to the Church of God.—The Doctrine of Repentance. 1668.—Heaven taken by Storm. 1669.—The Mischief of Sin. 1671.—A Divine Cordial; or, the Privilege of those that love God.—The Holy Eucharist.—The Duty of Self-denial.—A Fast Sermon before the Commons. 1649. Heb. iv. 14.—Religion our true Interest. Mal. iii. 16--18.—A Plea for the Godly; or, Excellence of the Righteous.—The Saints' Delight.—Sermons before the Lord Mayor, on public Occasions.—Funeral Sermons for Mr. Hodges; Mr. Jacob Stock; Mr. John Wells; and Mr. Henry Stubbs.—Four Sermons in the Morning Exercises.—Three Farewel Sermons. 1662.—A Body of Divinity. 1692.

CROSBY-SQUARE.—*Independent*, Extinct.

accompanied with a portrait of the author by Sturt; together with a Recommendatory Preface by the Rev. William Lorimer, and the attestation of twenty-five other ministers, of principal note in that day. A new edition of this work, in two volumes octavo, was published a few years since.

STEPHEN CHARNOCK, B. D. descended from an ancient family in Lancashire, was born in 1628, in the parish of St. Katherine-Cree, London, where his father, Richard Charnock, practised as a solicitor. At a proper age, he was sent to Emmanuel College, Cambridge, where he had for his tutor Dr. William Sancroft, Archbishop of Canterbury. Upon leaving the College, he went to reside in a private family; and, afterwards, spent some time in the exercise of his ministry in Southwark, where he was made very useful. About 1649, he went to Oxford, and in the following year, obtained a fellowship in New-College. In 1652, he was incorporated Master of Arts, as he had before stood in Cambridge. Two years after, he became senior Proctor of the University, " being then taken notice of (says Wood) by the godly party for his singular gifts, and had in reputation by the then most learned Presbyterians; and therefore he was the more frequently put upon public work." Upon the expiration of his Proctorship, in 1656, he went over to Ireland, and resided in the family of Henry Cromwell. In Dublin he continued the exercise of his ministry, about four or five years, being held in high esteem by the most serious and judicious Christians, of different denominations; and he had many persons of distinction for his constant hearers. While he resided in that city, it is apprehended, he received his degree of B. D. from Trinity College. The Restoration putting an end to his ministry in Dublin, he returned to London, where he spent fifteen years in retirement; and for his farther improvement, took a tour occasionally to France and Holland. At length, in 1675, he accepted a call to become joint-pastor of a con-

CROSBY-SQUARE.—*Independent*, Extinct.

gregation in Crosby-Square, with the Rev. Thomas Watson. In this connexion he continued about five years, till he was removed by death, July 27, 1680, in the 53d year of his age. On the 30th of the same month, his remains were conveyed from Whitechapel, the place of his decease, to his meeting-house in Crosby-Square, and from thence to St. Michael's church, Cornhill, where they were deposited, and where a funeral sermon was delivered upon the occasion, by his fellow-collegian in the university, the Rev. John Johnson.*

The character of Charnock is so well known, and his writings held in such general esteem, that we need say the less in his commendation. He was, as to manners and deportment, venerable and grave, like an aged person from his youth; a man of excellent abilities, strong judgment, and singular genius. His attainments in learning were of the first order; having been, throughout life, a most diligent and methodical student, and a great redeemer of time, rescuing not only his restless hours in the night, but even the time that was spent in walking, from those impertinencies and fruitless vanities, which so often fill up the minds of men, and steal away their hearts from those nobler objects that more justly challenge their regard. He constantly wrote down his thoughts upon those occasions, which furnished him with many materials for his most elaborate discourses. With the learned languages he had a very extensive acquaintance. Mr. Johnson, his intimate friend, says, " he never knew a man in all his life, who had attained near to that skill that Mr. Charnock had, in the originals of the Old and New Testament, except Mr. Thomas Cawton." In the talent of preaching he had few equals. His sermons were chiefly of a practical nature, yet rational and argumentative, reaching to the understandings, as well as the affections of

* Wood's Athenæ Oxon. vol. ii. p. 657, 658.

CROSBY-SQUARE.—*Independent*, Extinct.

his hearers. When controversies came in his way, he discussed them with great acuteness and judgment, and discovered no less skill in applying them to practice. Though his preaching was considered by some persons as too high for the vulgar, and better suited to the more intelligent sort of Christians, yet, if sometimes deep, he was never abstruse, and handled the great mysteries of the gospel with much clearness and perspicuity : " So that if he were above most, it was only because most were below him."

In his younger days, he delivered his sermons without notes, but as he grew in years, and his memory began to fail, he penned and read them verbatim. Though he was not popular, on account of his disadvantageous way of reading with a glass, yet his preaching was much esteemed by the more judicious sort of hearers. He spent most of his time in his study, which made him somewhat reserved in conversation; but where he was well acquainted, he could be very free and communicative; and he selected his Society from the more serious, as well as intelligent part of mankind. His library, furnished with a curious, though not a very large collection of books, was unfortunately destroyed in the fire of London. In such reputation was he held by his brethren, that many able ministers loved to sit at his feet, for the benefit of those instructions which they could not get by many books, or by the sermons of others. In the course of his ministry at Crosby-Square, he intended to have presented his hearers with a complete body of divinity ; but his sun was set at the threshold of this design. He had entered upon a set of discourses on the Existence and Attributes of God, which he did not live to finish. While he treated upon these subjects, they inspired him with so lively an interest as seemed to indicate his near and rapid approach to his everlasting rest. It was, for some time before his death, his longing desire to be in heaven, where there is the perfection of grace and holiness ; and he ex-

CROSBY-SQUARE.—*Presbyterian*, Extinct.

pressed a lively hope that he should quickly enjoy that felicity.*

Mr. Charnock published nothing in his lifetime excepting a single sermon on "The Sinfulness and Cure of Thoughts;" in the Supplement to the Morning Exercise at Cripplegate. His other valuable writings were given to the public after his death, by Mr. Adams and Mr. Veal, to whom he had committed his papers. The first piece they published was his excellent " Discourse on Divine Providence," in 1680; to which they prefixed some account of the life and character of the author. This was followed, in 1681, by his " Discourses on the Existence and Attributes of God," in one large volume folio; to which was afterwards added another volume, consisting of discourses on " Regeneration, Reconciliation, The Lord's-Supper," and various other important subjects. A second edition of his works, in two volumes folio, appeared in 1684; and a third edition in 1702. To these several expressions was prefixed a good portrait of the author, engraved by R. White. His " Two Discourses on Man's Enmity to God, and on the Salvation of Sinners," were printed separately in octavo, in 1699. These several discourses were left behind him in the same form he usually wrote them for the pulpit. It is no unfavourable sign of the present times, that the works of *Charnock* are rising in the estimation of the religious world, and consequently, becoming scarce. Their merit, indeed, can scarcely be rated too high; for though they may want that perfection and beauty of style which they would, doubtless, have received had the author himself prepared them for the press; yet for strength of reasoning, solidity of judgment, and sublimity of genius, they are equalled by few, and excelled by none. To these observations, we shall subjoin the testimony of

* Mr. Johnson's Sermon on the Death of Mr. Charnock—and Preface to Mr. Charnock's " Discourse on Divine Providence."

CROSBY-SQUARE.—*Presbyterian*, Extinct.

a late writer, Mr. Toplady; " I have met (says he) with many treatises on the Divine Perfections; but with none which any way equals that of Mr. Charnock. Perspicuity, and depth; metaphysical sublimity, and evangelical simplicity; immense learning, and plain, but irrefragable reasoning, conspire to render that performance one of the most inestimable productions that ever did honour to the sanctified judgment and genius of a human being. If I thought myself at all adequate to the task, I would endeavour to circulate the outlines of so rich a treasure into more hands, by reducing the substance of it within the compass of an *octavo* volume. Was such a design properly executed, a more important service could hardly be rendered to the cause of religion, virtue, and knowledge. Many people are frightened at a folio of more than 800 pages, who might have both leisure and inclination to avail themselves of a well-digested compendium." Few of our readers need be informed that this task was executed, in 1797, by the Rev. Griffith Williams. In the course of the present year (1808) the inestimable " Treatise on Divine Providence," was reprinted, in a neat manner, in crown octavo, and accompanied with a fine portrait of the author.

SAMUEL SLATER, M. A.—This pious and excellent Divine was a native of London, and had the honour to descend from pious parents. Of his father, the Rev. Samuel Slater, who was ejected from St. Katherine's, Tower, we have spoken in a preceding article.* After passing through the elementary principles of learning at the grammar-school, Mr. Slater was sent to complete his studies at the University of Cambridge, where he proceeded M. A. He there attained great proficiency in the most useful parts of knowledge, and upon his appearance in public, discovered that he was qualified for eminent usefulness in the sta-

* See the WEIGH-HOUSE, Little Eastcheap.

CROSBY-SQUARE.—*Presbyterian*, Extinct.

tion assigned him by Providence. The first place that was favoured with his stated labours, was Nayland, in Suffolk, where he continued several years. From thence he removed to Bury St. Edmunds, in the same county, a sphere of more extensive labours and usefulness. There he exercised his ministry with great diligence, faithfulness, and success, till disabled by those in power, whose spleen and malignity against persons of his spirit and temper, supplied the place of law. This evil disposition discovered itself at the first assizes after the restoration, when he, and Mr. Claget, his fellow-labourer in the same town, were prosecuted for not reading the book of common-prayer.* Thus early did he begin to feel that storm, which about two years afterwards, on Bartholomew-day, 1662, drove him, and many other excellent ministers, for some years, into obscurity.

Mr. Slater being vigorously opposed for nonconformity at Bury St. Edmunds, removed to London, where he took advantage of the indulgence granted by King Charles the Second, for the employment of his talents in the ministry, and cheerfully embraced every opportunity put into his hands for public service and usefulness. Upon the death of the reverend and learned Mr. Stephen Charnock, in 1680, he became joint pastor of a congregation in Crosby-Square, where he laboured with great acceptance and fidelity to the day of his death.

Mr. Slater possessed very considerable talents for the ministry. His public discourses, both as to the matter and style of them, were admirably suited to the great end of preaching—the edification of his hearers. As his composures were drawn up with great exactness, so his matter was solid and substantial; his style plain, pithy, and sententious; and he possessed a grave, natural elocution, calculated to leave impressions of seriousness upon those who heard him. He was thoroughly acquainted with the scriptures, which he

---

* Calamy's Account, p. 646.

CROSBY-SQUARE.—*Presbyterian,* Extinct.

studied with close attention; was well versed in practical divinity; and always kept a considerable stock of sermons beforehand. Though he enlarged upon most subjects beyond what is usual, yet, it was always with an useful and entertaining variety; and his applications were at once so mild and gentle, and at the same time so close and convincing, that they stole imperceptibly upon the hearts of his hearers. Being of a tender sympathizing spirit, he was enabled to discharge, with great advantage, one part of his ministerial work—visiting the sick. On those occasions his expressions were remarkably tender, his prayers fervent, and much to the purpose; for he possessed a singular felicity of adapting his petitions to the particular exigencies of the persons he prayed for. In the whole of his ministry, his great aim was to do good. And it pleased God to crown his labours with much success, making him an instrument of great usefulness, in his day; and though he lived to a good old age, he had a large congregation to the last. He adhered strictly to the good old Protestant doctrines, was a singular honour to the ministerial character, and much valued by all who knew him, or were acquainted with his writings.[*]

His natural temper was excellent and amiable; and the grace of God had rendered it much more so. In this particular he had few equals, and no superior. A cheerful serenity always sat upon his countenance, and pourtrayed the benignity of his disposition. In his behaviour he happily united the gravity of the Divine, and the good breeding of the gentleman. He was very easy of access, condescending to his inferiors, and obliging to all: not of a meddling or censorious temper, nor did he affect to intrude into the affairs of others. Instead of interfering with other men's vineyards, he took care to keep and dress his own. He was an extensive blessing to all who knew him; a bright orna-

[*] Mr. Alexander's Sermon on the Death of the Rev. Samuel Slater.

CROSBY-SQUARE.—*Presbyterian*, Extinct.

ment to religion in every relation of life; and a faithful, diligent, and laborious pastor, who watched for souls as one that must give an account. He studied, prayed, and preached with a sincere aim to promote the sanctification and salvation of his hearers—to ripen them by grace for glory; and he was always ready to instruct, comfort, and encourage any who were under spiritual distress. In short, his wise, prudent, and truly Christian conduct rendered him an eminent blessing to the church of Christ, especially to that part of it over which Providence had placed him.*

It pleased God to prolong Mr. Slater's life to an advanced period, and he descended the vale of death without feeling any of those acute pains which are the usual attendants of malignant diseases. The thread of life was gradually worn asunder, and his soul left its tenement without any apparent agony at parting. The excellent Dr. Grosvenor, who was present the last time he appeared in public, (at least on a sacramental occasion) has the following remarkable passage in his diary, concerning Mr. Slater:—" The last sacrament he administered (says the Doctor) I received with him. He looked upon himself as near his end. At the close, he took a solemn leave of the congregation, and ended with these words, which were delivered on his part with the solemnity of a dying patriarch blessing his children, and with the authority of an apostle : ' I charge you before God, that you prepare to meet me at the day of judgment, as *my crown of joy*, and that not one of you be found wanting to meet me there at the right hand of God."†

During his confinement, Mr. Slater was visited by several of his brethren in the ministry. The Rev. Mr. Alexander, his colleague, who attended him on one of these occasions, observes, " The last time I was with him, when I asked him what the inward frame and temper of his spirit was, he

---

* Mr. Alexander's Sermon, *ubi supra*.
† Mr. Barker's Sermon on the Death of Dr. Grosvenor, p. 31, *note*.

told me, He blessed God he had peace, though not joy—good hope through grace—supported, though not transported." Another minister who visited him a few days before he died, said to him, " Sir, you have served God very faithfully, and you may expect from him great supports in your illness." He answered, " It is true, but God owes me nothing—he is not in my debt." And, being told again, there were many excellent promises for him to lay hold upon; he answered, " But God must give me the hand to lay hold upon them with." During his long weakness, the Lord graciously favoured him with his presence; Satan was never suffered to molest him; but he enjoyed uninterrupted peace and tranquillity within, and his graces shined to the last.* Then, like the gentle expiring of a lamp that ceased to be fed, or like the bright luminary of the morning, who, after cheering us for awhile with his benignant rays, leaves us gradually at night; so did this good man calmly descend into the valley of death, and left behind him but the shadow of departed light. He died May 24, 1704. (g)

Two funeral sermons were preached and published upon occasion of his death. One by the Rev. William Tong, who observes concerning Mr. Slater, that " He passed through the world with as clear and unspotted a reputation as any one." The other discourse was by the Rev. Daniel Alexander, who bears a strong testimony to his singular worth. There are two portraits of Mr. Slater, one an engraving, the other a mezzotinto; but they are both scarce. His publications will be mentioned in the note below. (H)

* Mr. Alexander's Sermon, *ubi supra*.

(g) Mr. Slater married the widow of Mr. Hood, daughter of Mr. Harman Sheafe, of London, son of Mr. Harman Sheafe, of Cranbrook, in Kent. This lady survived him.

(H) A Discourse of Family Religion, in 18 Sermons.—A Discourse on Family Prayer.—Another on Closet Prayer.—A Discourse on the Preciousness of God's Thoughts towards his People.—A Thanksgiving Sermon on the Discovery of the horrid Plot.—A Sermon before Sir John Shorter, Lord

CROSBY-SQUARE.—*Presbyterian*, Extinct.

JOHN REYNOLDS.—As this person is not mentioned by Anthony Wood, it is probable that he received his education in the University of Cambridge. At the Restoration he was minister of Roughton, in Norfolk, where he was ejected for nonconformity. Coming afterwards to London, he was chosen colleague with Mr. Slater, at Crosby-Square. He was one of the ministers who, on the part of the Presbyterians, went up to King James II. with the address of thanks for his indulgence, in 1687.* Mr. Slater, who preached his funeral sermon, speaks of him as a person of considerable abilities and learning, and well accomplished for his work; as a truly gracious humble Christian, a profitable preacher, an able catechist, and a faithful friend. Also as a wise man, a maker of peace, unreprovable, and exemplary in his conversation. Mr. Reynolds died November 25, 1691.†

DANIEL ALEXANDER.—With the history of this gentleman prior to his settlement at Crosby-Square, we are entirely unacquainted. In 1693, he was chosen assistant to Mr. Slater, and was happy in this connexion till Mr. Slater's death, when some uneasiness arising in the congregation occasioned his leaving Crosby-Square. Of this circumstance he speaks thus: " I had the honour and advantage to be an assistant to him (Mr. Slater) near eleven years, in all which time not the least tincture of jealousy, or suspicion,

---

Mayor, 1688.—A Sermon to young Men. Dec. 25, 1688.—And Funeral Sermons for the following ministers: Mr. Thomas Vincent, 1678.—Mr. Thomas Gilson, 1680.—Mr. John Oakes, 1688.—Mr. John Reynolds, 1691.—Mr. Richard Fincher, 1692.—Mr. William Rathband, 1695.—And Mr. George Day, 1697.—Also, a Funeral Sermon for Mrs. Lobb, wife of the Rev. Stephen Lobb, 1691.—N. B. The above catalogue is a strong proof of Mr. Slater's respectability as a Divine, and popularity as a preacher.

* Biog. Brit. vol. i. Art. Alsop.
† Calamy's Account, p. 480. Contin. p. 622.—and Mr. Slater's Sermon on the Death of Mr. Reynolds.

CROSBY-SQUARE.—*Presbyterian*, Extinct.

obtained to hinder our usefulness, or mutual confidence; but I was always treated by him with that unparalleled candour, condescending affability, endearing kindness, and sincere respect, which rendered my work in that relation much more pleasant and desirable than otherwise it would have been, as is now manifest from the quite contrary treatment I have met with since his death."* About 1704, Mr. Alexander removed to Armourers'-Hall, where he preached to a congregation till his death, Sept. 3, 1709, when he was 49 years of age. He lies buried in Bunhill-Fields.

BENJAMIN GROSVENOR, D. D.(1)—This eminent and truly excellent Divine, was born in London, on the first of January, 1695. His father was an eminent upholsterer; but, in the latter part of his life, met with considerable difficulties, from which he was kindly relieved by his son. At an early age he discovered marks of a sprightly genius, and became impressed with the importance of divine things, which were strongly inculcated by his pious parents. When only ten years old, he had such an awful view of the evil of sin, and such terrifying convictions upon his tender mind, that his life became quite a burden; till, at length, through the providence of God, he was led to hear a sermon at a meeting in Gravel-lane, Southwark, from a minister, whose name he never knew, that satisfied his doubts, removed his fears, and gave him clear views of the gospel method of salvation. From this time, his soul found its true rest; and, henceforward, the duties of religion were his greatest delight. He no longer relished the diversions common to youth; but after school-hours, retired to his closet, spending many hours in prayer and devout meditation, and in reading books on divine subjects. To such a length did he carry these exercises, that his good parents,

* Mr. Alexander's Sermon on the Death of Mr. Slater. *Preface.*
(1) In some of his early publications, he spells his name GRAVENOR.

Pickersgill del.^t Hopwood Sculp^t

Benjamin Grosvenor, D.D.
From an Original Painting.
In Dr Williams's Library, Red-Cross Street.

London, Pub. Octr 1st 1808, by Maxwell & Wilson, Skinner Street.

CROSBY-SQUARE.—*Presbyterian*, Extinct.

who rejoiced at the eminent piety of their son, nevertheless, were apprehensive, lest he should impair his health, and hazard his constitution.

It will be easy to conceive that a mind so powerfully affected with the truth and importance of religion, would feel a strong bias to the profession of the ministry. Such was the ardour he possessed at this period, that he thought he should be able to convert all who heard him: that he could say so much concerning the love of God to mankind, the condescension and compassion of the Redeemer, the worth of the soul, the excellence and evidence of the gospel, the glory and dignity of heavenly things, and the vanity and insignificance of those trifles which commonly alienate the affections from God, together with the glorious or tremendous consequences of a timely acceptance, or total refusal of the gospel salvation, as would certainly fasten the arrow of conviction so deep in the heart of a sinner, that he should not be able to extract it.

At length, with the consent of his parents, he entered upon a course of studies suited to the profession he had chosen; and in 1693, was placed, for academical learning, under the tuition of the celebrated Mr. Timothy Jollie, at Attercliffe, in Yorkshire. Of this amiable man he speaks in terms of singular respect; and as a preacher, seems evidently to have formed himself upon his model. (K) In 1695,

---

(K) The Rev. TIMOTHY JOLLIE, son to the Rev. Thomas Jollie, ejected from Althome, in Lancashire, was born about the year 1660. He pursued his academical studies under the Rev. Richard Frankland, at Rathmill, in Yorkshire, and was ordained pastor of a congregational church at Sheffield, April 28, 1681. The following year, he had his goods distrained, and was thrown into rigorous confinement in the castle of York. Some years afterwards he succeeded Mr. Frankland in the care of the academy; and had the honour of furnishing our churches with a considerable number of Divines, who greatly distinguished themselves in their day. Of his amiable character, Dr. Grosvenor has left the following instructive account. " He was a man of an excellent spirit, of great spirituality and sweetness of temper. The orders of his house were strict and regular; and few tutors maintained them better, and with so little severity. Every thing here was syste-

CROSBY-SQUARE.—*Presbyterian*, Extinct.

he returned to London, and continued his studies under several masters, particularly the Hebrew language under Monsieur Capell, who had formerly been Professor of the Oriental languages at Saumur, in France, but had fled to England for that liberty of conscience which was denied him in his native land.*

This seems the proper place to notice a circumstance in Dr. Grosvenor's life, which has been passed over by his biographers. In very early life he appears to have connected himself with the Baptists. Such was the uncommon seriousness of his disposition, that at fourteen years of age, he was baptized by Mr. Benjamin Keach, became a member of his church, and continued so about seven or eight years. It seems that he began to preach privately at the house of Mr. Keach, who finding him a youth of promising abilities, encouraged him to pursue a course of studies for the ministry. Soon after his return from the academy, he declared his

* Mr. Barker's Sermon on the Death of Dr. Grosvenor, p. 23—29.

matical. But the defects in his institution, as to classical learning, free philosophy, and the catholic divinity, were made amends for to those who were designed for the pulpit, by something those pupils who had any taste, took from him in his public performances. He had a charming voice, flowing, and of a musical sound; a natural eloquence; his elocution and gesture were such as would adorn an orator. The pathetic was sometimes so heightened with that divine enthusiasm, which is peculiar to true devotion, that he would make our hearts glow with a fervour, which he kindled in the breasts even of those, who endeavoured all they could, not to be moved by him. There have been tutors of greater learning, who have been capable of laying out a greater compass of education; but, at the same time it must be acknowledged that the relish for practical religion; that devotional spirit which was so improved by his example; that sweetness of temper and benevolent turn of mind, which a soul of any thing the same make, insensibly catches from such an example, are things not every where to be met with; and yet have such an influence towards our usefulness and acceptance as ministers, as cannot easily be supplied by any other qualities."† Mr. Jollie died at Attercliffe, where he resided, April 28, 1714. His funeral sermon was preached by his assistant, Mr. John De La Rose, and contains a description of his excellent character.

† Mr. Barker's Sermon on the Death of Dr. Grosvenor, p. 27, 28.

CROSBY-SQUARE.—*Presbyterian,* Extinct.

opinion in favour of infant-baptism, and the Presbyterian form of church-government; also, that unordained persons ought not to preach. " These things (says Crosby) moved the church to deal plainly with him. They recommended to him the reading impartially Mr. Tombes' *Examen;* and appointed proper persons to discourse these points with him. After much time spent between the church and him in controversy upon these points, without any effect, he desired a dismission. But, not being determined where to fix himself, they were necessarily obliged to grant his request, and did dismiss him in a general manner from his membership with them."* (L)

It was about this time that his mind became exercised with serious doubts as to the propriety of undertaking the ministerial office. These scruples he ascribes partly to the disputes amongst Christians, and his natural aversion to controversy. He likewise saw a very ill taste among the people, exemplified in their crying up one minister at the expence of another. However, he blessed God that he at length recovered from these discouragements, though they cost him many anxious hours, and many prayers and tears.

Mr. Grosvenor entered upon his public work, in the year 1699, having first passed his trials before several ministers eminent for their soundness in doctrine, and gravity of manners: these were Mr. John Quick, Mr. John Spademan, Mr. Thomas Rowe, Mr. Robert Fleming, Mr. Joshua Oldfield, Mr. John Nesbitt, and Mr. William Harris. In the same year, he was chosen assistant to Mr. Oldfield, at Maid-lane, Southwark. But the distinguished abilities he displayed as a preacher were not confined long to this station. In the year 1700, he preached as a candidate for the

* Crosby's English Baptists, vol. iv. p. 203.

(L) From Crosby's account the reader will naturally conclude that Mr. Grosvenor received a peaceable dismission. The contrary, however, was the fact, and it afterwards operated to his injury. Most of the ministers of that period, at least of the Independent and Presbyterian denominations, considered him to have been treated with harshness and injustice.

pastoral office at Stepney, in the room of the celebrated Matthew Mead; (M) and in 1702, engaged in a lecture at the Old Jewry, in conjunction with his amiable friend Mr. Samuel Rosewell. It was supported by some of the most eminent citizens of London; and they conducted it for some time, with considerable reputation. After Mr. Grosvenor had been thus employed about two years, he was chosen to succeed the venerable Mr. Samuel Slater, as pastor of the Presbyterian congregation in Crosby-Square. He was ordained July 11, 1704, and soon raised the church to a flourishing state, in which it continued many years without any considerable declension. This increase rendered it proper for him to have an assistant, and several valuable ministers served him successively in that office.*

In the year 1703, Mr. Grosvenor married Mrs. Mary South, daughter of Captain Henry South, of Bethnal-green, a family of eminence among the Dissenters. Of this lady, he observes, "She was of a handsome fortune, a comelier person, and of the most excellent disposition." They lived happily together till 1707, when she was suddenly removed by death, soon after her supposed happy recovery on the birth of her second child. This marriage, produced one son, Benjamin South Grosvenor, who died many years before the Doctor; and a daughter who died an infant. In 1712, Mr. Grosvenor married his second wife, Mrs. Elizabeth Prince, by whom he had four sons, of whom the youngest only survived him. It appears from Mr. Barker's account, that the children inherited neither their father's prudence nor piety, which occasioned him very heavy affliction; but he supported it with a patience and resignation that religion alone could inspire.†

(M) This appears from the church books belonging to the Independent Society at that place. It is probable Mr. Grosvenor would have settled there, had it not been for the unfavourable impression derived from his excommunication by Mr. Keach's church.

* Mr. Barker's Sermon, *ubi supra*, p. 29—31.   † *Ibid.* p. 31—34.

CROSBY-SQUARE.—*Presbyterian*, Extinct.

The popularity of Mr. Grosvenor as a preacher; his singular acumen and lively imagination, his graceful utterance, and fervent devotion, recommended him to some of the most considerable lectures about London. Besides the one at the Old Jewry already mentioned, he was one of the first preachers of the Friday evening lecture at the Weigh-House, set on foot at the beginning of the eighteenth century. The subjects discussed at the outset related to some important parts of divine worship; and several discourses delivered in 1707, and some following years, were afterwards published. In 1716, Mr. Grosvenor was chosen into the merchant's-lecture, upon a Tuesday morning, at Salters'-Hall. The University of Edinburgh taking into consideration his extraordinary merits, conferred upon him, in 1730, in the most respectful manner, and without his previous knowledge, the degree of Doctor in Divinity. In 1735, when the nation was under the alarm of Popery, some dissenting ministers in London, chiefly of the Presbyterian denomination, undertook a course of sermons at Salters'-Hall, against the principal errors of the church of Rome. It fell to the lot of Dr. Grosvenor, who was of this number, to discuss the subject of persecution, which he exposed in very strong colours.

Dr. Grosvenor continued in the faithful discharge of the various duties of the pastoral office till 1749, when age and infirmities compelled him to relinquish his charge, having been a minister in London during the period of fifty years. At the same time he resigned his lectureship at Salters'-Hall. The remainder of his life he spent in a devout retirement; in the performance of good offices among his friends; and in reading the best authors; so that scarcely any new book, on the subject of religion, or polite learning, escaped his notice.

At length, the disorder that terminated his life, increased so fast upon him, that his constitution was quite worn out; but though many perceived his groans, he was never heard

CROSBY-SQUARE.—*Presbyterian*, Extinct.

to murmur or repine. His setting sun shone brilliant to the last, and, as he descended into the vale of death, he experienced those divine consolations which had supported him during an honourable and useful career. His views of death, while in the midst of health, are strikingly represented in the following anecdote. Being at the funeral of Dr. Watts, a friend said to him, " Well Dr. Grosvenor, you have seen the end of Dr. Watts, and you will soon follow; what think you of death ?"—" Think of it (replied the Doctor), why, when death comes, I shall smile upon death, if God smiles upon me."—" I never perceived him to express any fear of dying, (says Mr. Barker,) he viewed the darksome valley without any gloom or horror, he had long rejoiced in hope of the glory of God, firmly believing in Jesus as the resurrection and the life, and in that God *who raised up Christ from the dead, as a pledge and earnest that he would quicken the mortal bodies of his faithful servants, by his Spirit which dwelleth in them.* And this temper of mind, owing in part to a natural sweetness of disposition, but principally to the supports of a divine faith, he preserved to the last. I took an affecting leave of him the night he retired into his chamber, where he remained seven weeks; during which his pain was very violent, but his patience had its perfect work. In my last visit he told me, no body knew what he endured, but he did not murmur or complain. He lost his speech some days, but not his senses, till he slept in Jesus, on Lord's-day morning, August the 27th, 1758, in the 83d year of his age."* His remains were interred in Bunhill-Fields; and an excellent discourse upon occasion of his death, was preached at Crosby-Square, by the Rev. John Barker, who had been his assistant and intimate friend for near half a century.

Dr. Grosvenor was low of stature, but his appearance manly and graceful; and though his constitution was rather

* Mr. Barker's Sermon, *ubi supra*, p. 39, 40.

CROSBY-SQUARE.—*Presbyterian*, Extinct.

tender than robust, yet he was seldom laid aside from public work. His voice, though small, was sweet and melodious, especially till the year 1726, when, in consequence of a violent inflammation, he was obliged to submit to the painful operation of having the *uvula* cut out of his mouth. This, ever after, occasioned an impediment in his pronunciation. Nevertheless, he had so great a skill in managing his voice, owing, perhaps, in some measure, to his knowledge of music, that few preachers were more capable of affecting and commanding an audience. His judgment and faith in the doctrines of the Christian religion, were steady and unshaken. Upon the points disputed among Christians, he might be pronounced a moderate Calvinist, nor did his sentiments ever undergo any material alteration; yet, he detested censoriousness, and abounded in candour and moderation. He possessed great mildness of temper, and a lively brilliant wit; was of a friendly disposition, and enjoyed an habitual cheerfulness, which rendered his pastoral visits peculiarly acceptable.* As a writer, he is peculiarly engaging from his devotional turn, uncommon remarks, and deep acquaintance with history. His language is always pure, his sentences well formed, and his ideas embellished with the most appropriate decorations. A list of his publications shall be given in the note below. (M)

* Mr. Barker's Sermon, *ubi supra*, p. 35—38.

(M) HIS WORKS.—1. An Essay on Health.—2. The Convulsions of Nature subservient to the Interests of the Church : a Sermon occasioned by the dreadful Storm, Nov. 26, 1703, and accommodated to the Design of the public Fast, Jan. 19, 1704. Hosea viii. 7.—3. A Confession of Faith at his Ordination. 1704.—4. Piety triumphant over Wickedness : preached at Salters'-Hall, to the Societies for Reformation of Manners, July 2, 1705. Prov. xi. 11.—5. Exhortation to the Duty of Singing : at the Eastcheap Lecture. Psa. lvii. 8. 1708.—6. The Protestant Religion, and the Liberties of England : a Sermon at Crosby-Square, on Nov. 5, 1709, on occasion of our Deliverance from Popery and Slavery. Psa. xlviii. 8.—7. Rejoice with Trembling : a Thanksgiving Sermon, Nov. 7, 1710. Psa. xi. 2.—8. The Excellence of the Duty of Prayer : at the Eastcheap Lecture. Psa. lxxiii. 28.

CROSBY-SQUARE.—*Presbyterian*, Extinct.

SAMUEL WRIGHT, D. D.—Dr. Grosvenor's first assistant was Mr. (afterwards Dr.) Samuel Wright, who was chosen to that service in 1705. He continued in this situation till 1708, when, upon the death of the Rev. Matthew Sylvester, he removed to Black-friars, and afterwards to Carter-lane. There he became well known by his popular

1711.—9. Dying in Faith: a Discourse on the Funeral of Mr. Peter Huson, who died Dec. 29, 1711. Heb. xi. 13. 1712.—10. The Temper of Jesus towards his Enemies ; and his Grace to the Chief of Sinners. Luke xxiv. 47. 1712.—11. A Sermon on the Name Jesus, Matt. i. 21.—12. A Discourse on the Christian Name, Acts xi. 26.—13. The Dissolution of the earthly House of this Tabernacle: occasioned by the Death of Mrs. Mary Franklyn ; with some Account of her Life and Sufferings for Nonconformity, 2 Cor. v. 1. 1713.—14. The Obligations to Hearing the Word: at the Eastcheap Lecture, James i. 19. 1713.—15. The Preservative of Virtuous Youth: preached to a Society of young Persons, at the Old Jewry, May 17, 1714. Psa. xviii. 23.—16. The Influence of Christ's Intercession: preached Jan. 1, 1714, in Gravel-lane, Southwark. Luke xiii. 8.—17. Precious Death: a Sermon at Crosby-Square, Jan. 1, 1716, occasioned by the Death of Mrs. Susannah Rudge. Psa. cxvi. 15.—18. Directions for the Profitable Reading the Scriptures: at the Eastcheap Lecture. James i. 21. 1717.—19. The burning of London by the Papists ; or, a Memorial to Protestants on Sept. 2.—20. The Mourner Relieved.—21. God the Author of the Exaltation and Prosperity of Kings: preached to a Society of young Men in Jewin-street, Oct. 20, 1719, the Day of the Coronation of King George I. Psa. cxxxii. 18.—22. God's Good Will to Great Britain: at the Lord's Day Morning Lecture in Little St. Helen's, May 28, 1720, the Birth-Day of his Majesty King George I. Deut. xxxiii. 16.—23. Observations upon Sudden Death: occasioned by the late frequent Instances of it both in City and Country. 1720.—24. Preparation for Death, the best Preservative against the Plague: the Substance of two Sermons, preached at the Merchant's Lecture, at Salters'-Hall, Jan. 17 and 31, 1721. Luke xii. 47.—25. The Death of the Righteous improved: preached at Crosby-Square, Nov. 10, 1723, on the Death of John Deacle, Esq. Heb. vi. 12.—26. Persecution and Cruelty in the Principles, Practices, and Spirit of the Church of Rome: preached at Salters'-Hall, April 10, 1735.—27. God's Eternity the Mourner's Comfort: preached at Crutched-Friars, June 8, 1740, on the Death of the Rev. Williams Harris, D. D. Psa. cii. 27.—Dr. Grosvenor was one of the authors of the occasional paper, published in 3 vols, octavo, in 1716. He wrote the first number on " Bigotry ;" also the Essays on " Moral Reformation." It is probable that he also published some other things that

| CROSBY-SQUARE.—*Presbyterian*, Extinct. |

talents and useful preaching, of which we shall have occasion to speak more particularly when we come to that place.

JOHN BARKER.—Mr. Wright was succeeded in the office of assistant by the Rev. John Barker, who, for upwards of four years, continued to assist Dr. Grosvenor, " with whom, (says he) I lived in perfect harmony, and still review with pleasure, and account my honour."* In 1714, Mr. Barker removed to Hackney, to succeed the celebrated Matthew Henry. From thence, after several years, he accepted an invitation to Salters'-Hall; and at both places appeared with great respectability and usefulness. Of this excellent man the reader may expect a more particular account hereafter.

CLERK OLDSWORTH.—Dr. Grosvenor's next assistant was the Rev. Clerk Oldsworth. Of this gentleman, but little information can be procured. It appears that he received his education in the college of Glasgow, upon what may be called Dr. Williams's foundation. He was ordained at the Old Jewry, Jan. 11, 1721, at the same time with Mr. Obadiah Hughes, Mr. Thomas Newman, and Mr. John Smith. After this, he continued to assist Dr. Grosvenor till his death, which happened in the prime of life, about the year 1726. We find his name among the non-subscribing ministers at the Salters'-Hall Synod, in 1719.

have not come to our knowledge. " An authentic Account of several Things done and agreed upon by the Dissenting Ministers, lately assembled at Salters'-Hall," published in 1719, has been ascribed to him; though we know not upon what authority. It was the first publication in defence of the Non-Subscribing Ministers, of whom Dr. Grosvenor was one.——Some of the above pieces have been collected into one volume, octavo, and lately published, with a recommendatory preface by the Rev. David Bogue, of Gosport.

* Mr. Barker's Sermon on the Death of Dr. Grosvenor, p. 32.

CROSBY-SQUARE.—*Presbyterian*, Extinct.

EDMUND CALAMY, B. D. was son to the celebrated Dr. Edmund Calamy, of Westminster, author of the abridgment of Mr. Baxter's Life and Times. It is probable that he was educated for the ministry, first in Scotland, and afterwards in Holland, at both which places, his father possessed considerable connexions. Returning to London, he was chosen, in 1723, to preach a Tuesday lecture at the Old Jewry, in conjunction with several other ministers of the younger class. In the year 1726, he was chosen assistant to Dr. Grosvenor, at Crosby-Square; in which situation he continued till the Doctor's resignation in 1749, when he also declined preaching. After this, he lived a few years in retirement, till his death, which happened in St. John's-square, June 13, 1755. Mr. Calamy was a learned and ingenious man, of great worth, and much respected in his day. He had a brother, Mr. Adam Calamy, who was educated at Mr. Watkins's academy, Spital-square, and bred to the profession of an attorney. He was one of the earliest writers in the Gentleman's Magazine. The subjects on which he chiefly exercised his pen, were essays in polemical theology and civil liberty; and he distinguished himself by the assumed signature of " A Consistent Protestant."

JOHN HODGE, D. D. a learned and respectable minister of the Presbyterian denomination, of whose life it is not in our power to lay before the reader many particulars. He received his academical education at Taunton, under the learned Mr. Henry Grove, for whom he ever afterwards retained an affectionate remembrance. The place where he spent the first years of his ministry was, we believe, at Deal, in the county of Kent. From thence he removed to Glocester, where he continued to labour with great reputation, for a considerable period. Dr. Grosvenor being disabled for public service, which made it expedient for him to resign the pastoral office in 1749, Dr. Hodge accepted an invitation to succeed him at Crosby-Square. At the time of his

CROSBY-SQUARE.—*Presbyterian*, Extinct.

settlement in that place, the congregation was in a very low state. And notwithstanding his pulpit composures were very sensible and devotional, and his manner of delivery just, though not striking, he was not so happy as to raise the church; but as the old members died, or families removed, it continued sinking. At length, the infirmities of advanced life, obliged him to resign the pastoral relation, about the year 1761 or 1762. After this, he lived for some time in retirement, preaching only occasionally, till he was removed by death, August 18, 1767. As an acknowledgment of the benefits he received during the course of his academical studies, he bequeathed to the academy of Taunton, his valuable library of books. Upon the dissolution of that seminary, they were removed to Exeter.

Dr. Hodge was a learned and respectable man, of moderate sentiments, and an excellent preacher. He favoured the republic of letters with a valuable set of discourses, in one volume, octavo, upon the Evidences of Christianity. They are written in a comprehensive, judicious, and nervous manner, and have been highly spoken of by good judges. He also published several single sermons: as one upon New-year's Day, at St. Thomas's, Southwark—another at the morning lecture, Little St. Helen's, August 1, 1751—and a third occasioned by the death of the Rev. John Mason, author of the treatise on Self-knowledge; preached at Cheshunt, Herts, Feb. 20, 1763. Dr. Hodge also drew up an account of Mr. May's Life, prefixed to his sermons. 1755. (N)

(N) Dr. Hodge had a son educating for the ministry at Daventry, under Dr. Ashworth, but who was removed by death in the following affecting manner. A fire happening in the town, greatly alarmed the family at the academy. Mr. Hodge desirous of rendering his assistance, became extremely active at the scene of distress; but returned home greatly fatigued, and his clothes soaked with water. This occasioned a fever, and produced a train of disorders that issued in his death. Of this event he had a remarkable premonition, which he hinted to a friend several days before it happened; and taking a walk into the church-yard, fixed upon the spot where he desired to be buried.—*Private Information.*

CROSBY-SQUARE. *Presbyterian.* Extinct.

RICHARD JONES.—Upon the resignation of Dr. Hodge, the principal members invited the Rev. Richard Jones, formerly a pupil of Dr. Doddridge, but who had been settled some years with the Presbyterian congregation in Green-street, Cambridge. Hopes were entertained that the congregation in Crosby-Square would revive under his ministry, but the experiment did not succeed to the extent desired. The lease of the meeting-house expiring about five or six years afterwards, the state of the Society was too discouraging to warrant a renewal; so that they agreed to dissolve their church-state, and the remaining members dispersed into other societies. This affecting event took place October 1, 1769, when Mr. Jones delivered a farewell discourse, suited to the occasion, from Titus ii. 13. *Looking for that blessed hope, and the glorious appearing of the great God, and our Saviour Jesus Christ.*

In this sermon, which was afterwards printed, Mr. Jones takes leave of his church in the following words : " As we are now met together for the last time in this place, as a Christian Society, and in a mutual relation, there is a special propriety in my discoursing to you on that appearing of Christ, our preparation for which is the great end of all religious institutions ; and to which I hope all my ministrations have more or less had a reference. See that you be ready for this appearing of Christ ; and that none of you be wanting at his right hand when he shall come to judgment. I close my public services among you with the professions of my sincere respect and esteem for you, and with my wishes for your happiness, temporal and eternal. With this discourse, and the celebration of the Lord's-Supper, my relation to you, as a pastor and teacher, will expire; but there is one relation that I shall ever bear you, in whatever place or station of service I may be hereafter fixed : for I shall always be your's to the utmost of my power, in all the offices of friendship, love and gratitude. I have no doubt but that the future charges of my life will be under the direction of

CROSBY-SQUARE.—*Presbyterian*, Extinct.

that Great Being, in whose favour I hope to make my final remove out of it: and if I had been more useful to you during the short time of my connexion with you, it would have afforded me a very exalted pleasure amidst all the pain of our present parting. Make a serious business of religion, wheresoever you go, *now that our gates are desolate:* nor let it ever appear that you have hitherto heard in vain. The public devotions of this house have in past years been conducted by those who were ornaments to human nature, as well as to a particular denomination of Christians: approve yourselves the worthy disciples of such teachers. Such of you as knew this place in its prosperous days, must for many late years have experienced similar emotions with those old men amongst the Jews, who wept at seeing the sad difference there was between the second temple and the first. The church of Christ, though *not of this world*, will in some measure partake of its changes and variations : and we of this Society must be reconciled to the disagreeable alterations that time and death have made amongst us. Amidst all the instability of this world, as to both its civil and religious concerns, let me lead your thoughts forwards to a higher and a better : where all the connexions and relations that are founded in religion and virtue, shall be more permanent, as well as more delightful."*

Mr. Jones, soon after his leaving Crosby-Square, settled with the Presbyterian congregation at Peckham, where he preached for a considerable number of years, and was succeeded by the Rev. W. B. Collyer. Some further particulars relating to his life and character, will be given under that article.

* Mr. Jones's Sermon at Crosby-Square, p. 24—31.

RELLYANISTS.

The Rellyanists, or Rellyan Universalists, take their name from James Relly, the leader of a religious sect, whose distinguishing tenets have received the name of Antinomianism. They, however, disclaim the term, for which reason we have avoided using it upon the present occasion. It is no uncommon thing in controversies concerning the doctrines of grace; even where the differences have been much smaller than those between Mr. Relly and his opponents, for one party to brand the other with the opprobrious epithets of Antinomian, or Arminian. " Each may hold principles, (it has been very justly remarked,) the consequences of which may be thought to lead, or may really lead in theory, to the alleged issue: but, though it be just to point out the legitimate consequences of a principle with a view to evince the true nature of it, yet candour forbids the ascribing of any thing to a person beyond what he perceives or avows."* Were these sentiments more generally attended to, there would be less acrimony in our religious disputes, as well as greater unanimity among persons who avowedly differ in opinion.

Not long after the dissolution of the Presbyterian Society in Crosby-Square, the meeting-house was taken upon lease, by Mr. James Relly, of whom we are enabled to present the reader with the following authentic account. (o)

James Relly was born at Jefferson, in the county of Pembroke, North-Wales, in the year 1720. His parents were respectable persons; and placed him for education at the grammar-school in that town. At the usual age,

* Theol. Dict. Perth. Art. *Antinomians.*

(o) The substance of this narrative was received from a respectable member of the religious community, now under our notice, to whom the autho desires to return his acknowledgments.

CROSBY-SQUARE.—*Rellyanists.*

he was put apprentice to a cow-farrier, in which occupation he is said to have excelled, on account of his activity, and great bodily strength. Relly was a wild ungovernable youth, and addicted to bad company. The occasion of his reformation is said to have been as follows. On a certain Sunday, he agreed with some other lads of his own stamp, to go and hear Mr. Whitefield preach, that he might have an opportunity of laughing at the Methodists. They commenced their sport by making a noise, and ridiculing the preacher, to the disturbance of the congregation. At length, Mr. Whitefield's discourse, which was delivered with his usual energy, so rivetted the attention of young Relly, that, when his companions wished him to retire, he resolved to stay behind, and from that time became serious. He now had many conflicts with himself, on his past life and future expectations.

Mr. Relly having formed an acquaintance with Mr. Whitefield, became one of his most strenuous supporters; and, in a little time, commenced preacher. His first stated ministeral charge was at Ridllangiregg, near Nasboth, in South-Wales, where he continued to preach some years. During his residence at this place, he took frequent journies to Bristol; and, on his way, would often stop at Kingswood, and other places, to discourse with the colliers. At this period he was extremely popular; but a separation taking place between him and Mr. Whitefield, gave a new turn to his connexions. This breach has been attributed by Mr. Relly's followers, to jealousy on the part of Mr. Whitefield; but the character of that great man was formed upon principles of too noble and disinterested a nature, to admit of so degrading an idea. It was probably occasioned by an alteration in Mr. Relly's sentiments.

After this affair, Mr. Relly came to London, where he soon united himself with the Universalists. His first preaching-place, as far as we are acquainted, was Coach-Makers' Hall, where he had a numerous congregation. Notwithstanding the size of the place, which was far from being small, the court-yard was often filled with hearers; and his voice was so powerful, as well as impressive, that it was capable of being heard at a great distance. At this time, he wrote several of his books; and his preaching and writings created no small stir in the religious world. A variety of persons attacked his peculiar sentiments, which they considered to be direct Antinomianism; and the founder of the sect was charged with many scandalous practices. The term Antinomian is said to have been first applied to him by Mr. John Wesley, and it has been fixed upon his followers ever since. The odium attached to his opinions, on account of the immoral tendency which they were represented to have, produced a great influence upon his followers, who gradually deserted him till he had but few left. In process of time, he took the meeting-house, in Bartholomew-Close, where he continued till the expiration of the lease, at Midsummer, 1769; soon after which he removed into the old meeting-house in Crosby-Square, where he continued to preach till his death, which took place on the 25th of April, 1778, in the 58th year of his age. His remains were interred in the Baptist burial-ground, Maze-Pond, Southwark, where a neat monument is erected to his memory. There were two elegies written upon his death; one by the late Mr. Barrow—the other by Mrs. Mary Burton. He left a widow and one daughter, who is still living, and the mother of a numerous family.

James Relly was a man of plain rough manners, but of strong natural abilities, and of a generous disposition. Concerning the nature and tendency of his principles, it is probable that most of our readers have formed their opinions. He believed that Christ as a Mediator was so united to mankind, that his actions was theirs, his obedience and sufferings theirs; and, consequently, that he has as fully restored the whole human race to the Divine favour, as if all had obeyed or suffered in their own persons; and, upon this persuasion, he preached a finished salvation, called by the apostle Jude, *The common Salvation.* By this, Relly understood the final restitution of all fallen intelligences. He published a variety of pieces in defence of his peculiar sentiments, of which a complete catalogue shall be inserted in the note below. (P) There are two portraits of him; one engraved by June—the other by Sylvester Harding.

We shall close this account of Mr. Relly, with the inscription upon his tomb-stone in Maze-Pond burial-ground:

> Beneath this Stone are deposited the Remains of
> Mr. JAMES RELLY,
> Who departed this life, April 25th, 1778,
> Aged 56 years.
> Being honoured with a divine commission
> To Preach the Glad Tidings of the Great Salvation
> To all People,
> He made full proof of his ministry,
> By endeavouring to rejoice the minds of men
> With Heavenly Truth,
> Knowing, with the Apostle, what it was
> To be an Ambassador of Christ,
> By Honour and Dishonour,
> By evil Report and good Report,
> As Deceivers and yet True,
> As Unknown, yet Well Known,
> As dying and behold we live,
> As chastened yet not killed,
> As sorrowful yet always rejoicing,
> As poor yet making many rich,
> As having nothing, and yet possessing all things,
> 2 Cor. vi. 8—10.

(c) 1. Remarks on a pamphlet, entitled, "A Dialogue between a True Methodist and an Erroneous Methodist." 1751.—2. Christ the Covenant of the People. 1753.—3. The Trial of Spirits. 1756.—4. A Collection of Hymns.—5. Union; or, a Treatise on the Consanguinity and Affinity between Christ and his Church. 1759.—The Cherubimical Mystery.—7. Anti-Christ resisted. 1761.—8. Christ the Christian's Life: a Sermon January 30, 1762.—9. The Sadducee detected and refuted. 1764.—10. The Eunuch for the Kingdom of Heaven's Sake —11. The Salt of Sacrifice, or, the One Baptism.—12. An Elegy on the Death of the Rev. George Whitefield. 1770.—13. Christian Liberty. 1775.—14. Epistles: or, the Great Salvation contemplated. 1776.----He also left in Manuscript the following: 1. A Discourse on the Lord's-Supper.---2. The History of Prince Llewellyn, in 4 Parts; divided into Scenes, and adapted for the Stage.---3. The Ministry of the New-Testament: or, the Substance of a Discourse on that Subject.

GREAT ST. HELEN'S.

PARTICULAR BAPTIST.

THE Church of St. Helen, which gives name to the surrounding buildings, was founded in the reign of Henry II. by one Ranulph, who granted it to the dean and chapter of St. Paul's. It received its name from St. Helena, the mother of Constantine the Great, to whom it was dedicated. In the vicinity of this church stood formerly a meeting-house, used for that purpose in the time of the Long-parliament, by the famous Mr. Hansard Knollys. The only account we have of it is that related by Crosby:* " When Mr. Knollys found that his preaching in the churches, though but occasionally, gave so much offence, and brought so much trouble on himself, he set up a separate meeting in Great St. Helen's, London, where the people flocked to hear him, and he had commonly a thousand auditors. But this was rather a greater offence to his Presbyterian brethren, than his former method. Now they complained that he was too near the church, and that he kept his meetings at the same times that they had their public worship. And first they prevailed upon his landlord to warn him out of that place; next, he was summoned to appear before a committee of Divines at Westminster, who commanded him to preach no more." What became of the meeting-house after Mr. Knollys quitted it, we no where learn: but of this eminent man, and of the church he collected, we shall have occasion to make particular mention hereafter.

* History of the English Baptists, vol. i, p. 229, 230.

LITTLE ST. HELEN'S.

PRESBYTERIAN.—EXTINCT.

Little St. Helen's, immediately adjoining to Great St. Helen's, on the east side of Bishopsgate-street, stood on the site of the Priory of St. Helena, founded in the year 1212, by William Fitzwilliam, a goldsmith, for the order of Benedictine Nuns. At the dissolution of the monasteries, it was granted by Henry VIII. to Sir Richard Cromwell, alias Williams, great grandfather of Oliver Cromwell. In the reign of Queen Elizabeth, it was purchased by the Leathersellers' company, who, with part of the materials, erected on the site their beautful hall, the largest and most elegant at that time in London. This hall, together with the adjoining buildings, was lately taken down, to make way for the handsome range of new buildings, called St. Helen's Place.*

The meeting-house in Little St. Helen's, was erected about the time of King Charles's Indulgence in 1672. It was a moderate-size building, with three good galleries, and being conveniently situated, was often made use of for lectures, and other public services among the Dissenters. The first public ordination held by the Nonconformists, after the Bartholomew Act, was performed at this place, June 22, 1694. Of this extraordinary service, which was conducted with peculiar solemnity, and lasted from ten o'clock in the morning till six in the evening, we shall present the reader with a particular account hereafter. The Friday morning lecture founded by Mr. Coward, in 1726, was carried on at this place till the demolition of the meeting-house; when it was removed to Camomile-street. There was also a lecture

* Strype, Maitland and Pennant's Histories of London.

| LITTLE ST. HELEN'S.—*Presbyterian*, Extinct. |

here, for many years, upon a Lord's-day morning, at seven o'clock, during the summer season, in commemoration of the happy accession of King George the First, to the throne of these kingdoms. It was conducted by various ministers, without respect to denomination, and is, also, removed to Camomile-street. The catechetical lecture on a Wednesday evening, formerly at Lime-street, was removed to this place; and a casuistical exercise, on a Lord's-day evening, was conducted here, for some years, by Mr. Pike and Mr. Hayward. Several cases of conscience which they discussed upon these occasions, were published in two volumes, duodecimo, in 1755; and as they possess considerable merit, have since then been reprinted.

The church which assembled at this place for considerably more than a century, was collected in the reign of King Charles the Second, by Dr. Samuel Annesley, a celebrated nonconforming minister. In his time the congregation was considerable, both for numbers and property, and continued in a flourishing state for many years after his death. At length, the congregation so far declined, that after the death of Mr. Kello, in 1790, they dissolved their church state. The meeting-house in Little St. Helen's, was then occupied by Mr. William Brown, who after preaching there a short time, removed his people in 1792, to Cumberland-street, Shoreditch. The place was then taken by the Rev. Christopher Frederic Triebner, a German Lutheran Divine, who had raised a small society in Brown's-lane, Spitalfields; but, in consequence of a division, conducted part of the people, in 1792, to Little St. Helen's. Mr. Treibner was a man of respectable character, and occupied the place about two years, when the lease expiring, he removed to the meeting-house in Great Eastcheap, formerly occupied by a Society of Baptists. A Mr. Underwood then occupied it for about a twelvemonth, till the place was shut up. In October, 1794, a lecture on a Sunday evening, was opened at St. Helen's, by Mr. David Rivers, who, for a short

LITTLE ST. HELEN'S.—*Presbyterian*, Extinct.

time, entertained his hearers with some pulpit essays in this place, and then removed to Monkwell-street. The last sermon preached at St. Helen's, was at Mr. Coward's Friday lecture, May 15, 1795, by the Rev. Samuel Palmer, of Hackney. This ancient building was then shut up for a few years; but in 1799, was entirely taken down, and some handsome houses erected upon the site.

The ministers of the old Presbyterian congregation were as follows:

Ministers' Names.	As Pastors.		As Assistants.	
	From	To	From	To
Samuel Annesley, D. D.	16..	1696	—	—
John Woodhouse,	1697	1701	—	—
Benjamin Robinson,	1701	1724	—	—
Harman Hood,	—	—	17..	1720
Edward Godwin,	1722	1764	1721	1722
Thomas Prentice,	1764	17..	—	—
George Stephens, M. A.	17..	1780	—	—
James Kello,	1781	1790	—	—

SAMUEL ANNESLEY, LL. D.—This eminent nonconformist Divine was born of religious parents, at Kellingworth, near Warwick, A. D. 1620.* He descended of a good family, and could claim noble connexions; being first cousin to Arthur Annesley, Earl of Anglesey, and Lord Privy Seal in the reign of Charles II.† His father dying when he was only four years old, the care of his education

* Dr. Williams's Sermon on the Death of Dr. Annesley, p. 130.
† Calamy's Contin. p. 73.

LITTLE ST. HELEN'S.—*Presbyterian*, Extinct.

devolved upon his mother, a very prudent and pious woman. He was so early under serious impressions, that he often declared, " he never knew the time when he was not converted;" and this religious disposition strongly inclined him to the ministry, from his very infancy.* From this he was not discouraged by an affecting dream during his childhood, *That he was to be a minister, and should be sent for by the Bishop of London, to be burnt as a martyr.*† At Michaelmas term, 1635, being fifteen years of age, he was admitted a student in Queen's College, Oxford, where, at the usual times, he took his degrees in Arts. While at the university, he was particularly remarkable for temperance and industry. He usually drank nothing but water, and though he is said to have been but of slow parts, yet he supplied this defect in nature, by prodigious application.‡

There is some dispute with respect to his ordination; that is to say, whether he received it from a bishop, or according to the Presbyterian method: Anthony Wood asserts the former, and Dr. Calamy the latter; it is possible both may be right.§ In 1644, he became chaplain to the Earl of Warwick, the admiral of the parliament's fleet. In process of time, his exemplary conduct, united to the great interest he possessed with persons in power, procured him a very good establishment at Cliff, in Kent. This was a very valuable living; for besides a revenue of four hundred per annum, it is also a peculiar, a great jurisdiction belonging to the incumbent, who holds a court, in which every thing relating to wills, marriage contracts, &c. are decided.‖ Here he succeeded Dr. Griffith Higges, the sequestered minister. At the commencement of his labours, he met with considerable difficulties, the people being rude and ignorant.

* Dr. Williams's Sermon, *ubi supra*, p. 134, 135.
† Calamy's Contin. p. 64.   ‡ Wood's Athenæ, vol. ii. p. 966.
§ Wood, *ubi supra*.—Calamy's Contin.---Biog. Brit. Art. *Annesley*.
‖ Biog. Brit. Art. *Annesley*.

LITTLE ST. HELEN'S.—*Presbyterian*, Extinct.

So high did they carry their opposition, as frequently to assault him with spits, forks, and stones, often threatening his life. But he was fortified with courage, and declared, that, " Let them use him as they would, he was resolved to continue with them, till God had fitted them by his ministry to entertain a better, who should succeed him; but solemnly declared, that when they became so prepared, he would leave the place." In a few years his ministry met with surprising success, and the people were greatly reformed.*

In July, 1648, Mr. Annesley was called to London, to preach the Fast sermon before the House of Commons, which, by their order, was printed. But, though greatly approved by the parliament, it gave much offence to some other persons, as reflecting upon the King, then a prisoner in the Isle of Wight. This is the ground of Mr. Wood's bitterness against him; and it cannot be denied that the author went all the lengths of the Presbyterian party.† It was about this time that he was honoured by the University of Oxford, with the title of Doctor of Laws, conferred upon him at the instance of Philip Earl of Pembroke.‡ On the 25th of August, in the same year, he again went to sea with his patron the Earl of Warwick, who was employed in giving chase to that part of the English navy which went over to the then prince, afterwards King Charles II.§ After continuing at sea more than three months, he returned to London in the December following.

Some time after this, having procured a suitable successor, he resigned his Kentish living, much against the will of his parishioners, that he might fulfil his promise to them when they were in a different temper. Not long after, in 1652, Providence directed his removal to London, by the unanimous choice of the inhabitants of St. John the Evangelist,

* Dr. Williams's Sermon, *ubi supra*, p. 136.
† Biog. Brit. *ubi supra*.   ‡ Ibid.
§ Heath's Chronicle, P. i. p. 176.

LITTLE ST. HELEN'S.—*Presbyterian*, Extinct.

Friday-street.* In 1657, he was nominated by Oliver, Lord-Protector, lecturer of St. Paul's; and, in the following year, the Protector Richard presented him to the living of St. Giles's, Cripplegate.† But this presentation growing quickly useless, he, in 1660, procured another from the trustees for the maintenance of ministers,‡ being also a commissioner for the approbation and admission of ministers of the gospel, after the Presbyterian mode.§ His second presentation growing as much out of date as the first, he obtained, August 28, 1660, a third presentation, of a more legal nature, from King Charles II.‖ Yet even this did not keep him there long; for on Bartholomew-day, 1662, he was ejected for nonconformity; having been removed from his lectureship at St. Paul's, about two years before.¶ It is said that the Earl of Anglesey, who was his near relation, took some pains to persuade him to conform, and even afford him considerable preferment in the church, in case he complied.** But as the Doctor acted from a principle of conscience, he declined the offer; and continued to preach privately during that, and the following reign.

Upon the Indulgence in 1672, Dr. Annesley licenced a meeting-house in Little St. Helen's, where he raised a flourishing Society, of which he continued pastor till his death. After the division in the Pinners'-Hall lecture, in 1694, and the establishment of a new one at Salters'-Hall, Dr. Annesley was one of the ministers chosen to fill up the number at the latter place, in conjunction with Dr. Bates and Mr. Howe.†† After the death of Mr. Case, he undertook the chief management of the morning lecture, of which he had been the main support.‡‡

* Dr. Williams's Sermon, *ubi supra*, p. 137.
† Calamy's Contin. p. 68, 69.   ‡ *Ibid.* p. 70.
§ Wood's Athenæ, vol. ii. p. 967.   ‖ Calamy's Contin. p. 71.
¶ Dr. Williams's Sermon, *ubi supra*.   ** Calamy's Contin. p. 73.
†† *Ibid.* p. 972.   ‡‡ Account, p. 48.

LITTLE ST. HELEN'S.—*Presbyterian*, Extinct.

As Dr. Annesley possessed a considerable paternal estate, he was enabled to do much good; not only providing for the education and subsistence of several ministers, but devoting a tenth part of his income to charitable purposes.* Though his nonconformity created him many troubles, yet it produced no inward uneasiness. His goods were distrained for keeping a conventicle; but Dr. Calamy remarks it as a judgment of God, that a justice of peace died, as he was signing a warrant to apprehend him.† As he had a very strong constitution, so he laboured earnestly in the work of the ministry for no less than fifty-five years. In the early part of his life, he is said to have been under darkness of mind, but for the last thirty years he enjoyed uninterrupted peace, and assurance of God's covenant love. At length, he was attacked by a painful distemper, which, after seventeen weeks intolerable torture, put a period to his life.‡ He was perfectly resigned to the conduct of Providence during the whole of his illness, and departed triumphantly to his eternal rest, Dec. 31, 1696, in the 77th year of his age. Dr. Daniel Williams preached his funeral sermon, and afterwards published it, with an account of his life and character.

Dr. Annesley was a Divine of considerable eminence, and extensive usefulness. Of a pious, prudent, and liberal spirit; and a warm, pathetic, as well as constant preacher. Before he was silenced he often preached three times a day; and afterwards, twice every Lord's-day, even till his last sickness. The last time he entered the pulpit, being dissuaded from preaching on account of his illness, he said, " I must work while it is day." He was very eminent as a textuary, and had great skill in resolving cases of conscience. His zeal to do good was equal to his ability. When he heard of any minister oppressed with poverty, he immediately employed himself for his relief. He was also

* Calamy's Account, p. 48.   † Ibid.   ‡ Ibid.

LITTLE ST. HELEN'S.—*Presbyterian*, Extinct.

very useful in filling vacant churches, and was the means of introducing the gospel into many dark and benighted villages. The poor looked upon him as their common father; and he spent much in distributing bibles, catechisms, and other useful books. His assiduous labours, and extensive beneficence, were accompanied with many other amiable qualities, which rendered his character truly estimable. The celebrated Mr. Richard Baxter, who knew not how to flatter, or fear any man, passes this eulogium upon him. " Dr. Annesley is a most sincere, godly, humble man, totally devoted to God."*

Dr. Annesley left a son, Benjamin Annesley; and two daughters. Judith, the eldest, married a Mr. James Fromantle, whose son, Annesley Fromantle, was educated for the ministry, at the college of Glasgow. The other daughter, Ann Annesley, was married to the Rev. Samuel Wesley, father to the late celebrated John Wesley. She was a sensible and pious woman, and bore nineteen children, of whom three were ministers; Samuel, John and Charles. Of Dr. Annesley's writings, a catalogue will be given in the note below.(P)

---

* Dr. Williams's Sermon, *ubi supra*, p. 138—143.

(P) His Works.—1. A Fast Sermon before the House of Commons, July 26, 1648. Job xxvii. 5, 6.—2. Communion with God; two Sermons at St. Pauls: the first, September 3, 1654; the second, March 25, 1655. Psa. lxxiii. 25, 26.—3. A Sermon at St. Lawrence Jewry, to the Gentlemen, Natives of Wiltshire. Nov. 9, 1654. 1 Chron. xii. 38--40.—4. On the Covenant of Grace: and on being universally and exactly Conscientious: two Sermons in the Morning Exercise at Cripplegate; Acts xxiv. 16. and Matt. vii. 12.—5. A Sermon at the Funeral of the Rev. William Whitaker, late Minister of Magladen, Bermondsey. Zech. i. 5, 6. 1673.—6. How we may attain to Love God with all our Hearts, and Souls, and Minds: a Sermon in the Supplement to the Morning Exercise at Cripplegate, Matt. xxii. 37, 38. 1674.—7. A Sermon on Heb. viii. 6. in the Morning Exercise Methodized. 1676.—8. Of Indulgences: a Sermon on Heb. x. 4. in the Morning Exercise against Popery. 1675.—9. How the adherent Vanity of every Condition is most effectually abated by serious Godliness: a Sermon in the Continuation of the Morning Exercises. 1683.—10. How we may

LITTLE ST. HELEN'S.—*Presbyterian*, Extinct.

JOHN WOODHOUSE, an eminent tutor and minister among the Nonconformists, received his education in the University of Cambridge. It having pleased God to work effectually upon his heart in his tender years, he escaped the snares of a college life; and his remarkable seriousness procured his admittance into the society of some of the gravest Divines. From the University, while but young, he removed into the family of Lady Grantham, in quality of chaplain. There he resided several years, and spent much of his time in retirement, in the acquisition of knowledge, and in devotional exercises. As an early pledge of more extensive usefulness, his labours were happily successful to the conversion of some persons in the family where he resided. At this period, Providence directed him to a pious gentle-woman under great doubts and perplexities of mind, by whose conversation he was remarkably fitted to administer consolation to others under like circumstances.

When the Uniformity Act took place, Mr. Woodhouse appears to have resided in Nottinghamshire; among the silenced ministers of which county, he is enumerated by Dr. Calamy. He afterwards removed to Sherif-hales in Shropshire, where he opened an academy for training up young men to the ministry, among the nonconformists; and he supported it many years with great reputation. His merit in this particular is the more remarkable, as he did it not from necessity, having a good fortune with the lady he married. (q) But this he considered a farther obligation to use-

give Christ a satisfactory Account, why we attend upon the Ministry of the Word; a Sermon in the Casuistical Morning Exercise. 1690.—11. A Sermon at the Funeral of the Rev. Thomas Brand; with an Account of his Life: Joshua i. 2. 1692.—Dr. Annesley was the editor of four volumes of the Morning Exercises above-mentioned, and wrote a preface to each of them. He also wrote a preface to Mr. Richard Alleine's " Instructions about Heart Work;" and joined with Dr. Owen in a preface to Mr. Elisha Cole's " Practical Treatise of God's Sovereignty."——*Wood's Athenæ*, and *Biog. Brit. ubi supra*.

(q) She was the daughter of Major *Hubbard*, of Leicestershire; a lady of singular piety, as well as handsome fortune.

LITTLE ST. HELEN'S.——*Presbyterian*, Extinct.

fulness. His dexterity in governing, by a due mixture of gentleness and authority, gave him no small advantage over his pupils. Till enfeebled by a painful distemper, his diligence was extraordinary. He piously managed his house as a nursery for heaven, as well as a school for learning; and the many excellent persons, both in the ministry and other professions, who were educated under him, gave sufficient proofs of his ability for his office, as well as fidelity in the management of it. He recommended to his pupils a plain, warm, familiar way of preaching, as most adapted for usefulness; and while he impressed upon them the importance of the ministerial office, many acknowledged him for their spiritual father. In the exercise of his employment, he endured many threatenings, losses and imprisonments; but having counted the cost, these never diverted him from his designs. Among other eminent persons educated under his care, were the following: Mr. Benjamin Bennet, of Newcastle-upon-Tyne, author of the Christian Oratory; Mr. John Ratcliffe, of Rotherhithe; Mr. Matthew Clarke, of Miles's-lane; Mr. Benjamin Robinson, of Little St. Helen's; and Mr. John Newman, of Salters'-Hall, London.

Besides his employment as a tutor, Mr. Woodhouse exerted himself with great zeal and activity as a preacher of the gospel. In this he was encouraged by the seriousness and affection of his hearers. About the vale of *Beaver*, he diffused saving light with great success, and was instrumental in the conversion of some who were remarkable despisers of the gospel. In other places he had, also, many seals to his ministry. He would often say, " I am much afraid of my work, from a sense of my own indisposition and insufficiency; but when I looked up to God for help, I have found his presence warming and enlarging me: and yet, what I had thought best prepared hath had least success." He dreaded an useless life; and when some unhappy circumstances occasioned him to break up the academy, it was his frequent complaint, " Now every field is unplea-

Hopwood Sculpt

Benjamin Robinson.
From an original Painting
In Dr. Williams's Library, Red Cross Street.

London, Pub, Dec.r 1,st 1808, by Maxwell, & Wilson, Skinner Street.

LITTLE ST. HELEN'S.—*Presbyterian*, Extinct.

sant, for fear I shall live to no purpose." Not long afterwards, however, he received an invitation to succeed Dr. Annesley at Little St. Helen's, where he continued in the faithful discharge of his ministry, till his death. Within a few days of that event, he took a solemn leave of his people, in a sermon delivered with his usual warmth and affection. He enjoyed the exercise of reason till the last; prayed with great fervour; was full of inward comfort; and died without a groan, in the year 1700, but at what age does not appear. (R)

BENJAMIN ROBINSON, a learned and respectable minister among the Presbyterians, was born at Derby, of pious parents, in the year 1666. His mother died only a few days after his birth, but Providence designing him for eminent service in the church, watched over his tender years; and his good father took strict care of his education. At a proper age, he was sent to the grammar-school at Derby, under the superintendence of that polite scholar and valuable minister, Mr. Samuel Ogden. Having made considerable proficiency in the learned languages, he was placed under the tuition of the Rev. John Woodhouse, at Sherif-hales, in Shropshire, where he finished his academical studies.

From under the care of Mr. Woodhouse, he removed into the family of Sir John Gell, where he applied so closely to study, as greatly to injure his health. He there became personally acquainted with that great and good man, the venerable Mr. Richard Baxter, in whose defence, against the charge of Socinianism, he, many years after, wrote an accurate and learned *Plea*. After some time, he removed into the family of Mr. Samuel Saunders, of Normanton, as

---

(R) Mr. Woodhouse published, a Sermon on the Death of Mrs. Jane Papillon. Rev. xiv. 13. 1698.—A Catalogue of Sins, (highly useful for self-examination.) 1699.—And a Sermon to the Societies for Reformation of Manners.

LITTLE ST. HELEN'S.—*Presbyterian*, Extinct.

domestic chaplain. The conversation of this family, and a valuable library to which he had access, rendered his situation very agreeable; and he had the satisfaction of being greatly respected. Here, he also preached publicly in turn with several other ministers, (s) and his labours found great acceptance and success.

Mr. Saunders dying, and Mr. Robinson altering his condition, he removed to Findern, in Derbyshire. There he was solemnly ordained to the work of the ministry, Oct. 10, 1688, in conjunction with his much-esteemed friend, Mr. Nathaniel Oldfield. Notwithstanding the discouraging state of the times, he applied to his work with great zeal, and becoming seriousness of spirit. His labours were not confined to his own immediate charge, but extended to other places, and he established several lectures at considerable distances. His learning, piety, and good sense, united with a most obliging behaviour, introduced him to an acquaintance with many worthy persons among the clergy and others, from whom he received such offers of preferment in the national church, as were not to be resisted, except upon a principle of conscience. At Findern, he set up a private grammar-school, in the year 1693, for which he was cited into the bishop's-court; but upon personal application to Dr. Lloyd, the then Bishop of Litchfield and Coventry, with whom he was acquainted, he soon obtained relief. The good bishop took this opportunity of entering into an amicable debate with Mr. Robinson, on the subject of nonconformity, which continued till two in the morning; when Mr. Robinson was dismissed with particular marks of favour from that prelate, who afterwards held a correspondence with him in writing. About this time, if not sooner, he became acquainted with that great and excellent man, Mr. John Howe, who discovering his great worth, resolved to embrace the earliest opportunity of bringing him to London.

(s) The Rev. Mr. Whitlock, Mr. Barret, Mr. Reynolds, and Mr. Cross.

LITTLE ST. HELEN'S.—*Presbyterian*, Extinct.

From Findern, Mr. Robinson was called to Hungerford, in Berkshire. This invitation he accepted upon the recommendation of Mr. Howe, who meeting him there, conducted his settlement with a solemnity peculiar to himself. He exercised his ministry in that place, with great acceptance, for seven years; and, at the earnest request of some of his brethren, in 1696, set up a private academy. This procured him enemies; and complaint being made to Dr. Burnet, Bishop of Salisbury, he was sent for by that excellent prelate, then in his progress, on a visitation, through Hungerford. Mr. Robinson having waited on the bishop, gave him such satisfactory reasons for his nonconformity, and for that undertaking in particular, as laid the foundation of an intimate friendship ever after.

As he was well qualified for the work of a tutor, so he laboured in it with great constancy, and was favoured with remarkable success. He had the honour of training up many persons, who proved useful ornaments to the church; and was a skilful guide to many younger ministers, in private conversation, and upon public occasions.

Mr. Howe, who, from their first acquaintance, had entertained an uncommon esteem for Mr. Robinson, longed for an opportunity of bringing him to the metropolis. This he at length effected. For in the year 1700, upon the death of Mr. Woodhouse, who had recommended Mr. Robinson to his people, as a fit person to succeed him, he received an unanimous invitation to take the pastoral charge of the congregation in Little St. Helen's, which he accepted. When he removed to London, he was in the prime of life, and his mental powers in full vigour. Besides his stated work, while his strength permitted, he frequently engaged in lectures, and other occasional services; so that there were few pulpits in London, of any note, that were not sometimes favoured with his presence. Upon the death of that worthy minister, Mr. George Hammond, in 1705, he was chosen one of the preachers of the Merchants' Lecture, at Salters'-

LITTLE ST. HELEN'S.—*Presbyterian,* Extinct.

Hall; and he supplied his turn with great constancy, and encouraging success. In his declining state, when growing infirmities would not admit of constant labour, he has sometimes reserved himself for that pulpit; knowing that at Salters'-Hall he should not only meet with some of his own people, but have an opportunity of preaching to greater numbers, and to a mixed congregation. And it was remarkable with what zeal and fervency he would address so large, as well as serious an auditory.*

As this eminent man bore a faithful testimony for God by an honourable and useful life, so he was peculiarly favoured in the circumstances of his death. It is a mercy to some, who cannot so well bear a lengthened conflict with the king of terrors, that God takes them to himself by some critical distemper, that soon puts an end to the combat. This tried soldier of Christ had a long and sensible engagement with the last enemy, but his soul was always triumphant. For several months before his last confinement, he had a bad state of health, which frequently disabled him from public service. At this time, those who conversed with him, could not but observe, that the more he was oppressed with bodily indisposition, the more flourishing and vigorous were his Christian graces. When the great subjects of religion were the topics of conversation, the powers of his mind did not seem in the least impaired. His patience and resignation were surprising to all around him; for though he longed to be at rest, he was willing to wait God's time, and humbly submit himself to whatever awaited him.

A worthy minister who visited him a few days before he was taken speechless, gives the following account of their conversation. " I found him in a most heavenly frame. The grace that was in him shined forth with wonderful strength and lustre, as it had done all the time of his sick-

* Sermon on the Death of the Rev. and learned Mr. Benjamin Robinson, by John Cumming, M. A. p. 51—62.

LITTLE ST. HELEN'S.—*Presbyterian*, Extinct.

ness. Inquiring how it was with him, he replied, Exceeding weak in body, but as to the state of his soul, he could say it was well with him, and that matters had of a long time been settled between God and him, upon a good and solid foundation. He declared again and again, that he had no darkness, no not a cloud to interfere between him and the cheerful light of God's countenance; that he was full of peace, and felt an inward joy that was unspeakable. Upon his friend saying, Sir, this is heaven in the beginnings of it, he answered, with tears of consolation, It is heaven! and if so much is to be enjoyed here, what shall we enjoy in the celestial glory? Speaking of the use God had made of him in his ministry, he said, He had the witness in himself, that from the time of his first devoting himself to his Lord and Master Jesus Christ, in that honourable and blessed work, he had made it his business to serve him faithfully, to that very day. Reflecting on his great weakness, and approaching dissolution, he said, That as he found his infirmities increasing upon him, so he found his inward pleasures, from the prospect of that happiness which was before him, to grow in proportion. His friend observes, that all the faculties of his mind seemed as sprightly and vigorous as if he ailed nothing."

When taking his last farewell of his family, he left the following solemn charge with his children: " You are, (says he) to my knowledge, the children of the covenant, for four or five generations. Do not suffer the entail to be cut off. It would be a great surprise to me, if heaven could admit of such a thing, to find at last you have lost your way thither. I devoted you to God in baptism, when infants, and you have confirmed it by your public and solemn engagements to him at the Lord's table. Remember the vows of God are upon you. If you forsake him, you contract double guilt, and must expect a heavier doom and punishment. " To his youngest child, with the same fatherly

LITTLE ST. HELEN'S.—*Presbyterian*, Extinct.

affection and concern, he recommended the words of dying David to Solomon, " Know thou the God of thy father, and serve him with a perfect heart, and with a willing mind : for the Lord searcheth all hearts, and understandeth all the imaginations of the thoughts : if thou seek him, he will be found of thee ; but if thou forsake him, he will cast thee off for ever." The last words he was heard to speak, were those of Simeon, when he had his Saviour in his arms, with which he cheerfully and triumphantly commended his departing soul to God : " Now, Lord, lettest thou thy servant depart in peace, for mine eyes have seen thy salvation : and, with these eyes, I shall see thy glory." After this manner, he spent many wearisome days, and painful nights, continually rejoicing in God, till at length, after eight weeks confinement to his bed, he triumphantly departed to his eternal rest, April 30, 1724, aged 58 years. His remains were interred in Bunhill-Fields, and the Rev. John Cumming preached his funeral sermon, which was afterwards published, with a copious account of his life and character.*

Mr. Robinson was in person well-formed, of a sprightly constitution, and an agreeable aspect. His natural capacity was of a superior order, and he had acquired a large stock of the most useful learning. He was not satisfied with a superficial knowledge of things, nor carried away with mere sound ; but his penetration was deep, and his judgment solid. These qualifications rendered him an able champion for the faith. He could see through the disguises of error, and dispel those mists with which they are sometimes shaded, even by the learned. His thoughts were distinct, and his recollection easy. He possessed a nervous way of reasoning, and forced conviction, not by a deceitful eloquence, but by dint of argument. As he was eminently furnished for all the duties of the ministerial office, so no man was more faithful in the discharge of them. His sermons were

* Mr. Cumming's Sermon, *ubi supra*, p. 84—90.

LITTLE ST. HELEN'S.—*Presbyterian*, Extinct.

directed to the great and necessary points of Christian faith and practice, which he discussed upon evangelical principles. Being sensible, that, whatever pretences man may make to probity and virtue, upon common natural principles, yet that the grace and truth of the gospel are the only effectual springs of true holiness, he was careful to press these things upon the minds of his hearers. His manner of preaching, suited to the dignity of his subjects, was grave, serious, and affecting. He could compose with great ease and rapidity, insomuch that it was observed, " he could do more in an hour, than most men in a day." Yet his performances appeared the result of laboured study, and long reflection. His eloquence was natural and manly, well adapted to argumentation. He possessed a warm and steady zeal for the leading doctrines of Christianity; was a Dissenter upon principle; yet, of the most enlarged charity towards those who differed from him; and pleaded for a free and impartial toleration. As he was eminently distinguished for his gifts and graces, so his whole conduct was exemplary, and an ornament to his sacred profession.*

As an author, Mr. Robinson did not appear very frequently before the public, but the few pieces he produced gave strong indications of his superior abilities, and met with great acceptance in the world. His first publication was a sermon preached at Salters'-Hall, to the Societies for Reformation of Manners, June 30, 1701, the text, Psa. cvi. 30, 31.—In 1709, he published, " A Review of the case of Liturgies, and their imposition; in answer to Mr. Bennet's Brief History of pre-composed set Forms of Prayer, and his Discourse of joint Prayer." To this Mr. Bennet wrote a reply, which was answered by Mr. Robinson, and produced a second letter from Mr. Bennet. This was a controversy of some importance, and called forth no inconsiderable talent. Some sentiments advanced by Mr. Bennet, were

* Mr. Cumming's Sermon, *ubi supra*, p. 62—84.

LITTLE ST. HELEN'S.—*Presbyterian*, Extinct.

considered not only contrary to the general sense of Dissenters, but as a shock upon the reason of mankind. It is no wonder, therefore, that his book met with animadversion. Two pamphlets by way of answer to it, were written by Mr. John Horsley, ancestor to the late bishop of that name. It was also severely reprehended by some of his own brethren, particularly by Dr. Wainewright, Mr. Ollyffe, and Dr. John Edwards, in his " Christian Preacher."*—Another controversy that engaged the pen of Mr. Robinson, related to the Trinity, the defence of which doctrine occupied much of his thoughts in the latter years of his life. It is well known that he was one of the four London ministers who wrote the tract, entitled, " The Doctrine of the Ever Blessed Trinity stated and defended, 1719 ;" in which he discusses the scripture evidence with great clearness and ability. His zeal for the importance of this doctrine, he discovered on a variety of occasions, and took a considerable share in the disputes at Salters'-Hall, where he joined the subscribing ministers.—Another of his publications was, a sermon, entitled, " The Protestant Succession refused by Men, but owned by God ;" preached May 28, 1719, the anniversary of the King's birth-day. He also wrote prefaces to several books, such as to Mr. Bartlet's Discourse concerning the Pardon of Sin, 1704; to Hitchin's Infant's Cause Pleaded, 1706 ; to Brown's Real Christian ; and to Warner's Discourse on Salvation, &c. And it is not improbable that he published some other things which have not passed under our notice.

HARMAN HOOD.—Mr. Robinson was assisted several years by a Mr. Harman Hood, who also preached an evening lecture at St. Thomas's, Southwark, in conjunction with Dr. Wright. But increasing illness compelled him to relinquish both these services about the year 1720. He survived Mr. Robinson, and furnished Mr. Cumming with

* Biog. Brit. vol. ii. Art. *Bennet*.

LITTLE ST. HELEN'S.—*Presbyterian*, Extinct.

several particulars relating to his life. His name is among the subscribing ministers, at the Salters'-Hall Synod, in 1719. The above are all the particulars we know concerning him, excepting that he appears to have been some way related to Mr. Samuel Slater, mentioned in a foregoing article. That excellent person is said to have married the widow of Mr. Hood, daughter to Mr. Harman Sheafe, of London, son of Mr. Harman Sheafe, of Cranbrook, in Kent.

EDWARD GODWIN.—This respectable minister was born at Newbury, in Berkshire,* about the year 1695. Being designed for the ministry, he was sent, at a proper age, to an academy at Tewkesbury, superintended by the Reverend and learned Mr. Samuel Jones, at that time, a very eminent tutor among the nonconformists. (T) Under

* *Private Information.*

(T) Mr. SAMUEL JONES, who was of Welch extraction, received his education in Holland, under the learned Perizonius. He kept his academy first at Glocester, from whence, in 1712, he removed to Tewkesbury, where, we believe, he was also pastor of a congregation. Of his method of education, a very interesting account may be seen, in a letter written in 1711, by Mr. (afterwards archbishop) Secker, then one of Mr. Jones's pupils, to the celebrated Dr. Isaac Watts.† Mr. Secker speaks highly of the advantages he enjoyed at this seminary, which he calls " an extraordinary place of education." Mr. Jones obliged his pupils to rise at five o'clock every morning, and always to speak Latin, except when they mixed with the family.—" We pass our time very agreeably (says Mr. Secker) betwixt study and conversation with our tutor, who is always ready to discourse freely of any thing that is useful, and allows us either then, or at lecture, all imaginable liberty of making objections against his opinions, and prosecuting them as far as we can. In this and every thing else, he shews himself so much a gentleman, and manifests so great an affection and tenderness for his pupils, as cannot but command respect and love."—When Dr. Doddridge set on foot his academy, his friend Dr. Clark communicated to him, Mr. Jones's Lectures on Jewish Antiquities. A copy of these, very neatly written, in two volumes octavo, is preserved in Dr. Williams's

† See Gibbons's Memoirs of Watts, p. 346.

LITTLE ST. HELEN'S.—*Presbyterian*, Extinct.

the tuition of this excellent person, Mr. Godwin made considerable proficiency in learning, which he improved by long and close application. Such was the high opinion entertained of his abilities and worth, that, upon the death of his tutor, he received a pressing invitation to succeed him in the important province of educating young men to the ministry. This, however, he modestly declined.* Upon his leaving the academy, he settled with a congregation at Hungerford, in Berkshire; where he preached about a year or two, in the capacity of an assistant. He also officiated as joint-tutor of an academy in the same town.†

Mr. Godwin settled in London, in the year 1721, as assistant to Mr. Benjamin Robinson, at Little St. Helen's. In the following year, he was ordained co-pastor; and upon Mr. Robinson's death, in 1724, succeeded to the whole charge.‡ As Mr. Godwin was a very lively and ready preacher, the congregation which had declined under his predecessor, soon experienced a considerable revival.§ He had not been long settled in London, before he was chosen to preach at some of the most popular lectures among the Dissenters. The first he was called to engage in, was at the Old Jewry, on a Tuesday evening, about the year 1723. His associates in this lecture, were Mr. Nathaniel Lardner,

---

library. Of Mr. Jones's ability as a tutor, we cannot but form a very high opinion from the merit and eminence of many of his pupils, among whom were the following:—Dr. Samuel Chandler, and Dr. Andrew Gifford, of London; Mr. Thomas Mole, of Hackney; Mr. Richard Pearsall, of Taunton; Mr. Henry Francis, of Southampton; Mr. Jeremiah Jones, the learned author of " A new and full Method of setting the Canonical Authority of the New Testament;" Dr. Daniel Scott, well known to the world by his learned and valuable writings; Dr. Joseph Butler, afterwards Bishop of Durham, the author of that most learned and valuable performance, " The Analogy of Natural and Revealed Religion ;" and Dr. Thomas Secker, who also conforming to the Church of England, rose to the See of Canterbury.

* Dr. Langford's Sermon upon the Death of Mr. Godwin, p. 28.
† *Private Information.* ‡ Dr. Langford's Sermon, *ubi supra*, p. 29.
§ MS. *penes me.*

LITTLE ST. HELEN'S.—*Presbyterian*, Extinct.

Mr. Obadiah Hughes, Mr. Samuel Chandler, Mr. Thomas Harrison, and Mr. John Kinch. The latter resigned, after a short time, as did also Mr. Godwin; and their places were supplied by Mr. Calamy, and Mr. Mole.* Upon the institution of Mr. Coward's Friday lecture, at Little St. Helen's, in the year 1726, Mr. Godwin was among the first ministers chosen to conduct it. The lecture was opened by the celebrated Mr. Matthew Clarke, and his associates were Mr. John Hubbard, Mr. Thomas Hall, Mr. Philip Gibbs, Mr. James Wood, and Mr. Godwin.† After some considerable time, he was chosen one of the Merchants' lecturers upon a Tuesday morning at Salters'-Hall; and likewise into the Friday evening lecture, at the Weigh-House, in conjunction with Dr. Langford, Dr. Chandler, and Dr. Lawrence.‡

The latter years of Mr. Godwin's life, were imbittered by many bodily infirmities, which, nevertheless, he bore with Christian fortitude and resignation; continuing in his ministerial work, as long as he had any strength remaining. At length, after labouring in this part of the vineyard, for more than forty years, with reputation to himself, and usefulness to others, the lamp of life having gradually wasted, was, at last, almost insensibly extinguished, on the 21st of March, 1764, in the 69th year of his age.§ His remains were interred in Bunhill-Fields, and Dr. Langford delivered a funeral discourse to his afflicted church, from John xii. 26. *If any man serve me, let him follow me; and where I am, there shall also my servant be.*

The character of Mr. Godwin is well known to many persons still living. By great assiduity, and intense application to study, even to the injury of his constitution, he acquired a large stock of knowledge; and being much devoted to religious retirement, by the blessing of God, he became

---

* Kippis's Life of Lardner, p. 6. † Coward's Lecture Sermons.
‡ *Private Information.* § Dr. Langford's Sermon, *ubi supra*, p. 30.

LITTLE ST. HELEN'S.—*Presbyterian*, Extinct.

a scribe well instructed in the things of the kingdom. The great and peculiar doctrines of the gospel were his delight. These he opened with judgment, defended with zeal, and applied in lively addresses to the consciences of his hearers. In prayer he was concise, clear, and spiritual; and upon extraordinary occasions, remarkably copious, free, and excellent. He was a person of great humility, meekness, and patience; of few words in conversation, (u) but open and undisguised. As a Dissenter, he acted upon the principle of Christian liberty, and adorned his profession by a moderate and peaceable spirit. Besides attending to the concerns of his own particular flock, he took a lively interest in the welfare of other churches, particularly those in the country; which appeared by his unwearied diligence in the management of some public trusts, for the support of the Dissenting interest. In short, few persons passed through the world with a more fair and unspotted reputation, or more generally esteemed by good men of all denominations.* (x)

(u) Of his great taciturnity, we have heard the following anecdote related by a person who was well acquainted with the circumstance. Mr. Godwin falling into company one day with Dr. Gill, who was equally remarkable for his few words in conversation, and there being some other persons present, they expected to derive much instruction from what passed between two Divines of so much learning and gravity. They were, however, greatly disappointed. Suspecting that their presence was the cause of this taciturnity, they withdrew from the room, leaving the two Divines tete à tete, each occupying a corner of the fire-place. One of these persons having the curiosity to know what would pass between them now they were alone, took a convenient station near the key-hole of the door. The result of the observation, however, was, that they still continued sitting in the same posture, without breaking silence, Dr. Gill being employed in rubbing his legs, after his usual manner.

* Dr. Langford's Sermon. *ubi supra*, p. 29—30.

(x) Mr. Godwin printed the following single Sermons: 1. The wonderful Work of God, an Obligation to continual Gratitude: preached at the Morning Lecture, Little St. Helen's, August 1, 1727. Psa. x. 7, 8.—2. A Funeral Sermon on the sudden Death of Mr. William Voyce, Jan. 26, 1728, in the 56th year of his age: preached at Little St. Helen's. Mark xiii.

LITTLE ST. HELEN'S.—*Presbyterian*, Extinct.

Mr. Godwin married the widow of his excellent tutor, Mr. Samuel Jones. She was the daughter of Mr. John Weaver, a worthy ejected minister, who was a considerable loser by his nonconformity. By this lady, Mr. Godwin had two sons. The eldest, though not trained to the ministry, preached a short time in Mr. Whitefield's connexion, but died in early life. The other son was educated under Dr. Doddridge, at Northampton, and settled at Wisbeach, in Cambridgeshire, where he continued twelve years. In 1758, he removed to Debenham, in Suffolk, but not being settled so agreeably as could be wished, he removed, in 1760, to Guestwick, in Norfolk, where he continued till his death, in November, 1772, in the 50th year of his age. This gentleman was father to the present Mr. Godwin, well known to the world by his "Political Justice," and other writings.[*]

The following inscription is upon Mr. Godwin's tombstone, in Bunhill-Fields.

> To the Memory of the
> REV. EDWARD GODWIN,
> Who was Pastor of the Church of Christ
> At Little St. Helen's, London,
> For upwards of 40 years.
> He had uncommon natural abilities,
> Improved with close application,
> And attended with remarkable Humility,
> Piety, and Sincerity;
> Was an earnest promoter of the Truths of the Gospel,
> And was esteemed by good and learned men
> Whilst living,
> And now greatly lamented.
> He died March 21, 1764,
> In the 69th year of his age.

[*] *Private Information.*

35--37.—3. Christ's Glory in his Incarnation, and the Fullness of his Grace and Truth: two Sermons on John i. 14. preached at Little St. Helen's, Oct. 25, and Nov. 8, 1728: in the Collection of Coward's Lecture Sermons. 1729.—4. The Gain of the whole World, no Compensation for the Loss of the Soul: a Sermon for the Benefit of the Gravel-lane Charity-School, Jan. 1, 1733. Mark viii. 36.—5. A Sermon at the Ordination of the

LITTLE ST. HELEN'S.——*Presbyterian*, Extinct.

THOMAS PRENTICE.—Mr. Godwin being disabled from constant service, Mr. Thomas Prentice, who received his education at Mile-End, under Doctors Conder, Walker and Gibbons, was chosen his assistant in 1762. Not long after Mr. Godwin's death, in 1764, Mr. Prentice succeeded to the pastoral office. In this situation he continued but a short time, when embracing the Sandemanian sentiments, his connexion with this church became dissolved. After this, Mr. Prentice joined the Sandemanian Society in Bull-and-Mouth-street, now meeting at Jacob's Well; but after a few years, retired to Nottingham, where he is still living, and carries on a manufacturing concern.*

GEORGE STEPHENS, M. A.—After the departure of Mr. Prentice, the Rev. George Stephens, a Scotsman, was invited to undertake the pastoral office, which he accepted. In this situation he continued a few years, till his death, at the latter end of 1780, or the beginning of 1781. Mr. Stephens had the misfortune to be blind with one eye; but this was not his greatest defect. He was an imprudent man, and became involved in his circumstances. We could also subjoin some other particulars not greatly to his honour, which cast a cloud over the evening of his life; but as these can add neither to the instruction of the living, nor the benefit of the dead, it is best they should be suppressed.†

JAMES KELLO, brother to the present Mr. Kello, of Bethnal-green, was born about the year 1755, in the city of London; and pursued his academical studies at Homer-

---

Rev. William Langford, at the Weigh-House. 1742.—6. A Sermon, entitled, The Danger of delaying Sinners.—Mr. Godwin, who was the intimate friend of Dr. Doddridge, superintended the printing of the Family Expositor, and corrected the proof sheets from the press. He also inspected the manuscript before it went thither, and made several important alterations, which Dr. Doddridge acknowledges to be " very much for the better."

* *Private Information.* † *Ibid.*

CAMOMILE-STREET.—*Independent.*

ton, under Doctors Conder, Gibbons and Fisher. At his leaving the academy, he settled with a congregation at Hertford, from whence he removed to London, to succeed Mr. Stephens, at Little St. Helen's. Here he preached with some acceptance for the space of eight years, when he was removed by death, in the midst of his days, Feb. 4, 1790, aged but 35 years. He is said to have possessed but slender talents, and to have affected too much of the fop.* His remains were interred in Bunhill-Fields, and with his death, the church over which he was pastor, may be said to have died also. The succeeding revolutions that the meeting-house underwent, till it was entirely taken down, have been noticed at the commencement of this article.

CAMOMILE-STREET.

INDEPENDENT.

IN a former article, we have given a copious account of the rise and progress of the ancient congregational church, of which that in Camomile-street is a branch. The Society in Lime-street being obliged to quit their meeting-house upon the expiration of their lease, at Christmas, 1755, and Mr. Richardson, their pastor, having relinquished his charge, the church divided. That which was considered the largest branch, and who retained possession of the church books,

* *Private Information.*

CAMOMILE-STREET.—*Independent.*

removed to the meeting-house in Miles's-lane, with which they were accommodated on the morning of the Lord's-day, by Mr. Jollie's congregation. Within a few months after their removal, Mr. William Porter was chosen pastor, and continued to preach in Miles's-lane for about ten years. At the expiration of that period, the congregation erected a new meeting-house in Camomile-street. It was opened in the year 1766, and is a good brick-building, of a moderate size, with three galleries. In 1795, Mr. Coward's Friday-morning lecture was removed to this place from Little St. Helen's. In 1802, Mr. Buck's congregation assembled here for a short time, on the afternoon and evening of the Lord's-day, while their new meeting-house was building. The church in Camomile-street is upon the Independent plan, and before the settlement of the present minister, was at a very low ebb; but is now in a flourishing condition.

The following have been pastors of this Society since the division above-mentioned.

Ministers' Names.	From	To
William Porter, ...	1756	1773
John Reynolds, ...	1774	1803
John Clayton, ...	1805	18..

WILLIAM PORTER, the first minister of this Society, was born in the neighbourhood of Royston, in the county of Kent. He received his education at Mile-End, under Doctors Conder, Walker and Gibbons. Not longer after he finished his academical studies, he was chosen pastor of this church, and ordained at Miles's-lane, August 7, 1756. For the space of ten years, he divided his labours between two places; preaching in the morning at Miles's-lane, and in the afternoon at an ancient meeting-house in Hoxton-

CAMOMILE-STREET.—*Independent.*

square, to the same congregation. But the distance between the two places being very inconvenient, and the latter by far too small to accommodate the people, they erected a new meeting-house in Camomile-street, which was opened in the year 1766. In this new situation, Mr. Porter continued about seven years, when his faculties became somewhat disordered; which being attributed by some persons to a different circumstance, occasioned a ferment in the church, and obliged him to leave the place. He, in consequence, resigned his charge, in a letter to the church, dated Feb. 4, 1773. After this, Mr. Porter removed to Chesham, Bucks, but did not, we believe, undertake any ministerial charge. In younger life, he possessed a very handsome person, and striking address. As a preacher, he was lively and agreeable, and, at one time, amazingly popular. But he was never remarkably judicious, not taking sufficient pains with his sermons; by which means he contracted a loose and lazy habit of composition.* Mr. Porter published a sermon occasioned by the death of Robert Cruttenden, Esq. preached at Miles's-lane, Aug. 7, 1763, on Psa. xxxi. 5. To this sermon were affixed some poetical composures by the deceased (y)

* *Private Information.*

(y) Mr. Cruttenden was nephew to the Rev. Robert Bragge, pastor of the congregation in Lime-street. He was educated for, and called to the ministry; and preached frequently in his uncle's pulpit. At this time he received offers of a handsome provision in the established church; but these he declined. However, being destitute of the spirit of his office, and finding that his conscience would not permit him to believe the truths which he from time to time delivered from the pulpit, he had the honesty to desist from preaching, and betook himself to a secular employment. This he pursued with considerable success, and in process of time, was chosen the Lord Mayor's Common Hunt, a place of considerable profit. But, losing a great part of his substance in the South Sea bubble, he sold his place, and lived in a private manner, upon the property he had left, and the profits of a place in the Post-office. In this situation, and in the fifty-second year of his age, the Lord was pleased to pluck him as a firebrand out of the burning. In what manner he himself informs us, in the

CAMOMILE-STREET.——*Independent.*

JOHN REYNOLDS.—This respectable minister was born in London, in the year 1739. Being designed for trade, he was apprenticed to a watch-maker, and became a member of Mr. Hitchin's church, in White-row, Spitalfields. It seems that he had no regular education for the ministry, but the want of this was, in some measure, compensated by intense application to study; by which means he acquired a respectable acquaintance with the languages, with natural philosophy, theology, and other branches of science. After his entrance upon the ministry, he preached a short time at Newport, in Essex, but did not settle there. Afterwards, he had a call from the Dissenting congregation at Haverhill, in Suffolk, where he succeeded the Rev. Thomas Mildway. He continued there till September 1773, when he removed to London, to succeed Mr. Porter, at Camomile-street. He was set apart to the pastoral office in that place, March 2, 1774. In this situation, he laboured upwards of thirty years, till he was removed by death, December 7, 1803, in the 65th year of his age. Mr. Reynolds's health had been declining for at least a year or two before he died. He was able, however, though somewhat indisposed in body, to preach and administer the Lord's-Supper, the Sabbath before his death. On the Monday following, he went to Denmark-hill, to baptize a child of Captain James Wilson. In the evening, he returned in a carriage to Shoreditch church, and in walking from thence to his house in Hoxton-square, the cold seized his lungs. All efforts to restore accustomed heat proved in vain; and he departed about two

---

narrative of his experience, delivered before Mr. Richardson's church, at the time of his being admitted a member, June 4, 1743, and afterwards published, with a recommendation by the Rev, George Whitefield. He survived his conversion upwards of twenty years, and during that time, bore a noble testimony to the truth and power of religion. After the division in the church at Lime-street, Mr. Cruttenden adhered to the branch in Miles's-lane. He died happily June 20, 1763, aged 73.——*Mr. Porter's Sermon on the Death of Robert Cruttenden.*

CAMOMILE-STREET.—*Independent.*

o'clock on the Wednesday morning. On Wednesday, December 14, his remains were interred in Bunhill-Fields, when Mr. Brooksbank delivered an address at the grave; and on the ensuing Lord's-day, Mr. Thorpe preached the funeral sermon, to the bereaved church in Camomile-street, but did not publish it.

Mr. Reynolds was in person about the middle size, rather stout built, and of an agreeable countenance. As a preacher, he was extremely unpopular, and the congregation sunk under his care. His sermons, however, discovered marks of labour, were well composed, and stored with suitable ideas. On these accounts, though his preaching never attracted a croud, yet it was esteemed by the more judicious. To a clear judgment he united a sound understanding, and retentive memory; and his mind being enriched by habits of reading and reflection, he proved an agreeable and instructive companion. His judgment concerning the great truths of the gospel coincided with those of Calvin, and to those doctrines he expressed a zealous attachment. His inquisitive mind was directed to various objects of curious and interesting research; and he left behind him at his death, a well chosen library of books, and other curiosities, which he had diligently collected. In early life, he cultivated a close intimacy and friendship with the learned Mr. Samuel Pike. Mr. Reynolds had also formed an intimate friendship with the late celebrated Robert Robinson, of Cambridge; and notwithstanding their difference upon some points, frequently met together when the latter was in London, and debated their sentiments with much temper and good humour.* Mr. Reynolds, we believe, never appeared before the public, in the character of an author.

* *Private Information.*

Upon his grave-stone, in Bunhill-Fields, there is the following inscription:

In Memory of the
REV. JOHN REYNOLDS,
Late of Hoxton-Square,
And for Thirty years
Pastor of the Independent Church
In Camomile-Street,
He died Dec. 7, 1803,
Aged 64 years.

JOHN CLAYTON, Jun.—After the church in Camomile-street had been destitute a full twelvemonth, the Rev. John Clayton, Jun. was invited to the pastoral office. This gentleman is eldest son to Mr. Clayton, of the Weigh-House; received his education at Homerton, and settled first at Kensington, from whence he removed to Camomile-street. He was set apart in the latter place, April 4, 1805. Though at the time of his settlement, the congregation was in a very low state, yet his labours have been successful in raising it to a very flourishing condition.

HOUNDSDITCH.

PARTICULAR BAPTIST.—EXTINCT.

HOUNDSDITCH was anciently called the City-Ditch, from its being the general acceptance of filth, and especially dead dogs, conveyed from the city. In process of time it was enclosed with a mud wall; but was afterwards filled up, and the ground levelled, and built upon.*

* Maitland's History of London, v. ii, p. 1007.

HOUNDSDITCH.—*Particular Baptist*, Extinct.

In the reigns of Charles and James II. a Baptist church met somewhere about Houndsditch, in the neighbourhood of Aldgate, but the precise spot is not ascertained. Nor are we able to communicate many particulars concerning the pastors of this Society. Crosby informs us, that Mr. Henry D'Anvers was joint-elder of a baptized congregation, near Aldgate; but when and where, or who was his colleague, he no where mentions. We strongly suspect this to be the same church with the one we have mentioned at Crutched-Friars, in an early part of this work. If so, it is probable Mr. D'Anvers might have succeeded Paul Hobson.

It appears from Edwards's Gangræna, that the Baptists had a meeting-house about Aldgate, as early as 1646. That Gangræne author relates the following curious circumstance that transpired there. " About Aldgate, in London, there was a great meeting of many sectaries, and among others Master Knowles, and Master Jesse, for the restoring of an old blind woman to her sight, by anointing her with oil in the name of the Lord. It was conducted after this manner. The old blind woman was set in the midst of the room, and she first prayed aloud, (all the company joining with her,) to this effect : That God would bless his own ordinances and institutions for the restoring of her sight. After she had done praying, Master Knowles prayed for some space of time to the same effect, for a blessing upon this anointing with oil; and, after prayer, she was anointed with oil, the person who performed this ceremony, repeating these words: The Lord Jesus give, or restore thee thy sight."*

HENRY D'ANVERS, a writer of some note among the Anti-pædo Baptists of the seventeenth century, descended from respectable parents. Of his history but few particulars

---

* Edwards's Gangræna, Part iii. p. 19.

HOUNDSDITCH.—*Particular Baptist*, Extinct.

are known. He appears to have been a colonel in the parliament army, as also governor of Stafford, and a justice of the peace, sometime before the usurpation of Oliver Cromwell: and we are told that he was well beloved among the people, being noted for one who would take no bribes. It was at this time that he embraced the principles of the Baptists, and also of the fifth monarchy men, though, it is said, he could not fall in with their practices. After the restoration he appears to have suffered considerably on account of his nonconformity. As he possessed a considerable estate, of about four hundred per annum, he made it over to trustees, that it might not be claimed by his persecutors. (z) In the reign of Charles the Second, Mr. D'Anvers was joint-elder of a baptized congregation near Aldgate. But his principles rendering him obnoxious to the government, a proclamation was issued, offering one hundred pounds for his apprehension. He was, at length, taken and sent prisoner to the Tower; but his lady having great interest at court, and there being no charge of consequence against him, he was released upon bail, about the year 1675. In the reign of James II. he attended some private meetings at which matters were concerted in favour of the Duke of Monmouth; but the scheme of that unfortunate prince miscarrying, Mr. D'Anvers fled into Holland, where he died about a year after the Duke was beheaded, A. D. 1686. Crosby speaks of him as " a worthy man, of an unspotted life and conversation."*

As Mr. D'Anvers was engaged in a controversy of some importance, both as it regards the subject, and the persons who were concerned in it, the reader will expect some account of his writings. In 1674, appeared the second edition of his " Treatise of Baptism: wherein that of Believers, and that of Infants, is examined by the Scriptures. With

(z) Crosby's Account of Mr. D'Anvers is so confused that it is difficult to distinguish whether some of the above particulars refer to father, or son.

* Crosby's English Baptists, vol. iii. p. 90—97.

HOUNDSDITCH.—*Particular Baptist*, Extinct.

the History of both out of Antiquity; making it appear, that Infants' Baptism was not practised for near four Hundred Years after Christ: with the fabulous Traditions, and erroneous Grounds upon which it was, by the Pope's Canons (with Gossips, Chrysm, Exorcism, Baptizing of Churches and Bells, and other Popish Rites,) founded. And that the famous Waldensian, and old British Churches, Lollards and Wicklifians, and other Christians witnessed against it. With the History of Christianity amongst the Ancient Britons and Waldensians." We have given the full title of this book, in order to prepare the reader for much curious matter which he may expect in the perusal. Without deciding upon the merits of the argument, it is not too much to say, that in this performance Mr. D'Anvers displays great labour and ingenuity; a good knowledge of ecclesiastical history, and of the writings of the ancients; and that he takes such a comprehensive view of the subject, as to deserve the attention of those who are desirous of acquainting themselves with the controversy. This treatise of Mr. D'Anvers soon brought upon him a number of adversaries, particularly Mr. Wills, Mr. Blinman, and Mr. Baxter. To these he replied in three distinct treatises, in 1675. Mr. Wills having charged Mr. D'Anvers with misquoting his authors, and perverting their sense, appealed to the Baptists upon the subject. This occasioned some of Mr. D'Anvers's brethren to print a short paper in his vindication. It was signed by Hans. Knollys, Will. Kyffen, Dan. Dyke, Jo. Gosnold, Hen. Forty, Tho. De Laune.

Besides his pieces upon baptism, Mr. D'Anvers published, " A Treatise of Laying on of Hands, with the History thereof, both from Scripture and Antiquity. 1674." In his History of Baptism, is an advertisement to the following effect. " There is by the same author, a book lately printed, called, Theopolis, or City of God, in opposition to the city of the Nations: being a comment upon *Rev.* chap. xx. 21. In which the mystery

HOUNDSDITCH.—*Particular Baptist*, Extinct.

of the two states, worlds, and kingdoms, Christ's and Antichrist's; the two cities, Jerusalem and Babylon; the two women, the bride and whore; the two creatures, Lamb and Beast, are particularly unfolded. With a more distinct account than any yet extant, of the great battle of Armageddon, and the success thereof, in the taking and destroying, and imprisoning of Dragon, Beast, and False-prophet; and the thousand years reign succeeding the same. With the many scriptural arguments why those two prophecies of the great battle, and thousand years reign, in point of time, do precede, or are to be before the personal coming of Jesus Christ, whose said personal coming and appearing, with his kingdom and reign on the earth with all the saints, is described, particularly asserted, and treated on.—A piece which may be very useful to any that would have information into these truths, and are desirous of more distinct light and knowledge into that blessed book, and Prophecy of the Revelation, so fully declaring the condition and state of the church in these last times." None of the above pieces are mentioned by Crosby.

EDWARD MAN.—Mr. D'Anvers was succeeded by a Mr. Edward Man, in 1687. This circumstance we collect from an ancient manuscript; and is the only particular relating to his life that we are acquainted with. In the confession of faith put forth by the Particular Baptists, in 1689, Mr. Edward Man is mentioned as pastor of a congregation in Houndsditch. Respecting Mr. Man's successors, and the state of this church in after times, we are entirely in the dark. But though we hear of no farther mention of a church in Houndsditch, of this denomination, it is not improbable, but it removed to some other place; and if so, will fall under our notice, in the succeeding part of this work.

GRAVEL-LANE, HOUNDSDITCH.

PRESBYTERIAN.—EXTINCT.

THE meeting-house in Gravel-lane, Houndsditch, was erected about the time of the Revolution in 1688, for the well-known Mr. Samuel Pomfret. His former meeting was in Winchester-street, but that place giving way, his people built a new one in Gravel-lane. It was a wooden building, of very considerable dimensions, with three capacious galleries; and capable of accommodating 1500 people. Mr. Pomfret was a minister of uncommon popularity, a lively, awakening preacher, and an instrument of much good in his day. He had a larger number of communicants than any other church in London, and notwithstanding his immense labours, held out to a good old age. In the latter part of his life he was assisted by Mr. William Hocker, likewise an excellent minister. They died within a month of each other, in 1721-2; and were succeeded by Mr. Denham, from Glocester. About 1730, Mr. William May was chosen his assistant. The congregation being somewhat reduced, though still respectable both for numbers, and opulence, after assembling at this place for about half a century, erected a smaller, but more substantial meeting-house, in Great Alie-street, Goodman's-fields, to which place we refer the reader for a more particular account of the above valuable ministers. The meeting-house in Gravel-lane, was afterwards occupied as a wool-warehouse, and is still in existence. But nothing of its original state is now to be seen, excepting the wooden walls.

BISHOPSGATE-STREET.

PRESBYTERIAN AND INDEPENDENT.—EXTINCT.

THIS is among the many places in the early times of the Nonconformists which cannot now be identified. In the reign of Charles the Second, a Presbyterian Society met somewhere without Bishopsgate; but by whom it was collected, is unknown. All that we know respecting it is, that the last pastor was Mr. Abraham Hume, a Scotsman, whom we shall have occasion to mention under a future article. (A) The Society appears to have been dispersed by a storm of persecution, raised at the latter end of the reign of King Charles the Second, or the beginning of the reign of King James.*

Besides the Presbyterian Society above-mentioned, there was an Independent congregation met many years afterwards, in Bishopsgate-street; but we know as little of this interest as of the former one. In a list of Independent churches in London, in 1727, there is one mentioned in Bishopsgate-street, of which the pastor was Mr. John Cox, and his assistant Mr. Thomas Davies.† Of these gentlemen we know nothing beside their mere names; excepting that Mr. Cox left the ministry in 1730, when, it is apprehended, his church broke up. With respect to the origin of this Society, it must have been some years later than 1695. It probably arose out of a neighbouring congregation, continued for a short while, and then suddenly expired.

(u) See HANOVER-STREET, LONG-ACRE.
* Mr. Fleming's Sermon on the Death of Mr. Hume, p. 42.
† MS. *penes me.*

HAND-ALLEY, BISHOPSGATE-STREET.

PRESBYTERIAN.—EXTINCT.

HAND-ALLEY is situated on the south side of Bishopsgate-street, a little without the gate. Here stood, formerly, a large meeting-house, occupied near seventy years by a very respectable congregation of Presbyterians. It was erected soon after Bartholomew-day, 1662, for the famous Mr. Thomas Vincent, whose name will always be mentioned with honour, on account of his disinterested labours during the dreadful plague, in 1665. After the great fire, which quickly succeeded the former calamity, most of the parish-churches being burnt, Mr. Vincent's meeting-house was violently taken from him for the use of the parochial minister, while his church was rebuilding. Maitland, who mentions this circumstance, describes it as " a large place, with three galleries, thirty large pews, and many benches and forms."* After some time, Mr. Vincent recovered the use of his meeting-house, and preached there till his death, in 1678. He was succeeded by Mr. John Oakes, as he was, by the celebrated Dr. Daniel Williams; who was followed in the pastoral office by the pious and learned Dr. John Evans, author of those excellent discourses on the Christian Temper. A few months before the death of this excellent person, his congregation, which was very numerous and wealthy, built him a new meeting-house, in New Broad-street, Petty-France, to which place they removed in 1729. Not long after, the meeting-house in Hand-alley was pulled down, and houses erected on the site. The lives of the pastors of this church, will come more properly under our notice, in the article NEW BROAD-STREET, PETTY-FRANCE.

* Maitland's History of London, vol. i. p. 452.

DEVONSHIRE-SQUARE.

PARTICULAR BAPTIST.

Devonshire-Square stands on the site of what was called Fisher's-Folly, from Jasper Fisher, citizen and goldsmith, one of the six clerks in Chancery, and a justice of peace, who erected a large and magnificent mansion here. The owner being a man of no great birth or fortune, and involved in his circumstances, his building so sumptuous a house was considered a piece of extravagant ostentation. It, therefore, received the name of Fisher's-Folly. This mansion afterwards belonged to the Earl of Oxford, from whom it passed to the Earl of Devonshire, who gave name to the street and square, built upon its ruins.*

The meeting-house now under consideration, stands in a paved yard, behind Devonshire-square, called Meeting-house Yard. It is an oblong building, of moderate dimensions, and has two galleries. Notwithstanding the alterations it has undergone, it still carries the marks of an ancient structure, though the precise date of it cannot be ascertained. The probability is, that it was erected soon after the formation of the church, a little before the Protectorate of Oliver Cromwell. After the fire of London, it was wrested from the lawful owners, and converted into a tabernacle for an episcopal congregation, till the parish-churches were rebuilt; when the Baptists regained possession. In the time of Mr. Stevens, about half a century ago, it was new-fronted, and otherwise improved. The church assembling here, is one of the earliest of the Baptist denomination in London. In a former article we have traced the rise of the Baptist churches to Mr. Lathorp's congregation. The members of the first

* Strype's, Maitland's, and Pennant's Histories of London.

William Kiffin.

Ætat 50, Anno 1667.

From an original Painting.

In the Possession of the Revd. Richd. Frost, Dunmow.

DEVONSHIRE-SQUARE.—*Particular Baptist*

separation from his church settled in Wapping, and chose Mr. Spilsbury for their pastor. In process of time some disputes arose in this church, on the subject of mixed communion. Those who were against it withdrew, and formed a separate Society, under the care of Mr. William Kiffin. The separation is said to have taken place in 1653, soon after which the present meeting-house was built. There is a report very prevalent, that Sir Robert Tichborne, Knt. and alderman of London, preached here frequently during the inter-regnum. (B)

(B) Sir Robert Tichborne, Knt. was a native of London, but descended, most probably, from the Tichbornes of Hampshire, formerly Lords Ferrard, in Ireland, and another branch Baronets in England. During the civil wars, he entered into the army, became a colonel of militia, and obtained from Fairfax, the lieutenancy of the Tower. He appears to have been one of the greatest advocates for the death of King Charles I. presented a petition from the common council of London for his trial, was a commissioner of the high court of justice, gave judgment, and signed the warrant for execution. When the long-parliament was turned out, in 1653, he was appointed a member of the committee, and represented the city of London in the parliament which gave Oliver Cromwell the Protectorship. Before this, he was chosen alderman of London, and elected Lord-Mayor, Dec. 15, 1655. He was knighted by Oliver Cromwell, and made one of the Lords of the other house. This so attached him to the Cromwell interest, that he proposed restoring Richard to the sovereign power. He was, however, appointed one of the second committee of safety, in 1659. At the Restoration, he was a prisoner to the Serjeant at Arms, from whom he withdrew, but came in again, and was tried and condemned. He acknowledged his activity in the King's death, and that he signed the warrant for his execution; but, added he, "had I known then what I do now, I would have chosen a red-hot oven to have gone into, as soon as that meeting; I was led into the fact for want of years, and I beg that your lordships will be instrumental to the King and parliament on my behalf." This humiliation saved his life, but he never regained his liberty, dying in the Tower; but the time is not known.* It appears from Maitland, that he resided in a wooden-house, at the upper end of Fitche's-court, Noble-street, Falcon-square. This house strangely escaped in the dreadful fire of London, when the surrounding houses were entirely consumed.† He was author of an excellent book, entitled, "A Cluster of Canaan's Grapes."

* Noble's Memoirs of Cromwell, vol. i. p. 416, 417.
† Maitland's History of London, vol. ii. p. 762.

HISTORY AND ANTIQUITIES

DEVONSHIRE-SQUARE.—*Particular Baptist.*

For several years past there has been a lecture at Devonshire-square, on a Lord's-day evening, conducted by a number of ministers of different denominations. The Wednesday evening lecture, formerly at Great-Eastcheap, being removed to this place, was preached some years by Mr. Swain, who had a crouded audience; and after his death by Dr. Jenkins. The church in Devonshire-square is one of those that constitute the Particular Baptist fund, for the relief of poor ministers and churches, in England, Wales, &c.

The following is a list of the pastors and assistants in the church at Devonshire-square, from the origin of the Society to the present time:

Ministers' Names.	As Pastors.		As Assistants.	
	From	To	From	To
William Kiffin,	16..	1692	—	—
Thomas Patient,	1666	1666	16..	1666
Daniel Dyke,	1668	1688	—	—
Richard Adams,	1690	1716	—	—
Mark Key,	1706	1726	1703	1706
John Toms,	—	—	1722	17..
Charles Bowler,	—	—	1722	17..
Sayer Rudd,	1726	1733	—	—
John Rudd,	—	—	1726	1733
George Braithwaite, M. A.	1734	1748	—	—
John Stevens,	1750	1760	—	—
Walter Richards,	1762	1764	—	—
John Macgowan,	1767	1780	—	—
Timothy Thomas,	1782	18..	—	—

DEVONSHIRE-SQUARE.—*Particular Baptist.*

WILLIAM KIFFIN.—This celebrated person, who made so distinguished a figure among the Anti-Pœdobaptists of the seventeenth century, was, probably, a native of London, and born about the year 1616. The family of the Kiffins appears to have come originally from Wales, where the name signifies a borderer.* He had the misfortune to lose his parents at an early age; for it having pleased God to visit the metropolis with a dreadful plague in 1625, they were swept away by that dismal calamity, which proved nearly fatal to himself. Having six plague-boils upon his body, nothing but death was looked for; nevertheless, he wonderfully recovered. Being left an orphan at nine years of age, he was taken under the care of such friends as remained alive; who possessing themselves of the property left him by his parents, and afterwards failing, only a small part was recovered by Mr. Kiffin.†

In 1629, he was put apprentice to John Lilburn, of turbulent memory, who, during the reign of Charles the First, followed the profession of a brewer, in London; but after the commencement of the civil war, obtained a colonel's commission in the parliament's service. At this time, young Kiffin had no sense of religion upon his mind. Growing melancholy upon a view of his outward condition, he resolved to leave his master; and accomplished his intention early one morning, being then fifteen years of age. Wandering about the streets of London, he happened to pass by St. Antholin's church, and seeing some people go in, he followed them. The preacher was Mr. Foxley, who, discoursing upon the fifth commandment, unfolded the duty of servants to masters. This was so applicable to the case of young Kiffin, as to create his astonishment. He thought the preacher knew, and addressed him personally. The effect was, that

---

* Noble's Memoirs of the House of Cromwell, vol. ii. p. 454.

† MS. Account of Mr. Kiffin's Life, communicated by one of his descendants.

DEVONSHIRE-SQUARE.—*Particular Baptist.*

Kiffin returned immediately to his master, before his absence was discovered.*

The impression made upon his mind by this discourse made him resolve to attend the preaching of the Puritans. Accordingly, soon afterwards, he went to hear Mr. Norton, who was the morning-preacher at the same place. His text was Isa. lvii. 18. *There is no peace saith my God to the wicked;* from which he took occasion to shew what true peace was, and that no man could obtain it without an interest in Jesus Christ: " which sermon (says Mr. Kiffin) took very great impression on my heart, being convinced I had not that peace, and how to obtain an interest in Christ Jesus I knew not; which occasioned great perplexity in my soul. I every day saw myself more and more sinful, and vile. Pray, I could not, nor believe in Jesus Christ I could not, and thought myself shut up in unbelief; and, although I desired to mourn under the sense of my sin, yet I saw there was no proportion suitable to that evil nature which I found working strongly in my soul. I only took up resolutions to attend upon the most powerful preaching, which accordingly I did; by means of which, I found some relief (many times) from the sense of a possibility that, notwithstanding my sinful state, I might at last obtain mercy. I took up resolutions to leave sin; and, although to will was present sometimes, yet, how to perform I had no power."†

After some time, he went to hear Mr. Davenport, in Coleman-street. His subject was, 1 John, i. 7. *And the blood of Jesus Christ his Son, cleanseth us from all sin.* From which he shewed the efficacy of the blood of Christ both to pardon, and cleanse from sin, answering many objections that the unbelieving heart of man would raise against that full satisfaction, which Jesus Christ has made for sinners: " Many of which (says Mr. Kiffin) I found to be

* MS. *ubi supra.* † *Ibid.*

DEVONSHIRE-SQUARE.—*Particular Baptist.*

such that I made in my own heart: as the sense of unworthiness, and willingness to be better, before I would come to Christ for life, with many other of the like kind. Which sermon was of great satisfaction to my soul; and I thought I found my heart greatly to close with this riches, and freeness of grace, which God held forth to poor sinners in Jesus Christ. I found my fears to vanish, and my heart filled with love to Jesus Christ. I saw sin viler than ever, and my heart more abhorring it; and soon after hearing Mr. Norton, from Luke i. 69. *And hath raised up a horn of salvation for us in the house of his servant David;* he shewed that Jesus Christ was mightily accomplished with power and ability to save his people: my faith was exceedingly strengthened in the fulness of that satisfaction which Jesus Christ had given to the Father for poor sinners, and was enabled to believe my interest therein. Then I found some ability to pray, and to meditate upon the riches of this grace; that I could say with David, *When I awake, I am still with thee.* I found the power of inbred corruption scatter, and my heart on fire in holy love to Christ."*

Mr. Kiffin, like most young converts, having but a slender acquaintance with the deceitfulness of his own heart, thought that it would be proof against the power of sin and corruption. He, therefore, much wondered when he heard ancient Christians complain so much of the strength of sin in their hearts. " In this frame of peace and rest (says he), I continued for near three months, rejoicing in the grace of God, and was ready to say, that by his favour, he had made my mountain so strong that I should never be removed. But a new storm began to arise in my soul; for under the comfort and peace I enjoyed, I thought the power of inbred corruption had been so broken within me, that I should never have found it prevail over me any more. I began to feel my confidence in God to abate, my comforts to lessen,

* MS. *ubi supra.*

DEVONSHIRE-SQUARE.—*Particular Baptist.*

and the motions of sin to revive with greater strength than ever. In every duty I performed, my heart was so carnal that duties were a burden to me, and by reason thereof I was a burden to myself. My comforts were gone, and in all the duties of religion, I was as a man that had no strength; yet durst I not omit the performance of any, having some secret hopes that the Lord would not utterly cast me off in displeasure, although my fears were stronger than my hopes. I was daily questioning, whether all that I formerly enjoyed, might be any more than such a taste of the good word of God, and powers of the world to come, as those had enjoyed which fell away."*

Mr. Kiffin continued many weeks in great distress of mind, ashamed of opening his case to any person. And it was still further strengthened by a conversation he overheard in company with some Christians, whom he understood to assert that " the least measure of true grace, was for a man to know that he had grace." As he mistook their meaning, he unhappily drew the conclusion, that he had no grace; which confirmed him in his former dark thoughts. From these, however, he was in some measure relieved by a sermon at London-Stone church. It was a preparation for the Lord's-Supper, and the preacher Mr. Moline. "In the beginning of his sermon (says Mr. Kiffin) he laid down this for truth, that to prepare a man for the right receiving the sacrament, it was absolutely necessary he should have grace, and the least measure of grace was sufficient. He then fell upon that question, what the least measure of grace was? and before he gave a positive answer, proved that to know a man had grace, could not be the least measure, but a very large degree of grace, being a *reflect act of faith,* &c. and then gave several characters of the least measure of true grace. I greatly wondered within myself (continues Mr. Kiffin) to hear him fall upon that which did so greatly and

* MS. *ubi supra.*

DEVONSHIRE-SQUARE.——*Particular Baptist.*

particularly concern me; and also found, in my own soul, some small beginnings of those signs of true grace which he laid down. This wonderfully relieved my hopes again; God being pleased to give me some strength to depend upon his grace more than I had received for many weeks before; my resolutions being strengthened to follow God, and to wait upon him in every duty, whatsoever his pleasure might be towards me at the last."*

It would be tedious to follow Mr. Kiffin through all the variations of his experience. Those who are acquainted with the history of Mr. John Bunyan, and other eminent Christians, who have been exercised with temptations, will be able, in some measure, to anticipate the experience of Mr. Kiffin.

The famous Mr. John Godwin settling in London, about the latter end of 1632, Mr. Kiffin constantly attended his ministry, which he found much to his advantage. About the same time, also, he became acquainted with several young men, who being apprentices, had no other opportunity for conversation but the Lord's-day. It was their constant practice to attend the morning lecture, at six o'clock, at Cornhill, and Christ-Church; and they met together an hour before, for prayer, and religious conversation.†

Mr. Davenport, Mr. Hooker, and several other ministers, leaving the kingdom on account of religion, Mr. Kiffin was put upon studying the grounds of Nonconformity. To this end, he furnished himself with all the books and manuscripts upon the subject, that he could obtain; and consulted several ministers, who, instead of satisfying him, rather despised his youth, and discovered more passion than reason, though afterwards they saw occasion to condemn the very things concerning which he desired satisfaction. Disappointed in this quarter, he searched the scriptures more diligently, and received much satisfaction from the preaching of Mr. Glover,

* MS. *ubi supra.* † *Ibid.*

DEVONSHIRE SQUARE.—*Particular Baptist.*

and Mr. Burroughs, the former of whom went to New-England, and the latter to Holland.*

After some time, Mr. Kiffin joined himself to an ancient Society of Independents, under the pastoral care of Mr. John Lathorp; and afterwards of the celebrated Mr. Henry Jessey. Being now twenty-two years of age, he formed a resolution of going to New-England, but was prevented by a particular providence; and soon afterwards entered into the married state, with a person who belonged to the same congregation. This being a time of peculiar severity against Nonconformists, the congregation was forced to meet early in the morning, or late at night. It was about this time that Mr. Kiffin was desired to exercise his abilities in public; and though the meeting was often disturbed, yet he was preserved from the hands of his enemies. Being assembled one Lord's-day, at a house upon Tower-hill, as he was coming out, several rude persons were about the door, and assaulted him with stones; but he received no material injury, though one hit him upon the eye. About a year after, he was sent for to visit a poor man, in Nightingale-lane, who proved to be the very person that disturbed the meeting upon Tower-hill. He observed, that he was then as well as most men; but from that time was taken ill, and had since so wasted away, that his bones nearly came through his skin. He then desired Mr. Kiffin to pray for him, and died that day.†

Not long after, Mr. Kiffin was taken at a meeting in Southwark, and carried before some justices of the peace. The assizes happening the next day, Judge Mallet committed him to the White Lion Prison, where he remained for some time a prisoner, till the judge returned from his circuit in Kent. While in confinement, some of the prisoners conceiving a prejudice against him, carried their malice so far as to contrive his destruction. Their first plan was to murder him at once; but being deterred from this,

* MS. *ubi supra.* † *Ibid.*

DEVONSHIRE SQUARE.—*Particular Baptist.*

they accused him to Judge Mallet, of speaking treasonable words against the King. Notwithstanding the falsity of this charge, and the intercession of Lord Brooke, he was refused bail; and continued in confinement till the Judge was himself committed to the Tower, upon an impeachment of the House of Commons.*

Mr. Kiffin being deprived of his paternal fortune through the dishonesty of his relations, was left to his own exertions for a maintenance. When he quitted the service of "Freeborn John," to whom he was apprenticed, as above-mentioned, he embarked in trade as a merchant, on his own account; in which he was very successful. In 1643, he went over to Holland, with a small adventure; which proving advantageous, he returned home, and by persuasion of the church of which he was a member, intermitted his secular employment for the study of the scriptures. Having nearly spent the produce of his former speculation, he went again to Holland, at the latter end of 1645, and was so fortunate as to realize several thousand pounds. This enabled him, upon his return, to preach gratuitously, without being burdensome to the churches. After this, Mr. Kiffin had several opportunities of raising his fortune: As first, by the Act of Navigation, prohibiting the importation of all goods, excepting upon English bottoms; and afterwards, during the war that broke out between the English and Dutch, when an order of council passed, encouraging the merchants to import tar, hemp, and cordage, for the parliament's fleet, for which they were to be indulged with bringing home a proportionate quantity of prohibited goods. By these means, and by the blessing of God upon his lawful endeavours, he amassed a very considerable fortune.†

The credit acquired by Mr. Kiffin as a man of business, procured him to be entrusted by the parliament, in 1647,

---

* MS. *ubi supra.*   † *Ibid.*

as an assessor of the taxes to be raised for Middlesex. His great affluence, united with the general, and deserved esteem in which he was held, placed him amongst the foremost of his denomination in the city, and gave him great influence with the Dissenters in general. An instance of this kind occurred during Oliver's Protectorate, when he wrote to those of his persuasion in Ireland, exhorting them to live peaceably, and submit to the civil magistrate.* Of his influence with men in power, some instances will be mentioned in the progress of this narrative.

Having brought Mr. Kiffin to that situation in which he may be said to be at the pinnacle of worldly prosperity, we proceed to give some account of his religious connexions during this period. It has been already noticed, that he was in communion with an Independent congregation, under the care of Mr. Jessey. After he had been connected a few years with that Society, he embraced the principles of the Baptists, and in 1638, was dismissed with several other members, to the Baptist congregation in Wapping, under the care of Mr. John Spilsbury. In a course of time, a controversy arose in that church, on the propriety of admitting persons to preach, who had not been baptized by immersion. This produced an amicable separation, headed by Mr. Kiffin, who seems to have been averse to the plan of mixed communion; but the two Societies kept up a friendly correspondence.† To this separation, the church in Devonshire-square, owes its origin; but, in what year it took place seems not quite certain. We have seen a memorandum which places it in 1653. Mr. Kiffin, however, must have been a pastor much earlier, as his name is united with that of Patient, in the Confession of Faith, published by the seven Baptist churches in London, in 1644.

But Mr. Kiffin did not confine his labours to a single con-

* Noble's Memoirs of Cromwell, vol. ii. p. 462.
† MS. *ubi supra*.

DEVONSHIRE-SQUARE.—*Particular Baptist.*

gregation: He travelled with his colleague, Mr. Thomas Patient, into various parts of the kingdom, to propagate and establish his mode of faith. The Rev. Thomas Edwards, who was then the Presbyterian champion, and author of the " Gangræna," accuses him of many extravagancies, likening his conduct to that of a mountebank, and charged him with not only praying by the sick, but anointing them, as is practised by the Roman-Catholic clergy. (c) " Many such heathenish and atheistical passages with baseness, (says Edwards,) I could relate of this man, and some of his members, and some others, but it would too much intrench upon modesty, and your patience." (d) " But it is probable,"

(c) Edwards's account of this affair is as follows: " One thing more (and is most of all considerable) of Kiffin's new found light, so called, which I had from some eye and ear witnesses of his members, who were present at Kiffin's and Patience's visitation of one of their members, whose name is Palmer, living in Smithfield, and laying hands upon her, did also anoint her with oil. The woman recovering, came into their conventicle-house, and there, before many people, said, That physicians left her as they found her, but brother Kiffin and Patience anointing her, she suddenly recovered; for which, in that place, she desired thanks might be put up; which Kiffin did also relate, and did, according to the woman's desire, return thanks."——*Edwards's Gangræna*, Part i. p. 6.

(d) As a specimen of Mr. Edwards's style when speaking of the sectaries, that is, of those who were not Presbyterians, we will present the reader with an extract from his account of Mr. Kiffin. " Another of these fellows, who counts himself inferior to none of the rest of his seduced brethren, one, whose name is Will. Kiffin, sometimes servant to a brewer, (whose name is Lilburn, who was lately put into Newgate, upon occasion of scandalizing the Speaker of the honourable House of Commons,) this man's man is now become a pretended preacher, and to that end hath by his enticing words, seduced and gathered a schismatical rabble of deluded children, servants, and people without either parents' or masters' consent. (This truth is not unknown by some of a near relation to me, whose giddy-headed children and servants are his poor slavish proselytes.) For a further manifestation of him in a pamphlet called, " *The Confession of Faith of the Seven Anabaptistical Churches*, there he is underwritten first, as metropolitan of that fraternity. I could relate, if time would permit, of somewhat I have had to do with him, in which he appeared to me to be a mountebank."—*Edwards's Gangræna*, P. i. p. 6.

DEVONSHIRE SQUARE.—*Particular Baptist.*

says a more candid writer, " that this behaviour was nothing more than what men of his sentiments constantly practised; it is certain his conduct was the exact reverse of his accuser, whose bigotry and narrowness of mind *was* (were) excessive.(E) On the contrary, Mr. Kiffin shewed a most Christian patience and forbearance, answering all these railing accusations by a very meek and sensible letter, humbly requesting leave for himself and his followers to object to what they saw proper in Mr. Edwards's preaching."* (F)

* Noble's Memoirs of Cromwell, v. ii. p. 455.

(E) As a proof of this, we shall quote what he says of toleration : " Toleration (says Mr. Edwards) will make the kingdom a chaos, a Babel, another Amsterdam, a Sodom, an Egypt, a Babylon, yea worse than all these; certainly it would be the most provoking sin against God, that ever parliament was guilty of in this kingdom; it proves the cause and foundation of all kinds of damnable heresies, and blasphemies. Toleration is the grand work of the devil, his master-piece and chief engine he works by at this time, to uphold his tottering kingdom; it is the most compendious, ready sure way to destroy all religion, lay all waste and bring in all evil; it is a most transcendant, catholique and fundamental evil for this kingdom of any that can be imagined. As original sin is the fundamental sin, all sin having the seed and spawn of all in it; so toleration hath all errors in it, and all evils; it is against the whole stream and current of scripture, both in the Old and New Testament, both in matters of faith and manners, both general and particular commands; it overthrows all relations, both political, ecclesiastical, and œconomical, &c." And speaking of the various sectaries endeavouring to obtain freedom for their religious opinions, he says, " All the devils in hell, and their instruments, were at work to promote toleration."† If Mr. Edwards survived the Restoration, and the Act of Uniformity, he most probably altered his sentiments respecting religious liberty.

† Edwards's Gangræna, P. i. p. 57, 58.

(F) Mr. Edwards preached a lecture at Christ-Church, London, where he took occasion to declaim against the " Sectaries," with the same virulence that he does in his writings. On one of these occasions Mr. Kiffin sent the following letter to him in the pulpit.

To Mr. EDWARDS.

" SIR,

" You stand as one professing yourself to be instructed by Christ, with abilities from God to throw down error ; and therefore to that end do

DEVONSHIRE-SQUARE.—*Particular Baptist.*

On the 17th of October, 1642, Mr. Kiffin, and three other Baptists, held a disputation in Southwark, with that celebrated champion, Dr. Daniel Featly. The only account we have of this dispute, is that given to the public by the Doctor, about two years afterwards, in a book entitled, " The Dippers Dipt: or, the Anabaptists Duck'd and Plung'd over Head and Ears, at a Disputation in Southwark." Whatever of argument is contained in this book, the Doctor has loaded his adversaries with plenty of abuse. In order that the reader may not entertain too favourable an idea of their character, he relates some remarkable stories to prove them, 1. An illiterate and sottish sect. 2. A lying and blasphemous sect. 3. An impure and carnal sect. 4. A cruel and bloody sect. 5. A profane and sacrilegious sect. And he sums up the whole by recording some fearful judgments of God upon the ringleaders of the sect. In such repute was the Doctor's book held at that time, that it passed through no less than six editions in as many years.*

In 1645, was published, " A Looking-Glass for the Anabaptists, and the rest of the separatists: wherein they may clearly behold a brief confutation of a certain unlicensed, scandalous pamphlet, entitled, *The Remonstrance of the Anabaptists, by Way of Vindication of their Separation.* The Impertinencies, Incongruities, Non-consequences, Falsities, and Obstinacy of *William Kiffin*, the Author and grand Ringleader of that seduced Sect is discovered and laid open to the View of every indifferent-eyed Reader that will

---

preach every third day: May it therefore please you, and those that employ you in that work, to give them leave whom you so brand, as publicly to object against what you say, when your sermon is ended, as you declare yourself; and we hope it will be an increase of further light to all that fear God, and put a large advantage into your hands, if you have the truth on your side, to cause it to shine with more evidence, and I hope we shall do it with moderation as becometh Christians.   Your's,

WILLIAM KIFFIN."

* Featly's " Dippers Dipt." 6th edit. 1651.

DEVONSHIRE-SQUARE.—*Particular Baptist.*

not shut his Eyes against the Truth. With certain queries, vindicated from Anabaptistical Glosses, together with others propounded for the Information and Conviction, (if possible) Reformation, of the said *William Kiffin* and his Proselytes. By JOSIAH RICRAFT, *a Well-willer to the Truth.*" The curious tract to which this long title is prefixed, consists only of twenty-six pages, in the quarto form. It contains a number of queries, with Kiffin's answers, and Ricraft's replies. This " Well-willer to the Truth," was a merchant of London, a bigotted Presbyterian, and sufficiently conceited of his polemical abilities, as appears by the above piece. He also wrote " A Book of Alphabets;" and a small volume, entitled, " A Survey of England's Champions, and Truth's Faithful Patriots, &c." 8vo. 1645, called by Mr. Wood " a canting book."* It contains an account of twenty-one persons who distinguished themselves in the civil wars, with their portraits prefixed. A copy of this book is extremely valuable, and difficult to be procured.

When Mr. Kiffin was at Coventry, he held another public disputation in defence of his peculiar sentiments. The combatants were Mr. Kiffin and Mr. Knollys, on the side of the Baptists; and Dr. Bryan, and Dr. Grew, for the Pœdo-Baptists. The debate was managed with good temper, and great moderation. Both sides, as is usual in such cases, claimed the victory; and much to their honour, they parted good friends.†

Some time after, Mr. Kiffin was prosecuted on the ordinance of parliament for punishing blasphemies and heresies. He was convened before the Lord-Mayor of London, at Guildhall, on Thursday, July.12, 1655, and charged with a breach of the ordinance, by preaching, " That the baptism of infants is unlawful." But the Lord-Mayor being then busy, the execution of the penalty required by the act,

---

* Wood's Athenæ Oxon. vol. ii. p. 123.
† Crosby's History of the Baptists, vol. iii. p. 5.

DEVONSHIRE-SQUARE.—*Particular Baptist.*

was deferred till Monday following.* Mr. Kiffin seems to have been treated by the Lord-Mayor with particular marks of favour, and it is very likely that he afterwards heard no more of the prosecution.

General Monk coming to London a little before the Restoration, took up his quarters near Mr. Kiffin's house; but he proved a troublesome neighbour. For, soon afterwards, he sent some soldiers at midnight, to seize upon Mr. Kiffin, and some other persons, and carry them to the guard at St. Paul's. The pretence was, that they had arms concealed in their houses, and this was rumoured about the city, on the following day. But, as these persons were peaceable citizens, and no soldiers, they sent to Sir Thomas Almin, Lord Mayor, in order to disprove the scandalous report; and stated that they had no arms, excepting such as were usual for housekeepers. At the same time, they entreated a speedy examination into their case, that they might not be detained, unjustly, from their several callings. Upon this, the Lord Mayor ordered the letter to be read in common-council; and their innocence being evident, proper officers were sent to the general, requiring their release, and the restoration of their arms, which was complied with.†

After the Restoration, Mr. Kiffin, as might be supposed, became a very obnoxious character, both on account of the religious opinions he professed, and the ample estate with which Providence had favoured him. For about six months, he enjoyed tolerable repose; but the Princess of Orange dying, a plot was laid to his charge, which, if it had taken effect, would have been attended with the loss of his property and life. A letter was forged from Taunton, to this effect. "That the Princess of Orange being now dead, they were ready to put their design in execution; and that Mr. Kiffin, according to his promise, was to provide, and send down powder, match, bullet, &c. for they be-

* Crosby, vol. i. p. 215.   † MS. *penes me.*

DEVONSHIRE-SQUARE.—*Particular Baptist.*

lieved the word, That one of them should chase a thousand." This letter being put into the hands of the government, Mr. Kiffin was seized on a Saturday, at midnight, and carried to the guard at Whitehall. There he continued the whole of the next day, subject to many taunts and threats of the soldiers, and not suffered to speak with a single person. In the evening, he was ordered before General Monk, and others of the council, who questioned him upon the contents of the said letter. Mr. Kiffin alleged his ignorance of the person, from whom it was said to be written, and expressed his abhorrence of every attempt to disturb the peace of the kingdom. After examination, he was remanded into custody of the soldiers. On the following day, he was taken under a guard of soldiers to Serjeants' Inn, to be examined before Lord Chief Justice Foster. Mr. Kiffin having obtained liberty to speak for himself, told his lordship, that the very contents of the letter would prove it a forgery. For, in the first place, it dated the rise of the plot, from the death of the Princess of Orange; whereas the letter was dated at Taunton, three days before she died. This, his lordship acknowledged to be a considerable objection, and finding it correct, observed, that it was possible the date might be incorrect, and, nevertheless, the contents true. Mr. Kiffin replied, that he left this to his lordship's consideration; but he had another remark to make which could be no mistake. It was this: That it was morally impossible any letter could be written from London to Taunton, and from Taunton back again, between the time of the Princess's death, and his seizure; for, as the Princess died on the Monday night, no advice could be given of it by post till the next evening, nor could an answer be received before the Monday following. Now, as he was put in confinement the Saturday preceding, this circumstance must prove it a forgery. Upon this, the judge looking steadfastly at the lieutenant-colonel, whose prisoner he was, expressed great anger at so malicious a proceeding, and discharging Mr. Kiffin, told him

DEVONSHIRE-SQUARE.—*Particular Baptist.*

he was perfectly satisfied of his innocence; and that, if he could find out the authors of the letter, he would punish them severely. The famous Mr. Henry Jessey was, also, implicated in this letter, and discharged at the same time.*

Not long after this narrow escape, Mr. Kiffin was apprehended on a Lord's-day, at a meeting in Shoreditch. Being taken before Sir Thomas Bide, he was committed to the New-Prison, together with several other persons, but, after four days, was released. After this, it pleased God to grant him a short respite, till he was called to manage an affair that nearly occasioned his ruin. The Hamburg Company endeavouring to establish themselves at this time, obtained from the King a proclamation for an exclusive trade in woollen manufactures, to Holland and Germany. This greatly affecting the other merchants, several who resided at Exeter, and other parts in the West of England, wrote to their representatives in parliament, to counteract this measure; acquainting them that Mr. Kiffin was a very likely person to give information on the subject. A committee of the House of Commons being appointed to inquire into the business, Mr. Kiffin was ordered to attend, which he did several times; and the committee reported to the House, their opinion against the measure. It was then resolved to petition the King to call in his proclamation; but before he complied, he resolved to hear the matter discussed in council. Mr. Kiffin being summoned to attend, his enemies made themselves sure of having him in the Gate-house. To this end, they charged him with speaking against his Majesty's prerogative, and with disloyal practices in the late times. But the King and council being satisfied that an exclusive trade was prejudicial to the interests of the country, recalled the proclamation, and thus Mr. Kiffin's enemies were disappointed. Indeed, so apparent was his innocence,

* MS. *ubi supra.*

DEVONSHIRE-SQUARE.—*Particular Baptist.*

that the King ever afterwards entertained a good opinion of him, as did several members of the council. Lord Arlington told him, that in every list he received, of disaffected persons, proper to be secured, his name was inserted; yet the King would never believe any thing against him. The Lord Chancellor Clarendon, also, stood very much his friend.*

About a year after this event, Mr. Kiffin met with another trial, which greatly endangered his life. He was again seized at midnight by Mr. Wickham, one of the messengers of the council, at the instance of the Duke of Buckingham. Being conveyed to York-house, he continued there under a guard of soldiers till the next night; when he was convened before the Duke, who charged him with having hired two men to kill the King, and in case they failed, with an intention of doing the business himself. In order to extort confession, the Duke promised him safety if he would tell the truth. Mr. Kiffin surprised at the charge, expressed his greatest abhorrence of such a design, even towards the meanest man in the kingdom, much more towards his Majesty; and told the Duke, that he could not be the King's friend, if he offered to screen the life of any man in his wits, who entertained so wicked a thing. The Duke told him, that he knew he could speak fair enough for himself, as he had so often done before the privy-council; but the charge would be made good by two witnesses. He then remanded him to the custody of the soldiers, with strict orders not to suffer any communication with him; but about two hours after, he was committed to the care of Wickham, the messenger. Though Mr. Kiffin was conscious of his innocence, yet he was not a little terrified at the treatment he met with; but it pleased the Lord to comfort and strengthen him for the day of trouble. On the following day, Lady Ranelagh paid him a visit, and inquiring into his case, advised him to

* MS. *ubi supra.*

DEVONSHIRE-SQUARE.—*Particular Baptist.*

write a letter to the Lord Chancellor, to acquaint him with his circumstances, and offered to deliver it herself. She accordingly gave it into the hands of the Chancellor, who informed her that no such charge had been made before the council, but he would acquaint the King with it the next day. This he punctually performed, and an order was made for his discharge, without the payment of fees.

Mr. Kiffin now thought that the storm was blown over; and understanding how much he was indebted to the kindness of the Lord Chancellor, went to his house the next morning to pay his acknowledgments. As he was waiting without, the Lord Chief Justice Bridgeman, Sir Jeffery Palmer, his Majesty's Attorney-general, Sir Heneage Finch, Solicitor-general, and Sir Richard Brown, a judge, came to the Chancellor upon business. After a while, Mr. Kiffin was called in, and questioned how he, being a prisoner, came there. To which he replied, that he was come to return the Chancellor thanks for interceding with the King on his behalf, by which means he had gained his liberty. The Chancellor acknowledged that an order had passed to that effect; but observed, that the Duke of Buckingham had afterwards brought in his charge, and a subsequent order was made for his detention. The Chancellor then told him, that he must return into the messenger's custody, but he would use his exertions to obtain for him a fair and speedy trial. Mr. Kiffin, knowing his innocence, expressed his cheerful acquiescence. The Chancellor then desired him to go to Whitehall, in his name, and try if he could persuade the King to take bail for his appearance. But his Majesty being from home, Mr. Kiffin returned into the city, and having procured two substantial citizens for his bail, hastened back again. By the good providence of God, it happened that the Chancellor was now with the King; and Mr. Kiffin having sent in his name, received for answer, that he might go home, but must be ready to appear when called for. His deliverance at this time he ascribed

DEVONSHIRE-SQUARE.—*Particular Baptist.*

solely to the Lord Chancellor, as the page who brought him the message, told him that the King seemed very angry.*

Some time after, he was sent for by Sir Richard Brown, to know where he had been during the summer. Mr. Kiffin told him, chiefly in London, but sometimes with his family at a kinsman's house, in Hertfordshire. Sir Richard then asked him, if he had not engaged the people with whom he walked, to enter into a covenant against the government. Mr. Kiffin told him, that the end of their meeting was to edify each other in matters of religion, without concerning themselves with the government. To which the other replied, that he had a witness present who could substantiate the charge, which he would inquire farther into. He then told him, that as he came to him voluntarily, upon sending for, he might go home, till he heard farther from him; which never happened.†

It was about this time, that some soldiers broke into his house, ransacked his papers, and carried him prisoner to the guard at the Exchange. Sir Thomas Player, the commander, after asking him several questions, said, that he had a special order to secure him, but if he would pass his word to be forth coming when sent for, he would let him go. To this Mr. Kiffin consented, and, afterwards, enjoyed a long interval of peace.‡

The laws against Nonconformists being executed with severity, Mr. Kiffin was apprehended at a meeting, and prosecuted for the penalty of forty pounds, which he deposited in the hands of the officer. But finding a flaw in the proceedings, he obtained a verdict in his favour, though it cost him thirty pounds. It had, however, this good effect, that many poor persons, who were prosecuted upon the same account, were now relieved, the informers being afraid to proceed against them. About 1682, he was again prose-

* MS, *ubi supra*.   † *Ibid.*   ‡ *Ibid.*

| DEVONSHIRE-SQUARE.—*Particular Baptist.* |

cuted for fifteen meetings, in the penalty of three hundred pounds. The informers managed their matters so secretly as to get the record for the money in court before Mr. Kiffin was acquainted with the transaction. But it happened that there were some errors in this record also; and Mr. Kiffin having some friends in court, they moved, that the cause should be heard before an order was made to amend them. In the mean time, Mr. Kiffin being informed of the particulars, employed able counsel; and after several hearings, the informers let the suit drop.*

In 1684, when the discovery of the Popish Plot, gave the court an opportunity of sacrificing those noble patriots Lord William Russel, and Algernon Sidney, strong attempts were made to involve Mr. Kiffin in the common ruin. But nothing to his prejudice could be extracted from the witnesses. At this time several persons fled to Holland; and among others, Sir Thomas Armstrong, who was outlawed. Some of his friends having transmitted him money by means of exchequer bills, the court got scent of it; and the offence being laid at the door of Mr. Joseph Hayes, Mr. Kiffin's son-in-law, he was apprehended, and tried for his life. Hayes, whose circumstances were ruined by this affair, narrowly escaped the halter, which the court, under Charles the Second, earnestly desired to be put about his neck.† The trial was curious and important, as it struck at the root of mercantile liberty. A good account of it is given by Burnet.‡

Upon his return home from this trial, in which it may be supposed he took considerable interest, Mr. Kiffin found a packet of letters, which had been left at his house by some unknown person about half an hour before. Upon his opening them, he found one directed to the Lord Chief Justice

---

* MS. *ubi supra.*
† Noble's Memoirs of Cromwell, vol. ii. p. 462.
‡ Burnet's History of his Own Times, vol. i. p. 599.

Jeffries, and another to himself, full of threats and treasonable expressions. As he could not but suspect some malicious design, he immediately sent them to Jeffries, whose clerk told Mr. Kiffin's servant, that he knew the handwriting. This still further strengthened his suspicions; and it is not a little surprising that he never heard any thing further concerning them.*

Some particulars above related, will convince the reader, that Mr. Kiffin was in great favour with his sovereign, and with some of the most considerable persons about his court. Perhaps it may be difficult to account for this circumstance, unless we suppose his skill as a merchant, and the property he acquired, had any weight. His principles, certainly, were not in his favour, he being a Dissenter of the most obnoxious sort. Though we cannot vouch for the authenticity of the following anecdote, it is too curious to be omitted.— King Charles the Second, it is well known, was often in want of money, to defray the expences of his pleasures, and would sometimes condescend to borrow of his subjects. On one of these occasions, it was currently reported, that he sent to Mr. Kiffin, to borrow of him *forty thousand pounds*. Mr. Kiffin apologized for not having it in his power to lend his Majesty so much, but told the messenger, that if it would be of any service, he would present him with *ten thousand*, which was accepted; and Mr. Kiffin used afterwards to say, that in so doing, he had saved *thirty thousand pounds*.† It is certain that Mr. Kiffin had much interest with the King, and was often a successful advocate at court, for his persecuted brethren. One or two instances deserve mention.

When the laws against the Nonconformists made their appearance, several magistrates in Buckinghamshire discovered great zeal in executing them; and having filled the county jail, hired two large houses in Aylesbury, which they

---

* MS. *penes me*.   † Crosby, vol. iii. p. 5.

DEVONSHIRE-SQUARE.—*Particular Baptist.*

converted into prisons. Not contented with the ordinary process of imprisonment, and confiscation of property, they endeavoured to revive the old practice of punishing heretics with banishment and death. In this they were sanctioned by a clause in the 35th of Eliz. which enacted, That any person legally convicted of being present at a conventicle, if after three months imprisonment, he should refuse to conform, or abjure the realm, he shall suffer death as a felon, without benefit of clergy. An attempt was made to carry this severe law into execution; and, after a mock trial, these zealous magistrates passed sentence of death upon ten men and two women, all Baptists, who were remanded back to prison, till the time appointed for their execution. Immediately after their condemnation, the son of one of the condemned persons took horse for London, and acquainted Mr. Kiffin with the circumstances. Upon which, they proceeded with great expedition, to the house of Lord Chancellor Hyde, and entreated him to lay the case before his Majesty, which he readily did. The King seemed very much surprised that any of his subjects should be put to death for their religion, and inquired whether there was any law that authorized such proceedings. Being informed upon this point, he promised his pardon, and gave orders accordingly. But when it was considered, that the form of passing a pardon would require some time, and that those who had so hastily passed sentence of death, might be as rash in the execution of it, Mr. Kiffin applied for an immediate reprieve, which his Majesty readily granted; and it was dispatched to Aylesbury by the same messenger who brought the dismal tidings. At the next assizes, the judge brought down the King's pardon, and liberated the prisoners; which put some stop to the violent proceedings in that part of the country.*

Another occasion, upon which Mr. Kiffin exerted himself

---

* Crosby, vol. ii. p. 180—185.

DEVONSHIRE SQUARE.—*Particular Baptist.*

on behalf of his denomination, occurred in 1673, upon the publication of a libel against the Baptists, entitled, " Baxter baptized in Blood." This scurrilous pamphlet charged upon the Baptists, the murder of Mr. Josiah Baxter, a minister of New-England, for no other reason than because he had worsted them in disputation; and to render that party the more odious, it was written with a minuteness of detail that carried with it the most artful shew of plausibility. Mr. Kiffin, to counteract the ill consequences of such a publication, went in person to the King, and so effectually stated his complaint, that an order was issued to have the book examined in council. This was accordingly done, and the forgery being sufficiently proved, an order of council to that effect was published in the Gazette, and Dr. Parker, the licenser, compelled to publish a testimonial to the same purpose.*

King Charles the Second dying in February, 1684-5, was succeeded by his brother, James the Second. In the summer of that year, the Duke of Monmouth landed at Lyme, and setting up his standard, invited the people to take up arms against the gloomy tyrant. But this ill-judged expedition, soon afterwards, cost him his head. Among the unfortunate persons who attached themselves to his cause, were two grandsons of Mr. Kiffin, Benjamin and William Hewling; the latter of whom accompanied the Duke from Holland, whither he had been sent to complete his education. These interesting youths being taken prisoners, were conveyed to London, and lodged in Newgate. It having been reported, that the King meant to make examples only of a few, and leave his officers to make the best bargains they could for the remainder, Mr. Kiffin offered, through a great personage, three thousand pounds for the lives of his grandsons. But he missed the right door; for Judge Jefferies getting scent of these contracts, in which he was not

* Crosby, vol. ii. p. 278. and vol. iii. p. 4.

DEVONSHIRE SQUARE.—*Particular Baptist.*

included, was provoked to the greater cruelty, insomuch that but few escaped. Among the sufferers were these unfortunate youths. During their confinement, and at the place of execution, they behaved in the most resigned, yet dignified manner; and met their deaths with the most Christian fortitude. Of all the unhappy victims that were sacrificed upon this occasion, none were more pitied than these two brothers. Their youth, (one not quite twenty, the other only twenty-one,) their beauty, their being the only sons of their mother, and she a widow; their extraordinary piety, resignation, even excessive joy at their approaching fate, made all men look up with horror at a throne, which, instead of being that of mercy, was not only severe justice, but excess of cruelty. For these unfortunate youths were flattered with life; and while in prison, treated with the greatest inhumanity, nay, shameful barbarity. The flintiness of the King's heart cannot be more strikingly illustrated than in the fate of these two brothers. When their sister, Hannah Hewling, presented a petition to him on their behalf, she was introduced by Lord Churchill, afterwards Duke of Marlborough. While waiting in the anti-chamber for admittance, Lord Churchill, standing near the chimney-piece, assured her of his most hearty wishes for the success of her petition; " But, Madam, said he, I dare not flatter you with any such hopes, for that marble is as capable of feeling compassion as the King's heart."*

As Mr. Kiffin happened to be related to these unfortunate youths, it is not surprising that the Jacobite party looked upon him with jealousy and suspicion. At the trial of William Hewling, Jeffries observed in public court, that his grandfather Kiffin deserved, equally with him, that death which he was likely to suffer. This great storm being over,

* Mr. Kiffin's Life, *ubi supra.*—Noble's Memoirs of Cromwell, vol. ii.— Western Martyrology.—and Toulmin's History of Taunton.

DEVONSHIRE-SQUARE.—*Particular Baptist.*

there seemed to be less restraint upon the favourite court design of introducing **Popery.** For this purpose, before the sitting of parliament, the members were tampered with in order to extract a promise of voting for the repeal of the Test laws. Though, in general, they refused to pledge themselves upon the subject, yet the **Papists** held their public meetings, and their insolence grew to such a height as to alarm all true Protestants. The court observing this, set on foot a new project, which was to engage the Nonconformists on their side, by promising them an equal authority in the nation with other Protestants. By thus setting the Dissenters against the Church of England, they thought of strengthening the Popish interest. But though some persons, under a sense of their former sufferings gladly accepted this gleam of liberty, yet the majority refused to fall in with the design. Among the latter was Mr. Kiffin, who exerted himself strenuously against it. The King, however, persevered in his plans, and resolved to introduce some Dissenters into places of trust.

Mr. Kiffin was personally known to the marble-hearted James, who, no less than his brother Charles, was disposed to favour him. Having arbitrarily deprived the city of its old charter, and determined to put some Dissenters into the magistracy, he sent to Mr. Kiffin to attend him at court. When he went thither in obedience to the King's command, he found many lords and gentlemen. The King immediately coming up to him, addressed him with all the little grace of which he was master. He talked of his " favour to the Dissenters," in the court stile of the season; and concluded with telling Mr. Kiffin, " he had put him down as an alderman in his new charter:"—" Sire," replied Mr. Kiffin, " I am a very old man, and have withdrawn myself from all kind of business for some years past, and am incapable of doing any service in such an affair, to your Majesty or the city;—besides, Sire," continues the old man, fixing his eyes steadfastly upon the King, while the tears ran down

DEVONSHIRE-SQUARE.—*Particular Baptist.*

his cheeks, " the death of my grandsons, gave a wound to my heart, which is still bleeding, and never will close, but in the grave!" The King was deeply struck by the manner, the freedom, and the spirit of this unexpected rebuke. A total silence ensued, while the galled countenance of James seemed to shrink from the horrid remembrance. In a minute or two, however, he recovered himself enough to say, " Mr. Kiffin, I shall find a balsam for that sore," and immediately turned about to a lord in waiting.*(G)

Mr. Kiffin was now placed in a very awkward situation, from which there were no means of escape. Through some lords and gentlemen about the court, he interceded with the King to reverse his appointment, but without effect. He was told that the great interest he had in the city might be of service to his Majesty; and as to the death of his grandchildren, and loss of their estates, it should be made up to him by any honour or advantage he could reasonably desire. This, however, was no temptation to Mr. Kiffin, who was fully convinced that the court designed nothing less than the total ruin of the Protestant religion. As he delayed accepting the office, and six weeks had elapsed since the time he received the summons, Sir John Peake, the then Lord Mayor, declared publicly in court, that Mr. Kiffin ought to be sent to Newgate; and, in the course of a few days, he understood it was intended to put him into the Crown-office,

* Noble's Memoirs, vol. ii. p. 463.

(G) A reproof equally unexpected and equally deserved, this unfeeling monarch received, at an extraordinary council, which he called soon after the landing of the Prince of Orange; when, amidst the silent company, he applied himself to the Earl of Bedford, father to the beheaded Lord Russel, saying, " My Lord, you are a good man, and have great influence; you can do much for me at this time;" to which the Earl replied, " I am an old man, and can do but little;" then added, with a sigh, " I had once a son, who could now have been very serviceable to your Majesty;" which words, says Echard, struck the King half dead with silence and confusion.—*Echard's History of England.*

DEVONSHIRE SQUARE.—*Particular Baptist.*

and proceed against him with the utmost severity. Upon this he resolved to take the advice of able counsel, who told him his danger was very great. That if he accepted the office, it would cost him *five hundred pounds;* but if he refused, he might be fined from *ten* to *thirty thousand*, according to the pleasure of the judge. He, therefore, thought it better to comply. Not long after, the King was invited to dine in the city, when each of the aldermen were obliged to lay down fifty pounds to cover the expences. Mr. Kiffin was, also, put into the commission of the peace, and made one of the lieutenancy. But he meddled very little with civil concerns. During the nine months he continued alderman of Cheap Ward, he was held in great respect, and studied to promote the welfare of the city. At length he was discharged from the troublesome office.*

Mr. Kiffin continued in the exercise of his ministry, with various colleagues, to a good old age. Like the great apostle of the Gentiles, he passed through evil report and good report; and though greatly reviled by some men on account of the unpopularity of his opinions, yet this very circumstance occasioned his being held in high reputation by others. In estimating the characters of persons at this period of our history, there is great danger of misrepresentation, through the prejudice of party writers; and it requires no inconsiderable knowledge of human nature to avoid splitting upon this rock. Mr. Kiffin had the courage and integrity to avow his opinions at a time when it was dangerous to do so; and had they been as absurd, or as dangerous as they were represented, neither the weapon of abuse, nor the civil sword were proper instruments for his conviction. It is a distinguishing feature of truth, that it invites inquiry: to stifle it is the mark of a bad cause, and the certain resort of bigots. Though Mr. Kiffin spent the chief part of his life in a

* MS. *ubi supra.*

DEVONSHIRE-SQUARE.—*Particular Baptist.*

storm, it was his happiness to die in peace. This event took place December 29th, 1701, in the 86th year of his age.

Some of the outlines of Mr. Kiffin's character may be gathered from the preceding narrative. He possessed good natural talents, and the bent of his inclination led him to make theology his principal study. Crosby says, he was " a great disputant, and when joined with others, generally had the preference."* His temper appears to have been mild and amiable, and in propagating his peculiar tenets, he behaved with great moderation and decency. Though bigotry was the reigning vice of the times, he seems to have had as little of it as most men; and exerted his influence with persons in power, to repress it in others.

A noble instance of his generosity occurred when the French Protestants took refuge in England. He received under his protection, a family of considerable rank, fitted up and furnished a house for their reception, provided them with servants, and entirely maintained them at his own expence. Afterwards, when this family recovered some part of their ruined fortune, he would not diminish it a single shilling, by taking any retribution for the services he had rendered them.†

He was deservedly held in great esteem by his brethren; and the large property he acquired in business, gave him considerable weight in all their concerns. It also enabled him to do much good, and to dispense the word of life without being burthensome to the churches. His religious principles were strict Calvinism, and excepting upon the point of baptism, he does not appear to have deviated from the standards of orthodoxy in his time. His name is affixed to the two confessions of

* Crosby's English Baptists, vol. iii. p. 3.
† Noble's Memoirs of Cromwell, vol. ii. p. 464.

faith, set forth by the Particular Baptists, in 1644, and 1689.(H)

Though Mr. Kiffin but rarely meddled with politics himself, yet his connexions were amongst the warmest patriots of those warm times. One of his daughters married Mr. Benjamin Hewling, a Turkey merchant, of considerable fortune, in London, who, happily for himself, died before his two sons, the unfortunate youths above-mentioned. After his death, they were carefully brought up by a tender mother, and by their maternal grand-father, Mr. Kiffin.* Another of his daughters was married to Hayes the Banker, before-mentioned. He had, also, another daughter, married to Mr. Thomas Liddel; and several sons. The eldest died a young man, aged about twenty. His second son having an inclination to travel abroad, was accompanied by a young minister as far as Leghorn; and proceeding by himself to Venice, there entered too freely into conversation upon religious subjects, and was poisoned by a Popish priest. Mr. Kiffin lived happily with his wife, for the space of forty-four years. Concerning her he says, " I can truly say, I never knew her utter the least discontent under all the various providences that attended me, or her; but eyeing the hand of God in them, so as to be a constant encourager of me in the ways of God. Her death was to me the greatest sorrow that I ever met with in this world." She died October 5, 1682.† Mr. Kiffin's grand-daughter, Hannah Hewling, about a year after the execution of her brother, married Major Henry Cromwell, grandson to the celebrated Oliver. From this marriage is descended the present surviving branch of that once illustrious family.‡

(H) It is not known that Mr. Kiffin ever published any thing, excepting a single piece, entitled, " A sober Discourse of Right to Church-Communion;" in which he pleads for strict communion.

* Noble's Memoirs of Cromwell, vol. ii. p. 454.

† MS. *ubi supra.*

‡ Dr. Gibbons's Sermon on the Death of Wm. Cromwell, Esq. *Appendix.*

DEVONSHIRE-SQUARE.—*Particular Baptist.*

Upon his tomb-stone in Bunhill-Fields, was the following inscription; preserved by the industrious Mr. Strype, in his edition of Stow's Survey of London.

> WILLIAM KIFFEN,
> Eldest Son of William Kiffen of London, Merchant,
> (And an Anabaptist Preacher) (1)
> Died in the Lord, August the 31st, 1669,
> In the 21st year of his age.
> Also,
> PRISCILLA LIDDEL,
> Wife of Robert Liddel,
> And Daughter of William Kiffen,
> Who fell asleep in the Lord, March 15, 1679.
> Aged 24.
> And
> HANNA, late Wife of William Kiffen,
> And Mother to the above-named William and Priscilla,
> Who fell asleep in the Lord, the 6th of October, 1682,
> In the 67th year of her age.
> And
> HARRY KIFFEN,
> Son of the above-said William Kiffen.
> Dec. 8, 1698, aged 44.
> Also,
> HENRIETTA, late Wife of John Catcher.
> Aug. 15, 1698, aged 22.
> And
> WILLIAM KIFFEN, the Elder,
> Of London, Merchant,
> Husband to the above-said Hanna,
> And Father to the above-said William, Harry, and Priscilla,
> Dec. 29, 1701,
> In the 86th year of his age.

(1) The words in a parenthesis were, most probably, inserted by Strype.

THOMAS PATIENT, was some time an Independent minister in New-England, where, he embraced the sentiments of the Baptists. This was, probably, the reason he is not mentioned by Cotton Mather, who seems to have

DEVONSHIRE-SQUARE.—*Particular Baptist.*

possessed a portion of that bigotry which disgraced some of his countrymen. Patient not being suffered to live quietly on the other side of the Atlantic, crossed over to England about the time of the commencement of the civil wars, and became colleague with Mr. Kiffin. Their names are united in the confession of faith, put forth by the seven Baptist churches in London, in 1644. After this, he travelled about the country, and was very industrious in propagating his opinions. Crosby informs us, that he went over to Ireland, with General Fleetwood, Lord-Lieutenant of that kingdom, who having displaced Dr. Winter, appointed Patient to preach in the cathedral.* In Dublin, he was also chaplain to Colonel John Jones, who married the sister of Oliver Cromwell, and was one of the lords of his other-house. Colonel Jones is described as a person lost in fanaticism, which led him to prefer his favorite chaplain Patient before the regular clergy. Accordingly, he was appointed to preach before Jones and the council, in Christ-Church, Dublin, every Sunday.† It appears from Milton's State Papers, that Patient travelled into different parts of Ireland, along with the English army: He dates a letter from the head-quarters, Kilkenny, April 15, 1650. Crosby says, that he was very instrumental in promoting the interest of the Baptists in that country; and was probably the founder of the Baptist church at Clough-Keating, which, at the time he wrote, was very numerous.‡

We have no account in what year Mr. Patient returned to England, but it was, most probably, after the Restoration. Being chosen to the office of joint-elder with Mr. Kiffin, he was set apart in Devonshire-square, June 28, 1666; Mr. Harrison, and Mr. Knollys, assisting upon the occasion.§ In this office, however, he was not suffered to continue

---

* Crosby's History of the Baptists, vol. iii. p. 42.
† Noble's Memoirs of Cromwell, vol. ii. p. 215.
‡ Crosby, *ubi supra.*   § MS. *penes me.*

| DEVONSHIRE-SQUARE.—*Particular Baptist.* |

long, by reason of death; as appears by the following memorandum in the church-books belonging to the Society. " July 30, 1666, Thomas Patient was, on the 29th instant, discharged by death from his work and office, he being then taken from the evil to come; and having rested from all his labours, leaving a blessed savour behind him of his great usefulness, and sober conversation. This his sudden removal being looked upon to be his own great advantage, but the church's sore loss. On this day he was carried to his grave, accompanied by the members of this and other congregations, in a Christian, comely, and decent manner." Mr. Patient published nothing besides a single treatise in quarto, on the subject of Baptism.

DANIEL DYKE, M. A. a learned minister of the Baptist persuasion, was born about the year 1617, at Epping, in Essex, where his father, Mr. Jeremiah Dyke, a good old puritan, was the parochial minister. The famous Mr. Daniel Dyke, author of an excellent treatise on " The Deceitfulness of the Human Heart," and minister first at Coggeshall, in Essex, but afterwards at St. Alban's, in Hertfordshire, at the former of which places he was suspended by Bishop Aylmer, was the brother of this gentleman, and uncle to our Divine.

Mr. Daniel Dyke the younger, after being sufficiently instructed at private schools, was sent to the University of Cambridge, where he took the degree of Master of Arts. At his leaving the university, he received episcopal ordination, and had not long entered upon the ministry before he became noticed for his great learning, and useful preaching. It is not surprising, therefore, that he received suitable preferment. Accordingly, after some time, he was presented to Hadham *Magna*, in Hertfordshire, a living of considerable value. He was, also, made one of the chaplains in ordinary to Oliver Cromwell, Lord Protector, and in 1653,

DEVONSHIRE-SQUARE.—*Particular Baptist.*

one of the Triers for the approval and admission of ministers; an office for which his learning, judgment, and piety rendered him well qualified. Previously to this he had embraced the sentiments of the Baptists, and appears to have been the only one in this commission, with the exception of Mr. Tombes, and Mr. Jessey.

Upon the Restoration, Mr. Dyke discovered his great integrity, by refusing to conform to the episcopal government, and to the ceremonies of the Church of England. In contemplation, therefore, of the approaching storm, he voluntarily resigned his living. When his intimate friend Mr. Case, who was one of the ministers deputed to wait upon the King at the Hague, endeavoured to dissuade him from his purpose, telling him what a hopeful prospect they had from the King's behaviour, &c. Mr. Dyke told him plainly, " That they did but deceive and flatter themselves: That if the King was sincere in his show of piety, and great respect to them and their religion; yet when he came to be settled, the party that had formerly adhered to him, and the creatures that would come over with him, would have the management of public affairs, and circumvent all their designs, and in all probability not only turn them out, but take away their liberty too." The wisdom and justice of these remarks were fully justified by the King's subsequent conduct.

After Mr. Dyke had resigned his living, he preached as often as he had opportunity, and through some kind appearance of Providence, was generally preserved from the rage and malice of his persecutors. Though he lived in two or three great storms, and had several writs out against him, yet he never was imprisoned more than one night. After preaching a year upon trial, he was chosen colleague with Mr. Kiffin, at Devonshire-square, and set apart to the office of joint-elder, February 17, 1668; Mr. Knollys, Mr. Harrison, and Mr. Kiffin, officiating upon the occa-

DEVONSHIRE-SQUARE.—*Particular Baptist.*

sion.* In this station he continued a faithful labourer, till removed by death, in 1688, when he was about 70 years of age. His remains were interred in Bunhill-Fields, and his funeral sermon preached by Mr. Warner.

Mr. Dyke was a man of so much modesty, that he could never be prevailed upon to appear in print. His name, however, stands with some others in two or three printed papers, in the composing of which it is supposed he had some concern. These were, The Quaker's Appeal answered; or, a full Relation of the Occasion, Progress, and Issue of a Meeting at Barbican, between the Baptists and Quakers" 1674.—" The Baptist's Answer to Mr. Wills's Appeal." 1675, &c.—" Recommendatory Epistle before Mr. Cox's Confutation of the Errors of Thomas Collier." He also edited a volume of sermons by his father.†

RICHARD ADAMS.—As Mr. Adams is not mentioned by the Oxford historian, it is probable that he received his education in the University of Cambridge. We have no account of him before the Restoration, when he had the living of Humberstone, in Leicestershire; but which he was forced to relinquish by the act of uniformity, in 1662. After his ejectment, he married; and set up a meeting in his own house, at Mountsorrel, where he preached about fourteen years. As many persons resorted to hear him, it excited the jealousy of a neighbouring justice, of the name of Babington, who, though a sober man, was very severe with him, and oppressed the Dissenters more than all the other justices in that county. He fined Mr. Adams *twelvepence* per day, and sent to the officers of the parish to make distress for it. Though the consciences of these men smote them in their unhallowed work, yet the threats of the justice induced them to seize his pewter, and send it to the pew-

* MS. *penes me.*
† Crosby's History of the Baptists, vol. i. p. 355—359.

DEVONSHIRE-SQUARE.—*Particular Baptist.*

terer's, which, however, they refused to buy. After this, the justice sent for Mr. Adams, and told him he was not against his keeping school, if he would cease to preach; otherwise he must expect to be troubled. Crosby informs us, that this justice died soon after by excessive bleeding.* How far this may be considered a retaliation of Providence, we do not take upon us to say. But, though it may be presumption in us to determine precisely what are the judgments of God, yet it cannot be denied, that he has sometimes displayed his power in such a striking manner, and accompanied by so many remarkable coincidences, that it would argue extreme insensibility, were they to pass unnoticed. Though we are far from crediting all the numerous tales of this kind upon record, yet if we believe that the Almighty superintends the concerns of his church, we cannot suppose him indifferent to the sufferings of his people; more especially as he has set a particular mark upon persecutors. This will be a sufficient apology for our introducing such frequent references to the Divine interposition.

Towards the latter end of the reign of King Charles II. Mr. Adams removed to London, and was chosen minister of a congregation at Shad-Thames, Bermondsey. From thence, upon the death of the Rev. Daniel Dyke, he was called to be joint-elder with Mr. Kiffin, at Devonshire-square. He was ordained to that office in October, 1690, and the service was managed with great solemnity, by Mr. Knollys, Mr. William Collins, Mr. Hercules Collins, &c. For several years after his settlement in Devonshire-square, singing the praises of God in public worship, was a thing utterly unknown to the congregation. Indeed, most of the Baptist churches at this period, seem to have avoided it as an antichristian infection. It was not till December, 1701, that this enlivening part of devotion was introduced to Mr. Adams's church; and even then it was used, for some time, with

* Crosby's History of the Baptists, vol. iii. p. 38.

DEVONSHIRE-SQUARE.—*Particular Baptist.*

extreme caution. Mr. Adams, who was a man of great piety and integrity, lived to a very great age, but was disabled from constant preaching several years before his death, which happened in the year 1716.*

MARK KEY.—Of this worthy minister, but few memorials remain. His parents, though in poor circumstances, were pious persons, of the General Baptist persuasion, and members of the church in White's Alley, Moorfields. With this society Mr. Key was himself connected in the early part of his life, first as a member, and afterwards as a preacher. He was called into the ministry, April 1691, and in the same year, chosen assistant preacher to that church. This office he resigned, on account of ill health, in April 1695, and retired into the country for the benefit of the air. In the following year, we find him again in London, preaching to different societies in the Baptist connection, both of the General and Particular persuasion. On the 27th of February, 1701-2, he was received into communion with the church in Devonshire-square, and in June following, to adopt the praseology then in use, was called to exercise his gift; which being approved, he was unanimously chosen assistant to Mr. Adams, February 4, 1702-3. Upon this occasion, he was requested by the church, to remove his lecture from White's Alley to Devonshire-square, with which he complied.

It should seem that Mr. Key possessed popular talents for the ministry, as several attempts were made to remove him from the situation in which he was now fixed. Within a month after his settlement in the assistant's office at Devonshire-square, he received a call to be pastor of a church in Wapping. In the month of June following, the Baptist church at Warwick sent him a similar invitation; as did the church in Petticoat-lane, about six months afterwards. Such, however, was the affection of the people to whom he

* MS. *penes me.*

DEVONSHIRE-SQUARE.—*Particular Baptist.*

now ministered, that, at their earnest solicitations, he rejected these proposals. It was not long before the church in Devonshire-square testified their esteem, by calling him to the office of joint-pastor. Their invitation is dated December 27, 1705, and on the same day in the following year, he was ordained to the elder's office. The sermon upon the occasion, was preached by the Rev. Joseph Maisters. The ceremony of ordination was performed with laying on of hands, Mr. Adams saying, " I do declare by the authority of Christ and this church, that my brother Mark Key, is by the church appointed and ordained a joint elder, pastor, or overseer, with myself over her."

As Mr. Adams grew in years, the chief burden of the pastoral office devolved upon Mr. Key, who appears to have been an active and vigilant pastor, and much esteemed by the church. Mr. Adams dying in 1716, Mr. Key continued sole pastor till his death in 1726. The following account of his funeral is preserved in the church-books of the Society. " June 23, 1726. It having been reported that it hath pleased Almighty God, in the all-wise dispensation of his providence, to exercise this church with the loss of our well-beloved brother Mark Key, our late pastor, and that several of the brethren have had a meeting, to consider of the funeral, it was thought proper to propose, and agreed, (1.) That the corps be carried from the Meeting-house, and interred in the burial-ground, Bunhill-Fields, on Monday the 27th instant. (2.) That a sermon be preached on the occasion by Mr. Richardson, to begin at four o'Clock precisely. (3.) That Mr. Noble, or Mr. Wallin, be desired to pronounce a funeral oration at the grave. (3.) That the following ministers be invited to support the pall, viz. Mr. Noble, Mr. Wallin, Mr. Richardson, Mr. Rees, Mr. Ridgeway, and Mr. Arnold, all being pastors of churches. (5.) That the following pastors and ministers be also invited, viz. Mr. Barrow, Mr. Gill, Mr. Harrison, Mr. Wilson, Mr. Rudd, Mr. Mulliner, Mr. Bidle, Mr. Ring, Mr. Spencer, Mr. Towns-

DEVONSHIRE-SQUARE.—*Particular Baptist.*

hend, Mr. Townshend the seventh day minister, Mr. Sandford, Mr. Davenport, and Mr. Morton. (6.) That hatbands, gloves, and cloaks be provided for all the ministers. (7.) That all the brethren are desired to provide themselves hat-bands, gloves, and cloaks, for their more decent attendance at the funeral."* Though Mr. Key never appeared before the public as an author, nor does he appear to have possessed any literary endowments; yet, the above extract will serve to shew that he was held in very great respect by his church.

In February, 1722, Mr. JOHN TOMS and Mr. CHARLES BOWLER, members of the church in Devonshire-square, who had been called into the ministry, were desired to assist Mr. Key on the morning of the Lord's-day; to which they consented. Concerning these persons, we can furnish no particulars, excepting that the name of Mr. Toms appears upon the list of subscribing ministers, at the Salters'-Hall Synod, in 1719.†

SAYER RUDD, M. D. Upon the death of Mr. Key, the late Dr. Andrew Gifford, then assistant to his father at Bristol, was invited to the pastoral office at Devonshire-square, but declined. After this, the attention of the church was directed to Mr. Sayer Rudd, pastor of a congregation at Turners'-Hall; and in order to accomplish his removal, it was proposed that the two churches should unite. Several letters passed between them upon the occasion; and on the 25th of December 1726, it was agreed that the church at Turners'-Hall, should meet with that in Devonshire-square, on the following Lord's-day. One difficulty, however, remained. The people at Turners'-Hall enjoyed a considerable bequest, to which they were entitled only while a distinct church. In order to preserve this, it was finally agreed, that the church in Devonshire-square, then consisting of 158

* MS. *penes me.*   † MS. *penes me.*

DEVONSHIRE SQUARE.—*Particular Baptist.*

members, should dissolve, and afterwards be received into communion with the other society.

Tuesday, June 27, 1727, being the day appointed for consummating this business, Mr. Toms was chosen to be the mouth of the church in Devonshire-square. Having first engaged in prayer, he afterwards delivered a very seasonable and pertinent discourse concerning the nature and ends of church-fellowship, asserting the independence of every church and congregation, and its power to transact within itself, all affairs relating to the glory of God, and their own edification; for the promoting of which ends, they might not only form themselves into a body, but if they should see occasion, afterwards dissolve, and give themselves up to another community. After this, he reminded the church to which he stood related, of the several steps they had taken since the decease of their late pastor, in order to their settlement with another; at the same time, letting them know, that what they were now about to do, was not the effect of precipitancy and rashness, but of mature deliberation, conference, and prayer. He then acquainted them, that having, on the 7th of May last, come to a resolution to dissolve their present church state, they were now met to fufil their design; and putting it to the vote, it was unanimously agreed, that from that time, their church should be dissolved.

Mr. Rudd then addressed his own church as follows: My brethren and sisters—" I am now to address myself to you over whom the providence of God has placed me as overseer. You have been witnesses to what has passed on the part of the church, late under the pastoral care of Mr. Mark Key, deceased. They have dissolved their church state, and now offer themselves for communion to you; and forasmuch as you have already signified your readiness to receive them into your communion, by giving them an invitation thereto, your silence now is a sufficient testimony that you recognise and confirm your satisfaction in admitting them as members with you." After this Mr. Rudd pro-

DEVONSHIRE SQUARE.—*Particular Baptist.*

ceeded to declare that he did in the name of the Lord Jesus Christ, and as the mouth of the church, receive them into full communion, to partake of all the ordinances and institutions which Christ has appointed in his house. The two churches having then united, several regulations were drawn up for their mutual benefit; and the members present having signed their names, the Lord's supper was administered, and the congregation dismissed.

Mr. Rudd continued pastor of the united church, till 1733. In the April of that year, he signified his intention of taking a tour to France; which being disapproved by the church, they refused their consent. In the following month, however, it appears that he took which is commonly called " French leave :" For at a church-meeting held June 3, it was reported that Mr. Rudd was gone to France; and agreed, that his salary should be withheld till he gave satisfaction. From this time, Mr. Rudd's connection with the church in Devonshire-square was dissolved.* Of his after-history we shall have occasion to make mention in a future article.

JOHN RUDD, a member at Turners'-Hall, accompanied his brother to Devonshire-square, where he preached occasionally as an assistant. In 1732, he accepted an invitation to become pastor of the Particular Baptist church, in Broad-street, Wapping, at which place we shall make further mention of him.

GEORGE BRAITHWAITE, M. A.—Within nine months after Mr. Rudd's departure, the church was once more agreeably settled in the Rev. George Braithwaite. This worthy and respectable minister was born in the year 1681, at Fornacefells, in Lancashire. His parents, and indeed the whole of his relations were zealous members of the Church

* MS. *penes me.*

DEVONSHIRE-SQUARE.——*Particular Baptist.*

of England; and from his infancy, devoted him to the ministry in that church, with a view to his succeeding an uncle, who was a celebrated preacher in that part of the country. He was, accordingly, sent to a grammar-school near the place of his nativity; whence, after a while, he removed to a more noted seminary in Yorkshire, where he continued till such time as he was sent to the University. There he attended the several lectures, and the usual course of academical exercises; and prosecuting his studies with diligence, took his degree of Master of Arts. Not long after, some domestic occurrences obliged him to leave this seat of learning. In consequence of the illness of a near relation, who was supposed to be at the point of death, he was hastened home; and after this, had no opportunity of returning.

Mr. Braithwaite, in early life, became a subject of divine grace, and was made to experience the value of those blessings, which it was intended he should dispense to others. It was while a youth also, that he embraced the distinguishing tenets of the Baptists, before he knew that there were any people of that profession in the world. But it is presumed, that he did not long remain uninformed as to this particular. Some time after his leaving the University, he came to London, and joined a church of that persuasion under the care of the Rev. David Crossley, near Cripplegate. This was in the year 1706, when he was about twenty-five years of age.

But Mr. Braithwaite's talents were not designed to be concealed long in this state of comparative obscurity. Though he consented for a while to sit down as a private church-member, yet the furniture he had acquired, fitted him in no small degree to be an instructor of others. His abilities for the ministry were first tried and approved by the church with which he communicated; and after solemn fasting and prayer, he was recommended by them to the great work of preaching the everlasting gospel.

About this time he received considerable offers from his relations and friends, who were very desirous that he should

DEVONSHIRE-SQUARE.—*Particular Baptist.*

settle in the Church of England. But this not being agreeable to his judgment, he cheerfully sacrificed all outward advantages to the honour of Christ, and the peace of his own conscience. He had formerly determined, that if God should call him by his grace, and put him into the ministry, he would devote the first fruits of his labours to the poor ignorant people in his native place. He, accordingly, went down into Lancashire, where a divine blessing accompanying his preaching, he soon gathered a church, and for some time went on very comfortably. At length, a difference arising about the terms of communion, a separation became necessary. But it was a very amicable one; Mr. Braithwaite being enabled to conduct himself with that amiable and truly christian spirit, which so greatly distinguished him. Though his longer continuance with this people was impracticable, yet he was resolved to leave them with some mark of his affection. Accordingly, he generously confirmed to the congregation and their successors for ever, the place of worship, the burial-ground, and the baptistery which were all situated upon his own estate.

After this, he settled with a congregation at Bridlington, in Yorkshire, where he preached several years with reputation and success; and in all probability had ended his days there, had not his zeal against prevailing intemperance rendered his situation uneasy. It was with a view to serve the best interests of his people, that, on this occasion, he published a small treatise against unnecessary frequenting public houses, which gave great offence. His unsettled state being made known to his friends in London, they recommended him to the congregation in Devonshire-square, which he found no difficulty in accepting. He accordingly removed to London, and was set apart in that place, March 28, 1734, Dr. Gill gave the charge, and Mr. Wilson preached to the people. In this situation, Mr. Braithwaite continued to the time of his death.

In each of the above places, his ministry met with accept-

DEVONSHIRE SQUARE.—*Particular Baptist.*

ance and success. His preaching was plain, serious and affectionate; and he had a remarkable gift in prayer. In this exercise he was noted for a holy importunity; and expressed himself with so much fervour, that it was thought to injure his constitution. He was enabled to maintain a close walk with God; and for two and thirty years together, kept an exact account of the frame of his spirit, in the closet, the family, and the world. The reflections with which his account is interspersed, discover the breathings of a truly pious mind. In his conversation he was friendly, affable, and courteous; and took every opportunity of introducing something that might tend to edification. He possessed a natural warmth of temper, of which he was sensible, and would often acknowledge with regret. His circumstances in the former part of life, were easy and plentiful; but, as is often the case with Dissenting ministers, a large family, and confined income, greatly reduced them. In the latter part of his ministry, he met with some sharp, and unexpected troubles, which took great effect upon his spirits, and tended, in no small degree, to break a constitution naturally good. He lived, however, to see the clouds in a good measure disperse, for which he heartily thanked God, a little before his dissolution.

His decay was gentle and gradual; and for the most part without pain, or sickness: His understanding was clear and unclouded; his conversation heavenly; and his satisfaction as to a better world, full and uninterrupted. He would say to the honour of sovereign grace, he had no fears, no doubts, and longed to be at home, where the wicked cease from troubling, and where his weary soul would be at rest. At length, it pleased God to grant him his desire; and his death was so remarkably easy, that, without a figure, he might be said to fall asleep in Jesus.* He died July 19th, 1748, in the 67th year of his age. His funeral sermon was

---

* Mr. Wilson's Sermon on the Death of the Rev. George Braithwaite, p. 42.

DEVONSHIRE-SQUARE.—*Particular Baptist.*

preached at Devonshire-square, July 24th, by the Rev. Samuel Wilson, on 2 Tim. iv. 7, 8. *I have fought a good fight, &c.* a text chosen by the deceased.

In this discourse, Mr. Wilson says, " I persuade myself that every one who was acquainted with the remarkable modesty and humility of the Rev. Mr. George Braithwaite, deceased, will readily acquit him of the charge of vanity in the choice of these words as the subject of his funeral discourse. I shall not easily forget the serious and very affectionate manner in which, a little before his death, he spoke to me upon this head: My dear brother, said he, (for that was the manner of the good man, always warm and pathetic,) I have nothing to boast of, far be it from me; but I bless God, he has, through his grace, enabled me, in a measure, to be faithful. And I look upon it as a singular mercy, that I have not to charge myself with a single instance, in which I have been left to baulk my conscience, as to any one truth of the gospel, or ordinance of Christ, out of fear, or in favour to any man."—" Glorious mercy! adds Mr. Wilson, to have, in the view of eternity, the testimony of a good conscience, that in simplicity and godly sincerity, he had his conversation in the world; and at the same time to see his obligation to a higher hand, and thankfully to acknowledge that, by the grace of God he was what he was."* (K)

---

* Mr. Wilson's Sermon on the Death of the Rev. George Braithwaite, p. 29—33.

(K) Mr. Braithwaite's publications consist of, 1. The Nation's Reproach, and the Church's Grief; or, a serious needful Word of Advice to those who needlessly frequent Taverns, and Public-houses, and often spend the Evening there. In a Letter to my Neighbour, and Countrymen.—2. The Saint's Desire in Time, and Happiness in Eternity: a Sermon occasioned by the Death of Mr. Humphrey Trend; preached near Devonshire-square, Dec. 19, 1736. Psa. xvii. 15.—3. The Conflicts and Conquest of the born of God; or, Faith's Victory and Triumph over the World: a Sermon preached Aug. 30, 1741, on the Death of Mrs. Mary Newsham. 1 John, v. 4,

DEVONSHIRE-SQUARE.—*Particular Baptist.*

JOHN STEVENS.—A few months after the death of Mr. Braithwaite, Mr. Henry Lord, of Baccup, was requested to pay a probationary visit to the church in Devonshire-square; but he declining, Mr. John Stevens was invited in November, in 1749, to supply the vacancy for three months. At the expiration of that time, he received a call to the pastoral office, which he accepted; and was ordained in May 1750. Here his preaching attracted great notice, and he was amazingly popular. So great was his reputation, that, upon the resignation of Dr. Gill, he was chosen, in conjunction with Mr. Brine, to conduct the Wednesday evening lecture in Great-Eastcheap. For the space of ten years, he maintained a fair character, and was held in great esteem by his brethren. But, at the end of that period, an unhappy circumstance took place, which cast a cloud over his character for the remainder of life. He was, in consequence, dismissed from the office of pastor at Devonshire-square, and excluded the Society. Though the circumstances of the case were too well authenticated at the time, yet there were not wanting some persons who believed him innocent; and their attachment was strengthened by a pamphlet published by Mr. Stevens in his own vindication. As many of these persons adhered to him, he took the lease of a meeting-house, in Red-Cross-street, where he formed a new church, and preached till his death.* Some further particulars relating to his life and writings, may be expected in our account of that place.

WALTER RICHARDS.—The church in Devonshire-square remained destitute of a pastor for some considerable time after Mr. Stevens's dismission. At length, on the 12th of September, 1762, it was agreed to give Mr. Walter Richards, of Birmingham, a call to the pastoral office.

* *Private Information.*

DEVONSHIRE-SQUARE.—*Particular Baptist.*

This he accepted, and received the following letter of dismission from the Baptist church at Birmingham, dated Nov. 14, 1762.

"The baptized church of Christ, meeting in Cannon-street, Birmingham, holding the doctrine of particular election, and final perseverance, send their Christian and most respectful salutation to the church of Christ, of the same faith and order, meeting near Devonshire-square.

Dear and beloved Brethren, Whereas it hath pleased the all-wise God, in the course of his kind and good providence, (for he worketh all things after the council of his own will,) to cast the lot of our beloved brother, Mr. Walter Richards, amongst you, and as we are desired to give him a letter of recommendation to you, we cheerfully comply with the request, and would observe, That our brother Richards is a member in full communion with us, his principles and moral character agreeable to us, and as becometh the gospel of our Lord Jesus Christ. And we observe, moreover, that our brother before-named, was, at a time, appointed for that solemn purpose, approved and set apart as a minister of the gospel, or to preach the word of God, in which character he now resides with, and labours amongst you; and, therefore, we dismiss and recommend him to your communion as a member, and minister of the gospel. As to his abilities for the weighty and solemn work in which he is engaged, you are acquainted with them, which makes it needless we should say any thing on that head: And, therefore, we have only to say, that it will afford us all imaginable pleasure, to hear of his honour and prosperity amongst you. Our prayers to your God and ours, we hope, will be constant, and fervent, on his account. His name and memory are precious to us, and we trust ever will be. The Lord has done great things for him, and, we hope, hath still greater things in reversion for him. O! may he help you much who have believed through grace; and, also, be a happy means of large additions to you of such as shall be

DEVONSHIRE SQUARE.—*Particular Baptist.*

saved. He is sound in the faith; God grant he may continue so. In a word, may he be a workman that needeth not to be ashamed, rightly dividing the word of truth. May he continue faithful unto death, and the Lord grant him a crown of life. Finally, may the whole of his conduct and conversation, most evidently prove that he is a sincere lover of the Lord Jesus Christ, the Gospel, and you. We commend him and you to God, and the word of his grace, and conclude, your most affectionate brethren in the faith and fellowship of Jesus Christ our Lord. Signed,

JAMES TURNER, Pastor, &c. &c."*

Mr. Richards was ordained to the pastoral office in Devonshire-square, Dec. 16, 1762. Dr. Gill gave the charge, and Mr. Wallin preached to the people. Through some means or other, the preaching of Mr. Richards did not give general satisfaction to the church, which was the occasion of his continuing but a short time in this connexion. He, in consequence, resigned the pastoral office, April 23, 1764. After this, Mr. Richards went over to Ireland, and settled with a congregation at Cork, where we believe, he is still living.†

JOHN MACGOWAN.—A few months after the departure of Mr. Richards, the Rev. Richard Hutchings, pastor of a congregation at Long-Buckby, in Northamptonshire, preached for some time upon trial, and was near settling; but the church not being quite unanimous, he declined their call. Some time after, Mr. Macgowan, who had preached with great acceptance, was invited to undertake the pastoral office, with which he complied.

This gentleman was a native of Scotland, and born at Edinburgh, about the year 1726. Of his early life we possess but little information. After receiving a common school-educa-

* MS. *penes me.*   † *Private Information.*

DEVONSHIRE-SQUARE.—*Particular Baptist.*

tion, he was placed out to the trade of a weaver; but how long he followed this occupation we are not able to say. In early life he connected himself with the Wesleyan Methodists, amongst whom he received his first religious impressions. In this connexion he also became a preacher. Afterwards embracing the Calvinistic sentiments, he joined the Independents, and at length the Particular Baptists. For some years, he was settled with a congregation of that persuasion at Bridgnorth, in Shropshire; where he laboured under great discouragements for want of success. This induced him to embrace the earliest opportunity of removing to some other place. In July, 1766, the church in Devonshire-square, sent him an invitation to preach upon trial; and his ministry being approved, he was called, in the September following, to the pastoral office. He was received into communion Dec. 15; and set apart on the 29th of July, 1767. Mr. Clarke opened the meeting with prayer; Dr. Gill proposed the questions; Mr. Wallin preached to the minister; Dr. Stennett to the people; and Mr. Burford concluded with prayer. In this connexion Mr. Macgowan continued nearly fifteen years, till he was removed by death, Nov. 25, 1780, in the 55th year of his age.*

Of the frame of his mind, during his illness, we have the following particular account, drawn up by the Rev. John Reynolds. "I frequently visited him (says Mr. Reynolds) in his last sickness, when he took occasion, as opportunity offered, of opening to me his whole heart. At one time he was in great darkness of soul, and lamented exceedingly the withdrawings of the presence of God. Two things, he said, had deeply exercised his thoughts. The one was, how those heavy and complicated afflictions, which God had seen fit to lay upon him, could work so as to promote his real good. And the other was, that God, his best friend, should keep at a distance from his soul, when he knew how much his

* MS. *penes me.*

mind was distressed for the light of his countenance. ' O !' said he, turning to me, and speaking with great earnestness, ' my soul longeth and panteth for God, for the living God; his love-visits would cheer my soul, and make this heavy affliction sit light upon me. The wonted presence of Jesus, my Redeemer, I cannot do without,—I trust he will return to me soon;—yea, I know he will in his own time; for he knows how much I need the influence of his grace.' In this conversation he often mentioned the depravity of his nature, and what a burden he found it;—' My heart,' said he, ' is more and more vile,—every day I have such humiliating views of heart-corruption as weighs me down,—I wonder whether any of the Lord's people see things in the same light I do.' And then turning to me, he said, ' And do you find it so my brother?' Upon my answering him in the affirmative, he replied, ' I am glad of that.'

"The next time, which was the last of my conversing with him, I found him in a sweet and heavenly frame: His countenance indicated the serenity of his mind. On my entering the room, he exclaimed, ' O, my dear brother, how rejoiced am I to see you! sit down, and hear of the loving-kindness of my God. You see me as ill as I can be in this world, and as well as I can be whilst in the body. Methinks I have as much of heaven as I can hold.' Then tears of joy, like a river, flowed from his eyes; and his inward pleasurable frame interrupted his speech for a time. He broke silence with saying, ' The work will soon be over;—you see what you must soon experience;—but death to me, has nothing terrific in it;—I have not an anxious thought;—the will of God, and my will are one;—'tis all right, quite mysterious —We are to part here; but we shall meet again.—You cannot conceive the pleasure I feel in this reflection, viz. that I have not shunned to declare (according to my light and ability) the whole counsel of God;—I can die on the doctrines which I have preached,— they are true,—I find them so.—Go on to preach the gospel

DEVONSHIRE-SQUARE.—*Particular Baptist.*

of Christ, and mind not what the world may say of you.' All the while I sat silent; and rising up to take my leave, fearing he would spend his strength too much, he immediately took me by the hand, and weeping over each other, we wished mutual blessings. Upon parting, he said, ' My dear brother, farewell—I shall see you no more.'—Thus (continues Mr. Reynolds) I left my much esteemed friend and brother; and the next news I heard of him was, that on the Saturday evening his immortal spirit left the body to go to the world of light and bliss, and keep an eternal sabbath with God, angels, and saints."* His funeral sermon was preached by Mr. Benjamin Wallin, from Zech. iii. 2. *Is not this a brand pluckt from the fire?* a text chosen by the deceased. Dr. Stennet delivered the address at his interment in Bunhill-fields, where the following inscription may be seen upon his grave-stone:

Here lies
JOHN MACGOWAN, U. D. M.
Who at the hand of God
Merited nothing but final destruction
Yet through grace was enabled to hope
In a finished salvation.
He died Nov. 25, 1780, Aged 54 years.
Eph. ii. 8.
For by grace are ye saved through faith,
And that not of yourselves; it is the gift of God.

Mr. Macgowan possessed talents of a peculiar and striking nature, which might have been displayed with advantage in a very different station, had his natural inclination finally prevailed. But an ardent zeal for the gospel of Christ, engaged all the powers of his mind. He possessed good natural abilities, a lively imagination, and retractive memory. As a preacher, he was faithful, judicious, and affectionate. His humility was very remarkable. He experienced great

* Macgowan on Ruth. *Preface.*

conflicts in the discharge of the ministerial office, on account of an habitual sense of his guilt and corruptions, which frequently overwhelmed him with shame, when he appeared in public.* His sentiments upon theological subjects, harmonized in general, with those of Calvin. He was a zealous Trinitarian; but with regard to the sonship of Christ, and the pre-existence of his human soul, he deviated from reputed orthodoxy. He did not conceive the phrase " Son of God," to be properly a divine title; but rather understood it as an inferior or mediatorial character. Yet this did not lessen his esteem for his many worthy brethren who thought otherwise, and maintained what is called, " the eternal generation of the Son of God;" on the contrary, he read their works with pleasure. With regard to the human soul of Christ, he inclined to the pre-existent scheme.† As a companion and friend, he was highly spoken of, and held in great esteem by his brethren. Mr. Macgowan (says Mr. Reynolds) was one of the most valuable and improving companions I ever had the honour of an intimacy with. We visited often, and our conversation usually turned on important subjects, which proved very instructive to my own mind. The natural cheerfulness of his temper, the ease and familiarity with which he communicated his ideas, his great integrity and unaffected piety, rendered him the pleasant companion, the amiable Christian, and the sincere friend: no one more sensibly felt the loss of him than myself."‡ His constitution was naturally delicate, but greatly weakened by hard study, and frequent, laborious preaching, which brought on a lingering illness, that, after a few weeks confinement, terminated his life.‖

As an author, Mr. Macgowan is well known in the world, on account of the singular subjects he has chosen,

* Mr. Wallin's Sermon on the Death of the Rev. John Macgowan, p 29.
† *Private information.* ‡ Macgowan on Ruth. *Preface.*
‖ Mr. Wallin's Sermon, p. 30.

DEVONSHIRE-SQUARE.—*Particular Baptist.*

and the peculiarity of style with which he has treated them. In some of his pieces he has allegorized to an excess; his characters are distorted; and his colouring much too high. He also treats his opponents with unjustifiable severity; and endeavours to work upon the passions by those artifices which can only mislead the ignorant and inexperienced. We have better evidence for the doctrines of the gospel, than those afforded by ghosts and spectres. His writings, however, are in great esteem amongst a numerous class of readers; and it must be acknowledged, that some of his pieces are written with great smartness. Accordingly, they have passed through several editions. The titles of his publications will be given below.(L)

TIMOTHY THOMAS, the present minister at Devonshire-square, is a native of Leominster, where his father, the Rev. Joshua Thomas, was many years a worthy and respect-

---

(L) A Letter to the Rev. John Allen, on the Doctrine of the Trinity.—2. Death; a Vision: Or the solemn Departure of Saints and Sinners, represented under the Similitude of a Dream.—3. Familiar Epistles to the Rev. Dr. Priestley.—4. Socinianism brought to the Test; or Christ proved to be the adorable God, or a notorious Imposter. In a series of Letters to the Rev. Dr. Priestley.—5. A curious Letter to the Rev. Edward Brydges Blacket, LL. D. occasioned by his Sermon preached before the Bishop of Exeter, at the Consecration of St. Aubin's Chapel, in Dock-Town, Plymouth.—7. Infernal Conference; or Dialogues of Devils; in which the many Vices which abound in the civil and religious World, doctrinal and practical, are traced to their proper Sources. 12mo. N. B. There is also an edition of this book in one volume 8vo.—7. The Life of Joseph, the Son of Israel. In eight Books. Chiefly designed to allure young Minds to a love of the sacred Scriptures.—8. The Arian's and Socinian's Monitor.—9. Priestcraft defended; a Sermon occasioned by the Expulsion of six young Gentlemen from the University of Oxford, 1768.—10. The Sure Foundation; a Sermon on the Death of the Rev. Benjamin Messer; preached at Grafton-street, June 21, 1772. 2 Tim. ii. 19.—11. The Cleansing Fountain opened; a Sermon on John i. 7. occasioned by the Death of Mrs. Elizabeth Beusted, March 11, 1773.—12 A Looking-Glass, for the Professors of Religion; in seven Tracts on practical Subjects.—13. The Foundery Budget opened; or the Arcana of Wesleyanism, 1780.—14. Discourses on the Book of Ruth, and other important Subjects. Revised and prefaced by the Rev. John Reynolds, 8vo. 1781.

DEVONSHIRE-SQUARE.—*Particular Baptist.*

able minister, of the Anti-Pædobaptist denomination. In 1778, Mr. Thomas went to Bristol Academy, under the tuition of those excellent persons, Mr. Hugh Evans, and his son Dr. Caleb Evans, whose sister he married. In 1781, he was called to fill up the vacancy in the church at Devonshire-square, occasioned by the death of Mr. Macgowan; and was ordained on the 30th of September in that year. Mr. Wallin delivered the introductory discourse, and proposed the questions; his father Mr. Joshua Thomas gave the charge; and Mr. Booth preached to the people. The text selected for the charge was somewhat remarkable: *O Timothy, keep that which is committed to thy trust.* 1 Tim. vi. 20. In mentioning this circumstance it is but justice to observe that Mr. Thomas was not one of those ministers who love punning in the pulpit—who cannot forego a joke, even at the expence of decency of good manners. Though by these means too many gain the admiration of a gaping multitude, yet, they were arts that he abhorred; being as much unsuited to the gravity and dignity of the pulpit, as to the solemnity of divine worship. For several years past, Mr. Thomas has kept an academy at Islington, in which are taught the elementary principles of education. During the last administration, when a change took place in the allotment of the *Regium Donum*, the share falling to the Baptists, was made over to Mr. Thomas, and Mr. Dore; who have had the distribution of it ever since.

DEVONSHIRE-SQUARE.—*Particular Baptist.*

and the peculiarity of style with which he has treated them. In some of his pieces he has allegorized to an excess; his characters are distorted; and his colouring much too high. He also treats his opponents with unjustifiable severity; and endeavours to work upon the passions by those artifices which can only mislead the ignorant and inexperienced. We have better evidence for the doctrines of the gospel, than those afforded by ghosts and spectres. His writings, however, are in great esteem amongst a numerous class of readers; and it must be acknowledged, that some of his pieces are written with great smartness. Accordingly, they have passed through several editions. The titles of his publications will be given below.(L)

TIMOTHY THOMAS, the present minister at Devonshire-square, is a native of Leominster, where his father, the Rev. Joshua Thomas, was many years a worthy and respect-

(L) A Letter to the Rev. John Allen, on the Doctrine of the Trinity.—2. Death; a Vision: Or the solemn Departure of Saints and Sinners, represented under the Similitude of a Dream.—3. Familiar Epistles to the Rev. Dr. Priestley.—4. Socinianism brought to the Test; or Christ proved to be the adorable God, or a notorious Imposter. In a series of Letters to the Rev. Dr. Priestley.—5. A curious Letter to the Rev. Edward Brydges Blacket, LL.D. occasioned by his Sermon preached before the Bishop of Exeter, at the Consecration of St. Aubin's Chapel, in Dock-Town, Plymouth.—7. Infernal Conference; or Dialogues of Devils; in which the many Vices which abound in the civil and religious World, doctrinal and practical, are traced to their proper Sources. 12mo. N.B. There is also an edition of this book in one volume 8vo.—7. The Life of Joseph, the Son of Israel. In eight Books. Chiefly designed to allure young Minds to a love of the sacred Scriptures.—8. The Arian's and Socinian's Monitor.—9. Priestcraft defended; a Sermon occasioned by the Expulsion of six young Gentlemen from the University of Oxford, 1768.—10. The Sure Foundation; a Sermon on the Death of the Rev. Benjamin Messer; preached at Grafton-street, June 21, 1772. 2 Tim. ii. 19.—11. The Cleansing Fountain opened; a Sermon on John i. 7. occasioned by the Death of Mrs. Elizabeth Bensted, March 11, 1773.—12 A Looking-Glass, for the Professors of Religion; in seven Tracts on practical Subjects.—13. The Foundery Budget opened; or the Arcana of Wesleyanism, 1780.—14. Discourses on the Book of Ruth, and other important Subjects. Revised and prefaced by the Rev. John Reynolds, 8vo. 1781.

DEVONSHIRE-SQUARE.——*Particular Baptist.*

able minister, of the Anti-Pædobaptist denomination. In 1778, Mr. Thomas went to Bristol Academy, under the tuition of those excellent persons, Mr. Hugh Evans, and his son Dr. Caleb Evans, whose sister he married. In 1781, he was called to fill up the vacancy in the church at Devonshire-square, occasioned by the death of Mr. Macgowan; and was ordained on the 30th of September in that year. Mr. Wallin delivered the introductory discourse, and proposed the questions; his father Mr. Joshua Thomas gave the charge; and Mr. Booth preached to the people. The text selected for the charge was somewhat remarkable: *O Timothy, keep that which is committed to thy trust.* 1 Tim. vi. 20. In mentioning this circumstance it is but justice to observe that Mr. Thomas was not one of those ministers who love punning in the pulpit—who cannot forego a joke, even at the expence of decency of good manners. Though by these means too many gain the admiration of a gaping multitude, yet, they were arts that he abhorred; being as much unsuited to the gravity and dignity of the pulpit, as to the solemnity of divine worship. For several years past, Mr. Thomas has kept an academy at Islington, in which are taught the elementary principles of education. During the last administration, when a change took place in the allotment of the *Regium Donum*, the share falling to the Baptists, was made over to Mr. Thomas, and Mr. Dore; who have had the distribution of it ever since.

Dissenting Churches

IN THE

CITY OF LONDON.

SOUTHERN DIVISION.

CONTAINING,

1. GREAT-EASTCHEAP.
2. MILES'S-LANE.
3. DYERS'-HALL.
4. JOINERS'-HALL.
5. PLUMBERS'-HALL.
6. TALLOW-CHANDLERS'-HALL.
7. SALTERS'-HALL.
8. CUTLERS'-HALL.
9. BUCKINGHAM-HOUSE.
10. THREE-CRANES.
11. GREAT ST. THOMAS APOSTLE.
12. BOW-LANE.
13. BROKEN-WHARF.
14. CARTER-LANE.
15. FRIARS'-STREET.
16. MEETING-HOUSE COURT.

GREAT-EASTCHEAP.

PARTICULAR BAPTIST.—EXTINCT.

THE origin of this Church, like that of many others, particularly that of the Baptist denomination, is involved in great obscurity. Though we have taken some pains in examining manuscripts, and comparing lists of ministers, during the latter half of the seventeenth century, our researches, with regard to the article before us, have not met with the desired success. It seems, that about the year 1696, two societies of the Baptist denomination, then destitute of pastors, agreed to unite under the ministry of Mr. John Noble. One of these, very probably, was the church in Gracechurch-street, noticed in a former article. Mr. Noble, after labouring thirty-four years in this connexion, was gathered to his fathers. His successor was Mr. Samuel Dew, in whose time the congregation very much declined; and the lease of the meeting-house expiring about 1760, they dissolved their church state. Most of the surviving members joined themselves to the church in Horsleydown, under the care of Dr. Gill. During the chief part of Mr. Noble's time, the church assembled at Tallow-Chandlers'-Hall, Dowgate-hill, from whence they removed to Maidenhead-court, Great-Eastcheap. Though the exact date of this removal is not mentioned, it must have been between the years 1727 and 1730. For many years a lecture was carried on at this place on a Wednesday evening. Dr. Gill preached it alone nearly thirty years. After his resignation, Mr. Brine, and Mr. Stevens, conducted it jointly for a few years; after which it was removed to Cripplegate. There it was carried on for some time by four ministers: Mr.

GREAT EA·TCHEAP.—*Particular Baptist*, Extinct.

Brine, Dr. Stennett, Mr. Burford, and Mr. Clarke. The lecture was afterwards removed to Little St. Helen's, and from thence to Devonshire-square, where Mr. Swain preached it alone, with great popularity for a few years. He was succeeded in this lecture, as well as in his congregation, by Dr. Jenkins.

In pursuance of our plan, we proceed to give some account of the ministers of this Society, so far as our information reaches, and which we shall introduce with the following table.

Ministers' Names.	As Pastors.		As Assistants.	
	From	To	From	To
John Noble, ...	1690	1730	—	—
Samuel Wilson, ...	—	—	172.	1726
John Davenport, ...	—	—	1727	17..
Samuel Dew, ...	1731	1706	—	—

JOHN NOBLE.—This worthy minister was born about the year 1660, and had the advantage to descend from religious parents. When very young, he was accustomed to attend with them upon divine worship among the Dissenters. On one of these occasions, he was apprehended, and sent to the common jail, where he endured great hardship. But though he begun to suffer thus early for the profession of religion, yet, as himself has remarked, he was all this while destitute of its power. It pleased God, however, to make his confinement subservient to a saving change upon his heart. While in prison, he pursued his studies with diligence, and made a considerable progress in useful knowledge; so that, upon proper occasions, he was enabled to defend, as well is preach the gospel. Soon after his enlargement, he was

GREAT-EASTCHEAP.—*Particular Baptist*, Extinct.

baptized upon a profession of faith, and received into church-fellowship. In a little time, his abilities for the ministry became so apparent, that he was sent forth to preach the gospel, and his labours were accompanied with great success. For some time he preached to several churches in the country, only occasionally, not chusing to undertake a pastoral charge. He also taught grammar learning at this period, that he might be the less chargeable to poor churches. After spending some time in the country, where his ministry was both acceptable and useful, he received a call from two congregations in London, about the same time; but as he could not accede to both their requests, the high esteem they entertained of him, induced them to unite. In this situation Mr. Noble continued with great honour and usefulness, for about thirty-four years, till he was removed by death, June 12, 1730, in the 71st year of his age. His funeral sermon was preached by Mr. Edward Wallin, from Phil. i. 21. *For me to live is Christ, and to die is gain.**

In this discourse Mr. Wallin gives a particular description of Mr. Noble's religious character; from whence it appears that " his manner of recommending truth to others was not with excellency of speech, or wisdom of words, but he chose plainness of speech, and such a way of expression as was out of the common road, yet so enlivened with many striking sentences, as commanded attention, and carried with them much light and conviction." In his preaching he dwelt much on the free grace of God, which was his delightful subject. He, also, frequently insisted upon the leading doctrines of the gospel. The length to which he carried his speculations upon some subjects, occasioned many persons to charge him with loosening the obligations to moral duties; but though the manner in which he stated some doctrines might have this tendency, yet, the thing itself was the re-

---

* Mr. Wallin's Sermon on the Death of Mr. Noble, p. 31—32.

GREAT-EAS CHEAP.—*Particular Baptist*, Extinct.

motest from his intention. On the contrary, he laboured to improve the doctrine of grace to a strict regard for the precepts of the gospel. The zeal he discovered in defending the peculiarities of the supra-lapsarian scheme, sometimes led him into uncharitable censures of his brethren; but it was remarked, that when he took the chair at the monthly association of Baptist ministers, he behaved with great prudence and moderation. In his last illness, he expressed a cheerful resignation to the divine pleasure, declaring that the truths he had preached to others, were the comfort and support of his own soul in the near views of death and eternity. He was buried in the ground belonging to the Park-Meeting, Southwark.*

Mr. Noble was assisted in the latter part of his life by several ministers. One of these was the learned Mr. SAMUEL WILSON, afterwards of Goodman's-Fields, concerning whom we shall have occasion to make particular mention hereafter. Mr. Wilson removing to Broad-street, Wapping, about the year 1726, was succeeded by Mr. PETER DAVENPORT, to whose name we can add no particulars. Mr. Noble was succeeded in the pastoral office by Mr. Dew.

SAMUEL DEW.—Concerning this gentleman our information is extremely slender. His origin appears to have been humble, and he was bred to the trade of a stone-cutter; but how long he followed this profession, we are not able to say. His mind being seriously impressed, he applied in early life to the study of the sacred scriptures, and having embraced the principles of the Baptists, commenced preacher in that denomination. After spending a few years in occasional labours, he settled with a Baptist congregation at Mitchel-Dean, in Glocestershire, where he was very popular, and not a little useful. In 1731, he removed to London, to succeed Mr. Noble, at

* Mr. Wallin's Sermon, *ubi supra*.—Crosby's History of the Baptists, vol. iv, p. 375—390.

GREAT-EASTCHEAP.—*Particular Baptist*, Extinct.

Great-Eastcheap. Here his popularity abated, nor did his labours meet with that success with which they had formerly been attended. In consequence, his congregation greatly declined, and, at length, upon the expiration of their lease about 1760, dissolved their church state. After this, Mr. Dew did not assume any ministerial charge, but preached occasionally for his brethren, and communicated with the church upon Horsleydown, under the pastoral care of Dr. Gill. Mr. Dew was a man of respectable character, and esteemed a good preacher by the admirers of high Calvinism. But the manner in which he explained some doctrines, was considered by many persons as having an Antinomian tendency. Nothing, however, could be farther from his design. His only publication that we have met with, is a funeral sermon for Mrs. Mary Bevois, preached at Mr. Gill's meeting-house, April 1, 1735, on Job xix. 25. Mr. Dew survived the dissolution of his church only a few years.*

The meeting-house in Great Eastcheap, after the Baptists quitted it, was never occupied by a regular Dissenting church; but has passed through the hands of various adventurers. It was taken first by Mr. Richard Elliot, who was assisted by the late Mr. Thomas Tuppen, of Bath, and held it from 1760 to 1773, when he removed to Glass-house-yard. Mr. West, a builder, who afterwards erected a meeting-house at Hammersmith, then occupied it for a short time. Upon his removal, the Swedenborgians held it for some years. The meeting-house was afterwards taken by the Rev. Christopher Frederic Triebner, a German Lutheran Divine, who occupied it about two years. Mr. Waterman, also, preached here for some time before he settled at Ratcliff; but, we believe, his services were confined to an evening lecture. About eight years ago, the meeting-house was taken down,

* *Private Information.*

together with the adjoining buildings, and all traces, even of the court, are now lost in a large house and warehouse erected upon the site.

MILES'S-LANE.

INDEPENDENT.—EXTINCT.

First Church.

MILES'S-LANE, properly ST. MICHAEL'S-LANE, so called from the saint to whom the parochial church is dedicated, falls into Cannon-street, at the north end, and on the south into Crooked-lane, and so into Thames-street. The meeting-house stands in a paved court, called Meeting-house-yard, on the right hand side from Cannon-street. It is a large, substantial brick-building, with three good galleries; and is one of the oldest places of worship among the Dissenters. Though the exact date of the building is not now to be obtained, there is good evidence that it must have been erected very soon after the restoration of Charles the Second. Being a large and commodious place, it was fixed upon as a prey to the parish minister, when his church was consumed in the fire of London, A. D. 1666; nor could the rightful owners regain possession till the new church was built. This was the fate of many other meeting-houses, at that time, and places in a strong light the unprincipled power of the ecclesiastical government, during the reign of Charles the Second.

OF DISSENTING CHURCHES.

MILES'S-LANE.—*Independent*, Extinct. First Church.

The meeting-house in Miles's-lane, was occupied in its early state by two different congregations, both Independent. Each of them is become extinct; one in our own time, under the late Dr. Stephen Addington; the other nearly a century ago. These we shall take up separately in their proper order; beginning with the latter, as least known; and better suited to chronological precision.

The first church that falls under our notice, was collected soon after the act of Uniformity, by the Rev. Matthew Barker, the ejected minister of St. Leonard's, Eastcheap. Mr. Baxter mentions him among the Independent Ministers, who began to set up their separate meetings after the fire of London, in 1666. His congregation assembled at Miles's-lane on the morning of the Lord's-day; and he continued their pastor through successive persecutions, between thirty and forty years. He was succeeded in the pastoral charge, by the Rev. John Short, in whose time the congregation greatly declined; so that, at his death, which happened in 1718, they dissolved into other societies. About two or three years prior to this event, they removed to some other meeting-house. Both these ministers were Calvinists, and men of good learning and reputation, by which they helped to support the cause of Nonconformity, at a time when its enemies expected that it would sink into oblivion. We shall follow up our plan by giving a brief account of each of these Divines.

Ministers' Names.	From	To
Matthew Barker, ...	1662	1698
John Short, ...	1698	1718

MATTHEW BARKER, M. A.—This excellent minister was born about the year 1619, at Cransley, a small village

MILES'S-LANE.—*Independent*, Extinct. First Church.

near Broughton, in Northamptonshire. Being designed for the ministry, he was placed at a proper age, at Trinity College, Cambridge; and having taken his degrees, removed to Banbury, in Oxfordshire, where he superintended an academy. On the breaking out of the civil war in 1641, he was forced to leave that place, and retired to London. Soon afterwards, he was chosen minister of St. James's, Garlick-hill, in which situation he continued about five years. Thence, he removed to Mortlake, in Surry, being invited to the lectureship at that place, by some citizens who resided there in the summer. On the death of Mr. Robrough, in 1650, he was called to the living of St. Leonard's, Eastcheap, which he held till Bartholomew-day, 1662, when, not being able to satisfy himself in some things required by the act of Uniformity, he was forced to resign. He, however, continued in the ministry, though with many hazards and difficulties; preaching to a separate congregation of his own gathering, as the times would allow. It does not appear where his people first met for public worship, but as they were composed of some of his old parishioners, it, probably, was somewhere in the same neighbourhood. The meeting-house in Miles's-lane, being erected early in the reign of Charles the Second, they were allowed the joint use of that place, and Mr. Barker preached to them for many years with great acceptance, till the time of his death, which happened March 25th, 1698, being then in his 80th year.

From a MS. account of Mr. Barker's life, left behind him at his death, he appears to have been a person of great sincerity, and remarkable humility; much addicted to prayer, very diffident concerning the success of his ministry, and ardently concerned for the promotion of true godliness. He was a man of considerable learning, great piety, and universal candour and moderation. As he disliked controversy, he earnestly avoided it, laying but little stress upon points of inferior importance, in which he was sensible

MILES'S-LANE.—*Independent*, Extinct. First Church.

others were as much at liberty to differ from him, as he from them. This apprehension evidently governed his practice. He discovered a peculiar pleasure in conversing with young ministers; with whom he used great freedom, without regard to any difference of sentiment in smaller matters; cheerfully encouraging them in the work they had undertaken, and rejoicing in the prospect of their usefulness, when, through age, his own abilities visibly declined.* (M)

JOHN SHORT.—This learned Divine descended from a respectable family in the West of England. His grandfather, Mr. John Short, was a gentleman of good estate at Aishwater, in Devonshire, but a great enemy to the Nonconformists. So exasperated was he against his son for not conforming at the Restoration, that he resolved to disinherit him; and left his estate to another person. This was the Rev. Ames Short, who was ejected from Lyme-Regis, in Dorsetshire, and passed through many sufferings on the score of nonconformity. He was a grave and serious Divine, much the gentleman, and a pleasant companion. He died suddenly, July 15, 1697, aged 81. His son, Mr. John

---

* Calamy's Account, p. 45.—Contin. p. 63.—Nonconformist's Memorial, vol. i p. 144.

(M) WORKS.—Mr. Barker published, 1. Natural Theology; or, the Knowledge of God.—2. A Discourse on Family Prayer.—3. Reformed Religion; or, the right Use of Christianity described in its Excellency and Usefulness in the whole Life of Man. 1619.—4. *Flores Intellectuales;* or, select Notions, Sentences and Observations, out of several Authors, especially for the Use of young Scholars entering into the Ministry.—5. Three Sermons in the Morning Exercises.—6. Two Sermons, preached upon public Occasions.—7. Annotations on the two Epistles to the Thessalonians; in the Continuation of Mr. Poole.—Mr. Barker, also, had a hand in the English-Greek Lexicon.

MILES'S-LANE.—*Independent*, Extinct. First Church.

Short, of whom we are now to speak, was exposed, when a child, to all the severity of persecution, in common with his father. Dr. Calamy relates an affair which happened to him at that period, and places the barbarous proceedings of those times in a very strong light. Old Mr. Short being confined prisoner to his own house, by the Five Mile Act, in 1665, the county-troops often entered the town to search after him, and rifled his house. Being several times disappointed, they became enraged; and one of them caught his son, fixed a pistol to his breast, and threatened to kill him, if he did not tell where his father was. The child answered, " My father does not acquaint me whither he goes." As they were searching the chimnies, chests, boxes, &c. they threatened the servant-maid after the same manner. She said, " My master doth not hide himself in such places ; he has a better Protector." To which they made this reply, " The devil take him and his Protector too !"

Mr. Short was educated for the ministry among the Nonconformists, but at what seminary we are not able to say. It is highly probable that he passed some time in one of the universities of Holland. Having finished his studies, he set up an academy at Lyme, where he was very useful in training young men to the ministry ; and occasionally preached for his father, who had a private meeting in that town. He afterwards removed to Colyton, in Devonshire, where he followed the same profession. Upon the death of the Rev. Matthew Barker, in 1698, he was invited to London, to succeed him in his congregation at Miles's-lane. In this connexion he continued till his death, which happened about the year 1718. Mr. Short was a man of considerable learning, of great piety, and of a sound judgment. He had the misfortune to have an impediment in his utterance, which was a great denial to him, and occasioned his not being heard with pleasure in the pulpit; so that the congregation sunk under his administration. A few years before his death they removed to another meeting-house; and upon the decease of their pastor, dissolved their church-state, and mixed with other societies.*

MILES'S-LANE.

INDEPENDENT.—EXTINCT.

Second Church.

HAVING dismissed the former Society, we proceed to give some account of the other Independent church, to whom the meeting-house in Miles's-lane, properly belonged. It was erected in the early part of the reign of Charles II. as before-mentioned, for the use of the Rev. Stephen Ford, and the congregation under his care. The Society, however, existed many years prior to this. We strongly suspect that it was gathered during the long parliament, by the Rev. Sydrach Sympson, one of the Westminster Assembly, and an eminent Independent Divine, during the interregnum. In his time, the congregation met in St. Mary-Abchurch, Cannon-street; but where it assembled after his death, till the present meeting-house was built, we are not able to say. Mr. Short's congregation removing about 1715, the church now under consideration, which had hitherto met for public worship in the afternoon only, occupied the place on both parts of the day. This Society was originally very large and

* Calamy's Continuation, p. 418, &c.—Neale's Life of Matthew Clarke, prefixed to his Sermons, p. 33.

MILES'S-LANE.—*Independent*, Extinct. Second Church.

respectable, and composed of many persons of good substance. Towards the latter end of Mr. Ford's life, the congregation gradually declined; and was, at length, reduced so low, that though he was obliged to have an assistant, they could not raise for him a sufficient maintenance. After his death, however, the congregation greatly revived under the successful labours of the excellent Mr. Matthew Clarke, one of the most popular ministers of his day. Upon his decease, and the choice of Mr. Jollie for pastor, in 1726, an unhappy breach took place; when several of the members withdrew, and founded the present church in New Broad-street. Though this circumstance operated unfavourably for the Society in Miles's-lane, nevertheless, Mr. Jollie was enabled to stand his ground, and maintained a respectable congregation to the day of his death. A short time previous to this event, he relinquished the afternoon service to Mr. William Porter, whose congregation was accommodated with the use of the meeting-house on that part of the day, for the space of ten years, when they removed to a new place of worship, in Camomile-street. In the time of Mr. William Ford, who was Mr. Jollie's successor, the congregation was in a low state; and continued so under Dr. Addington, notwithstanding he attracted some notice for a short time after his settlement in London. At length, Dr. Addington's growing infirmities, and the necessities of a neighbouring congregation, led the way to an arrangement that gave mutual satisfaction, and eventually issued in the dissolution of his church. The congregation at the Weigh-House, under the pastoral care of the Rev. John Clayton, having determined to erect a new meeting-house, were looking out for a temporary place of worship, while their new one was building. At this time, Dr. Addington being disabled from engaging in more than one service on the sabbath, agreed to resign his pulpit on the other part of the day to Mr. Clayton. This was the state of things for several months. But the Weigh-House being finished at the begin-

MILES'S-LANE.—*Independent*, Extinct. Second Church.

ning of 1795, Mr. Clayton's congregation returned thither. This proved a discouragement to Dr. Addington's church; and his infirmities still increasing, he resigned the pastoral office, June 14, 1795. After this, his people kept together but a short time; for not agreeing upon the choice of a successor, and the Society being greatly reduced, they thought it best to dissolve their church-state. In point of religious sentiment, there does not appear to have been any material alteration in this Society, since the time of its commencement. The several ministers, whose lives we are about to record, have been distinguished by their zealous attachment to the doctrines of the gospel. For though the separation that took place upon Mr. Jollie's settlement, was occasioned nominally by a difference of sentiment, yet, it does not appear that he differed much from his predecessors. The cry of heterodoxy has often been raised against the most valuable ministers of Christ; and sported by bigots with more zeal to support the dogmas of a party, than to serve the interests of genuine religion.

Upon the dissolution of Dr. Addington's church, the meeting-house was taken by a Society of Scotch Seceders, whose history will pass under our revision in the next article In the mean-time we will present the reader with some account of the pastors in the Independent Society, whose names and succession may be seen at one view, in the following table.

Ministers' Names.	From	To
Sydrach Sympson, ...	164.	1658
Stephen Ford, ...	166.	1694
Matthew Clarke, ...	1692	1726
Timothy Jollie, ...	1726	1757
William Ford, Jun.	1757	1781
Stephen Addington, D. D.	1781	1795

MILES'S-LANE.—*Independent.* Extinct. Second Church.

SYDRACH SYMPSON, whom Mr. Neal styles "a meek and quiet Divine, of the Independent persuasion,"* received his education in the University of Cambridge. He afterwards became a celebrated preacher in London.† Being appointed curate and lecturer of St. Margaret, Fish-street, his preaching soon gave offence to Archbishop Laud, who, at a metropolitical visitation, in the summer of 1635, convened Mr. Sympson, and several other Divines, before him, for a breach of the canons. Most of them having submitted at this time, were dismissed.‡ But the intemperate bigotry of Laud, and the violent manner in which he exacted conformity, drove many eminent Divines out of the kingdom. Some retired to Holland, and others to New-England. Amongst the former were Dr. Thomas Goodwin, Mr. Philip Nye, Mr. Jeremiah Burroughs, Mr. William Bridge, and Mr. Sydrach Sympson. These were afterwards the five pillars of the Independent, or congregational party; and, in the Assembly of Divines, were distinguished by the name of the *Dissenting Brethren.*§

Mr. Sympson afterwards returning to England, was chosen in 1643, a member of the Assembly of Divines, at Westminster; and gave constant attendance.‖ In their debates he conducted himself with great temper and moderation. He was one of the Divines who published, and presented to the house, in 1643, An Apological Narration on the part of the Independents:¶ Bishop Kennet says, he was silenced for sometime from preaching, because he differed in judgment from the Assembly in points of church discipline; but was restored to his liberty, October 28, 1646.** In 1650, he was appointed, by the parliamentary visitors, Master of Pembroke-Hall, Cambridge, in the room of Mr. Vines, who refused the engagement.†† It being proposed by

* Neale's Puritans, vol. ii. p. 518.   † Ibid. vol. i. p. 623.
‡ Ibid. p. 585.   § Ibid. p. 623.   ‖ Ibid. vol. ii, p. 41.
¶ Ibid. p. 98.   ** Ibid. vol. i. p. 518.   †† Ibid. p. 395.

MILES'S-LANE.—*Independent*, Extinct. Second Church.

parliament to tolerate all who agreed in the fundamental doctrines of Christianity, a committee was appointed, in 1654, to draw up a catalogue of fundamentals. Mr. Sympson was a member of this committee, and had a principal hand in drawing up some articles; which, however, were not presented to the house; and, so, were never acted upon.* In the same year, he was constituted by an order of council, a commissioner for the approbation of public preachers. The commissioners were in all thirty-eight; selected from the three denominations; and are commonly known by the name of *Tryers*.† In 1655, he was appointed under a commission from Oliver Cromwell, one of the New Visitors to the University of Cambridge, in order to regulate and secure the education of youth.‡ In the time of the long parliament, he gathered a congregation in London, upon the Independent plan, which met in Abchurch, near Cannon-street. Mr. Sympson was a Divine of considerable learning; and of great piety and devotion. In his last sickness he was under some darkness, and melancholy apprehensions; upon which account, some of his friends, and brethren, assembled in his house, to assist him with their prayers. In the evening, when they took their leave, he thanked them, and said, he was now satisfied in his soul; and lifting up his hands towards heaven, said, "he is come, he is come;" and died that night, A. D. 1658.§

Mr. Sympson was succeeded in his living of St. Mary-Abchurch, by Mr. John Kitchin, a Presbyterian Divine, who was ejected at the Restoration. After this, his congregational church must have met privately; but the name of his successor we are not able to determine with certainty. We have before us the names of several Independent ministers who had congregations at this period; but it is difficult to assign them their particular spheres of labour. As

* Neal's Puritans, vol. ii. p. 443. † *Ibid.* p. 447.
‡ *Ibid.* p. 462. § *Ibid.* p. 518.

MILES'S-LANE.—*Independent*, Extinct. Second Church.

Mr. Ford came to London soon after Bartholomew-day, it is probable that not many years elapsed after Mr. Sympson's death, before he took charge of the church.

STEPHEN FORD.—He pursued his studies at Oxford, though at what College does not appear. Wood has passed him over in silence, and Calamy has done but little towards supplying that defect. He appears to have been a truly disinterested character, and influenced by the most ardent wishes to promote the best interests of the people of his charge. During the inter-regnum, he was presented to the living of Chipping-Norton, in Oxfordshire, where, in a short time, he had the satisfaction to find his labours crowned with eminent success. In an epistle to his people, still extant, he says, " When the blessed God inclined my heart to the ministry, my earnest request was, that he would be pleased to cast my lot in a place where I might be eminently useful in the church and cause of Christ.—At the time I became your minister, I had three places offered me: one of them was worth near twenty times as much as this poor vicarage. But I found my heart more inclined towards you than towards any of the said places ; and, through grace, I refused them all for your sakes."

When the black Bartholomew Act passed, August 24, 1662, he was obliged to quit his living because he could not satisfy himself to conform. He, however, still continued to preach privately, as he had opportunity ; and was instrumental in raising a congregation of Protestant Dissenters in that place, which exists to this day. He became their first pastor, was much beloved by them, and his labours were very successful. But he was sadly harassed on account of nonconformity, and, at length, some of his enemies threatened his life ; so that he was forced to fly to London, where he often preached in the time of the plague, when others fled into the country for escape. Upon his leaving Chipping-Norton, the interest of religion in that town visibly declined;

MILES'S LANE.—*Independent*, Extinct. Second Church.

He left an address with his people in the most faithful and affectionate terms, in which he says, " Now my beloved, the returns that I expect and desire of you, for all the sufferings that I have undergone, and am likely still to undergo, for your sake; for all my temporal losses, for my care and pains, labour and travail for your everlasting happiness, are, That you will be pleased to read, consider and practise these following duties." He then exhorts them to serious self-examination, watchfulness and prayer; and dissuades them from conformity to the world, &c.—Upon his coming to London, he settled with a congregation in Miles's-lane, Cannon-street, and continued to officiate as their pastor, nearly thirty years. He also set up a catechetical lecture, for young men, on Lord's-day mornings, at seven o'clock; but afterwards changed it to the evening, and, it was hoped, did much good.*

As Mr. Ford advanced in years, he grew infirm, and his congregation declined, which made it necessary to provide him an assistant. The Rev. Matthew Clarke, being in London, in 1689, gave Mr. Ford's congregation an occasional sermon, from which they conceived such great expectations, that upon his return home, they sent him an unanimous invitation to assist their aged pastor. This, after some deliberation, he accepted; and in the course of a year or two, was ordained joint-pastor. The Reverend and aged Mr. Ford, did not survive this last act more than two years. After seeing his congregation comfortably settled with a promising young minister, he resigned his spirit in peace, and was received to his reward, sometime in the year 1694, being then far advanced in life, though his exact age doth not appear.†(N)

* Calamy's Acc. p. 540. Contin. p. 705.—Noncon. Mem. vol. iii. p. 121.
† Neal's Memoirs of the Rev. Matthew Clarke, prefixed to his Sermon, p. 33.

(N) WORKS.—Mr. Ford published, Scripture Rules which Jesus Christ,

MILES'S-LANE.——*Independent*, Extinct. Second Church.

MATTHEW CLARKE, an eminent Divine among the Independent Dissenters, descended of a reputable family in the county of Salop. His father, the Rev. Matthew Clarke was ejected by the act of Uniformity in 1662, from Narborough in Leicestershire; and compelled by the violence of persecution to retire to a solitary house in Leicester Forest, where his only son Matthew was born, February 2, 1663-4. Upon the Five-mile act taking place in the following year, Mr. Clarke removed his family first to Stoke-Golding, and afterwards to little Bowden; but the times growing more favourable, he at length settled at Market Harborough, where he gathered a congregation of Protestant Dissenters, amongst whom he laboured with great acceptance and usefulness above forty years. But such was the severity of the times, that this reverend person, who was universally beloved by the whole country, suffered imprisonment three several times in Leicester jail, for no other crime than preaching: and in the latter end of the reign of king Charles II. was prosecuted upon the Oxford Act, and his goods seized for the payment of the fine. But under all these disadvantages, Mr. Clarke took particular care of the education of his son, whom he himself instructed in the learned languages; and on account of his eager thirst after divine knowledge, determined to dedicate to the work of the ministry.*

While Mr. Clarke resided in his father's house, he enjoyed the company of some other young gentlemen, who boarded there with a view to the University. Under the instruction of his excellent parent, he made himself master of the Latin, Greek, and several of the oriental languages, to which he afterwards added the Italian and French: the latter of which, he spoke and wrote with uncommon fluency and exactness.

hath given his Churches to walk by; which was approved of and consented to by all the members of the Church, at Chipping-Norton.—An Epistle to the People of his Care.—Discourses on a Gospel Church; and on Regeneration, 1675.

* Memoirs of the Rev. Matthew Clarke, prefixed to his sermons by the Rev. Daniel Neal, page 7—9.

MILES'S-LANE.—*Independent*, Extinct. Second Church.

Being prepared for academical learning, he was placed under the care of the Reverend and learned Mr. John Woodhouse, an eminent tutor at Sheriff-hales, in Shropshire, with whom he finished his preparatory studies. In order still further to fit him for the pulpit, he went to London for the benefit of conversing with learned men, and forming himself upon the model of the most celebrated preachers of that day. He continued in the metropolis nearly two years, and joined in communion with the church at Girdlers'-Hall, under the pastoral care of the Rev. George Griffith. After this, he returned into Leicestershire, and formed an acquaintance with the most experienced Christians in that part of the country. At this time, he was much noticed on account of his seriousness of spirit, his courteous behaviour, and that humility and prudence which distinguished him beyond his years.*

He entered upon his ministerial work, in the year 1684, a time of as great severity against Protestant Dissenters, as had been known since the restoration of King Charles the Second. At his first appearance in public, he met with great acceptance. Novelty drew many to hear him, and those whose prejudices were invincible, could not but admire his great abilities, and decent behaviour in the pulpit. During the three years he assisted his father at Market Harborough, large additions were made to the church; besides which, he laid the foundation of several Dissenting Churches in the neighbouring country. His engaging behaviour endeared him so much to the people in those parts, that they were very desirous of his continuance. Upon his coming to London in 1687, his friends persuaded him to supply the congregation at Sandwich in Kent, for a few Lord's-days. This was the church of which the excellent Mr. Pomfret had been pastor, till being imprisoned for preaching, he made his escape, and fled the country in disguise. After Mr. Clarke had been there about a month or six weeks, the people expressed

* Memoirs, &c. page 11, 12.

MILES'S-LANE —*Independent*, Extinct. Second Church.

such esteem for his ministry, and used such arguments as detained him for two years; and nothing but his father's pressing importunities prevailed with them to give up their interest in him at last. At Sandwich his labours were very successful, and he left behind him a name that was mentioned with respect for many years afterwards.*

In 1689, he returned to London, where there was a great demand for young ministers. But after a few weeks he returned to his father, and accepted the choice of the church to become his assistant. While in London, he preached an occasional sermon to Mr. Ford's congregation in Miles's Lane, by which they conceived such a favourable opinion of his abilities, as to send him an invitation to assist their aged pastor. The arguments and intreaties used on this occasion, procured his own and his father's consent; but being a member of the church at Harborough, and their assistant, he would not finally accept the call without their permission. The people were for some time unwilling to part with him, and used their best endeavours for his detention; but being at length satisfied with the call of Divine providence, they consented to his removal.†

Mr. Clarke settled in London under great disadvantages, his friends not having a pulpit to give him, for so much as one part of the Lord's-day. Mr. Barker's congregation assembled at Miles's-lane in the morning; and Mr. Ford preached to his own people in the afternoon, as long as his health would admit. This being the case, Mr. Clarke set up an evening lecture, which was very much frequented, and proved a young nursery to the congregation. To add to his discouragements, Mr. Ford's church and auditory were reduced so low, that they could not raise him a sufficient maintenance, with which they were almost ashamed to acquaint him; but they were surprised with his humble and modest reply: " That he had cast himself upon the provi-

* Memoirs, &c. page 12, 13.   † *Ibid.* page 14, 15.

MILES'S-LANE.——*Independent*, Extinct.   Second Church.

dence of God, which had always provided well for him; therefore as he had no reason to question their doing for him according to their ability, he should be satisfied with the will of God, and be content to fare as God should bless them together."

It was some time before the providence of God smiled upon this undertaking; for though Mr. Ford was in the decline of life, he was unwilling to be thought to have outlived his usefulness, and therefore filled the pulpit oftener than was desired. This hindered the increase of the congregation, and together with some other unkindnesses which Mr. Clarke met with, laid him under great discouragements. At length it was agreed, with Mr. Ford's consent, to choose him co-pastor, and admit him to stated service every other Lord's-day, as well as at other times when Mr. Ford was disabled. About this time, May 1692, he was solemnly ordained to the pastoral office, with imposition of hands, by several ministers, amongst whom were Mr. Ford, Mr. Griffith, and Mr. Barker. A few days previous to this service, he set apart some time to inquire into his spiritual state, humbly to confess his sins, and implore a blessing on his future labours. At the same time he entered into a solemn covenant with God; which together with the motives that influenced him in this affair, may be seen at length in the Memoirs of his life, published by Mr. Neal; and they afford eminent proofs of his sincere piety, humility, and entire devotedness to the will of God.

Mr. Ford dying in 1694. Mr. Clarke succeeded him in the whole of the service, and in a short time he had a crowded audience. About two years after this event, Providence directed him to the choice of a most agreeable wife, in the person of Mrs. Anne Frith, daughter of Mr. Robert Frith, who had been several times Mayor of Windsor. By this lady he left behind him a son and a daughter. In the year

* Memoirs, &c. page 15—23.

MILES'S-LANE.—*Independent*, Extinct. Second Church.

1697, three of the Pinners'-Hall lecturers died, within two months of each other.(o) This made way for the choice of Mr. Clarke, who preached in his turn at that lecture with great reputation till his death.*

The high esteem in which Mr. Clarke was held among Dissenters of all denominations, occasioned frequent applications to him for his occasional services. As he was at leisure on one part of the Lord's-day, and was ever ready to give his assistance, he frequently officiated for his brethren, so that he usually preached twice or three times on the sabbath, and several times in the week. His unwearied labours however, seem to have carried him beyond his strength; and he persisted in the same course till he had greatly injured his constitution. By constant preaching, his blood became so heated, that by degrees he lost his natural appetite and rest; but the imprudence of his conduct did not fully appear, till the spring of 1707, when he exhibited symptoms of a violent cold, and obstruction of his lungs. These being neglected at first, and happening at an unfavourable season of the year, produced a malignant fever, which was one and twenty days before it came to a crisis. Though he had the advice of the most eminent physicians, his disorder proved of that obstinate nature, that no hopes were entertained of his recovery. His whole mass of blood was corrupted, and the pores of his body dried up. In order to promote secretion, he had blisters, fresh pigeons applied to his feet every twelve hours, and bottles of warm water under his arms; but the symptoms were every day more threatening. His congregation, as might be supposed, was deeply affected with his case, and appointed seasons for public prayer and intercession upon his account; which were continued for nine several days, and assisted by most of the city ministers. Mr. Clarke himself was not insensible of the danger of his case, and therefore

(o) These were Mr. Thomas Cole, Mr. Nathaniel Mather, and Mr. Timothy Crusoe.

* Memoirs, &c. page 23—25.

| MILES'S-LANE.——*Independent*, Extinct. Second Church. |

while he had the use of his reason, settled his worldly affairs; and having taken a solemn leave of his wife, who was dissolved in tears by his bed-side, he resigned himself in humble devotion to the will of God. Being apprehensive that he was near his end, he desired Mr. Watts might be sent for to pray with him. That excellent person says, he observed in him a sweet calmness and composure of mind, a firm and steady reliance upon the merits of Christ alone for his salvation, and an humble resignation of himself to the will of God whether for life or death. He then assisted him in his devotions, and as a person departing out of the world, recommended him to the mercy of our Lord Jesus Christ, unto eternal life. Though the physicians gave no hopes of his recovery, they continued to watch the distemper, that they might be ready to assist any efforts of nature. When they apprehended that the next paroxysm would be his last; one of them proposed the use of bark, which the rest were afraid would hasten his death. Others advised the richest and highest cordial that could be prepared, which was ordered to be taken in a very large quantity, as the last assistance that could be afforded. The effect of this prescription was sudden and apparent. His fever gradually abated, nature discharged itself by degrees of the distemper, and after some weeks he recovered.*

Notwithstanding Mr. Clarke's recovery from this severe fit of illness, it so shattered his constitution, that though he enjoyed a pretty good state of health for some years after, he would frequently complain of disorders in his head, which at length, turned to a gouty humour, and settled in his feet. Upon his appearance in public, his church appointed April 23, 1707, as a day of solemn thanksgiving to God for his recovery. The Rev. William Tong, an eminent presbyterian minister, preached from Phil. ii. 27. *" For indeed he was sick and nigh unto death, but God had mercy on him;*

---

* Memoirs, &c. page 27—30.

MILES'S-LANE.—*Independent.* Extinct. Second Church.

after which Mr. Clarke with great humility and devotion first returned thanks to God, and then acknowledged with all affection and gratitude his obligations to his brethren, who had wrestled with God for so unworthy a life; assuring them it should be devoted, as God enabled him, to the service of Christ and his church. The first time he appeared in the pulpit, he preached a most affectionate sermon from Psal. cxviii. 18. *The Lord has chastened me sore, but has not given me over to death;* in which he expressed the temper of his mind upon his sick bed in the following words: " I had the sentence of death within myself, and concluded that I was deprived of the residue of my years, and should see the Lord no more in the land of the living, but under these apprehensions, I had some good hope through grace that I should see and enjoy him in the other and better world; having committed my soul into the hands of the Lord Jesus Christ, I was persuaded he would present it to the Father without spot and blemish. Though I had not those raptures which some have experienced upon a death-bed, yet I had so much faith as enabled me to stay myself upon God, trusting in the righteousness of my glorious Redeemer. When I was free from those confusions and disorders which the violence of my distemper brought upon me, I did not allow myself to speak or think hardly of God, but was enabled to acquiesce in his sovereign pleasure, saying, ' If the Lord has any further service for me, he will bring me back into his house, but if he has no further pleasure in me, here I am, let him do as seems good in his sight."—And so lasting were the impressions which this providence made upon him, that he noticed the anniversary return of it, in his family devotions, as long as he lived.*

When Mr. Clarke returned to his work, he abated nothing of his former labours, but preached as frequently as before his illness. In the year 1708, the nation sustained an unspeak-

---

* Memoirs, &c. page 30, 31.

MILES'S-LANE.—*Independent*, Extinct. Second Church.

able loss in the death of his Royal Highness George, Prince of Denmark, whose powerful influence over his royal consort Queen Anne, was not discovered till some time after his death, when her majesty gave into measures too apparently prejudicial to the interests of her people, and the Protestant succession. Upon this occasion, addresses of condolence were sent up from all parts of the kingdom, and Mr. Clarke, at the head of the Dissenters, waited on the Queen, and was received alone into the royal closet, clothed with mourning suitably to the solemn occasion.

After this, his reputation and usefulness continued to increase, till another melancholy providence befel him. In the month of November, 1715, as he was returning home out of Southwark, where he had been to visit a friend, his foot slipt over against the church in Tooley-street, and one of his legs bending under him, both the bones of it snapt asunder. He was immediately lifted into a coach, and went home in it alone to the surprise of his family. The bones being set by skilful surgeons, were healed in the usual manner, without any remarkable accident. He was obliged, however, to keep his bed for a month or six weeks, which so weakened his constitution, that though he retired into the country to recover his strength, and was entertained with cheerfulness at the country seats of several of his friends, in the neighbourhood of the metropolis, his spirits were apparently depressed, nor did he ever recover his former vivacity and briskness.*

Hitherto Mr. Clarke had preached but one part of the Lord's-day in his own pulpit, but the church which assembled there in the morning, removing to another place, the whole service devolved upon him. This he performed regularly for some time, to the manifest injury of his constitution; for instead of regular fits of the gout in his feet, which

* Memoirs of the Rev. Matthew Clarke, p. 31—33.

MILES'S-LANE.—*Independent*, Extinct. Second Church.

he used to have once a year, the humours began now to float into the noble parts, and to affect his head and stomach. He now lost his appetite, his bulk became considerably diminished, and though his legs would sometimes swell, it was not in the power of medical aid to expel the disorder to his extremities. In these unhappy circumstances, his church thought it high time to provide him an assistant. They accordingly, in 1720, chose, with great unanimity, and with his entire approbation, the Rev. Timothy Jollie, of Sheffield. This gentleman lived in great friendship with Mr. Clarke for six years, reverencing him as a father, and endeavouring to form his method of preaching upon so excellent a model. The assistance he now enjoyed, was not, however, of that service to him which it might have been, could he have been persuaded to resist the importunity of his friends, who were pressing him into their service upon every occasion. Instead of remitting his labours, he accepted in the same year that Mr. Jollie was chosen, a new lecture at Mr. Earle's meeting-house, Hanover-street, to be conducted by six ministers, on Thursday mornings, for the service of that end of the town. Here he gained fresh reputation, and spread his character into those parts of London and Westminster, where it was not so well known before. In 1722, he was chosen again to carry up the address of the Protestant Dissenters, congratulating his Majesty upon the discovery of the plot to bring in the Pretender and Popery.[*]

During this time there was something that sat very heavy upon Mr. Clarke's mind, and contributed not a little to impair his health. We allude to the unhappy divisions amongst his brethren, occasioned by their assembling at Salters'-Hall, to consult about advices for peace, to be sent into the West-country, where the harmony of the churches was disturbed by the revival of some disputes relating to the doctrine of the Trinity. When the London ministers met toge-

[*] Memoirs, &c. p. 33—35.

MILES'S-LANE.—*Independent*, Extinct. Second Church.

ther, it was debated, whether they ought not first to make a declaration of their own faith in that article, before they gave advice to their brethren. This was opposed by many, as foreign to the design of the assembly, and as that which might possibly lay the foundation of a division among themselves; and upon the question, it was carried by a small majority in the negative. But the brethren on the other side of the question, thought this an affair of such consequence, that they came to the next session of the assembly, determined to recal the former question, and if the majority did not consent, then to invite as many as would join them, to subscribe *the first article of the Church of England*, and *the answers to the fifth and sixth questions of the Assembly's Catechism*, as a test of their agreement in this article of faith. The warmth and passion with which the debate of that day was conducted, prevailed with some of the brethren to withdraw from so much noise and clamour, and unhappily divided the rest into two parties of subscribers and non-subscribers. Mr. Clarke sided with those who were for subscribing the articles, and after the breaking up of the assembly, thought it his duty to confirm the faith of his people in the important doctrine of the eternal Deity of our Blessed Saviour, by preaching on the subject; as did most of the Dissenting ministers in London, of all denominations, about that time. Having discharged his conscience in this particular, he would never allow himself to suspect those of heresy, or lukewarmness in the faith, who merely differed from him with respect to the expediency of subscribing. He was, therefore, ready to join with those of either party, whom he had reason to believe sound in the faith, upon all opportunities of worship; but this Christian temper gave occasion to some narrow-minded persons to spread reports to his disadvantage. These calumnies he would have neglected if he had been in perfect health; but being advanced in years, and depressed in his spirits, they filled his heart with the deepest concern. He mourned over

MILES'S-LANE.—*Independent*, Extinct. Second Church.

the unhappy state of the Dissenting interest, lamented the divisions amongst his brethren in public and private, and prayed earnestly that God would pour out a better spirit upon the contending parties. When he found that he could do but little service by his persuasions, he withdrew very much from public conversation, resolving to spend the short remainder of his days in silence and solitude.*

We have now brought this reverend person to the last stage of his existence. In the spring before his death, he spent a few weeks with his intimate friend, Mr. Coward, of Walthamstow; by which gentleman he had been employed, but a little before, in opening a lecture on a Friday morning, at Little St. Helen's. From Walthamstow, Mr. Clarke removed about Midsummer, to Tooting in Surry, where he was first seized with an asthmatic disorder, which, by the application of proper medicines, was quickly removed. He continued pretty well the remaining part of the summer; but being obliged to return to Tooting, in the dead of the following winter, on account of the death of the Rev. Francis Freeman, the Dissenting minister of that place, he was seized with the gout in his head and stomach. For a short time he was deprived of his senses, his complexion changed yellow, and his asthma returned with more violence than ever. From this time he had strong apprehensions of his approaching end; for though his friends encouraged him, and the physicians did every thing they could for his support, yet he felt such an inward decay of nature, and failure of spirits, as no medicine could reach. He never recovered his complexion, nor could the physicians drive the gout into his feet. However, he continued preaching, even when he had the greatest difficulty to get into the pulpit; and some of his last sermons, composed with a view to his own case, from Psa. xciv. 19. *In the multitude of my thoughts within me, thy comforts delight my soul,* were in the

* Memoirs, &c. p. 35—37.

MILES'S-LANE.—*Independent*, Extinct. Second Church.

opinion of some good judges, among the best they had ever heard.*

About the middle of February, he went with his family, for the benefit of the air and exercise, to Stoke-Newington; and rode out as often as the weather would permit. "Here, (says Mr. Neale,) I visited him, and observed that he endeavoured to be cheerful for the entertainment of his friends; though his spirits and strength were exhausted. When we were alone, he opened his heart, wounded with the divisions among his brethren, which he was satisfied, without some remarkable appearance of God, would end in the loss of the vital power of religion from among them; the glorious Spirit of God, in his converting and sanctifying operations, being already, in a great measure, departed from their assemblies.—*But*, says he, *I shall shortly be out of the way—I am not far from the place where the weary are at rest.* This was the last conversation I had with him; for a few days after, the humours which had already filled his legs, and floated about his body in different shapes and forms, seized his vitals, and put an end to his life in three days."—He had been very cheerful on Wednesday evening, and prayed in his family with unusual fervour and devotion; but about five o'clock on Thursday morning, he awoke and complained of a rising in his throat, which, upon his taking something, was removed. About seven it returned again, and after endeavouring in vain, to discharge his stomach, he was suddenly deprived of speech. His wife and family being alarmed, they immediately brought him in a coach to London. When he entered his own house, he was sensible, and seemed to be well pleased that he was at home. A few hours after he was in bed, he lost the use of one side of his body, and the next day fell into a kind of lethargy, in which he continued till about eight o'clock on the Lord's-day morning, when his pacific soul ascended to his great Redeemer,

* Memoirs, &c. p. 38.

MILES'S-LANE.—*Independent*, Extinct. Second Church.

March 27, 1726, after he had lived 62 years, seven weeks and two days.* His funeral sermon was preached by the Rev. Daniel Neal, from Matt. xxv. 21. *His Lord said unto him, Well done thou good and faithful servant, &c.*

Such was the end of that faithful and laborious servant of Christ, the Rev. Matthew Clarke. He was of a comely person, something taller than the middle size, and of proportionable bulk. He had a grave and venerable aspect; his features were strong and masculine; he had a piercing eye; and always an agreeable smile in his face. His likeness is strikingly represented in a large, well-finished mezzotinto portrait, by *George White*. Mr. Clarke united in an eminent degree the gentleman and the Christian. He was courteous and affable; and in his conversation so cheerful and entertaining, as made his company acceptable to all his acquaintance. In his life and manners he exhibited a pattern of uncommon piety and integrity; was humble and modest even to a fault; and in the latter part of his life, timorous and diffident of himself, which was his greatest foible. He passed through the world in a most inoffensive manner, without the least blemish upon his moral character, having as many friends, and as few enemies, as any man of his profession.†

His family was a well-governed society, in which the worship of God, and social duties were regularly performed. Though his circumstances in the world were not large, he always kept a hospitable table; which was often spread for the entertainment of his poor brethren in the ministry, and others, to whose necessities he continually ministered. Few men of his profession had fairer opportunities of making a large provision for their family; but he had an aversion to every thing that looked like covetousness, and therefore chose rather to do honour to religion, by living agreeably to his character, and station. The affairs of his church, which

* Memoirs, &c. p. 39—40. † *Ibid.* p. 40.

MILES'S-LANE.—*Independent*, Extinct. Second Church.

was numerous, and composed of persons of different tempers and dipositions, he managed with great prudence, and discretion; discharging the office of a vigilant and faithful pastor, by public instruction, and by an annual visitation of the families of his church, as long as his health would permit. He was extremely happy in composing differences; and in all church debates, moderated with that wisdom and pacific temper, as effectually gained him the hearts of his people. But Mr. Clarke's influence was not confined within the narrow limits of his family and church. He corresponded with his poor brethren in different parts of England, and by his great interest in the city, collected large sums of money for their support, which he carefully distributed to the most necessitous and deserving. He was an original member of the society of Congregational Ministers and Gentlemen, united for the support of the gospel in the country; and the welfare of this institution was upon his heart when he left the world; for the very last sermon he preached in his own pulpit, was an exhortation to his people to continue their encouragement of it, by a liberal contribution, which he received with great thankfulness and pleasure.*

Mr. Clarke possessed an extensive acquaintance with the oriental languages, which he derived as it were by inheritance; his father being one of the best critics of his age. To good learning he united a solid judgment in religious matters; and being addicted very much in his younger years to reading and meditation, he made himself complete master of the several controversies that were agitated in the Christian church. In his private judgment he followed the sentiments of the judicious Calvin, and was never wanting in a true Christian zeal for those points which he judged of most importance. It must be mentioned, however, to his lasting honour, that he was a person of great candour and modera-

* Memoirs, &c. p. 15—27.

MILES'S-LANE.—*Independent*, Extinct. Second Church.

tion; and in all the controversies of the age, was careful to avoid extremes. Though he constantly preached the doctrines he believed, and practised those forms of worship which appeared to him most consonant to the word of God; yet he never made his own judgment a standard of the faith and practice of his brethren. His soul was too generous, and his charity too extensive, to confine salvation within the limits of a single party; he was, therefore, willing to assist among societies of different denominations, and to give the right hand of fellowship to all who held the same glorious Head with himself. He loved the image of Christ wherever he beheld it; while he feared that an unbounded pretence to charity, would lessen a concern for the glorious truths of the gospel, he was no less fearful, lest an ungoverned zeal for truth, should make a shameful inroad upon Christian love.* It was the great desire of his life to see his brethren in the ministry, adorn the doctrines they professed, by a suitable walk and conversation. He would often say, " That men were to be esteemed as much for their manner of life, as for their art of preaching; and that an *orthodox head* would not atone for a *corrupt life*."†

Many of the younger candidates for divinity, applied to him for directions in their studies, and attended his ministry to form themselves by so excellent a model; for if Mr. Clarke triumphed any where, it was in the pulpit. His grave and majestic behaviour, his commanding voice, his agreeable pronunciation, attended with a proper fervency of spirit, struck his audience with an awful reverence. His method was just and regular, his subjects well chosen, and he spoke of the sublimest doctrines of our holy religion, in an intelligible manner. Having convinced the judgment of his hearers, he seldom failed of awakening their consciences, and touching their affections. Though his language was

* Mr. Neal's Funeral Sermon for the Rev. Matthew Clarke, p. 36—40.
† *Ibid.* p. 43.

MILES'S-LANE.—*Independent*, Extinct. Second Church.

plain and familiar, he carefully avoided low and vulgar expressions, which he used to say, exposed religion to contempt, and had a tendency to make men laugh, at a time when, above all others, they ought to be most serious.* In all his discourses he endeavoured to give every text its proper meaning : " For, (says he, in one of his printed sermons,) allusions may be, and are often made ; but to interpret scripture merely by the sound of words, is playing with our bibles, and trifling in the preacher, as it serves only to impose on the people, and induces them to think the text speaks what it never intended."† Upon the whole, he was an admired, as well as a useful preacher. An evidence of this was the great success that attended his ministry. In all places where he statedly laboured, he commanded a serious and crouded audience ; and left behind him at his death, one of the most numerous and flourishing congregations in the metropolis.‡ He was so happy as to have his ministerial usefulness continued to the very last; and though the croud of business which was always upon his hands, together with his natural modesty and diffidence, would not allow him to transmit his name to posterity, yet all who were acquainted with him bore this testimony, That he deserved to be ranked among the best and most useful Divines of the age in which he lived.§ (P)

* Memoirs, &c. p. 27. and Funeral Sermon, p. 41.
† Sermon at the Ordination of Mr. Hurrion, p. 11.
‡ Funeral Sermon, p. 42.   § Memoirs, &c. p. 40, 41.

(P) Works.—Mr. Clarke published in his lifetime, the following discourses : 1. A Sermon, preached to the Societies for Reformation of Manners, July 2, 1711, from Zech. iii. 8, 9.—2. The Wisdom of this World made foolish : a Sermon, preached at the Merchants' Lecture, in Broad-street, September, 1714, on 1 Cor. i. 20.—3. Zeal for God's House, expressed in a holy Resolution not to forsake it : a Sermon, preached at Little St. Helen's, May 28, 1715, on Nehem. x. 39.—4. The Nature and Advantage of trusting in God : a Sermon, preached at the Funeral of the Rev. Mr.

MILES'S-LANE.—*Independent*, Extinct. Second Church.

Mr. Clarke's remains were deposited in a vault at the East end of the burying-ground in Bunhill-Fields; over which a neat monument was erected at the expence of his church, with an inscription in Latin, composed by the ingenious Dr. Isaac Watts, who has likewise given an English translation. They are as follows:

M. S.

In hoc sepulchro conditur
MATTHÆUS CLARKE,
Patris venerandi filius cognominis,
Nec ipse minùs venerandus;
Literis sacris et humanis
A primâ ætate innutritus:
Linguarum scientissimus:
In munere Concionatorio
Eximius, operosus et felix:
In officio Pastorali
Fidelis et Vigilans:
Inter Theologorum Dissidia
Moderatus et Pacificus:
Ad omnia Pietatis munia
Promptus semper et alacris:
Conjux, frater, pater, amicus,
Inter præstantissimos:
Erga omes ominum ordines
Egregiè benevolus.

Quas verò innumeras invicta modestia dotes
Celavit, nec fama profert, nec copia fandi
Est tumulo concessa : Sed olim marmore rupto
Ostendet ventura dies; præconia cœli
Narrabunt; judex agnoscet, & omnia plaudent.

Abi, Viator, ubicunq; terrarum fueris,
Hæc audies.

Natus est agro Leicestriensi, A. D. 1664.
Obiit Londini, 27º die Martii, 1726.
Ætat. suæ 62.
Multùm dilectus, multùm desideratus.

Thomas Simmons, March 17, 1717-18, on Psa. lxxi. 1:—5. A Funeral Sermon for the Rev. Mr. Thomas Mitchell, preached at Stepney, Jan. 15, 1721, on Acts xiii. 36.—6. God seen in the Mount; or, Israel's Deliver-

MILES'S-LANE.—*Independent*, Extinct. Second Church.

plain and familiar, he carefully avoided low and vulgar expressions, which he used to say, exposed religion to contempt, and had a tendency to make men laugh, at a time when, above all others, they ought to be most serious.* In all his discourses he endeavoured to give every text its proper meaning : " For, (says he, in one of his printed sermons,) allusions may be, and are often made ; but to interpret scripture merely by the sound of words, is playing with our bibles, and trifling in the preacher, as it serves only to impose on the people, and induces them to think the text speaks what it never intended."† Upon the whole, he was an admired, as well as a useful preacher. An evidence of this was the great success that attended his ministry. In all places where he statedly laboured, he commanded a serious and crouded audience; and left behind him at his death, one of the most numerous and flourishing congregations in the metropolis.‡ He was so happy as to have his ministerial usefulness continued to the very last; and though the croud of business which was always upon his hands, together with his natural modesty and diffidence, would not allow him to transmit his name to posterity, yet all who were acquainted with him bore this testimony, That he deserved to be ranked among the best and most useful Divines of the age in which he lived.§ (P)

* Memoirs, &c. p. 27. and Funeral Sermon, p. 41.
† Sermon at the Ordination of Mr. Hurrion, p. 11.
‡ Funeral Sermon, p. 42. § Memoirs, &c. p. 40, 41.

(P) WORKS.—Mr. Clarke published in his lifetime, the following discourses : 1. A Sermon, preached to the Societies for Reformation of Manners, July 2, 1711, from Zech. iii. 8, 9.—2. The Wisdom of this World made foolish : a Sermon, preached at the Merchants' Lecture, in Broad-street, September, 1714, on 1 Cor. i. 20.—3. Zeal for God's House, expressed in a holy Resolution not to forsake it : a Sermon, preached at Little St. Helen's, May 28, 1715, on Nehem. x. 39.—4. The Nature and Advantage of trusting in God : a Sermon, preached at the Funeral of the Rev. Mr.

MILES'S-LANE.—*Independent*, Extinct. Second Church.

Mr. Clarke's remains were deposited in a vault at the East end of the burying-ground in Bunhill-Fields; over which a neat monument was erected at the expence of his church, with an inscription in Latin, composed by the ingenious Dr. Isaac Watts, who has likewise given an English translation. They are as follows:

M. S.

In hoc sepulchro conditur
MATTHÆUS CLARKE,
Patris venerandi filius cognominis,
Nec ipse minùs venerandus;
Literis sacris et humanis
A primâ ætate innutritus:
Linguarum scientissimus:
In munere Concionatorio
Eximius, operosus et felix:
In officio Pastorali
Fidelis et Vigilans:
Inter Theologorum Dissidia
Moderatus et Pacificus:
Ad omnia Pietatis munia
Promptus semper et alacris:
Conjux, frater, pater, amicus,
Inter præstantissimos:
Erga omes ominum ordines
Egregiè benevolus.

Quas verò innumeras invicta modestia dotes
Celavit, nec fama profert, nec copia fandi
Est tumulo concessa: Sed olim marmore rupto
Ostendet ventura dies; præconia cœli
Narrabunt; judex agnoscet, & omnia plaudent.

Abi, Viator, ubicunq; terrarum fueris,
Hæc audies.

Natus est agro Leicestriensi, A. D. 1664.
Obiit Londini, 27° die Martii, 1726.
Ætat. suæ 62.
Multùm dilectus, multùm desideratus.

Thomas Simmons, March 17, 1717-18, on Psa. lxxi. 1:—5. A Funeral Sermon for the Rev. Mr. Thomas Mitchell, preached at Stepney, Jan. 15, 1721, on Acts xiii. 36.—6. God seen in the Mount; or, Israel's Deliver-

MILES'S-LANE.—*Independent*, Extinct. Second Church.

Translation.

Sacred to Memory.
In this sepulchre lies buried
MATTHEW CLARKE,
A son bearing the name
Of his venerable father,
Nor less venerable himself;
Train'd up from his youngest years
In sacred and human learning:
Very skilful in the languages:
In the gift of preaching
Excellent, laborious, and successful:
In the pastoral office
Faithful and vigilant:
Among the controversies of Divines
Moderate always and pacific:
Ever ready for all the duties of piety:
Among husbands, brothers, fathers, friends,
He had few equals:
And his carriage toward all mankind was
Eminently benevolent.
But what rich stores of grace lay hid behind
The veil of modesty, no human mind
Can search, no friend declare, nor fame reveal,
Nor has this mournful marble power to tell.
Yet there's a hastening hour, it comes, it comes,
To rouze the sleeping dead, to burst the tombs
And set the saint in view. All eyes behold:
While the vast record of the skies unroll'd,
Rehearse his works, and spread his worth abroad;
The Judge approves, and heaven and earth applaud.

Go Traveller; and wheresoe'er
Thy wandering feet shall rest
In distant lands, thy ear shall hear
His name pronounced and blest.

He was born in Leicestershire, in the year 1664,
He died at London, March 27, 1726,
Aged 62 years,
Much beloved, and much lamented.

ance, and their Enemies' Destruction: a Sermon, preached at the Merchants' Lecture, in Broad-street, May 22, 1722, on Exod. xv. 9--11.—7. A Sermon, preached at the Funeral of the Rev. Mr. Jeremiah Smith, who

MILES'S-LANE.—*Independent*, Extinct. Second Church.

TIMOTHY JOLLIE.—If any men are supposed to be ennobled by the worthy deeds of their parents or ancestors, or by their sufferings in a righteous cause; surely the descendants of eminent saints and servants of God, have the best title to that honour. Such a claim had the Rev. Timothy Jollie, of Miles's-lane. Both his grandfathers were worthy ministers, confessors in the cause of nonconformity, and sufferers for conscience-sake; who, with about two thousand more, were obliged to quit their livings by the fatal Bartholomew Act, in 1662; because they could not comply with the terms that were imposed *not by the gospel of Christ, but by the act of Uniformity.* The Rev. Thomas Jollie was ejected from Altham, in Lancashire; and the Rev. James Fisher, his maternal grandfather, from Sheffield, in Yorkshire. They were both men of great piety and worth, and suffered much by fines and imprisonments, from the violent spirit of the times. Mr. Jollie's father, the Rev. Timothy Jollie, who, also, was a considerable sufferer in the cause of nonconformity, was an emi-

departed this Life, August 20, 1723, on 1 Peter, v. 4.—8. A Sermon, occasioned by the Death of the Rev. Mr. John Foxon, who departed this Life October 26, 1723, on John xix. 30.—9. Of being Blessed, and made a Blessing: a Sermon, preached on New-Year's Day, 1724, for the Benefit of the Charity-School in Gravel-lane, Southwark, on Gen. xii. 2.—10. Of rightly dividing the Word of Truth: a Sermon, preached at the setting apart the Rev. Mr. Hurrion, to the Office and Work of a Pastor in Mr Nesbitt's Church, 1724, on 2 Tim. ii. 15.—11. A successful Ministry the Blessing of God: a Sermon, preached at the setting apart the Rev. Mr. Wright, to the Office and Work of a Pastor in the late Mr. Foxon's Church, 1724, on 1 Cor. iii. 6.—The above eleven Sermons were collected together, and re-published after Mr. Clarke's death, by the Rev. Daniel Neal; who added three other Sermons from Mr. Clarke's Manuscripts, entitled, "The Gospel Invitation," preached at the Rev. Mr. Earle's meeting-house, Hanover-street, 1721, on Luke xiv. 23. To these are subjoined the discourse preached upon Mr. Clarke's death. The volume is introduced with some account of the author's life, and a good engraving of him by Pine, 8vo. 1727.

MILES'S LANE.—*Independent*, Extinct. Second Church.

nent tutor at Attercliffe, in Yorkshire, and pastor of a congregation at Sheffield, in the same county.

Mr. Jollie was born at Attercliffe, the place of his father's residence, in the year 1692. The advantages he enjoyed in early life, both with respect to human learning and religious instruction, may very well be conceived. After passing through a course of preparatory studies, he entered upon academical learning, under the direction of his father, who, we may be sure, would be particularly concerned for the improvement of his own son, and would spare no pains in furnishing him with suitable qualifications for the work of the ministry, both as a scholar, and as a Christian. Nor did Mr. Jollie disappoint the expectations of his friends; for he entered on his sacred employment with good acceptance, and with very considerable applause.

Some of the first years of his ministry were spent in assisting the Rev. John Wadsworth, at Sheffield, in Yorkshire, the same church of which his father had been pastor for many years. There he acquired great reputation as a preacher, and was greatly beloved and valued by all his connexions. His fame reaching London, he was invited in 1720, by the church in Miles's-lane, to assist their excellent pastor, the Rev. Matthew Clarke, with whom he lived in great friendship for six years. Upon Mr. Clarke's decease in March, 1726, Mr. Jollie was chosen by a majority of the church, to succeed him in the pastoral office, to which he was solemnly set apart in September following. Previous to his ordination, he was examined as to his faith, by the ministers who assisted in that work; amongst whom were Dr. Ridgley, Mr. Hurrion, and Mr. Sladen, who all jointly and separately expressed their full satisfaction in the frank and open declaration that he had made. But notwithstanding this, several persons were dissatisfied with the choice, which occasioned a melancholy breach in the church, on the charge of a defect in Mr. Jollie's orthodoxy. It was first promoted by a few persons who had more zeal for the interests of a

MILES'S-LANE.—*Independent*, Extinct. Second Church.

party than for the cause of real godliness; and what made the case more lamentable was, that they were countenanced by several ministers of reputation; who, however, had reason afterwards to bewail their conduct. The consequence was, that 63 members withdrew, 19 men, and 44 women, who formed themselves into a separate church, and chose Mr. Guyse, of Hertford, to be their pastor. After such a breach, and so many circumstances concurring to depress the church, it is no wonder that difficulties ensued; but Mr. Jollie overcame them all, and though his congregation was not so numerous as before, it still continued respectable, and his station was as easy as that of most ministers of his day.*

Mr. Jollie's character, in whatever view it be considered, presents us with an amiable transcript of those religious principles which so powerfully influenced his mind in health, in sickness, and at the hour of death. He was a sound, grave Divine; steadfast in his adherence to the truths of the gospel; and so unblamable in the whole of his behaviour, as to disarm the tongue of slander, and present an example truly worthy of imitation. In his temper he approved himself a true and genuine disciple of the meek and humble Jesus, a follower of the Lamb of God, a minister of the gospel of peace. The strain of his preaching was always to speak the truth in love; not to blow up the fire of contention, but to raise the flame of divine love in the hearts of his hearers. Few have maintained a more inoffensive behaviour—few have gone off the stage with a more unblemished character than he did.

This amiable man was afflicted almost from his earliest years, with a painful distemper,(Q) which often confined him

---

* MS. *penes me.*

(Q) Mr. Jollie's disorder was the gout. Notwithstanding it frequently interrupted him in performing the stated duties of his office, he maintained an unabated affection for the house of God, and was never more agreeably

MILES'S-LANE.—*Independent*, Extinct. Second Church.

for weeks together from his public work. This, no doubt, greatly obstructed his usefulness; but though he was prevented from labouring in the pulpit, such as visited and conversed with him in those seasons of confinement, might learn from him, and from his example, a very instructive lesson of patience, and of quiet submission to the will of God. He saw the rod as in his father's hand. He considered his afflictions not as judgments, but as trials; and he looked forward by faith to the happy and glorious issue of them. On these occasions he would often repeat those animating words, 1 Pet. i. 8. " That the trial of your faith being much more precious than of gold that perisheth, though it be tried with fire, might be found unto praise, and honour, and glory, at the appearing of Jesus Christ, whom, having not seen, ye love." And though the pains of nature, and other troubles that befel him, were sometimes difficult to bear, yet he was never permitted to faint in the day of adversity; but would often encourage himself as the Apostle Paul did, and say, " I can do all things through Christ who strengtheneth me."

When in the last weeks of his wearisome pilgrimage, he had received the sentence of death in himself, he not only possessed his soul in patience, under the pressing infirmities of a decaying body, and continued to exercise that meek and quiet submission to the will of God, for which he had all along been eminent, under the various and tedious afflictions of his life; but more than so, he rejoiced in the hope of the glory of God; for he knew and could assuredly say, that he, was going to Christ and to a better world; where he should feel pain no more, where he should no more meet with

employed than when proclaiming from the pulpit the unsearchable riches of Christ. The writer of this has been told that he used frequently to be brought into his meeting in a sedan chair, which remained at the bottom of the pulpit's stairs ready to convey him away when he had done preaching.

MILES'S-LANE.—*Independent*, Extinct. Second Church.

trouble, and from whence sin and sorrow are for ever excluded.

During the weeks of his last sickness, when he had the free use of his intellectual powers, prayers and praises were in a manner his constant employment. The two nights preceding his death were almost wholly spent in singing praises to his God and Saviour, though with a faint and feeble voice, yet with evident tokens of an elevated soul, enraptured with the flames of divine love : And so, he made an easy transit from the imperfect praises of this world, to the perfect praises of heaven. Thus honourably did this excellent man finish his mortal career, August 3d, 1757, in the sixty-sixth year of his age; having been a preacher for more than forty years, thirty-seven of which had been spent in connexion with the church in Miles's-lane. His intimate friend, Dr. Jennings, who had for many years exchanged pulpits with him twice in the month, preached his funeral sermon from Philip. i. 23. *For I am in a strait betwixt two, &c.** (R)

WILLIAM FORD, Jun.—This pious and amiable man had the honour to descend from ancestors, who, for several generations, distinguished themselves by their zeal and sufferings in the cause of primitive Christianity. Among them, he numbered several faithful ministers of the gospel, whose disinterested labours, and remarkable usefulness, have transmitted their names with veneration to posterity. His great-great-grandfather was the Rev. *John Vincent*, a minister in the North of England, who was so harassed for his nonconformity, that, though he had many children, not two of

---

* D. Jenning's Sermon on the Death of Mr. Jollie, p. 31--34.

(R) It is not within our knowledge that Mr. Jollie published more than a single Sermon, entitled, " Christ's dominion, the Christian's joy ;" preached August 1st, 1730, to the Society that support the Lord's-day morning lecture, at Little St. Helen's; on Psalm cxlix. 2.

MILES'S-LANE.——*Independent*, Extinct. Second Church.

them were born in the same county.* This venerable confessor left two sons, *Thomas* and *Nathaniel Vincent*, both ministers, and sufferers on the same account. The former is well known by his useful labours in London, during the time of the plague; and the latter, by his astonishing zeal and courage, amidst the most cruel persecutions. Of these excellent men, we shall have an opportunity of giving a more particular account in the progress of this work. A daughter of Mr. Nathaniel Vincent, was married to a Mr. Ford, a very respectable merchant in London, by whom she had two sons, *John* and *William Ford*, both Dissenting ministers. The former was settled some time at Sudbury, in Suffolk; and the latter at Castle-Hedingham, in Essex; where they lived greatly respected, for many years. Mr. William Ford left three sons: William, the subject of our present notice; John, a physician and preacher, who died a few years since; and Webb Ford.†

William Ford, Jun. was born at Castle-Hedingham, in the year 1736. While a youth, he is said to have discovered those amiable traits of character which distinguished him in after life. The example of his pious parents, connected with religious instruction, had a powerful influence upon his mind and conduct, which were regulated by habits of virtue and piety. As his inclination to the ministry was early and ardent, so it was greatly encouraged by his pious father, who afforded him every opportunity of becoming an able minister of the New-Testament. After passing through a preparatory course of education, he was placed under the care of the learned Dr. David Jennings, with whom he finished his academical studies. At his leaving this seminary, he was chosen to assist his tutor, in the ministry, at Old Gravel-lane, Wapping; and not long after, became assistant,

* Calamy's Contin. p. 30.
† Evangelical Magazine for Dec. 1806, p. 530, 531.

MILES'S-LANE.—*Independent*, Extinct. Second Church.

also, to Mr. Jollie, at Miles's-lane. Upon Mr. Jollie's death, he succeeded to the pastoral charge, at the latter place, and was ordained Dec. 14, 1757. Upon this occasion, Dr. Savage delivered the introductory discourse; Dr. Jennings gave the charge; and Mr. William Ford, Sen. preached to the people. In this situation Mr. Ford continued till the year 1781, when, in the meridian of life, he was compelled, through severe affliction, to relinquish the duties of the pastoral office; and he retired to Windsor. There, when not disabled, he continued to preached in a private house, till death removed him to a better world, on the 23d of January, 1783, in the 47th year of his age. His remains were removed to London, for interment in Bunhill-Fields: The Rev. Joseph Barber delivered the oration at his grave; and Dr. Addington preached a funeral sermon to the people of his late charge, from Psa. xxxvii. 37. *Mark the perfect man, and behold the upright; for the end of that man is peace.*

Though Mr. Ford was removed early in life, which was a source of affliction to his friends, yet, it was none to him. His mind had early received that pious tincture, which future years advanced to very considerable attainments in the divine life. He possessed a sweet natural temper, which was much improved by the Spirit and principles of the gospel. As a Christian he had few equals; and was, in an eminent degree, remarkable for a spirit of humility, which shone through his whole life and conversation. Though he possessed talents for the ministry, and his attainments in human and divine knowledge, well qualified him for his work, yet he was not so generally acceptable as a preacher, as some others, who did not possess his qualifications. His unpopularity was occasioned, doubtless, by an extreme heaviness in the pulpit. It is no disparagement, however, to his brethren, to introduce a remark of the late Dr. Gibbons, " That he had heard much worse sermons at Pinners'-Hall lecture, than those made by Mr. Ford."

MILES'S-LANE.—*Independent*, Extinct. Second Church.

And it may be further remarked, that he was held in great esteem by those who were acquainted with his worth. It was the will of God to visit him with a long and distressing illness, which, at length, carried him off; but he was, through the whole, very patient and submissive to the disposal of heaven, and very composed and happy in his soul. The fears of death were dissipated, and with a cheerful hope he waited, under great languor and pains of body, for his dismission to that rest which remains for the people of God.*(s)

Stephen Addington, D. D. the seventh son of Samuel and Mary Addington, was born at Northampton, on the 9th of June, 1729. His father, who was by trade a hatter, was a member of the congregation of Dissenters under the care of Dr. Philip Doddridge, who then kept his academy in that town. His mother was a Baptist, and belonged to the society of that denomination, at what was called the Little Meeting-house, of which Mr. Shepherd was minister.

The opening of Mr. Addington's life, was also the dawn of his character; for in his youth he was distinguished for his serious piety. It was this, especially, which introduced him to the notice of his father's minister, by whose recommendation he was designated to the sacred office, and under whose care, after receiving such advantages as the town afforded for grammatical learning, he was placed at about 17

* Dr. Addington's Sermon on the Death of Mr. Ford.—Mr. Barber's Address.—And *Private Information*.

(s) Works.—Mr. Ford published, 1. An Oration at the Interment of Dr. Jennings. 1762.—2. A Scripture Catechism.—3. Sermons to Tradesmen.—4. The Religious Care of Families recommended; in a Sermon to Young People, Dec. 25, 1769. Gen. xviii. 19.—5. Two Sermons on the Lord's-Supper—6. A Discourse on Religious Liberty. Acts iv. 19, 20.—7. A Sermon on the Death of his Wife, Mrs. Elizabeth Ford, who departed this Life, May 31, 1781, in the 51st Year of her Age. Psa. lxxiii. 24.

MILES'S-LANE.—*Independent*, Extinct. Second Church.

years of age. His family residing in the town, he did not become an inmate with that of Dr. Doddridge, but attended daily in his class at the lecture of the academy. This circumstance, though unfavourable to the establishment of a particular intimacy, does not appear to have prevented, on the part of that respectable tutor, during the remainder of his life, a degree of friendship for his pupil, which led him to take a kind, and almost parental interest, in all his concerns; nor did it prevent a suitable respect and affection on the part of the pupil. The extensive learning and extraordinary industry, the exemplary piety, the active benevolence, and steady friendship of that excellent man, and bright ornament of the Christian church, were not less the subjects of delightful conversation, in the privacy of Mr. Addington's life, than they have been the theme of just eulogium to an impartial posterity.

With such a model continually presented to his view, it is no wonder that Mr. Addington should have aimed at a resemblance, both in his deportment and manners. Accordingly, it is probable, that some foundation existed for the remark which was made at his first appearance in a public capacity, that there was a very observable imitation of his tutor. Of Mr. Addington's acquirements previous to his admission into the academy, there are no means of obtaining any satisfactory account. It was in this seminary probably, that he was furnished with most of the knowledge, both literary and professional, which was designed to qualify him for the office of the Christian ministry. Here too, it may be presumed, he formed those habits of industrious application, which afterwards prevailed in a remarkable degree through a large portion of his life.

At the close of the usual term of residence at Northampton, he received an invitation to settle with a small congregation of Dissenters at Spaldwick, in Huntingdonshire, with which, by the advice of his tutor, he complied. His father dying about the same time, the son became charged with the

MILES'S-LANE.—*Independent*, Extinct. Second Church.

care of his widowed mother ; and after settling the affairs of the family in the town of Northampton, removed with her in the year 1750, to his new residence at Spaldwick. This good woman continued in the house of her son till after his marriage, and under his immediate protection, till the time of her death ; which took place at Market-Harborough, in the year 1768.

At Spaldwick, Mr. Addington's ministry proved very acceptable. From this circumstance, and from the affection of the people, he was inclined to remain longer in that situation than had been at first proposed : For his worthy tutor, under whose direction he had the happiness of acting, had from the first suggested his desire of seeing him fixed at Market-Harborough, where he had himself exercised his ministry, and where he had commenced his academical labours some years before. The unsettled state of the Society in that place, also, presented the probability of an opening.

But the period was now approaching, when he was for ever to be deprived of the friendship and counsels of his affectionate guide and instructor, Dr. Doddridge. This illustrious man died at Lisbon, Oct. 26, 1751. Not many months after this afflictive event, Mr. Addington's thoughts were directed to the marriage state. The companion of his choice was a Miss Reymes, a young lady nearly of his own age, and the daughter of Mr. Robert Reymes, of Norwich, a descendant of a very ancient and respectable family, in the county of Norfolk. She likewise had the happiness of being a particular friend of Dr. Doddridge, and was on a visit at his house, when the acquaintance commenced. The union took place Feb. 13, 1752.

A few weeks only after this event, the situation was offered to Mr. Addington's acceptance, which had been chosen and marked out for him, in the wishes, at least, of his affectionate foster-parent. There had for many years existed at Harborough, a large and flourishing Society of Dis-

MILES'S-LANE.—*Independent*, Extinct. Second Church.

senters, first collected about 1673, by the Rev. Matthew Clarke, who was ejected from Narborough, in the same county. He was succeeded by an excellent minister, the Rev. David Some, who preached there a great number of years, and to whom Dr. Doddridge was assistant. From his death, in May, 1737, it does not appear, that the people had been satisfactorily settled with a minister. Upon the resignation of their pastor in the beginning of the year 1752, their choice was divided between two persons, who had been proposed by their respective friends. At length it was wisely agreed by both parties, to withdraw their suffrages from each, in favour of a third candidate, if one could be found who should be agreeable to the whole congregation. At this juncture Mr. Addington was recommended to them by a neighbouring minister; (T) and soon afterwards received an unanimous invitation to settle among them. With this he thought it his duty to comply; both as it opened to him a large sphere for exertion, and as it would probably enable him the better to provide for his now enlarged family demands. Accordingly, in the month of July, 1752, he removed to Harborough, and there established himself in the very house where his good friend had lived, and first commenced his academical instructions.

The first five years of his residence at Harborough were devoted, almost exclusively, to the duties of his pastoral office. He was ordained in the month of September, 1759; on which occasion the service was conducted by the Rev. Mr. Gilbert, of Northampton; Mr. Guthridge, of Oundle; Mr. Boyce, of Kettering; Mr. Gregson, of Rothwell; and Dr. Ashworth, of Daventry.

His congregation was considerable in number, and consisted very much of persons residing in the numerous villages around Harborough; some of them at the distance of

(T) The Rev. Mr. Gilbert, of Oakhampton, afterwards successor to Dr. Doddridge, at Northampton.

MILES'S-LANE.—*Independent*, Extinct. Second Church.

several miles. Amongst those persons he spent a large portion of his time, visiting and preaching in their houses; and taking a particular and most friendly share in all their interests. So entirely did he appear to possess the confidence and affection of his people, that he became scarcely less their friend and counsellor in their various secular concerns, than their spiritual guide and instructor. He was in the habit of performing for them the kindest offices; and was at some considerable pains to acquire such a degree of knowledge and skill in other professional departments than his own, as would render him capable of giving useful assistance to the poorer classes of his neighbours. It is really entertaining to recollect the eagerness with which these worthy people resorted to their minister for such direction in their little affairs, as would supersede the necessity of applying for legal or medical advice.

These, and many others of a similar kind which might be mentioned, are only incidental circumstances, arising out of the intimacy of the connexion which subsisted between the minister and his people. The grand and leading object of that connexion was, doubtless, their moral improvement, and spiritual welfare; but to the promotion of this object, the intimacy of the relation, and its various circumstances, were all happily subservient.

In pursuance of the same design, it was Mr. Addington's custom to distribute and associate as many of his people as he could into classes, according to their age, sex, and situation; with a view to their moral improvement. In those societies they were in the habit of meeting at stated times, for prayer and religious conference; often attended by their minister; but the societies were always under his superintendence; and once in every year, about Christmas, each of them spent a cheerful evening together at his house. Even the female servants had also their annual day; on which, after assembling in the meeting-house, and spending a part of the afternoon in cleaning and beautifying some of its furniture, they partook of a social and friendly entertainment provided for them.

Independently of his more common and frequent visits in the families of his people, to inquire into their health, and to assist them according to his ability and their necessities, he had stated occasions in the summer season of going into the neighbouring villages to preach in the houses of his friends, and to discharge such pastoral duties amongst them as became requisite. During these visits numbers would flock together, and listen with earnest attention to his familiar discourses and exhortations; while they testified their affection, by a marked attention towards his person and services. With a similar disposition did they receive his visits to them in sickness; and for himself he has often been known to declare in his family, the benefit and pleasure which he has enjoyed in attending to their conversation, and in witnessing their conduct under circumstances which are calculated to put both principles and characters to the proof. From persons in the humblest station, and of the meanest external attainments, under the pressure of poverty and severe afflictions, he has often confessed, that he derived such lessons of cheerful resignation to the appointments of Providence, and even of gratitude for mercies with which the condition of the sufferers did not prevent their perceiving themselves to be indulged, as he had not found in more apparently favoured situations, and as he hoped ever, for his own sake, to remember and to improve.

The services of the sabbath appear to have derived a more than usual degree of interest from the circumstances above related. It was pleasant to observe the zeal and regularity with which the congregation at Harborough, assembled to wait on the ministry of the gospel. Neither distance of abode, nor unfavourable seasons, were usually sufficient to prevent their attendance, nor their punctuality to the appointed hours of service. These particulars, as well as the seriousness of their demeanour in public worship, their

MILES'S-LANE.—*Independent*, Extinct. Second Church.

devout participation in sacred exercises, and their eager attention to the preaching of the word, were so remarkable, as commonly to excite the observation of strangers; whilst it rendered the office of the ministry peculiarly pleasant. " Of Mr. Addington's talents for the ministry, or the particular manner in which he discharged its duties, I do not (says his biographer) consider myself qualified to judge correctly. It will not, I believe, be too much to say, That amongst his own people, his labours were both acceptable and beneficial to the great purposes of the Christian ministry. His sermons, especially during the greater part of his residence at Harborough, appear to have been composed with considerable care, and are for the most part written nearly entirely in short hand; although in preaching he did not always confine himself to his notes. The subjects were chiefly of the experimental and practical kind; and his delivery would, I suppose, be considered as animated and affectionate. His manner was certainly less governed by the fashionable maxims of oratory, than by his own feelings, and the appearance of his hearers at the time: impressive perhaps, and not seldom successful in arresting their attention, and conveying to their minds, with considerable force, the truths he was solicitous to impart, or the sentiments and affections he wished to cultivate."

The foregoing view of Mr. Addington's character, exhibits the pastoral connexion in an amiable and engaging point of view; and forms a strong contrast to the manner in which it appears in too many instances in the present day; wherein, as far as relates to the generality of his flock, the minister knows but little more of them than what he collects, either from public report, or from their profession on the Lord's-day. The public ministration of the word and ordinances of the gospel are unquestionably principal means of salvation;

MILES'S-LANE.—*Independent*, Extinct. Second Church.

but these public services are considerably aided in their efficacy by private and individual intercourses. The familiar acquaintance which is thus obtained with the character and circumstances of the people, gives a suitable direction to the public counsels of their minister; whilst the confidence which they at the same time acquire in his friendship and affectionate regards for their best interests, cannot fail to assist the impression, and promote the salutary influence of these counsels on their minds.

In the sixth year of his residence at Harborough, Mr. Addington entered upon a new engagement, which necessarily demanded a considerable share of that time which had hitherto been devoted either to his family, or to ministerial and pastoral duties.

At Kibworth, a village distant about five miles from Harborough, a boarding-school for young gentlemen had been for many years under the care of the Rev. Mr. Aikin, father of the present distinguished writer, and philosopher Dr. John Aikin, and the no less celebrated Mrs. Barbauld. By the removal of Mr. Aikin, at this period, to Warrington, to take charge of the academy there, the school was necessarily relinquished; and it was recommended to Mr. Addington by Mr. Aikin, and others, to commence an undertaking of this kind at Harborough. Accordingly he offered himself to the friends of Mr. Aikin, as his successor; and opened his house for that purpose in the year 1758. From this time, he was more closely occupied than before, and his pursuits and engagements were diversified and increased. His habits of application, however, enabled him to keep pace with the multiplied demands; and besides these, we find him voluntarily entering on a variety of undertakings, in furtherance of his purposes in the different departments of his duty, which were not necessarily required of him. With an increasing family of his own; with the care of the education of youth, to the number of from thirty to forty; with the charge of a congregation, under circumstances which

MILES'S-LANE.—*Independent*, Extinct. Second Church.

required no small attention; and possessed at the same time of a constitution which, from his earliest years, to the close of life, could never be denominated healthy; it would not have been surprising if he had found neither leisure nor inclination for any other engagements, than such as were constantly to be expected of him. It appears, however, that whilst these several concerns were upon his hands, he published a considerable number of books on various subjects, connected with his profession as a minister and a tutor; many of which could not be executed without much labour and application. During a part also of this period, he extended his pastoral charge to the congregation at Kibworth. The number of his scholars rendered it necessary for him to keep two assistants; the one to teach writing and arithmetic, and the other to assist him in the classics: for the latter, he usually chose a young minister who had finished his theological studies, and commenced preacher; so that he availed himself of this gentleman's assistance on the Sabbath. It was the preaching assistant's business to officiate at Kibworth, three Sabbaths in every month, and on the fourth to take Mr. Addington's place at Harborough, whilst he went to supply the congregation in that village, and to administer the ordinances of baptism and of the Lord's-supper. This management was designed at first merely as a temporary accommodation to the people at Kibworth, till they should be provided with a suitable minister. From various causes, however, it was continued for a considerable time, not less than two years and a half, and added to Mr. Addington's regular engagements. Besides these, he was much in the habit of attending meetings of ministers, in different parts of the adjacent county; and was often called to take an active share in the services on these occasions.

It will be supposed, that, to accomplish such manifold purposes, no inconsiderable care in the management of time, and diligence in the improvement of it, became requisite. He was a truly diligent man; from six to seven hours

MILES'S-LANE.—*Independent*, Extinct. Second Church.

of the day he was constantly in his school; the duty of family prayer, morning and evening, occupied about another hour; the meals of the young gentlemen, which it was his custom to attend, at least an hour and half more;' making together nine hours of each day, devoted to the youth under his charge. The remainder, after deducting what was required for family meals, was divided between a certain portion of exercise usually taken on horseback, in the middle of the day; visits to his people, and other acquaintances; and his study. Throughout this period, he was by no means a strong and healthy man; he had many severe and dangerous sicknesses, which were attributed to excessive application to business. The same cause operating upon a constitution of an originally feeble texture, was assigned for that valetudinary state which was habitual with him; and which, at rather an early period of life, terminated in a sudden diminution of his active powers.

After continuing these exertions for nearly thirty years, reckoning from his first settlement at Harborough, he began to apprehend some failure, if not of his strength, at least of that activity in the application of it, which was requisite in the discharge of his various duties. Under this impression, it seemed prudent to contract the sphere of these duties; and the only method that presented itself of doing this was, by relinquishing his school, and confining his public services to the care of his congregation. Accordingly, after deliberating for a time, this resolution was adopted, and he was preparing to carry it into effect, when circumstances occurred, which eventually issued in a total change of situation.

At different periods of his life it had been proposed to ihm, to remove from Harborough, into situations which were supposed to open to him a more extensive sphere of usefulness. Once, indeed, he had been actually prevailed upon, to accept the charge of a considerable congregation in London; when the importunity of his people, between

MILES'S-LANE.—*Independent*, Extinct. Second Church.

whom and himself there had ever subsisted the most cordial affection, prevailed over the resolution he had adopted, and changed his determination to remove. Upon the present occasion, however, although this mutual affection had not suffered the smallest diminution, an invitation, which he received to settle in London, was recommended to his acceptance by a number of circumstances, rather singular in their concurrence at this juncture; and not only justifying his removal, but rendering it, though painful in the extreme to the separating parties, apparently an act of duty and propriety, which was confirmed by future reflections and experience.

It was not without the severest struggles that he resigned the connexion which had long been endeared to him, by every thing calculated to produce, and to cherish reciprocally in the parties, the most cordial esteem, and the liveliest affection. The connexion, indeed, might be said not even now to have been broken up; but rather exchanged for an intimacy, differing only in the mode, not in the degree of its friendship; and continued under its new modification with unabated sincerity and pleasure, to the end of his life. As long as his health allowed him to travel, and, indeed, when he was under the pressure of infirmities, which must have suspended every idea of visiting at a distance any but the dearest friends, he persisted in making frequent journies to Harborough; and keeping up that affectionate intercourse, which had proved, through the greatest part of his life, the source of some of his best gratifications. He left Harborough in the month of October, 1781; and was set apart to the pastoral office in Miles's-lane, London, on the 22d of November following: the service was conducted by the Rev. Mr. Ford, his predecessor; Mr. Towle, Mr. Olding, Mr. Winter, Dr. Gibbons, and Mr. Brewer.

From the commencement to the close of this connexion, which was at the same time the close of his ministry, he was uniformly happy in the kindness and generous friendship of

MILES'S-LANE.—*Independent*, Extinct. Second Church.

his people. The ministry was ever his favourite occupation; that to which he devoted the best of his powers, and the warmest of his affections; and he was never so happy as when he had reason to believe, that by the blessing of the Great Head of the Church, it was rendered successful to its important object and end. In this success, in various degrees, he had more or less occasion to rejoice in all the periods of his life; and the joy which it inspired, whilst accompanied with the liveliest gratitude, was at the same time productive of renewed zeal and activity in the pursuit.

Mr. Addington had not been settled in London a year and a half, before a new employment was opened to his views. The countenance of a few respectable friends to the furtherance of the gospel, had for some time been given to a plan of educating a select number of persons for the ministry, by appointing them to receive stated lectures in private, from certain gentlemen, themselves, also, ministers, of the necessary abilities and qualifications. The obvious inconveniences and imperfections of this plan were now proposed to be remedied, by designating the young men to a fixed abode, and more regular and systematic discipline, both literary and moral, in the academic form, and under the direction of a resident tutor. This office was proposed to Mr. Addington's acceptance; and it is difficult to state the grounds of his compliance in any other way, than by supposing him to be prevailed upon, equally by the solicitations of persons, whose judgment and whose friendship had a claim to his deference; and by the constant and active desire of his own mind to be useful. Indeed, it cannot be considered but with surprise, that after having, under some consciousness of declining strength, unequal to the extensive engagements which had been pressing upon him for a number of years, but recently resigned a part of these engagements, for the sake of confining himself to his principal object; he should

MILES'S-LANE.—*Independent*, Extinct. Second Church.

again be induced to venture upon a new and arduous employment.

In the month of January, 1783, a house was opened at Mile-End, for the purpose of academical instruction, under the name of the Evangelical-Academy. To the duties of this new engagement, however disproportionate his strength, Mr. Addington brought all his zeal, and devoted his abilities of every kind, suitable to the occasion. And it is so far satisfactory, that his diligence was crowned with a proportion of success, at least equal to every moderate and rational expectation. It was during this period, also, that his friends, desirous of testifying their esteem for his character, and of procuring for him a distinction suitable to his new and important function, obtained the requisite testimonials to entitle him to the degree of Doctor in Divinity. It happened that the badge of this intended honour arrived at a juncture when, if any thing was necessary to exhibit to him the vanity of such distinctions, the most striking admonition was full in his view, in a most severe and dangerous illness.

He had entered upon his situation as tutor, but ten months, when he was attacked by a violent disease, which laid him by for several weeks. It seized him in the form of a severe and painful hiccough; which, with very few intermissions, continued for no less than nine days, notwithstanding he had the best medical advice. From this illness, however, though exceedingly emaciated and weakened, he at length recovered, more completely than was expected; and afterwards resumed his application to business with his wonted activity. Of all his pursuits, the ministry was that which was ever most dear to him. He was already in the habit of preaching three times every sabbath regularly, besides occasional services in the week at his own and other places. But considering that a weekly service might be established at his house at Mile-End, with a prospect of benefit to a populous neighbourhood, he opened there a lecture, which was continued every Friday evening, became well attended, and proved, according to repeated assurances which he received, both acceptable and useful. So pleasant, indeed, was this service rendered both to himself and his hearers, that he maintained it with the utmost regularity as long as he was able to engage in public; and even after he had resigned every other official duty, he persevered in this engagement with constant assiduity and affection. Such was the zeal of Dr. Addington's mind, that it seemed as if the fresh excitement which was called up by his new employments, was, for a time at least, accompanied with something like a temporary renovation of his active powers. Amidst the various avocations into which he had again entered, he found both opportunity and inclination to prepare and publish different works. The principal of these was, his " Life of the Apostle Paul, with critical and practical Remarks on his Discourses and Writings;" published in 1784.

When he entered on the business of the academy, he was in the 54th year of his age; and nearly in the state of health which had been common to him throughout the greatest part of his life; only, as must necessarily be the case, with less of the vigour and activity which belong to life's early and meridian stages; and that naturally declining energy still further diminished by causes which have been already noticed. But under the circumstances in which he was now placed, a few years were sufficient to exhaust completely the residue of his strength. To effect this, afflictions and trials of various kinds contributed their share. Disease and death were making inroads into his family, and trenching most materially on his comforts and his hopes. The companion of his life, who had enjoyed rather a remarkable share of health and cheerfulness, and had even assiduously devoted them to his happiness; was now confined to her chamber by an illness of such extraordinary severity and continuance, as to render her ultimate recovery from it scarcely less mira-

MILES'S LANE.—*Independent*, Extinct. Second Church.

culous than merciful. Of one of his children he was already bereaved; and others were threatened by the approach of complaints which, in the issue proved fatal. Thus, his family, which had ever been the object of his cares, and the scene of his pleasures, he was now called to contemplate with pain and apprehension; and when he stood most in need of the assistance, the support, and the consolations of domestic society, its pleasures were withdrawn.

At length he was again severely visited in his own person. On the 10th of December, 1789, he was seized with a paralytic affection, which, though not violent enough to lay him at once totally aside from his employments, proved the melancholy introduction to an extended series of diseases and infirmity. By the aid of medicine, assisted by the repeated use of Bath waters, his various complaints were mitigated, and partial recoveries obtained for upwards of six years from the date of the attack; but during the whole time, he went through most of his labours under much weakness. The academy, which in his affliction became to him a source of many and vexatious trials, originating in the base misconduct of one or two individuals; he most gladly resigned at the close of the year 1790: but as some disappointment was likely to be experienced from his successor not being ready to take the office at the period fixed upon in his notice of resignation, he remained in the situation, at the request of the managers, for three months longer; but at Lady-day, 1791, the academy was removed to Hoxton, and placed under the care of the Rev. Robert Simpson. Still amongst his people his services continued to be received with kindness, and favoured with every accommodation, so long as he was at all capable of exercising his ministry. When his limbs, enfeebled by disease, were no longer able to support him in the pulpit, and his faultering voice could scarcely be heard through the place of meeting, he was encouraged by their candid and kind attentions, to devote the little remain-

MILES'S-LANE.—*Independent*, Extinct. Second Church.

der of his strength to the duties of the sanctuary. This was his consolation: for amongst all the painful circumstances which conspired to cast a gloom over some of his latter years, nothing appeared to distress him so much as the apprehension of being altogether disabled and laid aside—an useless, broken vessel.

The apprehension itself was in fact realized: but like many of the painful forebodings of mankind, the reality was unattended with the distress which had been anticipated. His last declining path was rendered smoother than he had feared. The comforts of his domestic life were mercifully restored to him by the unexpected recovery of Mrs. Addington. The resignation of his academic enagagement released him from an intolerable burthen; and though he had still to sustain an increasing weight of bodily affliction and infirmity; yet the habitual calmness and serenity of his mind were no longer disturbed by the fatigues and vexations which that appointment had brought upon him. It is thought that he was never more uniformly cheerful than in the interval between this period and the close of his life. He had attained to a degree of patience under his afflictions, and resignation to the will of Providence, which had ever been the object of his desire and prayer. His public services were continued; he was again happy in the bosom of his family; enjoyed his visits to his numerous friends; and, although unable to walk a step without assistance, undertook journies to a considerable distance, particularly to revisit his old and endeared connexions at Harborough. On these occasions, as well as at home, he was, in proportion to his strength, abundant in ministerial labours; which, it was remarked, were never more earnest, never more affectionate.

His cessation from these labours was gradual, and highly favoured by an arrangement with a neighbouring congregation, whose place of worship was about to be taken down and rebuilt. The evening service had been already relinquished; so that the duties of the morning and afternoon

MILES'S-LANE.—*Independent*, Extinct. Second Church.

were divided between himself and the minister of the other congregation. By the continuance of this plan, he remained in active employment many months longer than he would otherwise have been capable; and in the end, when the other congregation retired to their new place, the conviction of his being unable to resume an additional service, rendered his total withdrawment much less painful to him than it would have been, had he been compelled by his infirmities to abandon the whole together. His letter of resignation was dated June 14, 1795. It declares his grateful sense of the many kind offices, and affectionate regards which he had received from his friends during his residence in London; together with an assurance of continuing to them the best tokens of esteem and thankfulness yet in his power, by continual prayer on their behalf: adding his request, also, for that further testimony of their friendship, by supplicating the Almighty, that he might be kept in a waiting frame, and, whenever the Lord should come, be found ready.

Thus calmly closed upon him the scene of his stated ministerial and pastoral duties. Undoubtedly he was affected by the consideration of outliving the character in which he had ever most delighted; but it was far from proving to him the painful trial he had once supposed, when threatened with a sudden suspension, before his powers were so sensibly exhausted. Old age, in its characters, if not in its years, was now upon him; the season of activity was spent; he had long perceived that his earthly tabernacle was dissolving; and the energies of his mind were fast sinking into that state of declension, in which the busy scenes and offices of life cease to produce their wonted interest.

His regular engagements being now ceased, he felt himself at liberty to spend the rest of the summer in the country, amongst his children and acquaintances. The visits he made upon this journey were manifestly undertaken with the

MILES'S-LANE.—*Independent*, Extinct. Second Church.

impression of bidding adieu to his family and friends. The sentiment was strong in his own mind, and his appearance and manners could not fail of exciting a correspondent foreboding in theirs. It is true, he exerted himself to the utmost of his power in every situation; but all was evidently tending to dissolution. In the pulpit (for this was not yet totally relinquished) he discovered a great degree of animation; but his strength was gone. In company he was cheerful, and received much enjoyment from the society and affection of those about him; but conversation was become little more than a mere interchange of friendship. His disposition had always been kind and affectionate; and his kindness and affection were now more conspicuous than ever. There was a calmness also, and serenity in his mind, which it was interesting to observe; and he usually took leave of his friends, under the full persuasion that he was to see them no more on earth, with the expression of his earnest concern, that they might be prepared to meet in a better world.

He returned to London in October; and with the little strength which yet remained, continued to fulfil his few engagements; but the increasing cold of the winter as it advanced, affected him severely. He had projected a review of his sermons, with a design to select a volume for publication; but in this he made very little progress. " I feel, (says he, in a letter of January 24, 1796,) almost incapable of every exertion; at best, exertions which a while ago, seemed delightful and desirable, appear now formidable labour. Both my legs and arms seems to be losing all their elasticity; and to be little better than as heavy weights hanging to a body too feeble to move them. It is, however, my great mercy that they are seldom in much pain. The Lord strengthen my faith, and grant me grace to finish my course with joy; and to wait with a truly waiting frame, till my change come."

MILES'S-LANE.—*Independent*, Extinct. Second Church.

That change was near at hand. On the first three or four days of February, he had a slight attack of erysipelas in his face; which, however, did not then indicate any material alteration of his general health. The evening of the sixth he had spent as usual with his family, and after supper was rather remarkably cheerful. At a little before eleven, his accustomed hour of retiring, he was carried up towards his chamber; but had not reached the top of the stairs when he was perceived to be sinking in his chair. It was the stroke of death. With some more assistance he was laid upon his bed, and immediately expired. He was then in his 67th year.

His remains were interred in Bunhill-Fields, on Monday the 15th of the same month; and the funeral service was performed by his long-esteemed friend, the Rev. Samuel Palmer, of Hackney; by whom also, as well as by the Rev. Samuel Brewer, at his favourite lecture, at Mile-End, sermons were preached to assist such of the living as were interested, in the proper improvement of the event.

The character of Dr. Addington has been so interwoven in the preceding sketch, that little remains to be added. His personal habits were orderly and correct. He was grave in his deportment, and temperate in all his enjoyments; yet not indisposed to cheerfulness. In his dometic and social relations, he was amiable, friendly, and useful. As a husband and a parent, he was devoted to his family. As far as he was actuated in his habitual diligence, by what are commonly termed motives of interest, it was the interest of his family that prevailed. His anxiety for his children went far beyond their temporal advantages. It discovered itself in every conversation he had with them, and in every letter he wrote. Frailties and imperfections undoubtedly he had, but they were not such as to tarnish the lustre of his profession as a believer in Jesus Christ, or as a minister of the

MILES'S-LANE.—*Independent*, Extinct. Second Church.

gospel; in the faith and hope of which he lived and died.*(v)

* Theol. Magazine for Jan. Feb. and March, 1803, vol. iii.

(v) WORKS.—In the early part of his life, he appears to have projected a Work of considerable magnitude, in which he carried his design so far as to publish a prospectus; but which, as he elsewhere mentions, partly on account of ill health, and partly from want of time, he was obliged to relinquish. The prospectus was affixed to the first of the publications in the following list, and is entitled, " Some Account of a Greek-English Concordance to the New Testament, upon a Plan entirely new; with a Specimen of the Work, as it is now preparing for the Press."

1. A Dissertation on the Religious Knowledge of the ancient Jews and Patriarchs; containing an Inquiry into the Evidence of their Belief and Expectation of a Future State. 4to. 1757.—2. A Greek-Grammar, drawn up in Question and Answer, nearly on the Pan of Ruddiman's Rudiments of the Latin. 12mo. 1761.—3. A complete System of Arithmetic, vulgar and decimal; with a List of foreign Coins, and their Value in English Money; the Principles of Mensuration; and a short Appendix on Land-Surveying. 2 vols. 8vo.—4. Maxims, religious and prudential; with a Sermon to young People. 12mo.—5. The Youth's Geographical Grammar, with Maps; one large Index of Countries, and another of Towns; geographical Definitions and Problems on the Terrestrial Globe; with an Account of the different Religions, and Forms of Government, established in all the known Parts of the World. 12mo. 1770.—6. An Inquiry into the Reasons for and against enclosing the opening Fields.—7. Eusebes to Philetus; Letters from a Father to a Son, on a devout Temper and Life. 12mo. 1761.—8. The Christian Minister's Reasons for baptizing Infants; and administering the Ordinance by Sprinkling, or pouring of Water. 12mo. 1772.—9. A Summary of the Christian Minister's Reasons for baptizing Infants, &c. in Question and Answer.—10. The Importance of attending early upon public Worship.—11. Resignation the Duty of Mourners: a Funeral Discourse on the Death of Mr. Thomas Dawson, of Coventry; from Job ix. 12. 1773.—12. A practical Treatise on Afflictions and Recovery; with a Discourse on Visiting the Sick, and suitable Hymns. 12mo. 1779.—13. A Collection of Psalm Tunes for public Worship; to which are added, several other Tunes in peculiar Metre; with a short Introduction to Singing. 1780.—14. A Collection of Anthems. 1780.—15. A Letter to the Deputies of the Congregations of Dissenters in London, on the Test Act. 12mo.—16. Peace the End of the perfect Man. A Sermon, preached at Miles's-lane, on the Death of the Rev. William Ford. To which is added, the Oration at his Interment, by Joseph Barber. Psa. xxxvii. 37. 1783.—17. The Life of Paul the Apostle, with critical and practical Remarks on his Discourses and Writings. 8vo. 1784.—18. The Divine Architect: a Sermon, preached

MILES'S-LANE.—*Scotch Seceders.*

MILES'S-LANE.

SCOTCH SECEDERS.

UPON the dissolution of Dr. Addington's church, the meeting-house in Miles's-lane was shut up; but it did not remain long unoccupied. Mr. Easton's congregation of Seceders, being in want of a place of worship, entered into an agreement for a lease of this place, and have occupied it ever since. As some of our readers may possibly be unacquainted with the origin and distinction of this denomination of Christians, we will here give a brief account of them.

SECEDERS are Dissenters from the kirk, or church of Scotland. The term comes from the Latin word *secedo*, to separate, or withdraw, from any society. They originated in the two brothers, Messrs. *Ralph* and *Ebenezer Erskine,* and some other respectable ministers of the church of Scotland. The occasion was this; in 1732, more than forty ministers presented an address to the general assembly, specifying in a variety of instances, what they considered to be great defections from the established constitution of the church, and craving a redress of these grievances. A petition to the same effect, subscribed by several hundreds of elders, and private Christians, was offered at the same

---

before the Middlesex Society for educating Poor Children in the Protestant Religion, on laying the first Stone of a Building to be erected in Cannon-street, New Road, Whitechapel. 1785.—19. The Dying Believer's Confidence, in his exalted Redeemer: a Sermon, preached at Deptford, Oct. 16, 1785, on Occasion of the much lamented Death of the Rev. John Olding; Acts vii. 59. 1785.—20. The People of God imploring Appearances of his Work, &c. A Sermon, preached at laying the Foundation of the new Independent Meeting in Baddow-lane, Chelmsford.—21. A People perishing for Lack of Knowledge: a Sermon, preached at Salters'-Hall, before the Corresponding Board in London, of the Society in Scotland for propagating Christian Knowledge in the Highlands and Islands. 1786.

MILES'S-LANE.—*Scotch Seceders.*

time; but the assembly refused a hearing to both, and enacted, that the election of ministers to vacant charges, when an accepted presentation did take place, should be competent only to a conjunct meeting of elders and heritors, being Protestants. To this act many objections were made, both by ministers and private Christians. They asserted, that more than thirty to one in every parish were not possessed of landed property, and were, on that account, deprived of what they deemed their natural right to choose their own pastors.

Mr. Ebenezer Erskine, minister at Stirling, distinguished himself by a bold and determined opposition to the measures of the assembly. Being at that time moderator of the synod of Perth and Stirling, he opened the meeting at Perth, with a sermon from Psa. cxviii. 22. in which he remonstrated with great freedom against the act of the preceding assembly, with regard to the settlement of ministers. A formal complaint was lodged against him; to which Mr. Erskine gave in his answers; and after three days warm reasoning on this affair, the synod found him censurable. Against this sentence he protested, and appealed to the next general assembly. When this met in May, 1733, it affirmed the sentence of the synod, and appointed Mr. Erskine to be rebuked and admonished from the chair. Upon which he protested, that, as the assembly had found him censurable, and had rebuked him for doing what he conceived to be agreeable to the word of God, and the standard of the church, he should be at liberty to preach the same truths, and to testify against the same, or similar evils, on every proper occasion. To this protest Messrs. William Wilson, Alexander Moncrief, and James Fisher, all ministers, gave in a written adherence, under the form of instrument, and these four withdrew, intending to return to their respective charges, and act agreeably to their protest, whenever they should have an opportunity.

Had the affair rested here, there never would have been a

MILES'S-LANE.——*Scotch Seceders.*

secession; but the assembly resolving to carry on the process, cited them, by their officer, to compeer next day. They obeyed the citation, and a committee was appointed to persuade them to withdraw their protest; which they refusing, were ordered to appear before the commission in August following, and in case of non-compliance, they were threatened with suspension. The commission met in August accordingly, and the four ministers, still adhering to their protest, were suspended from the exercise of their office, and in November following, were deprived of their respective charges, and declared no longer ministers of their church; at the same time, prohibiting any other ministers to employ them. From this æra the secession may properly be dated. The ministers were supported by Messrs. Ralph Erskine, Thomas Mair, John M'Laurin, John Currie, James Wardlaw, and Thomas Nairn; who protested against the sentence of the commission, and that it should be lawful for them to complain of it to any subsequent general assembly of the church.

The ejected ministers now erected themselves into an ecclesiastical court, which they called, *The Associated Presbytery*, and preached occasionally to numbers of the people, who joined them in different parts of the country. Some time after, several ministers of the established church joined them; and had meeting-houses erected, where they preached till their deaths. In 1745, the seceding ministers were become so numerous, that they were erected into three different presbyteries, under one synod, when a very unprofitable dispute divided them into two parties. The burgess oath in some of the royal boroughs of Scotland, contains the following clause: " I profess and allow with my heart the true religion presently professed within this realm, and authorized by the law thereof; I will abide at, and defend the same to my life's end, renouncing the Romish religion, called *Papistry*."—The two Erskine's, Mr. Fisher, and others, affirmed, that this oath was not contrary to the principles of the secession, and might be lawfully taken; Messrs. Moncrief, Mair, Gib, and others, contended on the other hand, that it was a virtual renunciation of their testimony; and so keenly was this controversy agitated, that they split into two parties, the Burghers, who took the oath; and the Anti-Burghers, who condemned it. This rupture took place in 1747, since which time they have had separate communion, and have been under the jurisdiction of different synods.

The Seceders are now become very numerous, not only in Scotland, but also in Ireland and America. They adhere strenuously to the Westminster Confession of Faith; and if any of their ministers teach doctrines contrary thereto, they are sure of being thrown out of their communion. They believe that the people have a natural right to choose their own pastors, and the settlement of their ministers always proceeds upon a popular election. This, indeed, is the chief point in which they differ from the church of Scotland.*

It is lamentable to observe, that the church of the secession, imbibed much of the bigotry and intolerant spirit of the mother church. We have a remarkable instance of this during Mr. Whitefield's journey in Scotland, in 1741. His first labours were in Messrs. Erskines' meeting-house at Dumferlin. Great persuasions were used to detain him there, and as great to keep him from preaching for, and visiting the Rev. Mr. Wardlaw, who had been colleague to Mr. Ralph Erskine, above twenty years, but was looked upon as perjured for not adhering to solemn league and covenant. This was new and unintelligible language to Mr. Whitefield; it was, therefore, proposed that the members of the Associate Presbytery should be convened, in order to instruct him on the subject. Being assembled, he inquired the cause of their meeting; they answered to discourse, and

* Buck's Theol. Dict. Art. Seceder, vol. ii. p. 408--414.

MILES'S-LANE.—*Scotch Seceders.*

set him right about church government, and the solemn league and covenant. He replied, they might save themselves the trouble, for he had no scruple about it; and that settling church government, and preaching about the solemn league and covenant, was not his place; that he had not made the subject his study, being too busy about matters which he judged of greater importance. Several replied, that every pin of the tabernacle was precious. He answered, that in every building, there were outside and inside workmen; that the latter, at present, was his province; that if they thought themselves called to the former, they might proceed in their own way, and he would proceed in his. He then asked them seriously, what they would have him to do? The answer was, that he was not desired to subscribe immediately to the solemn league and covenant, *but to preach only for them*, till he had further light. He asked, *Why only for them?* Mr. Ralph Erskine said, " They were the Lord's people." He then asked, Were no other the Lord's people but themselves? If not, and if others were the devil's people, they had more need to be preached to; that for his part, all places were alike to him; and that if the Pope himself would lend him his pulpit, he would gladly proclaim in it the righteousness of the Lord Jesus Christ. It was afterwards proposed that he should take two of their brethren with him to America, to settle presbytery there. But he asked, Suppose a number of Independents should come, and declare, that after the greatest search, they were convinced that Independency was the right church government, and would disturb nobody, if tolerated; should they be tolerated? They answered, *No!*—Soon after the assembly broke up, when Mr. Whitefield retired in disgust, and an open breach ensued.*

There are but three congregations of Seceders in London. That at Miles's-lane, originated in an amicable separation

* Gillies's Life of Whitefield, p. 78 -77.

from the church in Wells-street, Oxford-street, under the pastoral charge of the Rev. Alexander Waugh. Many of his people residing in the city, and finding the distance too great, to attend constantly at their own place; thought it would be more convenient to open a meeting for their use at this end of the town, still preserving their connexion with the old church. They assembled for some years in an old building in Meeting-house-court, Redcross-street; where Mr. Waugh used to preach to them regularly once a month. In process of time they thought it would be better to have a minister wholly resident with them, and chose the Rev. Alexander Easton.*

ALEXANDER EASTON, a native of Scotland, and educated at the University of Edinburgh. He was ordained to the pastoral office over this church, September 17, 1792. For the sake of convenience, the service was conducted at the large meeting-house in Monkwell-street, which was obligingly offered to them for the purpose. The ministers engaged on the occasion were Doctors Rutledge and Hunter, and Messrs. Steven, Love, and Waugh; the latter of whom preached. It is remarkable that Mr. Easton's credentials did not arrive from Scotland till the morning of his ordination. About three years afterwards, the congregation began to look out for a more convenient place of worship, and the meeting-house in Miles's-lane being then vacant, by the dissolution of Dr. Addington's church, they entered into an agreement for a lease. After undergoing a thorough repair, it was re-opened on Friday evening, December 25, 1795. Mr. Easton preached a suitable discourse upon the occasion, from Isaiah iv. 5. In the course of a few years, Mr. Easton being incapacitated for preaching, retired into Scotland, in the year 1800, and is still employed there in the tuition of youth.†

* *Private Information.* † *Ibid.*

JOHN RAE, a native of Scotland, and educated for the ministry in the University of Edinburgh. Being licensed to preach the gospel, he was admitted to the pastoral charge of a congregation belonging to the Secession, at St. Andrews. From thence, in consequence of a deed of translation by the associate synod, he was introduced Oct. 21, 1805, to the pastoral charge of the church in Miles's-lane, after there had been a vacancy of nearly five years. Mr. Rae is the present pastor; and the congregation not very large.

DYERS'-HALL, THAMES-STREET.

EXTINCT.

DYERS'-HALL, before the fire in London, was situated near Old Swan-lane, on the south side of Upper Thames-street; but being destroyed in the great conflagration, in 1666, a number of warehouses was erected on the site. After this, the company converted one of their houses in Little Elbow-lane, into a Hall, where they have continued since then, to transact their business.* In the reign of Charles the Second, Dyers'-Hall, or, as is more probable, an adjoining building belonging to the Company, was used as a meeting-house for Nonconformists; but a particular history of it is not now to be obtained. It appears from Calamy,† that Mr. Thomas Lye, ejected from Alhallows, Lombard-street, had some property in this place, and pro-

* Maitland's London. † Continuation, p. 945.

bably preached to a congregation here. According to Wood,* he " held forth in conventicles" at Clapham; where he was buried in 1684. These accounts seem inconsistent; but it is possible both may be true. Calamy also informs us, that Mr. Jeremiah Marsden's church, from Founders'-Hall, met some time, by Mr. Lye's permission, at Dyers'-Hall.† This little is all we know concerning this place. Of Mr. Lye we shall have to speak more particularly under the article CLAPHAM.

JOINERS'-HALL, THAMES-STREET.

PARTICULAR BAPTIST.—EXTINCT.

JOINERS'-HALL, situated in Joiners'-Hall Buildings, formerly called Friars'-lane, and before that Greenwich-lane, was used as a meeting-house, towards the latter end of the seventeenth century, by a congregation of Particular Baptists. The origin of this society, like that of many others, is involved in obscurity. Though it is probable this was one of the early churches of that denomination, yet we can trace it no farther back than the reign of Charles II. when a Mr. John Harris was the pastor. In the time of his successor, the congregation removed to Pinners'-Hall, vacant by the removal of Dr. Watts's church to Bury-street, in 1708. There they continued to assemble in the afternoon of the Lord's-day only, till 1723, when they removed to Devonshire-square, where the church became extinct under Mr.

---

* Athenæ Oxon. vol. ii. p. 761.   † Calamy, *ubi supra.*

JOINERS'-HALL, THAMES-STREET.—*Particular Baptist*, Extinct.

Clendon Dawkes, about the year 1751. In its early state, this was one of the most considerable churches of the Baptist denomination, on account both of the number of members, and the many wealthy persons who belonged to it. But in aftertimes it greatly declined, so that there were but few members left at the time of its breaking up * The elders and ministers of this church, from the earliest period we can trace it, were as follows:

Ministers' Names.	As Pastors.		As Assistants.	
	From	To	From	To
John Harris,	16..	1691	—	—
Tobias Russell,	—	—	16..	16..
Thomas Mariot,	—	—	16..	16..
Joseph Maisters,	1692	1717	—	—
Thomas Richardson,	1718	1730	—	—
Clendon Dawkes,	1735	1751	—	—

JOHN HARRIS.—Of this gentleman our information is extremely brief. He was pastor of this church in 1679; and died about 1691. His name is affixed to the Confession of Faith put forth by the Particular Baptist churches in 1689, denying Arminianism. Crosby has no account of him, nor does he even mention his name. He was succeeded in the elder's office by Mr. Maisters.

TOBIAS RUSSEL, and THOMAS MARIOT, were ministers in this society, at the same time that Mr. Harris was elder. It should be remarked, that these offices were perfectly distinct, and prevailed very generally among the Bap-

* *Private Information.*

JOINERS'-HALL, THAMES-STREET.—*Particular Baptist*, Extinct.

tist churches in the seventeenth century. The office of elder was equal in dignity and power, and somewhat similar in nature, to that of bishop, or pastor, in the most strict Dissenting churches in the present day. It was his office to dispense all Christian ordinances, and to preside in all matters that related to the welfare of his flock. The office of minister resembled, in some measure, the modern one of assistant. He was generally chosen from the congregation, and his business was to preach, and to visit the flock. If he possessed talents for the ministry, and proved an acceptable preacher, it often happened that he was called to the pastoral office, either in his own church, or in some other society. The names of both the above ministers are affixed to the Baptist Confession of Faith, in 1689.

JOSEPH MAISTERS.—This worthy minister was born at Kingsdown, near Ilchester, in Somersetshire, Nov. 13, 1640. He received his education at Magdalen College, Oxford, under the tuition of the celebrated Dr. Thomas Goodwin, and continued there about four years, till the Restoration. The ceremonies then introduced, inclined him to remove to Magdalen Hall, being at that time standing for his degree of B. A. which was denied him purely for his refusing conformity. After such usage he had little heart to stay at the university; he therefore quitted it, and followed his studies in private, preaching occasionally as he had opportunity. At length he settled with a society of Christians at Theobald's, in Hertfordshire, being ordained Oct. 30, 1667. He continued to preach to them for a number of years, and at length accepted an invitation to become elder of a Baptist congregation, at Joiners'-Hall, in the city of London. His church in the country was then reduced to a very small number, and met in the Presbyterian meeting-house, the ministers of the two congregations dividing the work between them. As he was not willing to desert his little flock, it was agreed upon his removal, that they should

JOINERS'-HALL, THAMES-STREET.—*Particular Baptist*, Extinct.

join his church in London; and he went down once a month to preach, and to administer the Lord's-supper to them in the country. In this connexion he continued till his death, which happened April 6th, 1717, in the 77th year of his age. He was interred in Bunhill-Fields, and his funeral sermon preached by Mr. (afterwards Dr.) Jeremiah Hunt, on Prov. xiv. 32.

Mr. Maisters, in early life, became the subject of those religious impressions which had a happy influence upon his conduct in more advanced years. The force of his principles enabled him, at a critical period, to relinquish a station which promised considerable profit and applause. His good natural abilities qualified him for extensive service; and he was blessed with a native modesty and mildness of temper, which were improved by care, and heightened by religion. His fancy was clear and lively, and continued with him to an age, when usually it takes its flight; and he regulated it with so much judgment, as not to outrun correctness of thought. His memory was so strong that, though he lived to an advanced age, any abatement of it was scarcely discernible. He was a very plain, serious, and judicious preacher; in doctrinal sentiments a professed Calvinist; and though he never used a pompous style, or fervent delivery, yet his preaching was generally acceptable, and admired by many serious and judicious Christians of different persuasions. He wrote down in his study the chief part of his discourses, which he committed to memory; and as it was very retentive, he forbore the use of notes. As a Christian, he maintained an unblemished character; was mild and gentle, temperate and humble, to a degree not commonly attained. His candour was remarkable; and his love extended to all who bore the image of God, however they differed from him in opinion. "In a word, (says Dr. Hunt,) he was so happy as to pass a life of almost seventy-seven years without a blemish. Blessed saint! Uncommon

JOINERS'-HALL, THAMES-STREET.—*Particular Baptist*, Extinct.

instance! Worthy our imitation! So beautiful even is this imperfect sketch of so amiable a life."

His death was equally remarkable: When he had faithfully served his Lord above fifty years, a few months before his death, he fell under a decay of nature, without any considerable sense of pain, or uneasiness of sickness. " When I paid him a visit, (says Dr. Hunt,) three days before his decease, he appeared perfectly serene and calm: The hope he expressed of future happiness, was not the rapturous assurance of some Christians of less extent of thought; the humble and knowing saint owning his many imperfections, had recourse to the merits and intercession of his Lord. When I was going to take my leave of him, he took me by the hand, and gave me a steady and a piercing look, which had in it a mixture of concern; I am so weak (says he) that I cannot now so well pray in my family: The good man thought it strange that the intercourse he had maintained with God in his family so many years, should be interrupted, little thinking his kind Father would so soon turn his prayer into praise. The manner of his dying was such as literally agreed to the account scripture gives of the departure of true Christians, *Falling asleep in Jesus*."[*]

THOMAS RICHARDSON.—Mr. Maisters was succeeded in 1718, by the Rev. Thomas Richardson. In 1723, he removed his congregation from Pinners'-Hall to Devonshire-square, then occupied by another congregation of Particular Baptists, under the pastoral care of Mr. Mark Key. The two Societies met alternately on both parts of the day, during the whole of Mr. Richardson's time; but after his death, the morning service was wholly allotted to this Society. Mr. Richardson continued to preach there till his

[*] Crosby's Hist. Eng. Baptists, vol. iv. p. 348.—Calamy's Contin. p. 107. Noncon. Mem. vol. i. p. 246.—Dr. Hunt's Sermon on the Death of the Rev. Joseph Maisters.

JOINERS'-HALL, THAMES-STREET.—*Particular Baptist*, Extinct.

death, which took place early in 1730. He was one of the Non-subscribing ministers at the Salters'-Hall Synod, in 1719. His only publication that we have met with, is a sermon, entitled, " The Conflict and Crown of a Christian ;" occasioned by the death of Dame Mary Page, relict of Sir Gregory Page; preached at Devonshire-square, March 23, 1728-9, on 2 Tim. iv. 7, 8. Mr. Thomas Harrison, of Wild-street, also published a sermon on the same occasion, in which it was thought he did not use Mr. Richardson well.

CLENDON DAWKES.—After a vacancy of more than two years, Mr. Hugh Evans, of Bristol, was invited to become pastor of this church; but he declining, Mr. Dawkes was chosen in 1735. This gentleman is supposed to have come originally from Wellingborough, in Northamptonshire, and was well known in London, where he preached among the Particular Baptists a considerable number of years. He settled, in early life, with an ancient congregation in Broad-street, Wapping, where he succeeded a Mr. Edward Elliot, about the year 1719, or 1720. In this situation he continued till Christmas, 1726, when he resigned his charge, and accepted a call to become pastor of a newly constituted church in Collier's-Rents, Southwark. This connexion, however, was but of short duration, for Mr. Dawkes left his people early in 1730; though upon what account we can find no where mentioned. The probable reason, however, was his partiality to strict communion; the church in Collier's-Rents being formed upon the mixed plan.*

After spending about three or four years without any settled charge, Mr. Dawkes was chosen about 1734, or 1735, to succeed Mr. Richardson as pastor of the Society that met in the afternoon at Devonshire-square. With this people he continued above sixteen years; but their numbers being

* *Private Information.*

JOINERS'-HALL, THAMES-STREET.——*Particular Baptist*, Extinct.

greatly reduced by deaths and removals, they were, at length, under the necessity of dissolving their church state. This event is said to have taken place about the year 1751. After this, Mr. Dawkes accepted a call from the Baptist church at Hemel-Hempstead, in Hertfordshire, where he finished his course, December 12, 1758, but at what age does not appear.*

Mr. Dawkes was a learned man, and an acceptable preacher. His religious sentiments were high Calvinism, but he seems to have carried himself with moderation towards his brethren. Mr. Brine, of London, preached his funeral sermon, at Hemel-Hempstead, and afterwards published it. The text, which was chosen by the deceased, was 2 Cor. v. 1. *For we know that if the earthly house of this tabernacle were dissolved, &c.* That part of the discourse which relates to Mr. Dawkes, is as follows : " It may now be expected that I should give a character of him, and a beauteous representation might be given of him; but I must inform you, that he laid an injunction upon me, not to enlarge upon his character, and that he expressed a dislike of bestowing encomiums upon the dead ; however, a few words concerning him may surely be allowed. He was meek, humble, and modest; wise, and learned ; diligent in study, there is reason to think, to the prejudice of his constitution. He had an enlarged acquaintance with the evangelical scheme, and a spiritual savour of the truths of the gospel. In his last long illness, which issued in his death, he was remarkably favoured with the gracious presence of God, and filled with a holy adoration of sovereign grace and mercy. Those glorious truths, which, in the course of his ministry, he recommended to you, were the matter of his support, consolation, and unspeakable joy, in the views of his dissolution."†

* *Private Information.*
† Mr. Brine's Sermon on the Death of Mr. Dawkes, p. 28, 29.

PLUMBERS'-HALL.

Plumbers'-Hall is situated in Chequer-yard, Dowgate-hill. It is not within our knowledge that any Dissenting church ever met here statedly, but we notice the place on account of the following circumstance, mentioned by our respectable historian, Mr. Daniel Neal. It appears from that author, that in the reign of Queen Elizabeth, the Puritans held a meeting here; but were disturbed by the sheriffs, and many of them sent to prison. On the 19th of June, 1567, they agreed to have a sermon and communion at Plumbers'-Hall, which they hired for that day, under pretence of a wedding. But here the sheriffs of London detected and broke them up, when they were assembled to the number of about a hundred. Most of them were taken into custody, and some sent to the Counter. On the following day, seven or eight of the chief were brought before the Bishop of London, Dean Goodman, Archdeacon Watts, and Sir Roger Martin, the Lord Mayor. The Bishop charged them with absenting from their parish churches, and with setting up separate assemblies for prayer and teaching, and administering the sacrament. He told them, by these proceedings they condemned the Church of England, which was well reformed according to the word of God; and those martyrs who shed their blood for it. To which one of them replied in the name of the rest, that they condemned them not, but only stood for the truth of God's word. Then the Bishop asked the ancientest of them, Mr. John Smith, what he could answer? To which he replied, "That they thanked God for the Reformation; that as long as they could hear the word of God preached without the idolatrous *gear* about it, they never assembled in private houses; but when it came to this point, that all their preachers were displaced who would not subscribe to the apparel, so that they could hear

PLUMBERS'-HALL.

none of them in the church for the space of seven or eight weeks, except father Coverdale, they began to consult what to do, and remembering there had been a congregation of Protestants in the city of London, in Queen Mary's days, and another of English exiles at Geneva, that used a book framed by them there, they resolved to meet privately together, and use the said book." And finally, Mr. Smith offered in the name of the rest, to yield, and do penance at Paul's Cross, if the Bishop and Commissioners, could reprove that book, or any thing else that they held, by the word of God.

The Bishop told him they could not reprove the book, but that was no sufficient answer for his not going to church. To which Mr. Smith replied, that, " he would as soon go to mass, as to some churches, and particularly to his own parish church; for the minister that officiated there was a very papist." Others said the same of other parish priests. The Bishop asked, if they accused any of them by name; upon which one of them named Mr. Bedel, who was present; but the Bishop would not inquire into the accusation. After some conversation respecting the habits, the Bishop asserted that princes had authority to command what God had left indifferent, which some of them urged him to prove; but the Bishop would not enter into the debate, alleging the judgment of the learned Bullinger: To which Mr. Smith replied, That, perhaps they could shew Bullinger against Bullinger, in the affair of the habits. The Bishop asked them whether they would be determined by the church of Geneva. Mr. Smith replied, " That they reverenced the learned in Geneva, and in other places, but did not build their faith and religion upon them." After much warm debating, in which they defended their conduct as built upon the word of God, which was of higher authority than the command of earthly princes, they were sent to Bridewell, and closely confined there above a year. At length, their patience and constancy having been sufficiently tried, they

TALLOW-CHANDLERS'-HALL.—*Particular Baptists.*

were released by an order from the lords of the council, with an admonition to behave better for the future.* How far these severities were justifiable by the laws of God, or consistent with that universal rule of conduct laid down by our Lord, *Whatsoever ye would that men should do to you, do ye even so to them,* must be left to the judgment of the impartial reader.

TALLOW-CHANDLERS'-HALL.

PARTICULAR BAPTISTS.

TALLOW-CHANDLERS'-HALL, a large handsome building, with piazzas, adorned with columns and arches of the Tuscan order, is situated on the west side of Dowgate-street, Upper Thames-street. This is one of the many city halls, which, in the seventeenth century, were let out to the Nonconformists for meeting-houses. Our knowledge concerning it in this connexion, however, is not very extensive. We have notice of two congregations, both of the Particular Baptist persuasion, who successively occupied it. Mr. Elias Keach, son to Mr. Benjamin Keach, gathered a church, which met first at Wapping, and afterwards in Goodman's-fields. From the latter place they appear to have removed, but not in his time, to Tallow-Chandlers'-Hall, where they published a confession of their faith. They afterwards built a new meeting-house in Angel-alley, Whitechapel, where we shall give a more particular account of this church.—The other congregation that occupied

* Neal's Hist. of the Puritans, vol. i. p. 162, 163, 164.

TALLOW-CHANDLERS'-HALL.——*Particular Baptists.*

Tallow-Chandlers'-Hall, and met there a considerable number of years, was the Society under the pastoral care of the Rev. John Noble, who, about the year 1728, or 1729, removed his people to a new meeting-house, in Great Eastcheap. The eminent Mr. Samuel Wilson, of Goodman's-fields, commenced his ministry by a Lord's-day evening lecture, opened for him at Tallow-Chandlers'-Hall. This little is all that we know concerning the place.

END OF THE FIRST VOLUME.

R. EDWARDS, PRINTER, CRANE-COURT, FLEET-STREET.

Index
to all 4 Volumes
is in the back of
Volume 4.

THE BAPTIST STANDARD BEARER, INC.
A non-profit, tax-exempt corporation
committed to the Publication & Preservation
of The Baptist Heritage.

SAMPLE TITLES FOR PUBLICATIONS AVAILABLE IN OUR VARIOUS SERIES:

THE BAPTIST *COMMENTARY* SERIES
Sample of authors/works in or near republication:
John Gill - *Exposition of the Old & New Testaments (9 & 18 Vol. Sets)*
  (Volumes from the 18 vol. set can be purchased individually)

THE BAPTIST *FAITH* SERIES:
Sample of authors/works in or near republication:
Abraham Booth - *The Reign of Grace*
John Fawcett - *Christ Precious to Those That Believe*
John Gill - *A Complete Body of Doctrinal & Practical Divinity (2 Vols.)*

THE BAPTIST *HISTORY* SERIES:
Sample of authors/works in or near republication:
Thomas Armitage - *A History of the Baptists (2 Vols.)*
Isaac Backus - *History of the New England Baptists (2 Vols.)*
William Cathcart - *The Baptist Encyclopaedia (3 Vols.)*
J. M. Cramp - *Baptist History*

THE BAPTIST *DISTINCTIVES* SERIES:
Sample of authors/works in or near republication:
Abraham Booth - *Paedobaptism Examined (3 Vols.)*
Alexander Carson - *Ecclesiastical Polity of the New Testament Churches*
E. C. Dargan - *Ecclesiology: A Study of the Churches*
J. M. Frost - *Pedobaptism: Is It From Heaven?*
R. B. C. Howell - *The Evils of Infant Baptism*

THE *DISSENT & NONCONFORMITY* SERIES:
Sample of authors/works in or near republication:
Champlin Burrage - *The Early English Dissenters (2 Vols.)*
Albert H. Newman - *History of Anti-Pedobaptism*
Walter Wilson - *The History & Antiquities of the Dissenting Churches (4 Vols.)*

For a complete list of current authors/titles, visit our internet site at
www.standardbearer.org or write us at:

The Baptist Standard Bearer, Inc.
No. 1 Iron Oaks Drive • Paris, Arkansas 72855

Telephone: (479) 963-3831   Fax: (479) 963-8083
E-mail: baptist@arkansas.net
Internet: http://www.standardbearer.org

Specialists in Baptist Reprints and Rare Books

Thou hast given a *standard* to them that fear thee; that it may be displayed because of the truth. -- Psalm 60:4

www.ingramcontent.com/pod-product-compliance
Lightning Source LLC
Chambersburg PA
CBHW021713300426
44114CB00009B/130